American Folk Music and Musicians Series

Series Editor: Ralph Lee Smith
 1. *Wasn't That a Time!: Firsthand Accounts of the Folk Music Revival,* edited by Ronald D. Cohen. 1995.
 2. *Appalachian Dulcimer Traditions,* by Ralph Lee Smith. 1997.

Series Editors: Ralph Lee Smith and Ronald D. Cohen
 3. *Ballad of an American: The Autobiography of Earl Robinson,* by Earl Robinson with Eric A. Gordon. 1998.
 4. *American Folk Music and Left-Wing Politics, 1927–1957,* by Richard A. Reuss with JoAnne C. Reuss. 2000.
 6. *The Hammered Dulcimer: A History,* by Paul M. Gifford. 2001.

Series Editors: Ronald D. Cohen and Ed Kahn
 5. *The Unbroken Circle: Tradition and Innovation in the Music of Ry Cooder and Taj Majal,* by Fred Metting. 2001.

The Hammered Dulcimer
A History

Paul M. Gifford

American Folk Music and Musicians, No. 6

The Scarecrow Press, Inc.
Lanham, Maryland, and London
2001

SCARECROW PRESS, INC.

Published in the United States of America
by Scarecrow Press, Inc.
4720 Boston Way, Lanham, Maryland 20706
www.scarecrowpress.com

4 Pleydell Gardens, Folkestone
Kent CT20 2DN, England

British Library Cataloguing-in-Publication Information Available

Library of Congress Cataloging-in-Publication Data

Gifford, Paul M.
    The hammered dulcimer : a history / Paul M. Gifford.
        p. cm. — (American folk music and musician series ; no. 6)
    Includes bibliographical references (p.) and index.
    ISBN 0-8108-3943-1 (alk. paper)
      1. Dulcimer—United States. I. Title. II. American folk music and
      musicians ; no. 6.
    ML1041 .G54 2001
    787.7'4—dc21   00-061946

♾™ The paper used in this publication meets the minimum requirements of
American National Standard for Information Sciences—Permanence of
Paper for Printed Library Materials, ANSI/NISO Z39.48-1992.
Manufactured in the United States of America.

For My Father

Contents

Illustrations

Frontispiece. Woman playing dulcimer with men playing recorders. Detail from *The Prodigal Son Tempted by Music*, tapestry, Flanders, c.1525 (The Minneapolis Museum of Arts, acc. no. 37.17).

1   Angel playing psaltery on lap. Stained-glass panel from the Burgkirche, Lübeck, c.1420 (St. Annen-Museum, Lübeck, Germany).

2   Angel playing the *mezzo cannone* (half-canon). Detail from *Madonna and Child Surrounded by Eight Angels* by the Master of Santa Verdiana. Oil on wood, 1367-1400 (Musée du Petit Palais, Avignon, France).

3   Angel playing dulcimer (*hakkebord*). Detail from the Book of Hours of Catherine of Cleves, painted at Utrecht, c.1440-1445 (The Pierpont Morgan Library, New York. M. 917, p. 302).

4   Angel playing dulcimer (*Hackbrett*). Fresco at Church of St. Leonhard and St. Katharina, Dornbach, Austria, c.1463 (Courtesy of Fr. Josef Allmaier).

5   Women playing dulcimer, recorder, and portative. Detail from Breviary of René II of Anjou, Duke of Lorraine, c.1442-1453 (Bibliothèque de l'Arsenal, MS 601, f. 2, Bibliothèque Nationale de France).

6   Angel playing dulcimer. Detail from *Mary, Queen of Heaven by the Master of the Saint Lucy Legend*, Bruges, c.1485-1500 (Photograph ©Board of Trustees, National Gallery of Art, Washington. Samuel H. Kress Collection).

Figures

Maps and Tables

Musical Examples

Foreword

One of the results of the post-World War II Folk Revival has been a great expansion of our knowledge of the history of American folk instruments and the publication of major works that provide the first broadly based surveys of these subjects. A number of such books have been written and published, not by academic historians but by people who have built or played the instruments they write about. These volumes have the dual advantage of containing immense amounts of buried history and reflecting the authors' deep personal knowledge of the particular instrument's musical features. Paul Gifford's work, *The Hammered Dulcimer: A History*, is one of the best and most important of these books. It is the first full historical overview of the hammered dulcimer and gathers together so much information, including fugitive material that will be unavailable to future researchers and writers, that its place among books on the subject will remain permanent.

In writing the book, Gifford decided that the history of the hammered dulcimer in America cannot and should not be divorced from the history of the instrument elsewhere in the world. Readers will welcome this decision. Most makers and players of the instrument are aware that it has historical antecedents extending back to Europe and elsewhere over long periods of time. This past, however, has been tantalizingly and frustratingly inaccessible. With this book, the doors of information are opened wide.

A few supposed or actual facts about the dulcimer's past have become common currency among today's American players, largely through brief historical statements and summaries in instruction books for playing the instrument. These include the beliefs that representations of the dulcimer appear on Assyrian reliefs, that the ancestor of today's dulcimer arrived in Europe from the Middle East, and that the instrument known today as the dulcimer is referred to in the King James Bible. Others have been intrigued by the fact that the illustration on the title page of Jean Ritchie's pioneering work on the Appalachian dulcimer, *The Dulcimer Book* (New York: Oak Publications, 1963), is an old woodcut showing a Renaissance music ensemble with a young woman hammering away at what seems to be a bridgeless hammered dulcimer. In addition, a full-page illustration in the same book shows a young dandy playing some sort of hammered dulcimer, with the French caption, *Homme de Qualité jouant du Tympanum*. Many players have wished to know more and have been curious to separate fact from legend but have not known where to find more complete information—to the extent that it can be known today, this book provides what they are looking for.

Of equal interest is the arrival and geographical dissemination of the hammered dulcimer in America and the changes from European anteced-ents undergone in the hands of craftspersons and players in this country. Neither folk music, folk instruments, nor the musical uses to which instru-ments were put survived the voyage across the Atlantic and transplanta-tion to American soil unchanged, and the hammered dulcimer was no exception. The descriptions in this book of physical changes in the instru-ment, the music that was played on it, the ways that it was used in en-semble playing, and its role in American social and cultural environments provide an immense amount of information on subjects about which little has previously been known.

The hammered dulcimer thrived in New York State and Michigan in the latter half of the nineteenth and early twentieth centuries among craftspersons and players, including members of the author's family. Gifford's relatives were among the small number who continued to play the instrument after its popularity waned, beginning in the early years of the twentieth century. These family connections and Gifford's acquain-tance with others in Michigan who have knowledge of the instrument and the social contexts within which it was played add a uniquely valuable dimension of insight and authority to his historical account.

The emergence of the hammered dulcimer from virtual disuse to a new birth of national popularity exceeding anything it had ever known, a pro-cess that began in the 1970s, also throws a spotlight on the Folk Revival itself, about which, despite its recent occurrence, remarkably little is known and understood. Gifford's summary discussion of the Revival is among the clearest that have yet appeared in print.

It is impressive to recall that the dulcimer remained virtually unknown throughout the sixties, which are generally regarded as the heyday of the Revival. It shares its relatively independent time frame with other features of the Revival such as the great expansion in knowledge of fiddle tunes, the increasing interest in that vague entity, Celtic music, and the immense increase in popularity of contradancing that is continuing to this day. Other things, such as renewed interest in the tenor banjo, are probably still heading toward their day in the sun.

Reviewing major events and time frames of the Folk Revival, including that of revival of interest in the hammered dulcimer, Gifford correctly indicates that our understanding of the Revival is in need of differentiation and refinement. I strongly agree. I would go so far as to say that Gifford's evidence argues for a shakeup in our ideas, which have been distorted by the fact that for a few years in the approximate time frame 1958-1964, folk music became a leading form of commercial music. In view of things that have happened since 1964, one might be inclined to say that the brief blip of commercial prominence could be considered a minor rather than a major feature of the Revival.

This book rescues the story of the hammered dulcimer from obscurity and inaccessibility. It is an immense contribution to our knowledge of American folk instruments and their relatives around the globe.

Ralph Lee Smith

Acknowledgments

Since the process of compiling the information in this book has taken over thirty years, it is probably hopeless to try to acknowledge everyone who helped me. I want to thank the numerous, but often anonymous, people—here called by the unfortunate term "informants"—who I serendipitously encountered while playing the dulcimer in the 1970s and 1980s; their reminiscences and pieces of information are sources otherwise impossible to find. Other people, now deceased, were generous in passing on what they knew about the dulcimer and its traditions. My father, Norman Gifford, was the earliest. Bob Spinner had acquired a wealth of knowledge about the instrument in Michigan, as well as various American cimbalom traditions. Gus Horvath and Nicolae Feraru, both masters of their own cimbalom traditions, over the years taught me much about Slovak/Hungarian-American Gypsy music and Romanian Gypsy music. Paul Tyler, Jim Leary, and Jim Kimball, who have extensively researched musical traditions in Indiana, Wisconsin, and New York, respectively, generously helped with important pieces of information. Walter Feldman was kind to offer his expertise and insights into Ottoman and Jewish traditions, which proved very fruitful. For certain hard-to-get German sources and information, I would like to thank Belisa Mang, Birgit Stolzenburg, and Reinhard Hoppe. Similarly, for Russian sources, Nadya Mitsul was very helpful, and Andrei Denissenko provided translations. Joshua Horowitz, Robert Godfried, Rogerio Budasz, Leila Makarius, A. J. Bashore, and Sara Johnson all willingly shared information concerning our mutual interests. In years past, Patty Looman, Robert Wey, H. E. Matheny, Sterl Van Arsdale, and Robert Stykemain were very helpful. I would like to acknowledge Madeline MacNeil's referrals and permission to use extracts from my columns in the *Dulcimer Players News*. For the loan or gifts of photographs and permission to use them, Luther Battles, D. Eugene Brooks, Cathy McNally Dali, Dot Gudger, Ernest Eckerdt, and Melva Cox Ridgeway were all very generous. Closer to home, I would like to thank my friends William White, William Webster, and Robert Hubbach for their advice and help. Terry Swier, my former colleague at the University of Michigan-Flint Library, helped considerably with difficult interlibrary loan requests. Finally, I thank my bride, Mary Jo Kietzman, for her forbearance and patience that writing this history of the dulcimer required.

Introduction

This book's origins lie as far back as 1968, when my uncle brought an old dulcimer out of a closet. My father had talked about the instrument occasionally as long as I could remember, so I already had a vague idea what it was. He finally now was ready to resume his plan to make one, interrupted by war, moves, and raising a family, and he intended to borrow the dulcimer to use as a model. Its appearance and sound fascinated me immediately, and, with the help of my father and uncle, I learned to play "The Irish Washerwoman" the same afternoon. Much has passed since that day, exploring different traditions of the instrument; this book represents what I have learned in the intervening years.

Americans had almost completely forgotten the instrument by that time. The players my father or uncle had known were long dead. Within a few months, following an inquiry my father made to the Library of Congress about getting a photocopy of an old dulcimer method he had once seen, I learned of some elderly players encountered by folklorists and a recently made record of one of them. But "dulcimer" in the popular Folk Revival meant an entirely different instrument, and the traditional American use of the instrument, with which my father had been familiar in his native Chautauqua County, New York, was unknown to outsiders.

The instrument's use in other countries, however, had been described by some writers, and during my first year of college I combed the University of Michigan Library looking for references. One could find a few commercial recordings of cimbalom, *santur*, and *Hackbrett*, which opened new musical areas for exploration, but the dulcimers of certain other traditions still remained mysteries. From 1969 to 1971, I was in Europe and the Middle East and tried to learn what I could, yet in retrospect that experience only prepared the way for later investigation.

What soon became obvious was that, unlike most musical instruments familiar to the Western world, people regarded the dulcimer in each of its traditions as a "native" instrument. Americans, perhaps because of their Protestant tradition, regarded the dulcimer as a very old instrument, because it was mentioned in the Bible. When asked where the instrument "originated"—a common question to anyone who has played it in public—players frequently cited its reference in the Book of Daniel. That might establish its ancient origins, but begged the question of its cultural provenance, which is the real meaning of the question that people asked. Americans are hungry for tradition, yet they often prefer to see their roots in exotic locations. Although our families have been in this country for almost four hundred years, a period long enough to establish a nation full of regional peculiarities and local identities, we still move a lot and assume new lives. Perhaps that is the reason we frequently look elsewhere to find cultural origins.

The origins of the dulcimer, an instrument with a presence in America for almost three hundred years, do lie elsewhere. Yet because it found a home in the rural backwaters and was largely outside of popular fashion, it assumed a strong "native" identity, much as its relative the *yangqin* did during the same period in China and Asia. Like dance fiddlers, dulcimer players played tunes locally or regionally popular, which they mostly learned by ear. While a few entrepreneurs set out to produce and sell the instrument on a mass scale, the bulk of nineteenth-century dulcimers surviving today were made by forgotten individuals who sold them locally. Since most people rarely played them outside their homes or neighborhoods, few Americans became familiar with the instrument unless they happened to know someone who had one. All these factors produced characteristics which created a variety of dulcimer with specific American features.

My task in writing this book has been to identify the instrument's origins and to trace its subsequent history, addressing the question to an American audience. Although I have paid special attention to the dulcimer of the oldest American tradition, I have tried to examine the history of dulcimer traditions throughout the world. Not oniy do many of these traditions have representatives in America, but they are worthy of study in themselves. Some of those are well known, but others are forgotten and obscure. In one case, for example, that of the Volga German-Americans of Colorado and Kansas, the dulcimer tradition may be the sole survivor of an eighteenth-century central German style.

After considering various options for organizing the topic, I decided that the simplest and ultimately the most meaningful would be by the instrument's term. Other possibilities—by country or by stylistic period, for example—might initially seem more logical, since writing and research on musical topics are usually divided that way. However, if we consider dulcimers as dulcimers (in the English-speaking world), as *Hackbrett*s, as cimbaloms, as *salterio*s, as *santur*s, as *tympanon*s, and as *yangqin*s (this last subsuming varieties from cultures of East Asia and Turkestan), we can understand the instrument's origins better and how it spread so far and established itself in the music of each culture. Unlike other instruments, which entered new countries through the front door of high fashion, diplomacy (as with band instruments), or religion, the dulcimer largely entered through the back door, by means of wandering minstrels, ostracized minorities such as Jews and Gypsies, and even through association with prostitutes.

Each variety has assumed specific musical and cultural associations. The late fourteenth-century Western European aristocratic fashion for the instrument survived into the eighteenth century as a middle-class fashion in England and America, while a parallel minstrel tradition survived into the twentieth century in the form of street buskers in England and Gypsy musicians at restaurants and weddings in Hungary and Romania. The *Hackbrett* was used exclusively by rural musicians and itinerant beggars in German-speaking areas, while the *santur* was played by harem and court musicians in the capital cities of the Middle East. These cultural associations both have been determined by the sound of the dulcimer itself and have determined the traditional musical and cultural associations in which the instrument has played a role.

With the exception of the chapters on the American dulcimer, the organization of the book divides the subject into chapters according to the dulcimer's name (*Hackbrett*, cimbalom, *salterio*, etc.). Individual references to instrument names retain the original spelling used in the citations, which may cause some confusion but is necessary for accurate documentation. Each chapter includes a history and description of the design of that dulcimer variety, and each of those sections is further subdivided by geography, with some attention towards the history of that particular variety in the United States. Since the American dulcimer is covered in more detail, it is organized into six chapters, which break the

topic down by themes. Three are arranged chronologically and then geographically; one is a discussion of traditional designs; and two discuss
the revival of the instrument.

Scholars and professional and amateur performers generally approach
folk music, especially that of the instrumental variety, in an ahistorical
manner, despite the music's inherent tradition and historicity. This probably results from the fact that ethnomusicologists and folklorists largely
gather information about a tradition from living informants. Musicolo-
gists and performers of classical music rely on texts as their sources for
both music and performance practice of past eras. With orally transmit-
ted music, however, sound recordings often remain the major source
from which historical notions about the development of the music de-
rive. This has led, for example, to many American attempts at histories
of country music which only begin with the earliest recordings in the
1920s, virtually ignoring earlier developments.

Instruments and information about their makers do provide ready
sources for their history. This is the approach I took in an article I wrote
in 1974 for an obscure magazine, *Mugwumps' Instrument Herald*, and
which Nancy Groce generally followed in her book *The Hammered Dulcimer in America*. In dealing with instruments produced by industry or
by specialized makers for a wealthy or professional clientele, this approach is adequate. However, for the dulcimer, whose makers are frequently unknown amateurs, concentrating on manufacturers omits much
of the story.

I have thus chosen to use many of the kinds of sources historians use
to study aspects of life which are often difficult to document through
traditional sources. These include local histories, newspaper articles,
published travelers' accounts and diaries, novels and plays, and manuscript collections. The digitization of some sources—such as electronic
texts and internet webpages, Chadwyck-Healey's databases of English
drama and poetry, Bell and Howell's collections, and *The Performing
Arts in Colonial American Newspapers, 1690-1783*, a CD-ROM by Mary
Jane Corry, Kate Van Winkle Keller, and Robert M. Keller, among other
new sources—has allowed me to look for that proverbial needle in a
haystack, providing enough references to develop arguments in a way
that was hitherto impossible. These new methods, nevertheless, did not
exclude research done the old-fashioned way.

The largest sources for the American dulcimer, however, have been
the players themselves and the family members and neighbors who knew

them, as well as the instruments that they played. My research in this area, outside what I learned initially from my family, began in 1971, when I joined the Original Dulcimer Players Club and got to know several players, some of whom had been interested in the instrument since 1900. I traveled around the country in the early 1970s, looking up players and attending fiddler's contests and the like, in an attempt to learn the original distribution and traditions of the now-forgotten instrument. From 1975 to 1984 I played the dulcimer on the porch of the Murray Hotel at Mackinac Island, Michigan, which drew people from all over. Not infrequently, older listeners might mention a family member, neighbor, or acquaintance who played the instrument in the past. I kept a record of each of these conversations, although unfortunately I rarely noted the name of the person who provided the information. In an attempt to revive traditional fiddling in the state of Michigan, I was active from 1976 to about 1980 in organizing local jam sessions around the state, and I heard stories about players at these events.

While these encounters turned up many bits of information about the dulcimer tradition in all parts of the United States, my activity has resulted inevitably in a bias towards information on the tradition in my home state of Michigan. Since there has been substantial use and interest in the state, this is not necessarily a weakness, however, since the tradition can be covered in greater detail. Still, early in my research, I had direct contacts, through people my father or uncle knew or had met, with the dulcimer tradition in western New York and northwestern Pennsylvania and in northeastern Ohio. Similarly, through Patty Looman and later H. E. Matheny, I became acquainted with the West Virginia tradition in the early 1970s. Later, as I began to learn the Hungarian cimbalom, Bob Spinner and Gus Horvath shared their lengthy experience with Gypsy musicians and cimbalom traditions of various origins, and most recently, Nicolae Feraru, from Romania.

Although I have had some acquaintance with most of the traditions discussed in this book, some still remain familiar only through recordings and others almost completely unknown except through books and articles written by specialists. Inevitably I must rely on the work of authors who have studied the dulcimer's history and use in particular regions, such as David Kettlewell for the British Isles; Birgitte Bachmann-Geiser and others for Switzerland; Balint Sarosi for Hungary; Josephine Ng for China; and others whose books and articles appear in the bibliography and endnotes. Not all musical traditions involving a variety of dulcimer have been described in equal depth. Although I have tried to treat each tradition equitably, the literature varies in quantity and accessibility. For traditions which have been discussed in the literature, this book may thus serve as much as a guide to further reading. For those weakly documented traditions, the book makes available to an English-reading audience information from less accessible sources written in various European languages, such as German, Italian, Russian, Polish, Ukrainian, and Romanian. In each case, however, I discuss the incidence of the particular tradition in the United States. It is through examining the history of the different traditions that we are able to understand and identify them and the dulcimers which play a part in those tradtions.

At the start of the new millenium, thousands of people in the United States now play what only thirty years ago was a forgotten and almost extinct instrument, and tens of thousands more have some familiarity with it. No one could have forecast this change in 1970. Although I discuss the revival of the dulcimer, I leave the task for others to describe it, especially its later years, in more detail. Indeed there are many interesting questions to ask about the meaning of the revival, about the place of the instrument within a larger Folk Revival, and the changed nature of the instrument as it relates to society. My interest and purpose in writing this book, however, remains much what it was when it started in 1968: to examine, document, and describe the traditions. Since the connection of the players in the revival to older traditions is very weak and little has been documented on sound recordings or in books, the task that I have chosen to attempt will, I hope, prove useful.

· *2* ·

Forerunners

Then an herald cried aloud, To you it is commanded, O people,
nations, and languages,
That at what time ye hear the sound of the cornet, flute, harp, sackbut,
psaltery, dulcimer, and all kinds of musick, ye fall down and worship
the golden image that Nebuchadnezzar the king hath set up:
And whoso falleth not down and worshippeth shall the same hour be
cast into the midst of a burning fiery furnace.

Daniel 3:4-6

Perhaps it is appropriate to begin the discussion of the instruments which
led to the origin of the dulcimer with this quotation from the King James
Bible. Old-timers frequently referred to it when inquirers brought up the
question. For some, the three biblical references to the instrument, in
Daniel 3:5, 10, and 15, were sufficient evidence to demonstrate its existence in an unbroken line from the time of Nebuchadnezzar, ruler of the
Babylonian Empire (605-562 B.C.). However, the true story is much
more complicated.

The modern dulcimer first appeared much later, in the fifteenth century. But we must first discuss both its antecedents and various theories
which writers have proposed as its antecedents if we are to approach the
truth. Some older, long-discredited arguments are still current in popular versions of the instrument's origins. Other, more scholarly interpretations have been repudiated or revised, yet still find their way into print.
Our task is to review these theories in light of recent research, to define
the instruments in question, and to offer answers that will satisfy the
questions regarding its origins.

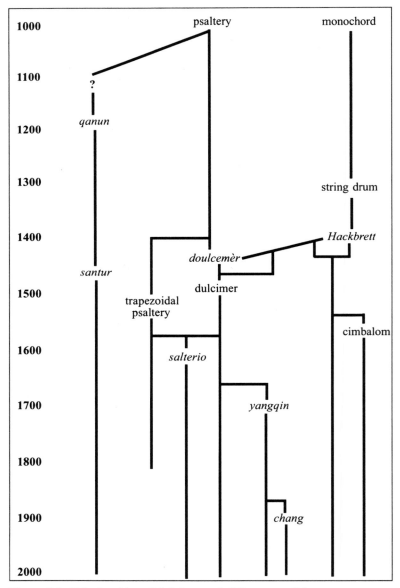

Figure 2.1: Relationships of dulcimers of different traditions.

Writers on music did not attempt to address the question until the nineteenth century. Carl Engel, in 1864, described an Assyrian bas-relief in the British Museum, known as the "Procession of King Assurbanipal," depicting a man playing what he regarded as a dulcimer.[1] He further considered such disparate instruments as the Chinese *qin*, Japanese *koto*, Finnish *kantele* and Russian *gusli* under this classification. Galpin later rejected Engel's interpretation of the instrument in question as a dulcimer.[2] We must concur with Galpin's argument.

By 1600, writers in English had begun to identify the dulcimer as a classical or biblical instrument. Perhaps these influenced later interpretations of the instrument's origins. The Geneva Bible (1560) and the Bishops' Bible (1568) were the first translations which used the word "dulcimer" in the third chapter of the Book of Daniel for the original Aramaic word *sumponyah*.[3] Modern writers such as Sendrey and Galpin have interpreted that instrument as a bagpipe,[4] while Sachs finds no bagpipe present in those times and suggests that the word meant a drum or an ensemble.[5] Edith Gerson-Kiwi concurs on the lack of bagpipes and offers the possibility that the instrument was a form of the *magrepha*, a bellows-blown organ used by priests in the last period of the Temple, the word *sumponyah* perhaps deriving from the Greek *siphon*, meaning "reed."[6] Whatever the original instrument was, however, the translators probably used the word "dulcimer" in the sense that John Maplet, in his dictionary of natural history, *Greene Forest* (1567), defined it: as a learned word for the "symphony" or common fipple flute, made of elderberry wood (see chapter 10). The common understanding of the word "dulcimer" reverted by the 1580s to what it had been earlier in the century, as a stringed instrument, and soon English writers began to evoke the dulcimer in classical contexts. Philemon Holland, in his translation of Livy published in 1600, chose to translate *psaltiriae* and *sambucae*, both stringed instruments, as "dulcimers."[7] Thomas Heywood, in *Troia Britanica* (1609), wrote "they in armes did kill: Vnto the Dulcimer first dance round."[8] Ironically the translators of the King James Bible, in retaining what was a reasonably accurate word in the 1560s for the instrument in the original text, influenced English speakers to regard the dulcimer as having an ancient origin. In fact, it was a relatively new instrument.

The Origins of the Psaltery

The instrument at Nebuchadnezzar's court listed in the Book of Daniel which interests us is not "dulcimer," however, but "psaltery." The word in the original Aramaic text was *pesanterin*, a term clearly deriving from the Greek *psalterion*. The Greek term itself was formed from the verb *psallein*, "to pluck." We can thus have little doubt that it was a plucked, stringed instrument.

This term appears in a bilingual Sumerian-Akkadian text dating from the Seleucid period, about 250 B.C. A cuneiform hymn to Ishtar, in the Temple of Ishtar at Agade, reads "The musician (Sumerian *nar*) [plays] the *sa-li-te-lu*." The corresponding Akkadian text for the instrument is *pagu*, which Galpin felt was cognate with the Hebrew *pg*, a technical term for playing stringed instruments with the fingers or plectra.[9] Greek influence was strong in the period following Alexander's conquests, and the *sa-li-te-lu* was undoubtedly a loanword from Greek.[10]

It is a difficult leap from the textual evidence of the *pesanterin* and *sa-li-te-lu* backwards to the iconographic evidence of an ivory box of Phoenician work dating from about 800 B.C., found at the Assyrian city of Nimrud, now at the British Museum. This depicts a procession of women with a double pipe, a frame drum, and two rectangular stringed instruments. Each of these instruments has about nine or ten strings stretched between their longer sides.[11] While it is tempting to link the design of these instruments to those which appear in Near Eastern and medieval European sources beginning in the tenth century A.D., the lack of iconographic evidence for the instrument in the long intervening period makes it difficult to accept a direct connection. Sachs interprets *pesanterin* as a harp and reminds us that the Aramaic text was composed about 165 B.C., several centuries after the reign of Nebuchadnezzar.[12]

We might define "psaltery" as an instrument, belonging to a European tradition, which consists of hollow box over which are stretched numerous, open strings which the player plucks. The term should not be regarded as a synonym for "box zither," using the Sachs-Hornbostel system, which groups together instruments of widely different traditions whose form and manner of playing are similar. Thus the modern *gusli* of northwestern Russia and its relatives in the Baltic Sea region, the *kantele* of Finland, the *kannel* of Estonia, the *kuokles* of Latvia, and the *kankles* of Lithuania, all of which have shallow boxes over which a number of open strings are stretched, are not psalteries, because they evolved from a five-stringed wooden lyre, medieval examples of which have been excavated at Novgorod and Gdansk.[13] The Chinese *qin* and other related instruments of the Far East, such as the Japanese *koto*, also evolved independently. Instruments such as the Bavarian zither and Ukrainian *bandura*, whose players pluck their numerous open strings, evolved from the monochord and lute respectively and for similar reasons do not belong to the family of psalteries.

No one has yet attempted to publish a detailed, historical study of the development of the European psaltery, and such a study is beyond the scope of this book. However, if we are to understand the history of the dulcimer, we need to look at its forerunners. The psaltery certainly contributed to the dulcimer's development. Writers have frequently confused the two instruments, and we cannot ignore it, especially since each instrument has influenced the other at different times in their histories.

Prior to 1000 A.D. it is difficult to verify the existence of a true psaltery in either the European or Islamic worlds. Isidore of Seville (c.570-636) compiled an influential treatise from late Roman sources, *Etymologiarum sive Originum libri*, listing terms used in various arts and sciences. He defined *psalterium* as an instrument with "latten" (i.e., brass) or silver strings stretched horizontally, struck, not plucked.[14] Whether or not his *psalterium* was truly a psaltery in the medieval sense it is impossible to say, due to lack of iconographic sources. Henry George Farmer felt that the Greek term *psalterion* was a "generic term applied to any musical instrument played with the fingers" and remarked on the lack of proof that the Roman *psalterium* was the psaltery.[15] Since Isadore's treatise remained influential for centuries, perhaps his definition was applied by scholars to the instrument presumably reaching Europe from the Islamic world in the eleventh century.

The *psalterium decachordum* (ten-stringed psaltery) appears in medieval texts, and two tenth-century illustrations of it, in a letter from St. Jerome to Dardanus, appear to depict a psaltery.[16] One is square and the other is triangular. As Stauder remarks, the number ten was symbolic (from the Ten Commandments), and the actual number of strings probably varied. King David appears with a triangular psaltery with eight tuning pegs, held vertically, in an eleventh-century Catalonian codex.[17] Farmer describes a tenth-century Syriac manuscript of Bar Bahlul in which the term *qithoro* was used for a different number of stringed instruments, including a trapezoidal psaltery of ten strings.[18] An eleventh-century Egyptian wood carving depicts a rectangular psaltery, though the number of strings is indistinct.[19]

Some of the earliest Western images of the psaltery, all not coincidentally in areas heavily influenced by Arab culture, depict rectangular instruments. A four-stringed psaltery appears in a carving on the south vestibule of the church at Jaca, Spain, and dates to the eleventh or twelfth century. A fresco in the Capella Palatine, at Palermo, Sicily, from the twelfth century, shows a rectangular instrument with six double courses, played with one hand holding a plectrum. Stauder illustrates ten other examples of stone carvings of psalteries from Spain and France, dating from the twelfth and thirteenth centuries. The most famous example is a carving in the Portico de la Gloria at the Cathedral of Santiago de Compostela, from the end of the twelfth century, depicting a triangular psaltery, with twelve strings, held on the lap and played with both hands.[20] However, others from this period appear to be played vertically, against the player's chest, as well as on the lap.

Qanun and Canon

An instrument distinct from the psaltery, the *qanun*, perhaps developed in Egypt by the tenth century or by the theorist al-Fārābī (died 950), was one of the chief instruments of al-Andalus (southern Spain), according to al-Shaqandī (died 1231).[21] The word itself means "law," deriving ultimately from Greek, and it would appear that its development was influenced by Pythagorean theory. It was described in a Hebrew manuscript of Abū i-Ṣalt (1067-1134) as an instrument for theoretical demonstration of intervals.[22] The European monochord, used to demonstrate intervals, developed out of similar philosophical origins. The *qanun* entered Christendom by the early part of the thirteenth century. The Spaniard Juan Gil of Zamora (fl. c.1265) wrote in his manuscript *Ars musicae* that the *canon* was an instrument of recent invention and that it was made in two varieties, full and half-size (*cano entero* and *medio cano*).[23]

The canon was in fashion from the thirteenth through the fourteenth centuries in Spain, Italy, and France. It was distinguished from the psaltery by the arrangement of its strings into courses, rather than the individual strings of the latter instrument. The full-sized instrument appears in an illustration in the thirteenth-century *Cantigas de Santa Maria*,[24] showing a rectangular box with one curved upper corner.

The half-size instrument, in the shape of a half trapezoid, with the oblique side holding tuning pegs set into holes at a plane with the instrument, was more popular.[25] Its presumably metallic strings were arranged into between thirteen and twenty-four courses of three or, rarely, four each. The player held the instrument against his chest, plucking the strings with a plectrum in his right hand. The left hand appears inactive in most illustrations, holding the instrument, or perhaps plucking the lowest courses as a bourdon. On some later illustrations, the left hand appears to hold a plectrum.[26] Juan Gil of Zamora mentioned both psaltery and canon, indicating that he regarded them as distinct instruments. Dick cites a thirteenth-century French poem, *Cléomadès*, which mentions *vièles et salterions / Harpes et rotes et canons* and *Vièles et sauterions / Harpes, et gigues, et canons*, which again supports the contemporary notion that psaltery and canon were different instruments.[27]

The half-canon was a minstrel's instrument. In *Reggimento e costumi di donna*, by Francesco da Barberino, written in 1318-1320, Lady Gienea dances to a *mezzo cannone* at an inn.[28] A minstrel of the King of Castile in 1327 played the *meo canon*.[29] One of the musicians employed in 1347 by John, Duke of Normandy, played a *demi canon*. In French, the word evolved into *micanon*, while it was *metzkanon* in Middle High German.[30] Despite its popularity in western Europe during the fourteenth century, the half-canon seems to have lapsed into extinction as the psaltery reasserted itself by 1400. Although an important instrument in its time and a significant development of the Arabic *qanun*, it played little or no role as a predecessor to the dulcimer.

The Psaltery in Medieval Europe

The psaltery, meanwhile, continued to enjoy favor in Europe. By 1200, instruments with two oblique incurved sides appeared. The earliest evidence seems to be English. A psalter in the Bodleian Library from the late twelfth century shows such an instrument, held on the lap and played with two quills.[31] Three further English illustrations, from the early thirteenth century, show the same shape and playing position.[32] A thirteenth-century carving from Amiens Cathedral shows an instrument in this form, with a central rosette and three smaller rosettes, held against the player's chest and played with a plectrum held in the right hand, the instrument's longer side upward.[33] An English example from the same century, but probably not realistically displayed, shows a psaltery with one rosette, and the side with the longer strings is downward.[34] Praetorius in 1619 described and illustrated an "old Italian instrument," called *istromento di porco* in common parlance, or "pig's head" instrument, which he said had thirty strings attached on one side to bone tuning pins with holes, somewhat longer than those on a harpsichord, and wooden pegs on the other side.[35]

Praetorius's description may refer to an instrument from a later period, but the name "pig's head" adequately describes the outline of the psaltery's shape in most of Europe during the fourteenth and fifteenth centuries. However, regional styles of construction and playing developed. In Bohemia, fourteenth- and fifteenth-century illustrations show players holding the pig's head psaltery so that the strings are in a vertical, rather than the usual horizontal position.[36] Perhaps through the influence of the canon, many psalteries appear to have been strung in double courses. Some illustrations show it being played by with a single hand holding a feather, while others show two hands in use. Although it was usually held against the player's chest with the longest strings upward, sometimes it appears in illustrations as played on the lap, with two feathers in each hand. Until a systematic analysis of illustrations appears, however, we will not fully understand these regional and temporal differences in construction and playing styles.[37]

The psaltery was an instrument used primarily by minstrels and troubadours. As a stringed instrument, it belonged to the category of "soft" or "low" music, played with other stringed instruments.[38] English literary evidence from the late fourteenth and fifteenth centuries links it with the harp, fiddle, lute, gittern, crowd, rebec, and citole.[39] French literary sources associate it with fiddles (*gige*, *vièle*, and *lire*), harp, rote, organ, gittern, and citole.[40] It was used in aristocratic environments. A French inventory of 1427 lists an "old psaltery enclosed in a wooden case painted in different locations with the arms of the Duke [of Orleans]."[41] Amateurs played it as well. In Chaucer's "Miller's Tale" (c.1386), we read of the poor Oxford scholar, who, among his herbs, books, astrolabe, and auguring stones, had a "gay sautrie,"

> On which he made a-nyghtes melodie
> So swetely that all the chambre rong
> And angelus ad virginem he song
> And after that he song the kynges noote.
> Ful often blessed was his myrie throte.[42]

The strings, at least on later varieties of the instrument, were metallic. Page notes that both Jean de Gerson and Bartholomaeus, in the early fifteenth century, mention silver, with bronze and brass as alternatives. Gerson, in another source, recommends both brass and gold strings.[43] LaPointe feels that the origin of the psaltery with the flared outline resulted from developments in wire drawing. He remarks that cold-drawn wire was available in France in the thirteenth and fourteenth centuries. The need for brass wire in the the carding process of the growing wool industry led Rudolf of Nuremberg to develop, about 1350, a process in which water-powered mills drew wire.[44]

Although the psaltery appeared regularly in fifteenth-century illustrations and literary sources, it rapidly declined during the next century. The reason probably had much to do with the growth of the harpsichord during the fifteenth and sixteenth centuries, as the tone was similar. Praetorius remarked that the virginal bore more resemblances to the psaltery than to the clavichord, in the way the sound was produced with a feather and in the shape of the case.[45]

Decline of the Psaltery

In Italy, France, and Spain, the psaltery remained in use through the sixteenth century. Psalteries were among the instruments used in *intermedi* for the wedding of Cesare d'Este and Virginia Medici at Florence in 1585 and for the wedding of Ferdinand I and Christine of Lorraine at Venice in 1589.[46] Alessandro Tassoni (1565-1635) wrote, about 1600, "I saw many years ago two things called *salterio*s in a board-like shape with cittern strings and saw one being played with a curved plectrum in the ancient manner, but, whether it came from the instrument or the performer, to me it appeared that it had not advanced much from the Moorish *dabbudà*."[47] Clearly by that time it had become rare in Italy. Zarlino in 1588 categorized the psaltery as a stringed instrument without keys played with both hands, like the harp, and Cerone, in 1613, mentioned it as a stringed instrument.[48] Inventories of the Medici, made in 1640, 1654, and 1664, mention them, although they were "in bad condition" in the last years.[49]

By the late sixteenth and early seventeenth centuries, the design of the dulcimer had begun to influence that of the psaltery. Praetorius illustrates a trapezoidal instrument, remarking that "such as it is still in use, I have never seen another, as triangular [i.e., trapezoidal]."[50] A woodcut

by the Swiss artist Tobias Stimmer (1539-1584) shows a woman plucking, with her fingers, a trapezoidal *Hakpret* with eight or nine double
courses and two bridges, with an inscription which declares "with women
it is very common."[51] Perhaps this was a Swiss fashion, as a painting
from about 1540, *The Castalian Fountain*, depicting an allegory of music, with both newer and older instruments, shows a woman plucking a
trapezoidal dulcimer on her lap, while elsewhere in the illustration a
woman plays a pig's head psaltery.[52] The presence of the two instruments in the same painting probably indicates that the painter regarded
them as distinct. See chapters 8 and 9 for further developments in psal-
tery-dulcimer hybrids in Italy and France.

Although rare, the psaltery survived into the eighteenth century in
England and Germany. Galpin illustrates a trapezoidal instrument, dated
1789, with eight single strings. He also cites a seventeenth-century he-
raldic manuscript by Randle Holme which depicts a rectangular
"shepherd's harp."[53] Adelung, in 1798, wrote that "there is still in some
regions [presumably in Germany], under the name of the *Psalter*, a type
of stringed musical instrument which accompanies the vocal part and
resembles the dulcimer, only that it is far narrower in proportion to its
breadth, has a deep sound box, and is struck with feather quills."[54]

Evidence for its use in the United States is also sparse, yet intrigu-
ing. It would appear that the "psalter" advertised by Michael Hillegas of
Philadelphia in 1764, which was listed between "violin d'amours" and
"guitars" among a variety of imported musical instruments, was an Italian *salterio* or French *psalterion* rather than a book of psalms.[55] In the
mid-1830s, the German lexicographer Gustav Schilling wrote

> in some areas, and namely in America, there also still exists at this
> moment an instrument with the name "psalter," "psalterion," or
> "salterion," although it is not exactly found very frequently. It consists
> of a four-inch high, trapezoidal case with soundboards; the upper is strung
> with three octaves of metal strings, which are played with the fingers. In
> playing, the instrument lays flat in front of the musician. It has much
> similarity with the dulcimer . . . only that it is not strung with multiple
> strings and is not struck with bats or little hammers.[56]

Schilling does not credit his source of information, and we are left to
wonder about the communities in which this instrument was played.
Perhaps a German-speaking correspondent may have described its use
in a German, or Pennsylvania Dutch, region. In any case, the detailed

description leaves little doubt that a psaltery was played in the United States at that time.

Certain surviving instruments also indicate the use of a psaltery in the United States in the early nineteenth century. The Winterthur Museum and Gardens has a "dulcimer" (M57.99.3), which the museum assigns a date from 1790 to 1825 and a Pennsylvania provenance. With its asymmetrical, incurved oblique sides, it recalls fifteenth-century instruments, although it is much bigger. Its length is 72 inches (183 cm), width is 20¼ inches (51 cm), and height is 4¾ inches (12 cm). Fifteen metal strings are stretched over a single bridge, which appears to divide them into octaves. Tuned diatonically, this would result in a three-octave range, just as Schilling describes. Cornelius Weygandt describes a half-trapezoidal instrument from York County, Pennsylvania, 30½ inches (77.5 cm) and 11 inches (27.9 cm) long, 20 inches (50.8 cm) wide, and 7½ inches (19 cm) high, with twenty pins set into the square end, holding metal strings.[57]

The Henry Ford Museum has a trapezoidal instrument, probably from the first half of the nineteenth century, which is lightly constructed and has metal pins on either pin block indicating 22 single strings. Wires and bridges, if any, are missing. It is 34 inches (86.3 cm) and 9½ inches (24.1 cm) long, 21½ inches (54.6 cm) wide, and 6 to 4 inches (15.2 to 10.2 cm) deep, the long side shallower than the short side. Another early nineteenth-century instrument of this type, at Old Sturbridge Village, is 20¼ inches (51.4 cm) on the long side, 13¼ inches (33.7 cm) on the short side, and 3¾ inches (9.5 cm) deep. It had eighteen single strings, of which one brass string survives, attached to wooden pegs on one side and nails on the other.

The provenance of these last two museum examples is unknown, so we cannot know what their makers actually called them. Yet there seems to be some evidence for limited use of either dulcimers that were exclusively plucked or homemade psaltery-like instruments with single strings. I was told by an informant in 1977 that his grandfather, a resident of Bradford, Illinois, who was born around 1847, played a trapezoidal instrument he called a "lyre," using celluloid picks. A half-trapezoidal "American zither" was manufactured by the Zither Manufacturing Company in the latter part of the nineteenth century, with fifteen single strings and measuring 18 inches (45.7 cm) on its longest side and 9 inches (22.9 cm) in width, but its name suggests influence from the Bavarian zither, then hugely popular among German immigrants, rather than from an older psaltery tradition.[58] Certainly that is true for the autoharp, guitar-zither, and other patented instruments manufactured by German-Americans in the late nineteenth and early twentieth centuries.

Around Tug Fork, West Virginia, at the middle of the twentieth century, an instrument called a psaltery was played by women in a Brethren church, before and after services, during the meditations between the sermons, and to accompany hymns. This was a rectangular stringed instrument with a lid and legs, resembling the "piano-harps" manufactured by James MacKenzie in Minneapolis.[59] Although no further information on this particular tradition has come to light, the German heritage of this denomination might indicate a survival of the instrument described by Schilling.

The folk singer Robert Beers acquired one of James MacKenzie's "piano-harps" in the early 1950s and devised his own method of playing it, calling it a psaltery after reading a description in a book.[60] He played it in performances with his wife and daughter until his death in 1972, including one at the White House, and inspired several people to learn to play it after his style. His use of the instrument, however, was not based in tradition.

The String Drum

The instrument which Sibyl Marcuse calls the "string drum" is a direct ancestor of the *Hackbrett,* which Herbert Heyde has demonstrated through a careful and systematic analysis of iconographic evidence.[61] According to illustrations dating from about 1360 to 1480, it was a long box, approximately 120 to 140 cm (47 to 55 inches) in length, but with shorter and longer examples as well, about 10 (4 inches) to 15 cm (9 inches) in width, and perhaps 4 (1½ inches) to 7 cm (2¾ inches) deep. It had two strings, presumably gut, which were struck by one or two sticks approximately 25 cm (10 inches) long. It rested on the player's shoulder when in play. If the player used one hammer, the free hand might hold up one end of the instrument. If played with two hammers, it rested on the ground. Its strings were undoubtedly tuned in fourths or fifths, and it acted as a bourdon instrument, much like its present-day descendant, the *tambourin à cordes*, used in the Pyrenees to accompany the performer's own flute playing.[62]

The "string drum" clearly was descended from the monochord, a long box over which one string was stretched. Scholars used it to demonstrate and teach the Pythagorean theory of intervals as well as to tune organs. One version became a minstrel's instrument, mostly in the south of France, and Heyde speculates that it was in that area that the string drum evolved. He makes a good case that the *chorus* or *choron*, mentioned by French authors during the fourteenth and fifteenth centuries, was this instrument. Aimeric de Peyrac, in the early fourteenth century, mentions "certain resounding *chori* strung with double strings."[63] In any case, the French author Jean de Gerson, writing about 1413, remarked that the *chorus* was the name given to an instrument by common people, which was an oblong, hollow piece of wood with two or three strings much thicker than those of a harp, which were struck by a stick, giving a harsh (*rudis*) sound.[64] Marcuse suggests that the term *chorus*, having been mentioned in a list of instruments by St. Augustine, was applied to several instruments capable of emitting two tones simultaneously.[65]

Figure 2.2: Drawing from an illumination of a fantastic creature playing a string drum, made perhaps about 1460 by a Dutch master. Source: Book of Hours, Ms. 234 ter, Bibliothèque Municipale, Laon, in Edouard Fleury, *Les instruments de musique sur les monuments du moyen age du Département de l'Aisne* (Laon: A. Cortilliot, 1882), opp. p. 58.

As Heyde comments, Gerson's remark about its "harsh" sound and "common" associations is consistent with that of Henri Arnaut of Zwolle, a Burgundian scholar, who described the *dulce melos* about 1440. The latter gave the instrument three meanings, one made in the "common and gross manner," which was struck by a "stick which produces contact with the strings, in the village manner," and the other two as forms of a keyboard instrument.[66] Arnaut's Latin term clearly links this instrument to the instrument that the French were beginning to call *doulcemèr* at this period. The links will be discussed in the next chapter.

Notes

1. Carl Engel, *The Music of the Most Ancient Nations* (1864; reprint, Freeport, N.Y.: Books for Libraries Press, 1970), 43-45.

2. Francis W. Galpin, *Old English Instruments of Music: Their History and Character*, 3rd ed., rev. (London: Methuen & Co., 1932), 66-67.

3. *Bishops' Bible, 1568: A Machine-Readable Transcript* (Cambridge: Chadwyck-Healey, 1996); *Geneva Bible, 1587: A Machine-Readable Transcript* (Cambridge: Chadwyck-Healy, 1996).

4. Alfred Sendrey, *Musik in Alt-Israel* (Leipzig: Deutscher Verlag für Musik, n.d.), 305; Galpin, *Old English Instruments*, 67.

5. Curt Sachs, *The History of Musical Instruments* (New York: W. W. Norton & Co., 1940), 84-85.

6. Sibyl Marcuse, *Musical Instruments: A Comprehensive Dictionary* (London: Country Life Ltd., 1964), 325, 501, citing Edith Gerson-Kiwi, "Musique," in *Dictionnaire de la Bible* (Paris, 1950).

7. Philemon Holland, *The Romane Historie Written by T. Livius of Padua* (London: Adam Islip, 1600), 1026 (Book 39, chapter 6).

8. Thomas Heywood, *Troia Brittanica* (London: W. Jaggard, 1609), 141 (Canto 7, line 39).

9. Eino Kolari, "Musik und ihre Verwendung im Alten Testament" (Ph.D. diss., University of Helsinki, 1947), 78-79; Francis W. Galpin, *The Music of the Sumerians and Their Immediate Successors, the Babylonians and Assyrians* (Cambridge: at the University Press, 1937), 36.

10. Kolari, "Musik," 79.

11. Galpin, *Music of the Sumerians*, pl. 8.

12. Sachs, *History of Musical Instruments*, 83-85.

13. See, for example, K. Vertkov, "Geschichte der russischen Guslitypen," *Studia instrumentorum musicae popularis* 1 (1969): 134-141; Dorota Poplawska, "String Instruments in medieval Russia," *RIdIM/RCMI Newsletter* 21 (Fall 1996): 63-70; Frederick Crane, *Extant Medieval Musical Instruments* (Iowa City: University of Iowa Press, 1972), 7-10. Joachim Braun, "Musical Instruments in

Byzantine Illuminated Manuscripts," *Early Music* 8 (July 1980): 319, interprets two eleventh-century Byzantine illustrations as psalteries, and suggests that one is a link to the *kantele-gusli* type. That appears likely, but the illustration is of a five-stringed lyre, not psaltery.

14. Robert Stevenson, *Spanish Music in the Age of Columbus* (The Hague: Martinus Nijhoff, 1960), 3, 8.

15. Henry George Farmer, "The Canon and Eschaquiel of the Arabs," *The Journal of the Royal Asiatic Society of Great Britain and Ireland*, Apr. 1926, 241.

16. Wilhelm Stauder, *Alte Musikinstrumente in ihrer vieltausendjährigen Entwicklung und Geschichte* (Braunschweig: Klinkhardt & Biermann, 1973), 83.

17. Codex fragment, Museu Diocesà, no. 8011, in Higini Anglès, *La musica a Catalunya fins al segle XIII* (Barcelona: Institut d'Estudis Catalans: Biblioteca de Catalunya, 1935), pl. 15.

18. R. Payne Smith, *Thesaurus Syriacus* (Oxford: e typographeo Clarendoniano, 1879-1901), 3613, in Farmer, "Canon and Eschaquiel," 245f.

19. Henry George Farmer, *Islam*, Musikgeschichte in Bildern, vol. 3: Musik des Mittelalters und der Renaissance, Lieferung 2 (Leipzig: VEB Deutscher Verlag für Musik, n.d.), 50-51.

20. Stauder, *Alte Musikinstrumente*, 84-85, 89. The Palermo fresco also appears in Farmer, *Islam*, 59. The Santiago de Compostela carving was incorrectly described as a dulcimer by Sachs, *History of Musical Instruments*, 258.

21. Farmer, "Canon and Eschaquiel," 245-247.

22. Israel Adler, *Hebrew Writings Concerning Music: In Manuscripts and Printed Books from Geonic Times up to 1800*, Répertoire international des sources musicales B IX2 (Munich: G. Henle Verlag, 1975), 8.

23. Stevenson, *Spanish Music in the Age of Columbus*, 47-48.

24. Stauder, *Alte Musikinstrumente*, 88.

25. For examples of illustrations of this, see Stauder, *Alte Musikinstrumente*, 86, pl. 126, showing a triptych from Piedra, Spain, dated 1390; and Sibyl Marcuse, *A Survey of Musical Instruments* (New York: Harper & Row, 1975), 212, showing an angel playing one with thirteen triple courses, in a detail of *The Coronation of the Virgin*, by Paolo and Giovanni Veneziano, dated 1478.

26. For example, in Turino Vanni the Second, *Madonna and Angels*, in the Louvre, in Raimond van Marle, *The Development of the Italian Schools of Painting* (1923-1938; reprint, New York: Hacker Art Books, 1970), 5: 251, fig. 164, and in a painting by Jacopo da Cione, illustrated in Claude LaPointe, "A Case Study in Iconographic Research," *RIdIM/RCMI Newsletter* 4 (Jan. 1979): 8, ill. no. 7.

27. Friedrich Dick, "Bezeichnungen für Saiten- und Schlaginstrumente in der altfranzösischen Literatur," *Giessener Beiträge zur romanischen Philologie* 25 (1932): 102.

22   *Chapter 2*

28. Francesco da Barberino, *Reggimento e costumi di donna* (Bologna: Romagnoli, 1875), part 1, chapter 5, paragraph 2.

29. Felipe Pedrell, *Organografía musical antigua española* (Barcelona: Juan Gili, 1901), 54n.

30. Dick, "Bezeichnungen," 41.

31. MS Gough Liturgy 2, f. 32, in Mary Remnant, *English Bowed Instruments from Anglo-Saxon to Tudor Times* (Oxford: Clarendon Press, 1986), pl. 28.

32. Remnant, *English Bowed Instruments*, pl. 29, 33, 36.

33. Stauder, *Alte Musikinstrumente*, 87, pl. 127.

34. Galpin, *Old English Instruments*, pl. 52.

35. Michael Praetorius, *Syntagma musicum*, vol. 2, *De organographia* (1619; reprint, Kassel: Bärenreiter, 1958), index.

36. Lukáš Matoušek, "Regional Signs of medieval Musical Instruments," *Hamburger Jahrbuch für Musikwissenschaft* 12 (1994): 209.

37. A preliminary report, based on 250 illustrations, was compiled by LaPointe, "Case Study in Iconographic Research," 3-12.

38. Robert Wangermée, *Flemish Music and Society in the Fifteenth and Sixteenth Centuries* (New York: Frederick A. Praeger, 1968), 198.

39. See, for example, Geoffrey Chaucer, *The Maunciple's Tale*, line 268; *Lybeaus Desconus*, line 147; *The Romance and Prophecies of Thomas of Erceldoune*, line 258; *Le bone Florence of Rome*, line 63; *The Romance of Guy of Warwick*, 635, line 11; *Sir Gawain and the Carl of Carlisle*, line 598; William Langland, *The Vision of Piers Plowman*, 13.233.

40. Dick, "Bezeichnungen," 36-40.

41. Archives nationales, K K 269, f. 26v., in Victor Gay, *Glossaire archéologique du moyen age et de la renaissance* (1887; reprint, Nendeln: Kraus Reprint, Ltd., 1967), 2: 276.

42. Geoffrey Chaucer, *The Miller's Tale*, lines 3213-3218.

43. Christopher Page, "Early 15th-Century Instruments in Jean de Gerson's 'Tractatus de Canticis,'" *Early Music* 6 (July 1978): 341.

44. LaPointe, "Case Study in Iconographic Research," 11.

45. Praetorius, *Syntagma musicum*, 2: 76.

46. Bastiano de'Rossi, *Descrizione del magnificentiss. apparato, e de' maravigliosi intermedi fatti per la commedia rappresentata in Firenze nelle felicissime nozze degl' illustrissimi, ed eccellentissimi Signori il Signor Don Cesare d'Este e la Signora Donna Virginia Medici* (Florence: G. Marescotti, 1585), 65; Cristofano Malvezzi, *Intermedii et concerti* (Venice: G. Vincenti, 1591), in Nino Pirrotta and Elena Povoledo, *Music and Theatre from Polizano to Monteverdi* (Cambridge: Cambridge University Press, 1982), 219.

47. Alessandro Tassoni, 1565-1635, *Paragone degli ingegni antichi e moderni*, M. Recchi, ed. (Lanciano: R. Carabba, 1915), 2: 126, in Salvatore Battaglia, *Grande dizionario della lingua italiana*, s.v. "Dabbudà."

48. Gioseffo Zarlino, *Sopplimenti Musicali* (1588; reprint, Ridgewood, N.J.: Gregg Press, 1966), 217; Pietro Cerone, *El Melopeo y maestro: tractado de musica theorica y pratica* (Napoles: Iuan Bautista Gargano y Lucrecio Nucci, 1613), 1038.

49. Frederick Hammond, "Musical Instruments at the Medici Court in the Mid-Seventeenth Century," in *Studien zur italienisch-deutschen Musikgeschichte* 10, Analecta Musicologia 15 (Cologne: A. Volk, 1975), 203, 207, 213.

50. Praetorius, *Syntagma musicum*, 2: 76.

51. Karl M. Klier, *Volkstümliche Musikinstrumente in den Alpen* (Kassel: Bärenreiter-Verlag, 1956), pl. 46.

52. *The Castalian Fountain*, in the Historisches Museum Basel, in Silvia and Walter Frei, *Mittelalterliche schweizer Musik*, Schweizer Heimatbücher 130 (Bern: Verlag Paul Haupt, 1967), 56.

53. Galpin, *Old English Instruments*, 61.

54. Johann Christoph Adelung, *Grammatisch-kritisches Wörterbuch der hochdeutschen Mundart* (Leipzig: Breitkopf und Härtel, 1798), pt. 3, 855.

55. *Pennsylvania Gazette*, 5 Jan. 1764.

56. Gustav Schilling, ed., *Encyclopädie der gesammten musikalischen Wissenschaften, oder Universal-Lexicon der Tonkunst* (Stuttgart: Franz Heinrich Köhler, 1840), 5: 566-567.

57. Cornelius Weygandt, *The Dutch Country: Folks and Treasures in the Red Hills of Pennsylvania* (New York: D. Appleton-Century Co., 1939), 301f. He calls it a "zitter," but, as he groups it with the true zitter, a fretted instrument related to the Appalachian dulcimer, he may be incorrect.

58. A label identifies the manufacturer as at "40 Court Sq.," but I have not learned the city.

59. Andrea Brisse, letter to author, 25 August 1982.

60. David Kettlewell, "The Dulcimer" (Ph.D. diss., Loughborough University, 1976), 298a.

61. Heyde, "Frühgeschichte des europäischen Hackbretts (14.-16. Jahrhundert)," *Deutsches Jahrbuch für Musikwissenschaft* 18 (1973-1977): 152-156; Sybil Marcuse, *A Survey of Musical Instruments* (New York: Harper & Row, 1975), 200-202.

62. Heyde, "Frühgeschichte," 155-156, sources 57 to 72. He explains his method for determining dimensions on p. 163.

63. Heyde, "Frühgeschichte," 155; Marcuse, *Survey of Musical Instruments*, 200, defines it as a string drum, while Galpin, *Old English Instruments of Music*, 73, quotes it in a discussion of the English crowd.

64. Marcuse, *Survey of Musical Instruments*, 200; Heyde, "Frühgeschichte," 160, source 12, quoting Jean de Gerson, *De canticorum originali ratione*, in *Opera* (Augsburg: Martin Fisch, 1494), 3: 191f.

65. Marcuse, *Survey of Musical Instruments*, 201.

66. G. Le Cerf, with E.-R. Labande, ed., *Instruments de musique du XVe siècle: les traités d'Henri-Arnaut de Zwolle et de divers anonymes* (Paris: Editions Auguste Picard, 1932), 19. The other forms of *dulce melos* have been debated in Sibyl Marcuse, *Musical Instruments: A Comprehensive Dictionary*, 158-159, and elsewhere.

· 3 ·

The Dulcimer's Origins

Iconographical and textual evidence contradict the widely influential writings of Curt Sachs, which claim that the dulcimer's origin was in the Middle East.[1] Subsequent articles have repeated his claim so much that it popularly has become fact. However, Sachs confuses the psaltery with the dulcimer in using the relief sculpture at the cathedral of Santiago de Compostela as evidence and provides no further sources for his claim. Chapter 4 demonstrates that in Iran the *santur* first appears in its modern form as a dulcimer only at the end of the fifteenth century and that in an earlier, Egyptian form it was a vertically held box-zither identical to the early *qanun*. The dulcimer, on the other hand, first appears in textual and iconographic sources from Western Europe during the early fifteenth century, prior to the earliest Islamic iconographic evidence of a struck dulcimer. Had it arrived in Europe from the Islamic world as a fully developed dulcimer, we would expect to find earlier evidence of the instrument. None, however, has surfaced. Therefore we must accept the thesis, argued well by both David Kettlewell and Herbert Heyde, that the dulcimer arose in Western Europe independently.[2]

A carved ivory panel on the cover of a psalter in the British Library (Egerton 1139), presumably written for Melisenda, daughter of Baldwin II, King of Jerusalem (1118-1131), and wife of Fulk, Count of Anjou and King of Jerusalem (1131-1134), has a medallion depicting King David playing a flat, trapezoidal, stringed instrument with two long sticks. This was probably carved by a Greek working at their court in Jerusalem.[3] Later Byzantine iconography depicts the *qanun*,[4] but no further evidence of a dulcimer in the Byzantine world has appeared. If the instrument depicted on the cover is a psaltery, we do have relatively early evidence that a trapezoidal psaltery was in use in the eastern Mediterranean during this period. It may be that the artist's attempt to render plectra resulted in their being too long and straight to be realistic. Perhaps the *kyusle*, a psaltery with symmetrical sides used one hundred years ago by native peoples along the Volga River, including the Chuvash, Udmurts, Tatar, and Mari, descended from this instrument.[5] Such instruments appear in Russian sources by the fourteenth century.[6] Given the strong Byzantine influence in medieval Russian culture, we should probably look to Byzantium as the source of that instrument. If we accept this instrument depicted in the ivory panel as a dulcimer—and it appears to be one—we must regard it, however, as a dead end in the instrument's development. Three hundred years would elapse before evidence of the instrument appears either in Western or Eastern sources. More likely this instrument was a version of the *kyusle*.

Heyde deserves credit in assembling a comprehensive body of evidence for the early history of the dulcimer and to make conclusions, from that evidence, on its development.[7] My discussion here departs from his treatment mainly in that it regards the *Hackbrett* and *dulce melos* as having appeared to develop independently of each other, the first in Germany and the second in France. Although Heyde recognizes the different designs, he fails to see their correlation to the terms used in the German and French languages. Viewing the development of the *Hackbrett* and *dulce melos* as separate instruments helps us understand both the differences in design and origins and the differences in the social milieus in which the instruments were found during the fifteenth and early sixteenth centuries.

The Origins of the *Hackbrett*

Certain early forms of the horizontally placed dulcimer, which was presumably strung with metallic strings and struck with two hammers in order to allow the melody to be played, resemble the string drum very closely in their general shape. Heyde classifies this design as "beam"-shaped. Other early dulcimers which appear in fifteenth-century sources from German-speaking territories are also rectangular, but are shallower, a design which Heyde calls "table"-shaped. However, the difference between the beam-shaped instruments and relatively long and narrow table-shaped instruments is only in the depth of the sound box.

The rectangular dulcimers of the fifteenth century, whether in the shape of a beam or table, appear in sources mainly of German, but also Flemish, Dutch, and Italian origin. The sources include manuscript illuminations, church frescoes, wooden and stone carvings in churches, stained glass panels, copperplate engravings, and tapestries. The earliest source that Heyde identifies is a carpet fragment, dated about 1420, from Alsace, depicting a gentleman in aristocratic dress playing a rectangular dulcimer with about five courses, with a woman playing a harp.[8] Other instances of illustrations of the instrument occur with regularity after 1440.

Heyde postulates that the development of the dulcimer played with two hammers began at the latest about 1375, perhaps in the Duchy of Burgundy. He argues that beginning at the middle of the fourteenth century, commerce in the Low Countries started to flourish, leading to a growth in leisure activities of the nobility and merchant class. At the same time, changes in economic relationships between the peasantry and the nobility permitted rural culture to enter the city and court. The string drum, presumably a peasant instrument, became transformed into a melodic instrument whose ringing, metallic strings evoked sounds thought to be of a higher order. The development of the dulcimer, Heyde argues, was probably concurrent with that of the clavichord, which was mentioned by 1404, since he notes that Arnaut of Zwolle regarded the hand-struck dulcimer as one expression of the *dulce melos*.[9] However this may be, it was the rectangular *Hackbrett* of German-speaking territories that resembled the string drum and thus must have evolved from it, rather than the *doulcemèr* of France.

The Spread of the Early *Hackbrett*

The term *Hackbrett* (German, "chopping block") first appears as a musical term in 1447, when a Zurich court book mentions that a merchant, Ackli, and some of his associates sat with their goods at a market, and Ackli played the *hackbrett*, "for nobody in pleasure, but in pain."[10] A Dutch lexicon published in 1477 mentions the term *hackbord*.[11] Subsequent literary sources which refer to it by the German word *Hackbrett* or its cognates occur during the later fifteenth and sixteenth centuries in Switzerland (especially Basel), Swabia, Saxony, Lower Rhine, Transylvania, the Baltic coast, Denmark, Alsace, and Silesia.

28   *Chapter 3*

Literary sources for the instrument which have been discovered are far rarer than illustrations of it from the fifteenth and early sixteenth centuries. Nevertheless, by correlating literary sources with iconographic sources originating in Germanic areas, which show the rectangular dulcimer with courses of multiple strings, we can conclude that the fifteenth-century *Hackbrett* was different than the *doulcemèr* (*dulce melos*) of France. In contrast to the rectangular instruments depicted in German, Netherlandish, and Italian sources, French illustrations from the fifteenth and early sixteenth century generally show a shallow, squarish instrument with incurved upper corners (thus retaining the shape of the pig's head psaltery) or a central bulge at the front of the instrument. Its strings are arranged individually, rather than in the courses of the *Hackbrett*. Although Heyde notes this shape, he minimizes its obvious connections with the psaltery.[12]

Artistic license, lack of detail, and careless restorations often render it difficult for us to identify many specific details concerning the design of the fifteenth-century *Hackbrett*, yet enough sources exist from which we can draw some conclusions. Examples include an altar carving made in 1425 in the cathedral at Minden; a choir stall carving in St. Stephen's Cathedral in Vienna, presumably from 1426; a copperplate engraving made by the monogrammist "b g," probably at Frankfurt am Main, at the Bibliothèque Royale, Brussels; illuminations in the Codex of Otto of Passau (1448), at the Gymnasium Casimirianum, Coburg; and frescoes in the parish churches at Görlitz, Saxony, Germany (c.1450-1460), Lovran, Croatia (1470-1479), Håtuna, Uppland, Sweden (1448-1467), Dornbach, Carinthia, Austria (c.1463) (see illustration 4), Haimburg, Carinthia, Austria (1473), Hermagor, Carinthia, Austria (c.1480), Kranj, Slovenia (1460-1470), Goropec na Ihanom, Slovenia (c.1480), Gluho Vrhovlje, Slovenia (c.1480), Gorica, Slovenia (beginning of the sixteenth century), Mirna, Slovenia (c.1490).[13]

The rectangular instrument was also current in the Low Countries, as one can see in illuminations in the Book of Hours of Catherine of Cleves (c.1440-1445), in the Pierpont Morgan Library (see illustration 3); in Jean Mielot's *Traité des quatre dernières chosé*, painted in 1455 at Bruges, and the Breviary of Philip the Good of Burgundy (1455-1460), both at the Bibliothèque Royale, Brussels; and in *Madonna with Angels*, by Geertgen tot Sint Jans, painted at Haarlem about 1488, at the Van Beuningen Museum, Rotterdam.[14]

Italian sources show that the rectangular instrument was in that country: *Madonna in Adoration of the Child*, by Giovanni Boccati da Camerino (c.1460), in the Galleria Nazionale, Perugia; a choir stall carving in Aosta Cathedral (1469); a painting from a tavern in Bellinzona (c.1470-1480), in the Museo Civico Bellinzona; a fresco in St. Dominic's Church, Cortona (late fifteenth century); and an illumination in the Sforza Book of Hours, made in Milan in 1494, at the British Library.[15]

The geographic range of the rectangular dulcimer (including the few examples of Heyde's beam-shaped instrument) thus ranges from Sweden and Holland through Germany, Bohemia, and Austria, south to northern Italy and Slovenia. Such a distribution suggests that the instrument that first developed from the string drum began to be played in the German-speaking area and spread outward from there.

Some of the illustrations are detailed enough to allow us to make inferences about the design of the rectangular *Hackbrett*. The number of strings is generally not meaningful, due to artistic license. However, two of the sources appear to be accurate. The instrument in the Dornbach fresco (see illustration 4) clearly has four courses of three strings each, while Kuret interprets the instrument in the Mirna fresco as having four courses of two strings each.[16] This is a logical number, for two reasons. First, the pitch of strings of the same length must stay within a narrow gambit, perhaps consisting of an interval of a fourth, to be playable,[17] because at the high register the strings break at a certain pitch, while at the low register they become slack and inaudible. Second, dividing the strings by a bridge into a ratio of 3:2 increases the range of what would otherwise only contain the tonic, major second, major third, and perfect fourth to a full diatonic octave. Thus:

do		fa
ti		mi
la		re
sol		do

The illustrations show the strings being divided by bridges, but again we must question their accuracy. The Boccati painting, the "b g" engraving, the Bellinzona tavern painting, and the Gorica fresco show three bridges, while the Book of Hours of Catherine of Cleves, the Codex of Otto von Passau, and the frescoes at Dornbach, Gluho Vrhovlje, and Mirna depict only two bridges.

The number of sound holes, however, might provide a more mean-ingful indication of sounding lengths and therefore bridges, since in later dulcimers they tend to be placed on either side of the treble bridge in order to give a sense of symmetry. Thus the "b g" engraving, the Minden carving, the Breviary of Philip the Good, the Boccati painting, the Aosta carving, and the frescoes at Håtuna, Gluho Vrhovlje, and Gorica all have two sound holes, mainly carved rosettes, implying one dividing bridge, while the Book of Hours of Catherine of Cleves, the Bellinzona painting and frescoes at Lovran, Cortona, Dornbach, and Mirna, have three sound holes, implying two bridges dividing the strings into differ-ent intervals.

It would appear, then, that the strings on some of these rectangular dulcimers were divided by one and on others by two bridges. Those in-struments depicted with three bridges may have a single dividing bridge and two bridges acting as nuts. The most productive division for an instrument with one bridge, as noted above, would be in a ratio of 3:2. For one with two division bridges, logic would indicate 9:6:4, so that the shortest group would be tuned a fifth higher than the middle group, thus providing the instrument with a diatonic range of an octave and a fifth:

sol	do	fa
fa	ti	mi
mi	la	re
re	sol	do

The bridges on the instrument depicted in the Dornbach fresco are arranged, however, so that the shortest division is on the right side of the instrument. This probably means that the tuning on that instrument was such that the lowest tone was on the bottom left.

Since angels or kings play most of these rectangular dulcimers in the illustrations, it is problematic to make conclusions about the place of the instrument in fifteenth-century German and Italian society. Neverthe-less, an angelic or regal portrayal must imply that the artists thought that it produced a quality of sound appropriate for the nobility, clerics, and those classes aspiring to gentility. Paulus Paulirinus, of Prague, writ-ing in Latin about 1461, remarked that the oblong instrument "makes the sweetest harmony by its ringing sound, and of all [instruments] its sonority is [most] pleasing to me."[18] The engraving by "b g" shows an aristocratically dressed woman entertaining herself by playing the

Hackbrett with a man on the lute. A German woodcut from about 1500-1510 shows a scholar playing on a rectangular dulcimer.[19] The Zurich reference from 1447 mentions a merchant playing it, and in that city in 1482 a man was prosecuted for having stolen a *hackbrett* from the schoolmaster at Gunzenhausen and having pawned it to the Jews.[20]

Instruments with a trapezoidal outline began to appear in Germanic areas during the latter part of the fifteenth century. This new shape was undoubtedly a result of experiments to increase the instrument's range. A stone carving of an angel playing a trapezoidal dulcimer with eight strings from 1473 appears in the monastery cloisters of Himmelkron bei Kulmbach, Bavaria.[21] Other early depictions of trapezoidal instruments include one played by an angel in *Mary, Queen of Heaven* by the Master of the Saint Lucy Legend, painted in Bruges between about 1485 and 1500 (see illustration 6); an illumination in the border of a gradual completed in 1494 at Einsiedeln, Switzerland; an altar carving from St. Mary's Church in Parchim, Mecklenburg (c.1500); and an engraving of a muse in Tritonius, *Melopoiae sive harmoniae tetracentiae* (Augsburg, 1507).[22] By the early sixteenth century, the *Hackbrett* had assumed its modern form, further developments occurring mostly in the number and placement of strings.

Origins of the *Doulcemèr*

The term *dulce melos* (combining Latin *dulce*, "sweet," with Greek *melos*, "song") first appears about 1440 in the Duchy of Burgundy, which included much of what is today Belgium and northeastern France. Arnaut of Zwolle's comment about its "harsh" sound contrasts with later descriptions and illustrations which indicate an acceptance by and a fashion for the instrument among the highest echelon of French-speaking society. The only way to reconcile his statement with this evidence is to interpret, as Heyde has, his first meaning of *dulce melos* as the string drum. In any case, *dulce melos* was rendered into French usually as *doulcemèr* and must have referred to the instrument with wire strings.

Just as we can link the development of the rectangular *Hackbrett* from the string drum to sources from German-speaking areas, we can discover the origin of the *doulcemèr* in France. Unlike early German illustrations, the shape of the earliest dulcimers which appear in French sources starting about 1440 do not resemble the string drum. Instead, the outline of most French instruments resembles those of contemporary psalteries—a shallow, rectangular box with two incurved, convex upper corners.

We may regard some examples, although resting horizontally and having the same general outline as the hammered instruments, as transitional, because the players plucked the strings with plectra. In an illumination in the Breviary of René II of Anjou, Duke of Lorraine, in the Bibliothèque de l'Arsenal (c.1442-1453), a woman holds plectra, perhaps three or four inches long, in each hand. Her instrument has two sound holes and two ranges of strings (see illustration 5). A virtually identical instrument appears in the Diurnal of René II of Lorraine in the Bibliothèque Nationale de France (L. 10.491), with two sound holes and upper and lower ranges of strings, but has the addition of a bridge which probably divided the strings into fifths.[23] Another example, from René II's Breviary, also in the Bibliothèque Nationale, shows a minstrel playing such an instrument holding, like a pencil, a straight plectrum in his right hand and what appears to be a slightly curved hammer in his left hand.[24] Perhaps not without coincidence, these three examples are all from the Lorraine ducal court.

Our earliest record of the word "dulcimer" comes from the Lorraine court, which could mean that this form of the psaltery first developed there. In 1449, Robinet le Francoys, player of a *doulz de mer* (!), was paid six florins by Duke René I for having played for several days for him, the duchess, and others.[25] A *doulce-mère* player who belonged to the Lord of Vergy played at Verdun in 1506 for René II, grandson of René I.[26]

Other French examples of the psaltery-shaped *doulcemèr* being struck include *Tres belles heures des Louis de Savoye* (1440-1465), ms. lat. 9473, Bibliothèque nationale de France, though this illustration is faint; *Champion des dames*, by Martin le Franc (c.1460), Bibliothèque Municipale, Grenoble, ms. 875, which depicts two different dulcimers clearly being struck by gently curved hammers held in the players' fists; a version of Filostrato de Boccace, by Pierre d'Amboise, for Mary of Cleves, Bibliothèque Nationale de France; and an illumination in *Livre des echecs amoureux*, attributed to Robinet Testard (c.1505), ms. fcr. 143, Bibliothèque Nationale de France.[27]

Despite the evidence from the Lorraine court which seems to show that the *doulcemèr* was played partly with plectra, contemporary Frenchmen must have regarded it as distinct from the psaltery. Jehan Molinet's

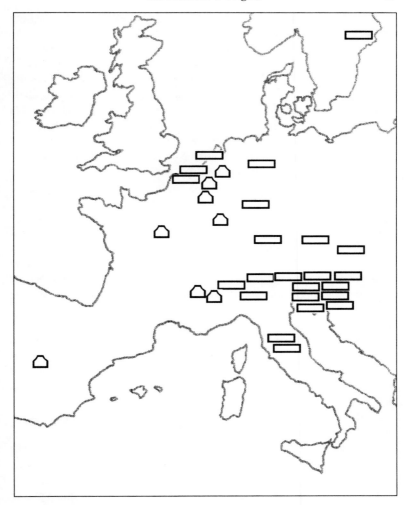

Figure 3.1: Distribution of fifteenth-century iconographic sources which depict rectangular dulcimers (*Hackbrett*s) and square dulcimers with incurved upper corners (*doulcemèr*s).

Les chansons Molinet de la journée guingaste (1479) mentions both *doulcemelles* and *psalterions* in a list of instruments.[28]

Evidence that the French instrument had gained popularity in Flanders by the end of the fifteenth century include an illumination by Master Guillebert in Augustine's *De civitate dei* (second half of the fifteenth century), ms. 9005, Bibliothèque Royale, Brussels; a tapestry, *Courtly Gathering in a Musical Conversation in the Open*, made at Brussels (c.1500), Germanisches Nationalmuseum; an altar painting (c.1500), by a Flemish master, in the Museu de Évora, Portugal; a tapestry from the beginning of the sixteenth century, Musée de Cluny; a tapestry made at Brussels (c.1520), in the Musées Royaux d'Art et d'Histoire, Brussels; and a tapestry, *The Prodigal Son Sets Out*, made at Brussels (c.1525), in The Minneapolis Institute of Arts (see frontispiece).[29]

The details of each of the instruments depicted in these sources vary, but they bear enough similarities for us to draw certain inferences. We have already noted Flemish examples of the rectangular instrument, but those are earlier, from the middle of the fifteenth century. This probably indicates that the French *doulcemèr* entered Burgundy and Flanders later than the *Hackbrett* and may have supplanted it. However, the earlier appearance in France of the instrument with this outline is undoubtedly an indication that the term *doulcemèr* referred to this instrument.

Unlike most of the Germanic examples, which are played by angels, the dulcimers in this group are mostly depicted as being played by actual people, although in some cases they might be muses. Of the thirteen examples, ten are played by stylish women; one is played by a man, presumably a minstrel; one is played by an angel; and one is unknown.[30] From this distribution we can be certain that the *doulcemèr* was, as Heyde remarks, one of the "lesdies instruments" of the aristocracy.[31]

Written sources confirm that the instrument was played at the highest social levels in French-speaking society. During the 1450s, Peter II, Duke of Brittany, conversed with Henri Guiot, a player of the *doulcemer*.[32] In 1454, Philip the Good, Duke of Burgundy, heard a *doulcemer* player at Wissembourg.[33] Musicians at the court of François II, Duke of Brittany (1458-1488) included "minstrels, trumpets, and *doulcemer* players."[34] Payments from the King of France were made in 1490 to Jehan de Tournou, *doulcemer* player, and to Jehan d'Avranches, *doulcemer* player.[35]

Some of the illustrations depict the dulcimer played in realistic situations. An ensemble of harp and dulcimer in the Musée de Cluny tapestry certainly depicts one, as Kettlewell remarks.[36] Others show dulcimer with portative, harp, lute, and two bells,[37] with recorder and portative,[38] fiddle, harp, and two recorders,[39] lute, rebec, harp, and bombard,[40] with recorder,[41] and with lute.[42]

Details of the design of the *doulcemèr* are more difficult to ascertain, due in part to the nature of the sources, several of which are tapestries. The Diurnal of René II of Lorraine shows a rather shallow instrument with two rosettes and a central bridge, perhaps resting at a ratio of 3:2. A lower group of about ten strings of equal length, attached to pins on the surface, is separated from an upper group of about six strings of varying length, which rest on the front of the instrument, against the convex corners.[43] The division bridge in this illustration, however, seems to be an early exception. Most of the illustrations of this instrument show only open strings which pass over nuts. The other transitional instrument, in the Breviary of René II of Anjou, depicts a very similar instrument, with two sound holes and two sections of strings, a lower one with five and an upper one with four, but with no central bridge (see illustration 5). Finally, in this transitional group, an illustration of a minstrel in the Breviary of René II of Lorraine shows an instrument with a single sound hole and about eight or ten strings of equal length which go over nuts on each side, held by pins on the surface. The player appears to hold a straight plectrum in his right hand and a curved hammer in his left.[44]

Most of the other illustrations of the *doulcemèr* indicate from five to twelve undivided strings of equal length. The *Champion des dames* illustration show dulcimers with three and four courses of two strings each. As we have seen with the discussion of early *Hackbretts*, the tuning of strings of equal length might allow a compass of a fourth, and these could be realistic. But it is difficult to understand how twelve strings of equal length could be tuned, unless many were in unison. Some instruments, however, must have been strung with strings of diminishing length, as the tapestry in the Musée de Cluny indicates.

From France, the *doulcemèr* spread to England, Spain, and Italy. Minstrels seeking service with foreign lords, as well as ladies-in-waiting to French and Burgundian princesses marrying foreign monarchs (such as René II of Anjou, Duke of Lorraine's daughter Margaret, who married Henry VI, King of England, in 1445), probably accounted for its spread. In France, however, it died out during the first part of the sixteenth century. The reference to the dulcimer player entertaining René II at Verdun in 1506 is the last. The Flemish tapestries from the 1520s, mentioned above, are the last to depict an instrument with the convex upper corners or central bulge at its front.

England

The earliest evidence for its use in England is the carving in the nave of Manchester Cathedral from about 1468, discussed by Galpin and Kettlewell, among others. This is an instrument with a trapezoidal outline—the earliest example of a dulcimer with that shape—about twenty strings, and no bridges, played by the angel with two slender hammers with the hooked ends downward.[45] In 1474, when Edward, Prince of Wales, visited Coventry, he was honored with a pageant at one station which featured three patriarchs and Jacob's twelve sons, "with mynstralcy of harpe and dowsemeris."[46] The *Squyr of Lowe Degre*, perhaps from about 1475, mentions "with fydle, recorde, and dowcemere."[47] A poem by the Welsh bard Gwaith Lewis Glyn Cothi, dated 1455-1485, mentions dulcimer (*dwsmel*) and harp (*thelyn*) together.[48]

Further literary evidence of the dulcimer in England includes a description of a pageant at Westminster in 1502 for Prince Arthur's wedding, which included

> all theise fresh apparelled Ladyes and women of honor having like Instruments of musicke as Claricordes, dusymers, claricimballs and such other; every each of them as well Lordes. . .as Ladyes. . .used and occupied and played uppon the Instrumentes all the waye comming from the lower end of Westminster Hall, till they came before the King and the Queenes Highnes and Majestie, so sweetly and with such noyse that in my mynde it was the first such pleasant myrth and property that ever was heard in England of longe season.[49]

The fact that women played "dusymers" at this pageant perfectly reflects the evidence from France and Flanders that society largely considered the dulcimer to be a woman's instrument. This use is further supported by John Barrett's *Alvearie or Quadruple Dictionarie* (1580), which defines "doulcimer" both as "an instrument of Musicke so called" and "a woman that plaieth on doulcimer."[50] Other English sources which mention the instrument do so in lists of instruments to emphasize sweet harmony. Stephen Hawes, in *The Pastime of Pleasure* (1509), writes "There sate dame musyke with all her mynstralsy / as taboures, trumpettes, with pypes melodyous / Sakbuttes, organs, and the recorder swetely /

Harpes, lutes, and crouddes ryght delycyous / Cymphans, doussemers w^t clarycymbales gloryous."[51] The romance *The Knyght of the Swanne* (1512) includes "pipes, taborins, doucimers, fidles, organs, psaltries, clavicordes, and mani other instruments there was in great nombre sowning al songes of armony" performing the day before the king's wedding.[52]

English iconography shows that minstrels also played it. The psalter of Henry VIII, from about 1540, includes an illustration of a minstrel playing a trapezoidal instrument with a lid and about ten or twelve strings; no bridges are visible.[53] An English stained glass panel, from the early sixteenth century, shows an angel playing a dulcimer in the shape of a book, a design which may be more figurative than literal. It has two rosettes, six strings, and two side bridges or nuts, and is played with two straight sticks.[54]

Spain

The evidence for its use in Spain is limited, but sufficient to demonstrate it had spread there from France. A Book of Hours in the Pierpont Morgan Library, probably illuminated at Toledo about 1470, contains an illustration of an angel playing an instrument with the characteristic central bulge at its front side and one central rosette, with long, straight sticks, but its eleven strings are stretched from front to back.[55] A poem by Juan del Encina, *El triunfo del amor*, from about 1496, mentions *dulcemelos, clavicordios, clavicimbalos, salterios, harpa, manaulo sonoro*.[56] An inventory of Queen Isabella's instruments in 1503 mentions a *dulçoemel* "for playing . . . in a case of wood."[57] As no later references appear, we can assume that it died out in Spain, as it did in France.

Italy

Italy appears to have had two distinct dulcimer traditions, an earlier one deriving from the *Hackbrett* and a later one deriving from the *doulcemèr.* The earliest Italian iconographic evidence, mentioned above and dating from about 1460 to 1494, shows long, rectangular instruments of the Germanic type. Heyde even recognizes, from these sources, pecularities of Italian design in the attachment of the strings to the side walls.[58]

The term *dolcemèle* appears in Italian sources from 1523 to about 1620. Lexicographers have equated the term *dabbuddà* with *dolcemèle*.[59] This may be based partly on an essay, *L'Ercolano*, by Benedetto Varchi (1503-1565), in which he distinguishes art from mere technical mastery: "The same breath and the same force seeks out to sound a horn that sounds a cornet, but not of course the same industry and mastery; it is still less the arms of the one who plays the *dolcemele* or the *dabbudà* as the one who plays the organs; it is, in short, art which gives perfection to things."[60]

Varchi's comments indicate that the *dabuddà* required two arms to play and thus was probably not the string drum (*altobasso*). But was the *dabbudà* just another word for the *dolcemèle*? This seems unlikely. The instruments clearly belonged to different social classes. The earliest reference to it, a sonnet by Domenico Burchiello (1404-1449), "Al medesimo Batista Alberti," with the opening lines "O, my Lord Sour, who poses as a poet / And who plays the *dabbudà* so well," obviously uses it sarcastically.[61] The disparaging comments about the psaltery, made about 1600 by Alessandro Tassoni (see chapter 2), that it "had not advanced from the Moorish *dabbudà* much," would at least seem to confirm its identity as a variety of dulcimer. The seventeenth-century poet Francesco Redi identifies it as a peasant instrument: "And among a hundred *colascioni* (long-necked lutes), a hundred raw country girls, playing the *dabbuddà*, the little song and dance the *bombababà*." Federigo Nomi mentions it in 1672 in a poem, "As drum here and there, a youth glances, striking the *dabbudà*."[62]

The term *dabbudà* definitely was a word for variety of dulcimer used in Italy from the fifteenth to seventeenth centuries, but it must have meant the dulcimer deriving from the rectangular instrument which probably entered from Austria. Obviously it retained its humble "chopping block" identity. Itinerant minstrels may thus have been responsible for its introduction to Italy. In 1691, a dictionary defined *dabbuddà* as an instrument "similar to the *buonaccordo* (clavichord), but without keys; today also called *ognaccordo*, and is played with two sticks, which strike the strings."[63] The instrument does not appear in later sources and probably went extinct about that time.

The *dolcemèle*, on the other hand, enjoyed a vogue among the patricians of northern Italy, especially in Venice, but also in Milan and Bologna, during much of the sixteenth century. Sabba da Castiglione, in his famous recommendations of 1560 to gentlemen on fashions, commented that some "rich, talented, not to say conceited, great lords and gentlemen . . . adorn [their rooms and studies] with musical instruments, like organs, harpsichords, clavichords, psalteries, harps, *dolcimele*, *baldosa*s, *pandora*s, and other similar ones."[64] Venetian inventories confirm his statement: one from 1549 lists a *dulcimello*, harpsichord, lute, and an old cittern, and another, from 1553, includes a *dulcimello*, "all framed and carved," along with five lutes, a *violon*, and two clavichords.[65] In the Bologna house of Felicini (died 1536) there were concerts of "lutes, viols, *dolsemelle*, harpsichords, clavichords, organs, *violunni*, recorders, cornets, and many other instruments."[66]

Italian writers on music in this period mentioned it in lists of stringed instruments. Pietro Aaron did so in 1523, as did Alessandro Citolini, in 1561, who described it as having metal strings, with rods, and Gioseffo Zarlino, in 1588, who classified it as a percussion instrument of hollow wood and metal strings.[67] Pietro Cerone, an Italian writing in Spanish in 1613, mentioned the *dulcemiel* as a stringed instrument.[68]

The evidence presented here suggests that the *dolcemèle* enjoyed a popularity among the upper classes in northern Italy after it had gone extinct in France and Spain and somewhat out of fashion in England. Likely it appeared as a domestic amusement, rather than as an instrument used in composed music for the church. It was used in a *mascherata* (masked procession) at Milan in 1574 along with many other instruments.[69] Michelangelo Buonarroti il giovane (1568-1646) poetically mentioned a consort which contained citterns, lutes, *pifferoni*, violins, and *dolzemeli*.[70] The *dolcemèle* must have died out during the seventeenth century, since literary references to it disappear.

Conclusion

Kettlewell and Heyde were the first to systematically study the origins of the dulcimer, thereby establishing that it originated in Europe. Although they recognized different types of dulcimers that were current in the fifteenth century, they did not understand that the *Hackbrett* and the *doulcemèr* had evolved independently, from two different instruments. As more iconographic sources for the instrument's history have surfaced in recent years, this separate evolution has become clearer. The status in society of the psaltery and the string drum appear to have determined that of the *doulcemèr* and *Hackbrett*, although at first each was embraced by the higher ranks. The *doulcemèr* soon went out of fashion in France and Burgundy, as the upper classes embraced keyboard instruments, while the *Hackbrett* became an instrument used by the middle classes and itinerant minstrels. This class division was illustrated most clearly in Italy. The subsequent history of the dulcimer, *Hackbrett*, and other dulcimer forms was determined in part by their social status at the beginning of their development.

Notes

1. Curt Sachs, *The History of Musical Instruments* (New York: W. W. Norton, 1940), 258.

2. David Kettlewell, "The Dulcimer" (Ph.D. diss., Loughborough University, 1976), 63-82; Herbert Heyde, "Frühgeschichte des europäischen Hackbretts (14.-16. Jahrhundert)," *Deutsches Jahrbuch für Musikwissenschaft* 18 (1973-1977): 135-172.

3. O. M. Dalton, *Catalogue of the Ivory Carvings of the Christian Era* (London: by Order of the Trustees, sold at the British Museum, 1909), 22-25.

4. For example, in sixteenth-century wall paintings at Varlaam Monastery, Meteora, and Philanthropinon Monastery, Ioannina, Greece, as illustrated in Fivos Anoyanakis, *Greek Popular Musical Instruments*, 2nd ed. (Athens: "Melissa" Publishing House, 1991), pls. 2, 56.

5. K. Vertkov, G. Blagodatov, and E. Yazovitskaya, *Atlas muzykal'nykh instrumentov narodov SSSR* (Moscow: Gosudarstvennoe Muzykal'noe Izdatel'stvo, 1962), 51, 53, 55, 57. In Mari, the name is *kyusle*; in Chuvash, *kyosle*; in Udmurts, *krez*; in Tatar, *gusli*.

6. Dorota Poplawska, "String Instruments in Medieval Russia," *RIdIM/RCMI Newsletter* 21 (Fall 1996): 65-66.

7. Kettlewell, "Dulcimer," 65-78, was the first to do so, but Heyde's body of evidence was larger.

8. Heyde, "Frühgeschichte," 166, source 76, citing Betty Kurth, *Die deutschen Bildteppiche des Mittelalters* (Vienna: A. Schroll, 1926), vol. 2, pl. 121.

9. Heyde, "Frühgeschichte," 152-153, 155-156.

10. *Schweizerisches Idiotikon* (Frauenfeld: Huber, 1905), 5: 901f., in Heyde, "Frühgeschichte," 161, source 33.

11. Gherard van der Schueren, *Theutonista of Duytschlender* (Cleve, 1477), 138, in Heyde, 161, source 34.

12. Heyde, "Frühgeschichte," 153.

13. Heyde, "Frühgeschichte," 165-166, sources 73, 77, 78, 79, 80, 85; Ingebjørg Barth Magnus and Birgit Kjellström, *Musikmotiv i svensk kyrkokonst: Uppland fram till 1625* (Stockholm: Svenska RIdIM-kommittén, 1993), 165;

Walter Salmen, *Katalog der Bilder zur Musikgeschichte in Österreich* (Innsbruck: Musikverlag Helbling, 1980), 100, no. 453; Uta Henning, "Musikikonographie in Kärnten," *Musicologica Austriaca* 10 (1991): 16-17, 23; Primo• Kuret, *Glasbeni instrumenti na srednjeveških freskah na Slovenskem* (Ljubljana: Slovenska Matica Ljubljana, 1973), 30, 42, 44, 56, 65, 112.

14. Heyde, "Frühgeschichte," 166, sources 81, 82, 86.

15. Heyde, "Frühgeschichte," 166, sources 83, 84; John Henry van der Meer, "Psalterium und Hackbrett," in *Das Hackbrett: ein alpenländisches Musikinstrument* (Herisau/Trogen: Verlag Schläpfer, 1975), 23, pl. 17; David Kettlewell, *All the Tunes There Ever Were: An Introduction to the Dulcimer in the British Isles* (Spoot, Glocs.: the author, 1976), fig. 48.

16. Kuret, *Glasbeni instrumenti*, 112.

17. This is a judgment based on experiments.

18. Standley Howell, "Paulus Paulirinus on Musical Instruments," *Journal of the American Musical Instrument Society* 5-6 (1979-1980): 15f. His choice of the word *dulce melos* may have been influenced by reading other Latin tracts, such as that of Henri Arnaut of Zwolle.

19. Heyde, "Frühgeschichte," 167, source 87; Alfred Quellmalz, "Musikdarstellungen auf Flugblattbildern," *Archiv für Musikforschung* 3 (1938): 24.

20. *Schweizerisches Idiotikon*, 34: 901f., in Heyde, "Frühgeschichte," 162, source 35.

21. Karl-Heinz Schickhaus, *Über Volksmusik und Hackbrett in Bayern* (Munich: BLV Verlagsgesellschaft, 1981), 145.

22. Heyde, "Frühgeschichte," 168-169, sources 110, 114, 115.

23. John Leach, "The Psaltery and Dulcimer," *The Consort* 34 (1978): 298-299.

24. Edmund A. Bowles, "Instrumente des 15. Jahrhunderts und Ikonographie," *Basler Jahrbuch für historische Musikpraxis* 8 (1984): 15; Nancy Groce, *The Hammered Dulcimer in America* (Washington: Smithsonian Institution Press, 1983), 14.

25. Albert Lecoy de La Marche, ed., *Extraits des comptes et mémoriaux du roi René pour servir à l'histoire des arts au XVe siècle* (Paris: A. Picard, 1873), art. 733, in Victor Gay, *Glossaire archéologique du moyen age et de la renaissance* (1887; reprint, Nendeln: Kraus Reprint, Ltd., 1967), 1: 567.

26. Albert Jacquot, *La musique en Lorraine* (Paris: A. Quantin, 1882), 28.

27. Heyde, "Frühgeschichte," sources 95, 99, 102, 103. These are illustrated in Jean Porcher, *L'Enluminure française* (Paris: Arts et métiers graphiques, 1959), pl. 85; Marc Pincherle, *An Illustrated History of Music* (New York: Reynal & Co., 1959), 26; David Munrow, *Instruments of the Middle Ages and Renaissance* (London: Oxford University Press, 1976), 24; and *La musique des origines à nos jours* (Paris, 1946), 121.

28. Jehan Molinet, *Les chansons Molinet de la journée guingaste*, lines 20, 22, MS fr. 1716, fols. 85v-86, Bibliothèque Nationale de France, in Edwin M.

42 *Chapter 3*

Ripin, "Towards an Identification of the Chekker," *The Galpin Society Journal* 28 (1975): 20. F. Godefroy, *Dictionnaire de l'ancienne langue française*, 2: 760, dates this poem at 1507.

29. Heyde, "Frühgeschichte," 167-168, sources 96, 97, 103, 104, 106, 108; Valentin Denis, *De muziekinstrumenten in de Nederlanden en in Italie* (Antwerp: Uitgeversmij. N. v. Standaard-boekhandel, 1944), pl. 146; Karel Moens, *Muziek & grafiek: burgermoraal en muziek in de 16de. en 17de. eeuwse Nederlanden* (n.p.: Pandora, 1994), pl. 24; Fabienne Joubert, *La tapisserie médiévale au Musée de Cluny* (Paris: Editions de la Réunion des Musées Nationaux, 1987), 121.

30. Heyde, "Frühgeschichte," 168, source 105, also notes an illumination in a Flemish manuscript from about 1520 depicting a woman playing a dulcimer at mealtime in the open, but I have not seen this illustration and cannot say whether the instrument belongs in this category.

31. Heyde, "Frühgeschichte," 149, citing Jeanne Marix, *Histoire de la musique et des musiciens de la cour de Bourgogne sous le règne de Philippe le Bon* (Strasbourg: Heitz, 1939), 102, 104.

32. Arthur Le Moyne de la Borderie, *Histoire de Bretagne* (Rennes: J. Pilhon et L. Hommay, 1906), 4: 384, in Heyde, "Frühgeschichte," 161, source 18.

33. Marix, *Histoire de la musique*, 69.

34. Gérard Lomenec'h, *Chantres et ménestrels à la cour de Bretagne* (Rennes: Editions Ouest-France, 1993), 163.

35. Archives nationales, KK 76, ff. 156, 502, in Gay, *Glossaire archéologique*, 1: 567.

36. Kettlewell, "Dulcimer," 74a.

37. Porcher, *L'Enluminure française*, pl. 85.

38. Breviary of King René II of Anjou, MS 601, f. 2, Bibliothèque de l'Arsenal; see illustration 6.

39. Breviary of René II, Duke of Lorraine, Bibliothèque Nationale de France, in Groce, *Hammered Dulcimer*, 14.

40. Tapestry, *Courtly Gathering in a Musical Conversation in the Open*, Brussels, c.1500 (Hampe-Katalog no. 813), Germanisches Nationalmuseum.

41. Tapestry, *The Prodigal Son Sets Out*, Flanders, c.1517-1530, Minneapolis Institute of Arts, in Candace J. Adelson, *European Tapestry in The Minneapolis Institute of Arts* ([Minneapolis]: Institute of Arts, 1994), 59.

42. Tapestry, Brussels, c.1520, *The Prodigal Son*, part of a series called *The Victory of Virtues*, in the Musées Royaux d'Art et d'Histoire, Brussels.

43. Leach, "Psaltery and Dulcimer," 299.

44. Groce, *Hammered Dulcimer*, 14.

45. Francis W. Galpin, *Old English Instruments of Music: Their History and Character*, 3rd ed. (London: Methuen, 1932), 64-65; Kettlewell, "Dulcimer," 71a. Kettlewell dates it at about 1460.

46. Mary Dormer Harris, ed., *The Coventry Leet Book: Or Mayor's Regis-*

ter, Early English Text Society, o.s., 134 (London: for the Society by Kegan Paul, Trench, Trübner & Co., 1907), 392.

47. Line 1075, in Galpin, *Old English Instruments of Music*, 64. The date of this poem is uncertain, but the *Oxford English Dictionary* assigns it as c.1475.

48. E. D. Jones, ed., *Gwaith Lewis Glyn Cothi* (Cardiff: Gwasg Prifysgol Cymru, 1953), 447, in *Geiriadur Prifysgol Cymru: A Dictionary of the Welsh Language* (Cardiff: Gwasg Prifysgol Cymru, 1950-1967), 1107.

49. Paul Reyher, *Les masques anglais* (Paris: Hachette, 1909), 500f., in John Stevens, *Music & Poetry in the Early Tudor Court* (London: Methuen, 1961), 250.

50. John Barrett, *An Alvearie or Quadruple Dictionarie*, 2nd ed. (London: 1580), n.p. The author died in 1578 and had begun work on it about 1555, but one must assume revisions appeared in the later edition. I have not seen the first edition.

51. Lines 1527 to 1531, Stephen Hawes, *The Pastime of Pleasure*, Early English Text Society, o.s., 173 (London: for the Early English Text Society by N. Milford, Oxford University Press, 1928), 61.

52. William J. Thoms, ed., *Early English Prose Romances*, new ed. (London: George Routledge and Sons, n.d.), 698. This was originally published in 1512 at London by Wynkyn de Worke.

53. Henry VIII's Psalter, Royal MS, 2A.XVI, f. 98v., British Library, illustrated, for example, in John Leach, "The Dulcimer," *The Consort* 25 (1968-1969): 392; Kettlewell, *All the Tunes That Ever There Were*, 9; Christopher Hogwood, *Music at Court* (London: The Folio Society, 1977), 31; and Groce, *Hammered Dulcimer*, 16.

54. "London Salerooms," *Early Music* 8 (July 1980): 381.

55. M. 1001, f. 139, Pierpont Morgan Library.

56. Higinio Anglès, *Historia de la musica medieval en Navarra* (Foral de Navarra: Institucion Principe de Viana, 1970), 424.

57. Felipe Pedrell, *Organografía musical antigua española* (Barcelona: Juan Gili, 1901), 91. Marcuse, *Musical Instruments: A Comprehensive Dictionary*, 159, interprets *dulçoemel para tañer* ("for playing") as the keyboard *dulce melos* described by Henri Arnaut of Zwolle.

58. Heyde, "Frühgeschichte," 166, source 75.

59. Francesco D'Alberti di Villanuova, *Dizionario universale* (Milan: 1825), 280; Battaglia, *Grande dizionario della lingua italiana*, s.v. "Dabbudà."

60. Benedetto Varchi, "L'Ercolano," in *Opere*, vol. 2 (Trieste: dalla Sezione Letterario-Artistica del Lloyd Austriaco, 1859), 148.

61. *Sonetti del Burchiello del Bellincioni e d'altri poeti fiorentini* (London: 1757), 127.

62. Battaglia, *Grande dizionario della lingua italiana*, s.v. "Dabbudà," citing Francesco Redi, *Opere* (Milan: Società tipografica de' classici italiani, 1809-1811), 1: 14, and Federigo Nomi, *I quattro libri delle poesie liriche d'Orazio Flacco* (Florence: All'insegna della Nave, 1672), 23.

63. *Vocabolario degli accademici della Crusca* (Florence, 1691), s.v. "Dabbudà."

64. Sabba da Castiglione, *Ricordi* (Venice: Paolo Gerardo, 1560), 56.

65. Stefan Toffolo, *Strumenti musicali a Venezia: nella storia e nell'art dal XIV al XVIII secolo* (Cremona: Editrice Turvis, 1995), 56.

66. Emilie Elsner, "Untersuchung der instrumentalen Besetzungspraxis der weltlichen Musik im 16. Jahrhundert in Italien" (Ph.D. diss., Berlin, 1935), 84.

67. Pietro Aaron, *Thoscanello de la musica* (1523; reprint, New York: Broude Brothers, 1969), book 1, chapter 4; Alessandro Citolini, *La tipocosmia de Alessandro Citolini* (Venice: Vincenzo Valgrisi, 1561), 493-494; Gioseffo Zarlino, *Sopplimenti Musicali* (1588; reprint, Ridgewood, N.J.: Gregg Press, 1966), 217.

68. Pietro Cerone, *El Melopeo y maestro: tractado de musica theorica y pratica* (Naples: Iuan Bautista Gargano y Lucrecio Nucci, 1613), 1038.

69. Elsner, "Untersuchung," 23.

70. Michelangelo Buonarroti il giovane, "L'Ajone," in *Opere varie* (Florence: Felice Le Monnier, 1863), 320.

1

2

3

4

5

6

7

8

9

10

11

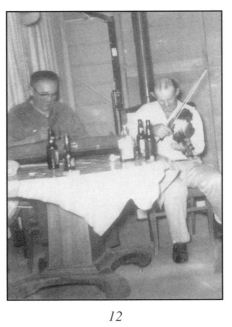

12

13

14

15

16

17

HEARING.

18

19

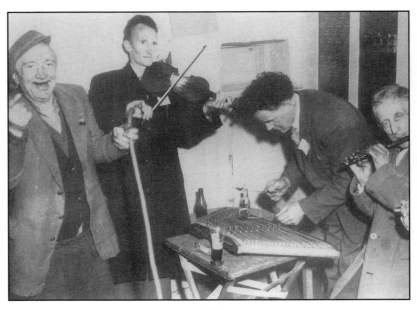

20

21

22

23

24

25

26

27

28

29

30

31

32

· 4 ·
The *Santur*

History

Although the European origin of the dulcimer and *Hackbrett* has been argued successfully by Kettlewell and Heyde and further expanded in chapter 3, writers who have not investigated the topic unfortunately will probably continue to echo the brief but false assertion by Sachs that the dulcimer originated in the Middle East. Even some writers on Islamic music, following authorities on the history of Western music, mistakenly follow the argument of Sachs and reiterate its alleged origin in antiquity.[1] Henry George Farmer, however, found no evidence of a dulcimer in Islamic writings on music or in iconography and suggested that it first appeared in Iran during the seventeenth century, perhaps through Turkish influence.[2]

Ibn Sīnā (980-1037), in his *Kitāb al-shīfāʻ*, describes an instrument, the *ṣanj jini* or *ṣini* ("Chinese *sanj*"), which was struck with sticks.[3] His disciple al-Huṣain ibn Zaila (died 1048), in *Kitāb al-kāfī fī'l-mūsīqī*, mentions the *ṣanj* and *shahrūd* as instruments with open strings, and describes the "Chinese *ṣanj*" as an instrument that "you play on with beating-rods (*maṭāriq*)."[4] While these descriptions might indicate a dulcimer, they also seem to describe a Chinese instrument of some sort, perhaps a type of *qin* or a version of the Korean *komun-ko*, which is played with a stick. In any case, there is no reason to assume a line of development connecting this instrument, whatever it was, to the *santur*.

The word *santur* derives ultimately from the Aramaic *pesanterin* and Greek *psalterion*. The form of the word in the oldest Arabic texts is *sanṭīr*. Farmer feels that the mention of the *sanṭīr* in "The Story of

Janshah" in *The Arabian Nights* is a "late fiction," but George Sawa
suggests that, since the *qanun* and *santur* were not in use at the time of
Harūn al-Rashīd (died 809), the term was interpolated at a later time or
that it referred to an open-stringed instrument, the *mi'zafah*.[5] A twelfth-
century Persian poem by Manucheri may mention the word *santur*, but
Zonis cites a hypothesis that this word could also be *shaypūr*, a trumpet,
as some manuscripts have it.[6] The earliest Islamic treatises on music do
not mention the *santīr*, and thus we can conclude that even if the word,
which had survived from antiquity, denoted an instrument in use, we
cannot be sure what the instrument was.

The earliest significant descriptive source for the *santīr* is a fourteenth-century Egyptian manuscript, *Kashf al-ghumūm*, in the collections of the Topkapi Palace Museum in Istanbul. This includes an illustration of a man holding a half-trapezoidal instrument in front of his
body, with its oblique side upward, plucking the strings with his right
hand and holding it with his left hand.[7] The manuscript says that Syr-
ians called *santīr* the same instrument known as *qanun* by Egyptians.[8]
Sawa feels that the illustration does not indicate its true playing position, since the text mentions that both left and right hands plucked it.[9]
However, numerous contemporary European illustrations of the canon
(actually the half-canon) show the instrument held in front of the body,
although the oblique end is usually to the player's left. Perhaps the player
used his left hand to alter the pitch of the strings or to pluck them occasionally.

The *kanun* had entered Persia by the fourteenth century, as the manuscript *Kanz al-Tuhaf* describes it as a half-trapezoidal instrument strung
with sixty-four strings in courses of three each.[10] Unfortunately the text
does not describe the material of the strings. Ibn Gaybī (died 1435) of
Herat described the *kanun* as trapezoidal, with strings made of "twisted
copper" arranged in courses of three, but he did not mention the *santur,*
despite references to many other instruments.[11] Sixteenth-century Persian illustrations depict the *kanun* played horizontally by women in ensembles with *chang* (harp) and *daire* (tambourine).[12] The *kanun* died
out in Iran later; the one played occasionally in that country today is a
relatively recent introduction from the Arab world.

Descendants of the fifteenth-century Persian *kanun*, however, survived in peripheral areas that were part of the Timurid Empire. In nineteenth-century Osha, Uzbekistan, there was an instrument called the *kalin*
or *kanun*, with thirty-six strings in courses of two each.[13] Although rare,

the Uighurs in Xinjiang province, China, in recent times played the
kalun, an instrument identical to the Uzbek *kalin*, with eighteen double
courses of steel strings. The technique involved plucking the strings with
a wooden or bamboo plectrum held in the right hand while the left hand
held an iron device which produced vibrato or glissandos.[14] Another
survival of the Persian *kanun* is the *svaramandala* or *kanuna*, known
mainly in the Punjab (Pakistan and India), with twenty-one brass and
steel strings. The few soloists play it vertically with two wire plectra,
each of which attach to the finger of each hand. The player holds in his
left hand an iron ring, which he uses on the strings to produce embellishments.[15] The survival of this technique in such places as far from
each other as Xinjiang and Punjab indicates a survival of an instrument
from Timurid culture and thus its age. No doubt players of the horizontally placed, metal-strung *kanun* of the fifteenth century used a similar
technique with the left hand.

The *santur*, in its modern form, probably developed from the metal-
strung *kanun*. Whether the word (a Persian or Turkish adaptation of the
Arabic *santīr*) was a regional term, as *Kashf al-ghumūm* says, or whether
it had become an alternative term for the *kanun*, the *santur* as dulcimer
appears first during the fifteenth century in Persia. Two illuminations in
a manuscript of Nizāmī's *Khamsah*, written in 1481 or 1482 in the court
Turcoman style, probably in Tabriz, Shiraz, or elsewhere in western Iran,
depict women playing *chang*, lute, and *santur* for Bahrām Gūr and a
princess.[16] The trapezoidal instrument rests on the floor with the side
containing the shortest courses nearest the player (see illustration 7).
Ibn al-Kayyāl's treatise, *Dhamm al-malā'ib wa'l-mahāhī*, written at
Damascus in 1486, mentions the *ṣintīr*.[17] Perhaps experiments by *kanun*
players, who probably used a plectrum in the right hand and an iron
device in the left and thus were not far removed from experimenting to
play with two wooden sticks, resulted in the development of the *santur*.

Ottoman Empire

The instrument starts to appear with greater frequency in other sources
during the late fifteenth and in the sixteenth centuries. Walter Feldman
notes that Ayni, a Turk who lived during the fifteenth century, included
it in one of his musical *gazel*s.[18] Sixteenth- and seventeenth-century
Turkish illustrations depict the *santur* in the same manner as the fifteenth-century Persian illustration mentioned above, played by women,

sometimes with the shorter end closest to the player.[19] Since two Turkish illustrations and the Persian illustration mentioned above both show the *santur* played in that unusual position, we may assume, first, that the apparently reversed position was not a mistake made by the artists and, second, that the instrument may have entered Turkey from Iran. Further, the *santur* began not as a court instrument played by male, professional musicians, but, like the contemporary *kanun*, as an instrument suitable for women of the harem.

In Ottoman Turkey, women musicians were either slaves confined to a harem or *çengîs*, meaning "players of the *çeng* (harp)," the instrument most closely identified with the harem. Feldman suggests that by the sixteenth century Gypsy women already performed as professional musicians and dancers (*çengîs*), available to be seen by men outside the harem.[20] Certainly this was the case in the seventeenth century. A French traveler named Quiclet heard, at Belgrade in 1658, Gypsy men and girls dancing and singing to the accompaniment of *kemânçes*, *santur*s, and *çögür*s (long-necked lutes with five strings).[21] The use of the *santur* by harem women, including those of the Seraglio, continued through the eighteenth century and into the early nineteenth century, as illustrations attest.[22]

Ottoman court musicians began to use the *santur* during the early seventeenth century. Wojciech Bobowski, a native of Galicia who wrote about Ottoman music during the middle of the seventeenth century, was known as Ali Beg el-Santûrî. During the eighteenth century, *fasıl* and *mehter-i bîrûn* ensembles, the former a formal ensemble performing suites of instrumental and vocal music, the latter an ensemble containing wind and percussion instruments used for outdoor dance music, both incorporated the *santur*. At the beginning of the nineteenth century, the sultan's court employed a *santur* virtuoso, Musâhib Santûrî Hüseyin, who received a salary larger than other, better known musicians.[23]

Regional courts of the Ottoman Empire also supported *santur* players. Thomas Shaw, about 1738, called the long-necked fiddle and the dulcimer, which, "with brass strings, is touched sometimes with the fingers, sometimes with small sticks, or else with a plectrum," the chief instruments of Turkish music in the Maghreb.[24] The instrument, along with *ney* (end-blown flute), *tanbûr* (long-necked lute), *mıskal* (panpipe), *müküm* (i.e., *kanun*), *kemâni* (spike fiddle), *sine kemân* (violin), and a reed instrument, was one of the instruments used at the courts of the hospodars in Moldavia and Wallachia during the second half of the eigh-

teenth century.[25] The English traveler Edward Daniel Clarke heard the
santur at Athens in 1802.[26] During the first part of the nineteenth century, Greeks and Jews in Egypt played the instrument.[27] In 1832, at
Alexandria, Edward Hogg watched a performance of dancers accompanied by men playing a "dulcimer," a single-stringed fiddle, and a small
tambourine.[28] These last two references, however, may refer to the *qanun*.

The *santur* continued to be played by Muslim Gypsies in Serbia after
independence in 1878, although there is some evidence that by the middle
of the nineteenth century the portable Hungarian cimbalom may have
supplanted the traditional *santur* (see chapter 6). Dilber Eda, a musician
apparently described by the Belgrade literary critic Ljubomir Nedić (1858-
1902), played *čočeks* (Gypsy dances) and *pevajčs* (songs) on the *santur*.[29]
Asan, a Turkish Gypsy living in Belgrade in 1910, the last player of this
instrument, was known for his performances of historical *sevdalinkas*
(love songs).[30] The Crimean Tatars continued to use the *santır* until
their expulsion from the Crimea during World War II.[31]

At mid-nineteenth century, a Constantinople musician, Hilmi Bey,
adapted a Romanian *ţambal* for use in Turkish music. This instrument,
the *santur fransız*, is discussed chapter 6. Although this new variety of
dulcimer enjoyed a certain fashion, other musicians continued to play
the *santur türk* into the twentieth century. In Constantinople they were
exclusively Jews; in eastern Anatolia they were Armenians.[32] The *santur*
of both varieties was in decline in Turkey by 1920, and today the instrument is almost completely forgotten.

Caucasus

Musicians in both what is now the Armenian Republic and Georgia
used the *santur*. The area was part of the Persian Empire during the
eighteenth century and earlier, and the instrument's introduction was
undoubtedly associated with the dominance of that culture. In Tbilisi,
"Persian" music was prominent until the 1840s, when Russians
introduced opera and other forms of Western music.[33] The *santuri*, as
Georgians call the instrument, must have been a part of that music. It
remained in use into the twentieth century as an accompaniment instrument in *sazandar* (professional musician) ensembles.[34] At mid-twentieth
century, urban ensembles in the Armenian Soviet Socialist Republic used
the instrument for the music of Sayat Nova, the eighteenth-century national poet.[35]

Iran

Scholars of Persian music have been unable to find illustrations of
the *santur* before the nineteenth century.[36] Persian manuscripts on music written from the sixteenth to early eighteenth centuries, such as
Fudūlī's (died c.1561) *Sāqiname*, Mīr Sadr al-Din Muhammad's (died
1598/9) *Risāla-ye-'ilm-e-musīqī*, Waqārī's *Goldaste andīshe*, and
Zuhūrī's (died c.1617) *Sāqiname*, which mention the *kanun* and many
other instruments, fail to mention the *santur*.[37] Perhaps it did disappear
from Persia after its fifteenth-century appearance, only to reappear later
from Turkey, as Farmer suggested.[38]

Europeans who left accounts of their travels to Persia indicate that
court musicians used the *santur* or the *kanun* during the seventeenth
century. Tavernier, who was there in the 1660s, mentioned it.[39] Kaempfer,
in Persia in 1684 and later, wrote that a less common, quadrangular

**Figure 4.1: Woman musician of the Persian court playing *santur*, early nine-
teenth century. Engraving after a painting in the Victoria and Albert Museum, London, in Carl Engel, *Musical Instruments* (London: Chapman and
Hall, 1873), 55.**

instrument was "played either with curved sticks or with quills,"[40] indicating that either he confused the *kanun* with the *santur* or perhaps that *santur* players at the time both plucked and hammered its strings (Shaw's remarks about the "dulcimer" of the Turks in the Maghreb are similar). More ambiguous is Chardin's mention of the *épinette* as a stringed instrument used in Persia.[41] Less so is Cornelis de Bruyn's mention of a "violin" and *hakkebert*, which he witnessed at the end of the century, although this word did not necessarily signify *santur*. The 1725 French edition of his travels says "there are also some *clavessins,*" but this word could mean *kanun*s.[42]

We might infer that Persian musicians used the *santur* during the eighteenth century, because of the presence of the instrument in the Caucasus. In any case, an eighteenth-century Persian manuscript, Al-Haqānī's *Risāla mūsīqī*, mentions both the *qanun* and *samtur*.[43] Its use was nonetheless obscure, probably limited to court music, especially of the royal harem. A painting from the early nineteenth century of a female musician of the court harem in Tehran (see figure 4.1) shows her playing the *santur*, the instrument resting on its case.[44]

The *santur* reached prominence at the court in Tehran during the late nineteenth century. It was played in ensemble with *kamāncha* (spike fiddle), *tār* (long-necked lute), *nay* (end-blown flute), and *zarb* (drum). Jean During mentions the earliest player known by name, Mohammed Hasan (Santur Khān), who was active during the middle of the century. Mohammed Sādeq Khān (known as "Soror-ol Molk") became head of the imperial ensemble during the reign of Nasreddin Shah (1848-1896). He taught the *santur* to several students, among them Sōma Hōzur (Habīb Santuri), who made some recordings.[45] The instrument was little known outside Tehran. At the beginning of the twentieth century, the instrument was said to be procurable only in the capital, and Sykes, an English investigator, even believed it to be of "foreign make."[46] The instrument then fell into decline, according to Caron and Safvate, until Somā Hōzur's son Somā'i (died 1946) appeared on the national radio. These broadcasts brought the instrument before a new audience, inspiring many to learn to play it.[47]

Traditional clerical hostility towards music relaxed during the Pahlavi era. The elite began to cultivate both Western and Iranian classical music. Abol Hosein Sabō, using modified Western notation, compiled volumes of the *radīf*, or repertoire on which improvisation is based, for the *santur*. Fayamarz Payvar wrote a method for the instrument.[48] Nevertheless, cultivation of art music was not widespread, it being largely limited to Tehran, Esfahan, and Tabriz. Musicians, according to During, tended to fall into four categories: amateurs of a middling level; amateurs who studied with well-known teacher, but who never played in public; professionals, who played in concerts and taught; and *motrebi*, who played music influenced by neighboring cultures in nightclubs.[49]

Iraq

The *santur* is a prominent part of the *chalghi al-baghdadi* ("Baghdad ensemble"). Its use is thus mostly confined to certain musicians in Baghdad, although the style also exists in Mosul and Kirkuk. This group consists of a singer (or "reciter"), *santur*, *joza* (spike fiddle), *dunbuk* (drum), and *daf* (tambourine). Its music is primarily vocal. In performance, an instrumental prelude is followed by singing in certain modes (*maqam*s), which the instrumentalists follow.

The history and development of this genre remain to be explained. Hassan remarks that some date its origin to the sixteenth century, but that the earliest writings on the subject date from the twentieth century.[50] He comments that before World War II, the musicians were frequently Jews. They played for weddings, circumcisions, and other private celebrations of the elite. In the decades before the war they began to play for a wider audience in cafes. In more recent years, musicians were both professional and amateur.[51] In 1973, the Musical Arts Department of the Ministry of Information and Culture began to sponsor an ensemble.

Afghanistan

In the western city of Herat, Persian music was in vogue during the 1920s, and some musicians played the *santur* and other Iranian instruments. This style of music, still in existence in 1940, went out of fashion, and by 1970 the instrument was only a memory.[52] In the early 1970s, a musician in the Radio Afghanistan Orchestra in Kabul played the *santur*. This was regarded as an imported, rather than native, instrument, but it is unknown whether the *santur* in use there came from Iranian or Kashmiri tradition.[53]

Kashmir and India

The *santur* is one of the instruments in the ensemble of Kashmir which performs *sufyana musiqi* ("Sufi music"). The other instruments are *setar* (long-necked lute) and *dokra* (drums), and formerly the *saz-e-kashmiri* (spike fiddle). The instrumentalists sing Persian and Kashmiri texts to their own accompaniment. They perform suites, with an instrumental prelude, followed by a series of songs, in a certain mode (*maqam*). This practice is common to other Islamic traditions, but in Kashmir, the musicians associate modes with time of day, a concept found in Hindustani music. The musicians are mostly professionals, but the style is in decline, and the number of musicians is small.[54]

Historical information concerning the *santur* in Kashmir is sparse and ambiguous. We can dispense with Day's fanciful notion that the *santur* and *qanun* developed from the *kattyayana vina* or *shatatantri* (hundred-stringed) *vina* mentioned in Sanskrit sources.[55] It clearly came from Iran or Iraq, but the period of its arrival is uncertain. The Persian-speaking Kashmiri court attracted musicians from elsewhere in the Islamic world as early as the fifteenth century. According to the memoirs of Jehangir, written in the early seventeenth century, Mirza Haider Dughlat, regent of Kashmir for eleven years in the 1540s and 1550s, had many musicians at his court, including those who played "lutes, dulcimers, harps, drums, and flutes."[56] However, the translator of this passage may have used the English word "dulcimer" for *kanun*. A manuscript by Mulla Togra, who died in 1667 at Kashmir, mentions *qanun*, but not *santur*.[57]

Day mentioned in 1891 that the *santur* could be found in India on occasion.[58] Without further details, we are left to wonder whether the instrument was used by Kashmiri musicians living elsewhere on the subcontinent, whether he referred to Kashmir, or whether it was a survival from an earlier period. In any case, its use in the classical music of North India today is due to the efforts of Shivkumar Sharma (born 1938). His father, Uma Dutt Sharma, a native of Kashmir, modified the tuning and taught his son to play the instrument. Shivkumar adopted a gliding, striking technique allowing a glissando-like ornament, *meend*, which for North Indian classical music is essential. He played the *santur* in a recital for the first time in 1955 and made his first recording in 1960. He subsequently made many more recordings, toured extensively, and taught several students, who follow in his footsteps.[59] To keep up with the grow-

ing interest in the instrument, musical instrument manufacturers began
to produce *santurs* in the 1970s.[60]

United States

The first *santur* players in the United States were Armenians. In
1892, Ignatius D. Bagdasarian, a subject of the Ottoman Sultan and a
resident of Cambridge, Massachusetts, received a patent for a "dulcimer."[61] He must have played it as well. Since he made the instrument,
other Armenians must have bought it and learned to play it. In Boston, a
man named Haigiz played the *santur* with a violinist named Stefan.[62]
Around 1940 in Detroit, an Armenian named Sam played the instrument. However, the *santur* remained rare among Armenian-Americans
and is now extinct.

Many Iranians came to the United States in the 1960s and 1970s to
enroll in universities. Among them were a number of *santur* players.
Nasser Rastegar-Nejad of Washington made several recordings in the
1960s. Kyu Hagigi of Chicago is active. Several other players and makers moved to the Los Angeles area, which has the largest concentration
of Iranians in the United States.

Design

Ottoman Empire

Although numerous illustrations of the *santur* from the sixteenth to
nineteenth centuries exist, few are detailed enough to allow many conclusions about the design of the instrument or its development. The best
technical descriptions are those of Bagdasarian's patent (1892) and Yekta
(1920). I have not learned of a surviving *santur türk* or of any clear
photographs of that instrument.

Feldman remarks that an illustration of a *santur* made before 1749 is
the most detailed. This shows an instrument of approximately the same
outline as modern Iranian *santurs*, with tuning pins placed on a horizontal plane into the right pin block, two round sound holes, and individual bridges probably placed inaccurately, with about six or seven on
the lower right and the same number on the upper left. It contains a hole
in the front rail, a detail common to some modern Iranian instruments.

Another illustration, from the 1720s, although less detailed, shows an instrument of comparable size, but with tuning pins placed vertically on the right.[63] In yet another illustration, from 1720, the *santur*'s tuning pins are upright, but set into the pin block on the left. The instrument appears to have fourteen triple courses which rest on rows of bridges which lay at the same angles relative to those of the oblique edges.[64]

Bagdasarian's patent depicts an instrument with 34 courses of four strings each resting on two rows of individual bridges. Each course, except the lowest in each row, is divided into octaves. The bridges on the lowest courses are placed nearer the outside edges of the soundboard. The tuning pins are set into the left pin block at a 45-degree angle to the plane of the instrument. Between the two rows of bridges, in the middle of the soundboard, is a single, round sound hole. For the tuning, we can infer from the string lengths that it took twenty-five succeeding courses to reach an octave.[65] Yekta describes an instrument with sixteen courses of five brass strings on each row of bridges, but only the left row dividing the courses into octaves.[66] Finally, a faint twentieth-century photograph of unknown provenance shows an instrument with probably eighteen courses on either side, the bottom five or six courses in the right row placed closer to the outside, with tuning pins set upright into the left pin block.[67]

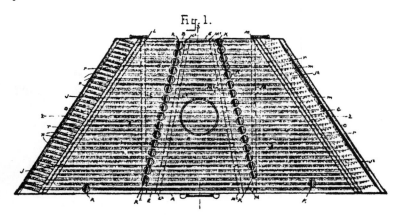

Figure 4.2: Diagram of *santur* (or "dulcimer") patented by Ignatius D. Bagdasarian, of Cambridge, Massachusetts, 19 July 1892. U.S. Patent number 479,323.

Chapter 4

From the information presented here, we can deduce that the eighteenth-century Turkish *santur*, which resembled modern Iranian instruments except perhaps in the placement of bridges and the placement of tuning pins into the left side, developed into a much larger instrument by the end of the nineteenth century. Feldman remarks that the octave consisting of twenty-five to twenty-seven notes in modern Turkish music developed at the end of the eighteenth and beginning of the nineteenth centuries.[68] Makers of the *santur türk* did make modifications to its design in order to make it compatible with the requirements of the new scale, but its resulting complexity may have rendered it difficult to play. Its extinction, however, may have resulted more from changes in musical tastes following World War I and the loss of the Armenian population in eastern Anatolia than from any inherent difficulty in playing the instrument.

Caucasus

The design of surviving *santur*s from Georgia and the Armenian Republic seems to be transitional between the nineteenth-century *santur türk* and modern Iranian instruments. The description given in Vertkov's *Atlas* indicates a smaller size than those of modern Iranian instruments. The Georgian instrument is 75 cm (29½ inches) and 26 cm (10¼ inches) long, 37 cm (14½ inches) wide, with sixteen courses. The Armenian instrument is 73 cm (28¾ inches) and 32 cm (12½ inches) long, 27 cm (10¾ inches) wide, 10 to 12 cm (3½ to 4¾ inches) high, with seventeen courses. The placement of bridges on the illustrated Georgian *santuri* indicates that both rows divide the courses into octaves. Its tuning pins fit into the left pin block, as on Turkish instruments, but on a horizontal plane, as with Iranian instruments.[69]

Iran

Nineteenth-century illustrations of the *santur* show instruments almost identical to those played today. The chief difference appears to be the smaller number of courses. The standard number today is nine courses over the left row of bridges and nine courses over the right row. During writes that Ali Akbar Shahi added three courses to the *santur* at the beginning of the twentieth century.[70] It appears, however, that nineteenth-

Figure 4.3: Modern Iranian *santur*. Author's collection.

century Iranian *santur*s normally had a total of sixteen courses. Such an instrument is illustrated by Sykes; however, a *santur* of unknown provenance in the collection of the Musée du Conservatoire National de Musique in Paris in 1884 contained 72 iron strings.[71]

The Iranian *santur* is usually made of walnut or beech. Its lower length is 90 cm (35½ inches), upper length 35 cm (13¾ inches), width about 25 cm (10 inches), with a depth of 5 to 6 cm (2 to 2½ inches). Two sound holes in the form of five-petaled flowers are cut into the soundboard. The row of individually turned bridges on the left divides each course of four steel strings into octaves, while on the bridges in the row on the right rest courses of four brass strings each. The courses on the right are tuned an octave below the neighboring courses resting on the right row. Although instruments with ten to twelve courses in each row exist, the standard number is nine on the right and nine on the left row. The player tunes the strings according to the mode (*dastgah*) in which he plays, and by moving bridges, he can modify the mode as necessary. The tuning pins are drilled into the right pin block at a horizontal plane with the instrument. The player holds light hammers (*mezrāb*) between first and second fingers.

Iraq

Two forms of *santur* exist today in Iraq. The basic difference is that the older variety is deeper than the newer one. Hassan gives the dimensions of the older form as 80 to 86 cm (31½ to 34 inches) at the lower length, 31 to 41 cm (12¼ to 16¼ inches) at the upper length, about 39 cm (15½ inches) in width, and 11.5 to 13 cm (4½ to 5 inches) in height. The corresponding dimensions for the newer variety are 89 to 91.5 cm (35 to 36 inches) and 31.5 to 41 cm (12½ to 16¼ inches) in length, 39 to 43 cm (15½ to 17 inches) in width, and 6.5 to 8 cm (2½ to 3¼ inches) in height.[72] There are a total of twenty-three or twenty-four courses of three or four steel or brass strings each. The row of bridges on the left divides each course into octaves, and the musicians plays on both sides of that row. On the right side, the lowest three or four bridges sit closer to the right edge than the rest. The other bridges on the right side sit in a row at a position which is one-third of the distance between the edges of the soundboard. The player strikes the strings which rest on the row of bridges only on their left side.[73] Except for the lowest three or four courses, the tuning of the courses on the right is in the same range as the right side of the strings over the left row of bridges. The player manipulates the position of the bridges to obtain the correct microtones. The hammers are light and similar to those used in Iran, except that the index fingers fit into holes, rather than open notches.

Kashmir and India

The Kashmiri *santur* differs in several respects from those of other traditions. One characteristic, the height of its corpus (about 11 cm), resembles that of the older Iraqi variety. Perhaps this is a clue to its origin. Its other dimensions set it apart from other *santur*s. Its lower length is 61 to 64 cm (24 to 25¼ inches), upper length 31 to 32 cm (12¼ to 12½ inches), and width is about 54 cm (21¼ inches). There are normally a total of thirty courses of four strings each, arranged in two rows, although in the past, instruments with less courses were common. According to Pacholczyk, various players use different tuning systems. If all the strings are of steel, the courses on the left side are tuned in unison with the neighboring courses on the right. Others use brass strings for the courses on the right and tune them an octave below the neighboring course on the left, as in the Iranian system. Only a few musicians tune the row of bridges on the left so that they divide the strings into octaves. Most only play on the strings to the right of the bridges in the left row and leave the left portion unplayable. The range is approximately from g^0 to g^2.[74] Shivkumar Sharma's modifications include adding another course, reducing the number of strings to three per course, and rearrangement of bridges.

Notes

1. For example, in Jean During, *La musique iranienne: tradition et évolution*, Institut Français d'Iranologie de Téhéran: Bibliothèque iranienne, no. 29 (Paris: Editions Recherche sur les Civilisations, 1984), 59.

2. *Dictionary of Music and Musicians*, Sir George Grove, ed., 5th ed., s.v. "Santir."

3. Amnon Shiloah, *The Theory of Music in Arabic Writings (c.900-1900)*: *Descriptive Catalogue of Manuscripts in Libraries of Europe and the U.S.A.* (Munich: G. Henle Verlag, 1979), 216.

4. Henry George Farmer, "The Canon and Eschaquiel of the Arabs," *Journal of the Royal Asiatic Society of Great Britain and Ireland*, Apr. 1926, 244f.

5. *Dictionary of Music and Musicians*, ed. Sir George Grove, 5th ed., s.v. "Santir"; George Dimitri Sawa, "The Differing Worlds of the Music Illuminator and the Music Historian in Islamic Medieval Manuscripts," *Imago Musicae* 6 (1989): 16 n. 36.

6. Ella Zonis, *Classical Persian Music: An Introduction* (Cambridge: Harvard University Press, 1973), 165 n. 26.

7. Shiloah, *Theory of Music*, 383. The manuscript is undated and Shiloah does not assign a date, but both Farmer and Sawa write that it is from the fourteenth century.

8. *Dictionary of Music and Musicians*, ed. Grove, 5th ed., s.v. "Santir."

9. Sawa, "Differing Worlds," 15-16.

10. Henry George Farmer, "Iranian Musical Instruments in the Ninth/Fifteenth Century," *Islamic Culture* 28 (July 1964): 180.

11. Abd al-Qadir ibn Ghaibī, *Jāmi al-alḥan fī 'ilm al-mūsīqī*, in Farmer, "Canon and Eschaquiel," 250.

12. B. W. Robinson, *Persian Paintings in the India Office Library* (London: Sotheby Parke Bernet, 1976), pl. 285, 383; Ivan Stchoukine, *Les peintures des manuscrits safavis de 1502 à 1587* (Paris: Librairie Orientaliste Paul Geuthner, 1959), pl. 61. Norah M. Titley, *Miniatures from Turkish Manuscripts: A Catalogue and Subject Index of Paintings in the British Library and British Museum* (London: British Library, 1981), 37, confuses a *kanun* with a *santur* in a six-

teenth-century Ottoman manuscript of Bâki's *Divan*, which includes an illustration of a young prince entertained by women musicians playing *mıskal* (panpipes,
not *çeng-i dehen*, or jew's harp), *çeng* (harp), *kemânçe* (spike fiddle), and *kanun.*
    13. Tamara S. Vyzgo, *Muzykal'nye instrumenty Srednei Azii* (Moskva:
Izdatel'stvo "Muzyka," 1980), pl. 84.
    14. Maurice Courant, "Chine et Corée," in *Encyclopédie de la musique et
dictionnaire du Conservatoire,* ed. Albert Lavignac (Paris: Librairie Delagrave,
1931), 1: 180; Xiang Zuhua, "An Examination of the Origin of the Yangqin,"
Chinese Music 4, no. 1: 17.
    15. C. R. Day, *The Music and Musical Instruments of Southern India and
The Deccan* (1891; reprint, Delhi: B. R. Publishing Corp., 1974), 133. Such
technique may be obsolete today.
    16. Ms. Per. 162, ff. 214v., 224v., Chester Beatty Library, Dublin; Dr. Elaine
Wright, Curator of the Islamic Collections, letter to author, 24 Nov. 1998. I wish
to thank Walter Feldman for pointing out his important discovery to me.
    17. Shiloah, *Theory of Music,* 184.
    18. Walter Feldman, *Music of the Ottoman Court: Makam, Composition,
and the Early Ottoman Instrumental Repertoire,* Intercultural Music Studies 10,
ed. Max Peter Baumann (Berlin: VWB - Verlag für Wissenschaft und Bildung,
1996), 160, quoting Agah Sirri Levend, *Divân edebiyati: kelimeler ve remizler,
mazmunlar ve mefhumlar* (Istanbul: Inkılap Kitabevi, 1943), 242-243.
    19. Pars Tuğlacı, *Osmanlı saray kadınları* (Istanbul: Cem, 1985), 110, 119.
I wish to thank Walter Feldman for making copies of this available to me.
    20. Feldman, *Music of the Ottoman Court,* 122-123.
    21. "Les voyages de M. Quiclet à Constantinople par terre, Paris, 1664,"
Glasnik istoriskog društva v Novom Sadu 7 (1934), in Stana Đurić-Klajn, *A
Survey of Serbian Music Through the Ages* (Belgrade: Association of Compos-
ers of Serbia, 1972), 26. This also appears in Josip Andreis, Dragotin Cvetko,
and Stana Đurić-Klajn, *Historijski razvoj muzičke kulture u Jugoslavija* (Zagreb:
Školska knjigov, 1962), 553.
    22. Tuğlacı, *Osmanlı saray kadınları,* 104, 123; *Türkische Gewänder und
osmanische Gesellschaft im achtzehnten Jahrhundert: Facsimile-Ausgabe des
Codex "Les portraits des differens habillemens qui sont en usage à Constantinople
et dans tout la Turquie" aus dem Besitz der Deutschen Archäologischen Insti-
tutes in Istanbul* (Graz: Akademische Druck, 1966), pl. 13.
    23. Feldman, *Music of the Ottoman Court,* 160-162.
    24. Thomas Shaw, "Travels or Observations, Relating to Barbary," in *A
General Collection of the Best and Most Interesting Voyages and Travels in All
Parts of the World,* ed. John Pinkerton (London: Longman, Hurst, Rees, Ormes,
and Brown, 1814), 15: 643.
    25. Franz Joseph Sulzer, *Geschichte des transalpinischen Daciens, das ist
der Walachey, Moldau und Bessarabiens* (Vienna: Rudolph Grässer, 1781), 2:
434.

26. Edward Daniel Clarke, *Travels in Various Countries of Europe, Asia and Africa* (London, 1816), 4: 4, in Fivos Anoyanakis, *Greek Popular Musical Instruments*, 2nd ed. (Athens: "Melissa" Publishing House, 1991), 300.

27. G. Villoteau, *La description de l'Égypte*, vol. 1, *État moderne* (Paris, 1809-1826), 898-900, E. W. Lane, *The Modern Egyptians* (London, 1860), 363, in *Dictionary of Music and Musicians*, ed. Grove, 5th ed., s.v. "Santir."

28. Edward Hogg, *Visit to Alexandria, Damascus, and Jerusalem* (London: Saunders and Otley, 1832): 1: 113.

29. *Rečnik srpskohrvatskog književnog jezika* (Novi Sad, 1973), 5: 642, quoting Ljubomir Nedić, *Celokupna dela*, vol. 2, Biblioteka srpskih pisaca (Belgrade: "Narodna Prosveta," 1932). This, however, seems to be in error, as a search of the source does not reveal the citation.

30. Tihomir Đorđević, "Cigani i muzika u Srbiji," *Bosanska vila* 25 (Mar. 1910): 77.

31. Selma Agat, "Kirim türk müziği," (thesis, Türk Müsikisi Devlet Konservatuvari, 1987), 83-85. Thanks to Walter Feldman for providing this rare piece of information.

32. Raouf Yekta Bey, "La musique turque," in *Encyclopedie de la musique et dictionnaire du Conservatoire*, ed. Albert Lavignac, 3: 3022. A photograph in the possession of Ara Dinkjian, from about 1910, shows four Armenians playing *santur*, clarinet, violin, and *tar*. He has a recording (Popular 700), made perhaps about 1930, of Harpoutte Karekin, with *santur* accompaniment.

33. Ronald Grigor Suny, *The Makers of the Georgian Nation* (Bloomington: Indiana University Press, 1988), 93.

34. K. Vertkov, G. Blagodatov, and E. Yazovitskaya, *Atlas muzykal'nykh instrumentov narodov SSSR* (Moscow: Gosudarstvennoe Muzykal'noe Izdatel'-stvo, 1963), 89.

35. Vertkov, *Atlas*, 91.

36. During, *La musique iranienne*, 59.

37. Mohammad Taghi Massoudieh, *Manuscrits persans concernant la musique* (Munich: G. Henle Verlag, 1996), nos. 27, 71, 115, 120.

38. *Dictionary of Music and Musicians*, ed. Grove, 5th ed., s.v. "Santir."

39. During, *La musique iranienne*, 59.

40. Engelbert Kaempfer, *Amoenitatum exoticarem politico-physico-medicorum Fasciculi 5* (Lemgo, 1712), in Frank Harrison, *Time, Place and Music: An Anthology of Ethnomusicological Observation c.1550 to c.1800* (Amsterdam: Frits Knuf, 1973), 141, 150.

41. Jean Chardin, *Voyages de Monsieur le Chevalier Chardin, en Perse* (Amsterdam: J. L. de Lorme, 1711), in Frank Harrison, *Time, Place and Music*, 125, 132.

42. Cornelis de Bruyn, *Reizen over Moskovie door Persie en Indie* (Amsterdam: W. and D. Goeree, 1711), 62b, in *Woordenboek der Nederlandsche Taal*, s.v. "Hakkebord"; *Voyages de Corneille le Bruyn par la Moscovie, en Perse, et aux Indes Orientales* (Paris: Jean Baptiste-Claude Bauche, 1725), 4: 122.

43. Massoudieh, *Manuscrits persans*, no. 41.

44. Carl Engel, *Musical Instruments* (London: for the Committee of Council on Education by Chapman and Hall, 1873), 55. Ruhallah Khāliqī, *Sar-guzasht-ī mūsiqī-i-Irān* (Tehran, n.d.), 1: 153, ascribes this painting to the period of Fath Ali Shah (1797-1834).

45. During, *La musique iranienne*, 66.

46. P. Molesworth Sykes, "Notes on Musical Instruments in Khorasan, with Special References to the Gypsies," *Man* 9 (1909): 162-163.

47. Nelly Caron and Dariouche Safvate, *Iran: collection de l'Institut International d'Études Comparatives de la Musique*, Les traditions musicales (n.p.: Buchet/Chastel, 1966), 173.

48. Farāmarz Pāyvar, *Dastūr santūr* (orig., 1340 = 1961; Tehran: Maqazeh Golbahār, 1346 = 1967).

49. During, *La musique iranienne*, 20-24.

50. Schéhérazade Qassim Hassan, "Survey of Written Sources on the Iraqi Maqam," in *Regionale maqam-Traditionen in Geschichte und Gegenwart*, edited by Jürgen Elsner and Gisa Jähnichen (Berlin, 1992), 252, 254.

51. Schéhérazade Qassim Hassan, *Les instruments de musique en Irak: et leur rôle dans la société traditionelle*, École des Hautes Études en Sciences Sociales: Cahiers de l'homme, n.s. 21 (Paris: Mouton, 1975), 109-110.

52. John Bailly, *Music of Afghanistan* (Cambridge: Cambridge University Press, 1988), 19-21; Lloyd C. Miller, "Aspects of Aghan Music with Special Emphasis on the Music of Herat from 1970 to 1975" (Ph.D. diss., University of Utah, 1979), 78, 91, 112.

53. Peter Ten Hoopen, notes to *Afghanistan: Music from the Crossroads of Asia*, Nonesuch H-72053. In 1969 in Kabul I met a member of the audience of a music hall who was familiar with the *santur*.

54. Jozef M. Pacholczyk, *Sufyana Musiqi: the Classical Music of Kashmir*, Intercultural Music Studies, ed. Max Peter Baumann (Berlin: VWB - Verlag für Wissenschaft und Bildung, 1996), 28-33.

55. Day, *Music and Musical Instruments of Southern India*, 102, 134.

56. Prithvi Nath Kaul Bamzai, *A History of Kashmir*, 2nd ed. (New Delhi: Metropolitan Book Co., 1973), 574.

57. Massoudieh, *Manuscrits persans*, no. 75.

58. Day, *Music and Musical Instruments of Southern India*, 133.

59. *Santoor*, website <http://www.santoor.com/santoory.htm>.

60. Such instruments were unavailable in and unfamiliar to music stores I visited in Delhi and Calcutta in 1970.

61. U.S. Patent no. 479, 323, patented July 19, 1892.

62. Walter Feldman, personal communication.

63. Feldman, *Music of the Ottoman Court*, 139, 161-162.

64. Andı Metin, *Gelenksel türk tiyatrosu: Kuka, Karagöz, Ortaoyunu* (Ankara: Bilgi Basımevi, 1969), n.p., citing III. Ahmet kitapliği, no. 3594, Topkapi Sarayi.

65. U.S. Patent no. 479,323, patented July 19, 1892.

66. Yekta Bey, "La musique turque," 3: 3022.

67. Mahmud Ahmad al-Hifni, *'Ilom al-âlât al-musîqîyah* (Cairo, 1971), 207.

68. Feldman, *Music of the Ottoman Court*, 163.

69. Vertkov, *Atlas*, 91, 98, pl. 426, 481.

70. During, *La musique iranienne*, 66.

71. Sykes, "Notes on Musical Instruments in Khorasan," 161; Léon Pillaut, *Le Musée du Conservatoire National de Musique: 1er supplément au catalogue de 1884* (Paris: Librairie Fischbacher, 1894), 38.

72. Hassan, *Les instruments de musique en Irak*, 64.

73. Habib Hassan Touma, *La musique arabe* (Paris: Editions Buchet/Chastel, 1977), 100-102.

74. Pacholczyk, *Sufyana Musiqi*, 34-35.

· 5 ·

The *Hackbrett*

The *Hackbrett* ("chopping block") has enjoyed a continuous presence among certain German-speaking peoples since the fifteenth century. It reached its greatest distribution during the eighteenth century yet, despite declines and persistent disparagement, has maintained itself through periodic revivals. By the end of the fifteenth century, a trapezoidal outline, needed to produce a wider tonal range, had replaced the earlier rectangular shape. Its design has remained essentially the same since that period, and, because of that, the year 1500 makes a good starting point for its history as developed in this chapter. This covers Germany, the Low Countries, Switzerland, Austria, Slovenia, Scandinavia, and German settlers in Russia and America.

History

1500-1800

The early *Hackbrett* with metal strings did migrate to a higher social position during the fifteenth century than that of its ancestor, the string drum, but it became more identified as an instrument of the middle class and of minstrels. This contrasted with the *doulcemèr* of France and Burgundy, where it was an instrument of highest fashion. To some extent the social division extended into the eighteenth century, but, for most of its history, the *Hackbrett* remained in the hands of minstrels and rural people.

Early in the sixteenth century, it probably was used by the same class as that which played the lute, since Bartelmo Schuster was listed as a lute and *Hackbrett* maker in Augsburg between 1499 and 1516.[1] In 1517, one could buy dulcimers, lutes, and harps at the market in Frankfurt am Main (see figure 5.1).[2] Johannes Jud recalled in 1574 that his father Leo Jud (1482-1542), an Alsatian priest who lived in Basel, Switzerland in his early years, played the *hakbröt* and the lute a little.[3] Bernhard Wyss commented on Ulrich Zwingli's musical talents, in his chronicle of the Reformation under the year 1519, writing that he played "fiddles, rebecs, recorders, flutes . . . the trumpet marine, *hackprätt*, the cornets."[4] The son of Thomas Platter (1499-1582), a printer in Basel, described hearing his father's amusement "on the jew's harp and on the *hackbret*, which at the time was very popular."[5] In northern Germany, this middling class also knew it; in 1561, the mayor of Stralsund, a Hanseatic city, wrote in his journal that "schoolmasters brought an instrument called *Hakkebraedt*, as he wanted to give me."[6] In 1590, an inventory of the Leipzig merchant Sebastian Cunrad's estate showed that he possessed two triangles, five hunting

Figure 5.1: Items which one could purchase at the market in Frankfurt am Main in 1517 included lutes, harps, and *Hackbret*s. Engraving from Johannes Geiler, *Die brösamlin Doct. Keiserspergs vffgelesen vo Frater Johan Paulin* (Strasbourg: Grüninger, 1517), 15, in Theodor Hampe, *Die fahrende Leute in der deutschen Vergangenheit* (Leipzig: Eugen Diederichs, 1902), 92.

horns, a *hölzernes Gelächter* (xylophone), a *Hackebret* in the case, and five flutes.[7] These references indicate that merchants, clerics, printers, and schoolmasters—all professions indicating a middle, if perhaps wealthy, class—played the instrument as a pastime. Women too played it in the sixteenth century, although Stimmer's comment that "with women it is very common,"[8] made perhaps about 1580, may refer mainly to a plucked version of the instrument. The chronicle of the Zimmern family, describing a maiden in service to Geroltzeck, living on the Lower Rhine during the end of the first half of the century, mentioned that she liked to "stand up and had to play the *hackbret* to the birds in cages."[9]

Most evidence for the instrument, however, points to increasing use among minstrels, who played it more and more for village dancing. This was especially true in Switzerland. Two minstrels, playing a shawm and a dulcimer presumably held by a neck strap, appear in an illustration playing for a carnival dance in 1509.[10] The Basel town council made payments in 1518-1519 to minstrels who played for the St. Veit's dancers, including one to *hackbretter* who played for a dance.[11] A minstrel on the *Hackbrett* was paid in 1524 for playing for Ulrich, Duke of Württemberg, at Montbéliard, now in France, so it did appear at the highest social level on occasion.[12] Minstrels outside Switzerland used it as well. In 1552 at Leipzig, an inventory of the estate of Wolff Schmit, a fiddler from Erfurt, included an old *Hackebred* and four unfinished ones.[13] A list of free musicians at Breslau in 1586 included a blind dulcimer player.[14]

Heyde remarks that the sound ideal of the urban middle class and nobility changed during the sixteenth century toward a "clearly delineated, sharply contoured, clean sound," and the dulcimer, with its ringing tone and sympathetic vibration, no longer met this ideal.[15] Othmar Luscinius, in 1536, reprinting Virdung's 1511 work on instruments, remarked about the instrument that it "is disgusting [*ignobile*], because of the great noise of sounds, each getting in the way of the others."[16] Despite this condemnation, however, the instrument lived on.

During the seventeenth and eighteenth centuries, the *Hackbrett* was clearly an instrument used in rustic situations, notably in Switzerland. Felix Platter wrote in 1612 "they celebrate the Feast of Sennes [July 30] in the name of Kilwo; all convene with drums, fifes, and *Hackbret*."[17] In 1631 it was reported of a carpenter in Lauperswill that he held a *Kilt* [party] nightly in his house, where the *Hackbrett* was played and danced.[18] Some of the musicians were itinerant and subject to local suspicion. In 1646, at

Appenzell, magistrates fined Hans Schwartz, from Tyrol, a *hackbrettler*, remarking that he also went around with his daughters improperly, and warned him out of the country.[19] Authorities suspected dancers as well. In 1677, at Grosshöchstetten, in Canton Bern, local authorities complained that Daniel Rüfenacht and Catharyna Küng "were together this past Christmas and, for an ample time, until in the evening, danced and frolicked to *Hackbrett* playing."[20] Jakob Schatzi played a *Hackbrett* and let his wife dance in 1700, at Erlach, Canton Bern.[21] Some of these references indicate that the *Hackbrett* was played alone, but fiddlers start to appear together with *Hackbrettler* in the early eighteenth century, as at Saanenländchen in 1719.[22]

Elsewhere in German-speaking territory, the *Hackbrett* was regarded as an "irregular" instrument that appeared at court on occasion. In 1643 at Nuremberg, it was included among hurdy-gurdies, bagpipes, citterns, castanets, flageolets, triangles, shawms, *Strofideln* (xylophones), crumhorns, jew's harps, *Octav-Geiger*, and cymbals in a "historical" concert.[23] The court of the Duke of Saxony at Dresden followed the custom of employing *Hackbrettierer*, a term which appears nowhere else in Germany. Philipp Hainhofer described a small dining chamber in the castle at Dresden in 1629, with five tables, one of them for the *Hackbrettierer,* "his musicians with dulcimer and *hültzines Glächter* (xylophone)."[24] Moritz Fürstenau remarks that the *Hackbrettierer*, usually four men, did not all play the instruments together, but used *Hackebret*, one or two lutes, a *Spitzharfe* (a vertical psaltery with strings on both sides of the box), and one or two violins.[25] Some *Hackbrettierer* advanced their social position and obtained regular employment, like Johann Stadermann, an oboist and court musician at Zeitz.[26]

However, polite society regarded the dulcimer with contempt. The musician Johann Mattheson wrote in 1713 that the "trifling *Hackbrett*s, except the large and gut-strung [instrument] named Pantalon, which is high-privileged, should be nailed to the houses of ill repute."[27] During the eighteenth century, wandering musicians, with whom people mostly associated the instrument, continued to be regarded by authorities with suspicion. At Waldeck, Upper Palatinate, in 1724, court books recorded that the "fiddler Hännerl Peter, who stays around Rötz, is in the habit of playing on the *Hackbredl,* may be a regular thief and robber."[28] A charter of the Swabian district government issued in 1742 identified itinerants as all foreign [i.e., not residents of the Swabian district] beggars and vagrants, be they Christians or Jews, deserters and discharged soldiers, peddlers or such people who carry around for sale all sorts of trifling silly things, as toothpicks, tooth powder, hair powder, bouquets of flowers, shoe polish, published songs and the like and really beg under this pretense, mainly also sing vile songs, wandering schoolchildren, hurdy-gurdy players, bagpipers and other pipers, *Hackbrettler*, pickpockets, safe porters, knick-knackers, etc.[29]

Authorities placed *Cimbal* players, fiddlers, and hurdy-gurdy players under penalty in Franconia in 1746, and they passed a law concerning hurdy-gurdy players, *Hackbrettler*, and bagpipers in 1747 in Württemberg.[30] Perhaps unrealistic as an ensemble, but instead idealized by the painter as rustic instruments, bagpipes, hurdy-gurdy and dulcimer accompany dancing in a painting from about 1770 by Johann Elias Nilson.[31]

The ensemble consisting of a violin, dulcimer, and bass (or, rather, a cello-sized instrument; it is variously designated as *Bassgeige, Brummbass, Bassetl*) nevertheless became popular as accompaniment for dancing at village weddings and festivals throughout German-speaking areas during the eighteenth century. The word *Cymbal* appeared during the seventeenth century and increased in frequency during the eighteenth century, especially in areas near Bohemia, such as Saxony, the Upper Palatinate, and Lower Austria, but also in Holland. As mentioned in chapter 6, Jewish musicians incorporated the *Cymbal* into ensembles with two violins and a bass by the middle of the seventeenth century. Since they also went in large numbers to Amsterdam, itinerant Jewish musicians may have had some responsibility for the spread of this instrumentation.

Horak's study of archival records from Upper Austria concerning dance musicians show that in 1724 the dulcimer was still a minor instrument, being mentioned four times. In contrast, the violin was mentioned twenty-three times, the bagpipes thirteen times, and the fife eight times, and groups of three musicians ranked third, after groups of two and single musicians.[32] However, the violin-dulcimer-bass ensemble was increasing in popularity in Austria. Such a group was described as playing for a wedding at Vienna in 1734.[33] By 1738, in Carinthia, records named six such ensembles, which Antesberger calls "probably the most customary combination" there.[34] At Weissenhorn, Württemberg, Franz Martin Kuen (died 1771) illustrated a scene at an inn with town musicians, including his grandfather, playing violin, *Hackbrett*, and bass.[35] In northern Germany,

Johann Heinrich Voss described a wedding dance to the music of the same grouping in a poem at Wandsbeck in 1776.[36]

During the eighteenth century the *Hackbrett* became closely identified as an instrument to accompany the violin. Many fiddlers also played the dulcimer. For example, of nine fiddlers from Auerburg im Inntal district, Upper Palatinate, between 1780 and 1794, six could play the dulcimer.[37] As the violin-dulcimer-bass combination became more popular, the image of the itinerant dulcimer player as individual beggar gradually disappeared. The ensemble gradually replaced the bagpipes-violin-shawm combination in that part of Germany. Joseph Hazzi reported in 1805 that dance music was mostly *Hackbrett*, two clarinets and violins and cello and that the bagpipes were no longer in use.[38]

Perhaps because of influence from France or of Hebenstreit's enlarged dulcimer, the *Hackbrett* experienced a brief fashion among upper-class northern Germans during the middle of the eighteenth century. Gilt instruments with an extra sound box added to the pin block on the right, on which single, gut bass strings were stretched, as illustrated in Verschure-Reynvaan's *Muzikaal Kunstwoordenboek* (1795), were made during the

Example 5.1: "Rakes of London," from *Tablature indrettet til Hakke-Bret*, a 1753 manuscript in the collections of the Musikhistorisk Museet, Copenhagen.

middle of the eighteenth century by such makers as Joachim Muntz, of Fronberg.[39] A Danish *hakke-bret* tablature of 1753 probably indicates the fashionable type of music played by this social class. It contains seventeen minuets, five arias, a number of marches and *Aufzüge* (processions), English country dances, and French dances (see example 5.1).[40] This was clearly not art music, but arrangements of popular music compiled for an amateur who could not read music. The lack of surviving German music composed for the dulcimer probably means that little formal teaching on the instrument took place, most players thus teaching themselves.

Decline in Germany

Although the *Hackbrett* and *Cymbal* were played in central and northern Germany, much investigation remains to be done on its use in those areas, in contrast to the extensive historical research that has been done in Austria, Switzerland, and southern Germany. In Mecklenburg, an old verbal wedding invitation mentions the *Hackbrär*, and a nineteenth-century dialect poem mentions *Fidel, Bass*, and *Hackebredd*.[41] Wrede's dictionary of the Cologne dialect makes reference to a bagpiper, *Hackbrett*, and drum in 1804, *Hackbrett*, flute, and shawm in 1806, and to a *Hackbrett* in 1826.[42] The daughter of an innkeeper in a story by the Frankfurt am Main writer Friedrich Stoltze, which appears to take place around 1835, tells her father "Papa, I miss a piano; you won't be burdened with playing the abominable *Hackbrett* in the sitting room for me."[43] Perhaps this part of Stoltze's story is a metaphor for the growth of middle-class values and the rejection of peasant culture.

In 1827, an encyclopedia entry remarked that the dulcimer "is completely out of use, only perhaps with common people here and there, for example still occurring in dance music."[44] In 1836, however, Schilling reported that in Thuringia "we heard highly skilled players of this underrated instrument, who performed far more and pleasingly than one would expect."[45] The Schleswig-Holstein writer Klaus Groth (1819-1899), in memories of his youth, describes a group of young musicians playing violin, clarinet, *Hackbrett*, and bass.[46] The *Hackbrett* was disappearing, yet even in 1880 Mendel reported that in central Germany "the *Hackbrett* is often seen in the midst of small bands of itinerant musicians," although he felt that the accordion could provide a better melodic line and a small, muffled drum could produce a better harmonic texture.[47]

Although the accordion may have dealt the final blow to the *Hack-brett* and *Cymbal* in Germany, it was the influence of urban instrumentation and the growth of wind bands that gradually ousted the dulcimer and the older ensemble from the dance floors. Komma sees two trends in Bohemia, which may be valid for German-speaking areas in general. One was the fashion for the Viennese waltz, with which string music, dominated by a pair of violins, was associated. The other was the development of brass instruments in military bands, especially after 1850.[48] The position of the dulcimer in dance music, filling the texture with rhythmic harmonic patterns, might be replaced by horns or the accordion. String-led ensembles persisted in Bavaria after World War II, but the instrumentation was two violins, clarinet, trombone, and bass.[49] The second violin in these ensembles played in thirds and sixths with the melody, rather than the double stops of the eighteenth-century second violin. That older style, however, survived among the Volga Germans, as they were isolated from these new trends.

Low Countries

Iconographic evidence suggests that the early, rectangular *Hackbrett* reached Holland and Flanders by the middle of the fifteenth century and that the early *doulcemèr* was played in Flanders in the late fifteenth and early sixteenth centuries. The Germanic word was rendered into Dutch as *hakkebord*, *hakkebert*, or *hakbord*, and it was the earlier word which lasted. It apparently remained in use for some time as an amateur's instrument played by women, as a painting by Pieter Claeissins the Young (c.1570-1623), *Parable of the Wise and Foolish Virgins*, depicts women in genteel dress playing cards to the accompaniment of women playing a fiddle, lute, and dulcimer. The player holds a hammer in her left hand and plucks a string with the third finger of her right hand.[50] Several well made Flemish instruments from the seventeenth and eighteenth centuries survive in museums. Their finely carved rosettes and elegant decoration are evidence that the instrument was played in relatively genteel, domestic settings.[51] A Dutch inventory from 1759 lists a *hakkebordt* by Johannes Couchet (1615-1655), an Antwerp harpsichord maker.[52] In the eighteenth century, the dulcimer continued to be played in a middle-class environment; a painting by J. P. Nollekens (1706-1748) depicts a woman of that class playing it with two men on the cello and violin.[53]

Despite the evidence of middle-class use, the dulcimer in the Low Countries seems to have been mainly an instrument of itinerant minstrels. It was already so by the sixteenth century. Gerhard de Jode's (1509-1591) engraving of musical instruments places classical instruments, such as clavichord, spinet, lute, cittern, on two panels, while his third panel contains a dulcimer, bagpipes, hurdy-gurdy, and tabor pipe.[54] Dyrck Rembrantz van Nierop, in an appendix to his *Wis-konsige Musyka* (Amsterdam, 1659), included a diagram of a *hackebort*, which he called a "crude and rustic instrument," and described a tuning system in use whereby four courses ran over two bridges in the ratio of 9:6:4 (evidently a survival of a fifteenth-century system; see chapter 3).[55] An archival record of 1765 listing vagabonds in Brabant, now in Belgium, mentioned "de Bruid, who makes music on the *hakkebord*."[56] Jacob Lustig, a Groningen organist, listed the *hakkebord* along with the *noordsche balk* (a relative of the zither and Appalachian dulcimer), in 1771.[57] By the middle of the nineteenth century, the dulcimer was obsolete in the Low Countries. Edmond Vander Straeten mentioned in 1892 having heard at Brussels forty years earlier a person named Jaekske, who played "all sorts of fantasies" on a *hakkebert* which he supported with a neck strap.[58]

Scandinavia

The earliest evidence of the dulcimer in Scandinavia is its depiction in a fresco at the parish church at Rynkeby, Denmark, painted about 1560.[59] A poem by Niels Bredal, published at Copenhagen in 1568, includes lines "Sing, chant, dance and spring / with *hakkebrætt*, drums and fiddles that ring."[60] The Danish cleric Anders Arebo, at the time Bishop of Trondheim, Norway, in the introduction to his psalter of 1623, invited his Norwegian audience to "fill their *krokharp*s, *hackebrett*s, and *langspil* with" the 150 psalms in his collection.[61] The hero in a Swedish translation of the Dane Ludvig Holberg's *Poema heroico-comicum* (1750) was a resident of Callundborg who was proficient on all percussion instruments, in particular the dulcimer and hurdy-gurdy.[62] Clearly these references indicate the dulcimer's humble social situation in Denmark. The Danish tablature from 1753, mentioned above, is evidence of a fashion for the instrument among the middle or upper classes, but this seems to have been a short-lived fashion. The instrument did last until the nineteenth century in Denmark. A story by Adam Oehlenschläger, written in 1813, includes a description of music played by men on the clarinet and triangle and a boy of eight on the *hakkebræt*.[63]

In Sweden, the *hackbräde* appears to have been reasonably popular from the seventeenth to the first part of the nineteenth centuries. Its social position was like that in Germany. In 1685, it was written that it was an instrument for farm workers.[64] The Musikhistoriska Museet has three eighteenth-century dulcimers from Transtrand, Dalecarlia, and Norrköping. Nineteenth-century local histories indicate that the instrument was known in Småland.[65] In the early nineteenth century it was still widespread in northern Svealand and southern Norrland.[66] Around the middle of the nineteenth century, fiddle and *hackbräde* provided music for parties on Boxing Day.[67] There is some evidence that the dulcimer was used in Norway during the eighteenth century,[68] but none for Finland or Estonia.

Switzerland

The two cantons in Switzerland where the *Hackbrett* tradition has persisted are Appenzell and Wallis (Valais). Although each has developed unique characteristics, they both belong to the wider Alpine *Hackbrett* tradition in the way the instrument is used in ensembles. As noted above, the *Hackbrett* began to be paired with the violin early in the eighteenth century. The two instruments still could be found together at the beginning of the next century. A traveler described a dance in 1804 at Innerrhoden, Appenzell, to the two instruments.[69] Although instruments from Wallis perhaps as old as the eighteenth century have survived, researchers have not discovered any literary evidence documenting use there earlier than the late nineteenth century.[70]

In the nineteenth century, the dulcimer was played in other cantons. About 1820, it was still played in a valley in Inner Switzerland, and a traveler who visited Entlebuch, in Luzern canton, in 1824, described it there.[71] Beggars played it in the Berner Oberland as late as 1925.[72] At Grindelwald, in 1830, a traveler commented on a group that played the shawm, *Hackbrett*, and violin at a dance.[73]

At the beginning of the nineteenth century Appenzell *Streichmusik* (string music) was merely a variety of a wider Alpine violin-dulcimer style. As the century passed, however, it became more distinctive. By the 1820s, musicians added a *Basset* (a small bass viol) to the combination, which a traveler heard in 1826, at an inn at Weissbad.[74] That year Ferdinand Huber published his setting of two schottisches from Appenzell "as they were played by the musicians with a violin, a *Hackbrett*, and a bass."[75] While the violin plays the melody, the *Hackbrett* plays a partly arpeggiated countermelody of considerable intricacy (see example 5.2).

The function of the *Hackbrett* in the ensemble remains the same today. The player improvises by ear an accompaniment part, using arpeggios, tremolos, and other figures.[76] By 1900, the instrumentation had increased to include a second violin, playing in parallel harmony with the first violin, a cello, playing double stops on the off-beats, and a full-size

Example 5.2: *Schottisch* **(first strain), one of several Appenzell dances performed on violin,** *Hackbrett,* **and bass, published in 1826 by Ferdinand Huber. Source: Alfred Tobler, "Der Volkstanz im Appenzellerlande,"** *Schweizerisches Archiv für Volkskunde* **8 (1905): 100.**

bass instead of the small *Basset*. There are numerous such groups today, playing both at traditional venues such as *Sennenballe* (cowherd's balls) and in more concertlike settings for tourists. Some are family-based, tracing their origins well into the nineteenth century, while others are of more recent formation. The musicians work in a variety of occupations, including farming, and regard music as a hobby, although they may make recordings and earn money from playing.[77] Hans Hürlemann, a string musician himself, has written a book on the Alder family, the best-known of the Appenzell groups.[78]

In Wallis, the *Hackbrett* survived into the twentieth century, although with a small number of players. In 1915, a player from that canton explained that there were so many individual tuning variations that they had to organize a congress in order to determine a single tuning, because of the need to accompany clarinets.[79] Some players may play alone, but usually the traditional function is as an accompaniment for a melody instrument. The instrumentation is variable, in contrast to Appenzell. It may accompany a clarinet, violin, trumpet, or an accordion.[80] The "Oberwalliser Spillit," founded in 1956, for example, features violin, diatonic accordion, *Hackbrett*, and bass.[81]

Austria

Although today the traditional *Hackbrett* is played mainly in Styria and East Tyrol, it existed in most of Austria through the nineteenth century. Around 1820, at Scheuchenstein, Lower Austria, Jakob Gauermann illustrated a wedding dance to the accompaniment of a violin, dulcimer, and a full-sized bass.[82] In Upper Austria, around 1810, weddings were accompanied generally by two violins and a bass, more expensive weddings including a *Hackbrett*, and in 1854 a writer reported the *Hackbrett* to still be in use.[83]

In 1796, it was reported that violin and *Hackbrett* were the most common instruments to accompany dancing at taverns in Salzburg.[84] At Pinzgau, Salzburg, during the 1870s, two clarinets, violin, and *Hackbrett* accompanied the *Perchtentanz*, a form of morris dancing, while in 1889 the fife (*Pfeife*) and *Hackbrett* did so.[85]

Strolz wrote in 1807 that a *Hackbrett* could be found in almost every Alpine hut, especially in the Zillertal, Tyrol. In that region, the fife (*Schwegel*) was added to the violin-dulcimer ensemble, as illustrations by Placidus Altmutter from about 1800 and 1815 show, or the ensemble might consist of a zither, *Hackbrett*, fife, two violins, bass, and jew's harp.[86] At a "butcher's jump" at Kufstein, Tyrol, in 1846, a march was played by two violins, *Hackbrett*, and *Bassett*.[87] In 1879, Sander wrote that youth in the Bregenzer Wald, in Vorarlberg, would neglect their cattle and hold spontaneous dances, using fiddlers, fifers, and *Hackbrettler*.[88]

In 1812 and 1813, at Lavanttal, Carinthia, common dances and small weddings usually featured a first violin (*Primgeiger*), *Hackbrettlist*, and bass, although larger weddings featured two fiddlers and occasionally wind instruments, if held outside.[89] In 1819, the customary music at rural weddings in Carinthia consisted of two violins, *Hakbretl*, and bass, and rarely wind instruments, the clarinet having been used then for twelve or fifteen years.[90]

The popularity of woodwind and brass instruments grew during the nineteenth century and gradually drove out the *Hackbrett* and violin from wedding music in most of Austria. In parts of Styria, East Tyrol, Tyrol, and Carinthia, however, the *Hackbrett* continued in use into the twentieth century. As late as the 1930s, in the Gailtal, Carinthia, the band at the annual *Lindentanz* consisted of two violins, clarinet, bass, and *Hackbrett*.[91] Field recordings made prior to 1960 in Tyrol and East Tyrol included items with the *Hackbrett* in various ensembles, including a wind band; flugelhorn, accordion, and bass; violin, hurdy-gurdy, and bass; accordion and bass; and harp and accordion. The recordings consisted of *Ländler*, polkas, waltzes, and other dances, as well as a yodel.[92] In East Tyrol, the *Hackbrett* continued to be made and played in the Iseltal and the Lienzer Becken into the 1970s and used in ensembles of varying instrumentation, the most common in the postwar period being clarinet, trumpet, trombone, *Hackbrett*, and bass.[93]

The area in which the traditional *Hackbrett* remains the strongest is Styria. At the beginning of the nineteenth century, the instrument was part of an ensemble consisting of one or two violins and bass. Such groups were reported at Neuberg in 1803, Kaisersberg in 1810, Fürstenfeld and Mariazell in 1811, and elsewhere.[94] In 1813, J. F. Knaffl wrote a detailed description of the wedding ritual in Styria, with transcriptions of dance tunes for two violins, *Hackbrett*, and bass, played in the Fohnsdorf district. He described the four musicians leading the wedding party to the church, playing a wedding march, and, following the ceremony, playing the same march to the tavern. Upon arrival at the tavern, the bride took part in three or four dances. The meal followed, lasting five or six hours, during which time the musicians played "table" music. At the conclusion of the meal, a toasting ceremony, with songs and instrumental accompaniment, followed. At about nine o'clock in the evening, dancing began, first with *Ehrentänze* ("honored dances"), where the bride danced the minuet and the *Deutsche* with guests. The ball continued into the night, with dances faster than the minuet and slower than the *Deutsche*. The first violin played the melody, the second violin played in parallel harmony in thirds and sixths, while the *Hackbrett* accompanied "by continuous arpeggios, in trills in thirds, sixths, and octaves, also in jumping tenths."[95]

As in other German-speaking areas, wind instruments began to replace string instruments in Styria during the nineteenth century. In 1843, at Teinbach, it was reported that musical instruments were mostly only winds, now and then a violin, bass, and *Hackbrettel*.[96] The older string ensemble also incorporated the clarinet or the trombone.[97] In western Styria especially, the *Hackbrett* nevertheless remained popular into the twentieth century. By the 1930s, its style had diverged somewhat from the diatonic accompaniment found in Salzburg and Tyrol, as players were using partly chromatic tunings and playing the melody.[98] Nevertheless, in 1979, a Styrian dance fiddler commented that the *Hackbrett* "makes its contribution to dance music somewhat in the background: it is contented with accompaniment [*Dazuschlagen*]."[99]

As the diatonic accordion increased in popularity, the *Hackbrett* became more associated with it, and by the middle of the twentieth century, its tuning followed that of the accordion. Its diatonic tuning allowed the keys of either F, B-flat, E-flat, and A-flat major or D, G, C, and F major to be played. After World War II, it began to be taught in state-sponsored music schools; in 1951, Walter Kainz, an instructor at Voitsberg, wrote a method. He commented in the introduction, however, that "playing music by note is, for a real *Hackbrett* player, an absurdity."[100]

Slovenia

Although the tradition is now extinct, Slovenians in central Slovenia, as well as in Carinthia, played the dulcimer. Except for the Hungarian-influenced *cimbal* played in Prekmurje, in eastern Slovenia, the instrument was identical to the diatonic *Hackbrett*. The German word was rendered into Slovenian as *oprekelj*, as well as other terms. In Primorskoj, it was variously called *aprikel, oprekelj, bretl, prekl* (from the Austrian diminutive *Brettl*), *cemele, cimprekelj* (combining *cimbal* and *oprekelj*), *opsase,* and *šenterija* (evidently from *santur*, once used in Serbia). In Gorenjskoj, *broma, pentek,* and *pretelj,* or *pretl,* were used.[101] Violin and *oprekelj* appear together in a painting from 1702.[102] The use of the dulcimer in Slovenia followed Alpine practice as an instrument to accompany the violin. In 1795, a traveler described an ensemble as consisting of *Zymbel,* violin, and bass.[103] Hacquet wrote in 1801 of the Krainer (the inhabitants of central Slovenia) that "violins, bass and *Zimbel* comprise their entire music."[104] By 1838, although the violin-dulcimer duo and violin-dulcimer-bass trio were still in evidence, instrumental combinations, consisting of three to five musicians, frequently included a clarinet, trumpet, or horn, both with and without the dulcimer.[105] The addition of wind instruments seemed to sound the death knell for the dulcimer, as in 1846, Matia Majar wrote that in the Zilja Valley in Carinthia, the current ensemble consisted of two violins, a bass viol, one or two clarinets, and a dulcimer, but the last instrument was often absent.[106]

Research by Mira Omerzel-Terlep has shown that the *oprekelj* was most popular in the late nineteenth century in western Slovenia, in Štajerska, Notranjska, Gorenjska, and Koroška, and around Gorizia (now in Italy) and Tolmin, as well. While it disappeared from wedding bands, it remained in use as an instrument for informal occasions. The last active player was Leopold Pivk (1912-1979), of Hotedrščica, near Goriška Brda.[107]

Volga Germans

Catherine the Great, Empress of Russia, issued a manifesto in 1763 designed to encourage Germans to settle along newly acquired land on the Volga. Immigration soon followed, especially from Hesse, but also from the Rheinland, Baden, Württemberg, Alsace, and the Palatinate, and by 1768 the immigrants had established 104 colonies.[108] Immigration then stopped; isolated from modernizing influences that touched the homeland, these farming colonists preserved many eighteenth-century customs that died out in Germany. One of these was the use of the dulcimer. They called the instrument both *Hackbrett* (or *Hackebrett*) and, to a lesser extent, *Zimbal.*

Weddings were important events in the social life of the Volga colonies, and music was intricately associated with the wedding ritual. Most of the information about wedding music that we have refers to the early twentieth century, so there is little with which to develop a history. Nevertheless, it would appear that many practices had changed little from the eighteenth century.

The musicians, often members of the same family, were, in Victor Klein's words, the "spirit and soul" of each wedding. One ensemble used until the end of the nineteenth century consisted of violin, *Hackbrett*, and bagpipes *(Dudelsack)*.[109] The size of the group varied, but the core consisted of violin and dulcimer. Two instruments might suffice, but more commonly the group had four musicians and might even be increased to as many as ten.[110] The most typical group during the first part of the twentieth century appears to have consisted of first and second violin, dulcimer, and a three-stringed cello (see illustration 11). The second violin, unlike that in Alpine ensembles which developed during the nineteenth century, seems to have been used for playing chords, like the Hungarian *kontra*.[111] Another instrument, such as the clarinet, trumpet, or accordion, might be added.[112] Wind instruments had replaced the stringed instruments for the wedding procession to and from the church, but not on the dance floor.[113]

The wedding ritual lasted for one to three days. On the eve of the wedding, close relatives and neighbors assembled at the bride's house and drank and danced, perhaps to only a small number of musicians. The next day a wind band assembled at the bride's house, leading the party to church with chorales or wedding marches and holding up the rear of the procession after the ceremony towards the groom's house or other location where the party was held. Sometimes the musicians exchanged their wind instruments for stringed instruments when they arrived. The first three dances, called the *Brautreihe* ("bridal series"), consisted usually of waltzes, danced only by the newlyweds. The crowd then joined in with other dances, including the polka, *Schleifer*, mazurka, galop, *Züricher Schwabtanz*, *Oira*, *Rusche*, *csardas*, *krakowiak*, *Mineon*, and fox trot, some being favored by older dancers, others by the younger people. The musicians gathered themselves around a table, near the groom's place. They were paid by the dancers, who often placed coins on the *Hackbrett* before they began to dance. Dances were interrupted regularly by toasts, which were accompanied by music. Dancing resumed after the meal and continued into the morning. Sometimes dancing would follow the next day.[114]

During World War II, the Soviet authorities ordered the Germans living in the Volga settlements to be evacuated. They went to distant locations in Kazakhstan and Siberia. Few would have been able to take *Hackbrett*s with them, and wedding customs could have been recreated in the new areas only with difficulty. Their descendants became somewhat russified, and many have recently emigrated to Germany. The survival of this dulcimer tradition thus rested with the descendants of those emigrants who found new lives in the United States and South America.[115]

Revival

By the early twentieth century, the *Hackbrett* had virtually disappeared from Salzburg. Tobi Reiser, a popular singer and guitarist, first saw one in a tavern in 1932 played by a Styrian woodsman. Later his group incorporated an East Tyrol *Hackbrett*, but its diatonic tuning and weight caused difficulties. Reiser, his son, Franz Peyer, and Heinrich Bandzauner, an instrument maker, designed a new, lighter instrument with a chromatic tuning, and by 1938 they had produced eighty instruments. By 1940 there were over a hundred players of the new *Salzburger Hackbrett*.[116] That year Cesar Bresgen included a *Hackbrett* part in his children's opera *Sommer und Winter*.[117]

In the postwar period, the *Salzburger Hackbrett* grew in popularity, both in Salzburg and in neighboring Bavaria. Teachers taught the *Hackbrett*, as well as zither, guitar, and harp, in state-sponsored music schools, mainly to children, who formed ensembles of stringed instruments and played from written music. The new *Hackbrett* thus became absorbed into the domestic tradition of *Hausmusik* associated with the zither and guitar. Methods were written by Otto Eberhard in 1951 and by Karl-Heinz Schickhaus in 1962.[118] Commercial firms as well as individual makers manufactured the instruments.

By the early 1980s, in just two districts in Bavaria (Miesbach and Bad Tölz-Wolfratshausen), Hans Halmbacher identified 102 ensembles which included from one to three *Hackbrett*s. Most consisted of teenagers, largely female, playing different instruments, including accordion, recorder, violin, bass, but mostly zither, guitar, or harp, in addition to the *Hackbrett*.[119] The success of the instrument was due in large measure to the Bavarian system of music schools. These began originally between 1923 and 1933 and continued to grow in the postwar period: in 1982, there were 91,300 pupils at 165 schools.[120] Today there are a few professional players and teachers employed at the schools. Rudi Zapf, who plays a variety of music on his instrument, has organized a festival in Munich for several years. A repertoire of "serious" music has developed in recent years as well, Karl-Heinz Schickhaus having encouraged composers to write for the instrument. In 1999, *Hackbrett* players in Baden-Württemberg formed an organization, the Landes-Hackbrett-Bund.

The *Hackbrett* in America

Lutheran and Reformed Germans who settled in Pennsylvania, Maryland, and other colonies in North America during the middle of the eighteenth century would certainly have brought the *Hackbrett* with them, just as did the Germans who settled along the Volga during the same period. Probably typical was the use of the instrument at a dance in 1808 at the house of John Glessner, in York County, Pennsylvania, which Lewis Miller illustrated thirty years later (see illustration 10). The artist indicated his lack of familiarity with the English word "dulcimer," as the inscription under the illustration reads "Stepfan a good violin player and his companion a German playing on the indulcimor, or barbiton neut. lyricum, ein hackbret."[121] Miller obviously copied this phrase from a dictionary. "Stepfan" appears to be Afro-American, as were many fiddlers in America at that time. From this we can assume that, while the Pennsylvania Germans preserved the *Hackbrett* tradition, they probably were absorbing the country dances of their English-speaking neighbors by the early nineteenth century. The word "dulcimer" was familiar to some Pennsylvania Germans: in 1797, one Dr. Dady, a German immigrant fluent in English, appeared in Shrewsbury Township, York County to sell something he called a "dulcimer elixir," which would allegedly rid purchasers of evil spirits.[122] In 1923, Henry Shoemaker wrote that the French Huguenots in Berks, Lehigh, and Lebanon Counties, Pennsylvania brought "the dulcimer, 'dulcimore,' or hackbrett, as it was variously called."[123] As these counties were settled primarily by Germans, who in part evidently called it *Hackbrett*, his Huguenot attribution must be wrong.

At Charleston, South Carolina, in 1778, Bartholomew Hobzl, "lately arrived here from Germany," advertised that he taught the "violin, dulcimer, French horn, bassoon, and clarinet after the most approved manner."[124] Hobzl clearly was a trained musician, and the dulcimer he taught must have been part of the middle- and upper-class fashion of central and northern Germany of the period. If he had any success in attracting pupils during the Revolution, they would more likely, in any case, to have been of English descent.

A specific German *Hackbrett* or dulcimer tradition, derived from eighteenth-century immigration, however, does not seem to have survived into the twentieth century. Little evidence of use of the instrument in the traditional German-speaking area of Pennsylvania is known to me, although one informant told me of his Pennsylvania "Dutch" ancestor, a Civil War veteran who settled in Kansas, who had one.[125] Several members of the Pittsburgh family of the music publisher Theodore Presser, born in 1848, played the "dulcimer"; his mother was from Gettysburg and their playing could represent a long-standing tradition of German origin.[126] Mrs. Ollie Knittle (c.1859-c.1953), of Adams County, Indiana, played a couple of tunes (including "King's Head") on a trapezoidal dulcimer, using corset-stay hammers, which was supposed to have been brought from Pennsylvania by her husband's grandfather.[127] This is some evidence for the survival of a Pennsylvania German tradition, but the corset-stay hammers indicate influence from Anglo-American tradition. Similarly, although Loy Swiger (1913-1981), who learned to play the dulcimer as a child in Doddridge County, West Virginia, from Jesse Ash, held his hammers between first and second fingers, it is likely that this was an individual aberration, rather than part of a wider tradition of German origin.

Some immigrants from Austria and Switzerland played the *Hackbrett*, but this was largely an individual phenomenon. John Kegel, of Appenzell, Switzerland, made his instrument in 1904 and afterwards emigrated to Albany, New York, where he continued to play it.[128] Elfrieda Bergman Haese, whose grandparents immigrated to Milwaukee, Wisconsin, from Styria, recalls a player among the Austrian immigrants there.[129] Hans Ofeld, an Austrian who settled in Yorkville, New York City, in the 1930s, played the *Hackbrett* and zither at private parties.[130]

The Germans coming from the Volga River colonies in Russia brought the most vigorous *Hackbrett* tradition to the United States. They began to immigrate in the 1870s, first to wheat-growing areas in Ellis and Rush Counties, Kansas, later to areas of sugar beet cultivation in Colorado, Nebraska, Wisconsin, and Michigan, and also to the San Joaquin Valley of California and to western Washington. World War I stopped emigration. As these immigrants had come from insular, rural areas and settled in rural areas, they preserved many customs, including weddings and wedding music.

The "dulcimer," as the Volga Germans called the *Hackbrett* or *Zimbal* once they learned English, was almost indispensable in the groups which played for weddings. Its countermelodies provided the rhythmic accompaniment for the ensemble. The instrumentation was variable, but its core was the violin and dulcimer. To this combination bagpipes might be added, as Sallet writes,[131] but more typical, at least in areas of substantial Volga German settlement, as in Kansas and Colorado, was first and second violin, dulcimer, cello or bass, and clarinet or accordion. Until World War II, weddings, which sometimes lasted for three days, remained the chief venue for the music. During the 1940s, however, the growth of popularity in the polka among the wider population seems to have caused the bands to appear more in public places, such as pavilions, bars, and lodge halls. The piano accordion grew in popularity in the 1930s and 1940s, gradually ousting the violins. With the addition of trombone or sometimes baritone horn or trumpet, the wedding music of the Volga Germans in Colorado now took on the label "Dutch Hop" music.[132]

In other areas of Volga German settlement, however, the dulcimer declined. In Ellis County, Kansas, S. J. Sackett wrote in 1962 that dulcimer playing was a "dying art," although he was able to meet four or five players.[133] In that region, dances had also moved out of homes in the 1930s into public halls. Bands, which earlier might consist of two or three violins and a dulcimer, or violin, dulcimer, cello, accordion or reed organ, and sometimes clarinet, increasingly used saxophone, guitar, trombone, and piano. This change in venues coincided with increasing marriage outside the Russian-German community during World War II. In Kansas, the term *Hochzeit* was used both for the wedding party and for a particular polka step used there. Sackett wrote that the wedding dances included waltzes, polkas, "hochzeits," schottisches, as well as fox-trots and rock-and-roll. Dulcimer players primarily played the traditional dance tunes, but also knew tunes like "Red Wing," "Listen to the Mockingbird," "Sioux City Sue," and "Lili Marlene."[134] By the 1970s, some dulcimer players, like Al Jacobs, of Menasha, Wisconsin, who had an instrument made by Wendelin Younger, of Hays, Kansas, no longer identified it as an ethnic instrument and played strictly "American" tunes.

Other areas of Volga German settlement, like Kenosha, Wisconsin, and the Saginaw, Michigan, area, included dulcimer players. Adam Clauss, Sr., came with his family to Michigan in 1912 as an eight-year-old, and he played the instrument on the ship sailing over the Atlantic. Later he played for weddings with his three children. The population of Volga Germans in the Saginaw area was much smaller than those of Colorado, Kansas, or Nebraska, and the distinctive music died out in the 1950s.

Example 5.3 (next page): "Filzstievel Polka" (first strain), played by Bob Schmer, piano accordion, Albert Fahlbusch, dulcimer, Andy Gentry, trombone, Roger Fahlbusch, bass guitar, Tim Sauer, drums, of Scottsbluff, Nebraska. Source: *Polka Play Boys*, LP PPB 100-1, early 1970s.

In Colorado and neighboring Nebraska, however, "Dutch Hop" music continued to grow in the postwar period. Local record labels, like Rocky Mountain, of Greeley, and Frontier, of Denver, issued recordings of local bands. Adolph Lesser's band even received a contract from Columbia in 1950. Regular dances were held in ballrooms, barns, and bars, in Denver, Greeley, Fort Collins, Windsor, Loveland, and elsewhere in northern Colorado, as well as Scottsbluff, Nebraska.[135] In the 1980s, a weekly radio show broadcast from Windsor, Colorado, featured the music, and weekly dances were held in Denver, Colorado Springs, Fort Collins, and Loveland.[136] Over twenty bands were active in Colorado and Nebraska, and most had issued recordings. Nearly all featured the dulcimer.

As with the *tsymbaly* of the Ukrainian-Canadians, the dulcimer of the descendants of the Volga Germans in Colorado, Nebraska, and Kansas stands as a distinctive ethnic symbol. Although violins have mostly disappeared from the ensembles and new instruments, like the ubiquitous electronic keyboard and drums have been added to them, the dulcimer remains. The instrument may be partly responsible for continued interest in the music. For example, Mike Gaschler, who had played rock music in high school, went to a wedding reception a few years afterwards and was impressed by the dulcimer in the band. His wife bought him one and soon he was playing with a band. In 1982, he started his own band, the "Polka Nuts," with his two daughters, and they continue to perform and tour.[137]

The role of the dulcimer in "Dutch Hop" music is to embellish the melody with broken chords, countermelodies, variations, and also occasionally to reinforce it. Its function thus is the same as in other *Hackbrett* traditions. The repertoire of the bands includes polkas, waltzes, and Russian and Polish tunes which were inherited from the immigrants who came from Russia, newly composed tunes in the same style, polkas and waltzes from the postwar pop tradition, and more recent country-western tunes.

Design

Before discussing regional *Hackbrett* designs, we might mention a few characteristics which seem to apply to most local traditions. The common name for the instrument implies a common origin, and, although later innovations may obscure it, it is possible to demonstrate characteristics which set the *Hackbrett* family apart from other dulcimer traditions. The tuning of most *Hackbrett*s, unlike most instruments of the cimbalom family, but like those of British and American traditions, is diatonic. Although regional innovations in bridge placement may obscure this basic design, the diatonic tuning necessitates the placement of the pin blocks at angles more acute than those of the most of the cimbalom family. Another characteristic is the use of four strings per course throughout, which is similar to British instruments but different from most eastern cimbaloms, which use five or more. Rosettes, either carved or set into the two to four sound holes, are common, which is also characteristic of Ukrainian and Polish *tsymbaly*, but unlike the simple holes of British dulcimers. Finally, hammers usually have upper and lower notches carved into the ends and are held between first and second fingers. This grip is similar to that used on instruments of the cimbalom family (whose hammers, however, often have only an upper notch), but different than that used in British and American traditions.

Germany

Museum catalogs and other sources have failed to distinguish the German *Cymbal* (also *Zimbel, Zimbal*, etc.) from the *Hackbrett*, although these names may represent traditions more than instrument types. Nevertheless, certain dulcimers from southern Germany surviving in modern collections, probably originally called *Cymbals*, display many similarities to older Hungarian *cimbaloms* and should be identified as such. Those are discussed in chapter 6.

*Hackbrett*s in traditional style from what is now Germany are rather rare. Four examples in the Heyer Collection of the University of Leipzig, said to be from the late seventeenth and eighteenth centuries, had dimensions ranging from 75 to 102 cm (29½ to 40 inches) at the lower length, 40 to 72 cm (15¾ to 28½ inches) at the upper length, and 36 to 47 cm (14¼ to 18½ inches) in width. One instrument had seven treble and seven bass courses, each with four strings per course, while the others, lacking bridges, had from nineteen to twenty-four courses, one with five strings per course, the other two with four per course.[138] A "rustic" German instrument, in the Snoeck Collection in 1894, but part of the collection of the Staatliche Hochschule für Musik in Berlin in 1922, was 106 cm (41¾ inches) at the lower length, 31 cm (12¼ inches) wide, and 6 cm (2½ inches) high, with eighteen courses of four each. Three other instruments of this type in that collection ranged from 106 to 109 cm (41¾ to 43 inches) at the lower length, 31 to 42 cm (12¼ to 16½ inches) in width, 6 to 10 cm (2½ to 4 inches) in height, and had sixteen to nineteen courses of four strings each.[139]

Low Countries

Surviving seventeenth- and eighteenth-century instruments provide our main source for the design of dulcimers in the Low Countries. Hubert Boone has analyzed seven examples, but the sample is too small and varied to draw general conclusions about the design of the dulcimer in Flanders and Holland.[140] The instruments he described have rosettes and painted decoration on the soundboards. Such instruments provide evidence of use in the middle and upper classes, but Boone did not identify any dulcimers which itinerant musicians would have used.

Scandinavia

Few dulcimers survive in Scandinavia. Kettlewell describes a *hackbräde* in the Historiskt Museum in Göteborg with eleven treble courses of four strings each, without sound holes.[141] An eighteenth-century dulcimer in the Tromsø Museum in Norway lacks bridges, but its fifteen lower courses have five strings each, and the remaining twelve upper courses have six strings each.[142] Its large size and the number of strings per course indicate that it probably was called a *cymbal*.

Switzerland

A Swiss clergyman, Johannes Hutmacher (born 1533), compiled a manuscript with a technical description of the design of the *Hackbrett* of his day. Even if he falls short in many details, he provides information of a sort not to be found anywhere else, especially since no dulcimers from that period have survived. From Brigitte Geiser's analysis, we can get a picture of a sixteenth-century Swiss dulcimer. Hutmacher gives dimensions for "large" and "medium-sized" instruments. These contained "stars," or rosettes, the diameter for the large instruments being 93 to 103 mm (3¾ to 4 inches), while those of medium instruments are given as 75-85 mm (3 to 3½ inches). The length of large instruments is 800 mm (31½ inches), the width 320 mm (12½ inches), and the angle of the pin blocks is given as 50 or 48 degrees. The pin blocks are 33 mm (1¼ inches) wide and 55 mm (2¼ inches) high and the bridges 20 mm (¾ inch) high. The tuning pin is 36 mm (1½ inches) long and shown with a "swallowtail" end, the same as the design of tuning pins used on Appenzell instruments as recently as the early twentieth century. For a medium-size *Hackbrett*, Hutmacher suggests a length of 720 mm (28¼ inches), a width of 280 mm (11 inches), pin blocks 27 mm (1 inch) high and 30 mm (1¼ inches) wide, with bridges 22 mm (.87 inch) high. He unfortunately does not mention the number and arrangement of strings nor materials.[143]

Appenzell and Wallis traditions are distinct, and the design of their instruments seems to have been so since the early nineteenth century. In Appenzell, brass strings are used, requiring a shorter string length, while Wallis instruments use steel strings. A *Hackbrett* made by John (Hans) Kegel in 1904, in the author's possession, appears identical to those in many photographs and may be regarded as typical of older Appenzell instruments.[144] It is 80 cm (31½ inches) and 48 cm (19 inches) long, 36.5 cm (14½ inches) wide, and 8 cm (3¼ inches) high, with a detachable lid. There are eleven treble courses, eleven bass courses, and one course on the left, each containing five strings per course. One bridge divides the five lower treble courses into fifths, and another bridge divides the upper six treble courses into sixths, providing a chromatic tuning. Two rosettes are set into two round sound holes. The pin blocks are nailed and glued to the sides, but not to the baseboard, making a very lightly built instrument. Appenzell hammers are relatively long and shaped so that the round shaft ends in a flat playing end. Johann Fuchs and other makers today have made innovations in the tuning, yet follow tradition in other ways.[145]

Amadé Salzmann's study of Wallis instruments, although limited to about fifteen, shows that they contain more individual variations than Appenzell instruments, yet still comprise a distinct variety. As they are strung with steel (earlier iron) strings, the length is longer, from 89 to 102 cm (35 to 40¼ inches) at the longer end and from 53 to 66 cm (21 to 26 inches) at the shorter end. Width ranges from 35 to 45 cm (13¾ to 17¾ inches), depending on the number of courses, and the height is 5 to 10 cm (2 to 4 inches). A single treble bridge carries eight to eleven courses of three to five strings each, most often four, and a single bass bridge carries five to eleven courses of the same number. The tuning is diatonic, and, in common with traditional Austrian *Hackbrett*s, jacks (called *Register*) are incorporated. When raised, these sharpen the course by a half-tone, allowing the instrument to be played in various keys. Instruments have two sound holes of different designs, and the pin blocks generally are not directly attached to the baseboard. The hammers are carved from fruit-wood or birch, about 21 cm (8¼ inches) long, with upper and lower finger notches and round shafts which are gently curved at the playing ends.[146]

Austria

Styrian instruments vary considerably in particulars of string arrangement and thus size. Instruments in two Graz collections, dating from the late eighteenth and nineteenth centuries, range from 83 to 103 (mostly about 100) cm (32¾ to 40½ inches; 39½ inches) at the longer length, 40 to 68 cm (15¾ to 26¾ inches) at the shorter length, and 26 to 45 cm (10¼ to 17¾ inches) in width. All have single treble and bass bridges, although the total number of courses varies from fifteen to twenty-eight, with three to five strings per course.[147] Some twentieth-century *Hackbrett*s contain fourteen to sixteen treble courses, with a smaller number of bass courses, as few as five and as many as fourteen, with four or occasionally five strings per course.[148] Sound holes vary in number from two to four and may be round or may have rosettes. Tuning is also variable, but it usually follows the diatonic "Styrian" accordion, allowing the *Hackbrett* to be played either in the keys of F, B-flat, E-flat, and A-flat, or in D, G, C, and F.[149] Jacks (*Leittonscharniere*) are sometimes found on the instruments, but seem to be exceptional. Hammers, writes Rosenzopf, are carved from the root of the spruce tree, but vary considerably in design.[150] Kainz shows two examples, both with shallow upper and lower notches in the handles. One is carved from a single piece of wood, with a curved playing end. The other uses a spring steel shaft and a round playing end, wrapped on one side with leather.[151]

In East Tyrol, according to Pedarnig, *Hackbrett*s are larger than the Styrian instruments, but the tonal range is smaller. He describes newer instruments being 154 cm (60¾ inches) and 88 cm (34¾ inches) long, 54 cm (21¼ inches) wide, and 9 cm (3½ inches) high. They are tuned diatonically and generally have nine treble and nine bass courses, each with three or four strings per course, although some may have ten treble and eleven bass courses. They contain two to four sound holes. Jacks (*Halbton-schneller* or *Halbtonheber*) are found on all instruments, although the number varies from two to fourteen.[152] The diatonic *Hackbrett* of Salzburg was about 116 to 125 cm (45¾ to 49¼ inches) at the lower length, 35 to 41 cm (13¾ to 16 inches) wide, and 6 to 7 cm (2½ to 2¾ inches) high, with a total of twenty or twenty-one courses (but sometimes more) of four (sometimes five) strings each. They had carved rosettes and a number of jacks.[153]

Slovenia

The Slovenian *oprekelj*, according to Mira Omerzel-Terlep, most often had twenty-one courses of five strings each, with three to eight half-step jacks, providing a diatonic range from A to e^2. However, nineteenth-century examples vary in design, and four strings per course are also common. The general dimensions are about 100 cm (39½ inches) at the lower length, 56 cm (22 inches) at the upper length, 43 cm (17 inches) in width, and 7 cm (2¾ inches) in height. Hammers were carved from wood, sometimes covered with cotton or yarn, and were also made from metal. Omerzel-Terlep writes that the size of Slovenian instruments was similar to that of East Tyrolian instruments, but the tuning was closer to the traditions of Styria and Salzburg.[154]

Volga Germans

Information on the dulcimers of this tradition comes from instruments made in the United States, as I am aware of only one Russian photograph (see illustration 11). One might consider them as falling into two types. The first has only treble and right bass bridges, while the second also has one or two bass courses over a bridge on the lower left side of the soundboard. These may correspond to eighteenth-century *Hackbrett* and *Cymbal* types, but, as two informants called instruments of the latter type *Hackebrett* or *Hackbrett*,[155] the distinction, if any, may have been lost. The second type was depicted by Johann Conrad Seekatz (1719-1768), a Hessian court painter, in his painting *Two Boys, One Playing a Dulcimer* (see illustration 9). This shows an instrument with nine treble courses, eight bass courses, and a single bridge on the lower left, played with long, slender hammers with hooked ends. The instrument has four semitone jacks on the left and one on the right.[156] Since the painter was active in the same part of Germany from which most of the Volga colonists came, this instrument probably represents the type brought to Russia. Semitone jacks are unknown in the Volga German tradition, however, so Seekatz probably depicted a recent innovation. Sackett reported that dulcimers in

Ellis County, Kansas, were of the first type, with seventeen, nineteen, or twenty-one courses of four strings each (in one case, three), with two to four sound holes, although three was normal.[157] A photograph of the dulcimer played by Anton Sauer, of Antonino, Kansas, made in 1903, shows eight treble and nine bass courses, with four strings per course; it thus belongs to the first type.[158] Instruments of the second type, with eight treble courses of four or five strings per course, nine courses of four or five over a bridge on the right, a course over a bridge on the lower right-hand side of the soundboard, and two courses of brass strings over a bridge on the lower left-hand side of the soundboard, were played by Henry Maser, of Au Gres, Michigan, and Alexander Eckerdt, of Flint, Michigan.[159] A diatonic tuning seems to be standard, playable in the violin keys of A, D, G, and C major.

The number of sound holes varies from one to four, although three is typical, and their design differs. Clusters of small holes seem to be characteristic. A central hole with six concentric holes is found, again suggesting a relationship to the Central European *Cymbal*, but six-petaled flower designs exist as well. Hammers are carved of hardwood, usually with both upper and lower finger notches, the playing end shaped, by means of a hole, so that the stem appears to curve backwards and join the stem again. Another characteristic of the Volga German design is that upper and lower lengthwise rails are mortised into the pin blocks, somewhat like the instruments of the Eastern European cimbalom family. The baseboard, however, is thicker, and extends to the edges of the instrument. A dulcimer made by Adam Deines in Flint, Michigan, about 1930 measures 47 and 22¾ inches (119 and 57.8 cm) in length, 20¾ inches (52.7 cm) in width, and 3¾ inches (9.2 cm) in height; its baseboard is 5/8 inch (1.6 cm) thick.

The design of the dulcimer of Volga German heritage probably retains the diatonic tuning of the old German *Hackbrett* and in some cases the left-hand bass bridge of the eighteenth-century Bohemian-German *Cymbal*. Since the latter term was in occasional use in the Volga colonies, it is likely that the *Cymbal* had entered Hesse by the 1760s, when the colonists emigrated. The number and design of the sound holes on some instruments also bears some resemblance to Bohemian and Hungarian members of the cimbalom family.

The Salzburg Chromatic *Hackbrett*

The unique feature of this dulcimer is its tuning. Its courses rest on bridges which lie parallel with the pin blocks. Each succeeding course is tuned a half-step higher than the neighboring course on the opposite bridge. It is thus possible to play a tune in any key with only two hammering patterns. Instruments have thirteen or fourteen courses, with three or four strings per course, over the left bridge and twelve or thirteen courses over the right bridge, although instruments with more courses also exist. The lower length is 83 to 85 cm (32¾ to 33½ inches), the upper length 33 to 38 cm (13 to 15 inches), the width 50 to 52 cm (19¾ to 20½ inches), and the height about 6 cm (2½ inches). Tuning pins are set into the left pin block. In the center of the soundboard is a single, round sound hole, often with a rosette. In recent years, a *Tenorhackbrett*, with a wider range, has become popular.

Notes

1. Willibald von Lütgendorff, *Die Geigen- und Lautenmacher vom Mittelalter bis zur Gegenwart* (Frankfurt am Main, 1924), 456, in Herbert Heyde, "Frühgeschichte des europäischen Hackbretts (14.-16. Jahrhundert)," *Deutsches Jahrbuch für Musikwissenschaft* 18 (1973-1977): 162 n. 37.

2. Johannes Geiler, *Die brösamlin Doct. Keiserspergs vffgelesen vo Frater Johan Paulin* (Strasbourg: Grüninger, 1517), 15, in Theodor Hampe, *Die fahrende Leute in der deutschen Vergangenheit* (Leipzig: Eugen Diederichs, 1902), 92.

3. Johannes Jud, *Historische Beschreibung von dem Leben und Tod, Hauss und Geschlecht, Kinder und Kinds-Kinderen des fürtrefflichen Manns Hrn. Leonis Judae* (1574) in Miscellanea Tigurina, part 3 (Zurich, 1724), 62, in Karl-Heinz Wyss, *Leo Jud: seine Entwicklung zum Reformator, 1519-1523*, Europäische Hochschulschriften, ser. 3, vol. 61 (Bern: Herbert Lang; Frankfurt am Main: Peter Lang, 1976), 56.

4. Georg Finsler, ed., *Die Chronik des Bernhard Wyss*, Quellen zur schweizerischen Reformationsgeschichte, vol. 1 (Basel: Basler Buch- und Antiquariatshandlung, 1901), 4f., in Heyde, "Frühgeschichte," 162 n. 38.

5. Felix Platter, Basel, 1612, in Heinrich Boos, ed., *Thomas und Felix Platter: zur Sittengeschichte des XVI. Jahrhunderts* (Leipzig: S. Hirzel, 1878), 134.

6. *Baltische Studien*, 19, in Troels-Lund, *Dagligt liv i Norden i det 16de Aarhundrede* (Copenhagen: Gyldendalske Boghandels Forlag, 1903), 6: 79.

7. Rudolf Wustmann, *Musikgeschichte Leipzigs* (Leipzig: B. G. Teubner, 1909), 1: 164.

8. Brigitte Geiser, "Das Hackbrett in der Schweiz," in John Henry van der Meer, Brigitte Geiser, Karl-Heinz Schickhaus, *Das Hackbrett: ein alpenländisches Musikinstrument* (Herisau/Trogen: Verlag Schläpfer, 1975), 33, quoting Georg Hirth, *Liebhaber-Bibliothek alter Illustratoren* (Munich: Hirth, 1880-1903), 4: 1084.

9. Karl August Barack, ed., *Zimmerische Chronik*, 2nd ed. (Freiburg: J. C. B. Mohr, 1881-1882), 3: 612, in Heyde, "Frühgeschichte," 162 n. 41.

10. Luzerner Chronik 1513, f. 259, in Geiser, "Hackbrett in der Schweiz," 29.

11. F. Ernst, "Die Spielleute im Dienste der Stadt Basel vom ausgehenden Mittelalter (bis 1550)," *Basler Zeitschrift für Geschichte und Altertum* 44 (1945): 204, in Geiser, "Hackbrett in der Schweiz," 25n.

12. Dr. Schneider, "Herzog Ulrichs Hofhaltung in Mömpelgart, der Schweiz und Hohentwiel," *Württembergische Vierteljahrshefte für Landesgeschichte* 9 (1886): 35.

13. Wustmann, *Musikgeschichte Leipzigs*, 1: 67.

14. Sibyl Marcuse, *A Survey of Musical Instruments* (New York: Harper & Row, 1975), 224.

15. Heyde, "Frühgeschichte," 147.

16. Ottomar Luscinius, *Musurgia seu praxis musicae* (Argentorati: apud Ioannem Schottum), 13. I am relying on the translation in Kettlewell, "Dulcimer," 97.

17. Karl Nef, *Historisches Museum Basel: Katalog No. 4: Musikinstrumente* (Basel: Emil Birkhäuser, 1906), 27, in Hanns in der Gand, "Volkstümliche Musikinstrumente der Schweiz," *Schweizerisches Archiv für Volkskunde* 36 (1937): 93.

18. Bern Chorgerichtsmanual, in Geiser, "Hackbrett in der Schweiz," 25.

19. Wochenrathsprotokoll, 26 Sept. 1646, in Margaret Engeler, *Das Beziehungsfeld zwischen Volksmusik, Volksmusiker und Volksmusikpflege: am Beispiel der Appenzeller Streichmusik* (Herisau/Trogen: Verlag Schläpfer, 1984), 31.

20. Bern Chorgerichtsmanual, 29 July 1677, in Geiser, "Hackbrett in der Schweiz," 26.

21. Erlach Chorgerichtsmanual, 2 June 1700, in Geiser, "Hackbrett in der Schweiz," 26.

22. Hanny Christen, "Unser Hackbrett," *Volkshochschule* 25 (1956): 39.

23. Willi Kahl, "Das nürnberger historische Konzert von 1643 und sein Geschichtsbild," *Archiv für Musikwissenschaft* 14 (1957): 287.

24. Philipp Hainhofer, *Des Augsburger Patriciers Philipp Hainhofer Reisen nach Innsbruck und Dresden*, ed. Oscar Doering, Quellenschriften für Kunstgeschichte und Kunsttechnik des Mittelalters und der Neuzeit, n.s., vol. 10 (Vienna: Carl Graeser & Co., 1901), 208.

25. Moritz Fürstenau, *Zur Geschichte der Musik und des Theaters am Hofe zu Dresden* (1861; reprint, Leipzig: Edition Peters, 1979), 1: 202.

26. Arno Werner, *Städtische und fürstliche Musikpflege zu Zeitz* (Leipzig: Siegel, 1922), 90, in Werner Braun, "The 'Hautboist;' an Outline of Evolving Careers and Functions," in Walter Salmen, ed., *The Social Status of the Profes-*

sional Musician from the Middle Ages to the 19th Century, trans. by Herbert Kaufman and Barbara Riesner (New York: Pendragon Press, 1983), 132.

27. Johann Mattheson, *Das neu-eröffnete Orchestre* (Hamburg: B. Schiller, 1713), 280.

28. Walter Hartinger, *Volkstanz, Volksmusikanten und Volksmusikinstrumente der Oberpfalz zur Zeit Herders*, Quellen und Studien zur musikalischen Volkstradition in Bayern, ser. 4, Studien zur musikalischen Volkstradition, vol. 1 (Regensburg: Gustav Bosse Verlag, 1980), 50.

29. Hampe, *Die fahrende Leute*, 102.

30. Hartinger, *Volkstanz*, 35; *Sammlung der württembergischen Gesetze*, 14: 306, in Hermann von Fischer, *Schwäbisches Wörterbuch* (Tübingen: H. Laupp, 1904-1930), 3: 1010f.

31. Karl-Heinz Schickhaus, *Über Volksmusik und Hackbrett in Bayern* (Munich: BLV Verlagsgesellschaft, 1981), 164.

32. Karl Horak, "Der Volkstanz in Oberösterreich und im Salzkammergut," in *Beiträge zur Volksmusik in Oberösterreich*, ed. Walter Deutsch (Vienna: A. Schendl, 1982), 131.

33. Helge Thiel, "Quellen und Nachrichten zur volkstümlichen Geigenmusik in Österreich," in *Die Geige in der europäischen Volksmusik*, ed. Walter Deutsch and Gerlinde Haid, Bericht über das 1. Seminar für europäische Musikethnologie, St. Pölten, 1971 (Vienna: A. Schendl, 1975), 111.

34. Günther Antesberger, "'Ain Groschen in die Geigen . . .': Kärntner Spielleute im 18. Jahrhundert," *Musicologica Austriaca* 10 (1991): 43-44.

35. Schickhaus, *Über Volksmusik*, 141, 143.

36. Johann Heinrich Voss, "Reigen," in *Sämtliche Gedichte*, 4: 55-57.

37. Reinhard Seitz, *Tanzmusikpatente*, in Hartinger, *Volkstanz*, 50n.

38. Joseph Hazzi, *Statistische Aufschlüsse* (Nuremberg: In der Steinischen Buchhandlung, 1805), 4: 256, in Hartinger, *Volkstanz*, 64.

39. Joos Verschuere Reynvaan, *Muzijkaal Kunst-woordenboek* (Amsterdam: W. Brave, 1795), 356-357. Muntz's instrument, dated 1757, is in the Germanisches Nationalmuseum, no. 731. A similar one is in the Braunschweig Städtisches Museum. An engraving by the genre painter Josef Munsch, *A Trio*, which appeared in *Der Hausfreund* 16 (1873): 393, depicting two eighteenth-century gentlemen playing violin and transverse flute, accompanied by a woman playing a large *Hackbrett* by ear, cannot be used as evidence of this fashion.

40. "Tablature indrettet til Hakke-Bret," Musikhistorisk Museum, Copenhagen.

41. Alfred Horn, *Zur Geschichte des Kirchspiels Selmsdorf im Fürstentum Ratzeburg* (Schönberg in Mecklenburg: Lehmann & Bernhard, 1909-1934), 1: 349, and Wilhelm Heyse, *Frische Kamiten ut Krischan Schulten sin Muskist* (Berlin, 1863), 17, in Richard Wossidlo, *Wossidlo-Teuchert mecklenburgisches Wörterbuch* (Berlin: Akademie-Verlag, 1958), 3: 346.

42. Adam Wrede, *Neuer kölnischer Sprachschatz* (Cologne: Greven, 1956), 1: 321.

96   Chapter 5

43. Friedrich Stoltze, "Der rothe Schornsteinseger" (1867), in *Gesammelte Werke* (Frankfurt: Heinrich Keller, 1892), 3: 17.

44. J. S. Ersch and J. G. Gruber, ed., *Allgemeine Encyclopädie der Wissenschaften und Künste* (Leipzig: Johann Friedrich Gleditsch, 1827), 45: 76.

45. Gustav Schilling, ed., *Encyclopädie der gesammten musikalischen Wissenschaften, oder Universal-Lexicon der Tonkunst* (Stuttgart: F. H. Köhler, 1835-1841), 3: 414.

46. Klaus Groth, *Uit min Jungsparadies* (Berlin: Georg Stilke, 1876), 21.

47. Herman Mendel, *Musikalisches Conversations-Lexikon*, 2nd ed. (Berlin: Robert Oppenheim, 1880), 4: 469.

48. Karl Michael Komma, *Das böhmische Musikantentum*, Die Musik im alten und neuen Europa, ed. Walter Wiora, vol. 1 (n.p.: Johann Philipp Hinnenthal-Verlag, 1960), 73.

49. Schickhaus, *Über Volksmusik*, 49.

50. Hubert Boone, "Beknopte Bijdrage tot de Geschiedenis van het Hakkebord in de Lage Landen," *Volkskunde: Tijschrift voor Nederlandsche Folklore* 77 (1976): 206; Richard D. Leppert, *The Theme of Music in Flemish Paintings of the Seventeenth Century* (Munich: Musikverlag Emil Katzbichler, 1977), 2: 32, 226. The painting is in the collections of the Klooster Zwart-Zusters Augustinessen, 136708B, in Bruges. Leppert's survey of 770 paintings revealed no other examples, which must indicate the relative scarcity of the dulcimer.

51. Boone, "Beknopte Bijdrage," 209-211, discusses these.

52. Peter Williams, "A Dutch Harpsichord Inventory of 1759," *The Organ Yearbook* 3 (1972): 82-83, in Boone, "Beknopte Bijdrage," 212; Hubert Boone and Wim Bosmans, *Volksinstrumenten in België* (Leuven: Peters, 1995), 23.

53. Boone and Bosmans, *Volksinstrumenten*, 27, 203.

54. Boone, "Beknopte Bijdrage," 207.

55. J. Murray Barbour, "Nierop's Hackebort," *Musical Quarterly* 20 (July 1934): 312-319. Barbour further discusses Nierop's theoretical octave of seven equal tones. The placement of the bridges, in any case, may be a survival of a fifteenth-century system.

56. M. J. van den Born, website, quoting Record 93, file 112-04, <http://www.xs4all.nl/~defonte/b.txt>.

57. Jacob Wilhelm Lustig, *Inleiding tot de Muziekkunde* (Groningen: H. Vechnerus, 1771), 82-83, in Boone, "Beknopte Bijdrage," 207-208.

58. Edmond Vander Straeten, *Les billets des rois en Flandre* (Ghent: J. Vuylsteke, 1892), 165, in Boone, "Beknopte Bijdrage," 208-209.

59. Mette Müller, "Der himmlische Lobgesang in Rynkeby: eine dänische ikonografische Quelle des 16. Jahrhunderts," *Studia instrumentorum musicae popularis* 4 (1976): 72.

60. Niels Bredal, *Børne-Speigel* (Copenhagen, 1568), 4, in Troels-Lund, *Dagligt liv i Norden i det sekstende århundrede* (Copenhagen: Gyldendal, 1969), 3: 3, in Bjørn Aksdal, *Med Piber og Basuner, Skalmeye og Fiol: Musikkinstrumenter: Norge ca.1600-1800* ([Trondheim?]: Tapir, 1982), 27.

61. Kettlewell, "Dulcimer," 105-106, quoting Anders Arrebo, K. *Davids Psalter, Sangviisz udsat, under hundrede og nogle Melodier og Toner* (Copenhagen, 1623).

62. Ludvig Holberg, *Baron Ludvig Holbergs Poema heroico-comicum, angående den beröomlige Peder Pårses hjelte-bedrifter* (Stockholm: Peter Jöransson Nyström, 1750).

63. Adam Oehlenschläger, "Eremiten," in *Poetiske Skrifter*, vol. 14-15, *Hrolf Krake. Oervarodds Saga. Eremiten* (Copenhagen: Nordiske Forlag, 1899), 231.

64. Haqvin Spegel, *Gudz werk och hwila* (Stockholm: Nicolaus Wankijf, 1685), in Kettlewell, "Dulcimer," 107.

65. Gunnar Olof Hyltén-Cavallius, *Värend och Virdarna: ett försök i svensk ethnologi* (Stockholm, 1863-1868), 2: 458, and Carl Viking, "Kråksmåla o Ålghult snr, Handbörd och Uppvidinge hdr, Småland," EU 19163, Nordiska Muséet Archives, in Kettlewell, "Dulcimer," 303.

66. *Svensk uppslagsbok*, s.v. "Hackbräde."

67. Gustav S. Eriksson, ed., *Julseder*, vol. 1 (Stockholm, 1928-1934), in Kettlewell, "Dulcimer," 303.

68. Aksdal, *Med Piber og Basuner*, 27-28.

69. J. R. Steinmüller, *Beschreibung der schweizerischen Alpen- und Landwirtschaft* (Winterthur: In der Steinerischen Buchhandlung, 1804), 2: 193, in Geiser, "Hackbrett in der Schweiz," 26.

70. Amadé Salzmann, *Das Hackbrett im Wallis: Instrumentenbau und Spielanleitung* ([Visp]: Rotten-Verlag, n.d.), 13-14, 34-37.

71. Christen, "Unser Hackbrett," 40; In der Gand, "Volkstümliche Musikinstrumente," 93.

72. Geiser, "Hackbrett in der Schweiz," 61.

73. F. J. Hugi, *Naturhistorische Alpenreisen* (Leipzig: Solothurn, 1830), 124-125, in In der Gand, "Volkstümliche Musikinstrumente," 93; Geiser, "Hackbrett in der Schweiz," 26.

74. Fr. K. von Kronfels, *Gais, Weissbad und die Molkenkuren in Canton Appenzell* (Konstanz: Wallis, 1826), 140, in Engeler, *Beziehungsfeld*, 31.

75. Alfred Tobler, "Der Volkstanz im Appenzellerlande," *Schweizerisches Archiv für Volkskunde* 8 (1905): 100-103. These appeared originally in Johann Rudolf Wyss, ed., *Sammlung von Schweizer-Kühreihen und Volksliedern*, 4th ed. (Bern: J. J. Burgdorfer, 1826).

76. Johannes Fuchs, son of the best-known maker in Appenzell, Johann Fuchs, stressed to me the difference of the Appenzell style, as opposed to the Salzburg *Hackbrett* or Belarusian *tsimbaly* schools, in *not* reading music.

77. Engeler, *Beziehungsfeld*, 146-152, 53-68.

78. Hans Hürlemann, *Brummbass, Geige, Hackbrett: 100 Jahre Appenzeller Streichmusik Alder*, Appenzeller Brauchtum, vol. 2 (St. Gallen: VGS, 1984).

79. In der Gand, "Volkstümliche Musikinstrumente," 93.

80. Geiser, "Hackbrett in der Schweiz," 4.

98   *Chapter 5*

81. Salzmann, *Hackbrett im Wallis*, 14-15.

82. Karl M. Klier, *Volkstümliche Musikinstrumente in den Alpen* (Kassel: Bärenreiter Verlag, 1956), pl. 87.

83. Franz Sartori, *Neueste Reise durch Österreich* (Vienna: Doll, 1811), 3: 356, and F. X. Pritz, *Überbleibsel aus dem hohen Alterthume im Leben und Glauben der Bewohner des Landes ob der Enns* (Linz, 1854), 81, in Klier, *Volkstümliche Musikinstrumente* 52, 100.

84. Walter Deutsch, Sepp Gmasz, and Maria Theresia Schimpfössl-Ager, "Dokumente und Literatur zur Volksmusik in Salzburg," in *Die Volksmusik im Lande Salzburg*, ed. Walter Deutsch and Harald Dengg, 11. Seminar für Volksmusikforschung, 1975, Schriften zur Volksmusik, vol. 4 (Vienna: A. Schendl, 1979), 34.

85. Klier, *Volkstümliche Musikinstrumente*, pl. 92; Deutsch et al., "Dokumente und Literatur," 30.

86. Walter Deutsch and Manfred Schneider, ed., *Beiträge zur Volksmusik in Tirol* (Innsbruck: n.p., 1978), ill. 3; Fritz Stradner, "Das Hackbrett: ein Beitrag zu seiner Entwicklungsgeschichte," *Jahrbuch des österreichischen Volksliederwerkes* 15 (1966): pl. 4; Johann Strolz, "Schnodahaggn, Unterinnthalische Volksliedchen," *Der Sammler für Geschichte und Statistik in Tirol* 2 (1807): 76, in Klier, *Volkstümliche Musikinstrumente*, 52, 72, and in Rainer Gstrein, "Tanzmusik-Ensembles in Österreich im 19. Jahrhundert: Ein Beitrag zur Frage der "Authentizität' der Besetzungspraxis instrumentaler Volksmusik," in *Tanz und Tanzmusik in Überlieferung und Gegenwart: Bericht über die 12. Arbeitsgang der Kommission für Lied-, Musik- und Tanzforschung in der Deutschen Gesellschaft für Volkskunde e. V. vom 12. bis 16. September 1990 in der Otto-Friedrich-Universität Bamberg*, ed. Marianne Bröcker, Schriften der Universitätsbibliothek Bamberg, vol. 9 (Bamberg,1992), 422.

87. *Das deutsche Volkslied* 28 (1926): 51, in Klier, *Volkstümliche Musikinstrumente*, 99.

88. Hermann Sander, *Ein Beitrag zur Geschichte der Volksschule in Vorarlberg* (Innsbruck: Wagner, 1879), 22-24, in Erich Schneider, "Spielleute und fahrende Musikanten in Vorarlberg," *Jahrbuch des österreichischen Volksliedwerkes* 26 (1977): 89.

89. Gstrein, "Tanzmusik-Ensembles," 424; E. v. G., "Die Hochzeitsfeyerlichkeiten im Lavantthale, *Der Aufmerksame* 2 (1813), no. 73, in Julijan Strajnar, "Geige und Geigenmusik in der slowenischen Volkstradition," in *Die Geige in der europäischen Volksmusik*, 421f.

90. Gerlinde Hofer, "Eine Kärnter Bauernhochzeit aus dem Jahre 1819," *Österreichische Musikzeitung* 25 (1970), issue 9.

91. Helge Thiel, "Quellen und Nachrichten zur volkstümlichen Geigenmusik in Österreich," in *Die Geige in der europäischen Volksmusik*, 109 n. 43.

92. *Katalog des Phonogrammarchives der österreichischen Akademie der Wissenschaften in Wien* (Vienna: Hermann Böhlaus Nachf., 1960), 60-64.

93. Florian Pedarnig, "Das Hackbrett in Osttirol," in *Beiträge zur Volksmusik in Tirol*, ed. Deutsch and Schneider, 171-172.

94. Description of Neuberg, 1803, Steiermärkisches Landesarchiv, MS no. 134, 94f., in Gstrein, "Tanzmusik-Ensembles," 421; Richard Wolfram, "Die Volkstanznachrichten in den statistischen Erhebungen Erzherzog Johanns," in *Volk und Heimat: Festschrift für Viktor von Geramb* (Graz: A. Pustet, 1949), 271ff., in Gstrein, "Tanzmusik-Ensembles," 424; Konrad Mautner and Victor von Geramb, *Steirisches Trachtenbuch*, vol. 2 (Graz: Leuschner & Lubensky, 1935), 97, in Klier, *Volkstümliche Musikinstrumente*, 99; color drawing in a dance manuscript of Karl Gspan, of Bruck an der Mur, in Klier, pl. 83; New Year's card for Archduke Johann, in Klier, pl. 90.

95. Josef Müller-Blattau, "Volksmusik in der Knaffl-Handschrift," *Zeitschrift für Volkskunde*, n.s. 10 (1939): 206-211.

96. Gstrein, "Tanzmusik-Ensembles," 424.

97. Walter Wünsch, "Die Volksmusikinstrumente der Steiermark," *Izvestiya na Instituta za Muzika* 13 (1969): 76.

98. Franz Hurdes, "Wesen und Bedeutung des Hackbrettes," *Heimatland*, 1934, 3.

99. Hermann Härtel, "Liebe zur Volksmusik," *Sänger- und Musikantenzeitung* 22 (1979): 275. He writes that *Dazuschlagen* means to think through a countermelody and to figure out pauses.

100. Walter Kainz, *Hackbrett-Fibel: Eine Anleitung zum Schlagen des steirischen Hackbrettes*, 2nd ed. ([Graz]: Verlag der Arbeitsgemeinschaft für Volksmusikpflege in Steiermark, 1954), 1.

101. Andrijana Gojković, *Narodni muzički instrumenti* (Belgrade: Vuk Karadžić, 1989), 37, 42, 50, 141, 144, 156, 182.

102. Mira Omerzel-Terlep, "Oprekelj na Slovenskem," *Muzikološki zbornik* 16 (1980): 97.

103. J. H. G. Schlegel, *Reise durch einige Theile vom mittäglichen, Deutschland und Venetianischen* (Erfurt: In der Hennischen Buchhandlung, 1795), in Zmaga Kumer, "Schriftzeugnisse und Bildquellen von Instrumentalensembles in Slowenien," *Studia instrumentorum musicae popularis* 2 (1972): 167.

104. Balthasar Hacquet, *Abbildung und Beschreibung der südwest- und östlichen Wenden, Illyren und Slaven*, part 1 (Leipzig: Industrie-Comptoir, 1801), 1: 25, in Kumer, "Schriftzeugnisse," 167.

105. B. Orel, "Novo gradivo o slovenski ljudski noši iz prve polovice 19. stoletja," *Slovenski etnograf* 2 (1949): 68ff., in Kumer, "Schriftzeugnisse," 168.

106. Matia Majar, *Pesmarica cerkevna* (Klagenfurt, 1846), xiii, in Kumer, "Schriftzeugnisse," 167.

107. Mira Omerzel-Terlep, "Cimbale - opsase ali orphica - na Goriškem in v Brdih," *Etnolog: glasnik Slovenskega Etnografiskega Muzeja* 53, no. 1 (1992): 208-209.

108. Richard Sallet, *Russian-German Settlements in the United States* (1931; reprint, Fargo, N.D.: North Dakota Institute for Regional Studies, 1974), 11; S. J.

Sackett, "The Hammered Dulcimer in Ellis County, Kansas," *Journal of the International Folk Music Council* 14 (1962): 61.

109. Victor Klein, *Unversiegbarer Born* (Alma Ata: Kasachstan, 1974), 68-69.

110. A. Kirschner, "Wie die Wolgadeutschen Hochzeit feierten," *Heimatbuch der Deutschen aus Russland*, 1956, 131, describes music with violin and *Zimbal*; J. Toepfer, "Verlobungs- und Hochzeitssitten im Wolgagebiet," *Deutsches Leben in Russland* 2 (1924): 115.

111. Eugen Kagarow, "Materialen zur Volkskunde der Wolga-Deutschen," *Zeitschrift für Volkskunde*, n.s. 3 (1931): pl. 3, shows one fiddler holding the violin in its normal position, while the other holds it sideways with the bow on the G and D strings, as in the Hungarian Gypsy *kontra* style; Mark Warren and Marilyn Hehr Fletcher, *Hochzeit: Dutch Hops: Colorado Music of the Germans from Russia, 1865-1965* ([Evergreen, Colo.: Shadow Canyon Graphics] printer, 1990), quotes Adolph Lesser, describing the Roths, of Wheatland, Wyoming: "one violin would lead, and the other would second."

112. Kagarow, "Materialen zur Volkskunde," pl. 3; Gottfried Habenicht, "Die wolgadeutsche Hochzeit," *Jahrbuch für ostdeutsche Volkskunde* 24 (1981): 161; Warren and Fletcher, *Hochzeit*, 24.

113. Habenicht, "Wolgadeutsche Hochzeit," 160.

114. This is a summary of the descriptions included in Kirschner, "Wie die Wolgadeutschen," 129-134; Habenicht, "Wolgadeutsche Hochzeit," 160-161, 172-173; Toepfer, "Verlobungs- und Hochzeitssitten," 114-116; Kagarow, "Materialen zur Volkskunde," 245-247; and Thomas Kopp, *Wolgadeutsche Siedeln im argentinischen Zwischenstromland* (Marburg: N. G Elwert Verlag, 1979), 145-153.

115. It would appear that the dulcimer has not survived among the Volga Germans who settled in Argentina, at least not to the same extent as with those who settled in Kansas and Colorado. The webpage of Casa Breyer S.A. <http://www.breypar.com.ar/cd1.html>, for example, offers recordings of seven different Argentinian bands of Volga German descent. The usual instrumentation of these bands is a lead accordion, second accordion or keyboard, bass, and drums.

116. Tobi Reiser, "Wie das Hackbrett zu neuem Leben kam," *Sänger– und Musikantenzeitung* 2 (Jul.-Aug. 1959): 51-53.

117. Cesar Bresgen, *Sommer und Winter* (Potsdam: L. Voggenreiter, [1940]).

118. Otto Eberhard, *Spielanleitung für das chromatische Hackbrett* (Salzburg, n.d.), in Klier, *Volkstümliche Musikinstrumenten*, 56 n. 26; Karl-Heinz Schickhaus, *Hackbrett-Fibel: Eine Unterweisung für das Spiel auf dem chromatischen Salzburger Hackbrett* (Munich: Josef Preissler, [1962]). Several others have since appeared.

119. Hans Halmbacher, *Sänger und Musikanten im bayerischen Oberland: aus Vergangenheit und Gegenwart der Landkreise Miesbach und Bad Tölz-Wolfratshausen* (Hausham: Fuchs-Druck, 198-?), passim.

120. Reinhard Loechle, "Sing- und Musikschulen in Bayern," *Sänger– und Musikantenzeitung* 25 (Sept.-Oct. 1982): 299-300.

121. *Lewis Miller: Sketches and Chronicles* (York, Pa.: The Historical Society of York County, 1966), 66; Groce, *Hammered Dulcimer*, 42.

122. "The York Daily Record Online," <http://www.ydr.com/forgotten/1700a.htm>.

123. Henry W. Shoemaker, *The Music and Musical Instruments of the Pennsylvania Mountaineers* (Altoona, Pa.: Mountain City Press, Times Tribune Co., 1923, printer), 4.

124. *South Carolina & American General Gazette*, 25 May 1778.

125. Informant, conversation with author, Mackinac Island, Mich., 1977.

126. J. F. Cooke, "Theodore Presser: Educator, Publisher, Philanthropist," *The Etude* 66 (July 1948): 404.

127. Harold Zimmerman, letter to author, 1985.

128. Letter from his daughter Ottilie Nieman to the Musical Museum, Deansboro, New York; the instrument and letter are now in the possession of the author.

129. James P. Leary, conversation with author, Mount Horeb, Wis., May 1999.

130. Informant, conversation with author, Mackinac Island, Mich., 1979.

131. Sallet, *Russian-German Settlements in the United States*, 84-85.

132. Warren and Fletcher, *Hochzeit*, 12, 14-15, 18-19, 24, 59.

133. Sackett, "Hammered Dulcimer," 63-64.

134. Sackett, "Hammered Dulcimer," 61, 63; Sr. Mary Eloise Johannes, *A Study of the Russian-German Settlements in Ellis County, Kansas*, The Catholic University of America Studies in Sociology, vol. 14 (Washington: The Catholic University of America Press, 1946), 114-116; Kansas State Historical Society, website, "Ethnic Folk Bands," section seven of "They're Playing Our Song," <http://www.ukans.edu/heritage/kshs/places/bands7.htm>.

135. Warren and Fletcher, *Hochzeit*, 20-22.

136. Marilyn Mehr Fletcher, "The Dutch Hop in Northern Colorado," *Viltis* 44 (May 1985): 17; "Colorado Dutch Hop," *The Polka News*, 23 Aug. 1989.

137. Marty Jones, "Going Nuts: The Polka Nuts Keep Music All in the Family," *Backbeat*, <http://www.westword.com/1996/072596/music2.html>.

138. Hubert Henkel, *Clavichorde*, Musikinstrumenten-Museum der Karl-Marx-Universität-Leipzig. Katalog, vol. 4 (Frankfurt am Main: Verlag Das Musikinstrument, 1981), 76, 78, 80-81.

139. C. C. Snoeck, *Catalogue de la collection d'instruments de musique anciens et curieux* (Ghent: J. Vuylsteke, 1894), 23; Curt Sachs, *Sammlung alter Musikinstrumente bei der Staatlichen Hochschule für Musik zu Berlin* (Berlin: Julius Bard, 1922), 38-39. Sachs classed the dulcimers in that collection into "older" and "newer" types, but it appears that "older" type consisted of German instruments, while the "newer" type mainly were Italian *salterios*.

140. Boone, "Beknopte Bijdrage," 208-213.

141. Kettlewell, *Dulcimer*, 304. The Musikhistoriska Museet in Stockholm has three Swedish instruments, two of them from the eighteenth century, one with three strings per course.

142. Aksdal, *Med Piber og Basuner*, 28.

143. Geiser, "Hackbrett in der Schweiz," 36, 38-39. Hutmacher's manuscript "Uffzeichnung der Künsten" (pages 176-177 have the description of the *Hackbrett*) is in the Kantonsbibliothek Baselland in Liestal.

144. Hürlemann, *Brumbass, Geige, Hackbrett*, contains photographs of identical instruments on 27, 33, 40-41, 80, 88-91.

145. For example, in the way the pin blocks rest on the lengthwise rails rather than being attached to the baseboard.

146. Salzmann, *Hackbrett im Wallis*, 28-29, 32, 34-60.

147. Gerhard Stradner, *Musikinstrumente in Grazer Sammlungen*, Tabulae Musicae Austriacae, vol. 11 (Vienna: Verlag der österreichischen Akademie der Wissenschaften, 1966), 49-50, 140-142.

148. Klier, *Volkstümliche Musikinstrumente*, pl. 45; *Austrian Folk Music*, vol. 2, *The Western & Southern Provinces*, Arhoolie 3003; an instrument I saw for sale in Graz in 1969; Max Rosenzopf, "Der Bau des steirischen Hackbrettes in Köflach 1970," *Instrumentenbau-Zeitschrift* 25 (Feb. 1971): 148-149.

149. Kainz, *Hackbrett-Fibel*, 2-3; Rosenzopf, "Bau des steirischen Hackbrettes," 149.

150. Rosenzopf, "Bau des steirischen Hackbrettes," 149.

151. Kainz, *Hackbrett-Fibel*, 5.

152. Pedarnig, "Hackbrett in Osttirol," 171-173; Fritz Stradner, "Das Hackbrett: ein Beitrag zu seiner Entwicklungsgeschichte," *Jahrbuch des österreichischen Volksliederwerkes* 15 (1966): pl. 6.

153. This is based on five instruments described in Kurt Birsak, "Anmerkungen zu den Volksmusikinstrumenten im Salzburger Museum Carolino-Augusteum, besonders zur Bundanordnung der alpenländischen Zither," in *Die Volksmusik im Lande Salzburg*, 213-214.

154. Mira Omerzel-Terlep, "Oprekelj na slovenskem etničnem ozemlju," *Traditiones: zbornik Inštituta za Slovensko Narodopisje* 19 (1990): 198-201, 210.

155. Mrs. Henry Maser, a native of Russia, conversation with author, Au Gres, Mich., 1977; Ernest Eckerdt, interview by author, Swartz Creek, Mich., 15 Mar. 2000.

156. In the Städelsches Kunstinstitut, Frankfurt am Main. Thanks to Belisa Mang for this information.

157. Sackett, "Hammered Dulcimer," 61-62.

158. Warren and Fletcher, *Hochzeit*, 24.

159. *Adolph Lesser: Old Time Wedding Favorites*, photograph on cover, LP record, 1970s.

• 6 •

The Cimbalom Family

From the point of view of history, it makes sense to group together all dulcimers called by cognates of the Latin term *cymbalum*. These have been found traditionally in central and eastern Europe, in an area from Latvia and the Russian borderlands of Belarus on the north, westward into Bohemia and Germany, and southward into Romania and Greece. Although modern forms of these instruments vary from each other, they share a history common enough to place them under a single heading.

Both Old and New Testaments mention *kynbalon*, a Greek term for a brass percussion instrument.[1] Isidore of Seville (c.570-636) defined *cymbala* (plural) as "hollow round metal plates, struck together."[2] By the fifteenth century, the term was conjoined with the Latin *clavis* ("key") to form *clavicymbalum*, a word for an early harpsichord. People who might attach such a biblical and classical term to an instrument had to come from an environment that was learned, not peasant or "folk."

History

By the mid-sixteenth century, the *Hackbrett* had penetrated as far east as the Transylvanian Saxon city of Kronstadt (now Brașov, Romania). Records of that city state that in 1546, an emissary of Mircea Ciobanu, voivode of Wallachia, came to procure a musical instrument, "called *Hack Bret*," for the children of the voivodess.[3] This record tells us several things: the *Hackbrett* had migrated to the easternmost frontier of German-speaking communities; it was fancied by the Byzantine-influenced court of Wallachia; and thus it must have been part of the instrumentarium of the upper class of Kronstadt. If the *Hackbrett* was known in that city, German communities in Hungary must also have known it.

However, in the same decade, the instrument was still unfamiliar to the Hungarian chronicler who described merry-making at the court of Queen Isabella at Vienna in 1543: "the finest 'Egyptian' [Gypsy] fiddlers played here. They did not pluck the strings with their fingers, but beat them with wooden rods, and accompanied this with singing at the top of their voices."[4] Since we have seen that the *Hackbrett* was well established with minstrels in Switzerland by this time, we should be surprised only by the writer's lack of familiarity with the instrument. Furthermore, we should not interpret this quotation to mean continuous Gypsy association with the instrument since that time.

Nevertheless, it seems that a fashion for the instrument among clerics and scholars developed in Hungary during the middle of this century. Emericus *literatus Cymbalista* (that is, in Hungarian, "Imre Cimbalmos, a student") appeared in a record at Sopron in 1564.[5] György Zrínyi, describing two Gypsy minstrels captured from the Turkish Bey of Pecs in 1596, wrote that one "has a *czimbaliom* of such a kind as that with which the students (clerics) sing mass, but does not strike it with sticks, only plucks it with his fingers, like a harp."[6] Perhaps this minstrel played a psaltery or *kanun*, as the latter instrument was still present in parts of the old Byzantine Empire, as a Greek fresco from that century attests.[7] Considering the early period in which the word is used to describe the instrument, these two references, indicating an association with clerics or seminary students, is probably good evidence that it was Hungarians who first applied the term *cymbalum* to the dulcimer.

Not only scholars played the instrument in Hungary. A Unitarian Bible, from Cluj (Koloszvar) in 1575, mentions "trumpeters, *cimbalomoknac*, fiddlers, and lutenists," and in 1578, Bishop Peter Bornemissza mentions "lute, *czimbalom*, organ, fiddle, trumpet, drum, and *sip* (flute)."[8] The first quotation suggests that it had become, like the others, an instrument used by minstrels.

The cimbalom probably spread from Hungary, carried by minstrels who sought patronage at foreign courts. A Russian list of foreign words published in 1596 defines *musikiya* as playing on *guslis*, *domras*, *lyras* (hurdy-gurdies), and on *tsinbals* and other stringed instruments.[9] This early evidence of its presence in Russia and its absence later may indicate that it was an aristocratic novelty there at the time, but failed to take hold there, either among the upper classes or with professional minstrels.

By the seventeenth century, the instrument was well established in the city of Lviv (Lwow, Lemberg), now in Ukraine. Professional musicians there consisted of two classes: musicians of "Italian music," that is, those who played the forms of music of the Catholic world on standard instruments of Western music; and *muzykants*, or minstrels, who played for weddings and banquets on the three-stringed fiddle of Byzantine origin called the *serbska* (i.e., "Sorb" or "Serb"), the hurdy-gurdy, the *cymbał*, and the flute (*szyposze*).[10] An ensemble of two *serbska*s and a *cymbał* seems to have been standard.[11]

Jewish minstrels in Lviv were using the instrument by the early seventeenth century. It is possible that Jews migrating from Germany had brought the instrument with them, as, according to Walter Feldman, the term *hakbretl* was a secret word in use among *klezmorim* in eastern Galicia in the early twentieth century for the instrument.[12] However, lacking earlier evidence of Jewish association with the instrument, we might also assume that they adopted the instrument from Christian minstrels there. In 1629, the musicians' guild in Lviv negotiated an agreement which permitted certain Jewish musicians to play at Catholic weddings and banquets and to hire extra guild musicians if the event fell on a Jewish holiday. Until that time, Jewish musicians, who, according to Bałaban, performed only as a sideline to their regular occupations, were not allowed to play at Christian weddings. The list of the thirteen approved musicians included Abus Cymbalista and Eizyk Bass, whose bynames indicate the instruments they must have played.[13]

Before we examine the Jewish tradition and its influence, we need to look at evidence of the instrument called by the word *cimbalom* and its cognates elsewhere during the seventeenth century. From Lviv, minstrels probably carried it further east. Pamva Berynda's *Leksykon slovenoros'kyi*, published at Kiev in 1627, mentions it, defining the word *bryatsalo* as "jingling, striking of anything like a *klepalo* (semanterion), cittern, organ pipe, *tsimbal*, harp."[14] In 1652, Bogdan Chmielnicki, hetman of the Ukraine, ordered that Gritska Ilyushenka-Makushchenka, a *tsymbalist*, lead a guild of musicians in the Dnieper River region, with the power to execute those who might disobey him.[15] With such limited evidence at our disposal, however, it is hard to learn whether the instrument was finding its way to the villages, where during the nineteenth century in parts of western Ukraine it was very common, or whether it was limited to minstrels who were patronized or owned by the aristocracy.

In the region now defined as Belarus, Nazina writes that the instrument was widespread in both villages and towns during the seventeenth century. Sources from that era mention the occupation of *tsimbalist*.[16] An anonymous play, *Alexei, chelovek bozhii*, includes a wedding scene with a line "The *tsimbaly* and fiddles are here! All men come here to listen to them and drink."[17]

References to it in Poland, except those concerning Jews or to the *serbska* minstrels of Lviv, are scarce. In 1643, the gallery of the dining hall in the Warsaw castle of the royal marshal, Adam Kazanowski, featured musicians which played fiddles, lute, viola, double harp, *cymbał*, harpsichord, and a woodwind instrument, *pozytywy*.[18] A tax law of 1673 mentions "fiddlers, *cymbalist*s, bagpipers and such village music,"[19] but this association with rural music appears to be exceptional.

In Hungary, the cimbalom appears to have found a place in the orchestras of magnates, in much the same environment as the Warsaw reference indicates, as well as with rural minstrels. A decree passed at Marosvásárhely in 1649 ordered that "whoever plays the fiddle, the cimbalom, the *koboz* (short-necked lute), or the pipe, either at houses or in taverns, on a Sunday and is caught at it will have the fiddle taken away from him and thrown to the ground and he himself be put in the pillory."[20] A fiddler and cimbalom player served the magnate Ádám Batthyány in 1656.[21] Count Erdődy's household orchestra included three violinists, one cimbalist, three pipers, four trumpeters, one bagpiper, and one drummer.[22] A poem written in 1695, describing a wedding, mentions *cimbalom*, virginals, fiddles, and bagpipes.[23] Although the cimbalom may have been played with fiddles, the standard Gypsy orchestra instrumentation had not yet appeared. The instrument was also familiar, in the plural form *czimbala*, to a Croat, Juraj Habdelić, who mentioned it in his 1670 dictionary, as well as the term *cimbalaš* for the player of the instrument.[24]

Central Europe

The Thirty Years' War (1618-1648) witnessed a large devastation of the population in Bohemia, and during this period many Jews settled in the German-speaking city of Prague. It appears that Jewish musicians developed a new type of ensemble there during this period. This incorporated elements of the instrumentation of Italian baroque music, with two violins and a bass, but used the *Cymbal* as well as harpsichord as a continuo instrument. It is likely that their use of the dulcimer (and the word *Cymbal* for it) resulted from a migration from Lviv or eastern Galicia, since few Jews lived in Hungary at that time. Perhaps Jews in Lviv had already developed the instrumentation as a hybrid of "Italian" and *serbska* music current in that city and brought the style to the Bohemian capital. The earliest record of a player in Prague is that of Chajim Zimbalista, a convert who served in Wallerstein's army and was buried in 1637.[25]

We can infer the instrumentation of the Jewish ensemble from a Prague document from 1651, in which a number of Jewish musicians petitioned to be allowed to play on Sundays and holidays. Each petitioner was identified by name and by instrument. There were nine fiddlers, four players of the harpsichord (*instroment*), four players of the dulcimer (*zimbal*, *zimbaldt*, *ziembalis*), and four bassists.[26] This rather neat division of instruments suggests that they formed a guild which comprised four ensembles. Except for the odd fiddler, the number divides into two fiddles, one harpsichord, one dulcimer, and one bass per group. From later descriptions and from an understanding of the instruments, it is unlikely that both harpsichord and dulcimer were used together. More likely, the harpsichord replaced the dulcimer when the group accompanied singing in the temple, while the sturdier dulcimer could be used for wedding processions and dancing and playing in taverns. An example of the substitution might be seen in the description of a procession of Jews in honor of the coronation of Emperor Leopold I of Austria in 1678. This included a woman playing the "cymbals" with two fiddlers, and a harpsichord with two fiddlers in another group.[27]

Christian musicians of Prague petitioned against the Jewish musicians in an undated (but from 1651 or soon after) document, complaining of the competition. They remarked that they "unfailingly attend and go daily into all taverns and other places," sold "lutes, violins, citterns, harpsichords, and dulcimers (*Hackbretter* is the word used in the petition), along with strings of all kinds," and "bargain down for engagements, weddings, banquets, and other festivities."[28] They further attacked the Jewish musicians for their lack of training, as the Christian musicians prided themselves on their knowledge of continuo, different keys, and rhythm, while the Jews played without formal rules.[29]

Jewish musicians in Germany and Bohemia were subject to various local laws which restricted the size of their ensembles. The cities of

Fürth and Worms (in 1708) limited their groups to three musicians, while Metz and Frankfurt am Main allowed four.[30] If the ensembles had three musicians, they likely consisted of two violins and bass, as illustrations from about 1700 depicting Jewish weddings in Alsace and Germany indicate,[31] but if four, a dulcimer was added. This is the instrumentation shown in an etching from 1714 of a group leading a Jewish wedding procession in Frankfurt am Main (see figure 6.1).[32] The same instrumentation, but lacking a second fiddle, is featured in an engraving of an Ashkenazic wedding at Amsterdam made in 1723. The dulcimer player, in this example, has his instrument resting on a chair in front of him, a music manuscript placed on the chair's back.[33]

Figure 6.1: Jewish wedding procession in Frankfurt am Main, led by musicians playing two fiddles, dulcimer, and cello. Engraving from Johann Jacob Schudt, *Jüdische Merckwürdigkeiten* (Frankfurt, 1714), in Georg Liebe, *Das Judentum in der deutschen Vergangenheit* (Leipzig: Eugen Diederichs, 1903), 77.

It is impossible to say whether the Bohemian Jewish *Cymbal* of the late seventeenth and early eighteenth centuries was significantly different in design from the contemporary *Hackbrett*. The Amsterdam illustration indicates not. But the spread of the name *Cymbal* for the instrument does appear to be associated with the spread of the Bohemian Jewish instrumentation. The word for the instrument had spread to Holland by 1685, when a poem published that year, *Krispyn, Muzikant*, included a line "I play the lute, the harp, the *Simbaal*, and the cittern."[34] Other Dutch authors mention "the noise of the *cimbel* strings" (about 1700) and the "pleasant tone of the good *cimbel* strings" (about 1710).[35] A painting from about 1700 by a Flemish artist, Hendrik Govaerts, *The Servants' Dance*, shows a large dulcimer on a pedestal with four feet in an ensemble with violin and cello. Kettlewell notes that this instrument has a small bass bridge on the left in addition to the normal treble and bass bridges.[36] Georg Philipp Telemann, a Saxon, described in 1704 hearing Pantaleon Hebenstreit play his "marvelous *Cymbal*."[37] In *Musicalisches Theatrum*, by J. C. Weigel (about 1720), the author illustrates a woman playing a *Cymbal*.[38] The term was also used in Sweden from the mid-eighteenth to mid-nineteenth centuries.[39] Since, as we have seen, the use of the Latin term *cymbalum* for "dulcimer" began in Hungary, the increasing incidence of the word in Germany and Holland during the late seventeenth and early eighteenth centuries must have resulted from an influence coming from that direction. Bohemian, and specifically Prague, Jews no doubt created the fashion for the style of music which incorporated the instrument, and the instrument spread west and north from there.

Ashkenazic communities even in England may have used the instrument by this time. In Thomas Baker's play *An Act at Oxford* (1704), a character announces "when you come to Town, Ladies, I'll present you with a Jewish Consort of Tongs, Dulcimers, and Catcalls."[40] In isolation, we might give that reference no significance, but during the first part of the eighteenth century, some Britons may have regarded the dulcimer as typically Jewish. An advertisement in a Dublin newspaper in 1738-1739 announced "THE JEWS MUSIC is to be had at the Sign of the Fiddle and Dulcimer in Copper Alley by Archibald Williamson, who Gentlemen are pleased to called the IRISH JEW. N.B. Said Williamson provides Bands of musick for Private Balls &c."[41] Williamson clearly was not Jewish, but one might surmise that his nickname carried some association with his dulcimer playing. In 1767, a German-born Jew, Isaac Isaacs (died 1791) arrived in Dublin from London, where he enjoyed a successful career playing Irish jigs and reels on his dulcimer in theatres and taverns; for several years he was under a retainer to play with a fiddler weekly for a well-known brothel operator, Mrs. Margaret Leeson.[42] Other individual Jewish musicians may also have wandered to the West and found similar employment in taverns and houses of ill repute.

Jews in German-speaking areas continued to use the dulcimer throughout the eighteenth century. In the early part of the century in Prague, the dulcimer was also used with violins to accompany *meshorerim* (singers) and *hazzanim*, as were flutes, organs, and percussion instruments, on the Sabbath.[43] The dulcimer appeared in a copperplate engraving of a Jewish procession in 1741, along with three violins, hautboy, bassoon, and cello.[44] An engraving published about 1770 in Nuremberg by Johann Peter Wolff shows a fiddler with a dulcimer player who has notes in front of him.[45] About 1778 at Deutz, near Cologne, violin, dulcimer, and bass could be heard in taverns there, played by Jewish musicians.[46] Around 1800, gentile dances in Märkisch-Friedland (now Mirosławiec, in western Poland) were accompanied by the music of five Jewish tradesmen, who played, as a part-time occupation, in an ensemble consisting of two violins, clarinet, cello, and dulcimer. The lead fiddler could play by note, but the others played only by ear, improvising the accompaniment.[47] In Leszno (Lissa), Posen, now in Poland, Ludwig Kalisch (born 1814) recalled that the (Jewish) *Cymbel* player in that town "was esteemed as a great talent. Like the Gypsies, [the Jewish musicians] were natural musicians and did not read music."[48]

In Bohemia, Christians also adopted the *cimbal*. Šimon Benda (1693-1735), a linen weaver and father of the composer František Benda, played several instruments, including the shawm, bagpipes, and dulcimer, in taverns.[49] We know little else about the instrument's use by Christians in Bohemia during the eighteenth century, but it would appear that the dulcimer was occasionally grouped with the popular bagpipes-shawm combination, as Benda's choice of instruments would suggest. In the Chrudim region, between about 1820 and 1835, the usual instrumentation for dance music was two violins, *cimbal*, and bass. Since the musicians came from the village Bystrék, they were known as *Bysteráci*. It was recalled, many years later, that the last dulcimer in Korouhue was played by a teacher about 1835.[50] About that time the ensemble, which consisted of violin, *cimbal*, bass, harp, and hurdy-gurdy, found in the upper Labe River region and "Bohemian Siberia," bordering with Moravia, died out.[51] Although the bagpipes (*dudy*)-clarinet-violin ensemble survived in places like the Chodsko region, in other areas bands consisting of woodwind and brass instruments replaced the string ensembles for dance music.[52] In Moravia, however, the dulcimer continued to find a place until World War II in the northern and eastern parts of the region.[53]

Although the main discussion of the dulcimer in German-speaking countries is to be found in chapter 5, we should note those areas where the term *Cymbal* (and variants, such as *Zimbel*, *Cimbal*, etc.) was used.

In addition to areas already noted, such as Saxony and Posen, it appears that in the eighteenth and early nineteenth centuries, the term was common in Franconia, the Upper Palatinate (Oberpfalz), and Bavaria. *Cimbal* players, fiddlers, and hurdy-gurdy players were subject to a penalty, according to a law passed in Franconia in 1746, at a time when authorities began to persecute itinerant musicians and other vagrants. Hartinger's study of licenses granted to folk musicians in the Upper Palatinate between 1778 and 1800 revealed that seventeen dulcimer players were

Figure 6.2: Musicians play violin, trumpet, shawm, dulcimer, and bass, in the Altenburgs, Saxony, at the end of the 18th century. Detail from engraving by Fried. Neiffen, in *Deutsche Jugendzeitung* 15 (1846): plate 15-16.

licensed, and the instrument was mostly called *Cimbal, Zimbal*, and *Zympal*, although it was also called *Hackbrett*.[54] At Rosenheim, Bavaria, a license to play at weddings and other dances was granted in 1825 to a player of the *Cymbal*.[55] Saxon peasants used the *Cymbal* at their dances in the late eighteenth century, as an 1846 engraving depicts musicians with violin, dulcimer, trumpet, shawm, and bass, in the Altenburgs some fifty years earlier (see figure 6.2).[56] By 1843, however, the *cymbal* had "completely disappeared" from the music of the Lusatian Sorbs.[57] Still, it lingered in some places. Schickhaus writes that Maria Perreiter, the only traditional dulcimer player in Bavaria that he ever met, called her instrument *Zimbal*. This had five strings per course and three bridges.[58]

In Austria, the parish register of Henndorf am Wallersee, Salzburg, during the period of the Thirty Years' War (1618-1648) contains occupational descriptions of individual minstrels, including *Hackprötler* (*Cymbalista*).[59] Leopold Mozart, writing in 1755 about his new work, *Bauernhochzeit* ("Peasant Wedding"), suggested that a *"Hackebrettl* or *Cymbal"* might be located at the carnival on Shrove Tuesday, in order to be added to the orchestra.[60] In Styria, the dulcimer was usually called *Hackbrett*, but several references from the early nineteenth century refer to the dulcimer as *"Hackbrett* or *Cymbal."*[61] Although it may appear that contemporary observers regarded the two words as synonyms, it is more likely that the terms represented dulcimers of two traditions, with different tuning systems. Indeed a description of dance music at Neuberg, Styria, from 1803 calls the *Hackbrett* a *"Zimbal* of a smaller sort."[62] By the late eighteenth century, the *Cymbal* of Bohemia and neighboring German and Austrian regions had acquired characteristics which survive in the contemporary Hungarian cimbalom, which are discussed below.

Hungary and Slovakia

Many Jews migrated to Hungary and Slovakia from Bohemia and Moravia during the eighteenth century. Among them were musicians. Aron Cymbalista and Seligh Cymbalista appear in a list made in 1709 at Stupava, Slovakia; Jacob Löhl, *cymbalista*, at Vitencz, in 1735/1736; and Moises Salomon, *musicus czimbalista*, at Szentgyörgy in 1736.[63] Although the cimbalom had already been known in Hungary, it is likely that the particular tradition with which the Hungarian instrument has been most closely associated—that of Gypsy music—derives from the Bohemian Jewish tradition. Sarosi remarks that the first "renowned" Gypsy musician, Mihály Barna, played violin around 1737 with a second violin, harp, and bass, the others being non-Gypsies. He reminds us that the first Gypsy orchestra with what became its standard instrumentation—a *primas*, or leader, playing violin, another violin playing *kontra* (chordal accompaniment), cimbalom, and bass—was led by a woman, Panna Czinka (died 1771).[64] A Hungarian painting from about 1760 depicts Hungarians dancing to two ensembles, one a Jewish group with two violins and cimbalom, the other a Gypsy trio with two violins and cello.[65] This may illustrate a period of transition in which Gypsies adopted the instrumentation and elements of a style of music from the Jews.

Although Hungarian Jews continued to play the cimbalom and what became known as Gypsy music until the early part of the twentieth century, sedentary Gypsies rapidly developed their musical talents and developed a strong identification with the music. From the last two decades of the eighteenth century until the middle of the nineteenth century, which Sarosi calls the "*verbunkos* period," Gypsy music evolved into its present

Figure 6.3: Hungarian Gypsy musicians playing violins, clarinet, cimbalom, and cello, at a *csárda* (inn), mid-nineteenth century. Engraving in Thomas Powell, ed., *Illustrated Home Book of the World's Great Nations* (Chicago: People's Publishing Co., 1888), 292.

form and identity. Virtuosic playing and the transition of the *verbunkos*, a recruiting dance, into the *csárdás*, a social dance with a distinctive Hungarian feeling, satisfied both the Romantic ideal and the need for a national identity.[66] During the nineteenth century, Gypsy orchestras found patronage both among the aristocracy and urban elite as well as among the peasantry. They absorbed stylistic elements both from Austrian classical music and from the music of the peasants.

At the middle of the nineteenth century, Liszt commented that the Hungarian cimbalom was played exclusively by Gypsies.[67] He felt that the violin and cimbalom provided the foundation of the Gypsy orchestra and that the cimbalom shared "with the first violin the right to develop certain passages and to prolong certain variations indefinitely according to the good pleasure of the moment."[68] Gypsy musicians had already developed the instrument's technique to the point where a Scottish traveler who heard a trio play in an inn at Izak in 1834 could remark that the instrument was "by far the most effective instrument of the band."[69] The improvisatory nature of cimbalom accompaniment was well established by this time, and Liszt incorporated elements of cimbalom style into his

Figure 6.4: Showroom of the cimbalom manufacturer Gyula Mogyoróssy of Budapest, as depicted in his catalog from about 1917.

Hungarian Rhapsodies. He particularly liked the instrument; when entertaining guests in his later years, Liszt frequently hired Gypsy musicians, more often a cimbalom player like Pál Pintér, rather than a violinist.[70] Throughout most of the nineteenth century, the Hungarian cimbalom was a portable, although somewhat heavy, instrument. The player placed it on a table or barrel when in play, and the player dampened the vibrating strings with his hands or forearms, sometimes with a velvet cloth attached, with each change in chords.[71] In 1874, the Budapest instrument manufacturer Joszef V. Schunda (1845-1923) patented a cimbalom with weighted dampers, published a method, and by 1906 had produced ten thousand instruments. These rapidly found favor with Hungary's bourgeoisie and gentry and eventually with Gypsy musicians. The instruments featured a chromatic range from D^1 to e^3 and an internal cast iron frame. Competitors like Sternberg Ármin és Testvére and Antal Habics continued to manufacture the portable, wood-braced cimbalom as well as the large model.[72] Gyula Mogyoróssy, who started his Budapest firm in 1892, like other manufacturers, offered, in his 1917 catalog, fifty-one models, ranging from a portable, "three-quarter" size instrument with thirty courses, costing sixty korona, to a full-size instrument with elaborate legs and pin block covers acting as dampers, for five hundred korona.[73]

Although still chiefly played by Gypsy musicians, the cimbalom had now become a "national" Hungarian instrument, with an appeal that went beyond the bounds of Gypsy music. Methods and transcriptions, mostly of popular Hungarian songs, songs from operettas, and salon music, were written by Géza Allaga, who initiated a cimbalom course at the National Conservatory in Budapest in 1890, and others, like László Kun, who began teaching the instrument at the Royal Academy of Music in 1897.[74] Aladar Rácz, whose playing at a restaurant in Geneva, Switzerland, in 1914 inspired Stravinsky to incorporate the cimbalom in his *Ragtime* and *Renard*, returned to Budapest in 1938 to teach at the Academy of Music and inaugurated a new school of playing.[75] He made arrangements of works by Couperin, Bach, and others. In the 1960s and 1970s, Márta Fabian inspired many new compositions by Hungarian composers in a contemporary idiom.[76] Viktoria Herencsár is active as a teacher and performer, and she organized the Cimbalom World Association, an organization for dulcimer players from countries around the world. The organization's first congress was held in Budapest in 1991;

subsequent congresses have been held every two years, in Bratislava, Slovakia; Brno, Czech Republic; Mogilev, Belarus; and Chişinău, Moldova. Members from more than fifteen countries have performed at these events.

The Hungarian cimbalom today is taught in music schools in the Czech Republic, Slovakia, Serbia, Romania, Moldova, and Ukraine, as well as Hungary. There are also a number of professional percussionists in France, Britain, and the United States who have learned the classical repertoire, including Kodaly's *Hary Janos Suite*, Stravinsky's pieces, and newer compositions by Hungarian and Slovak composers.

Under socialism the employment of Gypsy orchestras in restaurants was subsidized by the government. Since the demise of Communism, Gypsy music has somewhat declined, because few restaurants can afford to employ many musicians. Some musicians have emigrated to Canada and Western Europe, so Hungarian Gypsy music continues to live outside of Hungary.

In Slovakia, Gypsy orchestras use the *cimbal* in the same way as those in Hungary. Although found all over, it is more frequent in the western and eastern parts of the country. Regional variations in its use include its absence among the music of the Highlanders; larger ensembles of six to eight musicians in the Kopanice area; smaller groups in the counties of Zemplin and Šariš; and four-piece groups around Gemer.[77]

Austria, Slovenia, Croatia, and Serbia

The Austrian province of Burgenland and the Prekmurje region in eastern Slovenia were part of Hungary before 1918. The Hungarian cimbalom is played in those areas. In Prekmurje, the *banda* (ensemble) may consist of two violins, viola, two clarinets, *cimbal*, and bass, and follows the Hungarian Gypsy style. The repertoire includes older Slovenian dances as well as waltzes, tangos, fox-trots, and other standards. There were many more such groups before World War II than in the 1970s.[78] Omerzel-Terlep reports that one *cimbalist* in Ćakovec called the small instrument (*oprekelj*) a "Jewish *cimbal*."[79]

The *cimbal* is played to a limited extent in the northern parts of Croatia. Peasants in Hrvatsko Zagorje (the hills north of Zagreb) used to make it themselves.[80] In Serbia, it is played by Gypsies in Hungarian-speaking and Romanian-speaking areas of Vojvodina and the Banat. In the 1920s, Stevo Nikolić's Gypsy orchestra of Novi Sad used the instrument. It is possible that in the nineteenth century Turkish Gypsies in Serbia, despite calling it a *santur*, played the portable Hungarian cimbalom. Famintsyn illustrates such an instrument, which he described as played by Mustafa, who wandered from about 1850 to 1875 in Croatia, Slavonia, Serbia, Bosnia, and Hungary.[81]

Poland, Ukraine, Belarus, Lithuania, and Latvia

Let us return to Eastern Europe, in order to follow the development of the other members of the cimbalom family. Although the traditions are distinct and have been so for many years, an investigation into their history reveals some of the reasons for the similarities. However, much research still remains to be done.

Jewish association with the instrument in this region remained strong until the nineteenth and even twentieth century, especially in Poland, where it is still to some extent regarded as a "Jewish" instrument.[82] This historical association accounts for similarities in both the design and tuning of traditional dulcimers found today in locations as disparate as Latvia and Greece. However, it would be incorrect to link the dulcimer exclusively to them. Although we can demonstrate the Jewish link to later Gypsy association with the instrument in Hungary and Romania, it is harder to make the connection to the peasant tradition in Ukraine and to some extent to that in Belarus.

The singular Hungarian *cimbalom* and Yiddish *tsimbl* became the plural words *cymbały* in Polish, *tsymbaly* in Ukrainian, and *tsimbaly* in Byelorussian.[83] The Hutsul people of the Carpathian Mountains in western Ukraine must have adopted the instrument by 1700. Their surnames became hereditary by the middle of the eighteenth century, and the surname Tsymbalistyi is found among them. Since there is evidence from the mid-seventeenth century of Christian *tsymbalist*s in the Dnieper River region, we might reason that the Hutsul tradition derives from the playing of *serbska* musicians in Lviv and vicinity from that era. In the 1780s, Rigelman wrote that Ukrainian musicians played many instruments, among them *tsymbaly*.[84] In 1817, a writer mentioned an ensemble consisting of violin, violoncello, and *tsymbaly*.[85]

Further references indicate that the instrument was in common use throughout the nineteenth century in western Ukraine. In 1831 Gołębiowski wrote that the *tsymbaly* was in use in Rus Czerwona, Volhynia, and Podolia.[86] The ensemble known as *troista muzyka* ("trio music"), with violin, *tsymbaly*, and bass, was popular in 1836 in Galicia, Old Pokutia, Kolomyya, and Stanyslaviv districts.[87] Liszt remarked in 1859 that it was "well spread amongst the peasants of Little Russia [Ukraine], who generally suspend it by a strap round the neck."[88] A Russian ethnographic survey made in the 1860s noted that in the Novogradvolynia district, Volhynia gubernia, the *tsymbaly* accompanied the violin, the only location where the survey mentioned the instrument.[89] M. V. Lysenko wrote in 1874 about *troista muzyka* with violin, *tsymbaly* and tambourine (*buben*).[90] In 1880, Oskar Kolberg's ethnographic survey of Kolomyya and Pokutia (Sub-Carpathian Rus) mentioned the violin, *tsymbaly*, three-string *basetla* (a cello-sized bass), and the *sopilka* (fipple flute).[91]

In the twentieth century, the peasant *troista muzyka* ensemble in Ukraine varied in instrumentation. The *tsymbaly*, however, was found only in the western part of the country. In addition to the instruments already named, the ensemble might include second violin, clarinet, trombone, bass drum with cymbals, and accordion or bayan (chromatic but-

Figure 6.5: Fiddler and *tsymbalist* play for a group of people dancing the *kolomyjka*, at Chortovets, near Obertyn, in western Ukraine, before 1880. Source: Oskar Kolberg, *Dzieła wszystkie*, 31: *Pokucie*, 3: xiii.

ton accordion).[92] The *tsymbalist* follows the melody line fairly closely, perhaps simplifying it, or plays an accompaniment, which varies in texture.[93] These groups are closely involved with the wedding rituals in the villages, and the neck strap allows the *tsymbalist* to play in the processions to and from the church.

During the Soviet period, the traditional use of the *tsymbaly* in western Ukraine continued, but new forms of the instrument developed, as in other parts of the Union. In the 1920s, ensembles of players of the *bandura* began to include the *tsymbaly*. Oleksandr Nezovibatko designed a *tsymbaly* family, consisting of soprano, alto, bass, and contrabass instruments, and, starting in 1951, the Chernihiv Musical Instruments Factory produced over ten thousand instruments of this design. A *tsymbaly* course at the Kiev Conservatory also began that year, and, by 1970, classes were taught in Lviv, Chernivtsi, Kherson, Lutsk, Kharkiv, Chernihiv, and Ternopil. Graduates taught the instrument and organized amateur ensembles. Nezovibatko wrote a method.[94] In recent decades, the Hungarian cimbalom has become popular as an instrument taught in conservatories, the influence coming from Romania and Moldova; unlike those in Belarus, most of the students are male.[95]

The traditional range of the *tsymbaly* north of Ukraine actually follows the Tsarist-era Pale of Settlement, in which Jews were allowed to live, quite closely. Although there were examples of gentiles playing the instrument in Poland and Belarus in the eighteenth and nineteenth centuries, for most of this period it was largely in the hands of Jews. Evidence of Jewish musicians and their instruments in this region is rather sparse until the latter half of the eighteenth century. A mural on a synagogue wall in Przedbórz, Poland, from about 1760, featured a *tsimbl* and violin.[96] At mid-eighteenth century, Marcin Matuszewicz, castellan of Brest-Litovsk, wrote that poorer nobles occasionally hired Jewish bands from the smaller towns.[97] The artist Jan Piotr Norblin de la Gourdaine made a pen and ink drawing in 1778 of a Jewish fiddler and *tsimbler*, and in 1819 he painted a watercolor depicting two fiddlers and a *tsimbler*.[98] A description of a Jewish wedding in Podolia, Ukraine, from the 1790s, mentions the musicians as playing two violins, dulcimer, and violoncello.[99]

The reasonably common Ashkenazic family names of Zimbler, Cymbler, and Zimbalist, adopted at the end of the eighteenth and beginning of the nineteenth centuries, indicate that the instrument was in wide use among the *klezmorim* at that period. The most famous Polish image of the klezmer is that of Jankiel Cimbalist, a character in Adam Mickiewicz's epic poem *Pan Tadeusz*, which takes place in Lithuania in 1811-1812. Jankiel had wandered as a musician in his younger days, but now ran an inn. Since he played Polish music, critics have proposed that Mickiewicz incorporated this character as a way to include Jews as Poles in their national struggle for independence.[100] Since every Polish school-child studies this poem, the association of the *cymbały* with Jews lives on, although the instrument today is rare in that country. Various writers have claimed Mickiewicz's model for Jankiel Cimbalist to be Yankel Liberman of St. Petersburg, whom Mickiewicz heard in the 1830s, or Mordko Fajerman (1810-1880), of Warsaw, a performer of mazurkas and polonaises, said to be the last *cymbały* player in that city.[101] Mikhail Yosif Guzikov (1806-1837), a native of Shklov, Belarus, played the flute and *tsimbl* before learning the xylophone, which impressed audiences from Odessa to Paris.[102]

Some of the *klezmorim* wandered far outside the Pale. Famintsyn recalled a Jewish *tsimbler* who played for the dances of the landowners of Meshchovsk district, Kaluga gubernia, Russia, in the 1840s.[103] Rimsky-Korsakov wrote that a Jewish trio of violin, *tsimbaly*, and tambourine appeared in his native town of Tikhvin, Russia, in the 1850s and soon became fashionable with the landowners.[104]

An ethnographic survey made in the 1860s noted that, in the Western Province [Lithuania, Latvia, Belarus] "mainly Jewish musicians played *tsimbaly*," using it with violin, clarinet, bass, and tambourine.[105] In 1861, Moses Berlin remarked that "Jewish *tsimbalist*s were popular with the people since time immemorial," playing at Jewish weddings and occasionally at synagogues during Simhat Torah and Hanukkah.[106]

However, by this time, a general decline in the use of the instrument by Jewish musicians had set in. In Kujawy, Poland, in the 1850s, Kolberg wrote that the *cymbały* was almost obsolete, appearing only, but rarely, at Jewish weddings.[107] Beregovskii's inquiries with Ukrainian *klezmorim* in the 1920s and 1930s revealed that of nine he had asked, only one remembered the *tsymbaly* being in use. That person recalled that his grandfather, in Makarov, Kiev gubernia, played, the band also including violin and clarinet.[108]

Nevertheless, in other locations, Jews continued to play the *tsimbl* into the twentieth century. It was in use at Daugavpils, Latvia, in the early years of the century,[109] and in 1908 an American wrote that it was played by "old people" in many parts of Poland.[110] Jewish recordings made in Lviv and Warsaw from 1908 to about 1911 featured it.[111] In the 1910s and 1920s, Iosif Isayevich Lepyansky (born 1873), of Vitebsk, Belarus, and his three sons organized a ensemble with four *tsimbaly*, playing Jewish wedding music by ear, dividing the parts into first violin, second violin, accompaniment, and bass.[112]

Gypsies in Belarus, Poland, and Ukraine have also played the instrument. During the middle of the nineteenth century, Shpilevskii commented that in Mir and Nyasvizh, Belarus, they played *tsimbaly*, guitar, jew's harp, and tambourine.[113] In his village in western Ukraine around 1910, Dmytro Prosyniuk recalled only Gypsies playing the *tsymbaly*, not ethnic Ukrainians. A displaced group of Gypsies from Volhynia who survived the Holocaust was wandering in western Poland in the late 1940s, playing harp and *cymbały*.[114] Sedentary Gypsies from the village of Turka, near Kolomyya, Ukraine, played violin, *tsymbaly*, and *baraban* (bass drum) for weddings at mid-twentieth century.[115]

In Poland during the twentieth century, peasants have played the *cymbały* only rarely and only in certain areas. Its use among ethnic Poles has been limited to some players in northern Poland, mostly postwar refugees from Vilnius province in Lithuania and Belarus, and to peasants in the county of Rzeszów in southeastern Poland.[116] Noll feels that the tradition in the latter regions began only in the second half of the nineteenth century or beginning of the twentieth century. He notes the absence of any evidence to the contrary and theorizes that it spread from Jews in the market towns to peasants living near those towns.[117] Czekanowska concurs that the tradition in Rszezowskie and Nowosadeckie is historically connected to Jewish tradition and also to Gypsy ensembles, which were popular in the areas of Orawa and Spisz.[118] Noll mentions a player who learned the *cymbały* from a Jewish musician in Łańcut during World War I.[119] Piotr Dahlig suggests that the instrument spread from the mountainous regions up the San and Wisłok Rivers, as well as from towns to nearby villages in the region and from Jewish and Gypsy musicians to Polish peasants.[120]

An example of a traditional peasant ensemble in southeastern Poland was that of the Sowa family of Piątkowa. The family tradition began with Piotr Sowa, a fiddler and *cymbalist* who lived in the early nineteenth century. Jozef Sowa (1904-1983) played an accompaniment part on the *cymbały* with a first violin, a second violin (playing chords, essentially the same as the Hungarian *kontra*), and a double bass. Together with a male singer, the group played polkas, waltzes, *wolne* (slow dances), and other dance tunes, such as the *sztajerek* and *krakowiak*.[120]

Dahlig writes that peasant musicians in Rzeszowskie felt a need to increase the instrumentation of the traditional fiddle-bass fiddle combination at the end of the nineteenth century and early twentieth century by adding a second violin and *cymbały*. The introduction of the latter instrument took place especially in the years before and after World War I. In the 1930s, the *cymbały* could be a cheap substitute for the fashionable but costly accordion, as it was possible for the players to make it themselves. Following World War II, the *cymbały* became more identified as an instrument characteristic of the region. Perhaps fifty players were active in the 1980s. An annual contest, held in Rzeszów, began in 1981. One could hear ensembles that used the instrument at local festivals in Krosno, Rzeszów, and Przemyśl, as well as at the national festival in Kazimierz nad Wisłą. In addition to these public presentations, *cymbały* players appeared at certain local harvest festivals, at clubs, and of course in music making at home.[122]

Belarusians today regard the *tsimbaly* as a "national" instrument. This status, however, is a recent development, dating from the 1930s or 1940s. In the early and mid-nineteenth century, as we have seen, it was mainly, though not exclusively, a Jewish instrument. As in southeastern Poland, it would appear that peasants largely adopted it from Jewish tradition in the late nineteenth century.

Nevertheless, there is some evidence to show that gentile musicians played it in earlier years. Krzysztof Zawisza, voivode of Minsk, wrote that, about 1712, he had "Łeba music and Minsk music with a *cymbal*; they played the old-fashioned dances well. "[123] A religious tract from the first half of the eighteenth century mentions violins and *tsimbaly* and other instruments.[124] In 1784 a "rural violin and *tsimbaly*" played for Mateusz Butrimowicz, lord of Pinsk.[125] About 1863, music at weddings in Polesie (now western Belarus) was provided by violin, *basetlya* (a portable bass viol), tambourine, and *cymbały*.[126] The *tsimbaly* had been used by peasants in the Pripiat River region in the early nineteenth century, although the instrument was not encountered in an ethnographic study of that region made a century later.[127]

The *tsimbaly* was very popular in village ensembles in much of Belarus during the first half of the twentieth century. These groups were an integral part of the wedding ceremony, and they played wedding marches and dance tunes, such as polkas, waltzes, quadrilles, and others. The size of the ensemble was variable, partly depending on the financial generosity of the wedding party. While one or two violins, *tsimbaly*, and diatonic accordion (*garmonika*) was typical in most of Belarus, other combinations included accordion and *tsimbaly*; *tsimbaly* and tambourine; violin, *tsimbaly*, accordion, and drum (*baraban*); bayan, *tsimbaly*, violin, and clarinet; or large ensembles, such as two bayans, three *tsimbaly*, two violins, and zither (*tsitra*), or diatonic accordion, *tsimbaly*, violin, clarinet, trumpet, bass, and drum. The *tsimbaly* was most popular in Vitebsk, Minsk, Grodno, Gomel, and Mogilev regions.[128]

One unique development in Belarus was that of ensembles which included numerous *tsimbaly*. This had begun with the Lepyanskys of Vitebsk by the 1910s, but it reached greater popularity later in the century. In 1928, Iosif Zhinovich (born 1909), who had learned the instrument from his family, organized a *tsimbaly* ensemble, basing the parts on the string quartet, like the Lepyansky family had done. He used a new design by the instrument maker K. Sushkevich, in soprano, alto, bass, and contrabass sizes. The new instrument was the foundation of the State Folk Orchestra of the Byelorussian Soviet Socialist Republic, organized in 1937. Following World War II, Zhinovich wrote a method and started a *tsimbaly* course at the Minsk Conservatory. Music schools around Belarus began instruction in the new instrument, and factories, schools, and "houses of culture" sponsored amateur *tsimbaly* ensembles.[129]

In the post-Soviet period, music students, largely female, continue to study the *tsimbaly* in the Zhinovich tradition. In addition to arrangements of Belarusian folk music, they play a variety of classical and popular music, both arranged and specially composed. The usual instrument is the soprano instrument manufactured by the Belarusian Industrial Amalgamation of Musical Instruments in Minsk. They do not play for weddings. Amateur *tsimbaly* ensembles, using both the traditional and the Sushkevich instrument designs, exist in various parts of the country.

The traditional dulcimers of Lithuania (*cimbolai*) and Latvia (*cimbole*) appear to be of the same type as that used in Belarus. Poles in Lithuania had adopted the instrument as early as 1831.[130] In 1863, Kolberg mentioned a band in Ukmerge which consisted of violin, *cymbały*, and tambourine (*bęben*).[131] In the twentieth century, its use by Lithuanians was mainly in the southern and eastern parts of Lithuania, as an instrument for accompaniment in village ensembles consisting of such instruments as violin, *cimbolai*, and tambourine; two violins, *cimbolai*, and bass drum with attached cymbals (as in Suwałki province, now in Poland); two violins and *cimbolai*; diatonic accordion and *cimbolai*; or violin, diatonic accordion and *cimbolai*.[132] In Latvia, the *cimbole* is found in the southern and eastern portions of the country.[133] In 1947, S. Krasnoperovs, a Latvian composer, helped form an orchestra of folk instruments, which included the *cimbole*, for the Latvian song and dance ensemble "Šakta."[134]

In Russia itself, traditional use of the *tsimbaly* is limited to the southern part of Pskov district and to the northwestern part of Smolensk district, where the typical ensemble in the early part of the twentieth century consisted of violin, *tsimbaly*, and tambourine (or bass).[135]

Romania and Moldova

In Romania, the *ţambal* tradition derives partly from the Hungarian Gypsy tradition, established in Transylvania in the eighteenth century, and partly from the Jewish tradition in Moldavia. It represents to some degree a convergence of both traditions, yet the two still remain somewhat distinct. The *ţambal* is almost exclusively played by *lăutar*s, Gypsies who follow music as a hereditary occupation.

Although, as we have noted, the *Hackbrett* was present in Kronstadt (now Braşov) as early as 1546, the *ţambal* arrived more recently. In the late eighteenth century, when Transylvania was part of Hungary, Gypsies played the instrument. Sulzer wrote in 1781 that the dulcimer was sometimes used in an ensemble which might consist of one or two violins and jew's harp or panpipes (*moscal*).[136] In the last decades of the eighteenth century, villages in Vojvodina (now in Serbia), like Grebenac and Vrsac, included Romanian Gypsies who played the *cimbul*.[137] A writer commented in 1814 that Transylvanian Gypsy bands in the past had included violins, violoncello, *Cymbal*, and sometimes panpipes, but more recently had shifted to wind instruments, especially the clarinet, which had displaced the *Cymbal*.[138]

Jewish migration into Moldavia during the eighteenth century resulted in the introduction of the dulcimer. In 1744, Solomon, the Jewish *ţămbălar* ("the *tsimbler*"), of Iaşi, received a tax redemption.[139] In 1835, the guild of Jewish musicians in Iaşi, led by Iţic Ţambalagiu, had its own synagogue.[140] *Klezmorim* who were officially registered in the northern town of Botoşani in 1845 included four fiddlers, four clarinetists, four bassists, and four *ţambalar*s, as well as three *badkhonim* (wedding jesters).[141] This neat division of instruments must have indicated the standard instrumentation of Jewish ensembles in that region, which would have included one of each of the instruments.

Evidence from the 1850s indicates that *klezmorim* and *lăutar*s played together on occasion.[142] This was, without doubt, the means by which the *ţambal* was introduced to the much larger number of Gypsy musicians in Moldavia and eastern Wallachia. It was a gradual process, taking place in the second half of the nineteenth century and early twentieth centuries. In 1864, Filimon, in describing the instruments of the *lăutar*s, mentioned the *canon*, "an ancient Jewish instrument . . . introduced to our country by a Jew." He remarked that it was rectangular, with many strings, and served, together with the *cobză* (a small lute), to accompany the melody.[143] Filimon, however, in confusing the Turkish *kanun* with the *ţambal*, demonstrated his lack of familiarity with the new instrument, as, even by the 1880s, it was only starting to establish itself. An ethnographic survey made in 1884-1885 indicated that it was found mainly in Ialomiţa county, where it was played in ten villages, and in one village each in Dimboviţa, Prahova, Buzău counties (all in Muntenia), Tulcea (in Dobrogea), and Iaşi counties (in Moldavia).[144] Alexandru writes that it was not until the early twentieth century that Gypsies in Moldavia adopted the instrument.[145]

The *ţambal* tradition is strongest in Muntenia, in the southeastern part of Romania, which is more or less the area where it was found in the 1880s. It is somewhat weaker in Oltenia, Dobrogea, Moldavia, and Bucovina. Players use it primarily as an instrument for accompaniment, in ensembles with varying instrumentation, such as violin, *ţambal*, bass; accordion, violin, *ţambal*, bass; and violin, accordion, clarinet, *ţambal*, and bass. As it was adopted, it tended to replace the *cobză* by assuming its musical role. The *ţambalagiu* plays patterns of accompaniment called *ţiituri*, which vary according to the type of music being played, such as *cîntece batrîneşti* ("old peoples' songs"), or dances such as the *horă*, *sârbă*, *geampara*, *brâu*, and others. In the regions of Romania which were part of Hungary before 1918, the *ţambal mare* (large *ţambal*) is played mainly in the larger towns by a declining number of Gypsy musicians; here players rely more on broken chords and countermelodies, as in Hungary, rather than on the *ţiituri* of Wallachia and Moldavia.

By the late nineteenth century, a stationary *ţambal* on legs had appeared in some of the leading Bucharest ensembles.[146] The Hungarian cimbalom gradually entered the Bucharest tradition after the union with Transylvania, although Scheffler, a local firm which in the early part of the century manufactured the small *ţambal*, also imported the large instrument.[147] Since that time, it has been replacing the *ţambal mic* (small *ţambal*) in both urban and village traditions. The "Romanian" tuning used on the *ţambal mic*, which bears a close resemblance to tuning systems used in Ukraine, Poland, and Belarus, has also gradually disappeared, most of the instruments having been converted to "Hungarian" tuning. Village *lăutar*s, nevertheless, continue to play the *ţambal mic*. While the cimbalom's primary function remains as an instrument for accompaniment, a virtuoso solo tradition was developed in this century by Nitza Codolban, Iancu Cârlig, Iani Ciuciu-Marinescu, Gheorghe Pantazi, Toni Iordache, and others. In the Communist period, both small and large instruments were manufactured by the "Doina" factory in Bucharest. Today, instruments are made only by individual craftsmen.

In the Republic of Moldova, the *ţambal mare* has developed a pedagogical tradition, being taught in music schools, in contrast to Romania, where instruction is carried on among *lăutar*s in private. Non-Gypsies play it in amateur and state-sponsored ensembles.

Turkey

The discussion of the obsolete *santur türk* is found in chapter 4. Another dulcimer, called *santur fransız* (European *santur*) in order to distinguish itself from the older *santur türk*, was introduced to Turkish musicians in Constantinople, according to Rauf Yekta, during the reign of Sultan Mejid (1839-1860), by Romanian musicians. A court musician, Hilmi Bey, adapted it for use in Ottoman art music, and it enjoyed a certain fashion thereafter.[148] The most famous player of this tradition was Santuri Edhem Efendi (1855-1926), who composed many pieces.[149] This *santur* school continued through Santuri Ziya and his pupil Hüsnü Tüzüner, but ended with the latter's death in 1975. The decline of Ottoman art music was only partially responsible for the decline of the *santur*. Its design, with fixed tones, rendered modulation into different *makam*s (modes) difficult or impossible.

Yekta's comment that the instrument was introduced by Romanian musicians may be only partly true, because Turkish instruments bear some resemblance to those of Ukraine.[150] The Crimean War produced many Jewish refugees from Kerch and elsewhere in Ukraine who settled in the Ottoman capital in 1854,[151] but there is also evidence that *klezmorim* and *lăutar*s from Romania played there during that decade.[152] They undoubtedly were responsible for introducing the *santur fransız* to Constantinople.

Greece

Although there is evidence to demonstrate that the Turkish *santur* was played on Greek soil,[153] the modern Greek *santouri* (also transliterated as *sandouri*), despite its name, most likely derives from the Romanian *ţambal*. This is evident from its design, tuning, and padded hammers. Authorities such as Chianis agree that the *santouri* is a relatively recent introduction to Greek music, but they have not determined the specific details regarding its establishment among Greeks.[154]

The *santouri* is most closely associated with a style of music known as *zmirneika*, that is, music of Smyrna, now the Turkish city of Izmir, which until 1922 was predominantly Greek in population. One possible means of transmission of the instrument to Smyrna was through the introduction of the *santur fransız* from Constantinople.[155] However, a better explanation may be through a direct transfer from *klezmorim*, probably from Romania, who settled in Smyrna. Several hundred Jews, following pogroms in Russia and Romania, did settle there in 1892,[156] and, of course, some may have been musicians. This settlement may account for several practices associated with the *santouri* which have direct parallels in Eastern European, especially Jewish, tradition, but which would be unlikely to be associated with an instrument used for art music. These include the use of the shoulder strap when playing the *santouri* in wedding processions; the term *kompania*, used to describe an ensemble of musicians (which has a direct cognate in the Yiddish *kompanye*); the ensemble consisting of violin, *santouri*, and violoncello, found in some of the earliest Gramophone Company recording sessions made in Smyrna in 1910; and the use of the *santouri* to accompany dances at weddings.[157]

Following the exchange of populations in 1922, refugees from Smyrna and elsewhere in Asia Minor flooded into Greece. They brought the style of music familiar in the *café-chantants* of Smyrna, which featured a singer, usually female, with instrumental accompaniment, including *santouri*. This style dominated Greek entertainment for two decades.[158] With the subsequent popularity of the bouzouki-dominated *rebetiko*, however, *zmirneika* and the *santouri* declined in the 1940s. In the 1970s, some singers began a small revival of *zmirneika* and, with it, the *santouri*. Today the instrument is taught in a few music schools. Kofteros lists four currently active makers.[159]

The *santouri* is a part of the *kompania*, or ensemble, which contains a varying number of instruments, including violin, clarinet, and *laouto*.

It can double the melody heterophonically or play a chordal accompaniment. It is most significant in the music of the islands close to Turkey, especially Lesvos, where the ensembles at weddings play such dances as the *ballos, kalamatianos, sirtos, zeibekiko, karsilamas, sousta, hasapiko, hasapikoserviko,* and *tsifte-telli.* Soloists may also play a Turkish *taksim* or modern Greek popular music.

In Bulgaria, Gypsy musicians have made very limited use of a dulcimer, called *tsimbal.*[160] A photograph in the author's collection, made in the Balkan Mountains in the 1920s, depicts three Muslim Gypsies, one playing clarinet, another a tambourine (*daire*), and a third with a portable dulcimer with nine treble courses and nine bass courses, each with five strings, and evidence of a neck strap. It resembles the contemporary Greek *santouri* more than the Romanian *ţambal.* The design may suggest the instrument's origin, although the name indicates a northern source. In any event, its history in this country is completely obscure.

Traditions in North America

The Moravian *cimbal* tradition in America was represented by that of the Baca family, of Fayetteville, Texas, and a few other players in that vicinity. Czechs began to settle in south Texas in the 1850s. Joseph Bača and his family, from Bordovice, settled near Fayetteville in 1860. His son Frank J. Baca, who played clarinet, organized a band in 1892, consisting of himself and some of his thirteen children. The same year, Ignac Krenek made a dulcimer (as they now called it), which Frank Baca's children incorporated into their orchestra. It would appear that in the 1890s and 1900s the Baca family ensemble organized itself into a brass band, playing for parades, funerals, festivals, and band contests, while their orchestra, which included stringed instruments, played for dances. Instrumentation of the orchestra, about 1908, was violin, clarinet, dulcimer, trumpet, trombone, and violoncello (see illustration 13); another grouping from about the same time shows three violins, two cornets, two clarinets, trombone, dulcimer, bass viol, and drums.

Ray Baca (1893-1980) played the dulcimer with the Baca Orchestra for many years. The repertoire of the orchestra consisted mainly of Czech-American polkas and waltzes, with the odd schottische and other American or Mexican tune (like "El Rancho Grande," "Jole Blonde," and "Dixie"). He played the melody rather than accompaniment. In 1967, he traveled with his orchestra to Washington, to play at the Festival of

American Folklife. A few others in this region played the dulcimer with Czech bands, like Anton Kulhanek (with John R. Baca's Orchestra, about 1935), Johnny Stastny (with Anna Baca Stastny's family band, about 1937), and Ray Krenek, of Wallis, Texas. The dulcimer used in this tradition consists of eleven treble courses, twelve bass courses, and one left-hand bass course, each with five strings per course, with four rosettes or round sound holes.[161] Hammers are notched above and below, for the index and middle fingers, and resemble varieties of hammers that Kunz depicts from the region around Brno and Chodsko.[162]

German or German-Czech immigrants from Bohemia who settled in Wisconsin in the latter half of the nineteenth century also played the dulcimer. John ("Poopmaker") Zwiefelhofer (1850-1918) played it in a band with Joseph Hable, violin, Joseph Grill, clarinet, and Mr. Svoboda, horn, in the 1880s and 1890s in the Bohemian settlement around Bloomer, Chippewa County. They were all from southern Bohemia, near Česke Budejovice, where the instrument may have lasted longer than in other areas.[163] In the 1920s a man named Rubenzer, whose family was from southern Bohemia, still played the dulcimer in that area for dances, sometimes with an accordion or clarinet.[164] Although later generations dropped the word *Cymbal* in favor of "dulcimer," the immigrant generation likely called the instrument by that name.

In the nineteenth century, Hungarian Gypsy orchestras achieved fame outside Hungary, and, after 1860, many began to tour abroad. Mihály Farkas (1829-1890) and Náci Erdélyi (died 1893) led such orchestras on tours to America.[165] The earliest to settle permanently, however, were Gypsies from the depressed county of Saros (now Šariš, in eastern Slovakia), who followed the general emigration of Slovaks from that region to Pennsylvania, beginning about 1880 and continuing until 1914. The immigrant coal miners and steel mill workers came initially without wives and families and spent much time in the saloons. The Gypsy musicians followed them and played in the saloons for tips, as well as for banquets in fraternal halls and weddings.[166] They lived in such towns as Johnstown, Uniontown, McKeesport, and Lyndora, but congregated in Braddock, where Andrew Carnegie's U.S. Steel Corporation had a huge mill. By 1914, more than five hundred lived in what Irving Brown called "small, congested quarters." Another settlement of Gypsies, from larger towns in Zemplen, now in eastern Slovakia, settled in Homestead, Pennsylvania, following earlier migrations to New York City and Cleveland.[167] Sometime prior to 1924, Brown encountered "some forty or fifty families living in shanties grouped about a sort of square" in Braddock, where he heard a makeshift orchestra which included two cimbaloms.[168]

Other immigrant Gypsy musicians settled in New York City and Cleveland. In 1903, Edward Steiner described the houses in "Little Hungary," on Manhattan's Lower East Side, which sold liquor and "everywhere one hears the sound of the cymbal . . . out of which the gypsy hammers sweet music." He also mentioned a saloon in Cleveland, owned by a Gypsy, which featured the music of two violins, "cymbal," and bass.[169] Bercovici in 1924 described the "disputes" between the Gypsy musicians in the restaurants of New York's "Little Hungary" over whether the cimbalom player Janos Barti, who had recently died, was better than one still living.[170] Perhaps the experiences of the immigrant Gypsy cimbalom player of this period may be illustrated by those of Stefan Tuleja, interviewed in Romany by A. T. Sinclair in 1909. This person was born in a Gypsy community near Eperješ, now in Slovakia, and at sixteen, emigrated to New York City, where he had lived for seventeen years, playing for the Astors and other socialites.[171] Evidently the immigrant musicians playing Hungarian Gypsy music found some success by seeking such patronage. Meyer Davis, a Jewish "society" dance band leader for many years, started out with a Hungarian Gypsy orchestra, which included a cimbalom, in the 1910s, and, in the 1920s, Alexander Haas and his group were popular at Long Island parties.[172]

The generation of Gypsy children born or raised in the United States who learned the cimbalom in some cases studied formally with other Gypsies, using the Allaga method and transcriptions of Chopin and other composers.[173] The best-known player was Veronica Mikova, "Gypsy Countess Verona," who toured on the vaudeville circuit in the 1910s and 1920s. From Braddock, but resident in Cleveland, she recorded four sides for Columbia in 1916, mostly light classical music.[174] According to Gus Horvath, her act featured phosphorescent painted hammers which glowed in ultraviolet light. Although it was unusual, it was not unknown for Gypsy girls to become musicians;[175] likely this was a new response to American conditions.

The community in Braddock, which had already experienced the loss of members to Cleveland, Detroit, New York City, and Chicago, was devastated by the Great Depression.[176] Detroit's Hungarian community, in the enclave of Del Ray, had an active life, with numerous restaurants, churches, and fraternal organizations. Gypsies from Braddock and Homestead moved there and settled on Burdeno Street, replicating the Gypsy neighborhood of Braddock as well as those of Hungarian villages. In 1936 the Gypsy population there amounted to 163.[177] Cleveland, whose population of Hungarian Gypsy musicians was estimated in 1959 at about 200,[178] was the home of John Brenkacs and his Gypsy orchestra, which made a number of recordings on Columbia in 1924; the cimbalom player was Louis ("Bum") Ballog. In 1939, Brenkacs moved to Detroit, to play at the Hungarian Village Restaurant, and Gus Horvath joined him on the cimbalom. Horvath continued to play in Detroit restaurants until the early 1990s.

Although restaurants provided regular venues for Gypsy music, the Hungarian communities of Cleveland and Detroit offered many other opportunities. These included "grape harvest" festivals, picnics, banquets, New Year's Eve dances, concerts, and weddings. However, these declined, as the immigrants who arrived before the restrictive immigration policies adopted in 1924 aged and second-generation Hungarian-Americans moved outside the immigrant neighborhoods. In Cleveland, "grape harvest" festivals sponsored by churches numbered six in 1940, but declined to one in 1973; ten picnics were sponsored by societies in 1940, but none were held in 1973.[179] In Del Ray, about 1958, there were four or five bars and restaurants with cimbaloms, but the last place closed in 1993. The gradual decline in demand for the music meant that few young Gypsies learned the instrument after 1935. Today, Alex Udvary of Chicago is the last active player from this community. The large number of Hungarians who came to the United States following the revolution in 1957 included a number of cimbalom players. They settled in New York, Washington, D.C., and California.

Not all professional cimbalom players were Gypsies. In New York City, a number of Hungarian Jewish immigrants played the instrument. Joseph Kun played with Aladar Sio's Gypsy orchestra, a Jewish ensemble.[180] Julius Klein went from New York to Hollywood in the 1930s and thereafter appeared in many motion pictures. In other Hungarian settlements, the children of ethnic Hungarian immigrants learned to play the instrument. Dick Marta learned it in Pennsylvania and went to New York City, where he played in restaurants in the 1950s (see illustration 14). Most, however, regarded themselves as amateurs, even if they might join the musicians' union and earn extra money by playing. For example, George Simon, who learned to play the violin soon after he immigrated to New Jersey about 1905, later moved to Flint, Michigan, where he worked in an automobile factory, and organized a Hungarian orchestra. He bought a cimbalom for his son Joe, who taught himself and played with his father and other children of immigrants at restaurants, fraternal-organization and church affairs in the 1930s and 1940s. Learning music was a sign of upward mobility for Hungarian immigrants, and many learned Gypsy music, which in America did not seem to carry the stigma it had in Europe.

Cimbaloms were brought over in immigrant ships, imported from Hungarian manufacturers, and built in America by immigrants and their children. In 1907, Ferdinand Wagner, of New York City, received a patent for cimbalom dampers.[181] John Koleszar had a music store on Sixth Street in New York City from the 1910s until the 1940s and, besides offering violins, accordions, and a general line of instruments, made "cimbals." His undated catalog, which appears to have been printed during World War I, features eleven models, ranging in price from $85 to $400.[182] Alex Sagady, of Detroit, made about fifteen cimbaloms from the 1940s to the 1960s. Bela Somsak in California makes them today. Many other individuals made them as well, as one can see from homemade examples found in communities where Hungarians settled.

Although mass immigration of Jews from Poland, Galicia, the Russian Empire, and Romania began after 1880, when their use of the *tsimbl* was generally in decline, some did use it in America. As early as 1823, advertisements for a menagerie touring through Hamilton and Dayton, Ohio, promised "good music on the ancient Jewish Cymbal and other instruments,"[183] probably indicating that a Jewish musician from Germany or elsewhere in Europe may have already arrived. In New York City, one Goldberg played it with Max Yankowitz, an accordionist, on recordings made in 1913, and a Mr. Silver accompanied Max Leibowitz's violin playing on recordings made in 1919.[184] A vaudeville performer whose act was called "Uncle Sam and His Singing Strings" toured across North America and Australia in the 1910s and 1920s, using a dulcimer, which he had learned in his native Kiev. He placed it inside a piano-case prop, and, following the opening notes of Beethoven's Fifth Symphony, the prop would collapse, and he would play the dulcimer, as well as xylophone and other instruments.[185]

By the turn of the century, Romanian music had become fashionable in Lower East Side restaurants and wine cellars catering to Jewish immigrants.[186] Joseph Moskowitz, born in 1879 in Galaţi, Romania, learned the *ţambal* from his father, Moyshe Tsimbler, from whom he also learned to read music. From the age of fourteen, he began to tour, accompanying a Jewish singing group. He played in a tavern in Lemberg (Lviv), then toured until 1906 with Osher Feierstein and Moyshe der Blinder through Galicia, Romania, Hungary, and Constantinople. In 1907 or 1908, he came to America with the Matus "Gypsy" ensemble, playing in hotels on a Schunda cimbalom he had purchased in Budapest. In 1914, he opened a restaurant in the Lower East Side, at which he played regularly.[187] Moskowitz and Lupowitz's Restaurant, which, in the early 1930s featured a sign depicting the cimbalom, became an establishment well known for its "Gypsy" music and Romanian atmosphere.[188] He sold out his share in 1936 and from 1943 until his death played at Michel's Restaurant in Washington, D.C., with the namesake owner's "Gypsy" orchestra. Moskowitz made several recordings, with piano accompaniment, in 1916 for Victor, in 1927 for Columbia, and in 1954 on a long-playing record.[189] He died soon afterwards.

Ukrainians settled in huge numbers on the western plains in Canada, as well as in neighboring North Dakota and the coal fields of Pennsylvania, starting in the 1890s. Most came from western Ukraine, the area with a rich *tsymbaly* tradition. In their rural settlements in the New World, they retained many of their village practices, including weddings with *troista muzyka*. The *tsymbaly* was among the instruments brought over by the first immigrants. John Maga, who settled near Wostok, Alberta, in 1898, brought a violin and *tsymbaly* from his home in Bukovina.[190] Other immigrants, like Dmytro Prosyniuk, who left Ukraine in 1913, learned it after their arrival in the New World; in his case, in Winnipeg, Manitoba.[191] In either case, *tsymbaly* were made in Canada by many different immigrants during this first wave of immigration (1890-1930) and reflected the variety of traditional designs and tuning systems used in the old country.

In the United States, rural Ukrainian settlements in North Dakota, as across the border in Manitoba, fostered traditional Ukrainian wedding music. Bill Namyniuk, of Belfield, who learned to make his first "dulcimer" in 1926, at the age of twelve, from his uncles and brother, played it at Ukrainian weddings, dances, and anniversaries, in an ensemble consisting also of violin and accordion.[192] Migrants from Manitoba and Alberta who settled in Detroit played it at dances at the Ukrainian Hall, although it should be noted that not all the Ukrainian orchestras there used *tsymbaly*.[193] Pawlo Humeniuk, the New York City fiddler who made many Ukrainian and Polish recordings between 1925 and 1940, used *tsymbaly* accompaniment in only three of sixty-eight sessions. However, other recordings made in New York City during this period, including those of the Ukrainska Selska Orchestra in 1929 and 1930, feature it, as well as one with two solos by John Grychak, who was from around Easton, Pennsylvania.[194]

By the 1970s, the *tsymbaly*, or "dulcimer," as it was now widely called, had become an emblem of Ukrainian ethnic identity in Canada, at least for descendants of the first wave of immigration. As the children of the immigrants who came during that wave aged, their music and instrumentation gradually changed. Metro Radomsky's orchestra, when it began around 1930, consisted of violin, *tsymbaly*, and drum. As years passed, saxophone, accordion, and trumpet were added.[195] In the 1970s, instrumentation of Ukrainian-Canadian wedding bands might consist of violin, *tsymbaly*, and electric guitar, or violin, *tsymbaly*, accordion, electric guitar and bass, although the older violin, *tsymbaly*, and drum set was still in use. The older dances, like *harkan*, *kolomyjka*, and *hutsulka* gradually faded, while newer polkas and waltzes were introduced, as well as dances familiar to a general Canadian audience, like the schottische, two-step, fox-trot, and "Latin."

Weddings remain the chief venue for the music, although reduced in length to one day from the three-day affair of the 1930s. Independent record companies, such as V Records, Ltd., of Winnipeg, produce recordings of Ukrainian Country Music, including *tsymbaly* players, and radio shows promote the music. In 1970s and 1980s, *tsymbaly* contests were organized in Edmonton and Winnipeg, modeled after old-time fiddling contests, which promoted the instrument, and included both experienced Ukrainian-Canadian players playing traditional tunes identical in style to those played in Ukraine and even a few new players not of Ukrainian background playing such tunes as "Amazing Grace."[196] The National Ukrainian Festival at Dauphin, Manitoba, and the Pysanka Festival at Vegreville, Alberta, are the major events for *tsymbaly* playing and buying today.

Elsewhere in North America, members of Ukrainian communities have occasionally shown interest in the instrument, importing the newer, manufactured *tsymbaly* from the Ukraine. Graduates of *tsymbaly* courses in Ukraine and Belarus have recently immigrated to both the United States and Canada.

Although Polish and Lithuanian immigration to the United States has been very large, dulcimer players from those countries have left little evidence of any existence.[197] The same is true for Orthodox emigrants from Belarus.

Romanian immigration to the United States has mostly been from Transylvania and Banat, where the *ţambal* is little played. Nevertheless, some players, mostly from Muntenia, have been active in Romanian communities. Selvestru Cherchel came to Detroit before 1920 and played his cimbalom, made in 1924 in Detroit by a Greek named Stratos Vatsardis, in a tavern at the corner of Russell and Hancock Streets. In Indiana Harbor, Indiana, the Transylvanian fiddler Nicu Hanzi was accompanied by his daughter Victoria on cimbalom. Iancu "Borcea" Cârlig came to play at the Romanian Pavilion at the 1939 New York World's Fair and stayed in New York, Detroit, and Chicago, before returning to Romania in the 1950s. Nicolae Feraru, a virtuoso from Bucharest, came to Detroit in 1988 and plays for Romanian weddings and dances in Chicago.

Immigration to the United States from Greece was heavy just before and after World War I. The dislocation caused by the loss of Smyrna to Turkey led to further emigration. The largest settlements were in New York City and Chicago, but Greeks migrated to other cities and small towns all over the country. This era coincided with the popularity of the *santouri* and Smyrna-style music, and Greek music performed at weddings and at taverns in American cities frequently included the instrument.

Some indication of the popularity of the *santouri* in the Greek immigrant community can be gleaned from the numerous recordings made by Greek musicians in New York City and Chicago between 1917 and 1940. Spottswood lists fifty-one main entries (out of 194) which included at least some *santouri* or cimbalom playing. The leading singers in the Smyrna style, as Madame Coula, Marika Papagika, and Amalia Bakas, almost always recorded with *santouri* or cimbalom accompaniment. The most active players on record included Louis Rassias in New York City and Spyros Stamos (1893-1973) in Chicago.[198]

Although it is unfashionable today to talk of the "melting pot," the concentration of immigrants in American cities did affect Greek *santouri* players. As professional musicians, they came into contact with Gypsy cimbalom players, and many—perhaps most, if we judge by recordings made between 1918 and 1950—adopted the Hungarian instrument. Feldman mentions a *santouri* player in New York City who apprenticed himself to a Hungarian master after his arrival.[199] Already in 1927, cimbalom player Mano Zervelly recorded a "Gypsy Serenade."[200] Frank Gazis (1901-1980) played a Schunda cimbalom at Vanessi's Restaurant

Figure 6.6: Distribution of the cimbalom family in Europe, 20th century.

Eastern variety (incl. Romanian)

Hungarian-Central European variety

Area of greater use or familiarity

Area of greater use or familiarity

in San Francisco for over thirty years, until the 1970s. His 1960s recording includes only popular American standards.[201]

Although some Greek-Americans learned the cimbalom or *santouri*,
the instrument largely died out with the gradual deaths of the immigrants who arrived in the 1910s and 1920s. Continued immigration did
bring some new players, but they did not necessarily play it actively.[202]
The popularity of *rebetiko* music, and the associated bouzouki and guitar, drove out Smyrna-style music from Greek *tavernas* in America, a
process starting in the 1930s and continuing until the early 1970s. An
interest in the *santouri* among younger Greek-Americans has caused,
since the 1980s, a small revival of the instrument in the United States,
probably reflecting similar activity in Greece. John Roussas, of Philadelphia, Peter Kyvelos, of Boston, and others have made them, and Roussas
plays and teaches the instrument.

Design

Central European-Hungarian

The earliest illustrations of a dulcimer probably carrying the name
Cymbal with fairly accurate representations of their string arrangement
are the painting by Govaerts (c.1700), mentioned above, and Picart's
engraving of a Jewish wedding in Amsterdam (1723). Hubert Boone's
interpretation of the former painting indicates a large instrument with
eight treble courses of four strings each and nine or ten bass courses with
four or five strings each, with a small bass bridge on the lower left.[203]
Picart's illustration shows an instrument with two carved rosettes and
two bridges, the treble bridge having seven holes and the bass bridge
eight holes, indicating, if accurate, eight treble courses and nine bass
courses. The hammers are thick at the end where the player holds them,
with thin round shafts bent into sharp hooks at the playing end. J. C.
Weigel's engraving of a German woman (c.1720) is less accurate, but
still useful. It has two bridges; the hammers are straight rods with sickle-
shaped ends.[204] Schudt's engraving (see figure 6.1) of a Jewish wedding
procession in Frankfurt (1714) is useful only to show that the instrument
was light enough to be carried with a neck strap and that its hammers
ended in hook-shaped, unwrapped ends, as in the Amsterdam illustration.[205] Seekatz's painting from about 1760 (see illustration 9) shows an

instrument, probably from Hesse, with nine treble and eight bass courses, with a bridge for a single course on the lower left. Whether he called this a *Hackbrett* or *Cymbal*, this instrument bears similarities to the ones depicted earlier in the century, but the lower bridge on the left may show the influence of the *Cymbal*.

By the late eighteenth century, the Central European *Cymbal* had acquired characteristics which survive in the contemporary Hungarian cimbalom. These include a bridge on the left side which carries some of the bass courses, a tuning which retains a diatonic scale over the treble bridge but which also incorporates a chromatic range, pin blocks which are fastened to the baseboard, and an outer case which attaches to the baseboard.[206] South German or Austrian instruments which survive in museums exhibit these characteristics, such as numbers 693 (end of eighteenth century) and 694 (by Joseph Weixelpamer, 1811) in the collection of the Musikinstrumenten-Museum of the University of Leipzig and number 14 in the musical instrument collection of the Oberöster-reichisches Landesmuseum in Linz. The dimensions of such instruments were relatively large: the lower length ranged from 110 to 130 cm (43½ to 51¼ inches); upper length from 60 to 80 cm (23½ to 31½ inches); width from 42 to 60 cm (16½ to 23½ inches); and height from 7 to 12 cm (2¾ to 4¾ inches). Nine or ten courses ran over the treble bridge, nine to thirteen (usually twelve) courses ran over the right bass bridge,

Figure 6.7: Dulcimer (*Cymbal*) played by John ("Poopmaker") Zwiefelhofer, who immigrated to Chippewa County, Wisconsin, in the late 1880s from Bohemia. The bridge on the lower left (to the viewer, the upper right) side is missing. Courtesy of Peter Hable.

and three or four courses ran over the lower left bass bridge. Unlike later Hungarian instruments, the number of strings per course ranged from five to eight. These instruments generally had two or four rosettes. The tuning of one instrument, presumably from Upper Austria, has been preserved, showing a diatonic-chromatic range (see appendix 1).[207]

Kunz's description of the Czech and Moravian *cimbal*, based on a small number of nineteenth-century examples in museums and in descriptions, indicates that they bore the same characteristics as those in Germany and Austria: a lower left bass bridge with one to three courses; a diatonic-chromatic tuning; and dimensions ranging from 108 to 123 cm (42½ to 48½ inches) at the lower length, 63 to 75 cm (24¾ to 29½ inches) at the upper length; 45 to 60 cm (17¾ to 23½ inches) in width. He writes that courses consisted generally of three or four strings, but sometimes had six or seven, as with the German variety. His description of hammers shows three or four types. In Valašsko, they had hooked ends (as in the early eighteenth-century German and Dutch Jewish illustrations) or resembled Hungarian hammers; in Chodsko and the area around Brno, the handles were notched above and below and the playing ends widened vertically (the type of hammer used by the Texans Ray Baca and Ray Krenek); and an example from Kyjov bears a closer resemblance to Ukrainian hammers, with a deep upper notch in the handle and a thicker knob at the playing end.[208]

Until the middle of the nineteenth century, some Hungarian instruments were light enough to be carried with a neck strap. Unfortunately, one can glean few details concerning the string arrangement from illustrations.[209] In general, the hammers appear to be unwrapped, slender rods, the ends turning up slightly. Older instruments in the Néprazi Múzeum in Budapest are as small as 74 to 95.8 cm (29¼ to 37¾ inches) at the lower length, 54 to 70.5 cm (21¼ to 27¾ inches) at the upper length, and 31.5 to 43.5 cm (12½ to 17¼ inches) in width.[210]

Clearly, by the middle of the nineteenth century, the design of Hungarian instruments had been influenced by those of Moravia and Bohemia. A late nineteenth-century "three-quarter" size cimbalom, manufactured in Budapest by Sternberg (see figure 6.8), may be typical of Hungarian cimbaloms at the time of Schunda's development in 1874 of the large, pedal cimbalom. Its dimensions are 122 cm (47¾ inches) at the lower length, 80 cm (31¼ inches) at the upper length, 53 cm (20¾ inches) wide, and 12 cm (4½ inches) high, very similar to dimensions of the German and Austrian instruments mentioned above. The tuning is iden-

Figure 6.8: Three-quarter-size cimbalom manufactured by Ármin Sternberg és Testvére, of Budapest, late nineteenth century. Collection of William T. White.

tical to the Schunda instrument, except that the range ascends upwards from A^1. The four sound holes, as with other late nineteenth and early twentieth-century Hungarian cimbaloms, consist of a central hole surrounded by six concentric holes. The internal structure includes two wide pine braces glued to the baseboard at the middle and upper points; wooden bars are glued to the soundboard directly under the bridges and are intersected by two wooden bars placed lengthwise. Like modern cimbaloms, round soundposts rest on the baseboard under the bridge braces which are glued to the soundboard. The courses contain four strings each, except for the overspun courses, which rest in groups of three on the lower right and left bass bridges and are tuned from A^1 to $f\sharp^1$.[211]

The larger instruments manufactured by Schunda and his competitors starting in the 1870s had a chromatic range of D^1 to e^3. Pin blocks were bolted, screwed and glued to the baseboard and were supported by a free-standing cast-iron brace, held in place by the tension of the strings. Soundposts between the baseboard and intersecting wooden bars on the underside of the soundboard supported the downward pressure of the bridges. The optional dampers were operated by a pedal, which, when in operation, pulled two levers screwed to the underside of the instrument which pushed two rods through it, raising the weighted dampers. The firm of Lajos Bohak introduced a slightly different design in the 1920s, which soon won favor. Instead of a cast-iron A-frame brace, the pin blocks were braced with two steel bars which fit into steel plates bearing

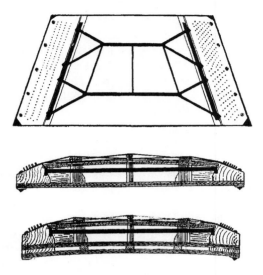

Figure 6.9: Diagrams of Gyula Mogyoróssy's cimbaloms, showing the cast-iron inner frames. Source: Mogyoróssy Gyula Hangszergyáros, *Cimbalom-árjegyzéke* **(Budapest: Mogyoróssy, 1917?).**

against each pin block. The soundboard, lacking sound holes, was free-standing, with open areas between it and the pin blocks. The angle at which the pin blocks lay decreased, allowing the string length of the bass strings to increase. Finally, Bohak enlarged the range, from C^1 eventually to a^3.

Poland, Ukraine, Belarus, Lithuania, and Latvia

Although they exhibit a great variety of tunings, details, decoration, and other characteristics which allow them to be further divided into subtypes, traditional dulcimers in Poland, Ukraine, Belarus, and neighboring regions display enough similar characteristics to form a common type. These include tuning schemes, string arrangements, and structural design.

In contrast to the Central European-Hungarian variety, these instruments are lighter in weight and lack the lower left bass courses. The basic structure consists uniformly of two horizontal rails mortised into the pin blocks at their ends, often acting as the outer sides on the front and rear of the instrument.[212] The baseboard, rather than being fundamental in the design in resisting the tension of the strings, is thin and added to the basic frame of two pin blocks and two rails. Although the Hungarian design of a central hole surrounded by six concentric holes also exists in Belarus, more typically sound holes are geometric rosettes cut in the soundboard. Hammers are heavier and shorter than the Hungarian type and are unwrapped at the playing ends. A common, although not universal, tuning characteristic is for a course tuned g♯¹ | c♯¹ to precede the g¹ | c¹ course. Another feature of this type is that the courses contain five to eight strings each, although some instruments may have three or four strings per course.

In general, the width of instruments in Belarus, Lithuania, and Latvia is narrower than those in Ukraine and southern Poland, due to a higher frequency of instruments with fewer courses. Nazina describes the dimensions of traditional *tsimbaly* in Belarus as ranging from 91 to 115 cm (35¾ to 45¼ inches) at the lower length, 71 to 94 cm (28 to 37 inches) at the upper length, 20 to 43 cm (8 to 17 inches) in width, and 5.5 to 9.3 cm (2¼ to 3¾ inches) in height.[213] For Lithuanian instruments, Baltrieniene and Apanavičius give the corresponding dimensions as 91 to 112 cm (35¾ to 44 inches) and 66 to 88 cm (26 to 34¾ inches) in length and 30 to 66 cm (11¾ to 26 inches) in width.[214] Priedite describes Latvian instruments as generally ranging from 75 to 110 cm (29½ to 43¼ inches) in length, 22 to 35 cm (8¾ to 13¾ inches) in width, and 6 to 15 cm (2½ to 6 inches) in height, while Dahlig, describing those played by Poles from Lithuania and Belarus, gives dimensions as about 90 and 75 cm (35½ and 29½ inches) long by about 30 cm (11¾ inches) wide.[215] Although the exact design varies from player to player, Belarusian, Lithuanian, and Latvian hammers are carved from single pieces of wood, with upper and lower notches for the finger grip, and the playing ends hook slightly upward.[216]

Older Belarusian instruments typically have only six or seven treble courses and a corresponding number of bass courses, but the latter may range in number from four to eight. It is not unreasonable to assume that *tsimbaly* with the smaller number of treble courses indicate an older design. Other Belarusian instruments frequently have eight, nine, and ten treble courses and a like number of bass courses, although sometimes the number of bass courses is less or greater by one.[217]

Tuning schemes on traditional Belarusian instruments are extremely varied. Zhinovich's survey revealed that the lowest treble course often began at g^1 | c^1 and continued upwards partly chromatically and partly diatonically, but might start as low as d^1 | g^0. Bass courses started often at c^0 or d^0. Frequently the top one or two treble courses had another bridge on the right, which changed the fifth interval to a minor or major second.[218]

The *tsimbaly* designed by Sushkevich and manufactured in Minsk has a chromatic tuning and, unlike most traditional Belarusian instruments, has a bass bridge on the lower left. Its three strings per course are fewer in number than most traditional instruments. Taught in schools, its players use a uniform hammer design, shorter than the traditional hammers, with padded ends.

Certain varieties found in the Ukraine have fewer strings than the ones generally made today. These instruments, with six treble courses, have a similar arrangement to those found on certain older Belarusian instruments. Because of this relationship, one might assume that the design is conservative and resembles *tsymbaly* made two or three hundred years ago. The Lemkos of Volovets district, Transcarpathia oblast, use a so-called "Verkhovyna" *tsymbal* (the survival of the singular form of the word in this district, incidentally, could indicate the long establishment of the instrument in local tradition), with six treble and six bass courses, each with three strings, which measures 50 to 70 cm (19¾ to 27½ inches) in length and 25 to 30 cm (10 to 12 inches) in width. Similar instruments are used in Mizhirya district and by the Boikos of Turkiv district, Lviv oblast.[219] A nineteenth-century instrument from Poltava has eleven courses of four each and is 78.6 cm (31 inches) and 57 cm (22½ inches) long and 24.3 cm (9½ inches) wide, while another one from that region has thirteen courses of four each and is 89 cm (35 inches) long and 29 cm (11½ inches) wide.[220] Such a relatively short length was probably characteristic through the entire region until the late nineteenth century. A *cimbolai* made about 1875 in northern Lithuania measured 64 cm (25¼ inches) in length, 27 cm (10¾ inches) in width, and 13 cm (5 inches) deep.[221] The instrument with which the *tsimbler* Mordko Fajerman of Warsaw posed for a photograph, probably in the 1870s,[222] is also short in length compared to modern instruments. Presumably the use of steel strings resulted in longer instruments.

Hutsul instruments, however, generally feature more courses. Vertkov illustrates an elaborately decorated instrument from 1890 with eleven treble and eleven bass courses, each with six strings, and Mierczynski describes one with 27 courses of seven strings each, 115 and 63 cm (45¼ and 24¾ inches) long and 50 cm (19¾ inches) wide.[223] Mark Bandera writes that Ukrainian immigrants to Canada brought two types of *tsymbaly*, one, called "Galician" or "Ukrainian," with four or five strings per course and with sixteen or eighteen courses, and another, called variously "Gypsy," "Bukovinan," "Hutsul," or "Romanian," with six strings per course and twenty or twenty-two courses.[224] Two older Ukrainian *tsymbaly* from Detroit that I have seen have nine treble and nine bass courses, each with five strings per course, one of them having many brass wires.[225] An instrument made in 1929 by Ignace Bronicki of Winnipeg has twelve treble and twelve bass courses, each with seven strings, and features diamond-shaped wooden inlays, much like the Hutsul instrument Vertkov illustrates.

Features of contemporary Ukrainian-Canadian *tsymbaly* may be illustrated by seven instruments made between 1957 and 1975 by Alberta makers in the collections of the Canadian Centre for Folk Culture Studies, Museum of Civilisation. The lower lengths range from 95 to 128.5 cm (37½ to 50½ inches), the widths from 36 to 73 cm (14¼ to 28¾ inches), and the heights from 7 to 11 cm (2¾ to 4¼ inches). Four have ten treble and ten bass courses, two have twelve treble and twelve bass courses, and one has thirteen treble and twelve bass courses. Five have five strings per course, while two have six per course.[226]

Although a study of traditional Ukrainian tunings has not been published, the situation is likely to be comparable to that in Belarus, with many individual and regional variations. Bandera describes two basic systems used in western Canada, the "Galician" and the "Gypsy" (and various other terms corresponding to the instrument designs mentioned above), as well as another one used by Nick Mischi, an immigrant from Bukovina. All three systems have the characteristic g♯¹ | c♯¹ course which precedes the g¹ | c¹ course.[227] This seemingly idiosyncratic feature is met with in Jewish tradition, as with the Lepyansky family of Vitebsk, in some tunings in Rzeszowskie, Poland, as well as in the standard Romanian *ţambal mic* tuning.[228] Such a wide distribution suggests a very old pattern, perhaps dating to the seventeenth or eighteenth century. Although Ukrainian peasant use of the *tsymbaly* began by the early eighteenth century and perhaps entered the villages by means of Galician *serbska* minstrels by the previous century, we cannot rule out persistent Jewish influence emanating from the towns which may have influenced the tuning.

Certain other characteristics also distinguish Ukrainian from Belarusian *tsymbaly* traditions. Instead of upper and lower notches for the fingers, Ukrainian hammers have either an upper notch or a hole through which the index finger goes, and they tend to be shorter. Older Ukrainian instruments have a cut-out area in the lower right corner of the soundboard, which allowed coins earned as tips to be removed, as well as a place to put the hammers. The baseboard on Ukrainian instruments often does not reach to the outer edges, as with Belarusian instruments, but is recessed away from them.

The *tsymbaly* manufactured after 1951 bore certain similarities to the traditional instrument, such as a relatively thin baseboard, but its designers added elements from the design of the Hungarian cimbalom, such as pedal-operated dampers, composite bridges, and cotton-wrapped hammers.

The *cymbały* of Rzeszowskie and southeastern Poland bears many similarities to Ukrainian instruments, but certain characteristics distinguish it from them. The number of treble courses ranges from seven to ten, with bass courses ranging from seven to nine, with four to six strings per course, although the most common arrangement seems to be nine courses of five strings each for treble and bass rows.[229] Dahlig notes that older instruments are smaller, typically measuring 82 cm (32¼ inches) and 53.5 cm (15½ inches) long and 35 cm (13¾ inches) wide, but instruments from the 1930s and later, in which the tuning began to be more chromatic and thus required more courses, measure 96 and 74 cm (37¾ and 29 inches) long and 40.5 cm (16 inches) wide.[230] Unlike Ukrainian and Belarusian instruments, which have long bridges, southeastern Polish instruments more often use individually turned bridges over which rest common rods. Sound holes are round, with geometric rosettes attached underneath. Another characteristic, also common to some Ukrainian instruments, is that frequently coves are cut out along the edges on the underside of the pin blocks. Hammers used by players in the region east of Rzeszów have the finger holes of the Ukrainian design, but, instead of being straight, are carved so that the shafts curve in a downward direction, while players in the Jaslo and Krosno areas tend to use longer and narrower hammers with notches cut out on both sides of the handle ends.[231] Tunings, although variable, are comparable to the "Galician" system used in Canada.[232] Jozef Sowa tuned his apparently so that the highest four treble courses were divided into major thirds.[233]

Romania and Moldova

The Romanian *ţambal mic* is relatively uniform in design. It resembles the Ukrainian and Belarusian instruments in its thin baseboard and its lengthwise rails mortised into the pin blocks. Often the rails, which act as side walls, are cut into a convex curve. Sound holes usually consist of a center hole with six (rarely four) concentric holes. Bridges are normally of the chessman type, supporting common lay rods, although composite bridges of the Hungarian type also occur. The older "Romanian" tuning system utilizes the $g\#^1$ | $c\#^1$ course which precedes the g^1 | c^1 course. Nine or ten courses go over the treble bridges, while eight to eleven courses go over the right-hand bass bridges. The older instruments often had five and even six strings per treble course and four strings for the upper eight or nine bass courses, but newer instruments use four strings per treble course.[234] Brass wire is still used for both treble and bass strings. However, unlike Ukrainian instruments, the bottom two to four bass courses on the right and one to three bass courses over bridges on the lower left have two (rarely three) overspun strings per course. Due to the preference for brass wire, the length of Romanian instruments is shorter than those of Ukraine, approximately 80 to 84 cm (31½ to 33 inches) and 56 to 63 cm (22¼ to 24¾ inches) long and 35 to 41 cm (14 to 16 inches) wide. The strings are commonly dampened by the use of pieces of leather inserted at the point where they rest on the bridges and nuts or by felt or cloth woven between the courses of strings. Hammers are of the Hungarian type, with an upper notch at the handle and cotton wrapped at the playing ends. Players use shorter hammers for the small *ţambal* than those they use on the large instrument, although in Wallachia hammers tend to be longer and thicker than those commonly used in Hungary. Like the instruments of Ukraine and Belarus, neck straps are usually attached.

The small *ţambal* could be purchased in music stores in the 1930s and was manufactured during the Communist period by the "Doina" factory in Bucharest. As the Hungarian cimbalom gained in popularity and availability during the mid-twentieth century, players converted the tuning on most of the small instruments to "Hungarian" tuning, by adding an agraffe to divide the second highest treble course and tuning the other strings accordingly. Today the small instrument, although still in use, is no longer manufactured, although there are individuals who can make it.

The "Doina" factory also manufactured the Hungarian-style cimbalom, although Romanian players preferred either Hungarian-made instruments or instruments made privately by workers in the factory, who took parts and materials home to produce instruments of a higher quality.[235] During the Soviet years, a factory in Kishinev, Moldavian Republic, manufactured copies of the Bohak cimbalom.[236]

Turkey

Two examples of the nineteenth-century *santur fransız* that I have examined had in one case eleven treble and eleven bass courses of five brass strings each, resting on long bridges and in another case, nine treble and nine bass courses, each with six strings per course.[237] The first one had four carved rosettes, two larger and two smaller. Hammers were relatively thick and short, with upper notches in the handle and cloth wrapped at the playing ends. Rauf Yekta Bey describes an instrument with twenty-one courses of five brass strings each, of which there were nine treble courses, ten bass courses, and apparently two bass courses over a bridge on the lower left. He describes a tuning scheme wherein the two uppermost courses are, like Romanian and some Belarusian and Polish instruments, divided into major seconds.[238]

Greece

The Greek *santouri*, though larger, bears many resemblances to the small Romanian *ţambal*. Some instruments often have inversely bowed lengthwise rails and, on certain instruments, rails appear to be mortised into the pin blocks and the joints covered with plates, as on Romanian instruments.[239] The two sound holes usually consist of center holes with six concentric holes, although round holes and center holes with four concentric holes also exist. Unlike most Romanian instruments, bridges are either long pieces or composite bridges, like those of Hungarian cimbaloms. Although brass wire is sometimes used, the length of the *santouri* is longer than that of the Romanian instrument, requiring the use of steel strings.

Older instruments seem to have five strings per course, although the standard today is four per treble course, with the addition of overspun strings for the lower courses. Overspun strings are grouped in courses of two or three and may rest on all the bass bridges, or only a portion, for

example, from g♯⁰ downward.²⁴⁰ Instruments from the early twentieth
century lack overspun strings. Commonly there are ten treble courses
and a varying number of right-hand bass courses. The number depends
on how low the bass range is. One to four courses go over the left-hand
bass bridges, and the corresponding number of courses on the right-
hand bass bridge would be twelve to fifteen.²⁴¹ Supplementary bridges,
to alter the fifth interval, are added to the upper treble courses. Hammers
are like the Hungarian variety, with padded ends, but a bit shorter. Older
hammers had thicker shafts, with a deeper notch for the finger.²⁴²

The *tsimbalo*, according to Anoyanakis, rests on four legs and often
has a pedal.²⁴³ However, a somewhat portable instrument with the appearance of a *santouri*, but with Hungarian tuning, also exists.²⁴⁴ In the
United States, a small instrument with Hungarian tuning and three legs
was made by A. Politis, of New York City. At least one player, Emmanuel
Piculas, of Detroit, converted a Schunda cimbalom to Greek tuning by
adding two bridge posts to the treble bridges and making other slight
modifications to the tuning.

Notes

1. 1 Cor. 13:1.
2. Robert Stevenson, *Spanish Music in the Age of Columbus* (The Hague:
Martinus Nijhoff, 1960), 7.
3. *Quellen zur Geschichte der Stadt Kronstadt in Siebenbürgen* (Kronstadt:
Theochar Alexi, 1896), 3: 360.
4. Janos Manga, *Hungarian Folk Song and Folk Instruments*, Hungarian
Folk Art, no. 2 (Budapest: Corvina Press, 1969), 60.
5. Bence Szabolcsi, *Népzene és történelem* (Budapest: Akadémiai Kiadó,
1954), 115; Manga, *Hungarian Folk Song*, 58, citing accounts of Nádasdy; Balint
Sarosi, *Gypsy Music* (Budapest: Corvina Press, 1978), 53.
6. Manga, *Hungarian Folk Song*, 58; also Sarosi, *Gypsy Music*, 53; Kornél
Bárdos, *Magyarország zenetörténete II: 1541-1686* (Budapest: Akadémiai Kiadó,
1990), 453-454.
7. Fivos Anoyanakis, *Greek Popular Musical Instruments*, 2nd ed. (Athens:
"Melissa" Publishing House, 1991), ill. 2, 36.
8. Bárdos, *Magyarország zenetörténete*, 148, 453; Manga, *Hungarian Folk
Song*, 58.
9. St. Petersburg, Pogodinsky Collection, no. 1642, in K. Vertkov, *Russkie
narodnye muzykal'nye instrumenty* (Leningrad: Muzyka, 1975), 252. The context clearly shows the *tsinbaly* as a stringed instrument. Earlier references in
Slavic literature to the term, as František Skarina's translation of the First Book

of Kings in 1518 (F. Skarina, *Vtoraya kniga Tsarstv*, A: 76, B: 77, in I. D. Nazina, *Belorusskie narodnye muzykal'nye instrumenty: strunnye* [Minsk: Nauka i Tekhnika, 1982], 54) are likely to be cymbals or bells, as discussed in Barbara Szydłowska-Ceglowa, *Staropolskie nazewnictwo instrumentów muzycznych* (Wrocław: Zakład Narodowy Imienia Ossolińskich Wydawnictwo Polskiej Akademii Nauk, 1977), 219-221.

10. Aleksandra Szulcówna, *Muzykowanie w polsce renesansowej*, Poznańskie towarzystwo przyjaciół nauk, Wydział historii i nauk społecznych: Prace komisji historii sztuki, vol. 6, pt. 2 (Poznan, 1959), 35. The mention of the *szyposze* is significant, as this Hungarian term (*sipos*) did not establish itself in Polish-speaking territory and thus supports the theory of Hungarian origin. Sorbs called the instrument *husla* in their language, although there is no reason to assume that the musicians were Sorbs. In the sixteenth century, Mateusz Strikowski wrote that Moldavians and Wallachians played the "Serbian fiddle" (see Anca Florea, "String Instruments in Romanian Mural Paintings between the 14th and 19th Century," *RIdIM/RCMI Newsletter* 19 [Fall 1994]: 60-61, but she misinterprets the word to mean the Serbian *gusla*).

11. Examples include "A pair of *serbska*s and *cymbał* dance in a circle" (Karol Badecki, *Polska komedia rybałtowska* [Lwow: Wydawnictwo Zakładu Narodowego im. Ossolińskich, 1931], 350, in Szydłowska-Ceglowa, *Staropolskie*, 224), which appears also in *Słownik języka polskiego* (Warsaw, 1900), s.v. "Cymbały," citing *Zwirscenie Mathyasza z Podola*; and "another group which accompanied dancing was made up of stringed instruments: two *serbska*s and *cymbał*" (Wacław Maciejowski, *Pismiennictwo polskie* [Warsaw: S. Orgelbrand, 1851-1853], 3: 77, in Szulcówna, *Muzykowanie*, 50).

12. Walter Feldman, personal communication.

13. Majer Bałaban, *Żydzi Lwowscy na przełomie XVIgo XVIIgo wieku* (Lwow: Nakladem Funduszu Konkursowego im H. Wawelberga, 1906), 533f.

14. Pamva Berynda, *Leksykon slovenoros'kyi* (Kiev: Vydavytstvo Akademii Nauk, 1961), 12.

15. *Dokumenti Bogdana Khmelnits'kogo* (Kiev: Akademii Nauk Ukrains'koi RSR, 1961), 275.

16. A. P. Gritskevich, "Chastnovladel'cheskie goroda Belorussii v XVI-XVIII," in *Sotsial'no-ekonomicheskoe issledovanie istorii gorodov* (Minsk: Nauka i tekhnika, 1975), 83. The author does not indicate the ethnicity of holders of the occupation of *tsimbalist*, however.

17. T. Livanova, *Ocherki i materialy po istorii russkoi muzykal'noi kul'tury* (Minsk, 1938), 1: 249, in Nazina, *Belorusskie instrumenty*, 55.

18. Adam Jarzębski, *Gościniec abo krotkie opisanie Warszawy* (1643; reprint, Warsaw: Państwowe Wydawnictwo Naukowe, 1974), 113.

19. Jan Stanisław Bystroń, *Dzieje obyczajów w dawnej Polsce: wiek XVI-XVIII* (Warsaw: Państwowy Instytut Wydawniczy, 1960), 2: 222.

20. Bárdos, *Magyarország zenetörténete*, 449; Balint Sarosi, *Folk Music: Hungarian Musical Idiom* (Budapest: Corvina, 1986), 137.

150	Chapter 6

21. Bárdos, *Magyarország zenetörténete*, 117.

22. Manga, *Hungarian Folk Song*, 58.

23. Bárdos, *Magyarország zenetörténete*, 461; translation in Manga, *Hungarian Folk Song*, 58.

24. Stanislav Tuksar, "Kajkavian Music Terminology in Juraj Habdelić's Dictionary (1670)," in *Glazbena baština naroda i narodnosti Jugoslavije od 16. do 19. stoljeća = The Musical Heritage of the Nations and Nationalities of Yugoslavia from the 16th to the 19th Century* (Zagreb: Vara•din, 1980), 182-183.

25. *Zeitschrift für hebräische Bibliographie* 6 (1902): 75, in Albert Wolf, "Fahrende Leute bei den Juden," *Mitteilungen zur jüdischen Volkskunde* 27 (1908): 91.

26. Paul Nettl, *Beiträge zur böhmischen und mährischen Musikgeschichte* (Brno: R. M. Rohrer, 1927), 78f., in Walter Salmen, *Jüdische Musikanten und Tänzer vom 13. bis 20. Jahrhundert* (Innsbruck: Edition Helbling, 1991), 156.

27. Alfred Sendrey, *The Music of the Jews in the Diaspora (up to 1800)* (New York: Thomas Yoseloff, 1970), 350. The ultimate source is probably *Judaeorum Morologia, oder Jüdisches Affen-Spiel* (Leipzig, 1678).

28. Nettl, *Beiträge*, 78f., in Salmen, *Jüdische Musikanten*, 162-165.

29. Salmen, *Jüdische Musikanten*, 59.

30. Salmen, *Jüdische Musikanten*, 66.

31. Judith Kaplan Eisenstein, *Heritage of Music: the Music of the Jewish People* (New York: Union of American Hebrew Congregations, 1972), 254; Georg Liebe, *Das Judentum in der deutschen Vergangenheit*, Monographien zur deutschen Kulturgeschichte (Leipzig: Eugen Diederichs, 1903), 77.

32. Johann Jacob Schudt, *Jüdische Merckwürdigkeiten* (Frankfurt, 1714), in Liebe, *Judentum*, 108.

33. Bernard Picart, *Céremonies et coutumes religeuse de tous les peuples du monde* (Amsterdam: J. F. Bernard, 1723), 1: 239, in Herman Pollack, *Jewish Folkways in Germanic Lands (1648-1806): Studies in Aspects of Daily Life* (Cambridge: M.I.T. Press, 1971), 30; Salmen, *Jüdische Musikanten*, ill. 29, 216; and Mozes Herman Gans, *Memorbook: History of Dutch Jewry from the Renaissance to 1940* (Baarn: Bosch & Keuning, 1977), 167.

34. Pieter de la Croix, *Krispyn, Muzikant* (Amsterdam: Albert Magnus, 1685), 18, in *Woordenboek der Nederlandsche Taal*, s.v. "Cimbaal."

35. Elisabeth Hoofman van Koolaart, *De naagelaatene Gedichten* (Haarlem: J. Bosch, 1776), 26, and Lukas Schermer, *Poëzy* (Haarlem: W. van Kessel, 1712), 118, in *Woordenboek der Nederlandsche Taal*, s.v. "Cimbaal."

36. David Kettlewell, "The Dulcimer" (Ph.D. diss., Loughborough University of Technology, 1976), 125. He suggests because of its size and arrangement and that because the artist worked in Prague, Hungary, and Vienna, it may represent an instrument from that region; Hubert Boone, "Beknopte Bijdrage tot de Geschiedenis van het Hakkebord in de Lage Landen," *Volkskunde: Tijdschrift voor Nederlandsche Folklore* 77 (1976): 206 n. 10, echoes the same thought. The painting was in a private collection and I have not seen a copy of it.

37. Hans Engel, *Musik in Thüringen* (Cologne: Böhlau Verlag, 1966), 14f.

38. Johann Christoph Weigel, *Musicalisches Theatrum*, ed. Alfred Berner, Documenta Musicologica, 1st ser.: Druckschriften-Faksimiles, no. 22 (facsimile ed., Kassel: Bärenreiter, 1961), f. 26.

39. Fredric Hasselquist, *Iter Palaestinum eller Resa til Heliga Landet förrättad ifrån år 1749 til 1752* (Stockholm: L. Salvii, 1757), 44, in *Ordbok öfver svenska språket*, s.v. "Hackbräde"; L. N. Synnerberg, *Svenskt waru-lexicon* (Göteborg: Sam. Norberg, 1815), 2: 136, in *Ordbok öfver svenska språket*, s.v. "Cymbal." A player in the 1860s is mentioned in Kettlewell, "Dulcimer," 303, quoting "Landsmalsför-eningarnas fest i Upsala," *Svenska Landsmal*, Nov. 1879, 581.

40. Thomas Baker, *An Act at Oxford* (London: for Bernard Lintott, 1704), 33.

41. Seán Donnelly, "A German Dulcimer Player in Eighteenth-Century Dublin," *Dublin Historical Record* 53 (Spring 2000): 84, quoting *Dublin Newsletter*, 30 Dec. 1738-2 Jan. 1739.

42. Donnelly, "German Dulcimer Player," 77-86.

43. Abraham Levy, "Reisebeschreibung, 1719-1724," *Israelitische Letterbode*, 1884, in Abraham Zevi Idelsohn, "Song and Singers of the Synagogue in the Eighteenth Century," in *Hebrew Union College Jubilee Volume (1875-1925)* (1925; reprint, New York: Ktar Publishing House, 1968), 403 n. 17. The translation uses "cymbals."

44. Original in Israel Museum, Jerusalem, ill. in Salmen, *Jüdische Musikanten*, 215.

45. Original in Germanisches Nationalmuseum, ill. in Salmen, *Jüdische Musikanten*, ill. 33, 218.

46. Anton Henseler, *Jakob Offenbach* (Berlin: Schöneberg, 1930), 19, in Salmen, *Jüdische Musikanten*, 67.

47. *Zeitung der Judentum*, 1875, 324, in Wolf, "Fahrende Leute," 154.

48. Ludwig Kalisch, *Bilder aus meiner Knabenzeit* (Leipzig: E. Keil, 1872), 141.

49. "Franz Benda's Autobiography," in Paul Nettl, *Forgotten Musicians* (New York: Philosophical Library, 1951), 204, which says he played dulcimer, oboe, and shawm; Charles Burney, *An Eighteenth-Century Musical Tour in Central Europe and The Netherlands*, ed. Percy A. Scholes (London: Oxford University Press, 1959), 176, which says he played "hautbois, bagpipe, and dulcimer."

50. Čeněk Holas, *České národní písne a tance*, vol. 5, *Chrudimsko a polabí* (Prague: B. Kočik, 1910), 76.

51. Holas, *České národní písne*, 5: 83f.

52. Karl Michael Komma, *Das böhmische Musikantentum*, Die Musik im alten und neuen Europa, ed. Walter Wiora, vol. 3 (n.p.: Johann Philipp Hinnenthal-Verlag, 1960), 72-74.

53. Ludvik Kunz, *Die Volksmusikinstrumente der Tschechoslowakei*, Handbuch der europäischen Volksmusikinstrumenten, ser. 1, vol. 2 (Leipzig: VEB Deutscher Verlag für Musik, 1974), 65.

54. Walter Hartinger, *Volkstanz, Volksmusikanten und Volksmusikinstrumente der Oberpfalz zur Zeit Herders,* Quellen und Studien zur musikalischen Volkstradition in Bayern, ser. 4: Studien zur musikalischen Volkstradition, vol. 1, (Regensburg: Gustav Bosse, 1980), 35, 50.

55. Karl-Heinz Schickhaus, *Über Volksmusik und Hackbrett in Bayern* (Munich: BLV Verlagsgesellschaft, 1981), 140.

56. *Deutsche Jugendzeitung*, 15, no. 8 (1846): 120-121.

57. L. Haupt and J. E. Schmaler, *Volkslieder der Wenden in der Ober- und Nieder-Lausitz* (Grimma, 1843), 2: 219.

58. Schickhaus, *Über Volksmusik,* 146-147.

59. Tobi Reiser, *Die zweite 25,* in Walter Deutsch, Sepp Gmasz, Maria Theresia Schimpfössl-Ager, "Dokumente und Literatur zur Volksmusik in Salzburg," in *Die Volksmusik im Lande Salzburg*, ed. Walter Deutsch and Harald Dengg, 11. Seminar für Volksmusikforschung, 1975 (Vienna: A. Schendl, 1979), 32.

60. Schickhaus, *Über Volksmusik,* 163.

61. Richard Wolfram, "Die Volkstanznachrichten in den statistischen Erhebungen Erzherzog Johanns," *Volk und Heimat: Festschrift Viktor von Geramb* (Graz, 1949), 271ff., in Rainer Gstrein, "Tanzmusik-Ensembles in Österreich im 19. Jahrhundert," in *Tanz und Tanzmusik in Überlieferung und Gegenwart: Bericht über die 12. Arbeitsgang der Kommission für Lied-, Musik-, und Tanzforschung in der Deutschen Gesellschaft für Volkskunde e. V.,* ed. Marianne Bröcker, Schriften der Universitätsbibliothek Bamberg 9 (Bamberg, 1992), 424, which describes a dance in 1810 at Kaisersberg to two violins, dulcimer, and bass; a description of dance music at Wildon in 1812 consisting of one or two violins, clarinet, bass or *violon*, and dulcimer, Gstrein, "Tanzmusik-Ensembles," 424; Karl M. Klier, *Volkstümliche Musikinstrumente in den Alpen* (Kassel: Bärenreiter-Verlag, 1956), 99, quoting Klier, *Schatz österreichischen Weihnachtslieder* (Stift Klosterneuburg bei Wien: Augustinus-Druckerei, n.d.) 3, no. 117, which mentions music in Judenburg district in 1819 on violin or clarinet, cello, and *Cimbal*.

62. Description of Neuberg, 1803, Steiermärkisches Landesarchiv, MS no. 134, p. 94f., in Gstrein, "Tanzmusik-Ensembles," 421.

63. *Studia Musicologica Academiae Scientiarum Hungaricae* 10 (1968): 199.

64. Sarosi, *Gypsy Music*, 53, 71-72.

65. András Borgó, "'Pharao barna ivadékai' és a klezmorim," *Muzsika* 39 (Sept. 1993): 38-39.

66. Sarosi, *Gypsy Music,* 85ff.

67. Franz Liszt, *The Gipsy in Music*, trans. Edwin Evans (London: William Reeves, n.d.), 312.

68. Liszt, *Gipsy in Music*, 313.

69. James Baillie Fraser, *A Winter's Journey (Tâtar): from Constantinople to Tehran* (London: Richard Bentley, 1838), 1: 51.

70. Dezső Legány, *Ferenc Liszt and His Country, 1869-1873* (Budapest: Corvina Kiádó, 1983), 43, 205, 257n.

71. Gus Horvath, of Detroit, born 1916, was familiar with this style of playing on a portable instrument.

72. Sternberg also made full-size instruments, and a Louis XV-style cimbalom made in 1895 by this company is in the collection of the Cincinnati Art Museum.

73. Mogyoróssy Gyula Hangszergyáros, *Cimbalom-árjegyzéke* (Budapest: Mogyoróssy, 1917?).

74. Arthur Hartmann, "The Czimbalom, Hungary's National Instrument," *Musical Quarterly* 2 (1916): 600.

75. Ethel Tauszky, "Aladar Racz: the Cymbalist," *Journal of the Gypsy Lore Society*, 3rd ser., 27 (Jan.-Apr. 1948): 43-46.

76. See Emőke Pintér, "The Hungarian Dulcimer," *The New Hungarian Quarterly* 20, no. 76 (Winter 1979): 217-220; György Kroó, "The Hungarian Cimbalom," *The New Hungarian Quarterly* 16, no. 59 (Autumn 1975): 218-220; John Leach, "The Cimbalom," *Music & Letters* 53 (Apr. 1972): 140-142; Laurence Kaptain, "The Hungarian Cimbalom," *Percussive Notes* 28 (Aug. 1990): 10-14, for more discussion.

77. Lýdia Mikušová-Ukropcová, "Das Hackbrett: zur Erforschung der instrumentalen Volksmusik in der Slowakei," *Musikforum* 33 (1988): 41.

78. Julijan Strajnar, "Geige und Geigenmusik in der slowenischen Volkstradition," in *Die Geige in der europäischen Volksmusik*, ed. Walter Deutsch and Gerlinde Haid (Vienna: A. Scheindl, 1975), 52.

79. Mira Omerzel-Terlep, "Oprekelj na Slovenskem," *Muzikološki Zbornik* 16 (1980): 103.

80. *Muzička enciklopedija*, 2nd ed. (Zagreb: JLZ, 1977), 1: 333, in Tuksar, "Kajkavian Music Terminology," 182f.

81. Aleksandr Sergeyevich Famintsyn, *Gusli—russkyi narodnyi muzykal'nyi instrument'* (1890); reprinted in *Skomorokhei na Rusi* (St. Petersburg: Izdvo "Aleteia," 1995), 295.

82. For example, I once talked to a native of Cracow who related that Jewish merchants in the nineteenth century played the instrument to attract business; the epic poem *Pan Tadeusz*, featuring the Jewish *cymbalist* Jankiel, is learned by Polish schoolchildren; and wooden carvings of *klezmorim*, playing violin, clarinet, flute, *cymbały*, and bass, are sold to tourists in Polish cities today.

83. Barbara Szydłowska-Ceglowa, "Die ältesten Namen der polnischen Volksmusikinstrumente auf Grund altpolnischer Sprachdenkmäler," *Studia instrumentorum musicae popularis* 6 (1979): 140.

84. Aleksandr Rigelman, *Lietopisnoe poviestvovan-ie o Maloi Ross-ii i eia narodie i Kozakakh voobshche*, Imperatorskoe obshchestvo istor-ii drevnostei ross-iiskikh (Moscow: v universitetskoi tipografii, 1847), pt. 2, 87, in Famintsyn, *Skomorokhei na Rusi*, 293n.

85. *Uteniya v Imperatorskom Obshchestve istorii Drevnosti*, 1870, no. 2, 86, in Andrei Ivanovych Humeniuk, *Ukrain'ski narodni muzychni instrumenti* (Kiev: Naukova Dumka, 1967), 159.

86. Lukasz Gołębiowski, *Gry i zabawy: róznych stanów w kraju całym, lub niektórych tylko prowincyach* (Warsaw: Druk N. Glücksberga, 1831), 240.

87. Kazimierz Wladysław Wojcicki, *Pieśni ludu: Biało-Chrobatów, Mazurow i Rusi znad Bugu* (Warsaw: n.p., 1836), 2: 360, in Famintsyn, *Skomorokhei na Rusi*, 295n. Alexander Fedoriouk, from Kolomyja, says that the original *troista muzyka* consisted of violin, *tsymbaly*, and *sopilka*.

88. Liszt, *Gipsy in Music*, 312.

89. *Etnograficheski zbornik Imperatorskogo Russkogo Geograficheskego Obshchestva*, 1: 307, in Famintsyn, *Skomorokhei na Rusi*, 298n.

90. M. V. Lysenko, *Kharakterystyka muzychnykh osoblyvostei ukrains'kikh dum i pisen'*, *vikonuvanikh kobzarem Veresaem* (Kiev, 1955), 12-13, in Humeniuk, *Ukrain'ski instrumenti*, 160.

91. Oskar Kolberg, *Dzieła wszystkie*, vol. 31, *Pokucie*, vol. 3 (Warsaw: 19—), 9.

92. Examples are given in Humeniuk, *Ukrain'ski instrumenti*, 157-162.

93. For notated examples, see Stanisław Mierczynski, *Muzyka huculszczyzny* (Cracow: Polskie Wydawnictwo Muzyczne, 1965), 80, 96; Humeniuk, *Ukrain'ski instrumenti*, 163; K. A. Vertkov, G. Blagodatov, E. Yazovitskaya, *Atlas muzykal'nykh instrumentov narodov SSSR* (Moscow: Gosudarstvennoe Muzykal'noe Izdatel'stvo, 1963), 175.

94. Oleksandr Nezovibatko, "All about the Dulcimer," in unidentified periodical (perhaps *Ukraine Illustrated Quarterly)*, vertical file, Archive of American Folklife, Library of Congress; Oleksandr Nezovibatko, *Ukrains'ki tsymbaly* (Kiev: Muzyka Ukraina, 1976), 14-16.

95. Alexander Fedoriouk, telephone conversation with author, 1999.

96. Maria and Kazimierz Piechotka, *Wooden Synagogues* (Warsaw: Arkady, 1959), in *Jewish Encyclopedia*, s.v. "Music," 12: 622.

97. Andrzej Ciechanowski, *Michał Kazimierz Ogiński und sein Musenhof zu Słonim: Untersuchungen zur Geschichte der polnischen Kultur und ihrer europäischen Beziehungen im 18. Jahrhundert* (Cologne: Böhlau Verlag, 1961), 17.

98. Halina Nelken, *Images of a Lost World: Jewish Motifs in Polish Painting, 1770-1945* (Oxford: Institute for Polish-Jewish Studies, 1991), i, ii; the earlier painting is also in Zygmunt Batowski, *Norblin* (Lwow: H. Altenberg, 1911?), 27. The earlier drawing is in Norblin's album, no. 386, in the Zbiory Czartoryskich at the Muzeum Narodowe in Cracow.

99. "Briefe über den jetzigen Zustand der Musik in Russland: zweyter Brief," *Allgemeinische musikalische Zeitung* 22 (24 Feb. 1802): 361-363.

100. See Bozena Shallcross, "'Wondrous Five': Adam Mickiewicz's *Pan Tadeusz* and the Romantic Improvisation," *East European Politics and Societies* 9 (Fall 1995): 523-533; Simon Schama, *Landscape and Memory* (New York: Vintage Books, 1995), 31-32.

101. Wladylsaw Nehring, *Studya literackie* (Poznan: A. Cybulski, 1884), 316, in Wolf, "Fahrende Leute," 154; Marian Fuks et al., *Polish Jewry: History and Culture* (Warsaw: Interpress Publishers, 1982), 67; also Zygmunt Gloger, *Encyklopedia staropolska* (1900-03; reprint, Warsaw: Wiedza Powszechna, 1974), 1: 255-256, in William Henry Noll, "Peasant Music Ensembles in Poland: A Culture History" (Ph.D. diss., University of Washington, 1986), 201.

102. Abraham Z. Idelsohn, *Jewish Music in Its Historical Development* (New York: Schocken Books, 1967), 458-459. Although he may have made changes to its design, it is unlikely that Guzikov "invented" his xylophone. Samson Jakubowski discovered the "wood harmonica" at St. Petersburg in the 1820s and toured with it. See Albert Sowinski, *Les musiciens polonais et slaves* (Paris: Librairie Adrien Le Clere, 1857), 270-271. Since Sowinski calls the instrument by an English name and because Jakubowski first saw it at St. Petersburg, the "wood harmonica" was probably not the *hölzernes Gelächter* of German tradition or the *facimbalom* of Hungarian tradition, but rather a sort of experimental instrument in the social tradition of Franklin's glass harmonica and the sticcado pastorale, a metallophone which interested both Franklin and Jefferson.

103. Famintsyn, *Skomorokhei na Rusi,* 297.

104. Nikolay A. Rimsky-Korsakov, *My Musical Life,* trans. from 5th rev. ed. by Judah A. Joffe, ed. Carl Van Vechten (New York: Vienna House, 1972), 6.

105. *Etnograficheski zbornik Imperatorskogo Russkogo Geograficheskego Obshchestva,* 4: 43, in Famintsyn, *Skomorokhei na Rusi,* 298n.

106. Moses Berlin, "Ocherk etnografii evreiskogo narodo-naseleniya v Rossii," *Zapiskakh Imperatorskogo Russkogo Geograficheskego Obshchestva: Etnograficheskii zbornik* (1861), issue 5, in N. F. Findeizen, "Evreiskie tsimbaly i tsimbalisty Lepianskie," *Muzykal'naia etnografie,* 1926, 39.

107. Kolberg, *Dzieła wszystkie,* 4: 209.

108. Moisey Beregovskii, *Evreiskaia narodnaia instrumental'naia muzyka* (Moscow: Sovetskii Kompozitor, 1987), 23.

109. Wolf, "Fahrende Leute," 155.

110. A. T. Sinclair, "Gypsy and Oriental Musical Instruments," *The Journal of American Folk-lore* 21 (1908), 207.

111. Joel Rubin, "The Romanian-Jewish Doina: A Closer Stylistic Examination," *Proceedings of the First International Conference on Jewish Music* (London: City University, 1997), 155.

112. Findeizen, "Evreiskie tsimbaly," 40-41.

113. P. M. Shpilevskii, "Puteshestvie po Poles'yu i belorusskomu krayu," *Sovremennik,* 1853, no. 8: 63, in Nazina, *Belorusskie instrumenty,* 55.

156   *Chapter 6*

114. Jerzy Ficowski, "The Polish Gypsies of To-day," *Journal of the Gypsy Lore Society*, 3rd ser., 29 (July-Oct. 1950): 93-94.

115. Alexander Fedoriouk, telephone conversation with author, 1999.

116. Piotr Dahlig, "Das Hackbrett im Nordosten Polens," *Studia instrumentorum musicae popularis* 8 (1985): 118-121.

117. Noll, "Peasant Music Ensembles," 195-204.

118. Anna Czekanowska, *Polish Folk Music: Slavonic Heritage—Polish Tradition—Contemporary Trends* (Cambridge: Cambridge University Press, 1990), 171-172.

119. Noll, "Peasant Music Ensembles," 198.

120. Piotr Dahlig, "Das Hackbrett und Hackbrettspieler im Südosten Polens," in *Chetverta konferentsiya doslidnykiv narodnoi muzyky chervonorus'kykh (halyts'ko-volodymyrs'kykh) ta sumizhnykh zemel'*: *Materialy* (Lviv, 1993), 53.

121. Jadwiga Sobieska, notes to Rodzinna Kapela Sowów, *Polish Folk Music: Rzeszowskie-wieś Piątkowa*, Muza SX 2348-2349.

122. Dahlig, "Das Hackbrett und Hackbrettspieler im Südosten Polens," 52-56.

123. Bystroń, *Dzieje obyczajów*, 2: 223. The author thinks this was a Jewish band, but the names of the dances—*Albo mene barszczu dajte* ["Or give me some borsht"], *Czerniec czernicu zawiow w pywnicu* ["The *Czerniec* took the baneberry to the cellar"], and *Anusiu serdenko, palisz moju duszu* ["Dear Anusia, you burn my soul"]—probably indicate otherwise.

124. *Polymia*, 1965, no. 2, 166, in Nazina, *Belorusskie instrumenty*, 55.

125. "Dyaryusz bytności Najj. Króla IMci Stanisława Augusta w Pińsku: Krystynowie w miesiącu Septembrze 1784," *Biblioteka Warszawska* 3 (1860): 253-282, in O. V. Dadiomova, *Muzykal'naya kul'tura gorodov Belorussii v XVIII veke* (Minsk: Nauka i Tekhnika, 1992), 37.

126. Kolberg, *Dzieła wszystkie*, 52: 207, in Noll, "Peasant Music Ensembles," 195.

127. Noll, "Peasant Music Ensembles," 196.

128. Nazina, *Belorusskie instrumenty*, 41-46.

129. G. C. Glushchenko, ed., *Istoriya belorusskoi muzyki* (Moscow: Muzyka, 1976), 232.

130. Gołębiowski, *Gry i zabawy*, 241.

131. Kolberg, *Dzieła wszystkie*, 53: 183.

132. Marija Baltrėnienė and Romualdas Apanavičius, *Lietuviu liaudies muzikos instrumentai* (Vilnius: Mintis, 1991), 159-160, 167-169.

133. Trisa Priedite, *Tautas mūzikas instrumenti*, Latvijas etnogrāfiskais brīvdabas muzejs (Riga: Arots, 1988), 47, 94-95.

134. *Muzykal'naya kultura Latviiskoi SSR* (Moscow: Muzyka, 1976), 256.

135. Tatiana Kazanskaya, "Traditsii narodnogo skripichnogo iskusstva Smolenskoi Oblasti," in *Narodnye muzykal'nye instrumenty i intrumental'naya muzyka*, vol. 2 (Moscow: "Sovetskii Kompozitor," 1988), 81; Ulrich Morgenstern,

Volksmusikinstrumente und instrumentale Volksmusik in Russland, Studia Slavica Musicologica, vol. 2 (Berlin: Verlag Ernst Kuhn, 1995), 34.

136. Franz Joseph Sulzer, *Geschichte des transalpinischen Daciens, das ist: der Walachey, Moldau und Bessarabiens* (Vienna: Rudolph Grässer, 1781), 2: 417. As the *mocaneşte*, one of the dances Sulzer mentioned, was danced in 1884 in Neamţu county, perhaps he refers to Bucovina.

137. *Etnološka grada: o Romima-Ciganima u Vojvodini*, vol. 1, Posebna izdanja 6: Vojvodanski Muzej (Novi Sad: Vojvodanski Muzej, 1979), 143, 302.

138. [Samuel Friedrich Stöck], "Geschichte der Musik in Siebenbürgen," *Allgemeine musikalische Zeitung* 16, no. 47 (23 Nov. 1814): 786-787.

139. I. Kara, "Lăutari evrei din Moldova," *Revistă cultului mozaic*, 15 Apr. 1974, 3. I would like to thank Joshua Horowitz for informing me of this article.

140. Mihail Gr. Posluşnicu, *Istoria musicei la Români* (Bucharest: "Cartea Românească," 1927), 587.

141. Kara, "Lăutari evrei din Moldova."

142. Kara, "Lăutari evrei din Moldova."

143. Nicolae Filimon, "Lăutarii şi compoziţiunile lor," in *Opere* (Bucharest: Editură Minerva, 1978), 2: 270.

144. Ion Muşlea, Ovidiu Bîrlea, *Tipologia folclorului din răspunsurile la chestionarele lui B. P. Hasdeu* (Bucharest: Editură Minerva, 1970), 572.

145. Tiberiu Alexandru, *Instrumentele muzicale ale poporului romîn* (Bucharest: Editură de Stat pentru Literatură şi Artă, 1956), 99.

146. Viorel Cosma, *Figuri de lăutari* (Bucharest: Editură Muzicală, 1960), 18, depicts a late nineteenth-century Romanian ensemble in Baku, with an instrumentation of two violins, viola, cello, panpipes, *ţambal*, and bass.

147. Nicolae Feraru, conversation with author.

148. Raouf Yekta Bey, "La musique turque," in *Encyclopédie de la musique*, ed. Albert Lavignac (Paris: Librairie Delagrave, 1922), 3: 3021.

149. Yilmaz Öztuna, *Türk musikisi ansiklopedisi* (Istanbul: Milli Egitim Basimevi, 1969-1976), 1: 180-183.

150. In addition to an instrument with six strings per course at the Cincinnati Art Museum, a characteristic not seen in Romanian instruments, the photograph of Santuri Edhem Efendi shows coves cut out along the outer edges on the underside of the pin blocks (see Öztuna, *Türk musikisi ansiklopedisi*, 1: 181).

151. Avram Galante, *Histoire des juifs de Turquie* (Istanbul: Editions Isis, 1984), 2: 203f.

152. Kara, "Lăutari evrei din Moldova," which mentions a contract from 1856 in which a Gypsy, Gheorghe Păun, played with Mendel, a Jew, in Constantinople.

153. Edward Daniel Clarke, *Travels in Various Countries of Europe, Asia and Africa* (London: T. Cadell & Davies, 1816), mentions a *santur* in Athens in 1802.

154. Sotirios Chianis, notes to *Epirotika with Periklis Halkias*, Folkways

Records FSS 34024 (New York, 1981), 15-16, who writes that it had been part of Greek music for less than a century; Anoyanakis, *Greek Instruments*, 360, says it was introduced to the *kompania* about 1920.

155. The hero in Nikos Kazantzakis's *Zorba the Greek* learned the *santouri* from a Turkish master in Salonica in the 1890s. Such a means of transmission of a Turkish instrument to a Greek may have seemed realistic to the author, but does not reflect the probable method by which the instrument generally entered Greek wedding music.

156. Galante, *Histoire des juifs*, 3: 118, 177ff.

157. For the shoulder strap, see the film "Guns of Navarone" (1961), featuring wedding musicians on the island of Lesvos; Dimitris V. Kofteros, *Dhokimio yia to elliniko santouri* (Athens: Ekdhoseis "Dhodhoni," 1991), 63, 65, 71, 74. Anoyanakis, *Greek Instruments*, 360 n. 15, gives the etymology of *kompania* as coming from the Italian *compagnia*, but this may be unlikely, as the Italian word means a theatrical company. Rudolf Brandl, "Die Struktur traditioneller Volksmusik-Ensembles in Griechenland," *Studia instrumentorum musicae popularis* 10 (1992): 107, says that the *kompania* derives from the "Asia Minor urban Greek-Jewish-Armenian *café aman* ensemble." Recordings made in Smyrna in 1910 with violin, *santouri*, and violoncello include an anonymous "instrumental quartet" playing *Kalamatianos* and *Sirtos politikos*, Victor 63514 (matrix numbers 12029b and 12030b) and *Smyrneiko amanes tzivaeri* and *Ali Passa*, sung by Despinis Maria, Victor 63424 (matrix numbers 12827b and 12828b).

158. Roderick Conway Morris, "Greek Café Music," *Recorded Sound*, no. 80 (July 1981): 81; Gail Holst, *Road to Rembetika: Music of a Greek Sub-Culture, Songs of Love, Sorrow and Hashish* (Athens: Denise Harvey & Co., 1975), 25, 35-36.

159. Kofteros, *Dhokimio yia to elliniko santouri*, 125.

160. *Tsigansko lyato: razkazi za otselyavane = Gypsy Summer: Tales of Surviving*, Kuker Productions KP/R 01, features the playing of Milan Aivazov-Mutsi (born 1922), of Plovdiv. His instrument, played undampened, appears to have a range of g^0 to c^3, higher than either the Romanian or Greek instruments.

161. Cleo R. Baca, *Baca's Musical History* (LaGrange, Tex.: LaGrange Journal, 1968), passim; Chris Strachwitz, notes to *Texas Czech-Bohemian Bands: Early Recordings 1928-1953*, Folklyric Records 9031; Ray Krenek, telephone conversation with author, 1984.

162. Kunz, *Volksmusikinstrumente*, 63.

163. Peter Hable, personal communication, 25 July 1999.

164. Rosemary Menard and Agatha Watson, interview by Jim Leary, transcript, 11 May 1985. I would like to thank Jim Leary for this reference and for introducing me to Peter Hable. The informants used the term "dulcimer," but the players probably used *cimbal* when speaking in German or Czech.

165. Sarosi, *Gypsy Music*, 130, 134-135.

166. Alex Shandor and Emil Shandor, conversations with author, 1980s.

167. Andrew A. Marchbin, "The Gypsies of Western Pennsylvania," *Journal of the Gypsy Lore Society*, 3rd ser., 12 (1933): 205-210.

168. Irving Brown, *Gypsy Fires in America* (New York: Harper & Brothers, 1924), 214-215.

169. Edward A. Steiner, "The Hungarian Immigrant," *The Outlook* 74 (29 Aug. 1903): 1040-1041.

170. Konrad Bercovici, *Around the World in New York* (New York: The Century Co., 1924), 203.

171. A. T. Sinclair, "A Hungarian Gypsy Tzimbal-Player," *Journal of the Gypsy Lore Society*, new ser., 3 (Jan. 1910): 228-232.

172. Spottswood, *Ethnic Music on Records*, 3: 1245; Joseph Alsop, "The WASP Ascendancy," *The New York Review of Books*, 9 Nov. 1989, 51.

173. Boldie Garber, born in 1899, used the Allaga method and was proud of the Chopin transcriptions he had learned.

174. Richard K. Spottswood, *Ethnic Music in America* (Urbana: University of Illinois Press, 1990), 3: 1289; Brown, *Gypsy Fires*, 214.

175. Brown, *Gypsy Fires*, 184-189, describes a family with a daughter "Mirishka," "a good cembalo player." Giggy Fransko of Detroit told me that this family would have been that of John Matuka.

176. Marchbin, "Gypsies of Western Pennsylvania," 207-208;

177. Erdmann Doane Beynon, "The Gypsy in a Non-Gypsy Economy," *American Journal of Sociology* 42 (Nov. 1936): 364-365.

178. Endre de Spur, "Gypsies in the Borough of Braddock, U.S.A.," *Journal of the Gypsy Lore Society* 38 (July-Oct. 1959): 91.

179. Karl Bonutto and George Pupic, *Selected Ethnic Communities of Cleveland: A Socio-economic Study* (Cleveland: Cleveland Urban Observatory, 1974), 44.

180. Spottswood, *Ethnic Music*, 3: 1279, 1284. Martzi Kallao, long-time Gypsy cellist in New York City, told me that Sio's group was Jewish. Laszlo Kun played cimbalom on a 1921 recording with Sio, but his relationship to or identity with László Kun, who taught at the Budapest Academy, is unknown to me.

181. U.S. Patent, no. 871,463.

182. John Koleszar, *Catalogue of Musical Instruments* (New York, n.d.). He may actually have constructed them from imported parts.

183. *A History and Biographical Cyclopaedia of Butler County, Ohio* (Cincinnati: Western Biographical Pub. Co., 1882), 309; *The History of Montgomery County, Ohio* (Chicago: W. H. Beers, 1882), 533. I would like to thank Sara Johnson for pointing out the second reference.

184. Spottswood, *Ethnic Music*, 3: 1424, 1546-1547.

185. Nephew, conversation with author, Mackinac Island, Mich., 1977.

186. D. M. Hermalin, "The Roumanian Jews in America," *The American Jewish Year Book 5662* (1901-1902): 101.

187. Zalmen Zilbercweig, ed., *Leksikon fun yidishn teater* (New York: Farlag Elisheva, 1931), 1: 231f. I wish to thank Jeffrey Wollock for translating this entry. According to Mike Gold, *Jews without Money* (New York: Horace Liveright, 1930), 114, Moskowitz first kept a wine cellar on Rivington Street.

188. Gus Horvath, who, in the early 1930s, studied the cimbalom in New York with Bela Zsiga, recalled the sign; Gold, *Jews without Money*, 114-118; Bercovici, *Around the World in New York*, 260; Gary Craig, "A Tribute to My Grandfather's Restaurant," <http://www.garycraig.com/classic/index.htm>.

189. Spottswood, *Ethnic Music*, 3: 1449-1450.

190. Lillian Semeniuk, ed., *Dreams and Destinies: Andrew and District* (Andrew, Alta.: Andrew Historical Society, 1980), 443f., in Brian Cherwick, "Ukrainian *Tsymbaly* Performance in Alberta," *Canadian Folk Music Journal* 23 (1995): 21.

191. Dmytro Prosyniuk, conversation with author, Detroit, Michigan, 1975.

192. Troyd A. Geist, *From the Wellspring: Faith, Soil, Tradition: Folk Arts from Ukrainian Culture in North Dakota* (Bismarck, N.D.: North Dakota Council on the Arts, 1997), 23, 25.

193. Linda Zajac said that her grandfather, who played the violin in a Ukrainian wedding band in Detroit, came from a part of Ukraine where the *tsymbaly* was not used, and his group did not have one.

194. Spottswood, *Ethnic Music*, 2: 1071-1083, 1112; Anisa H. Swyckyj, notes to *Ukrainian-American Fiddle & Dance Music: The First Recordings, 1926-1936*, vol. 1, Folklyric Records 9014.

195. Mark Jaroslav Bandera, *The Tsymbaly Maker and His Craft: The Ukrainian Hammered Dulcimer in Alberta*, Canadian Studies in Ukrainian Ethnology, vol. 1 (Edmonton, Alta.: Canadian Institute of Ukrainian Studies Press, 1991), 12. On recordings made in the early 1950s of the Radomsky Trio (Stinson 202, 221, 225), the instruments are violin, *tsymbaly*, and drum set.

196. Cherwick, "Ukrainian *Tsymbaly* Performance," 23-24; Mark J. Bandera, "'The Western Canadian Championships': *Tsymbaly* Competitions at the Red Barn," *Canadian Folk Music Journal* 11 (1983): 28-33; *V-Records Ltd. Annual Cymbaly Contest 1972*, V Records SVLP 3102; *Cymbaly Highlights 1973*, V Records SVLP 3107; *Award Winning Dulcimer Sounds*, Heritage Records HR-16.

197. Jozef Jankowski, a Pole from Baranovichi, Belarus, immigrated to Buffalo, New York, in the postwar period and now lives in Florida, where he makes *cymbały* after his father's pre-war design. Thanks to Pete Rushefsky for this information.

198. Spottswood, *Ethnic Music*, 3: 1133-1234.

199. Walter Feldman, "Middle Eastern Music Among Immigrant Communities in New York City," *Balkan-Arts Traditions*, 1975, 22.

200. Spottswood, *Ethnic Music*, 3: 1233.

201. Frank Gazis, *San Francisco Moods*, Capitol T 2206.

202. John Tsipouras, who lived in Detroit in the 1970s, was one.
203. Kettlewell, "Dulcimer," 125.
204. Weigel, *Musicalisches Theatrum*, f. 26.
205. Schudt, *Jüdische Merckwürdigkeiten*, in Liebe, *Judentum*, 108.
206. The diagram shown in Kunz, *Volksmusikinstrumente*, 69, however, shows pin blocks not fully attached to the bottom, which is more characteristic of *Hackbretts*, and no separate outer frame. Perhaps a more systematic survey would reveal regional exceptions to these general characteristics.
207. Hubert Henkel, *Clavichorde*, Musikinstrumenten-Museum der Karl-Marx-Universität-Leipzig. Katalog, vol. 4 (Frankfurt/Main: Verlag Das Musikinstrument, 1981), 86-87; Othmar Wessely, *Die Musikinstrumenten-Sammlung des oberösterreichischen Landesmuseums* (Linz, 1952). All examples are incorrectly called *Hackbretts*. Other examples of this type in European museums are described in: Carl Claudius, *Carl Claudius' samling af gamle musikinstrumenter* (Copenhagen: Levin & Munksgaards Forlag, 1931), no. 42 (51); Heimatmuseum, Steingaden, mentioned in Schickhaus, *Über Volksmusik*, 136; Neuen Bachgesellschaft zu Leipzig, *Verzeichnis der Sammlung alter Musikinstrumente im Bachhause zu Eisenach* (Leipzig: Breitkopf & Härtel, [1939]), no. 63; Curt Sachs, *Sammlung alter Musikinstrumente bei der Staatlichen Hochschule für Musik zu Berlin* (Berlin: Julius Bard, 1922), nos. 234, 2150; Thomas Jürgen Eschler, *Die Sammlung historischer Musikinstrumente des Musikwissenschaftlichen Instituts der Universität Erlangen-Nürnberg* (Wilhelmshaven: Florian Noetzel Verlag, 1993), no. 7.
208. Kunz, *Volksmusikinstrumente*, 59-65.
209. Sarosi, *Gypsy Music*, pls. 8, 9, 10, 12, 13, 15, 16, 19, 21, 22. These date from about 1790 to 1860.
210. Four instruments in their collection in 1969 fit into this range, but three others approach the Sternberg instrument in size.
211. This instrument is possessed by William T. White, who purchased it from Gus Horvath, of Detroit. It may have been brought by immigrant Gypsies from what is now Slovakia.
212. A drawing of this feature can be seen in Bandera, *Tsymbaly Maker*, 25-26.
213. Nazina, *Belorusskie instrumenty*, 24-25.
214. Baltrėnienė, *Lietuviu liaudies muzikos instrumentai*, 159.
215. Priedite, *Tautas mūzikas instrumenti*, 94; Dahlig, "Hackbrett," 120.
216. Nazina, *Belorusskie instrumenty*, 40; Baltreniene, *Lietuviu liaudies mūzikas instrumentai*, 159, 167; Priedite, *Tautas muzikas instrumenti*, 94.
217. These statements are based on my observation in 1997 of the twelve instruments in the collections of the Dzyaslaue (Zaslavl) Museum as well as on Zhinovich's collection of tuning schemes in Nazina, *Belorusskie instrumenty*, 32-39.

162   Chapter 6

218. Nazina, *Belorusskie instrumenty*, 32-39. Vladimir Berberov of Minsk showed me similarly variable tunings he had collected in the 1990s from about a dozen players.

219. I. Shramko, "Z istorii tsymbaliv," *Muzyka*, 1983, no. 6, 14; Victor Sostak, "The Cymbaly," *Carpatho-Rusyn American* 8 (1985): n.p.

220. The first is in the Smithsonian Institution, no. 96,464 (30,688); the second is in the Latvijas PSR Vēstures Muzejs, no. 162252, described in Priedite, *Tautas mūzikas instrumenti*, 95.

221. Vytautas Jurkštas, "Žemaičiu cimbolai," *Mokslas ir gyvenimas* (1977), no. 7: 36. This instrument was made by Jonas Bubokas, of Pieveniai, Mažeikiai district, in the Žemaitija region.

222. Marian Fuks, *Muzyka ocalona: judaica polskie* (Warsaw: Wydawnictwa Radia i Telewizji, 1989), n.p.

223. Vertkov, *Atlas*, pl. 144; Mierczynski, *Muzyka huculszczyny*, 150-151.

224. Bandera, *Tsymbaly Maker*, 42.

225. Instruments owned by Silas Braley, Midland, Mich., in the 1970s and William T. White, Okemos, Mich. The latter instrument came from Dmytro Prosyniuk, of Detroit, and probably was made in Canada.

226. Roy W. Gibbons, *The CCFCS Collection of Musical Instruments*, vol. 3, *Chordophones*, Canadian Centre for Folk Culture Studies, Paper no. 45 ([Ottawa]: National Museums of Canada, 1984), 10-21, 24-25. A nineteenth-century dulcimer of Canadian or American manufacture, no. 12 (73-644), is misidentified as a *cymbaly*.

227. Bandera, *Tsymbaly Maker*, 46-47.

228. Findeizen, "Evreiskie tsimbaly," 40; Noll, *Peasant Music Ensembles*, 207-208; Alexandru, *Instrumentele muzicale*, 103.

229. This is based on my observation of eight instruments from southeastern Poland, dated 1880 to 1970, in the collection of the Państwowe Muzeum Etnograficzne, Warsaw.

230. Dahlig, "Das Hackbrett und Hackbrettspieler im Südosten Polens," 54-55, 59.

231. Dahlig, "Das Hackbrett und Hackbrettspieler im Südosten Polens," 55, 60.

232. Noll, "Peasant Music Ensembles," 207-209.

233. *Polish Folk Music: Rzeszowskie wieś Piątkowa*, Muza SX 2348-2349, cover photograph.

234. Nicolae Feraru says that Moldavian instruments tended to have more strings per course than Muntenian instruments.

235. Nicolae Feraru, conversations with author.

236. Zhan Vizitiu, *Moldavskie narodnye muzykal'nye instrumenty* (Kishinev: Literatura Artistică, 1985), 196-223, includes detailed technical drawings of the Bohak model. Alexander Fedoriouk says that Ukrainians purchase instruments manufactured in Chişinău.

237. A *santur* for sale in the bazaar in Istanbul in 1970 and one in the collection of the Cincinnati Art Museum, 1977.

238. Raouf Yekta Bey, "La musique turque," 3: 3021.

239. Kofteros, *Dhokimio*, 66, 69, 74, 77; Walter Feldman's Greek instrument had the plates covering the rail-pin block joint, which is universal with Romanian instruments but apparently rare with Greek instruments.

240. Anoyanakis, *Greek Instruments*, 301.

241. Kofteros, *Dhokimio*, 96; Anoyanakis, *Greek Instruments,* 301.

242. Anoyanakis, *Greek Instruments*, 299.

243. Anoyanakis, *Greek Instruments*, 300.

244. Nikos Karatasos, *Laïkoi orghanopaikhtes*, Intersound 2098, cover photograph.

The Pantaleon

A survey of world dulcimer traditions would not be complete without a discussion of the pantaleon. Though its players were few and its life short, it remains significant in the history of Western music as an influence on the development of the piano. Its developer was Pantaleon Hebenstreit (c.1667-1750), whose playing impressed kings and eminent musicians.[1]

Hebenstreit was born in Eisleben, Saxony, the son of a town musician. While studying in Leipzig around 1690, where he earned his living as a dancing and music master, playing the violin and teaching harpsichord, he fell into debt. To avoid imprisonment, he found refuge in a village near Merseburg. There he spent evenings at an inn where one of the musicians played a dulcimer. The instrument attracted his interest, and, with the help of a pastor skilled in woodworking, he built an enlarged dulcimer, with both gut and metal strings. In time, according to Jacob von Stählin, a courtier who happened to hear him play this new instrument told Frederick Augustus I, Elector of Saxony, about this new instrument and its player, and the Elector invited Hebenstreit to appear at court.

Hebenstreit probably performed in the same context as the *Hackbrettierer* who apppeared on occasion at the Dresden court earlier in the century. However, it seems likely that the dulcimer player at the village inn called his instrument a *Cymbal* rather than a *Hackbrett*, and that the dance music ensemble Hebenstreit heard there owed its style to that developed by Prague Jews some forty or fifty years earlier. Although the difference in design between the contemporary *Hackbrett* and *Cymbal* is uncertain, Pantaleon's particular tradition probably came from the latter instrument, and he probably called his instrument a *Cymbal*, since all contemporary accounts of his instrument refer to it as such.

Whether Hebenstreit performed at court in 1697 or not, he did get out of debt, and he returned to Leipzig, plying his trade as a dancing master. There he played for Count Logi, an amateur lutenist, and Johann Kuhnau, Bach's predecessor at St. Thomas' Church, who later acquired one of Hebenstreit's enlarged dulcimers. In a 1717 letter to Johann Mattheson, Kuhnau recalled Hebenstreit's performer twenty years earlier. After he had played "preludes, fantasies, fugues, and all sorts of caprices with the bare sticks, he then bound his sticks with cotton and played a *partita*." Count Logi was beside himself, and, with astonishment, remarked "the likes of this my ears have never heard."

In 1698, Hebenstreit received an appointment as dancing master at Duke Johann Georg's court at Weissenfels. In 1703, Frederick Augustus heard him play, probably for the first time, according to Berner, on his "completely newly invented *Cymbal.*" The following year Telemann described hearing his "marvelous *Cymbal*" at Sorau.[2] In 1705, Hebenstreit travelled to Paris, where he performed for King Louis XIV. According to Abbaye François de Châteauneuf's *Le dialogue sur la musique des anciens* (Paris, 1725), the instrument and its player made such an impression on the king that he ordered that the instrument be henceforth called "pantaleon" (or "pantalon").

His life during the next few years is uncertain, though he appears to have received an appointment as a musician at the Eisenach court. He made a concert tour to Vienna, where he played before the Emperor, who presented him with a gold chain and locket with the imperial portrait. In 1714, Elector Frederick Augustus appointed Hebenstreit as a chamber musician and pantaleonist to his court, at the large annual salary of 1200 thalers, with 200 thalers as an allowance for maintenance of his instrument. As years passed, he seems to have played the pantaleon less. In 1729, he received an appointment as director of Protestant church music, not a prestigious position within the Catholic court, but one which provided him an income for the rest of his life.

A number of other musicians learned Hebenstreit's instrument, made concert tours, and received appointments as musicians at various European courts. Johann Christoph Richter (1700-1785) succeeded Hebenstreit, whose eyes had failed, as court pantaleonist at Dresden in 1733. Georg Gebel (1709-1753) became pantaleonist in the orchestra of Saxon Prime Minister Brühl after 1735. Christlieb Siegmund Binder, organist to the court at Dresden, showed his pantaleon, out of repair, to Burney in 1772. Maximilian Hellmann (1703-1763), who was a *Cymbalist* and percussionist at the Viennese court and Johann Baptist Gumpenhuber of Vienna were others.[3] A musician named Osbruk performed on the pantaleon in Paris in 1772.[4] Georg Noelli (1727-1789) toured in Italy, England, Denmark, and Sweden, before accepting an appointment as pantaleonist to the court at Mecklenburg-Schwerin in 1776. He was the last court pantaleonist, and with him the use of the instrument ended.[5]

As music written specifically for pantaleon apparently has not survived, we are left to make assumptions on its musical role in the Dresden court orchestra. Berner suggests, because Hebenstreit's strength was not in composition, that he freely improvised or played transcriptions of other works, especially keyboard pieces.

Kuhnau's 1717 letter to Mattheson, published in the latter's *Criticae musicae* (Hamburg, 1725), provides many details about the instrument, no example of which survives. He had been infatuated by the *Pantaleon-cymbal*, as he called it, for twelve years. His instrument began at a sixteen-foot E, continued diatonically to an eight-foot G, then had a chromatic range to e[3]. Although he felt its drawbacks were its long body, necessary for the proper length of the gut strings, the bridge arrangement of the lowest courses, and the "Herculean" effort and expense required to maintain it, he appreciated its sustained bass notes, arpeggios, and the ability to play *piano* and *forte*.[6]

Keysler in 1716 described it as thirteen and one-half spans (about 9 feet, 9 inches, or 297 cm) long and three and one-half spans (about 31 inches, or 78.7 cm) wide, with gut strings on one side and steel wire on the other, containing a total of 185 strings, and "so loud that it is fit only for very large rooms."[7] His description closely matches that of Charles Burney, who in 1772 described it as being more than nine feet long and having 186 gut strings.[8] The instrument Diderot heard in 1774 must have resembled these others, as he wrote that it was nine feet long, four feet wide, with 74 tones.[9] The Abbaye de Châteauneuf adds the detail that more than two hundred lute strings were attached to pins placed in a plank six feet long and an inch thick.[10]

As time passed, certain makers changed the number of strings. The instrument played by Noelli on his tour of England in 1767 was eleven feet long and had 276 strings.[11] Johann Adam Hiller, however, indicates that makers had "finally happened upon doubled courses of strings on both sides of the soundboard . . . namely of steel and brass strings on one and of gut strings on the other."[12] Hiller's comment suggests that makers reduced the number of strings per course on the side of the instrument with metal strings but increased those with gut. Noelli's instrument would have had a lower range than that of Hebenstreit, but it certainly had more strings.

Without surviving instruments or accurate illustrations, we are left to conclude that the pantaleon's length was over nine feet, with an oblique pin block about six feet in length. The overspun gut strings could not have stretched the entire length of the instrument, as they would have covered the side with the metal strings and thus have interfered with the ability to play on that side. The pantaleon, then, must have consisted of two separate dulcimers arranged side by side, as Kettlewell argues.[13]

Notes

1. This account, unless otherwise noted, relies on the following articles: *Die Musik in Geschichte und Gegenwart*, s.v. "Hebenstreit, Pantaleon," by Alfred Berner; Sarah E. Hanks, "Pantaleon's Pantalon: an 18th-Century Musical Fashion," *Musical Quarterly* 55 (1969): 215-227; Annedore Egerland, "Das Pantaleon," *Die Musikforschung* 23 (1970): 152-159; David Kettlewell, "The Dulcimer," (Ph.D. diss., Loughborough University, 1976), 168-179; Christian Ahrens, "Pantaleon Hebenstreit und die Frühgeschichte des Hammerklaviers," *Beiträge zur Musikwissenschaft* 29 (1987): 37-48.

2. Hans Engel, *Musik in Thüringen* (Cologne: Böhlau Verlag, 1966), 14f.

3. Karl-Heinz Schickhaus, *Über Volksmusik und Hackbrett in Bayern* (Munich: BLV Verlagsgesellschaft, 1981), 180.

4. D. Diderot, *Lettres à Sophie Volland*, ed. A. Babelon (Paris: Gallimard, 1950), 2: 86.

5. Lenz Dibiasio, "Pantaleon Hebenstreit und das Hackbrett in der höfischen Musik des 18. Jahrhunderts," unpublished paper. I wish to thank Birgit Stolzenburg for this.

6. Kettlewell, "Dulcimer," 170-171.

7. Johann Georg Keysler, *Travels through Germany*, 2nd ed. (London, 1756-1757), 4: 125-126, in Hanks, "Pantaleon's Pantalon," 220.

8. Charles Burney, *An Eighteenth-Century Musical Tour in France and Italy*, ed. Percy A. Scholes (London: Oxford University Press, 1959), in Hanks, "Pantaleon's Pantalon," 223.

9. Diderot, *Lettres*, 2: 86. Converting the *pied-de-roi* to the English foot, the measurements are 9 feet, 7 inches (292 cm), and 4 feet, 3 inches (129.5 cm). I

am unable to reconcile the number of 74 tones with Kuhnau's description of the range, unless many were duplicated.

10. Kettlewell, "Dulcimer," 169.

11. Hanks, "Pantaleon's Pantalon," 222. The same number was confirmed in a source from 1790 (224).

12. Johann Adam Hiller, *Musikalischen Nachrichten und Anmerkungen* (1770), in Ahrens, "Pantaleon Hebenstreit," 41.

13. Kettlewell, "Dulcimer," 174.

· 8 ·

The *Salterio*

The *salterio*, played today only in Mexico, developed as a hybrid of the medieval psaltery and the early dulcimer. As we have seen, musicians continued to play the psaltery in Italy until the late sixteenth century, but by the early seventeenth century the instrument was only a memory in that country. The *dolcemèle* enjoyed a certain fashion among the urban elite during the middle of the sixteenth century, but disappeared during the early part of the following century. The new psaltery, or *salterio* (also *saltèro*, in Italian), apparently developed during the first half of the seventeenth century in Italy. Its unknown designer retained the name and the method of playing the old psaltery but assimilated the trapezoidal shape and arrangement of strings of the *dolcemèle*. The resulting instrument drew from both traditions yet was new.

History

Italy

Athanasius Kircher, the German polymath who lived at Rome, was the first to describe the instrument. In *Musurgia universalis* (1650), he enthusiastically recommends it, as "if it is assigned to an experienced hand, like no others, [it] seems to yield a variety of harmonic proportions or a remarkable pleasantness of harmonious sound." Kircher calls it an instrument of professional musicians and describes an instrument belonging to a "noted" Roman musician, Giovanni Maria Canario, as having 148 strings. He provides a diagram for a trapezoidal instrument with two rosettes and two bridges, the left dividing the courses into fifths. He even includes a sample of tablature for the instrument. He writes that the musician strikes the strings with quills and uses the rest of his fingers to dampen the vibrating strings.[1]

Surviving *salterio*s have many fewer strings than Kircher describes, so perhaps later makers reduced the instrument's size. Luigi Valdrighi mentions the names of Alessandro Lodovico Veraldi, of Bologna (1616), and Brother Giuseppe, of Mirandola (1666), and David Kettlewell mentions Gion Zino, of Brescia, as makers, but little further evidence of the *salterio* in Italy during the seventeenth century seems to exist.[2]

The *salterio* reached its peak of fashion during the middle of the eighteenth century. Both professional musicians and male and female amateurs played it. Skilled makers produced richly decorated, carved, and gilt instruments in the latest fashion. They sold such instruments to wealthy amateurs, who, like the patricians of the sixteenth century with their *dolcemèle*s, intended to use them to decorate the rooms of their palaces. As an example of their cost, the Pièta, a school and orphanage in Venice which educated young women in music, paid five ducats and six grossi to Lodovico Forsato for a *salterio* for its chapel in 1706. The price paid for this instrument was almost the same amount as that paid by the school to the well-known maker Matteo Goffriller for two violins.[3] Collectors bought Italian *salterio*s in the nineteenth century and many are now in musical instrument museums in Europe and the United States.

Italian composers used the *salterio* on occasion in music written for the theater and church. The earliest dated music using the instrument seems to be in an aria in Vivaldi's opera *Giustino*, written in 1724.[4] Leonardo Leo used it in *La Contesa de Numi*, a secular cantata he wrote in 1729 for the birth of Louis, the royal Dauphin.[5] Girolamo Chiti, a Roman, composed various religious works for soloists, choir, orchestra, and organ, with *salterio*, some of them dated 1737.[6] Some of the better known composers who made use of it include Giovanni Battista Martini, who wrote a motet, *Ex tractatu Sancti Augustini*, for harpsichord and *salterio* obligato and alto and soprano solo, with continuo; Nicola Porpora, who used it in an aria in *Oratorio per la nascità di Gesu Cristo*, written at Dresden in 1748; Giuseppe Sarti, who composed a *Miserere* for five and six voices, with horns, flutes, *salterio*, oboes, and strings; and Niccolo Piccini, who composed *Matribus suis dixerunt*, for soprano with *salterio* and organ.[7] Gluck included the instrument in an aria from the opera *Le*

Cadi dupé, produced at Hamburg in 1761, evoking the Arabic *qanun*.[8] Most of the other surviving manuscripts containing music for the instrument are by relatively obscure or anonymous composers. The monastery of San Lorenzo at San Severo contains mostly anonymous lessons, lamentations, antiphons, and motets, some written for services during Holy Week, for soprano, *salterio* (or violin), and organ or continuo.[9]

Since the *salterio* often appears only in a single aria of an opera or oratorio, it is likely that it was played mostly as a secondary instrument by professional musicians. Such was the case with the best-known virtuoso, Juan Bautista Pla, a Catalonian oboist who was employed by court orchestras in Germany and Portugal and who made tours in France, England, and Italy, between 1752 and 1773.[10] Giovanni Battista Dall'Olio (1739-1832), a student of Padre Martini, an organist and music theorist, made *salterio*s in the 1760s and taught the instrument.[11] Other touring *salterio* players remain anonymous. Certainly Henry Brooke, in his novel *The Fool of Quality* (1765), must have based his fictional "Marmulet the famed Genoese Musician, who performed on the Psaltery, the Viol d'Amor, and other Instruments not known till then in England," on some real, touring performer.[12] Paolo Salulini, director of the theater at Siena, composed two concerti, one in 1751, undoubtedly for a professional, and Sebastiano Nasolini's concerto, probably written in the 1790s, demanded the skill of a virtuoso.[13]

Example 8.1: Measures 9-12 from the Largo movement of the Concerto for *salterio* and orchestra in C major by Sebastiano Nasolini (born 1768). Source: Manuscript in the library of the Istituto Musicale Nicolo Paganini, Genoa.

Despite its origins as an instrument played by professional musicians, the *salterio* seems to have been more popular with upper-class amateurs. Prominent among them were churchmen. Some made them, like Father Grazioli, of Lodi, who about 1775 manufactured models with gut strings, in the shape of an extended harp, or Brother Carlo Giacinto Longhi, of Novara, who made one at Viglevano in 1754.[14] Abbot Franciosi, of Florence, applied movable jacks to his instrument in order to raise and lower the tone of the strings, but because of its imperfect tuning, his system did not find followers. The abbots Carise (died 1782), of Naples, and Fabrizio Pasquali, of Rome, were also well-known players.[15] Pietro Franceschi, dean of the Livorno Cathedral, posed for his portrait in 1770 in front of a *salterio* (see illustration 15).[16]

Other dilettantes included noblemen, such as Cavaliere Parisio, who played a concerto of his own composition in Rome at an academy in the house of Henry Stuart, Cardinal York. Dall'Olio reported that a friar was so taken by the concerto that he absconded with it.[17] Cavaliere Vincenzo Olivieri, of Pesaro, composed a concerto for the instrument, which survives.[18] Saverio Mattei, an advocate of Naples, according to Dall'Olio, was a "true prodigy," able to play toccatas and arias in the keys of B, E, and A, the bass part with one hand and the violin part with the other. Women also played the *salterio*, as Dall'Olio wrote that he gave lessons to Countess Parisetti, of Rubiera.[19] A collection of music for *salterio*, written mostly by an obscure composer named Filippo Sugarelli in 1749 and 1750, was possessed by one Anna Maria Grazziani, and another manuscript was written for Maria Lucia Lancellotti.[20]

The third category of players of the *salterio* consisted of professional popular musicians, who performed in the streets of Italian cities. Charles Burney, describing the music he heard in the main piazza in Turin in 1770, mentioned "a man and woman [who] sang Venetian ballads, in two parts, very agreeably, accompanied by a dulcimer."[21] Goethe, visiting Verona in 1787, described the street sounds he heard in the evening: "Marlborough's little song is heard on all streets, then a dulcimer, a violin."[22] The "dulcimer" in these references can only be a *salterio*.

The last compositions for the *salterio* date from the 1790s. An oratorio by Bonaventura Furlanetto, *Moyses in Nilo* (1797), makes use of *salterio*s.[23] Nasolini's concerto dates no earlier than the 1790s, although he could have composed it a bit later. The instrument then went into a steep decline after 1800, as styles changed. Perhaps it remained in the hands of popular musicians somewhat longer, however, as they were less vulnerable to the whims of upper-class taste. Gregorovius described watching musicians tune a mandolin and dulcimer in a small orchestra playing for a "model ball" for common people at Rome in 1853.[24] Nevertheless, by 1879, Valdrighi could write that it was "now relegated to silence among the dust of old castles, in museums, near some mountain parish, in granaries, and very often among the goods of antique dealers."[25]

Dall'Olio wrote *Avvertimenti pei suonatori di salterio* ("Recommendations for *salterio* players") in 1770, which provides our most detailed description of Italian technique. He touches on twenty points, including posture, a free bearing, position of fingers, ornamentation, and observing tempo. However, in our discussion of dulcimer traditions, Dall'Olio's observations on the technique of producing sound are the most salient. He writes that the player should use the thumb, index and middle fingers of each hand, but that normally the player uses only the index fingers. To play fast, ascending passages, the performer may use the middle finger, but only as an aid, and he uses his thumbs only for some arpeggios and chords. Dall'Olio also remarks that the *ditali* [thimbles] should tend to be hard rather than soft, as ones that are too soft produced an "irritating" crack.[26] Lichtenthal, writing fifty years later, remarks that the *salterio* "is played with the two hands furnished with *ditali*, or they may be flat rings out of which comes a metal tip like the cannon of a pointed pen."[27] Carena, writing still later, notes that the *saltèro* is played "by striking with two little wooden rods, one for each hand; or else with *ditali*, which are like so many rings for sewing, fitted at the tips of the fingers of the hands, into each of which is fastened a pointed quill; also it is played by hand, that is, with the fingertip."[28] Clearly the usual method involved metal "thimbles" or rings which held quills in place, but hammers may have appeared later as an alternate method, perhaps through the influence of itinerant Alpine musicians.

Spain and Portugal

The term *salterio* today occasionally denotes the string drum, still in use in Aragon and among the Basques, and Cervantes, in *Don Quixote* (c.1600) clearly meant that instrument when he described *salterio*s, flutes, and tambourines playing for dancing at the wedding of Camacho.[29] Thus we need to look critically at any mention of the word *salterio* in Spanish sources prior to 1750 when examining the history of this instrument.

The dulcimer-like *salterio* reached considerable popularity in Spain, Portugal, and Latin America during the late eighteenth century, but its introduction and early history remain obscure.

Italian musicians probably introduced it to Spain during the first part of the eighteenth century. Indeed, Iberian musicians may have regarded it as an Italian instrument, as Luis Vidal, formerly hornist in the court orchestra at Lisbon, advertised in Charleston, South Carolina, in 1774, to teach "several instruments in the Italian taste, such as the mandoline, psaltery, English and French guitars."[30] Nevertheless, despite its Italian origin, musicians rapidly adapted the *salterio* to Spanish musical style. When Pablo Minguet y Irol published his *Reglas y advertencias generales* for different instruments at Madrid in 1754, he included the *psalterio*, as well as other instruments which must have been popular in polite society at the time, the guitar, *tiple*, *vandola*, cittern, clavichord, organ, harp, *bandurria*, violin, transverse flute, recorder, and *flautilla*.[31]

The earliest known Spanish player was also the best-known virtuoso in Europe, Juan Bautista Pla, mentioned above. He and his younger brother Josep were oboists at Madrid and Lisbon before 1751, when they embarked on a concert tour in Europe. In 1752 they played at a *concert spirituel* for the Queen of France, the elder brother playing "many pieces" on the *salterio*.[32] The Pla brothers then became engaged as oboists in the famous orchestra of the Grand Duke of Württemberg led by Niccolo Jommelli. Jommelli composed a *sinfonia* for *salterio* and orchestra for Pla during this period, which he rewrote from memory in January 1770.[33] The brothers toured Italy in 1762 and influenced *salterio* players in that country, as Pla's tuning for the instrument favorably impressed Dall'Olio.[34] Juan Bautista Pla played several concerts on the bassoon and *salterio* at London in 1769, before returning to Lisbon and then Madrid.[35]

The only other touring *salterio* virtuoso mentioned in the annals of European concert music was a Madame Bauer, the German wife of a German violinist. She performed at an opera concert in Spain between 1787 and 1790 and at a concert at Hamburg in 1792 with her husband. A critic commented that she played "the most difficult violin and clavier concertos with the greatest ease and expression." Her husband had been at Lisbon, and she may have learned the instrument there.[36]

Certainly other professional musicians in Spain played the instrument, as its use in theatrical music suggests. Don Blas Laserna scored an arieta and minuet for voice, *salterio*, and piano, in his tonadilla *Los amantes chasqueados* (1779).[37] Pablo del Moral wrote *seguidilla*s for *salterio* and guitar in his tonadilla *La tia burlada*, and the libretto of another tonadilla indicates use of the instrument.[38] Beryl Kenyon de Pascual mentions that several *salterio*s are preserved in, or came from, convents and monasteries and suggests that they may have replaced the organ during Holy Week, as some of the Italian manuscripts mentioned above indicate, or were played by nuns during their free time.[39] She has found little evidence, however, of manuscripts containing music for the instrument in archives of such institutions. Perhaps the fondness of Italian clerics for the *salterio* was not replicated in Spain to the same extent.

Figure 8.1: Detail of the *salterio* player in the frontispiece engraving of Pablo Minguet y Irol, *Reglas y advertencias generales que enseñan el modo de tañer* (Madrid: Jochin Ibarr, 1754).

Most of the surviving Spanish manuscripts of *salterio* music consist of easy sonatas, divertimentos, and dance tunes, such as minuets, fandangos, and contradanzas. The composers are either anonymous or obscure, like Vicente Adan, who wrote several divertimentos which survive.[40] The composers or music masters who wrote these manuscripts clearly intended them for amateurs, and women seem to have comprised many of these players. Kenyon de Pascual cites a 1788 article which recommended different instruments for people at various social levels, and the author suggested "a keyboard instrument, viola, *salterio*, etc. for polite society."[41] However, as in Italy, the fashion for the instrument declined after 1800.

Minguet y Irol discusses the technique of playing. He suggests that only the index fingers and the thumb of the right hand plucked the strings and describes slurs, appoggiaturas, trills, and harmonic accompaniment.[42] However, clearly some players used two fingers on each hand, since, for example, a passage in *Obra de Psalterio No. 1*, in M. 2249, Biblioteca Nacional, Madrid (see example 8.2), involves repeated thirty-second notes which would be facilitated by the use of both index and middle fingers.

Example 8.2: Measures 32 and 33 from *Obra de Psalterio No. 1*, in the first and presumably Allegro movement, in M. 2249, Biblioteca Nacional, Madrid.

France, Switzerland, and England

Touring performers may have created a brief fashion for the *salterio* in France and England. Frederick Hintz, a guitar maker to the Queen, advertised in 1763 that he made "Solitaires" as well as other stringed instruments.[43] This strange instrument can only be a *salterio*. In 1775, a man named Benoit, in Geneva, advertised that he made the *psalterion* as well as dulcimer, harpsichord, and pianoforte, and described, for readers unfamiliar with the instrument, that it was a "stringed instrument like the dulcimer, but instead of its strings played with hammers, they are plucked."[44] Laborde wrote in 1780 that some played the modern *psalterium* with their fingers and others with little rings attached to their fingers holding quills and added the familiar "this instrument is very agreeable when it is well played."[45] During the Revolution in 1789, a "small dulcimer, called *psalterion*" was confiscated from the Comte de Maillebois.[46] A. Jacoby, active between 1800 and 1820 at Auch, made a *psaltérion*; with courses of five and six strings each, it shows Spanish influence.[47]

Latin America

The economic, cultural, and personal ties between Spain and Portugal and their colonies in the New World remained very strong. We should not wonder, then, that the same fashions which prevailed among the aristocracy in the Iberian Peninsula followed them to the colonies. The taste for the *salterio* was one such fashion.

In Chile, the clavichord and *salterio*, introduced about 1765, were the instruments *par excellence* of aristocratic society, according to Pereira Salas. A German instrument maker named Enrique Kors had settled at Lima and produced *salterio*s for wealthy colonists. One richly decorated instrument, with case and stand, made in Lima for Isidora Riveros de Aguirre in 1785, is in the Museo Histórico Nacional in Valparaiso, Chile.[48] Other *salterio*s from this era exist in Jesuit churches in Bolivia, in the Casa de la Cultura in Quito, Ecuador, and in a private collection in Colombia.[49] A new *salterio* was advertised for sale in a newspaper at Havana in 1795.[50] Clearly wherever there were Spanish colonists, *salterio*s were likely to follow.

A remarkable Brazilian tablature for *salterio*, written in 1805 by a Portuguese-born lawyer, Antonio Vieira dos Santos, has been studied and transcribed by Rogerio Budasz. It contains numerous popular minuets and other dances, including some of Afro-Brazilian origin, such as *lunduns* and others, providing a rare source for secular colonial Brazilian music.[51] This instrument soon became naturalized in the Portuguese colony, as a *salterio* made in Brazil in 1762 is in the Martins Sarmento Museo in Guimaraes, Portugal, and in 1797 a *salterio* "made by Indians of Rio Janeiro" was advertised as for sale in a Madrid newspaper.[52] Budasz writes that the instrument was popular among the aristocracy during the early nineteenth century but today is completely forgotten.

The country where the *salterio* survives, although perhaps somewhat in decline, is Mexico.[53] We can presume that the *salterio*s mentioned as in use there in the seventeenth century were string drums,[54]

and that, as in Spain and elsewhere in Latin America, the modern instrument was introduced and became popular during the second half of
the eighteenth century. The colonial aristocracy may have abandoned it,
but by the middle of the nineteenth century peasants had adopted the
instrument. Harp, vihuela, and *salterio* accompanied a style of song
known as *cancion norteña*. The instrument was also used at mid-cen-
tury in an orchestra from Huamantla consisting also of guitar, violin,
double bass, clarinet, cornet, and flute.[55] In 1871, an American described
peons dancing to the accompaniment of harps, *salterio*, *bajo* (bass guitar), and *janarita* (a small guitar).[56]

Beginning in 1884, with the organization of the first such ensemble,
the *orquesta típica* grew in popularity. Its instrumentation was variable,
but the *salterio* was prominent, and the orchestras might have three to
six of them (see illustration 16). Other instruments might include flute,
marimbas, violins, guitars, *bajos sextos, mandolas, bandolone*, harp,
and *guitarróns*.[57] By this time, the *salterio* was made in two sizes, the
higher-pitched *salterio requinto* and the lower-pitched *salterio tenor*,[58]
and the *orquestas típicas* included both. The musicians read music, and
the *salterio* played the equivalent of the violin part in a standard orchestra. The repertoire consisted of popular Mexican waltzes, polkas, marches,
paso dobles, and standard songs by popular composers. Although some
orquestas típicas still exist, their popularity declined after the 1930s.

Today, one can hear the *salterio* played by a few professionals in
restaurants in Xochimilco and other locations. Dressed in formal wear,
they play Mexican standards to the accompaniment of guitar and bass.
They play the instrument with tortoise-shell picks attached to both index
fingers and the right thumb by silver rings. Although some have appeared on recordings, the instrument is generally hard to find. In March
1999, a *salterio* festival, sponsored by a government agency, was held in
Querétaro and may lead to a revival of the instrument.[59]

United States

Luis (or Lewis) Vidal, who claimed to have been a horn player at the
court of Portugal, toured the English Colonies in 1774. He was presumably the anonymous person who was to play a "sonada of the salterio;
and D'Exaudet's Minuet, with echos" at a concert on 17 May, which
featured vocal music and "different solos, upon various instruments,
unknown in this country."[60] At Philadelphia, on 17 June, at a concert

organized by Sodi, a dancing master who had been active in Paris and London, Vidal was to play "a solo on the psaltery, and a minuet imitating the echo," as well as solos on the guitar and mandolin.[61] He then went to Charleston, where he advertised in September and October that he offered to teach the mandolin, psaltery, and English and French guitars, although he spoke no English. He apparently decided that South Carolina offered little opportunity and left for the West Indies in December.[62] That colony may have had the richest planters in the Colonies, but evidently they had little interest in Continental fashions.

In 1935, a fourteen-piece *orquesta típica*, led by *salterio* player Angel Mercado, played for a weekly broadcast under Mexican government sponsorship for WJZ in New York City. The group had three *salterio*s, and in 1937, Sara Mercado was still in the city.[63] Other Mexican *salterio* players have appeared in the United States on occasion. One appeared in a movie directed by John Ford, *My Darling Clementine* (1946).

Design

Kircher illustrates a *salterio* with twenty-three treble courses, over bridge(s) dividing them into fifths, and twenty-four courses over the bridge(s) on the right. No surviving instrument has such a large number, which makes his description seem unrealistic, but he mentions an instrument with 148 strings.[64] Such an instrument might have an arrangement where some of the twenty-three treble courses had three strings and others four strings per course, while some of the bass courses had two and others three strings per course.

The surviving Italian *salterio*s from the first half of the eighteenth century vary somewhat in design, but certain characteristics are common. An undated tuning diagram in the Civico Museo Bibiografico Musicale in Bologna (figure 8.2) shows an instrument with nine treble courses resting on four bridges, a single course on a bridge on the lower left, and ten bass courses, the highest resting on a single bridge to the right of the main bass bridge. This corresponds to the diagram in the Lancellotti manuscript, except that the latter shows ten treble and eleven bass courses.[65] The common characteristic in the tuning system is that the lowest treble bridge divides the courses into a diatonic G-major scale, the next bridge divides two courses into minor sixths, followed by a bridge dividing one course into a perfect fifth. The course over the lower left bass bridge is tuned to g^0, an octave below the lowest treble course. The bass courses on the right start at a^0 and ascend diatonically to f^1 or $f\sharp^1$, and the remaining courses above provide the chromatic intervals lacking in the treble courses, starting at $c\sharp^1$ or $d\sharp^1$. Antonio Battaglia of Milan, active between 1757 and 1785, added another bridge, containing five courses, to the right of the right bass bridge, allowing a fully chromatic tuning.[66] The manuscripts I have examined require a chromatic range from $f\sharp^0$ or g^0 to e^3, minus $d\sharp^3$, but only a few later works, such as a sonata by the Milanese composer Melchiorre Chiesa and the Nasolini concerto, require $g\sharp^0$ and $a\sharp^0$.

Surviving Italian instruments are richly ornamented. Their bridges and moldings are often gilt, and their two sound holes sometimes contain gilt parchment roses. Instruments usually have four carved feet, allowing the back of the instrument to resonate freely. Many have cases, with a hinged front panel, suggesting that they remained in them while in play. The lower length ranges from about 63 to 82 cm (24¾ to 32¼

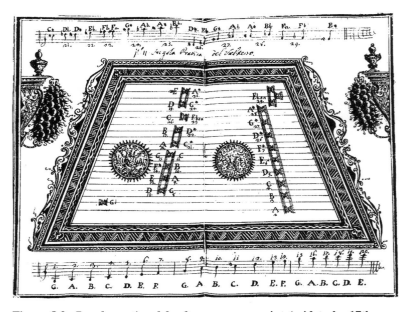

Figure 8.2: *Regola pratica del saltero*, a manuscript (said to be 17th century, but probably from the 18th) showing the tuning and arrangement of its strings. **Source: Civico Museo Bibliografico Musicale, Bologna.**

inches), the upper length from 34 to 46 cm (13½ to 18 inches), the width from 29 to 43 cm (11½ to 17 inches), and the height (minus feet) 7 to 8 cm (2¾ to 3 inches). Since museum examples frequently have improperly arranged bridges or lack them entirely, it is somewhat difficult to make generalizations about the number of courses and the number of strings per course. Nevertheless, it appears that nine to eleven treble courses, with four strings per course, was standard. Ten to twelve courses, with three or four strings per course, ran over the right-hand bass bridge(s), and one or two courses ran over the lower left-hand bass bridge. Both brass and steel wire were used.[67]

Italian makers also experimented with other designs. Gut-strung instruments are mentioned above. A small instrument, made by Michel Carlo Florindo of Rome in 1706, measures 39.2 cm (15½ inches) and 23.2 cm (9¼ inches) in length by 16 cm (6¼ inches) in width.[68] Battaglia made one measuring 44 cm (17¼ inches) long, 22 cm (8¾ inches) wide, and 3 cm (1 inch) high, with twenty-five triple courses and three bridges.[69] This was probably the *salterio in ottava alto* mentioned on a label advertising his gut-strung *salterio* attached to one of his instruments made in 1779.[70] Battaglia made a *salterio in ottava basso*, with an extended sound box on the right side with overspun gut strings, two examples of which are in the Museo degli Strumenti Musicali in Milan.

In her detailed study of Spanish *salterios*, Beryl Kenyon de Pascual notes the characteristics of eighteenth-century Spanish instruments which distinguish them from Italian instruments. She remarks that decoration is generally less luxurious, although bridges and the molding around the soundboard are often gilt, painted designs on the soundboard being common. She finds Spanish instruments to fall into two categories, one with twenty-six or fewer courses with the same dimensions as the Italian instruments, and another with twenty-eight or more courses measuring 90 to 100 cm (35½ to 39½ inches) long by 35 to 40 cm (13¾ to 15¾ inches) wide. Another characteristic is for Spanish instruments to contain more strings per course, often five and six.[71]

Mexican *salterios*, though plainer in decoration than their eighteenth-century predecessors, retain many characteristics of the Spanish design. The arrangement of bridges is similar, but the chief change is that the core G-major scale on the treble bridge has evolved into a D-major scale. The *salterio tenor* uses the D scale below the G scale of the eighteenth-century instruments, while the *salterio requinto* is tuned an octave higher than the *salterio tenor*. The lowest treble bridge segment holds four courses divided into fifths, the next segment holds three courses, and the upper segment holds six or eight courses. The middle segment is placed so that it divides the courses into minor sixths and the upper segment so that it divides them into diminished fifths. In order to change the string lengths to allow the proper tuning on some of the upper courses, metal nuts rest on the pin blocks. The right bass bridge contains thirteen courses and the left bass bridge four courses. The *salterio tenor* has four steel strings per treble course and three brass strings per bass course, while the *salterio requinto* uses three steel strings per course throughout.[72] A nineteenth-century Mexican *salterio* in the Brussels Conservatory collection measures 97 cm (38¼ inches) and 39 cm (15½ inches) in length and 41 cm (16 inches) in width and has the characteristics of the *salterio tenor*.[73]

Notes

1. Athanasius Kircher, *Musurgia Universalis* (1650; reprint, Hildesheim: G. Olms, 1970), 495-496.

2. Luigi Francesco Valdrighi, *Nomocheliurgografia antica e moderna* (Modena: coi tipi società tipografica, 1884), 125; David Kettlewell, "The Dulcimer" (Ph.D. diss., Loughborough University, 1976), fig. 87.

3. Denis Arnold, "Instruments and Instrumental Teaching in the Early Italian Conservatories," *Galpin Society Journal* 18 (Mar. 1965): 77.

4. Beryl Kenyon de Pascual, "The Spanish Eighteenth-Century *Salterio* and Some Comments on Its Italian Counterpart," *Musique-Images-Instruments* 3: (1997): 40.

5. Cantate 305, in the library of the Conservatorio di Musica S. Pietro a Maiella, Naples.

6. These are in the archives of San Giovanni di Laterano, Rome.

7. HH.57, 5, c.28-31, Civico Museo Bibliografico Musicale, Bologna; Add. 14124, British Library; Ms. 11, c.56, Biblioteca Comunale, Faenza; MS 212, Monastero di San Lorenzo, San Severo.

8. Karl-Heinz Schickhaus, *Über Hackbrett und Volksmusik in Bayern* (Munich: BLV Verlagsgesellschaft, 1981), 154-155. Schickhaus describes (174-177) the use of the *salterio* in an oratorio by Johann Ernst Eberlin and in a work by Maximilian Hellmann, both in the Italian style.

9. MSS 82, 83, 155, 168, 169, 172, 182, 184, 205, 220, 1162.

10. Josep Dolcet, "Katalonische Oboenvirtuosen am Hof Karl Eugens von Württemberg: die Brüder Pla," *Tibia* 17 (1992): 33-36.

11. Luigi Francesco Valdrighi, *Musurgiana: scràndola-pianoforte-salterio*

(Modena: Tipografia Cesare Olivari, 1879), 41-47; Kenyon, "Spanish Eighteenth-Century *Salterio*," 56; *The New Grove Dictionary of Music and Musicians*, s.v. "Dall'Oglio, Giovanni Battista."

12. Henry Brooke, *The Fool of Quality* (Dublin: Dillon Chamberlaine, 1765), 4: 233.

13. Ms. Mart. 2.5, 29 c.91-96, Civico Museo Bibliografico Musicale, Bologna; Mss.N.476/7, Biblioteca Communale, Assisi; M.3.22.15, Istituto Musicale Nicolo Paganini, Genoa.

14. Pietro Lichtenthal, *Dizionario e bibliografia della musica* (Milan: Antonio Fontana, 1826), 2: 173; Hubert Henkel, *Clavichorde*, Musikinstrumenten-Museum der Karl-Marx-Universität-Leipzig, Katalog, vol. 4 (Frankfurt am Main: Verlag Das Musikinstrument, 1981), 84f., pl. 82.

15. Valdrighi, *Musurgiana*, 39-40.

16. Luigi Crespi, *Portrait of Pietro Franceschi*, Pinacoteca, Bologna.

17. Valdrighi, *Musurgiana*, 45.

18. MS, c.(4), Convento di S. Francesco, Bologna.

19. Valdrighi, *Musurgiana*, 44, 48.

20. M2.5 v.55, ff. 85-114, Frank V. De Bellis Collection, San Francisco State University; Rés. 985, Bibliothèque Nationale de France, mentioned in Kenyon de Pascual, "Spanish Eighteenth-Century *Salterio*," 38.

21. Charles Burney, *An Eighteenth-Century Musical Tour in France and Italy*, ed. Percy A. Scholes (London: Oxford University Press, 1959), 58.

22. Johann Wolfgang von Goethe, *Italienische Reise*, Autobiographische Schriften, vol. 3, *Goethes Werke*, 7th ed. (Hamburg: Christian Wegner Verlag, 1967), 11: 50.

23. Autograph score, c.116, 105 (Correr, 85-92), Conservatorio di Musica "Benedetto Marcello," Venice.

24. Ferdinand Gregorovius, *Wanderjahre in Italien*, vol. 1, *Figuren: Geschichte, Leben und Scenerie aus Italien*, 3rd ed. (Leipzig: F. M. Brockhaus, 1870), 245. He uses the word *Hackebret*.

25. Valdrighi, *Musurgiana*, 33.

26. Valdrighi, *Musurgiana*, 51-54. An English translation appears in Nelly van Ree Bernard, *The Psaltery: an Annotated Audio-Visual Review of Different Types of Psaltery* (Buren: Frits Knuf Publishers, 1989), 80-82.

27. Lichtenthal, *Dizionario*, 2: 173.

28. Giacinto Carena, *Nuovo vocabolario italiano d'arti e mestieri*, ed. Ernesto Sergent (Milan: Francesco Pagnoni, 1868-1869), 17f.

29. Cervantes, *Don Quixote*.

30. *South Carolina and American General Gazette*, 23-30 September 1774.

31. Pablo Minguet y Irol, *Reglas, y advertencias generales para tañer el psalterio*, Reglas y advertencias generales que enseñan el modo de tañer (Madrid: Jochin Ibarra, 1754).

32. Balatasar Saldoni, *Diccionario biografico-bibliografico de efemerides de muscos españoles* (Madrid, 1881), 4: 256.

33. Niccolo Jommelli to Bottelho, 16 Jan. 1770, 23 Jan. 1770, in Marita P. McClymonds, *Niccolò Jommelli: the Last Years, 1769-1774*, Studies in Musicology, no. 23 (Ann Arbor: UMI Research Press, 1978), 500, 505. The *Sinfonia* survives as Mss. 38.1.4 and 24.1.1, Biblioteca del Conservatorio di Musica S. Pietro à Maiella, Naples.

34. Giuseppe Tartini to Padre Martini, 7 May 1762, in Anne Schnoebelen, *Padre Martini's Collection of Letters in the Civico Museo Bibliografico Musicale in Bologna: an Annotated Index* (New York: Pendragon Press, 1979), 613; Valdrighi, *Musurgiana*, 40-41, 44-45, 54.

35. Dolcet, "Katalonische Oboenvirtuosen," 35-36.

36. Mary Neel Hamilton, *Music in Eighteenth Century Spain* (New York: Da Capo Press, 1971), 138, where she is named as "Madame Baber"; Robert Eitner, *Biographisch-bibliograpisches Quellen-Lexikon der Musiker und Musikgeschichte der christlichen Zeitrechnung bis zur Mitte des neunzehnten Jahrhunderts* (Leipzig: Breitkopf & Härtel, 1900-1904), 1: 381.

37. Rafael Mitjana, "La musique en Espagne (Art religeux et art profane)," in *Encyclopédie de la musique et dictionnaire du Conservatoire*, Albert Lavignac, ed. (Paris: Librairie Delagrave, 1920), 2242-2244.

38. José Subirá, *La tonadilla escénica* (Madrid, 1929), 2: 480-481, 494.

39. Kenyon de Pascual, "Spanish Eighteenth-Century *Salterio*," 42.

40. Ms. 900, Monastery of Aranzazu, mentioned by Kenyon de Pascual, "Spanish Eighteenth-Century *Salterio*," 39; MS 297, Royal Academy of Music, London.

41. Kenyon de Pascual, "Spanish Eighteenth-Century *Salterio*," 42.

42. Minguet y Irol, *Reglas, y advertencias generales para tañer el psalterio*, n.p. This is reproduced, with an English concordance, in Bernard, *Psaltery*, 70-79.

43. "Mortimer's London Universal Directory, 1763," *Galpin Society Journal* 2 (1943): 50, in Kettlewell, "Dulcimer," 190.

44. *Almanach Musical* 1 (1775): 130.

45. Jean Benjamin de Laborde, *Essai sur la musique ancienne et moderne* (Paris: Ph.-D. Pierres, 1780), 1: 302-303.

46. Antonio Bruni, *Un inventaire sous La Terreur: état des instruments de musique* (Paris: Georges Chamerot, 1890), 87.

47. Curt Sachs, *Sammlung alter Musikinstrumente bei der Staatlichen Hochschule für Musik zu Berlin* (Berlin: Julius Bard, 1922), 40; Kenyon de Pascual, "Spanish Eighteenth-Century *Salterio*," 49.

48. Eugenio Pereira Salas, *Los origenes del arte musical en Chile* (Santiago: Imprento Universitaria, [1941]), 40-42, 327.

49. Leila Makarius, personal communication, 19 Nov. 1998; Kenyon de Pascual, "Spanish Eighteenth-Century *Salterio*," 54 n. 73; *Historia de la música en Colombia*, 3rd ed. (Bogotá: Editorial ABC, 1963), n.p.

50. Alejo Carpentier, *La musica en Cuba* (Havana: n.p., 1961), 62.

51. Antonio Vieira dos Santos, *Cifras de música para saltério*, ed. Rogério Budasz (Curitiba, 1996).

52. Rogerio Budasz, "A Nineteenth Century Brazilian Dulcimer Tablature," *Electronic Musicological Review* 1 (Sept. 1996): 1; Beryl Kenyon de Pascual, "Los salterios españoles del siglo XVIII," *Revista de musicología* 8 (1985): 321.

53. I have heard reports that the *salterio* may still be played in Lima, Peru, and in southern Chile, but I have been unable to confirm them.

54. Julio Estrada, ed., *La música de México*, vol. 1, *Historia*, by José Antonio Guzmán Bravo and Robert Stevenson (Mexico City: Universidad Nacional Autónoma de México, 1986), 129.

55. Claes af Geierstam, *Popular Music in Mexico* (Albuquerque: University of New Mexico Press, 1976), 46, 84.

56. W. R. Turnbull, "A Peep at an Hacienda," *Overland Monthly and Out West Magazine* 7 (1871): 520.

57. Geierstam, *Popular Music in Mexico*, 84.

58. Jorge Alberto Jara de León, personal communication.

59. "Más de 150 músicos demuestran que el salterio no está eb vías de extinción," Consejo Nacional para la Cultura y las Artes webpage, <http://www.cnca.gob.mx/cnca/nuevo/diarias/120399/infsalte.htm>.

60. *New York Mercury*, 9 May 1774.

61. *Pennsylvania Journal*, 15 June 1774.

62. *South Carolina & American General Gazette*, 23-30 Sept. 1774, 21-28 Oct. 1774, 9-16 Dec. 1774.

63. *New York Sun*, 20 Apr. 1935. Thanks to Bob Godfried for this article. She is listed in the American Federation of Musicians, Local 802, directory for 1937.

64. Kircher, *Musurgia Universalis*, 495-496.

65. Kenyon de Pascual, "Spanish Eighteenth-Century *Salterio*," 38.

66. Examples of this design are nos. 540 and 541, *Museo degli strumenti musicali*, Musei e gallerie di Milano (Milan: Electa, 1998), 424-425; and an example from 1766 in the Victoria and Albert Museum. Kenyon de Pascual, "Spanish Eighteenth-Century *Salterio*," 60, notes that an example by Longhi from 1754 in the Leipzig University collection is the earliest example of the use of this bridge.

67. Lichtenthal, *Dizionario e bibliografia*, 2: 173.

68. *Museo degli strumenti musicali*, Musei e gallerie di Milano, 423.

69. Sachs, *Sammlung alter Musikinstrumente bei der Staatlichen Hochschule für Musik zu Berlin*, 40.

70. Kenyon de Pascual, "Spanish Eighteenth-Century *Salterio*," 55. The same label is described in Edwin M. Ripin, *The Instrument Catalogs of Leopoldo Franciolini*, Music Indexes and Bibliographies, no. 9 (Hackensack, N.J.: J. Boonin, 1974), 61.

71. Kenyon de Pascual, "Spanish Eighteenth-Century *Salterio*," 43-45, 49.

72. Jorge Alberto Jara de León, personal communication.

73. V. C. Mahillon, *Catalogue descriptif et analytique du Musée instrumental du Conservatoire royale du musique du Bruxelles*, 2: 182-183.

• *9* •

The French *Psalterion* and *Tympanon*

Following a period during the latter part of the fifteenth and early part of
the sixteenth centuries in which the *doulcemèr* developed from the psaltery and enjoyed a fashion at French courts and among aristocratic women,
the instrument declined and disappeared. It spread to England, where it
survives to the present, and Italy, where it experienced a certain vogue
before dying out in the seventeenth century. However, the last French
reference to the instrument is to a performance on it at Verdun in 1506.

The psaltery then reasserted itself in France. A play written by
Barthélemy Aneau in 1542 at Lyons mentions *psalterion*s, virginal, spinet,
and other instruments.[1] The psaltery of this period, however, was probably not the pig's head instrument of the fifteenth century, but a trapezoidal instrument placed horizontally while in use, more like those illustrated by Stimmer and Praetorius. A manuscript from about 1585
which illustrates and describes the *psalterion* says that there were "several types." The anonymous author does not mention hammering, but
comments that the ones which were played with two feathers in two
hands are "more imperfect," because only two strings could be played at
the same time, while those plucked with fingers could play three or four
at a time.[2] Possibly the "several types" could include one played with
hammers. The illustration in this manuscript depicts a trapezoidal instrument with a central rosette and nineteen strings, arranged individually rather than in courses. As the artist appears to have rendered the
illustrations of other instruments accurately, we can assume that the
French *psalterion* of this period resembled earlier psalteries more than
the dulcimers of contemporary England or Germany.[3]

Marin Mersenne, in his *Harmonie universelle* (1636), illustrates and describes the *psalterium*. His instrument is a trapezoidal box with a lid, with thirteen double courses tuned in octaves or in unison played with a single stick curved upward at its striking end. In contrast to the author of the manuscript described above, he does not mention plucking as a technique. He gives a tuning which starts with a bourdon course tuned in G, resting on a separate bridge, then continues with a course tuned in C, going upward diatonically to a G two octaves above the first bourdon course. Mersenne remarks that it "is very agreeable, because of the clear and silvery tones that its steel strings produce," and comments that it "has this privilege above the other instruments, that one learns to play it in the space of one or two hours." The instrument he describes was small enough to be carried in a pocket and was cheap enough to be bought for a crown. However, he mentioned that others "can be made of all sorts of sizes" and that some placed another bridge in the middle "to have two *psalterium*s to one" and used two hammers to play it.[4]

Apart from Mersenne's description, our knowledge of the use of the *psalterion* in France during the seventeenth century is very limited. Towards the end of the century, the instrument grew in popularity. The word *tympanon* or *timpanon*, originally a Greek word for a kind of drum, began to be used for the dulcimer, in addition to the word *psalterion*. Richelet in 1679 defined *timpanon* as a "kind of very harmonious musical instrument which comes from Germany, which is made of wood, mounted with brass strings which are played with a feather."[5] It would appear that Richelet's instrument was the folk psaltery, described in chapter 2, which survived into the late eighteenth century in Germany.

However, during the beginning of the eighteenth century, the *tympanon* was played with hammers, and it found acceptance in fashionable society. An engraving from the late seventeenth century shows two men playing a transverse flute and lute accompanied by a woman playing a *tympanum* resting on a table. She holds slender sticks with curved ends between her index and third fingers.[6] The Bibliothèque Nationale de France holds a manuscript, *Air's propres pour le tympanon*, containing a large number of pieces arranged for the instrument. It appears to date from the first quarter of the eighteenth century, with songs and airs from operas and ballets, and minuets and other dances, especially by Lully and composers such as Philidor le père, Delalande, Aine Philidor, Favier, and many others.[7] Such music was probably typical of that played by the genteel amateur *tympanon* player of eighteenth-century France.

Example 9.1: *Menuet en chaconne,* by Philidor le père [presumably Jean Danican Philidor, c.1620-1679], from *Air's propres pour le tympanon.* Rés. F. 845, p. 15, Bibliothèque Nationale de France.

Although surviving instruments and contemporary descriptions seem to indicate that the *tympanon* was mainly an instrument of wealthy amateurs, the Abbé Carbasus declared in 1739 "I do not deign to speak of some vulgar instruments . . . like the *tympanon,* the *psalterion,* the shawm, the *flute à l'oignon* [ocarina?], the jew's harp."[8] His comments provide our only evidence that in France the dulcimer was played by any social group besides the wealthy.

Indeed, most evidence suggests that the instrument was fully acceptable to proper society. For example, an anonymous oil painting, *Singerie,* in the National Gallery of Art, Washington, shows a dulcimer with such instruments as lute, harpsichord, oboe, and bassoon. Diderot, in a 1762 letter, described an informal social occasion where his acquaintance Schistre played his mandore and *timpanon,* giving us an idea of the kind of situation where one might have heard the instrument.[9] Stéphanie, comtesse de Genlis, already an accomplished harpist, spent some time secretly learning the dulcimer (after 1765), planning to surprise her friend by playing it while wearing an Alsatian costume; evidently the French must have in part regarded it as a German instrument.[10] Inventories of noblemen's estates confiscated by revolutionaries in 1789 included *tympanons.*[11]

Although *tympanon* became the standard French word for "dulcimer," the word *psalterion* for the instrument continued in use during the eighteenth century. Laborde described in 1780 a *psalterion* that was played by plucking,[12] which probably indicates the presence of the Italian and

Spanish *salterio*. However, Savary, in 1748, in a list of instruments made at Paris, mentioned both the *psalterion* and *timpanon* as stringed instruments played by striking with sticks.[13] The *Encyclopédie* of Diderot and d'Alembert (1751/1765) describes the *psalterion* as a dulcimer, as does Framery (1791), who calls it a type of *tympanon*.[14] It is not clear what characteristics distinguished a *tympanon* from a *psalterion*, however.

In France, dulcimers were made by harpsichord makers such as Jean Marie Galland, of Paris, whose 1755 inventory included two "folding" *tympanons* and two "square" *tympanons*.[15] French instruments surviving in museum collections display a high degree of craftsmanship, with gilt details and soundboards with painted decoration. Their outside dimensions vary, but the length of the front tends to be longer than on contemporary dulcimers of other traditions, ranging from about 97 to 130 cm (38¼ to 51¼ inches). The number of courses is variable, from eighteen to thirty-two, and the number of strings per course varies as well, from two to five, although three or four are most common.[16] The Bibliothèque Nationale manuscript mentioned above indicates a range from a^0 to $a\sharp^2$, completely chromatic upward from c^1. Contemporary descriptions of hammers include that of Savary, who calls them "long brass rods"; Diderot's *Encyclopédie,* which says that they are made of boxwood, cornel, ebony, etc., curved at the ends, sometimes with rings at the other end for the fingers to hold them; and Framery, who describes them as made of ivory or wood trimmed with leather.[17]

The *tympanon*, being associated with the nobility, did not survive the changes in society brought about by the French Revolution. Surviving instruments in the late nineteenth century were bought by collectors.[18] One was a Kiev-born musician, Sacha Votichenko (1888-1971), who performed in recitals on a 1705 *tympanon* in Europe and the United States, where he settled.[19] In addition to his fantasies and rhapsodies on Russian melodies, he played arrangements of pieces by Rameau and other eighteenth-century French music, making use of hidden spotlights which illuminated the instrument's gilt case.[20]

Notes

1. Frank Dobbins, *Music in Renaissance Lyons* (Oxford: Clarendon Press, 1992), 65.

2. Susi Jeans and Guy Oldham, "The Drawings of Musical Instruments in MS Add. 30342 at the British Museum," *The Galpin Society Journal* 13 (1960): 30.

3. MS Add. 30342, f. 145v., British Library.

4. Marin Mersenne, *Harmonie Universelle: The Books on Instruments*, trans. Roger E. Chapman (The Hague: M. Nijhoff, 1957), 224-226.

5. Pierre Richelet, *Dictionnaire françois* (Geneva: Jean Herman Widerhold, 1679), 2: 451.

6. Nicolas Bonnart, *Simphonie du Tympanum, du Luth, et de la Flûte*, in Catherine Massip, "Les personnages musiciens dans les gravures de mode parisiennes de la fin du XVIIe siècle: intérêt et limites d'un genre iconographique," *Imago Musicae* 4 (1987): fig. 14.

7. Rés. F. 845, Department de la Musique, Bibliothèque Nationale de France.

8. Abbé Carbasus, *Lettre de Monsieur l'abbé Carbasus sur la mode des instruments de musique* (Paris: Vve. Allouel, 1739), in Pierre Monichon, *Petite histoire de l'accordéon* (Paris: Entreprise générale de fabrication et de publicité, 1958), 30, in Hubert Boone, "Beknopte Bijdrage tot de Geschiedenis van het Hakkebord in de Lage Landen," *Volkskunde: Tijdschrift voor Nederlandsche Folklore* 77 (1976): 208.

9. Denis Diderot, *Lettres à Sophie Volland,* ed. A. Babelon (Paris: Gallimard, 1950), 1: 150.

10. Austin Dobson, *Four Frenchwomen* (London: H. Milford, 1923), 142.

11. Antonio Bruni, *Un inventaire sous La Terreur: état des instruments de musique* (Paris: Georges Chamerot, 1890), 125, 176.

12. Jean Benjamin de Laborde, *Essai sur la musique ancienne et moderne* (Paris: Ph.-D. Pierres, 1780), 1: 302-303.

13. Jacques Savary, *Dictionnaire universel de commerce* (Paris: La veuve Estienne, 1748), 239, in Edmond van der Straeten, *La musique aux Pays-Bas avant le XIXe siècle* (Brussels: G.-A. van Trigt, 1872), 397-398.

14. Denis Diderot and Jean Le Rond d'Alembert, *Encyclopédie*, 13: 537; Nicolas Etienne Framery, Pierre Louis Ganguené, and Jerome Joseph de Momigny, *Encyclopédie méthodique: musique* (1791 and 1818; reprint, New York: Da Capo Press, 1971), 2: 290.

15. Pierre J. Hardouin, "Harpsichord Making in Paris, Part 1," *The Galpin Society Journal*, 10 (1957): 26.

16. This is based on descriptions in *Collection de Bricqueville à Versailles: Anciens instruments de musique* (Paris: D. Jouaust, 1893), 13; G. Thibault, Jean Jenkins, and Josiane Bran-Ricci, *Eighteenth Century Musical Instruments: France*

---

194 — Chapter 9

and Britain (London: Victoria and Albert Museum, 1973), 112; Hubert Henkel, *Clavichorde*, Musikinstrumenten-Museum der Karl-Marx-Universität-Leipzig, Katalog, vol. 4 (Frankfurt am Main: Verlag Das Musikinstrument, 1981), 83; V. C. Mahillon, *Catalogue descriptif et analytique du Musée instrumental du Conservatoire royale du musique du Bruxelles*, 4: 324, 445; Curt Sachs, *Sammlung alter Musikinstrumente bei der Staatlichen Hochschule für Musik zu Berlin* (Berlin: Julius Bard, 1922), 38-39; C. C. Snoeck, *Catalogue de la collection d'instruments de musique anciens ou curieux* (Ghent: J. Vuylsteke, 1894), 21-24; Carl Claudius, *Carl Claudius' samling af gamle musikinstrumenter* (Copenhagen: Levin & Munksgaards Forlag, 1931), 45-46; William Skinner, *The Belle Skinner Collection of Old Musical Instruments: A Descriptive Catalogue* (n.p., 1933), 108-109; Gustave Chouquet, *Le Musée du Conservatoire national de musique: catalogue raisonné des instruments de cette collection* (Paris: Firmin-Didot Freres, 1875), 40-41; Metropolitan Museum of Art, *Catalogue of the Crosby Brown Collection of Musical Instruments of All Nations*, Hand-Book No. 13 (New York: The Metropolitan Museum of Art, 1904), 58; Musée de la musique, website, <http://servsim.cite-musique.fr/museedelam>.

17. Savary, *Dictionnaire universel*, 239, in Straeten, *La musique aux Pays-Bas*, 398; Diderot and d'Alembert, *Encyclopédie*, 2: 14; Framery, *Encyclopédie methodique*, 2: 290.

18. Adolphe de Pontécoulant, *Histoires et anecdotes, Musée instrumental du Conservatoire de musique* (Paris: Michel Lévy Frères, 1864), 49-56, relates a story concerning the purchase of an antique *tympanon*.

19. *The Arizona Republic*, 25 Oct. 1971.

20. *New York Times*, 9 May 1917, 11; 15 Feb. 1920, 23; 16 Aug. 1931, section 8, 7.

· *10* ·

The *Yangqin* Family

Today there are undoubtedly more dulcimers in China than in any other country. No other Western instrument was introduced as early and has penetrated the musics of different Asian cultures so thoroughly. Its point of entry was southern China, but it gradually spread to other parts of China, Korea, Mongolia, Tibet, Central Asia, and Southeast Asia. While the dulcimer declined and went extinct in much of Western Europe, it prospered in Asia.

History

China

The term for "dulcimer" is the word *yangqin* (in the pinyin system of transliteration, used in the People's Republic of China since 1959; *yang ch'in* is the form in the Wade-Giles system). Although folk etymologies have arisen to explain the meaning of the term and a new character for *yang* has obscured its origin, the word derives from *yang*, meaning "foreign" or "Western," and *qin*, the name of an ancient board-shaped instrument whose seven strings are plucked.[1] This "foreign *qin*," like dulcimers in other cultures, found its way into native tradition long ago. Names for the instrument in the past included *tong-si qin* or *tongxien qin* ("brass-stringed *qin*") and *tong qin* ("copper instrument"). Names descriptive of its shape include *hudieqin* ("butterfly *qin*") and *shan-mian qin* ("fan-shaped *qin*"). Other names include *daqin* and *qiaoqin*, derived from verbs for "to beat," and *yaoqin*, used by the Qaozhou people of southern China.[2]

There is no question that the *yangqin* at one time was most popular in southern China, as Moule wrote in 1908, and particularly in Guangdong, Guangxi, and Yunnan provinces, as Soulié remarked in 1911.[3] This region of China was the earliest to witness significant direct contact with Europeans, and the instrument's concentration there suggests how it entered the country. We can dismiss the putative Persian origin for the instrument which Moule and others have suggested[4] on that basis. Had the instrument entered from Persia, we would not only expect the *yangqin* to resemble the *santur* instead of the Western European dulcimer, we would expect to find it more concentrated in areas along the Silk Road. Other writers, in attempting to explain its transmission, have pointed to missionaries, including Matteo Ricci, who demonstrated a spinet before the Emperor about 1600, or to others, such as Pereira and Pedrini.[5] The problem with this explanation is that the *yangqin* was used by amateurs, not by court musicians, and not, in any case, in Beijing. An introduction by Europeans arriving by sea is now generally accepted by Chinese scholars.[6] Remaining questions about its origin, then, concern the nationality of the ship's crews which entered Guangzhou (Canton) and the date of the introduction of the instrument.

Portuguese vessels began to trade in southern China as early as 1515, but the dulcimer was never established in that country. We must thus consider the ships from Holland or England, where the instrument was played during the seventeenth century, when ships from those countries first appeared in southern China, as the likeliest sources. If we used the flexible, bamboo hammer held between thumb and forefinger, as used in China, as a piece of evidence, we might favor English ships, since English hammers traditionally were made of flexible material and held in the same manner, while Dutch players seem to have followed the Continental practice of holding them between first and second fingers. The hammer is rather slender evidence, however, since the original transmission of the instrument was probably by an individual, rather than by a group of people, and individual players might follow practices exceptional to tradition.

A European must have played a dulcimer while in China for the instrument to have been adopted so readily. Had it appeared in a cargo of goods, it probably would not have particularly impressed the Chinese except as a curiosity. However, the Chinese regarded Westerners with trepidation, and, as Josephine Ng comments, traders "who held dealings with foreigners were regarded as the lowest of this grade."[7] The earliest

British convoy to enter China was commanded by John Weddell, who in 1637 was with two ships for six months near Macao.[8] Other British ships attempted to trade in 1658 and 1664, but it was not until 1699 that ships were allowed at Canton, remaining for the entire monsoon season to complete their lading.[9] By reasoning that a resident European, from a country where the dulcimer was in use, must have been responsible for the introduction of the instrument to southern China, we might assume that the introduction took place at the earliest about 1700.[10]

This date, however, is contradicted by a reference that Zhang Xuexha, a Chinese envoy to the Ryukyu Islands in 1663, used a *yaoqin* to accompany singing.[11] It also seems unlikely that a person of such high social status would be associated with an instrument recently adopted from foreigners. Ng, on the other hand, suggests that prostitutes, who were among the earliest documented players, may have learned the instrument from sailors.[12] Sailors, however, were drawn from the lowest social classes. Although the wandering minstrels and "dulcimer men" of eighteenth-century England and Holland belonged to the poorest class, amateur players might be better described as middle class. Ship's officers would thus be our prime suspects. However, further evidence will be necessary to support or modify this speculation concerning the dulcimer's introduction into China.

The *yangqin* was certainly in use during the eighteenth century. A Korean source says that the instrument was introduced to that country during the early part of the reign of King Yong-jo (1725-1775) from the China of Emperor Shih Tsung's reign (1723-1736).[13] Another source ascribes its introduction to Hong Dai-yong (1731-1783).[14] Since the *yangqin* has never been part of the Chinese court instrumentarium, the introduction of the instrument to Korean court music is rather curious.

Ng cites a 1751 reference describing an instrument with brass strings played with beaters, used in Macao.[15] Xiang Zuhua, in describing the history of the *yangqin* in Sichuan, mentions a story of a military officer, exiled to that remote province in the Qianlong period of the Qing dynasty (c.1770), who brought the instrument with him.[16] An American, John Francis Davis, described in 1836 a Chinese instrument as a "sort of harmonicon of wires, touched with two slender strips of bamboo."[17] In 1879, Alexandre Kraus wrote that the dulcimer, called *taakan*, was part of the orchestra of the Chinese theater in Japan.[18]

Ng describes several genres of Cantonese music which used the *yangqin* during the nineteenth and early twentieth centuries. "Courtesans," or female entertainers regarded as prostitutes, were prominent players. One well-known courtesan was Yang Fuling, active in the period from 1796 to 1820, who played the *pipa* (lute) and *yangqin*. These women, sometimes blind, learned to play the instrument as girls of seventeen or eighteen in order to prepare themselves for their profession. They entertained patrons at private houses and restaurants.[19] Other *yangqin* players were blind men, hired to perform by poorer families at festive occasions such as birthdays. Soulié mentions that blind men in tea houses accompanied their singing with the instrument.[20] Ng cites a book, *Ch'ing pai lei ch'ao*, which describes the use of the *yangqin* in several types of music: "Wood-Wind Music," of Tingzhou, Fujian province, with a nose flute; "The Eight Harmonious Joyful Ensemble," during Hsien Feng's era, in which eight musicians played in a circle, one hand playing one instrument, the other playing the instrument next to him; "Flowery Singing," dramatic music in Hangzhou involving *pipa*, *yangqin*, drum, and clappers; and "Blind-Girl Singing and Playing," blind girls who accompanied their songs with *yangqin* at private celebrations.[21]

The *yangqin* had entered other forms of regional Chinese music by the early twentieth century. Each of these had their own particular repertoire and techniques. In Chaozhou, in eastern Guangdong province, it was used in opera and popular folk music.[22] Use of the *yangqin* in Sichuan seems to have begun in the late eighteenth century. During the next century, a theatrical style called *Dagu Yangqin* developed, in which singers accompanying themselves on *yangqin*, *sanxian*, *huqin*, *erhu*, and *huaigu*, performed. *Yangqin* players in Chengdu, the provincial capital, also entertained in the private houses of the wealthy before the 1911 Revolution and in tea houses afterwards.[23] "Silk and Bamboo" music of Jiangnan was popular in Shanghai and medium and small cities in Jiangsu and Zhejiang provinces. Players of this style were amateurs of different classes who formed clubs, some of which had roots stretching back for hundreds of years. The size of the clubs varied, and they performed in ancestral halls, in Confucian temples, in tea houses, or restaurants. Such organizations grew rapidly in Shanghai after the 1911 Revolution.[24]

During the twentieth century the use of the *yangqin* expanded into other areas of China. The instrument accompanied singers in *Shandong Qinshu* (narrative singing of Shandong) and *Yulin Xiaoqu* (narrative singing of Yulin).[25] A Manchurian school of playing, with special techniques, developed in the 1920s.[26] Many new musical developments followed the 1949 Revolution. Over forty conservatories of music were established, and musicians and instrument builders experimented with new designs. In 1954 the first *yangqin* using a tempered tuning was built at the conservatory in Tientsin, following study of various regional *yangqin* and a Soviet instrument, and in 1956 a factory began to produce it.[27] In 1959, Yang Jingming, a player in the Central Broadcasting Orchestra, developed a system in which the strings rested on small rollers set into metal troughs, allowing for quick tuning. These soon won general favor.[28]

The conservatories taught both Western and Chinese instruments to students who enrolled either at the ages of twelve to sixteen or seventeen to twenty-two. Graduates joined professional troupes or became teachers in the conservatories. Mao's China regarded musicians as soldiers in the political struggle, and they performed in both professional and amateur troupes. *Yangqin* players, though mostly playing accompaniment, developed more and more solo pieces of great virtuosity. According to Edward Ho, during the Great Proletarian Cultural Revolution (1966-1979) one of the few ways middle-school graduates might avoid manual labor in the rural areas was to perform the "Model Plays" in propaganda troupes. Thus, starting in the early 1970s, the number of children learning musical instruments began to rise sharply. By the late 1970s, conservatories, which had in previous years admitted annually only a handful of *yangqin* students, now witnessed extreme competition among students wishing to gain entry. The result was a rise in the level of playing, with students displaying much virtuosity.[29]

Today, older musicians continue to play the traditional *yangqin* tea houses in Shanghai and Guangzhou, but the new, conservatory-developed style has become dominant. The new *yangqin* is well adapted to the Western tempered scale and, while it retains its Chinese character, it suits the contemporary desire for Western influence. Professional players learn to read Western notation but also to improvise. One of the leading *yangqin* teachers in China, Xiang Zuhua, expresses the post-Mao attitude when he writes "as long as we have our feet firmly planted in the foundation of our nation, take life as our source, and seek the new things and different individuality of our age, we can make our artistic works reach the level of nationalization, modernization, and individuality."[30] Today, the growth of the *yangqin* in China is the most dynamic development of any dulcimer tradition in the world. In 1991, Chinese factories had difficulty keeping pace with increased demand for traditional instruments, including the *yangqin*.[31]

Although some of the first *yangqin* teachers in the conservatories had learned the instrument through their families or through "Silk and Bamboo" clubs, a pedagogical tradition had developed by 1900. Some teachers taught aspiring "courtesans." A system of notation, known as *kung-ch'ih*, aided instruction, and the *kung-ch'ih* characters were printed on sheets attached to the soundboard next to the bridges. By 1920, Qiu Hechou, of Taishan, Guangdong province, had published a book, *Yuediao qin-zue xin-bian*, systematically describing hammering techniques, such as moderate strikes, slow strikes, and fast tremolos, using *kung-ch'ih* characters.[32] Later a system using Western numerals was introduced. Today, teachers in conservatories also use Western notation in teaching. Players in different regions have developed special striking techniques which constitute an important element in defining regional styles.[33]

Korea

Korean musicians adapted the Chinese dulcimer to the music of the court during the eighteenth century, as mentioned above. The Korean name is *yanggum* (*yangkeum*), a direct borrowing from Chinese, but in the past it was also called *kurach'olsa gum* ("European wire zither").[34] Its form, with seven treble courses of four brass strings each and seven bass courses of the same number, probably has changed little since its introduction to Korea. It is unique among dulcimers in that it is played with a single stick, although players in North Korea use two.[35] The earliest musical score of a *si-jo*, or lyric poem, is called *kurach'olsa gum* ("dulcimer"), written by Lee Kyu-geong during the reign of King Sun-jo (1801-1834).[36] The *yanggum* is used in the traditional genre of *Yongsan Hoe-sang* and to accompany classical lyric songs.[37] In South Korea, the *yanggum* remains as an instrument used in court music, but in North Korea, makers and musicians have modified its design and technique. Before World War II, courtesans (*kisaeng*) played the instrument (see illustration 8).

Xinjiang, Uzbekistan, and Tajikistan

The *chang* of Xinjiang province of China, Uzbekistan, and Tajikistan belongs to the *yangqin* family. The term denoted a harp in wide use in Central Asia before 1800. Its vertically placed tuning pins and fixed, fifth-interval treble bridge clearly indicate that it is not derived from the *santur*. Because of the geographic distribution of the instrument, the *yangqin* is the likely source. The penetration into Islamic art music traditions by a Chinese instrument of European origin thus is rather astonishing.

During writes that the *chang*, used in the *muqam*, or classical music, of the Uighurs of Xinjiang is a relatively recent introduction from China.[38] This introduction, however, must have taken place during the nineteenth century, and, as During remarks, musicians in the Kashgar region must have used it, since the spread of the *chang* to Tajikistan and Uzbekistan must have followed trade routes to those territories recently acquired by the Russians.

At the end of the nineteenth century, according to Lykoshin, a musician appeared in Tashkent with a heretofore unknown instrument. After the musician was invited to a party, a local musician bought his instrument and learned to play it.[39] Subsequently, the instrument became part of the Uzbek stringed instrument ensemble, especially in Tashkent and the Ferghana Valley. In line with other developments in the officially sponsored music of the Soviet republics, the *chang* was "reconstructed" into four sizes and incorporated in 1938 into a state orchestra which played arrangements of Western pieces.[40]

Mongolia

Mongolians, in Mongolia and in the Buryat Autonomous Region of Russia, as well as Inner Mongolia, appear to have incorporated the *yangqin* into professional ensembles during the early twentieth century. It is called *yochin*, *yochen*, or *yenchin*. The *yochin* is played both solo and in ensemble with other instruments as *sudrag* (a plucked lute), *yihor* (a large fiddle), and *telhengreg* (rattle).[41]

Tibet

The *yangqin* had entered Tibet by the middle of the nineteenth century, since H. A. Jäschke, who resided in Tibet for several years beginning in 1857, mentioned that the *yan-ljin* was a musical instrument used in Tsang, a province in central Tibet.[42] Geoffrey Samuel reports that some exiled Tibetan musicians prefer the name *gyümang* to the Chinese term. He describes the instrument being used in professional, secular ensembles with *damnyen* (large lute), small lute, and small and large fiddles. It is identical to older Chinese instruments, with seven or eight treble and bass courses each, and one instrument seen by Samuel was made in Tibet.[43]

Vietnam

Trân Van Khê wrote in 1962 that, while certain musicians in northern Vietnam played the dulcimer as a solo instrument, the number was small, and south Vietnamese regarded it as a Chinese instrument. It was called *dàn ban nguyêt* ("half-moon-shaped instrument"), *da câm* ("struck zither"), *duong câm* ("overseas zither"), or *tam thâp luc*, ("zither with 36 strings"). It had not entered Vietnamese ensembles.[44] Phong T. Nguyen, however, writing in 1998, remarked that the *dan tam thâp luc* was used in the *chèo* ensemble, a form of musical theater originating in the north.[45]

Thailand

Thai musicians began to use the *yangqin*, called *khim* in Thai, during the reign of Rama VI (1910-1926).[46] The instrument was undoubtedly adopted from Chinese living in Bangkok. The Thai heptatonic scale (seven equal parts to an octave) has been applied to the older, fourteen-course *yangqin* with success, although it appears that Thais still to some degree regard it as a foreign instrument. Nevertheless, Thai musicians play classical music on it, and the *khim* is one of the Thai instruments taught at the Music Department of Payap University.[47] Terry Miller writes that the instrument is the most popular stringed instrument in Thai music, used primarily for solo playing, mainly by women, but sometimes added to the *khrüang sai* and *mahori* ensembles. *Khim* players commonly learn from notation.[48] A number of Thai immigrants in the United States play the instrument.

Laos

In 1991 Terry Miller witnessed the use of a *khim* with ten treble and ten bass courses in a performance of a *khap thum* ensemble, a vocal genre, in Luang Prabang.[49]

Cambodia

The Cambodian name is *khimm*. The name of the instrument may indicate that it was introduced from Thailand, but Sam-Ang Sam remarks that its use, which had begun by 1900 and possibly thirty years before that, resulted from "Chinese opera." Cambodians adapted a Chinese theatrical form, which they called *basakk*. The two prominent instruments in the ensemble are the *khimm tauch* and *khimm thomm*, the former with a higher range than the latter. Sometimes the *khimm* is used in the *mahori*, or traditional string ensemble.[50] Cambodian music, like that of Thailand, uses a heptatonic scale.

Burma

Judith Becker reports that the Burmese name for the *yangqin* is *don-min*, and that it is a "popular instrument for traditional music or for newly composed tunes."[51] Resident Chinese may have introduced it, or perhaps it entered from Thailand.

Japan

Although the dulcimer was played in the Chinese theater in Japan in the nineteenth century, the instrument was never adapted for use in traditional Japanese music. On the other hand, in recent years, a number of Japanese have become interested in various forms of dulcimers, including the cimbalom, *yangqin*, the chromatic *Hackbrett*, and the dulcimer of the American revival. Playing styles are probably influenced by recordings of foreign players and by their visits to the country. By the late 1970s, Japanese bluegrass fans were learning of the American instrument.[52] Because of the nature of this interest, Japanese dulcimer playing should probably be grouped with recent Western European, North American, and Australian playing as a kind of transnational school with little basis in local tradition.

Overseas Chinese

The spread of the *yangqin* to southeast Asia resulted from Cantonese migration to those countries during the nineteenth and early twentieth

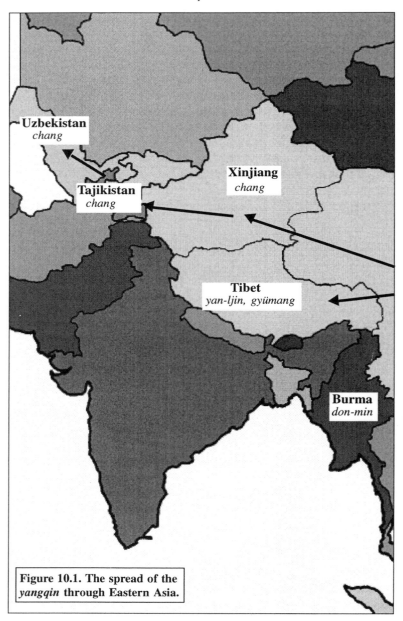

Figure 10.1. The spread of the *yangqin* through Eastern Asia.

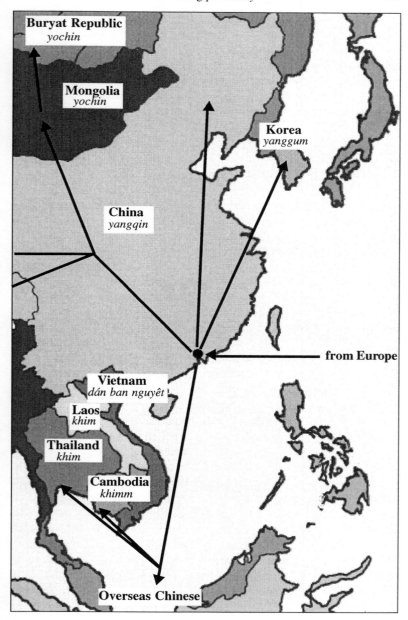

Buryat Republic
yochin

Mongolia
yochin

Korea
yanggum

China
yangqin

from Europe

Vietnam
dán ban nguyêt

Laos
khim

Thailand
khim

Cambodia
khimm

Overseas Chinese

centuries. In this regard, the presence of the instrument in Malaysia, Singapore, Indonesia, the Philippines, and elsewhere is associated with Chinese settlement. Similarly, Chinese immigrants to the United States and Canada have played the *yangqin* since the nineteenth century. Clubs of Chinese musicians, which use the instrument, exist in San Francisco and New York and elsewhere. In recent years, graduates of Chinese conservatories have introduced the new *yangqin* to American audiences.

Design

Chinese and Other Asian Forms

The oldest dulcimer traditions in Asia are those of China and Korea. The spread of the instrument into other Asian countries is relatively recent and, except for modifications in tuning, the forms of the instruments used in those traditions remain those of early twentieth-century China. Therefore we will restrict the discussion of the design of Asian instruments to those of China, Korea, and Central Asia.

As noted above, Chinese terms sometimes describe the *yangqin* by its shape—"fan-shaped," that is, with the outer edge of the pin blocks being convex, forming a half-round shape (see figure 10.2), and "butterfly-shaped," or pin blocks whose outside outline is convex. Other older ones are also trapezoidal, with pin blocks having straight edges. Moule wrote in 1908 that "no Chinese instrument probably is more varied in form, size, and arrangement than the *Yang Ch'in*."[53] Nevertheless, in comparison to dulcimers of most other traditions, the design of *yangqins* of the nineteenth and early twentieth centuries is relatively uniform.

Most older instruments are fan-shaped, with removable lids. The outline is usually scalloped, with the outer edges of the pin blocks following a convex curve. Every surface except the soundboard is usually finished with black or brown lacquer. Delicately carved bone or ivory rosettes fit on top of two round sound holes. There are two bridges, often with ivory or bone caps, the left one dividing the treble courses into fifths and the other one for the bass courses. It is likely that older instruments used brass wire, although by the late nineteenth century steel wire was in use. The treble bridge carries seven or eight courses of two, three, or four (usually three) strings each, while the bass bridge supports the same number of courses as the treble bridge, except that the lowest two or three courses may have only one or two strings each. Seven courses

Figure 10.2: *Yangqin* **manufactured at Guangzhou (Canton), about 1930. Author's collection.**

per bridge was standard, but by the 1880s, eight courses per bridge were in evidence.[54] Instruments range in size from about 71 to 78 cm (28 to 30¾ inches) at the lower length, about 46 cm (18 inches) at the upper length, about 26 cm (10¼ inches) in width, and about 5 cm (2 inches) in height. Hammers, called *quqin,* are made of bamboo, about 23 cm (9 inches) in length, with heads formed from the same piece of bamboo. They are held between thumb and forefinger, as in British and American traditions.

Factories in Beijing, Shanghai, and Guangzhou manufacture the *yangqin,* with the adjustable rollers for tuning, in five or six models. Since the 1960s these models have gradually replaced the traditional *yangqin* in the People's Republic. Instruments have two, three, or four bridges, the one with four bridges being the most popular. The smallest model has the traditional two bridges, each with ten courses, providing a range from e^0 to d^3. The medium model has another bridge between the traditional treble and bass bridges, with a chromatic range from d^0 to $d^{3.}$ The largest model has four main bridges, the left bridge dividing twelve courses of four strings each into fifths, the two middle bridges carrying nine courses of three each, and the bridge on the far right carrying ten courses of three each. Except for those resting on the bridge on the left, the courses are playable only on the left side of each bridge. The range is fully chromatic from G^1 to e^3, except for the bottom $G\sharp^1$ and $A\sharp^1$. The tuning of each course is a fifth lower than the neighboring course on the bridge to its left.[55]

Korea

The *yanggum*, because of its use in conservative court music, may retain the dimensions and design of the *yangqin* of the early eighteenth century. The dimensions of a nineteenth-century instrument, in the Stearns Collection of Musical Instruments, University of Michigan, are 64 and 44 cm (25¼ and 17¼ inches) long, 16.6 cm (6½ inches) wide, and 3.1 cm (1¼ inches) high.[56] Those of a South Korean instrument made in 1973 are 77 cm (30¼ inches) long, 26 cm (10¼ inches) wide, and 10 cm (4 inches) high,[57] the longer length of the newer one probably reflecting the use of steel, rather than brass strings. The *yanggum* is trapezoidal, with two bridges, the treble bridge dividing seven courses into fifths, the bass bridge carrying seven courses, each course having four brass or steel strings. The range is approximately from $d\sharp^0$ to $g\sharp^2$, tuned to the traditional Korean scale.[58] North Korean instruments today have a wider range, from c^0 to g^3.[59] In that country, two hammers are used to play an instrument which has twenty-five or twenty-six courses and a chromatic tuning, and some models are equipped with a damper pedal.[60]

Uzbekistan and Tajikistan

Sources for the description of the design of the *chang* are limited. Beliaev in 1933 described one with seven treble courses (divided by bridges into a 3:2 ratio) and seven bass courses, with a total number of forty strings.[61] Vertkov illustrates one with eleven treble courses, with three strings per course, and an uncertain number of bass courses, resting on connected bridges. He gives the dimensions as 85 cm (33½ inches) and 63 cm (25 inches) long, 30 cm (12 inches) wide, and 5 cm (2 inches) high.[62] Vyzgo shows one with chessman bridges and triple courses.[63] During writes that in Xinjiang the *chang* has fourteen courses of four strings each,[64] just like the *yangqin* of the nineteenth century.

Notes

1. Josephine Ng, "The Chinese Dulcimer: Yang-ch'in" (master's thesis, University of Washington, 1978), 4; Xiang Zuhua, "An Examination of the Origin of the Yangqin," *Chinese Music* 4, no. 1: 15.

2. Ng, "Chinese Dulcimer," 4-5; Xiang, "Examination," 15.

3. A. C. Moule, *A List of the Musical and Other Sound-Producing Instruments of the Chinese* (1908; reprint, Buren: Frits Knuf Pubs., 1989), 118; Georges Soulié, *La musique en Chine* (Paris: Ernest Leroux, 1911), 53.

4. Moule, *List*, 118.

5. Xiang, "Examination," 17-18; Louis Laloy, *La musique chinoise*, Les musiciens célebrés (Paris: Henri Laurens, n.d.), 78; Maurice Courant, "Chine et Corée," in *Encyclopédie de la musique et dictionnaire du Conservatoire*, ed. Albert Lavignac, 1: 180.

6. Xiang, "Examination," 15, 17.

7. Ng, "Chinese Dulcimer," 18.

8. Hosea Ballou Morse, *The Chronicles of the East India Company Trading to China, 1635-1834*, vol. 1 (Taipei: Ch'eng-wen Pub. Co., 1966), 14-30.

9. Morse, *Chronicles*, 33, 89, 147.

10. This date, however, conflicts with Xiang's statement that musicians of Guangdong province during the late Ming (1368-1644) and early Qing (1616-1911) dynasties "usually carried a *yangqin*" (Xiang, "Examination," 18). He does not cite a source for this statement, which may have been written long after the fact.

11. Xiang Zuhua, "The Tradition and Development of the Music of the Chinese Dulcimer—Yangqin," *Chinese Music* 15 (Dec. 1992): 65. Ng, "Chinese Dulcimer," 5, writes that *yaoqin* was the term used by the Chaozhou people of southern China.

12. Ng, "Chinese Dulcimer," 18-19.

13. Chang Sa-hun, "On the Interpretation of the Dulcimer Score and the Problems of Phyeong-Si-jo," *Asea Yon'gu* 1 (Dec. 1958): 126.

14. *Korean Music* ([Seoul]: Ministry of Culture and Information, n.d.), 67.

15. *Historia de Macau*, in Ng, "Chinese Dulcimer," 16-17.

16. Xiang Zuhua, "The Development and Schools of Performing Arts of the Chinese Yangqin," *Chinese Music* 5, no. 3: 51.

17. John Francis Davis, *The Chinese: A General Description of the Empire of China and Its Inhabitants* (New York: Harper & Brothers, 1836), 2: 249.

18. Alexandre Kraus fils, *La musique au Japon* (Florence: L'Arte della Stampa, 1879), 78.

19. Ng, "Chinese Dulcimer," 24-28.

20. Soulié, *Musique en Chine*, 53.

21. Ng, "Chinese Dulcimer," 23, 32-33.

22. Ng, "Chinese Dulcimer," 34-35.

23. Xiang, "Development and Schools," 51.

24. Xiang, "Development and Schools," 53; Lee Yuan-yuan, "Instrumental Music in the Chinese Society," *Chinese Music* 4 (Dec. 1981): 69.

25. Xiang, "Development and Schools," 74.

26. Edward Ho and Xu Pingxin, "The Manchurian Yangqin," *Chinese Music* 18 (1995): 51.

27. Ng, "Chinese Dulcimer," 136-137.

28. Mao Chi-tseng, "Reform of Traditional Musical Instruments," *Chinese Literature*, 1965, 111-112.

29. Edward Ho, "Yangqin and Its Music in China in the Period of 1949-1979," *Chinese Music* 20 (1997): 17-20, 24-31.

30. Xiang, "Tradition and Development," 68.

31. "Traditional Instruments Industry Needs Preferential Treatment," Xinhua General Overseas News Service, May 27, 1991, item no. 0527066.

32. Ng, "Chinese Dulcimer," 24, 28-29, 62-64, 150; Xiang, "Development," 52.

33. Edward Ho and Xu Pingxin, "The Manchurian Yangqin II," *Chinese Music* 19 (1996): 9-11.

34. *Survey of Korean Arts: Traditional Music* (Seoul: National Academy of Arts, 1973), 37.

35. Chang Sa-hun, "On the Interpretation," 126.

36. *Korean Music*, 67.

37. Keith Howard, *Korean Musical Instruments* (Hong Kong: Oxford University Press, 1995), 41.

38. Jean During and Sabine Trebinjac, *Introduction au muqam ouïgour*, Indiana University Research Institute for Inner Asian Studies: Papers on Inner Asia, no. 17 (Bloomington: Indiana University Research Institute for Inner Asian Studies, 1991), 39.

39. Tamara S. Vyzgo, *Muzykal'nye instrumenty Srednei Azii: Istoricheskie ocherki* (Moscow: Izdatel'stvo "Muzyka," 1980), 165, quoting N. S. Lykoshin, *Pol zhizni v Turkestane ocherki byta tuzemnago naseleniya* (Petrograd: Sklad T-va Berezovskii, 1916), 354-355.

40. Tamara Vyzgo and A. Petrosyants, *Uzbekskii orkestr narodnykh instrumentov* (Tashkent: Gosudarstvennoe Izdatel'stvo Khudozhestvennoi Literatury UzSSR, 1962), 30-31; Nezovibatko, *Ukrains'ki tsymbaly*, 8-9.

41. *Mongol népzene*, Hungaroton LPX 18013-14. One of the *yochin* players recorded was Dasdeleg, aged 71 in 1967, which indicates that the introduction of the instrument could not have been recent. K. Vertkov, G. Blagodatov, E. Yazovitskaya, *Atlas muzykal'nykh instrumentov narodov SSSR* (Moscow: Gosudarstvennoe Muzykal'noe Izdatel'stvo, 1963), 144.

42. H. A. Jäschke, *Tibetan-English Dictionary* (1881; reprint, Richmond, Surrey: Curzon, 1998), 506.

43. Geoffrey Samuel, "Songs of Lhasa," *Ethnomusicology* 20 (Sept. 1976): 415-417.

44. Trân Vân Khê, *La musique vietnamienne traditionelle*, Annales du Musée Guimet, Bibliothéque d'études, vol. 66 (Paris: Presses Universitaires de France, 1962), 143-144.

45. Phong T. Nguyen, "Vietnam," in *Southeast Asia*, edited by Terry E. Miller and Sean Williams, The Garland Encyclopedia of World Music, vol. 4, 490 (New York: Garland Publishing, 1998).

46. Jarernchai Chonpairot, conversation with author, 1975.

47. Payap University, website, <http://www.payap.ac.th/academic/music/music.htm>.

48. Terry E. Miller, "Thailand," in *Southeast Asia*, Garland Encyclopedia of World Music, vol. 4, 239-240, 282.

49. Terry E. Miller, "Laos," in *Southeast Asia*, Garland Encyclopedia of World Music, vol. 4, 350.

50. Sam-Ang Sam, notes to *Traditional Music of Cambodia*, (Middletown, Conn.: Center for the Study of Khmer Culture, 1987), 8; Sam-Ang Sam, "Cambodia," in *Southeast Asia*, Garland Encyclopedia of World Music, vol. 4, 169. The "dulcimer," a "harmonicon," and ceramic drum accompanied a performance of dancers at the royal court, described in "Campuchia Royal Theatricals: The King's Dancers, and His Harem," *Appleton's Journal*, 11, no. 270 (23 May 1874): 662. This may have been a stringed instrument of another sort, but a postcard dated 1902 shows a young *khimm* player in a group of Cambodian musicians.

51. *The New Grove Dictionary of Music and Musicians*, s.v. "Burma."

52. Akiko Yoshida, "Hammer Dulcimer Introduction," *Bluegrass and Old Time Package* [in Japanese], undated article, c.1979.

53. Moule, *List*, 119.

54. J. A. Van Aalst, *Chinese Music* (1884; reprint, New York: Paragon Book Reprint Corp., 1964), 68.

55. Lee Yuan-yuan, "Yangqin," *Chinese Music* 4, no. 1: 10-11; Ng, "Chinese Dulcimer," 49; Xiang, "Tradition and Development," 67-68.

56. Albert A. Stanley, *Catalogue of the Stearns Collection of Musical Instruments* (Ann Arbor: University of Michigan, 1918), 173.

57. Roy W. Gibbons, *The CCFCS Collection of Musical Instruments*, vol. 3, *Chordophones*, Canadian Centre for Folk Culture Studies, Paper no. 45 ([Ottawa]: National Museums of Canada, 1984), 34-35.

58. *Korean Music*, 67; *Survey of Korean Arts: Traditional Music*, 37; Andre Eckhardt, *Musik Lied Tanz in Korea* (Bonn: H. Bouvier, 1968), 55.

59. Howard, *Korean Musical Instruments*, 41.

60. "Introduction: Korean Musical Instrument," website, <http://www.korea-np.co.jp/pk/037th_issue/98040808.htm>.

61. Viktor Beliaev, *Muzykal'nye instrumenty Uzbekistana* (Moscow: Muzgiz, 1933), n.p.

62. Vertkov, *Atlas*, 22, pl. 601.

63. Vyzgo, *Uzbekskii orkestr narodnykh instrumentov*, 30.

64. During, *Introduction*, 39.

The Dulcimer in the British Isles

Like the traditions in Switzerland and Austria, the dulcimer has enjoyed a continuous presence in England since the fifteenth century, when it entered from France. Unlike the Alpine *Hackbrett*, however, the instrument has led a more obscure existence. Nevertheless, we can identify two somewhat distinct traditions associated with the dulcimer in England and, to a lesser extent, in Ireland: use by amateurs of middle-class or higher social status, and use by low-status professionals or beggars. Both traditions began in the fifteenth century. The first had its origins in the use of the instrument by women of high social status and relates to the later use of the *tympanon* in France, while the second originated in the use of the instrument by minstrels and relates to the use of the *Hackbrett* in Germany. As the fashion for the dulcimer declined during the early sixteenth century, as evidenced by its rarity in contemporary texts, it left the halls of the nobility and worked its way to the houses of rural gentry and residents of smaller cities.

History

The earliest English literary references to the instrument are mentioned in chapter 3. Based on these and on contemporary French, Flemish, and Spanish literary and pictorial references, we can assume a decline after about 1530. This was probably also true in England, yet it somehow survived there into the next century. Although Barrett's secondary definition of the word as "a woman that plaieth on doulcimer" suggests the stringed instrument, perhaps by the middle of the century the word started to also denote a woodwind instrument. John Maplet, in his *Greene Forest* (1567), writes that from the elder shrub people made "a kind of Symphonie whiche the common sort call a Pipe: the learned and more civil kinde of men name it a Dulcimer."[1] It seems likely during this period that the word began to be used for the fipple flute earlier called "doucet" or "dulceuse" or may also have been equivalent to the French *douçaine*, Spanish *dulzaina*, and Italian *dolzaina*, a double-reed instrument.[2]

Nevertheless, by the end of the century, the word certainly again meant the dulcimer that is the subject of this book. Thomas Thomas's Latin-English dictionary (1587) defines *pecten* as "a sticke wherewith they play on dulcimers" and *plectrum* as a "quill, bowe, or such like thing to play withall vpon the strings of a harp, rebeck, or dulcimer."[3] Subsequent literary allusions to the instrument indicate that the gentry remained familiar with the dulcimer, whatever it was, and held it in some regard. John Rhodes, in a poem "A Song in Commendation of Diuers Instruments of Musicke," written in 1588, mentions the dulcimer, along with over twenty other contemporary instruments (including the psaltery).[4] Although Shakespeare failed to mention it, his contemporaries Gabriel Harvey and Thomas Rogers did. Harvey describes "O the sugar candy of the delicate bagpipe there: and o the licorise of the diuine dulcimers there" in *Pierces Supererogation* (1593).[5] Rogers, in *Celestiall Elegies* (1598), writes "in mutuall loue her bodie and her soule, My dulcimers shall make no more delight."[6] In *The Teares or Lamentations of a Sorrowfull Soule* (1613), Sir William Leighton rhapsodizes "Praise him upon the claricoales, the Lute and Simfonie: With dulsemers and regalls, sweete Sittrons melody."[7] Similarly, Thomas Dekker, in "Paul His Temple Triumphant" (1632), lists it with stylish instruments: "And heard others strike harpe, Cimball, Clarion, Shaulme, Viall, harpsichord, Flute, Clarigall, The dulcimer, psaltry & Virginall."[8] Such references, while useful in informing us that Englishmen knew the dulcimer, unfortunately provide little evidence either for its description or for the circumstances in which musicians played the instrument.

During this period it appears that English speakers occasionally used the term "dulcimer" to denote a harpsichord. Randle Cotgrave's *Dictionarie of the French and English Tongues* (1611) translates *harpechorde* as "Arpsichord or Harpsicord; a Dulcimer."[9] Undoubtedly the "Consort of 22 Violins, with Flutes, Recorders and Dulcimores" mentioned in Edward Howard's comedy *The Six Days Adventure* (1671) refers to a keyboard continuo instrument.[10]

Descriptions of the more humble dulcimer began to appear with the restoration of the monarchy in 1660, when society began to accept frivolity. The instrument appeared with regularity in London places of entertainment. The Dutch traveler William Schellinks went to a music hall in Southwark in 1661 which was "divided into alcoves, and people go there to dine and listen to the music of an organ, dulcimers, bass violins, etc."[11] After attending a play, the diarist Samuel Pepys and his wife went to a puppet show in Covent Garden in 1662, and he wrote "here, among the fiddlers, I first saw a dulcimere played on with sticks knocking of the strings, and is very pretty." A month later, Pepys and some friends went to a tavern to drink beer, and, so he entered in his diary, "in the next room one was playing very finely of the dulcimer, which, well played, I like well."[12] After hearing it the first time only a month before, Pepys now felt comfortable to criticize it. Perhaps the relaxed moral restrictions of the Restoration created conditions for a renewed fashion for the instrument, at least among professional musicians of popular music. Covent Garden was full of music halls, taverns, and houses of prostitution; the dulcimer was clearly associated with places of ill repute. In Thomas Duffett's play *The Mock-Tempest* (1675), the character Stefania, a "baud," remarks "there are more of our Dulcimers thump'd ev'ry Night in Covent-Garden, then there are Ghittars scrap'd in a Week, in Madrid."[13] Kettlewell quotes a researcher, describing Sadler's Wells about 1683: "Mr. Sadler sold the water from the well on the strength of its medicinal qualities; he provided entertainment—music room, dancers, tumblers, ropewalkers, etc., and musicians, and each evening Mr. Pearson played the dulcimer from five till eight."[14]

At a slightly later period, we have evidence of the dulcimer being used in domestic settings. A study of probate inventories made between 1661 and 1714 of the citizens of Lincoln, for example, revealed that dulcimers appeared in two of them. This number contrasts with ten virginals, eight violins, five viols, three harpsichords, three citterns, two bass viols, organs, and spinets each, and one reference each to a lute, sackbut, triangle, and viol bandero.[15] While hardly a match for the popular virginals, viols, or even citterns, all popular instruments for amateur music making, the dulcimer clearly held a certain degree of popularity in that city. Indeed the instrument did not always invite derision, as in contemporary Germany. In 1710, Joseph Addison's metaphoric essay on different musical instruments called the dulcimer "a certain Romantick instrument," evoking "shady Woods, flowry Meadows, and purling Steams, Larks and Nightingals, with all the Beauties of Spring, and the Pleasures of a Country Life. This Instrument hath a fine melancholy Sweetness in it, and goes very well with the Flute."[16]

Perhaps the choice of a dulcimer for domestic, amateur use, rather than the far more common "pair" of virginals or spinet, was partly economic: it was cheaper and did not normally require the services of a music master. Thus, once a person learned how to tune it, he or she could play tunes by ear. In Colley Cibber's 1707 comedy *The Double Gallant*, the parsimonious character Sir Squabble Splithair, "Knight, and Citizen of London," declares the care in which he has given to raising his adult sister:

> I still keep her Fortune carefully in my own hands, for fear she shou'd idly throw it away upon some beggarly young Fellow: Not but I give her a good Gentlewomanly Education; for I have taught her several Tunes, my self, upon the *Dulcimer*; and to save the charge of a Singing Master, I let her go once a Week, with her Maid, in the Upper Gallery, to learn the Songs out of the *Opera*.[17]

Cibber may have introduced the reference to the dulcimer in order to make the audience laugh, but, in any case, the instrument's social situation seems plausible. Two years later, in Cibber's play *The Rival Fools*, he mentioned it in association with its other social tradition. When one knight asks another about a consort of music to woo a lady, the character responds jokingly, "O! a curious Noise as ever you saw, Sir—Indeed, I wou'd have had the lame Woman with the Dulcimer, and old Gratears the Blind Cymbal [hurdy-gurdy], but they sent me word they were just hir'd to Play Country Dances at my Lord Mayors."[18] As absurd as the playwright intended this statement to be, it is significant as the earliest reference to English street musicians using the instrument.

The dulcimer was indeed used for dancing during the first part of the eighteenth century, as Cibber implies. In James Miller's *The Mother-In-Law* (1734), a servant suggests to a lady that at "Christmas-time you'll have a Ball in his Worship's great free-stone Hall, accompany'd with a fine Concert [consort] of a Dulcimer, Bass-Viol, and two Pair of Bagpipes."[19] Here it appears that although the character speaking these lines was lower-class and the statement was intended for comic effect, the instrumentation may have been realistic.

The instrument also appeared occasionally on stage. Horace Walpole described a vaudeville-like show, or "oratory," that took place at Castle Tavern in 1751. This featured musicians imitating farts on the French horn, bagpipes on the flute, another playing the violin and trumpet simultaneously, and an actor mimicking well-known actors and singers, as well as less elevated instruments like the jew's harp, salt box, and an "admired" dulcimer.[20]

The genteel domestic use of the dulcimer continued in eighteenth-century England. An anonymous and somewhat primitive painting from about 1740, formerly in the collections of the Nassau County Museums, *A Musical Gathering,* shows an anomalous group of men posed with instruments: two with violins, the others with oboe, trumpet, and dulcimer.[21] Since each person is identified and some names are rare, it is probable that rural Essex, rather than Virginia, as Phyllis Braff tentatively proposed, was the home of the gentlemen.[22] The dulcimer player, "I. Elliston, Esqr," must have been a landed proprietor, as "Esquire" indicates. His instrument rests on a short table, and he holds, between his index and middle fingers, long, slender hammers with hooked ends and thicker handles.

David Kettlewell's research shows that dulcimers were commercially available in eighteenth-century England. Frederick Hintz, guitar maker to the Queen and royal family, advertised in 1763 that he also made "Mandolins, Viols de l'Amour, Viols de Gamba, Dulcimers, Solitaires [probably *salterios*], Lutes, Harps, Cymbals, the Trumpet Marine, and the Æolian Harp."[23] Clearly his customers, while not all royal, had fashionable taste. "Dulcemores" were among a large variety of instruments and musical merchandise available from Robert Bremner, a London dealer, about 1765.[24]

In much the same vein as in Cibber's *The Double Gallant,* Sir Tunbelly Clumsey, a character in Richard Brinsley Sheridan's 1777 play *A Trip to Scarborough,* had a daughter who was cloistered in a "lonely old house, which nobody comes near. She never goes abroad, nor sees company at home; to prevent all misfortunes, she has her breeding within doors; the parson teaches her to play upon the dulcimer; the clerk to sing, her nurse to dress, and her father to dance."[25] Here it appears that the dulcimer represented merely a typical domestic instrument for a girl's education, however, rather than Cibber's object associated with genteel parsimony.

The Anglo-Irish gentry followed English fashion, and an eighteenth-century reference also indicates its use there by that class. In 1782-1783,

Arthur O'Neill visited Parson Phibbs, of Arlaharty, near Ballymote, County Sligo, who, he wrote, "loved music: he encouraged it and he himself played well on that wired instrument called the dulcimer."[26] Many of these eighteenth-century references, both fictional and factual, demonstrate that the dulcimer was associated during this period with gentility, if not nobility: London knights and their sisters or daughters, a landed gentleman in Essex, and an Anglo-Irish vicar all played the instrument, and makers of fashionable instruments sold it. Other references, however, indicate that society regarded it as a lower-class instrument. Although we need more evidence, it would appear that the fashion for the instrument had partly shifted between 1660 and 1700 from minstrels, or lower-class professional musicians who plied their trade in taverns, to amateurs of higher status.

In the eighteenth century, Italian opera and musical forms such as the sonata were taught by music masters, both English and foreign, to those prosperous enough to afford lessons on the harpsichord, violin, and flute. Since people learned the dulcimer informally, as the references above show, from perhaps a brother or a local parson, they would have played song airs and popular dance tunes, such as minuets and country dances, rather than music specially composed for the instrument by professional, trained musicians. This popular association of the dulcimer with "native" music, rather than the more prestigious and fashionable Italian music, is illustrated by a scene in George Colman's 1762 play *The Musical Lady*. The character Mask praises Sophy's singing in Italian, who hopes "it is a little better than the horrid English ballad singing." Mask exclaims:

English ballad-singing! O the ridiculous idea! To hear a huge fellow with a rough horrible voice roaring out, *O the roast beef of old England*! Or a pale faced chit of a girl, when some country neighbour asks her in company, "Pray Ma'am, could you favour us with *Go Rose*!" "No Sir, not that, but another if you please;" and then begins screaming, *If love's a sweet passion*, squalling to the antient British melody of the bagpipe, the Welch harp, and the dulcimer.[27]

The late eighteenth and early nineteenth centuries were the age of the itinerant "dulcimer man." Colman's reference clearly shows a popular association with instruments used by other lower-class musicians. This is further supported by a scene in John O'Keeffe's play *Tony Lumpkin in Town*, from 1780, which satirizes the same clash in musical tastes between upper and lower classes found in Colman's play. The servant Tim talks at a party to a music master who has composed "two oratorios, ten serenatas; three sets of overtures, concertos for Signior Florentini's violoncello, songs for the Capricci of Palermo, and solos for Madam Sirmen's violin, grand ballets for Signor Georgettini." Tim responds "Damn you Signioras and your Signiors . . . can you play, Water Parted, or Lango-lee?" and invites him to a party with a hurdy-gurdy player and a dancing bear, and adds "Squire will have the dulcimer man."[28] Further evidence of the use of the dulcimer by itinerant musicians in this period is provided by an engraving from 1784, which shows a dulcimer player and a fiddler entertaining people outside their house (see illustration 18), puppets being mounted to sticks on the upper corners of the dulcimer.[29]

Maria Edgeworth, an Anglo-Irish writer, includes a "dulcimer man" as a character in her story "The Good French Governess" (1801), set in a fictional town, Leicester Fields, in England. A blind man, with an "extremely thin and hungry" boy, plays the dulcimer in the street. Herbert, the story's eight-year-old hero, has no money to give him, but offers two buns to the boy. In gratitude, the "dulcimer man" comes later to play in the back parlor to accompany the dancing of the girls of the house. Later the story includes a narrative which describes how a mob had confronted the musician with the accusation that the "dulcimer boy" had stolen the buns and then broke his dulcimer. The boy helps him repair it with wire purchased from an ironmonger.[30] Edgeworth's sympathetic portrayal illustrates the poverty of the street musician of her age.

Sir John Graham Dalyell (1775-1851) remarked that, "though very rarely seen," the dulcimer, "always one of the humblest character, remained as an amusement of the populace." He mentioned having heard a young man playing "favourite airs of the day" on the streets of London. Thus he was impressed by two young Londoners named Nelson, who in 1842 performed on two dulcimers, one playing the melody and the other an accompaniment, at public concerts in Edinburgh. They played "melodies of all kinds, and even whole symphonies," with "leathern muffled rods" striking four strings per course. Earlier they had toured through parts of the British Empire.[31]

Henry Mayhew, in his pioneering study, *London Labour and the London Poor* (1851), discussed street musicians active at that period. He considered them as part of a larger class of street performers, which included puppeteers, jugglers, blackface minstrels, exhibitors of trained animals, artists, dancers, singers, and proprietors of street games. Mayhew described street musicians as consisting of street bands, both English and German, and "players of the guitar, harp, bagpipes, hurdy-gurdy, dulcimer, musical bells, cornet, tom-tom, etc."[32] Charles Knight, in 1860, reiterated that the dulcimer was "now used by street musicians, to whom it is confined."[33]

Some of the itinerant "dulcimer men" included Gypsies, whose association with the instrument, we should note, was related to Gypsy use of its relatives in Eastern Europe only in the sense that they took up an instrument already locally popular with itinerant, lower-class musicians and not in the sense that their wanderings in the Middle Ages spread it. Watkin Ingram (born about 1800, died 1863), a Welsh Gypsy, and his sons Lewis and Robert played the instrument and traveled in England.[34] In 1908 a woman recalled that the dulcimer was among the instruments used by Gypsies hired to play for farmers' dances in Northamptonshire years earlier.[35] The English-born evangelist Gypsy Smith (1860-1947) remarked of his people that they "love to dance in the lanes to the music of the harp, the dulcimer, and violin."[36]

Although such "professional" street performances caught the public's eye, the dulcimer was also played at dances in the early nineteenth century by amateurs in what we today would call a semi-professional context. In 1874, local historians in Sheffield reminisced about a shoe-polish manufacturer, William Walmsley, active in the 1820s, who played the dulcimer at night and "was in request at parties and balls along with blind Jonathan, the fiddler and wait."[37] Perhaps Walmsley's use of the instrument in both amateur and professional situations anticipated later practice.

It appears that the dulcimer's popularity increased during the second half of the nineteenth century. In parts of England and Scotland many individuals (mostly men) played the instrument. A decline did not set in until after World War I. Although most instruments were made by the players themselves, commercial firms met the increased demand for the instrument by producing them. Between 1885 and 1920 several people wrote tutors for the dulcimer. The increased interest in the instrument contrasts sharply with the situation in Germany, where the dulcimer largely died out, and differs from that in parts of the United States, which experienced a similar boom some thirty years earlier.

Kettlewell describes a series of over three dozen letters to the magazine *Design and Work: A Home and Shop Companion*, appearing between 1876 and 1879, which discussed various aspects of dulcimer construction. Charles Gray, in a reply to these queries, wrote an article, "The Dulcimer: How to Make It," in *Amateur Work Illustrated*, in 1883.[38] Then in 1885, Ihlee and Sankey, of London, printed a tuning diagram, which called it an "exceedingly Popular Instrument."[39] Charles Roylance, who wrote and published tutors for various instruments, followed in 1886 (see figure 11.1) with *How to Learn the Dulcimer: Without a Master* (London: C. Roylance, [1886]), and *How to Play the Chromatic-Dulcimer* (1890), the latter for an instrument whose bridge divided the courses into half-steps. Paul Hasluck's *Violins and Other Stringed Instruments: How to Make Them* (1906) included a chapter on making dulcimers.[40] Further tutors for the dulcimer were written between about 1890 and 1920 by A. Dobigny, Havelock Mason, Nicola Podesta, and Walter Webber.[41]

The publication of articles on making dulcimers indicate that many individuals made them at home for their own use. Some commercial firms also produced them, however. Kettlewell writes that the names John Grey & Sons and Douglas & Co. occur most often on dulcimers of

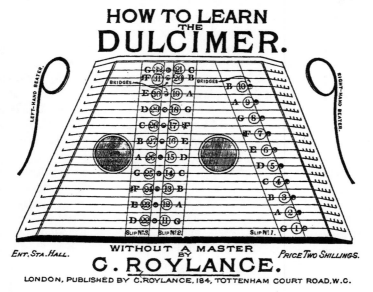

Figure 11.1: Title page of Charles Roylance's *How to Learn the Dulcimer: Without a Master* (London: C. Roylance, [1886]).

this era.[42] Perhaps more typical, though, were players who made them and sold them on occasion, like Will Lawrence, of Comberton, Cambridgeshire, who, as Russell Wortley reports, might sell the instrument he was playing in public and build himself another one during the winter.[43]

The tradition of street playing evident in the eighteenth and early nineteenth centuries continued in urban areas during this period of popularity. Jeffrey Pulver, for example, recalled someone who, about 1898, played "a rather shabby dulcimer in the suburban trains of the Great Eastern Railway."[44] In early twentieth-century Norwich, Dolly Gray pushed his dulcimer around on a cart, and Billy Bennington played his dulcimer with a banjo player in front of theaters during the early 1920s.[45]

In rural areas, the dulcimer appeared as an accompaniment for dancing, with touring puppet shows and circuses, and as entertainment in pubs. Some years before 1880, Mr. Howard, of Halesworth, Suffolk, won a dulcimer contest against a circus clown by covering the instrument with a handkerchief and playing it backwards.[46] Billy Cooper (1883-1964), of Hingham, Norfolk, recalled two men who toured around Norfolk, one operating marionettes and the other playing a dulcimer.[47] T. L. Southgate wrote in 1904 that the instrument "was common in private houses, and was often heard at fairs, dancing on the village green, and in our quiet streets."[48] Around the turn of the century, Will Lawrence traveled on a bicycle with his dulcimer to annual, week-long village feasts, playing in pubs and in the dancing booths at the fairs.[49] Charlie Philpott (born about 1877), played with his father James at servants' balls and "concert parties" in Suffolk.[50] At least one soldier carried his dulcimer to the front in World War I; in France an American volunteer ambulance driver heard three men playing banjo, violin, and dulcimer, amidst bombs.[51]

David Kettlewell's investigation of the dulcimer in the British Isles during the early 1970s led him to identify six separate traditions. He found three in England: London, East Anglia (Norfolk, Suffolk, and Cambridgeshire), and Birmingham; one in Scotland; and two in Ireland, Ulster and around Dublin. He found evidence, in the form of old instruments, that the dulcimer had been played elsewhere, but living players seemed to fall into those categories.

Regional Traditions

England

In East Anglia, some individuals continued to play the dulcimer in public after World War II. Reg Porter, of Ipswich, Suffolk, led a "dulcimer band." Lennie Pearce, of Woodbridge, Suffolk, who had played drums and sometimes dulcimer for dances with a group consisting of himself and a violin, piano, and banjo-mandolin, appeared with his dulcimer on a television show.[52] Billy Cooper, who first began playing on his father's dulcimer in 1893, was playing regularly at a pub in Hingham, Norfolk in the early 1960s. A recording of his playing, with fiddler Walter Bulwer and others, with whom he had played regularly in the 1920s, was made by Bob Davenport and Reg Hall in 1965 and issued in the 1970s, proved influential to a new generation of listeners in discovering traditional English dance music.[53] Billy Bennington, of Barford, Norfolk, who learned to play the dulcimer from Cooper, was still active into the 1980s, and a recording featured his playing.[54]

In their use of split-cane hammers with the ends tapered, pulled back around, and wrapped with wool and the design and tuning of their dulcimers, Kettlewell remarks that the East Anglia players' tradition corresponded to the descriptions of hammers and tunings given by most of the authors of the tutors and articles on construction mentioned above.[55] Billy Cooper also plucked his instrument with his bare fingers, but this technique was exceptional.[56] The recorded repertoire consists of older dance tunes, including polkas, waltzes, step-dance tunes (hornpipes), two-steps, marches, schottisches, and others.

Kettlewell based his identification of a London tradition, which, as noted above, was familiar on the city's streets by the middle of the nineteenth century, mostly on the playing of a single London player, Ted Carr. He had learned the dulcimer from his father, but discarded the hammers in favor of plectra. His repertoire consisted of breakdowns and recent popular songs, arranged in medleys and played for listening rather than dancing.[57]

A number of dulcimer players lived in the Birmingham area at mid-twentieth century. Like the London players Kettlewell interviewed or heard about, they used plectra of various kinds to play their instruments, although at least one began to play using the usual cane hammers with the ends looped around. They played older dance tunes and marches, popular songs, hymns, and light classical tunes. A commercial firm there manufactured dulcimers sometime in the nineteenth century, but the players also made them themselves. Buskers in that city appeared with the dulcimer as well.[58]

Scotland

Although the dulcimer gained substantial popularity in Scotland, especially in the area around Glasgow, during the early twentieth century, its early history there is obscure. Dalyell's two examples were both of Englishmen, and since he had an interest in the instrument, it would seem that if there had been any dulcimer playing in Scotland during the first half of the nineteenth century, he would have mentioned it. Thus we are left with the conclusion that the fashion for the instrument in evidence about 1900 was either related to the general upswing in English interest during the late nineteenth century or, perhaps more likely, to the industrial migration of Irish, who mainly came from Ulster, to the Glasgow region during that period.

Jimmy Cooper, who learned to play the dulcimer in 1918 or 1919 at Coatbridge, near Glasgow, recalled that "most of the dulcimer players that I found were nearly all of Irish descent."[59] The Murphy brothers, who played dulcimer and melodeon at that time in Cambuslang, a coal-mining village, must have had forebears who came from Ireland.[60] The best-known player of his era, William McNally (1870-1954), of Glasgow, claimed that the instrument had been played in his family for several generations. His Irish parents, who may have been from County Wexford, worked as itinerant entertainers, traveling through the British Isles with circuses. McNally's mother taught him the dulcimer by the age of ten. He played on the boats that in the summer went up the Clyde and made a command performance for King Edward VII in 1907, advertising himself as the "Royal Scottish Dulcimer King" and the "Paderewski of the Dulcimer."[61] McNally also recorded two sides for Regal-Zonophone and one side for Beltona in the early 1930s.[62] His records indicate that he plucked as well as hammered the strings.[63] Unlike most of the dulcimer players in the region who played at dances, McNally, a professional, preferred to entertain in theatres and at private parties.

Although players were most numerous in Glasgow and in neighboring Lanarkshire and Ayrshire, one could hear the dulcimer during the early twentieth century in other parts of Scotland. The father of Peter Henderson lived in Inverness and, about 1910, used to play with a fid- dler.[64] I also met a person in the 1980s who recalled dulcimer players who appeared at fairs around Aberdeen in the early 1930s. Although rare or unknown elsewhere in Scotland, the dulcimer was popular enough around Glasgow around 1910 or 1920 for contests to be held.[65] Playing continues in that city, where a dulcimer club perpetuates local tradi- tion.[66]

Musicians played melodies on the dulcimer, but more typically they "vamped" an accompaniment to the button accordion, or "melodeon." Jimmy Cooper recalled that about 1920 all the local dances were accom- panied by melodeon and dulcimer.[67] The melodeon player Daniel Wyper (born 1872), of Hamilton, brother of the recording star Peter Wyper, frequently was accompanied at dances by a dulcimer player named Jimmy Greenhorn.[68] The typical style was recorded about 1931 by Alec Bissett on melodeon, with accompaniment on dulcimer and piano by Bob Smith and J. B. Andrews, and in 1934 in Boston by emigrant Scots Donald Cummings on accordion and Eddy Holmes on dulcimer.[69] The recorded repertoire from this period includes Scottish songs and dance tunes ar- ranged in medleys for listening, as well as more dance-oriented medleys of waltzes, hornpipes, highland marches, eightsome reels, and Irish jigs. Jimmy Cooper in his later years played more modern popular tunes.[70]

Ireland

The earliest reference to the dulcimer in Ireland, noted in chapter 6, dates from 1738: Archibald Williamson, the "Irish Jew," advertised "the Jews music" at the Sign of the Fiddle and Dulcimer in Copper Alley, Dublin, and again in 1744 at a tavern by the same name in Dame Street.[71] Williamson's name, however, is certainly Scottish in origin; perhaps he came from Ulster. Seán Donnelly suggests that the dulcimer may have been "particularly associated with Jewish musicians at the time," and that his "nickname was a tribute to his skill" on the instrument. Cer- tainly a German-born Jew, Isaac Isaacs, who moved to Dublin in 1767, played Irish tunes at taverns and theatres. However, the ranks of profes- sional dulcimer players also included Irishmen. Donnelly mentions John Dowling, who lived in Dublin in 1761 and 1768, and one O'Kelly, who succeeded Isaacs in 1791 as the dulcimer player at Loughlin's Long Room in Rathfarnham.[72] While these Dublin dulcimer players all were professionals, in all probability the instrument also found a place as a domestic instrument among the Anglo-Irish gentry, such as with Parson Phibbs. The Anglo-Irish author Maria Edgeworth's 1801 story, although set in England, could indicate the existence of itinerant buskers in Ireland by that time. In any event, the instrument seems to have been used to accompany dancing in the early nineteenth century, as Charles J. Lever's 1843 novel *Jack Hinton, the Guardsman* includes a description of a gentleman's ball in Dublin taking place thirty years earlier: "mothers screamed, fathers swore, footmen laughed, and high above all came the measured tramp of the dancers overhead, while fiddles, French-horns, and dulcimers, scraped and blew their worst."[73] The music which accompanied the dancing at the wedding party at a Munster country gentleman's house in Gerald Griffin's 1829 novel *The Collegians* consisted of bagpipe, violin, and dulcimer.[74]

As the style of instruments used in Ulster that David Kettlewell discovered was different from those used in Scotland or England, it seems likely that the tradition there goes back well into the nineteenth century or earlier. Robert Douglass left Londonderry in 1830 and brought a dulcimer with him to Buctouche, New Brunswick.[75] Perhaps the relative concentration of the instrument in Ulster has to do with the large proportion of its population which is descended from Scots who came in the seventeenth and eighteenth centuries. The Ulster Scots were economically better off than the native Gaelic-speaking population and may have been more inclined to follow middle-class English or Anglo-Irish fashion.

In the early twentieth century, however, the dulcimer was played further south in Ireland. James Stephens, writing in 1916, mentioned that a friend "had promised to present me with a musical instrument called a dulcimer," and, when the author left the country, "with this dulcimer I shall be able to tap out our Irish melodies when I am abroad, and transport myself to Ireland for a few minutes, or a few bars."[76] As in contemporary London, Birmingham, and Glasgow, pedestrians in Dublin about 1920 could hear buskers playing the dulcimer. Andy Dowling, who later learned to play the instrument, heard John Barton, a Dublin street musician, play at fairs in Rathdowney about that time.[76] Perhaps Barton or others like him introduced the instrument to James Joyce, who, in his *Ulysses* (1922), includes a character who "carries a silverstringed inlaid dulcimer and a longstemmed bamboo jacob's pipe" as well as a "girl playing one of these instruments what do you call them: dulcimers."[78] From the references of both Joyce and Stephens, we can infer that, while the dulcimer was not exactly an instrument of great familiarity, it was hardly unknown to Dubliners of the early twentieth century.

Kettlewell provides evidence that the dulcimer seems to have been fairly well known in County Antrim, as he discovered a number of people in the 1970s who were said to have them and play them on occasion.[79] John Rea (1915-1983), an Ulsterman who appeared on record in the 1970s, played local dance tunes, such as jigs, reels, "highlands," and hornpipes, using hammers made of metal rods. There were players in County Tipperary and possibly in Donegal and Wexford earlier in the century as well.[80] Andy Dowling, of the Dublin region, played both popular songs and dance tunes on his instrument.[81] Today, however, the dulcimer is a forgotten instrument in Ireland, with little evidence of a revival.

Revival in England

In the 1970s a renewed interest in the instrument began. David Kettlewell, who first became interested after seeing one in an antique store, wrote a book, organized programs, performed in various places, and wrote a dissertation on the instrument, which provides much of the basis of my discussion. He produced a record of Jimmy Cooper, which led to his appearance at folk festivals. During this period there was a renewed interest in English traditional music, and the newly available recordings of the East Anglian players and others made the dulcimer familiar to a wider audience. An American singer, Jim Couza, who had discovered the instrument through American Folk Revival sources, toured around "folk clubs" in the late 1970s and 1980s with his dulcimer. Other players appeared in similar contexts.

Enough interest in the instrument existed by 1993 to form an organization, the Nonsuch Dulcimer Club. Like most dulcimer clubs in the United States, the organization took in players of both the mountain and the hammered dulcimers. The organization's activities were associated in part with folk festivals.

British and Irish Dulcimers Overseas and in America

The dulcimer clearly entered the American colonies by the early eighteenth century mainly from England. As this developed into an identifiably different tradition, however, its story appears elsewhere. Emigration from Britain to the United States, Canada, Australia, and New Zealand during the nineteenth and early twentieth centuries did include dulcimer players. The grandfather of Dave Cloughley, of New Zealand, emigrated to that country from Scotland, and his playing was passed down to his grandson, who in the 1970s appeared at folk festivals in New Zealand. Other players went to Australia. In the 1970s, influence from the American and British folk revivals introduced the instrument to that country, and Australians began to adopt it. Gillian Alcock of Canberra was one of the main forces in promoting the instrument there; she makes dulcimers of different varieties and holds instructional workshops. There was enough interest there for players to form the Australian Dulcimer Organization in 1999.

Nineteenth-century dulcimer players who emigrated from England to the United States assimilated rapidly into local musical life. Henry Clegg, born in 1825 in Bamber Bridge, Lancashire, became a Mormon convert and in 1855 emigrated to Utah, where he regularly played for dances. He described in his diary playing the dulcimer on the ship that brought him and other converts across the ocean: "at 5, 4 couples were married but if they were as sick as I was they would not have thought of marriage. I went and got my Dulcimer and played "The Girl —." It cured me of sea sickness. Lots that were sick in bed got up and danced."[82]

Thomas P. Mann (1833-1909) emigrated from England to Adel, Iowa, bringing his dulcimer with him. He taught his son Thomas B. to play, and in 1937 Sidney Robertson Cowell recorded the son's playing for the Library of Congress. Although the younger Thomas considered his playing to be American, his playing of "Nancy's Fancy," a tune not in traditional circulation in America, indicates that he retained some of his father's repertoire.[83] Perhaps other nineteenth-century English immigrants brought over tunes in a similar manner. Certainly some made them. Robert Humphries, a resident of Wilkinsburg, Pennsylvania, made a rather large one, with fourteen treble and thirteen bass courses, each triple-strung, in 1866.[84] Roland W. Everton (born 1857) and William Frost (born 1860), of Troy, New York, both immigrants from England, received a U.S. Patent (no. 625,663) in 1899. Their dulcimer resembled the type found in Birmingham, with twelve treble courses of five strings each and twelve bass courses of four each and one of three and single-piece bridges and hinged pin-block covers. Frost had immigrated in 1887 and Everton even more recently, both settling in a city whose heavy industry resembled that of Birmingham.[85]

A depression following World War I led many to emigrate from the Glasgow region. Charles Gordon left his coal-mining village in 1922 for Canada with a newly made dulcimer. Bill MacArthur came to Detroit, where he accompanied Patrick Allan's melodeon playing at annual Robert Burns Day parties for other immigrant Scots.[86] Eddy Holmes accompanied Donald Cumming's melodeon playing on dulcimer on fourteen sides recorded in Boston for Decca in 1934. Dominic McNally (1909-1974), son of William McNally, went to New York, where he played and sang on Morton Downey's radio show and recorded two sides in 1932 for Columbia's Irish series.[87] Peter Henderson left Inverness for Chicago in 1921 and within a few years made a dulcimer from memory. His wife Johan learned it and they played dance tunes and hymns at home, one playing the melody and the other vamping.

Some Irish players settled in the United States. The Philadelphia group "Four Provinces Orchestra" used a "piano-dulcimer" with violin, flute, banjo, and piano, at a recording session in 1926.[88] Paddy Needham, whose instrument bore the inscription "dulcimore" on its front side, played regularly at Irish affairs in Pittsburgh in the late 1930s and early 1940s.[89]

Design

A history of the design and structure of the dulcimer in the British Isles must begin with illustrations and other indirect sources. The earliest surviving instrument that David Kettlewell could find, in the York Museum, dates from the eighteenth century;[90] most other older instruments seem to date from the late nineteenth century. Nevertheless, we can identify certain characteristics which distinguish English dulcimers from other European varieties and at the same time link them to early American designs.

One of these links may be a lid. An illumination in Henry VIII's psalter, from the first half of the sixteenth century, shows a trapezoidal dulcimer resting on a table. Although details about the arrangement of its strings are not meaningful, it does have a flat lid with painted decoration on its interior.[91] A nineteenth-century example with a lid is in the collections of the Liverpool Museum (accession number 1969.201.2).[92] Kettlewell discusses a Derbyshire dulcimer built into a rectangular case with a lid.[93] Sally Whytehead owns an old dulcimer built into a case with a lid. While rare in surviving instruments, the use of a lid is rare or nonexistent in other traditions, except Appenzell and China, where older instruments almost always had them, and the United States, where it was not uncommon on nineteenth-century dulcimers.

A copy of John Playford's *Select Musicall Ayres* (1653) in the Glasgow University Library contains a contemporary tuning diagram with the inscription "The names of the strings of the English Dulcimur." It shows a tuning for an instrument with ten treble courses and ten bass courses, with an extra low bass course, and another for one with eight treble and eight bass courses, also with a single extra low bass course. The first is tuned so that the lowest four-course section over the treble bridge gives a D-major scale. The bass courses are tuned a fifth lower than the treble courses immediately above, and they contain the chromatic intervals above C. The eight-course tuning starts with a C scale in the lowest four-course treble group, with the bass courses a sixth lower than the treble course immediately above.[94]

The anonymous painting *A Musical Gathering*, from about 1740, depicts a trapezoidal dulcimer resting on a short table with cabriole legs (see illustration 17). Its soundboard is decorated with painted designs and two gilt rosettes. Single, long bridges support the strings, whose number is uncertain. The player holds, between his first and second fingers, hammers consisting of straight rods with their striking ends hooked backwards, with thick handles.[95] Although gilt rosettes are unknown on later English or American dulcimers, the stenciled decoration using bronze leaf, common on nineteenth-century American instruments, may hark back to such eighteenth-century dulcimers.[96]

Kettlewell's study and the tutors and articles on construction from the late nineteenth and early twentieth century remain the best sources on traditional British dulcimer design. These show that in East Anglia and elsewhere in southern England the most common design was one that used a G-major scale for the lowest four treble courses. The tuning given by Roylance in 1886 was diatonic, with the bass courses an octave below the treble course immediately above.[97] During this period of popularity, it appears that tuning innovations allowing a chromatic scale spread, and subsequent tutors and articles show the modified tuning.[98] Since these dulcimers had individual bridges, the placement of certain ones could be altered in order to permit other intervals, besides the fifth, to provide a chromatic range (see appendix 1).

The dulcimers tuned so that the first treble course is g^1 on the right and d^2 on the left have a lower length of 31 inches (79 cm) or 32 inches (81 cm), an upper length of 14 to 19 inches (36 to 48 cm), a width of 12 to 16 inches (30 to 41 cm), and a height of 2 or 3 inches (5 or 8 cm). An instrument made by Will Lawrence, of Comberton, Cambridgeshire, owned by Russell Wortley, has a lower length of 41 inches (104.1 cm) and was intended to be tuned a fourth lower.[99] Most have four strings per treble and bass course, although some have five. Ten (sometimes eleven) treble courses and the same number of bass courses are standard. Kettlewell writes that brass wire was preferred for the bass courses, but that steel was often used because of the difficulty in obtaining brass. Two round sound holes, sometimes with a turned ring as a border, are common, although some have four. Little decoration appears on these dulcimers. Hammers are made of split cane, the ends soaked in hot water, looped back and tied with twine or wool.[100]

The two London players described by Kettlewell both used a diatonic tuning, rather than the diatonic-chromatic tuning favored in East Anglia. One instrument had eleven treble courses of four strings each and the same number of bass courses with three strings each, while the other had twelve treble and ten bass courses, both with four strings per course.[101]

Distinguishing characteristics of dulcimers in the Birmingham tradition, according to Kettlewell's research, include a diatonic tuning, single-piece bridges, and a longer length than East Anglian dulcimers. The length results from the first four-course group being in D major; Kettlewell gives examples of such instruments ranging from 40 to 44½ inches (101.6 to 113 cm) long. The examples he cites had eleven to fourteen treble courses of four strings each and ten or eleven bass courses of three strings each. The tuning of Bill Fell's dulcimer, starting at $g\sharp^1$ ǀ $c\sharp^1$ on the treble bridge, but with most bass courses tuned a ninth lower than the treble course immediately above, is similar to the most common traditional American tuning. Most players exclusively pluck their dulcimers with plectra.[102]

Scottish dulcimers are more disparate in their design. Peter Henderson, making them in Chicago during the 1920s from the memory of his Inverness father's instrument, followed the southern English pattern fairly closely, with ten treble and ten bass courses, each with four strings, but used single-piece bridges and a diatonic tuning. He used split-cane hammers with looped ends. A Glasgow-area dulcimer in the author's collection, made about 1922, measures 37¼ inches (94.6 cm) and 23¼ inches (59 cm) in length and 19¼ inches (48.9 cm) in width and has thirteen treble and fourteen bass courses, each triple, which lie on long, single-piece bridges. The relatively obtuse angles of the pin blocks mean that the intended tuning was probably partly chromatic. Such a tuning was used by James Rodger, formerly of Glasgow.[103] Other Scottish instruments, in the collection of the University of Edinburgh, measure 37½ inches (95.3 cm) and 40½ inches (102.9 cm) at their lower lengths and have nineteen and twenty-six triple courses respectively.[104]

Jimmy Cooper's main instrument had nine treble and eight bass courses, each with four strings, resting on individual bridges. He tuned it diatonically, with the first four-course treble bridge scale in D major, but with an initial $g\sharp^1$ | $c\sharp^1$ course, and with bass courses tuned an octave below the treble course immediately above.[105] He considered the addition of the c-sharp course his own "alteration." William McNally used diatonic dulcimers with the initial scales of C and G, with bass courses an octave below the neighboring treble courses, but changed the location of the bridge under the highest two courses, to create an interval of a diminished fifth.[106]

Despite all these individual variations, it appears that we can identify some characteristics typical of Scottish, especially Glasgow-area, dulcimers. Bridges are mostly single-piece rather than individual. Three strings per course are most common. Different sizes existed, but it appears that the initial four-course treble group in D major is most typical. A full investigation of the tradition, however, has yet to appear.

Ulster dulcimers, according to Kettlewell's study, are remarkable in their unusually small number of courses. Those he examined had from six to nine treble and from five to eight bass courses, mostly with three strings per course. John Rea tuned his diatonically, the lowest treble course being e^2 | a^1, with the bass courses a fifth below the treble course immediately above. He made his hammers of thick steel wire.[107] The dulcimer that Robert Douglass brought from Londonderry to New Brunswick in 1830 is 38 inches (96.5 cm) and 19 inches (48.5 cm) long, 18 inches (45.5 cm) wide, and 4 inches (10.3 cm) high and has eight treble courses and nine bass courses, each with three strings. Hitch-pins indicate that there was originally one more treble course, although its single-piece bridge indicates not, or perhaps a bass course on the lower left side. The black instrument's sound holes are covered with light-colored round overlays in which a six-petal floral design is cut.[108]

Notes

1. John Maplet, *A Greene Forest, or a Naturall Historie* (London: Henry Denham, [1567]), 42.

2. Francis W. Galpin, *Old English Instruments of Music: Their History and Character*, 3rd ed., rev. (London: Methuen & Co., 1932), 143; Sibyl Marcuse, *Musical Instruments: A Comprehensive Dictionary* (London: Country Life Ltd., 1964), 149, 155, 160.

3. Thomas Thomas, *Dictionarium Linguae Latinae et Anglicanae* (1587; facsimile, Menston: Scolar Press, 1972).

4. John Rhodes, "A Song in Commendation of Diuers Instruments of Musicke," line 19, in *The Covntrie Man's Comfort* (1588; London: M.D., 1637).

5. Gabriel Harvey, *Pierces Supererogation, or a New Prayse of the Old Asse*, in *The Works of Gabriel Harvey* ([London], 1884-1885), 164.

6. Thomas Rogers, "Qvatorzain 5. Terpsichore," line 11, in *Celestiall Elegies of the Goddesses and the Muses* (London: by Richard Bradocke for I.B., 1598).

7. Sir William Leighton, "A Thankesgiuing to God, with Magnifing of His Holy Name Vpon All Instruments," in *The Teares or Lamentations of a Sorrowfull Soule* (London: Ralph Blower, 1613), 70.

8. Thomas Dekker, "Paul his temple triumphant," in F. David Hoeniger, "Thomas Dekker, the Restoration of St. Paul's, and J. P. Collier, the Forger," *Renaissance News* 16 (Autumn 1963): 197.

9. Randle Cotgrave, *A Dictionarie of the French and English Tongues* (London: A. Islip, 1611), n.p.

10. Edward Howard, *The Six Days Adventure* (London: for Tho. Dring, 1671), act 4, scene 1.

11. *The Journal of William Schellinks' Travels in England, 1661-1663*, translated and edited by Maurice Exwood and H. L. Lehmann, Camden Fifth Series, vol. 1 (London: Royal Historical Society, 1993), 51.

12. Samuel Pepys, *Diary*, 23 May 1662, 23 June 1662.

13. Thomas Duffett, *The Mock-Tempest* (London: for William Cademan, 1675), 22.

14. Winifred Phillips, British Broadcasting Corporation, letter to David Kettlewell, 27 August 1974, in Kettlewell, "Dulcimer," 186.

15. J. A. Johnston, ed., *Probate Inventories of Lincoln Citizens*, Publications of the Lincoln Record Society, vol. 80, 1989 (n.p.: Lincoln Record Society, The Boydell Press, 1991), lxxiii.

16. [Joseph Addison] *The Tatler* (8-11 April 1710), no. 157, para. 12.

17. John Whitley Bruton, *Colley Cibber's The Double Gallant: A Critical Old-Spelling Edition* (New York: Garland Press, 1987), 70. The italics are in the original.

18. Colley Cibber, *The Rival Fools* (London: for Bernard Lintott, [1709]), 30. "Cymbal" meant the hurdy-gurdy.

19. James Miller, *The Mother-In-Law* (London: for J. Watts, 1734), 41.

20. Horace Walpole to Montagu, 12 May 1752, W. S. Lewis, ed., *Horace Walpole's Correspondence* (New Haven: Yale University Press, 1937), 9: 131, in Lance Bertelsen, "Journalism, Carnival, and *Jubilate Agno*," *ELH* 59 (1992): 368.

21. Phyllis Braff, "*A Musical Gathering*: Investigative Steps and Preliminary Conjectures," in *Music in Colonial Massachusetts 1630-1820*, vol. 2, *Music in Homes and in Churches* (Boston: The Colonial Society of Massachusetts, 1985; distributed by University Press of Virginia), 515-545. The Nassau County Museums sold this painting at a Christie's auction in 1996.

22. Braff cautiously suggests, on the basis of its simple style, that the painting was done in Virginia, although she notes the presence of the names in Essex. Further investigation into genealogical sources, especially the International Genealogical Index, reveals both a cluster of the rare names Wending, Godbold, Rippingale, and Elliston around Terling, Essex, and an absence of those names in Colonial America.

23. "Mortimer's London Universal Directory, 1763," *Galpin Society Journal* 2 (1943): 50, in David Kettlewell, "The Dulcimer" (Ph.D. diss., Loughborough University of Technology, 1976), 190.

24. Eric Halfpenny, "An Eighteenth Century Trade List of Musical Instruments," *Galpin Society Journal* 17 (1964): 100, in Kettlewell, "Dulcimer," 191.

25. Richard Brinsley Sheridan, *A Trip to Scarborough*, Act 1, Scene 1, in *The Plays & Poems of Richard Brinsley Sheridan*, ed. R. Crompton Rhodes (New York: Russell & Russell, 1962), 1: 295.

26. Donal O'Sullivan, *Carolan: The Life and Times and Music of an Irish Harper*, vol. 2, *The Notes to the Tunes and the Memoirs of Arthur O'Neill* (London: Routledge and Kegan Paul, 1958), 167. I would acknowledge Sara Johnson for this reference.

27. George Colman, *The Musical Lady: A Farce*, in *The Plays of George Colman the Elder*, ed. Kalman A. Burnim (1762; reprint, New York: Garland Press, 1983), 1: 20.

28. John O'Keeffe, *Tony Lumpkin in Town: A Farce* (London: for T. Cadell, 1780), 17.

29. John Nixon, "Hearing," hand-colored line engraving (London: William Wells, 1784), in the collection of the John D. Rockefeller, Jr., Library, Colonial Williamsburg Foundation.

30. Maria Edgeworth, "The Good French Governess," in *Tales and Novels*,

vol. 1, *Moral Tales* (1801; reprint, New York: AMS Press, 1967), 317-318, 320, 347-348, 356-357.

31. Sir John Graham Dalyell, *Musical Memoirs of Scotland* (1849; reprint, Norwood, Pa.: Norwood Editions, 1973), 260f.

32. Henry Mayhew, *London Labour and the London Poor*, vol. 1, *The Street-Folk* (London: Griffin, Bohn & Co., 1861-1862), 6.

33. Charles Knight, ed., *The English Cyclopaedia: A New Dictionary of Universal Knowledge* (London, 1860), in Kettlewell, "Dulcimer," 198.

34. John Sampson, "The Wood Family," *Journal of the Gypsy Lore Society*, 3rd ser., 51 (1932): 64-65.

35. Lucy Broadwood, "English Gypsy Musicians," *Journal of the Gypsy Lore Society*, n.s., 1 (Jan. 1908): 287.

36. Gypsy Smith, *Gypsy Smith: His Life and Work* (1901?; etext version at <http://www.revival-library.org/smithgypsy/04.htm>).

37. Robert Eadon Leader, *Reminiscences of Old Sheffield: Its Streeets and Its People*, 2nd ed. (Sheffield: Leader and Sons, 1876), chapt. 8, website <http://dove.mtx.net.au/~exy/fth_material/reminiscences_8.html>.

38. Kettlewell, "Dulcimer," 200-201a.

39. "Diagram and Scale of the Dulcimer, with 32 Notes" (London: printed for Ihlee & Sankey, 1885), British Library.

40. Paul N. Hasluck, ed., *Violins and Other Stringed Instruments: How to Make Them*, Cassell Work Handbook Series (London: Cassell, 1906; Philadelphia: David McKay, 1907, 1912, 1914), chapter 11, "Dulcimer Making," 141-158.

41. A. Dobigny, *Self-Instructor for the Dulcimer*, Dobigny's Popular Self-Instructors (London: E. Donajowski, [1885-1892]); Havelock Mason, *Turner's Universal Tutor for the Dulcimer* (London: J. A. Turner, [1908]); Nicola Podesta, *The National Dulcimer Tutor* (London: Ascherberg, Hopwood & Crew, [191-?]); Walter Webber, *Dallas' Complete Tutor for the Dulcimer: Ordinary, Chromatic and Chords* (n.p., c.1920?). A copy of the first is in the British Library. Kettlewell, "Dulcimer," 214a-215a, discusses the tutors by Mason and Webber, but neither he nor I have seen the others.

42. Kettlewell, "Dulcimer," 205a. The Boston Museum of Fine Arts has a dulcimer (1917.1780A) made by John Grey & Sons, Ltd., of London, labeled a "dulcetta."

43. Russell Wortley, "The Traditional English Dulcimer," *Folk Review* 5 (Nov. 1975): 15.

44. Jeffrey Pulver, *A Dictionary of Old English Music & Musical Instruments* (London: Kegan Paul, Trench, Trubner & Co., 1923), 75.

45. Billy Bennington, "Billy Bennington," interview by John Howson, *English Dance and Song* 46 (1984): 3-4.

46. Keith Summers, "Sing, Say or Pay! A Survey of East Suffolk Country Music," *Traditional Music* 8 & 9 (late 1977/early 1978): 29.

47. Wortley, "Traditional English Dulcimer," 15.

48. T. L. Southgate, "Evolution of the Pianoforte," in *English Music [1604 to 1904]: Being the Lectures Given at the Music Loan Exhibition of the Worshipful Company of Musicians, Held at Fishmongers' Hall, London Bridge, June-July 1904* (London: Walter Scott Publishing Co., 1906), 8.

49. Wortley, "Traditional English Dulcimer," 15.

50. Summers, "Sing, Say or Pay!" 29.

51. Leslie Buswell, *With the American Ambulance Field Service in France: Personal Letters of a Driver at the Front* (n.p.: for private distribution, 1916), website, <http://raven.cc.ukans.edu/~libsite/wwi-www/Buswell/AAFS1.htm>.

52. Summers, "Sing, Say or Pay!" 48, 52.

53. *English Country Music*, Topic 12T296.

54. *English Country Music from East Anglia*, Topic 12TS229.

55. Kettlewell, "Dulcimer," 224.

56. Bennington, "Billy Bennington," 3.

57. Kettlewell, "Dulcimer," 218-222.

58. Kettlewell, "Dulcimer," 233-248.

59. Jimmy Cooper, "Jimmy Cooper," interview by Alan Ward, *Traditional Music* 7 (1977): 21.

60. John McGreevy, a native of Cambuslang, conversation with author, Mackinac Island, Mich., 1970s.

61. Andrew McNally, e-mail to author, 24 Feb. 2000; Cooper, "Jimmy Cooper," 22; Cathy McNally Dali, letters to author, 1997, e-mail, 7 Dec. 1999, 17 May 2000.

62. Regal-Zonophone MR 1089, "The Road to the Isles: Scottish Dulcimer Medley," parts 1 and 2, featuring Over the Sea to Skye, The Campbells Are Coming, March—Miss Drummond of Perth, Strathspey—Reel of Tulloch, and Beltona BL 1881, "Ravelled Lines." This information is from Keith Chandler.

63. Picking was exceptional, but not unique to McNally. In 1984 I talked to a man in his seventies whose grandfather, who lived in the Glasgow area, played the dulcimer with a "pick" as well as with hammers.

64. Peter Henderson, conversation with author, Coloma, Mich., 1975.

65. Patrick Allan, conversation with author, Hamtramck, Mich., 1974.

66. Sally Whytehead, personal communication, 1997.

67. Kettlewell, "Dulcimer," 261.

68. Keith Chandler, "Early Recordings of Traditional Dance Music: Peter and Daniel Wyper, Champion Melodeon Players of Scotland," *Musical Traditions*, article MT005, website <http://www2.prestel.co.uk/mustrad/articles/wypers.htm>.

69. "Medley of Popular Reels" / "Medley of Popular Waltzes," Beltona BL 1685; "Medley of Irish Waltzes," / "Medley of Scottish Songs," Beltona BL 1651; "Liverpool and Sailors' Hornpipes" / "Strathclyde Hornpipes," Beltona BL 1688 (information from Keith Chandler). The recordings of Cumming and

Holmes are listed in Richard K. Spottswood, *Ethnic Music on Records* (Urbana: University of Illinois Press, 1990), 5: 2872f.

70. *Jimmy Cooper: Dulcimer Player*, Forest Tracks FTS 3009.

71. Seán Donnelly, "A German Dulcimer Player in Eighteenth-Century Dublin," *Dublin Historical Record* 53 (Spring 2000): 84. Galpin, *Old English Instruments of Music*, 68, suggests that the *timpan* of medieval Irish texts may have been a dulcimer, but Ann Buckley, "What Was the Tiompan? A Problem in Ethnohistorical Organology: Evidence in Irish Literature," *Jahrbuch für musikalische Volks- und Völkerkunde* 9 (1978): 53-88, concludes it was a variety of lyre with three metallic strings. See also Ann Buckley, "Notes on the Tiompán in Irish Literature," *Studia instrumentorum musicae popularis* 5 (1971): 84-90.

72. Donnelly, "German Dulcimer Player," 77-79, 84.

73. Charles J. Lever, *Jack Hinton, the Guardsman* (1843; London: George Routledge and Sons, 1872), 73.

74. Gerald Griffin, *The Collegians* (London: Saunders and Otley, 1829), 3: 280.

75. Andrea Kirkpatrick, Curator, New Brunswick Museum, letter to author, 15 Nov. 1999.

76. James Stephens, *Insurrection in Ireland* (Dublin: Maunsel & Co., 1916), 1.

77. Kettlewell, "Dulcimer," 252f.; John Feeney, "The Dulcimer Player of Clonmeen," *Treoir* 10, no. 5 (1978): 11.

78. James Joyce, *Ulysses* (New York: Modern Library, 1946), 57, 506. He mentions the dulcimer in another passage on page 269.

79. Kettlewell, "Dulcimer," 274. In 1969 I met a woman who had emigrated from Belfast and remembered the dulcimer from her younger years, about 1920.

80. Robin Morton, notes to *Drops of Brandy*, Topic 12TS287; Caomhain MacAoidh, personal communication, 1997, mentioned a photograph he had seen of a dulcimer player in Tipperary; Kettlewell, "Dulcimer," 260.

81. Kettlewell, "Dulcimer," 258.

82. Henry Clegg, Diary, 1 Apr. 1855, MS 6613, Historical Archives of The Church of Jesus Christ of Latter-Day Saints, Salt Lake City, Utah, website, <http://www.cclegg.com/family/history/voyage htm>.

83. [Benjamin A. Botkin], notes to Library of Congress, Music Division—Recording Laboratory AAFS 41; "Nancy's Fancy" appears in Peter Kennedy, ed., *The Second Fiddler's Tune-Book* ([London]: The English Folk Dance and Song Society, 1954), 27.

84. Henry C. Gilchrist, *History of Wilkinsburg, Pennsylvania* ([Pittsburgh]: n.p., 1940), 77; Elizabeth M. Davison and Fullen B. McKee, ed., *Annals of Old Wilkinsburg and Vicinity: The Village, 1788-1888* (Wilkinsburg, Pa.: The Group for Historical Research, 1940), 412, calls the maker Hutchinson and says that

the dulcimer was in the collections of the Historical Society of Western Pennsylvania.

85. U.S. Patent no. 625,663; 1900 census, New York, Rensselaer Co., City of Troy, enumeration district 78, sheet 2, line number 58; 1900 census, Soundex index, New York.

86. Patrick Allan, conversation with author, 1974.

87. Spottswood, *Ethnic Music on Records*, 5: 2672f., 2813; Cathy McNally Dali, personal communication, 1997.

88. Spottswood, *Ethnic Music on Records*, 5: 2770; Philippe Varlet, personal communication.

89. Silas Braley, conversation with author, 1970s.

90. Kettlewell, "Dulcimer," 191.

91. Henry VIII's psalter, Royal MS, 2A.XVI, f. 98v., British Library.

92. Pauline Rushton, *Catalogue of European Musical Instruments in Liverpool Museum* ([Liverpool], 1994), 128. Unfortunately the author calls it "probably eastern European."

93. Kettlewell, "Dulcimer," 249a.

94. Kettlewell, "Dulcimer," 184a-184b.

95. *Music in Colonial Massachusetts 1630-1820*, vol. 2, *Music in Homes and in Churches*, flyleaf.

96. Kettlewell, "Dulcimer," 223a, suggests this possibility.

97. Roylance, *How to Learn the Dulcimer*, title page.

98. Kettlewell, "Dulcimer," 224.

99. Wortley, "Traditional English Dulcimer," 14; personal communication, 1969.

100. Kettlewell, "Dulcimer," 223a-224; Wortley, "Traditional English Dulcimer," 13-14.

101. Kettlewell, "Dulcimer," 220, 222.

102. Kettlewell, "Dulcimer," 241-248.

103. Kettlewell, "Dulcimer," 269.

104. *A Checklist of the Plucked and Hammered Stringed Instruments in the Edinburgh University Collection of Historic Musical Instruments* (Edinburgh: Edinburgh University Collection of Historic Musical Instruments, Reid School of Music, 1982), nos. 314.122.4 (1092), 314.122.4 (836).

105. John McCutcheon, "Jimmy Cooper: Dulcimer Player: A Review and Musings," *Dulcimer Players News* 4, no. 3 (Summer 1978): 17.

106. Kettlewell, "Dulcimer," 267, 268c.

107. Kettlewell, "Dulcimer," 273a-277.

108. Andrea Kirkpatrick, letter to author, 15 Nov. 1999.

· 12 ·

The Dulcimer in America, 1717-1850

The boom in dulcimer manufacturing and playing of the mid-nineteenth century was largely a rural phenomenon. The proprietors of the factories, to the extent that we know, were natives, descendants of colonial immigrants. The purchasers and players of the instruments were mostly of the same ethnic stock as the manufacturers. Thus the design of the instruments and the styles of playing probably represent a continuation of designs and styles followed in the British colonies during the eighteenth century.

The dulcimer was not a common instrument in Colonial America. Although much research remains to be done, certain systematic surveys have not revealed the instrument. Barbara Lambert's research in estate inventories in three Massachusetts counties from 1645 to 1734 shows citterns, virginals, viols, and various other instruments, but no dulcimers.[1] Although more limited in scope, Nancy Baker's study of Anne Arundel County, Maryland, estate inventories from 1746 to 1759 shows mostly violins, with four estates with flutes, and one each with a spinet and trumpet.[2] Research by Mary R. M. Goodwin in eighteenth-century Virginia newspapers, inventories, diaries, and letter books reveals many harpsichords, violins, and other instruments, but no dulcimers.[3]

Nevertheless, based on evidence that suggests a renewed interest in the instrument in England after 1660, we should not be surprised if some future researcher discovers the existence of a dulcimer in the colonies in the latter half of the seventeenth century.[4] The relatively undeveloped American ports, however, could not support a tavern culture as extensive as that of London. The professional "fiddlers" who appeared in Covent Garden would not have been able to support themselves with their music in New York or other American cities. If a dulcimer found its way to the colonies during the seventeenth century, it would probably have done so as a household instrument.

The earliest record of a dulcimer in America indeed shows it as a domestic instrument. On 23 May 1717, Samuel Sewall, a judge of the high court of Massachusetts, traveled from his home in Boston and entered in his diary: "To Salem, Meadford, Lodge at Cousin Porter's: See and Hear the Dulcimer."[5] The instrument apparently was at the home of the Rev. Aaron Porter (1689-1722), the minister of Medford, Massachusetts, who was married to Susan, the daughter of Samuel's brother Stephen Sewall, a merchant in Salem. Perhaps the dulcimer was played by a guest of the Porters, but, in this private setting, it seems more likely that it may have belonged to Mrs. Porter. The owner of two slaves, Porter, like his uncle, was a graduate of Harvard College and one of the colony's elite.[6]

Sewall's reference to the dulcimer is the first of several eighteenth-century American references to the instrument, most of which indicate a rather genteel environment in which the instrument was played. Such a social situation, however, seems to have been characteristic for owners of most musical instruments.[7] Lacking trained music masters, other Colonial gentry of the first part of the eighteenth century may have turned to the dulcimer as an instrument suitable for the women of the household to teach themselves to play. This fits well with the fictional characters of parsimonious knights and their female relatives mentioned in plays by Colley Cibber and Richard Brinsley Sheridan in contemporary England.

One music master living in Philadelphia, however, offered to teach the dulcimer. On 21 March 1749, John Beals, "musick-master, from London," advertised in the *Pennsylvania Gazette* that "he teaches the violin, hautboy, German flute, common flute, and dulcimer by note. Said Beals will likewise attend young ladies, or others, that may desire it, at their houses. He likewise provides musick for balls or other entertainments."[8]

Beals continued the same advertisement for three further issues.[9] Despite this man's versatility on several instruments, demand for a music master in Philadelphia was evidently not sufficient for him to earn a living, as he advertised in February 1752 that he made a variety of nets in addition to offering lessons on instruments, this time omitting the dulcimer.[10] However, in January and February 1753, Beals ran another, similar advertisement, this time adding the dulcimer.[11] Although we have no further evidence of dulcimer playing in Philadelphia in this period, its inclusion in the list of instruments that he taught indicates that some families probably had them.

In 1752 and 1753, a professional dulcimer player appeared in the colonies. Richard Brickell, a promoter of puppet shows and demonstrations of electricity, magic lanterns, and clockworks, advertised in the *New York Gazette and Weekly Post Boy* on 27 April 1752 the appearance of a contortionist and magician, adding "to make the entertainment more agreeable, the company will be diverted with the musick of the dulcemer." A week later, Brickell announced that the show would be in the theatre on Nassau Street, and that "there will be a variety of musick, such as the dulcimer, violin, &c."[12] The advertisements do not reveal the name of the dulcimer player, but we can presume it was the same player who appeared in 1753 in Charleston, South Carolina, in one of Brickell's shows. The promoter ran five successive advertisements in July 1753 announcing an exhibition of wax sculptures of the Austro-Hungarian empress, her son, and a courtier, adding that, "during the time of seeing these beautiful curiosities, the company will be entertained with the best pieces of Music, or any of the favourite tunes in vogue, performed on the Dulcimer, by Mr. Richardson."[13]

The Tuesday Club, an organization of gentlemen in Annapolis, Maryland, with an interest in music, heard Thomas Richison play the dulcimer with Alexander Hamilton on the cello, on 21 November 1752.[14] The similarity of the name as well as the date of the performance would seem to indicate that Thomas Richison or Richardson was the same person who played for Brickell's shows in New York and Charleston as well as for the Tuesday Club. Even if we regard dulcimer playing in eighteenth-century England as practiced by lower-class professionals on the one hand and by middle-class amateurs on the other, we need to realize that these are ideal situations. This man's playing or demeanor may have been unusual enough to allow him to appear in a gentlemen's club as well as the theatres and streets to which he was probably more accustomed.

Other evidence shows that the dulcimer was in use in the American colonies. In 1770, a "second-hand" dulcimer was one of the items advertised in the *Boston Gazette* to be sold by auction.[15] Such an instrument may have even been made in Massachusetts, since advertisements of music merchants of the period do not mention the dulcimer as one of the types of instruments they imported. In 1775, Richard Lightfoot, from Dublin, a pin manufacturer in New York, advertised in the *New York Mercury* that he "draws harpsichord, spinnet, fortipiano, dolsemor [*sic*], and all other kinds of music wire."[16] Obviously he must have felt that there were local dulcimer owners who needed to replace broken strings or makers of the instrument who needed new wire. Stephen Spelman, a Revolutionary soldier in a Connecticut unit, wrote in his journal that on 30 September 1776, after arriving at New Haven in the morning and attending "meeting" in the afternoon, the soldiers "marched through old Milford to Stratford; at evening heard the dulcimer and organ."[17] We can only speculate on the circumstances surrounding the dulcimer at Stratford; perhaps Spelman heard it in church.

Immigrants arriving in the eighteenth century may have brought dulcimers to the Colonies. Although it is difficult to accept traditional accounts as accurate, perhaps some may contain truth. John C. Conley, of Nashville, Michigan, born in 1836 in Northboro, Massachusetts, played a dulcimer which he claimed was brought from Ireland by his ancestor in the eighteenth century.[18] Less believable, however, is the statement of J. R. Cantrell, of McMinnville, Tennessee, that each generation of his Cantrell ancestors had played the instrument since their arrival in Jamestown, Virginia, in the early seventeenth century.

Evidence for the dulcimer in the nation's early period, although scarce, indicates that it was a domestic instrument largely played by young women. J. E. Wright and Doris S. Corbett write that, as the frontier began to leave western Pennsylvania, people had time to pass evenings "singing to the accompaniment of the violin, spinet, or dulcimer."[19] In 1812, the Mexican aristocrat José Bernardo Gutierrez de Lara met at New Orleans "a very beautiful young woman of an illustrious family of Baltimore," noting that "she plays the dulcimer admirably."[20] Clearly the latter is an example of the instrument in the hands of the wealthy, the same class of people who earlier might have employed John Beals to teach their daughters. Orlando Bolivar Willcox's novel *Shoepac Recollections* (1856), set in his native Detroit during the 1820s, includes an Army major and veteran of the War of 1812 who is charmed at an evening party by Miss Maud, who "sat at a species of dulcimer, singing some sweet ballad of olden time."[21] Since military officers dominated the frontier elite, the author thus places the dulcimer firmly within the same social environment as that of de Lara's New Orleans woman. As the century passed, however, this upper-class domestic use declined, as pianos became more readily available.

Merchants in the newly independent United States now had to pay tariffs on imported musical instruments. This may have spurred an increase in local manufacture of instruments. Nevertheless, in 1821 a Boston dealer could advertise recently imported instruments, including pianofortes, bugles, clarinets, flutes, fifes, violins, guitars, flageolets, military cymbals, aeolian harps, harp lutes, tambourines, French horns, trumpets, trombones, bassoons, bass viols, and double basses, all selected in London.[22] Dulcimers, because of their relative ease of construction, as well as learning, may have benefited from independence. In addition, as a sturdy instrument less prone to problems caused by humidity that the early pianos faced, it may have found suitable conditions for its popularity to grow.

Sometime between 1800 and 1805, a person in recently settled Seneca, Ontario County, New York, made a dulcimer for Elizabeth Garbutt (1781-1838), who had immigrated with her family from England in 1798. This instrument, now in the Scottsville, New York, Library, may be the oldest surviving American-made dulcimer in existence. It appears to have originally had nine treble and nine bass courses, each with four strings, laying on long bridges. Two round sound holes may have been decorated with wooden rosettes. The outer measurements of its trapezoidal body are 43½ inches (110.2 cm) and 21¾ inches (55.2 cm) in length.[23]

In this period, most dulcimer manufacture would have been carried out on a small-scale, individual basis. In 1879, a cousin recalled that Henry Powell (1811-1835), an itinerant portrait painter from Fairfield County, Ohio, active in Lancaster and Columbus, Ohio, as well as Kentucky, "manufactured bass and tenor drums, dulcimers, and a variety of musical instruments."[24] His short and active life would have precluded an opportunity to make many dulcimers, but perhaps he was typical of such makers in this period, producing a variety of instruments.

One maker, however, carried on a larger trade. In 1828, Richard Vernon (1789-1877), a native of Stokes County, North Carolina, settled in Jefferson County, Indiana. A woodworker who made everything from horse fiddles (an idiophone used at shivarees) to carriages and coffins, dulcimers were his chief product for a while. He brought loads of them on flatboats down the Ohio and Mississippi Rivers, selling them at New Orleans and returning home on foot. Vernon's dulcimer business was not small; his granddaughter related that one of his loads consisted of seventy-five instruments. Extant dulcimers made by Richard Vernon are unknown, but they had four strings per course, and the hammers had whalebone shafts with chamois-covered wooden heads.[25] This probably took place in the 1830s or perhaps 1840s. River traffic provided ready markets in the prosperous South for the producers of such manufactured goods, but Vernon's product was unusual for the time and certainly one of the first mass-marketed dulcimers.

Other evidence from the early nineteenth century indicates that people living far from the Eastern seaboard used the dulcimer, or at least an instrument called by that name. Since the evidence is literary and there seems to be no knowledge of the traditional use of the hammered dulcimer in some of these areas, the instrument called "dulcimer" in these references more likely refers to the Appalachian dulcimer. Certainly by the 1820s the word "dulcimer" did describe this instrument. Baynard Rush Hall, who lived in southern Indiana during that decade, wrote a book, *The New Purchase*, in 1843, based on his experiences there. He includes a chapter about a fictionalized character, Vulcanus Allheart, a blacksmith and native of Virginia, who played the "dulcimer," which the author describes as "a monotone instrument shaped like an aeolian harp, and done with a plectrum on wire strings."[26] Pulaski County, Kentucky, seems to have been one location where there were several players. Allen Smith does mention rectangular examples (which were called "dulcimers") made in Metcalfe and Cumberland Counties and heard of similar ones made in Burnside, Pulaski County.[27] In any case, the inventory of the estate of William Matherly, of Pulaski County, made in 1825, shows one "Dulcimore," appraised at $3.[28] William McGinnis (died 1838), who lived in Pulaski County from the 1820s until 1836, when he moved to Clark County, Missouri, played the flute, fife, and sang and accompanied himself on the dulcimer.[29] The inventory of the estate of Conrad Staines, of Pulaski County, made in 1842, lists one "Dulcime" valued at $.50 and a "school harp and case" at $3.[30] In neighboring Casey County, Kentucky, the inventory of the estate of Isaiah Clifton, made in 1840, lists a dulcimer, appraised at $1.[31] Although these south-central Kentucky dulcimers were probably not hammered dulcimers, systematic research in probate inventories in other areas may offer further evidence of the use and spread of that and other instruments during this period. In Rockbridge County, Virginia, Susan Roadcap purchased a dulcimer at the sale of the estate of Christian Roadcap in 1848.[32] Again, however, the nature of this instrument is uncertain. Perhaps it is more likely that the dulcimer appraised at $1 in the inventory of the estate of William Moon, who died in 1844 in Madison County, Alabama, and purchased by Rachel Moon, was the instrument of this study.[33]

Other evidence of early nineteenth-century American dulcimers comes from surviving instruments themselves. A problem is that few bear inscriptions of their makers' names and dates. Their provenance may be unknown or incompletely known. We may be able to assign dates to some instruments, based on design, decoration, appearance, and elements of provenance, but it is difficult to place some instruments neatly into a chronological arrangement such as this. Nevertheless, certain dulcimers clearly date from the early nineteenth century.

One unusual dulcimer is in the collections of the Metropolitan Museum of Art (accession no. 1978.369). It was originally part of the estate of an elderly woman who died in the 1920s in Darrtown, Ohio. Assigned a date of about 1815, the instrument has pin blocks arranged asymmetrically, so that the row of individually turned treble bridges forms a right angle to the strings. It has seven treble and seven bass courses, each with two strings per course. The treble bridges divide each course into octaves, rather than the usual fifths, and notes marked on the bridges indicate a tuning of C-major scales on the row of bass bridges and both sides of the treble bridges, for a three octave range of c^0 to b^2. A painted cardboard "rose" attached to the underside of a single square soundhole and carved outward scrolls on the acute corners decorate the instrument, which is of cherry with a reddish stain. It rests inside a specially made case with a cover and spiral, turned legs. A hammer with a whalebone shaft belonged to the dulcimer. The dulcimer measures 57½ (146.5 cm) and 30¾ inches (78.1 cm) in length, 15 inches (38.1 cm) in width, and is 3¾ inches (9.5 cm) deep.[34]

Such a design, with a case on legs specially made to hold the dulcimer, seems to anticipate later American designs where the dulcimer is an integral part of a rectangular case, often with a lid. It resembles certain dulcimers from northern England with rectangular cases or dulcimers built into cases and may recall a common eighteenth-century design. This likely was intended for use as a stationary household instrument, rather than as a portable instrument to take to dances. The elegant, if provincial, design of the Metropolitan Museum dulcimer also appears to be appropriate to the middle-class or upper-class frontier family who likely owned it originally.

Gerald Milnes examined an old dulcimer in Monroe County, West Virginia, which dates from the early nineteenth century or even earlier. Its corners are decorated with inward scrolls. Individual, turned bridges support twelve treble courses of four each and eleven bass courses of two each. The instrument has only a single, round sound hole.[35]

The Historic Michie Tavern Museum, Charlottesville, Virginia, has an early nineteenth-century dulcimer. The trapezoidal instrument fits snugly into a rectangular case, with a hinged lid, which rests on a table with four turned legs. The dulcimer is 42 inches (106.7 cm) and 21 inches (52.3 cm) long, 15 inches (38.1 cm) wide, and has twelve treble courses of four strings each and three bass courses of two strings each. The placement of the bass courses is between the first and second, second and third, and fourth and fifth treble courses. Bridges are individually turned. The two sound holes consist of a center hole surrounded by six small holes.[36] The provenance of this instrument is unknown, but the style of its stenciled decoration on the instrument's side facing the player and interior of its lid and its legs suggest a probable date of about 1825 to 1835. The string arrangement, individual bridges, and sound hole design are all similar to the design used by later makers in Ohio and elsewhere.

A dulcimer built into a rectangular case, with a hinged lid, the whole supported by lyre-shaped legs, once belonged to a Richmond, Virginia, estate. This instrument has fourteen treble courses of three strings each resting on a bone-topped single-piece bridge, with no bass courses. Its soundboard contains two larger sound holes, forming a six-pointed petal star, and two smaller round sound holes. Its case is veneered with mahogany. The lyre form of its legs suggests a late Empire style, and, with its hand-forged pins, we can safely place it within this chapter and assign a date of about 1835 to 1845.[37]

A store in Boston had for sale in 1980 a dulcimer with an inscription "James Young, Fayette, Maine, Mar. 1, 1841."[38] This instrument had hand-forged tuning pins, but unfortunately no other details about this instrument are available.

The earliest dulcimers which appear to have been made for others on a regular basis came from western New York State. The Ontario County Historical Society, Canandaigua, New York, possesses one with an inscription "Presented to Sophia L. Hall by her friend P. Cogswell, 1830." This trapezoidal dulcimer measures 45¾ (116.3 cm) and 28 inches (71.3 cm) in length and 15¼ inches (38.8 cm) in width. Although its bridges are missing, marks on the soundboard, which lacks sound holes, indicate that it had individual bridges, with ten treble courses of three each and nine bass courses of two each. Stenciled letters next to the bridge locations indicate its tuning. The dulcimer's sides are decorated with grain painting, and an American eagle is painted on its soundboard. The

Figure 12.1: Dulcimer made by P. (probably Philander) Cogswell, of Steuben County, New York, 1830. From the Collections of the Ontario Historical Society.

instrument rests in a rectangular, cherry case, with a hinged lid and turned legs.

Another instrument, in Hedgesville, New York, appears to have been made by the same person. A round, stenciled inscription on its soundboard reads "I. Cogswell." As it is worn, the "I." could easily have originally been "P." The dulcimer was altered in recent times, a restorer having installed new tuning pins and bridges and probably cut new heart-shaped soundholes. The original string arrangement was ten treble courses of three strings each and nine bass courses of three strings each. The front and back sides are contoured and decorated with grain painting.[39]

The maker of these last two dulcimers was undoubtedly Philander Cogswell, the only Cogswell in the 1830 and 1840 censuses in western New York whose given name began with "P." Born 1 June 1798 in New Milford, Connecticut, he moved with his parents to LeRaysville, Pennsylvania, in 1812. In 1830, he lived in Bath, and in 1840, in Reading, both in Steuben County, New York.[40] The fact that two dulcimers bearing his name exist, in addition to the pitch names being stenciled on one of them, indicate that he must have made them on a commercial, if small-scale, basis. This activity would imply an increased demand for the instrument in western New York at this time. Such a demand probably led to full-scale commercial dulcimer manufacturing in the years before the Civil War.

The evidence presented here suggests that dulcimers were brought from England and Ireland, as well as Germany (see chapter 5), during the eighteenth century and that they were present in most parts of the country during the first half of the nineteenth century. Certain designs used later in the century were already present at this period. Nevertheless, American dulcimer playing and making in the early nineteenth century remain somewhat cloudy. The picture would change, however, at the middle of the century.

Notes

1. Barbara Lambert, "Social Music, Musicians, and Their Instruments in and around Colonial Boston," in *Music in Colonial Massachusetts, 1630-1820*, vol. 2, *Music in Homes and in Churches* (Boston: The Colonial Society of Massachusetts, 1985; distributed by University Press of Virginia), 422-431.

2. John Barry Talley, *Secular Music in Colonial Annapolis: The Tuesday Club, 1745-56* (Urbana: University of Illinois Press, 1988), 26, table 2, citing data compiled by Nancy Baker, housed at Historic Annapolis, Inc.

3. Mary R. M. Goodwin, "Musical Instruments in Eighteenth Century Virginia," Early American History Research Reports, microfiche ed. (Williamsburg, Va.: Colonial Williamsburg Foundation, 1989), 1x.

4. Here I regret to mention that the alleged bill of lading of 1609 that mentions a dulcimer, for which I cited Franklin George, in Phyllis Lehmann, "Give Me That Old Time Music," *Cultural Post*, no. 9 (Jan.-Feb. 1977), in my article, "Development of the Hammer Dulcimer," in *The Hammer Dulcimer Compendium* (Silver Spring, Md.: MIH Publications, 1977), 8, is without any factual basis. David Kettlewell, in his article "Dulcimer," in *The New Grove Dictionary of Music and Musicians*, unfortunately repeated this statement, and it has found its way into further secondary and tertiary sources.

5. Samuel Sewall, *The Diary of Samuel Sewall: 1674-1729*, vol. 2, *1709-1729*, ed. M. Halsey Thomas (New York: Farrar, Straus and Giroux, 1973), 855.

6. Clifford K. Shipton, *Biographical Sketches of Those Who Attended Harvard College in the Classes 1701-1712*, Sibley's Harvard Graduates, vol. 5 (Boston: Massachusetts Historical Society, 1937), 441-444.

7. Lambert, "Social Music," 422-431, shows a predominance of merchants, mariners, ministers, schoolmasters, and innkeepers among owners of musical instruments.

8. *Pennsylvania Gazette*, 21 March 1749.

9. *Pennsylvania Gazette*, 28 March 1749, 5 April 1749, 13 April 1749.

10. *Pennsylvania Gazette*, 18 February 1752, 25 February 1752, 3 March 1752.

11. *Pennsylvania Gazette*, 30 January 1753, 6 February 1753.

12. *New York Gazette and Weekly Post Boy,* 27 April 1752; 4 May 1752.

13. *South Carolina Gazette,* 2 July 1753, 11 July 1753, 16 July 1753, 23 July 1753, 30 July 1753.

14. Talley, *Secular Music,* 29.

15. *Boston Gazette,* 19 Feb. 1770.

16. *New York Mercury,* 10 July 1775.

17. Fannie Cooley Williams Barbour, *Spelman Genealogy: The English Ancestry and American Descendants of Richard Spelman of Middletown, Connecticut, 1700* (New York: Frank Allaben Genealogical Co., 1910), 147.

18. Fred Conley, "Genealogy of Fay Oliver Conley," typescript, Burton Historical Collection, Detroit Public Library.

19. J. E. Wright and Doris S. Corbett, *Pioneer Life in Western Pennsylvania* (Pittsburgh: University of Pittsburgh Press, 1940), 214, 244. They do not provide their source for this statement, but they based their work on many primary sources.

20. "Diary of José Bernardo Gutierrez de Lara, 1811-1812: II. Year of 1812," *American Historical Review* 34 (Jan. 1929): 291.

21. Walter March (pseud.), *Shoepac Recollections: A Way-side Glimpse of American Life* (New York: Bunce & Brother, 1856), 127.

22. *New England Galaxy,* 2 Feb. 1821.

23. Mitzie Collins, "The Elizabeth Garbutt Reed Dulcimer," *Dulcimer Players News* 10 (Spring 1984): 22-24.

24. John Powell, *Authentic Genealogical Memorial History of Philip Powell of Mifflin Co., Pa.: and His Descendants and Others, with Miscellaneous Items and Incidents of Interest* (Dayton, Ohio: for the author, 1880), 133, 213, 216.

25. Unidentified clippings, entitled "Made Old Dulcimer," "Regarding the Dulcimer," and "More about the Dulcimer," probably from the *Madison Herald* and *Madison Courier* from the late 1920s or early 1930s, in Vernon file, Madison Jefferson County Library, Madison, Ind. Thanks to Janice Barnes for communicating this.

26. Robert Carlton (pseud.), *The New Purchase, or Seven and a Half Years in the Far West* (New York: D. Appleton & Co., 1843), 2: 33.

27. L. Allen Smith, *A Catalogue of Pre-Revival Appalachian Dulcimers* (Columbia, Mo.: University of Missouri Press, 1983), 27-30.

28. Pulaski County, Kentucky, will book 2: 172.

29. Autobiographical sketch of James Crain McGinnis (1830-1893), written in 1876-1877, in "The Kelly Family Book, 1972," website <http://www.gps.caltech.edu/~gdunn/KellyBook.htm>.

30. Pulaski County, Kentucky, will book 3A: 630.

31. Casey County, Kentucky, will book 1: 287; website <http://www.jadecat.com/famdocs/icliftonsrinv.htm>.

32. Rockbridge County, Virginia, will book 11: 147-154, website <http://www.99main.com/~jrothgeb/readers.txt>.

33. Madison County, Alabama, probate record 11: 168, 171.
34. Laurence Libin, *American Musical Instruments in The Metropolitan Museum of Art* (New York: The Metropolitan Museum of Art, 1985), 100-102. I also examined this in 1975, when it was in private hands.
35. Gerald Milnes, personal communication, 24 Nov. 1999.
36. Gregory L. MacDonald, General Manager, Historic Michie Tavern Museum, letter to author, 24 Oct. 1979.
37. Owned by John J. Kleske, Binghamton, New York, in 1977.
38. Bill Webster, conversation with author, 1980.
39. Bob Wey, letter to author, 19 Nov. 1977.
40. E. O. Jameson, *The Cogswells in America* (Boston: Alfred Mudge & Son, printers, 1884), 434; 1830 census, Steuben County, New York; 1840 census, Steuben County, New York.

The Dulcimer in America, 1850-1900

Local histories and pioneer reminiscences frequently describe the rarity of musical instruments in the early nineteenth century.[1] Fiddlers played for dancing, both at informal "frolics" and formal balls. Church music popularized the bass viol in some regions, while military music spread the fife, clarinet, drum, and even bassoon. Men of means played the flute or violin, and their wives and daughters favored the piano, as well as the guitar and harp. Slaves played the fiddle, banjo, and various impromptu percussion instruments, and by the 1840s, blackface minstrels had begun to introduce these to new audiences. American firms in the 1830s and 1840s began to manufacture various newly invented free-reed instruments, such as the lap organ, seraphine, melodeon, flutina, and accordion, which found eager buyers.

Where did the dulcimer fit into this scheme? We have seen how its use during the eighteenth and early nineteenth centuries resembled somewhat that of the piano, as an instrument played at home, both by women and men. It seems also likely that an increase in its popularity occurred in the 1830s and 1840s in western New York and probably in other places, such as West Virginia. But three elements differentiate the dulcimer and its use from the piano and other instruments: First, interest in the instrument was native, rather than caused by international fashion. Second, its players lived mainly in rural areas or near the frontier, rather than in cities. Third, the makers who supplied the demand and created a demand for the instrument were both native and rural, in contrast to manufacturers of the piano and banjo, who were located in the major cities and often were immigrants.[2] The dulcimer, unlike most of the other instruments mentioned above, had not been imported as an item of commerce from England or Europe during the eighteenth and early nine-teenth centuries. It was a fashion from below, the emerging American commercial culture both responding to and creating the demand for the instrument.

Although not the earliest American dulcimer maker, C. Haight may have been the first to promote the instrument in a commercial way. In 1848, his *Complete System for the Dulcimer* was published by William Hall & Sons, New York. I have been unable to identify him, but he prob-ably lived in New York State. The name was common in Westchester and Dutchess Counties. None of the C. Haights in the 1850 census in New York or other states were earning their living as manufacturers or musicians, but the author must have produced the book in order for cus-tomers to learn to play the instruments that he probably manufactured. The only clue to his instruments is the "gamut" or diagram of the dulci-mer, which shows eleven treble courses of four each and seven bass courses of two each, with two sound holes shaped like tildes (~).[3] The same string arrangement was used by three manufacturers in Chautauqua County, New York, in the late 1850s, and one of them almost certainly used the tilde-shaped sound hole as well. Haight thus may have lived in that county or in western New York; in any event, his dulcimers prob-ably influenced those manufactured in Chautauqua County.

Whatever influence Haight's manufacture may have had on the use of dulcimers, in certain areas people had already begun to use it to ac-company the fiddle for dancing. This function was its most characteris-tic use in most of the region bordering the Great Lakes during the latter half of the nineteenth and beginning of the twentieth century. On New Year's, 1849, at Whigville, near Flint, Michigan, the opening of a hotel was celebrated by a ball, to which four hundred people were invited. They danced to "a fiddle or a dulcimer."[4] Nearly all the settlers in that vicinity had come from western New York, and the fiddle-dulcimer com-bination undoubtedly had been used there. However, the dulcimer as an instrument played at balls was far from the rule in contemporary Michi-gan. The diaries of Henry Parker Smith, of Schoolcraft, for example, mention ensembles consisting of two fiddles, post horn, and trombone (1848), three fiddles, clarinet, and bass viol (1850), while Smith, a fid-dler himself, seems to have usually played for balls together with a sec-ond fiddle and a bass viol.[5]

People played the dulcimer at dances in early Wisconsin, also heavily settled by migrants from New York State. Balls at the Steele Tavern at

Newport were accompanied by violin, dulcimer, and bass viol.[6] Ellen Sweet (1849-1937), of rural Verona, began to play a dulcimer made at her home in 1857 by Orrin Sweet (no relation), who came from New York State to make and sell dulcimers to the pioneers and who had left a dulcimer with Ellen's family as payment for use of a building. She accompanied her brother James, who played second fiddle, and her sister Addie, who played the melodeon, first playing at the age of nine for a Fourth of July ball at Arnold's Tavern at Polkerville (later Blue Mounds), and in the years following, at the Plow Inn near Madison, the Fitchburg town hall, and the tavern at Verona.[7]

Clearly an interest in the dulcimer increased in the years before the Civil War, at least in some areas. The anonymous dulcimers which appear to have been made during this period, such as some with tuning pins marked "W. Wake," presumably the mark of William Wake, a manufacturer of piano supplies in New York City active in the 1850s, testify to this growth.[8] Manufactured tuning pins probably indicate a transition to commercial production, although some dulcimers which are probably from this period still have hand-forged tuning pins. The labor involved in making them by hand would preclude mass production, but the availability of manufactured pins (usually one-quarter inch in diameter and between 1.875 and 2.0625 inches in length and intended specifically for dulcimers) now reduced the time necessary to make a dulcimer and eased the way for people to make them commercially.[9]

The identity of many makers eludes us. Only a minority of instruments bear makers' inscriptions, which may be stencil-painted, stamped, or on printed labels pasted to the back or interior. We know the names of other makers or manufacturers from patent applications or from information passed down by their descendants, but we cannot always identify their instruments. While most older American dulcimers probably date from about 1850 to 1890, with a concentration from 1855 to 1875, very few bear dates, so dating is mostly by estimate.

During the 1850s, Morgan H. Sackett (1827-1919) and his brother Hiram B., of Irving, New York, made a small number of dulcimers, said by family tradition to number seven, probably sold to people in the local area.[10] The Sacketts lived in Chautauqua County, New York, and may have responded to an increased demand for the instrument in the western part of the state, already indicated by the earlier activity of Philander Cogswell in Steuben County. Philip N. Woliston (born about 1823 in Adams County, Pennsylvania), a woodworker, pattern maker, and machinist of Springfield, Ohio, made an attractive dulcimer in a rectangular case, probably in this period, and stamped "P. N. Woliston" on a pin block, indicating he probably made the instrument commercially.[11] Smith Beecher (1808-1875) a cabinetmaker who opened a shop in Southbridge, Massachusetts in 1842, had a musical bent and built dulcimers as well as other instruments.[12] Such makers had already begun producing dulcimers for others before the manufacturing boom began, but they did so on a small scale.

If the number of surviving instruments is any indication, the first serious dulcimer manufacturing venture begin with two firms in Chautauqua County, New York. Brothers Lewis S. Wade (1824-1912) and Harrison Wade (1825-1900) started a factory in 1855 or slightly earlier at Stedman, in the town of North Harmony. That year, the Wade brothers reported that they had invested $80 in real estate, $100 in tools and machinery; had $1400 worth of lumber, which amounted to 70,000 board feet, and veneer, wire, glue, and other materials; intended to produce 500 dulcimers annually, for a product of $4000; and employed six men at an average monthly salary of $23.[13] My great-grandfather, Augustus C. Gifford (1836-1920), a fiddler and woodworker, worked there. Two dulcimers attributed locally to this factory indicate they manufactured at least two different models until 1860, when the factory burned down.[14] Dulcimers identical to these were sold in Pennsylvania, Ohio, and Michigan, and probably other states. The Wades employed salesmen who traveled and demonstrated their product. One of them, Charles C. Cowles, sometimes received cattle for payment, instead of cash, which he would sell in Chicago before he returned home.[15] By 1859, the Wade brothers had established a second factory at Milton, Kentucky, probably to gain better access to markets near the Ohio and Mississippi Rivers. They appear to have had an agent in Missouri, R. J. Rudisill, who wrote *Music for the Piano Dulcimer, Containing Airs, Marches, Polkas, Hornpipes, &c.: Also Directions for Tuning* (Stedman, N.Y. and Milton, Ky.: L. S. & H. Wade, 1859; Mayville, N.Y.: John E. Phelps, printer).[16] After 1860, with the fire having closed the Stedman factory and the Milton enterprise out of existence, as it was not listed in the U.S. census of manufactures for that year, the Wade brothers went on to other ventures, Harrison into the booming oil business near Warren, Pennsylvania.

Henry Ransom (1809-1863), husband of the Lewis S. and Harrison Wade's sister Temperance, was a merchant in nearby Sherman, New York, in 1850, and perhaps an investor in the Wades' enterprise. He must have sensed profit, as in 1856 he opened a rival factory in Sherman.[17] This enterprise was successful, since instruments similar to one donated by his granddaughter to the New York Historical Association are in Pennsylvania, Ohio, Michigan, Missouri, and elsewhere. Charles W. Stanton, Jr., of Sherman, New York, a fiddler and dulcimer player, exhibited one of Ransom's instruments in 1903 and wrote that "many thousand" had been manufactured by Ransom and sold by him and his agents.[18] One Ransom instrument was said to have been transported in 1854 by oxcart from New Lebanon, Illinois, to Siskiyou County, California.[19] One in Michigan has its original shipping case, perhaps indicating that Ransom's salesmen demonstrated and took orders, then shipped them to customers accessible by railroad. Ransom left Sherman, and by 1859, like the Wade brothers, he had opened a factory at Newport, Kentucky, across the Ohio River from Cincinnati. In 1860, he reported that he had invested $3000 in capital, used $1565 worth of "musical articles," employed three men at monthly wages of $105, and produced $4730 worth of dulcimers annually.[20] Ransom's instruments normally lacked maker's identification, but the back of one example is stamped "H. Ransom / Manufacturer / Newport Ky."[21] Active in 1861, the Civil War probably put a close to Ransom's operation. Following his death, his sons Martin (1839-1866) and J. Monroe (1843-1874) went to Nunda, New York, and seem to sold off the stock of dulcimers manufactured at Newport. The latter published a broadside with tunes written in a numerical tablature with which he seems to have instructed purchasers of his instrument.[22] The particular model of rectangular dulcimer that he sold around Nunda matches ones found in locations as far apart as Michigan, Tennessee, Kentucky, and California, indicating extensive sales activity.[23]

Following Ransom's departure from Sherman, New York, Lafayette Chesley manufactured dulcimers identical to the model that Ransom had produced, as they are identified with a label on the back: "L. Chesley, Manufacturer and Wholesale and Retail Dealer of Dulcimers, Sherman Chaut. Co., N.Y."[24] One of these was bought in Oklahoma recently, so this factory's sales must also have been widespread. Chesley was active in 1860, as he reported his occupation as "dulcimer," but did not report his factory in the census of manufactures, which may indicate a relatively small operation.[25] By 1865, if not earlier, Chesley was out of business.[26]

John Low (born 16 September 1816, Lancaster, Massachusetts), from a family of comb makers, manufactured dulcimers in Clinton, Massachusetts.[27] He had begun by 1858, when he wrote and published *An Instructor for the Dulcimer, Containing Airs, Marches, Waltzes, Schottisches, Hornpipes, &c.: also, Directions for Tuning* (Boston: Oliver Ditson & Co., 1858). As his daughter was born in Pennsylvania about 1858 and the tuning diagram in his method indicates a tuning identical to the Chautauqua County instruments, Low may have been involved as a salesman for Ransom's firm. In 1860, his occupation was recorded in the census as "musical instrument manufacturer."[28] His book, which was the most popular dulcimer tutor and was sold by other makers as well,[29] shows a diagram of a rectangular dulcimer with the same tuning as that of C. Haight. Low was issued a patent (no. 28,811, dated June 19, 1860) on a rectangular dulcimer with eleven treble courses divided by a bridge into minor seconds and ten bass courses. Low assigned this patent to Nathan Bruce (1792-1876), of Southborough, Massachusetts, who must have at least intended to manufacture the new chromatic dulcimer. Low was a partner with his nephew Albion W. Gibbs in the manufacturing enterprise,[30] but despite his apparent initial efforts, I have never seen any instruments which follow the patent nor know of any rectangular dulcimers in New England with eleven treble and seven bass courses that Low presumably manufactured. As he estimated his personal estate

AN

INSTRUCTOR

FOR THE

CONTAINING

AIRS, MARCHES, WALTZES, SCHOTTISCHES, HORNPIPES, &C.

ALSO,

DIRECTIONS FOR TUNING.

BY J. LOW.

BOSTON:
Published by OLIVER DITSON & CO., 277 Washington Street.
NEW YORK: C. H. DITSON & CO.

Figure 13.1: Title page of John Low's *An Instructor for the Dulcimer* (Boston: Oliver Ditson, 1858).

at only $300 in 1860, his output must have been relatively small and local.

The Civil War may have halted Ransom's border-state business, but dulcimer manufacturing continued elsewhere. Mortimer DeLano (1823-1898), of Oxford, Oakland County, Michigan, with the assistance of his brother Oscar (1827-1904), was active, according to Oscar's granddaughter, for about eight or ten years, but is listed in the *Michigan Business Gazetteer* only in 1863.[31] Some of his instruments are identified with the stenciled label "M. DeLano," while other instruments resembling the two I have seen with the maker's label lack it. Another commercial instrument, resembling the known DeLano design in every characteristic except the shape of the sound holes, exists in multiple examples in Michigan and elsewhere and may also have been produced by DeLano. He sold his instruments in southern Michigan and Ontario, where a later maker, Emerson Kelly, of Mount Forest, produced dulcimers almost identical to this second design.[32] William Thurston (born about 1832), of Farmington, Oakland County, Michigan, made dulcimers commercially around 1860 or slightly later, when he can be located there.[33] Perry Wight (1831-1862), of South Alabama, Genesee County, New York, produced a fairly large number of trapezoidal dulcimers around 1860. The instruments made by Thurston and Wight can be identified by stenciled labels. All of these makers had a smaller production than the Wade and Ransom factories and probably sold their instruments in a limited area themselves.

What may have been the largest dulcimer manufacturing enterprise, if surviving instruments are any indication, began during the Civil War. Ezra Durand (born 8 March 1833, Seneca Falls, New York) was a music teacher, probably conducting singing schools, in Dowagiac, Michigan, in 1860, where he probably met William Vogel (born about 1823), an immigrant German cabinetmaker with a shop in the city of Niles, Michigan.[34] Durand probably also was an agent for George A. Prince and Company, of Buffalo, a large manufacturer of melodeons. By 1862, Durand had returned to the neighborhood of his parents' home, Chelsea, Michigan, where in that year he held a peddler's license.[35] The following year both he and William Vogel lived in Chelsea, where Durand paid tax as a peddler and Vogel as a "retail dealer."[36] In 1864, both still lived there, but Durand now had licenses as both peddler and manufacturer, and Vogel as a peddler.[37] Although one might assume that Durand was the entrepreneur and salesman and Vogel the builder, the relationship of the two is unclear. In any case, it appears probable that Durand had begun manufacturing dulcimers at Chelsea by 1864. Their partnership seems to have come to an abrupt end, however, as Vogel sold lots there in 1864 and 1865.[38] A label inside a dulcimer indicates Vogel's activities during this period:[39]

> William Vogel
> manufacturer of
> Piano-Stools
> and Dulcimers.
> Also Agent for Prince & Co.'s Single and
> Double Reed Melodeons!
>
> ——
>
> Dulcimers and Melodeons Tuned and Repaired. All orders attended to promptly. Shops in Mechanics Block,
> Niles, - - - - - - - - - - - - - - - - - - Mich.

Durand was listed in the *Michigan State Gazetteer and Business Directory for 1867-8* as a dealer in "music and musical instruments" in Chelsea.[40] He sold property in Chelsea at the end of 1866 and by February 1867 had moved to Stonington, Connecticut.[41] On 31 December 1867, Durand was issued a United States patent (no. 72,824) on a dulcimer, and that year his book, *Dulcimer without a Master: Containing the Elements of Music, and Complete Instructions; to Which is Added a Choice Selection of Popular Music Adapted to the Instrument* (Boston: Oliver Ditson & Company, 1867), was published. Clearly a major manufacturing initiative was underway in Stonington. In 1868, the local directory listed William Vogel's business as musical instrument manufacturing, with a shop on Myers Alley, and Ezra Durand's brothers David and John E. listed separately as dulcimer maker and music dealer respectively, while Ezra was a piano tuner.[42] Vogel received a patent on another dulcimer, with dampers, on 10 November 1868 (no. 84,027), but assigned it to Durand. Ezra Durand left Norwich in 1869, although his brother David stayed until 1871, and in the latter year, William Vogel was an accordion manufacturer in Stonington; two years later he was a partner with one Hughes as a manufacturer of cabinet and parlor organs in Taftville, Connecticut.[43] Ezra Durand's movements are unknown until 1882, when he sold organs and pianos at St. Joseph, Missouri; in 1884 and later he sold or manufactured organs in Portland, Oregon.[44]

Evidence thus shows that William Vogel manufactured dulcimers in Niles, Michigan, about 1865, and in Stonington, Connecticut, probably from 1867 to 1869. Ezra Durand clearly manufactured them in Chelsea, Michigan in 1864. The period of their dulcimer manufacturing thus ranged from 1863 to 1869 in three different locations. But their business relationship is not clear. In any event, more dulcimers made by Vogel and Durand are found in museums than any dulcimer of any other manufacturer, and many are in private hands as well. Those in Michigan and neighboring states may have been produced during their Michigan years, while others found in New England and along the Eastern seaboard as far south as North Carolina probably were produced in Connecticut.

The activities of the dulcimer salesmen resembled in some ways those of the manufacturers of the autoharp, guitar-zither and other patented play-by-number instruments popular from about 1890 to 1920. To aid learning tunes on the dulcimer, some of the manufacturers included strips of paper or even glass, sometimes called "scales,"[45] with numbers or syllables representing the notes of the scale. Other makers stenciled numbers on the soundboard next to the note names under each course. It is difficult to say, however, whether the books and broadsides, either in standard notation or in numerical tablature, helped the salesman or the purchaser more. It seems likely that offering such aids to learning would promote the sale of a dulcimer to a potential customer doubtful of his or her musical ability. Since few copies of these tutors and broadsides have survived, it is more likely that those who really learned the instrument soon abandoned them if they ever used them at all. The oral tradition, in short, won out.

From the various methods and broadsides we can get an idea of the type of music that the manufacturers thought appropriate for the instrument. By far the biggest category is that of dance tunes. These include ones like "Money Musk," "Fisher's Hornpipe," "Copenhagen Waltz," "Haste to the Wedding," "Jenny Lind Polka," "Union Waltz, or Buy a Broom," "Durang's Hornpipe," "The Devil's Dream," as well as others suitable for contradances, cotillions or quadrilles, waltzes, schottisches, and polkas. Another sizeable category is that of marches and patriotic tunes, such as "Yankee Doodle," "Hail to the Chief," and "Washington's March." These would have been familiar through local fife-and-drum and military bands who performed on the Fourth of July and other civic occasions. Songs popularized by touring blackface minstrels, such as "Oh, Susannah" and "Dandy Jim," form another type of tunes found in

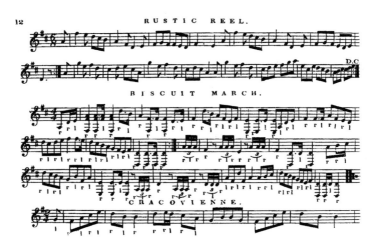

Figure 13.2: "Rustic Reel," "Biscuit March," and part of "Cracovienne," in C. Haight, *Complete System for the Dulcimer* (New York: William Hall & Sons, 1848), 12.

Figure 13.3: "The Celebrated Opera Reel," "Durang's Hornpipe," and "Charley over the Water," in John Low, *An Instructor for the Dulcimer* (Boston: Oliver Ditson, 1858), 29.

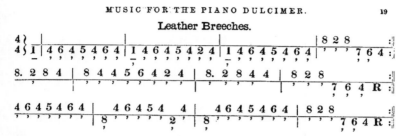

Figure 13.4: "Leather Breeches," in R. J. Rudisill, *Music for the Piano Dulcimer, Containing Airs, Marches, Polkas, Hornpipes, &c., also Directions for Tuning* (Stedman, N.Y., and Milton, Ky.: L. S. & H. Wade, 1859), 19.

Example 13.1: Transcription of "Leather Breeches" from the version in Rudisill's book. It probably represents an orally learned version of the tune.

the books. A few operatic airs and popular songs, like "Auld Lang Syne," also appear. Durand's book was the only one which included hymns, probably reflecting his background as a singing-school teacher and a desire to make the dulcimer more appealing and respectable to middle-class purchasers.

    Unlike the authors of the other methods, who used standard notation, the Missourian Robert J. Rudisill wrote his tutor using tablature. Most of the tunes he included were dance tunes, and one was the well-known tune "Leather Breeches," a version of the eighteenth-century Scot-

tish tune "Lord Macdonald's Reel." His version (see example 13.1) pre-
dates other known published versions of the tune under that name[46] and
likely reflects how he played it.

Many of the purchasers of these factory-made dulcimers, to the extent that we know, seem to have bought them in part for the same reason
that wealthier people bought pianos—as a way for their daughters to
learn music. Earlier in the century, some of the frontier elite bought
dulcimers, but by the 1850s improved transportation and manufacturing
made the more desirable piano widely available. Similarly the much
cheaper, mass-produced dulcimer now became available to families with
less means, and many used it in the same domestic context. Ann Branson,
an orthodox Quaker minister, boarded one evening in November 1859
with a family of non-Quakers as she traveled from Pennsville to Stillwater,
Ohio. Her host asked if she would like to hear his daughter play on the
dulcimer. The dour Quaker woman responded that she had no use for
music, nor did she even want to look at the instrument.[47] One day in
1858 Jane M. Tillotson, of Brunswick Township, Medina County, Ohio,
wrote in her diary that "Lib and I went over to hear Lottie play on the
Dulcimer."[48] In the same year, Mary Hollowell, of Preble County, Ohio,
a single woman in her thirties, willed her dulcimer to her brother and
her accordion to her sister.[49] Annie R. Stuart, a young woman teaching
in a district school near Tiffin, Ohio, made two entries in her diary for
May, 1861 that she "played on the dulcimer," evidently for her own
amusement, once on a Saturday and once on a Monday after school.[50]
During the Civil War, the instrument evoked pleasant thoughts of domestic bliss to certain Ohio soldiers. Robert S. Dilworth described in his
journal how he and other soldiers serenaded their colonel at Fort Wood,
Tennessee, one day in 1862 with four violins and two flutes, but when he
went to sleep, he "was present with one with whom my heart is always
and hearing the dulcimer played as I have heard it when my heart was
light."[51] Jacob Bruner, an officer writing from Louisiana in 1863 to his
wife Martha at her home in Antwerp, Paulding County, Ohio, remarked
"How I wish you were here to kiss Old Dan Tucker on my lips as you
used to do. That would be better and sweeter music to me than Rebecca's
dulcimer!"[52] Julia Ellen Smith (born 1845), of Orange or Solon Township, Cuyahoga County, Ohio, had a dulcimer probably manufactured by
the Wade Brothers which she played alone.[53] Martha M. Town (born
1841), of Washington, Pennsylvania, also owned the same type of dulcimer.[54]

Probably also typical were purchasers, like the Sweets mentioned above, who bought a dulcimer to enrich family music making. A child, for example, might be able to accompany his father's fiddling. With instruments scarce, families relatively large, and a need to be self-reliant, a dulcimer might allow a group of family members to play for local parties. James Swan (1824-1913), a farmer, fiddler, and dancing master of Ingham Township, Ingham County, Michigan, played for dances at his home and around the area with members of his family who played the organ, dulcimer, cello, and other instruments.[55] William Wells (1830-1899), of Stow, Chautauqua County, New York, owned a dulcimer made by the nearby Wade Brothers factory which his son Merle played, as well as the fiddle.[56] Charles W. Barnes (born 1840), of Meridian Township, Ingham County, Michigan, owned a dulcimer similar to the Wells instrument; his children Elizabeth and Archie learned to play it.[57] Other examples of families who played the dulcimer will be mentioned later, but these will suffice to show how the purchasers of these commercial dulcimers used them.

At this time the instrument appeared occasionally on stage. Minstrel shows occasionally featured it. Hans Nathan mentions a playbill of Messrs. Howes and Company, dated March 27, 1848, describing an ensemble consisting of dulcimer, banjo, tambourine, and bones.[58] The Snowden Family Minstrels, of Mount Vernon, Ohio, who were Afro-Americans, used the violin, "triangular," dulcimer, and castanets in their performances during the 1860s.[59] In 1866, P. T. Barnum described a thirteen-year-old spiritualist "boy medium," Henry B. Allen, touring to Boston and Portland, who, with the help of an assistant, managed to make sounds on a dulcimer, guitar, bell, and small drum, without the use of his hands.[60] In her 1884 novel *Old Caravan Days*, set in Ohio in 1857, Mary Hartwell Catherwood describes a tavern which had a dulcimer left behind as payment for use of the barroom by a traveling showman. This person also played the flute and harmonium and sang songs such as "Lily Dale" and "Roll On, Silver Moon," but despite his advertisements, he failed to draw an audience and, to pay his debts, left the less portable dulcimer at the tavern.[61] In contrast to the ever-present banjo of the minstrel shows, which popularized that instrument, the dulcimer was only rarely a stage instrument during this period. The spread of the instrument was probably only minimally affected by its occasional use among touring performers.

Regional Patterns

Before 1840 or 1850 it appears unlikely that much difference in the prevalence of dulcimers existed in different areas of North America. A fashion for the instrument had apparently developed in western New York State by this time, and it spread to those areas to which residents of this area migrated, especially northern Ohio, Michigan, and Wisconsin. Nevertheless, dulcimers made in the nineteenth century existed in areas as disparate as Maine, Virginia, West Virginia, southern Ohio, Indiana, Missouri, Tennessee, North Carolina, and elsewhere. The spread of the instrument resulted partly from the commercial activity of manufacturers both large and small and partly from migration to new regions.

The North

Great Lakes Region

The area where the dulcimer was best integrated into dance music ensembles was in the Great Lakes region, especially the lower part of the region, stretching westward from New York State and the northern tier of Pennsylvania through northern Ohio and Indiana into the Lower Peninsula of Michigan, continuing into Wisconsin and parts of Minnesota and Iowa. The exact boundaries of this region are unclear, but "Great Lakes Region" is an apt enough description, since the Great Lakes form the center of the region. Perhaps the eastern boundary starts approximately in the Binghamton, New York-Williamsport, Pennsylvania, area, where several players lived early in the twentieth century. It corresponds to the region defined by Wilbur Zelinsky as "New England Extended."[62]

Manufacturers certainly were responsible for some of the popularity of the instrument, but the characteristic use of the dulcimer in this region must have resulted from migration patterns, since the chief style of playing was the use of somewhat improvisatory accompaniment patterns, known as "chords" or "chording," or, less specifically, "playing second." Whether such playing was used elsewhere during the nineteenth century is impossible to say, but traditional players in North Carolina, West Virginia, and Tennessee living at the middle of the twentieth century seemed unaware of this style.[63] Most of the dulcimer tutors do not mention it, which implies that "chording" was spread orally. For such a style to spread, the region must have had enough players living near each other to pass such a tradition.

This style of accompaniment playing on the dulcimer probably had roots in English playing, although German influence is possible. We have noted Dalyell's description of two English brothers who appeared in 1842 in Edinburgh, one playing the melody and the other the accompaniment.[64] This musical role, however, likely appeared much earlier, probably in the seventeenth century, and was common to all the known dulcimer traditions in German-speaking countries as well. Some of the earliest American evidence appears in manuscripts of the Wight family, of South Alabama, New York, in the possession of James W. Kimball. One page features the very popular tune "Money Musk" followed by eight bars in common time of a "Dulcimer Second."[65] Another early source is a broadside from the years after the Civil War which accompanied a dulcimer probably manufactured by Elon Hackett, of Liberty Center, Ohio, with the heading "A Collection of Choice Tunes Prepared Expressly for the Dulcimer!"[66] This includes, in numeric tablature, examples of an "Accompaniment in D" and an "Accompaniment in A." Transcriptions of twentieth-century "chording" appear on later pages.

Ensembles using the dulcimer varied in instrumentation to some extent, but usually the melody (or "lead") was carried by a fiddler. A second fiddle might fill with rhythmic chordal playing, and a cello or bass viol might play the bass line. Towards the end of the century, an accordion or mouth organ might substitute for the fiddle, while a banjo, guitar, or reed organ might substitute for the second fiddle and the bass. The most common grouping, however, was fiddle and dulcimer alone.

In the vicinity of the two dulcimer factories in Chautauqua County, New York, the usual dance ensemble in the 1880s consisted of fiddle, dulcimer, and bass viol. My grandfather remembered Merritt Barnes, John Hitchcock (1841-1890), and Silas Taylor playing in that combination at local dances in the town of North Harmony.[67] Malchart (Mep) D. Mason (1836-1925), of Bemus Point, played the fiddle and dulcimer with those men and others as well.[68] Three sisters in Viroqua, Wisconsin, during the latter half of the century played the three instruments regularly.[69] In the vicinity of Ross's Corners and Honeyville, Jefferson County, New York, a group of young men formed an organization which they called the "Happy Band," consisting of Robert D. Loveland, first violin; Homer J. Oatman (1858-1936), second violin; Clarke W. Oatman (1859-1901), dulcimer; Mottie Lewis, flute; and Frank Oatman (born 1860), bass viol.[70]

Although more or less formal quadrille bands played for balls in Eaton Rapids, Michigan, W. Scott Munn recalled that the rural youth in nearby Hamlin Township in the 1880s relied on fiddler Eli Saumns and his dulcimer accompanist Clyde Jefferies and later Wilbur Post for a "hoe-down" at the Red Ribbon Hall.[71] In the 1870s and early 1880s, Frank Roberts, a fiddler, played for dances in Byron, Michigan, with a piccolo, organ, and sometimes a dulcimer.[72] William F. Shaw (born about 1867), of Kingston, Wisconsin, played his homemade dulcimer for barn dances, housewarmings, and weddings until about 1906, in combinations such as fiddle and dulcimer, cornet, fiddle, and dulcimer, and cornet, first and second fiddles, and dulcimer. When Helene Stratman-Thomas contacted Shaw in 1946 about making a recording, he declined, responding that he had not played for forty years and commenting "furthermore it should have a leading instrument as this Dulcimer never was intended as a leading instrument but to fill in a accomplementry [sic] playing."[73]

Most players in these ensembles using the dulcimer were farm boys who might earn a little extra money at parties. Shaw generally received about three dollars a night, the same that Albert Ives (born 1853), a dulcimer player of Casnovia Township, Muskegon County, Michigan, earned at dances.[74] A photograph of Curtis O. Render (1874-1950), posed with his dulcimer and accordion, fiddler A. Otis Fish (1878-1949), and guitarist Lewis Dunlap, taken at Mount Pleasant, Michigan, in 1899, typifies many such groups consisting of young men.[75] Their reputations were local, and they played close to home. As a boy, Edwin F. Baxter (1881-1949), of Cheboygan County, Michigan, put his dulcimer in a grain bag and carried it over his shoulder to dances.[76] Even if they drove a sleigh or rode a horse, they could not leave their farms for long.

One exception, notable for the impression it made on the young Henry Ford, was a duo which lived in Detroit. Albert B. Race (1845-1895) was a confectioner and stationer. He played the dulcimer regularly with Wesley Phelps, and in 1883 they advertised the "Race & Phelps Orchestra" at Race's business address, 609 Michigan Avenue.[77] Ford's sister Margaret Ruddiman recalled that Race (she remembered his first name as George) was a "cripple" who put his instrument on a table and called the dances while he played "beautiful music."[78] William Finzel, recalling dances at the Bryant (Ford's in-laws) home in Dearborn, probably in the early 1890s, remembered a "little crippled violinist," which must mean that Race also played that instrument.[79] Race's urban residence probably allowed him better access to transportation than what the typical rural musician had, and his urban occupation probably meant more freedom to travel, so he came closer to fitting the profile of a professional musician than most rural dulcimer players.

In much of this region in the period under consideration, many young men found employment during the winter as lumberjacks. They worked long hours, but evenings and Sundays found them in their shanties relaxing, playing cards or checkers and entertaining themselves with songs, jokes, fiddling, and occasional stag dances.[80] Given that dulcimers were often played by young men, it is no surprise that they appeared in the lumber camps. John S. Weeks (born about 1844), came from Springfield Center, New York, to Morley, Michigan, in 1868, and found work as a blacksmith in local lumber camps, ferrying his "shop" up and down the Muskegon River. He brought a dulcimer with him, on which he would accompany his fiddling wife Martha. Weeks made six violins for his children and several dulcimers as well, his son James playing the latter instrument more than the others.[81] Arch Bristow related that fiddlers often accompanied lumber rafts down the Allegheny River from Warren County, Pennsylvania, towards Pittsburgh. A local lumber company sponsored a trip in June 1881, unusual in that two fiddlers, Hugh Sutherland and Sid Bullock, accompanied by Jesse R. Martin on the dulcimer, played for two sets of dancers on the raft.[82] In other areas of heavily forested northern Pennsylvania, the dulcimer was used at dances, such as at Frenchville, Clearfield County, around 1878.[83] Henry Shoemaker wrote in 1931 that dulcimers had been found in lumber camps near the Sinnemahoning Creek and in the Black Forest, in Lycoming County, Pennsylvania, though less frequently than fiddles, mouth organs, or accordions.[84]

During the revival of the 1970s, players sometimes introduced the dulcimer as the "lumberjack's piano."[85] The origin of this euphemism is uncertain—its use derives from Patrick Murphy's liner notes to Chet Parker's 1966 recording—but Murphy's source may have referred to the use of the instrument in a troupe called the "Michigan Lumberjacks," active from the 1930s to the 1950s, which E. C. Beck, an English professor at Central Michigan College, organized. Nevertheless, its popularity in Michigan, especially near the Muskegon and Manistee Rivers, was contemporary with the lumber boom in that state (roughly 1850 to 1900), and dulcimers must have found their way to the camps. John Brown (born 1851), of Banks Township, Antrim County, made several, on which he played lead.[86] He taught it to Jay Mudge (1876-1948), of Kewadin, who began playing in 1900. Mudge told a reporter in 1947 that "when he was a youngster, working in the lumber camps of this region, the dulcimer was a popular instrument at dances. At that time . . . it was used to accompany other instruments."[87] About the turn of the century, William Hogan, of Hubbardston, Michigan, took his dulcimer with him to a lumber camp in the Upper Peninsula, where he worked a season or two.[88] James G. Baxter (1854-1939), a dulcimer player, worked in lumbering operations in northern Michigan, especially around Alpena and Lewiston, where he was employed by the Michelson and Hanson Lumber Company.[89] Martin E. Crump (1875-1949), a native of Berrien Springs, Michigan, played chords on a rectangular dulcimer to accompany fiddler Rob Gilbert, as well as tunes like "Turkey in the Straw" and "Red Wing." Crump worked in the woods for twenty-one winters around Littlefield Township, Emmet County, and must have played it in the camps.[90] Although there was no special association of the dulcimer with lumber camps, any more with than other instruments, such as the fiddle, mouth organ, accordion, banjo, or guitar, workers in the camps did play the instrument. In the years after 1900, when most of the virgin lumber in Michigan had been cut and former lumberjacks might recall their youth, their reminiscences of the dulcimer might have caused some, like Beck, to associate the instrument with the camps.

During the latter half of the nineteenth century some makers continued to produce dulcimers in quantity, although their distribution was not as widespread as that of the Durand-Vogel and the two Chautauqua County, New York, factories. The most prolific manufacture was carried on by Elon Hackett (1804-1892), a native of Maine, who had moved from Dryden, New York, to Ripley Township, Huron County, Ohio, in 1838, where in 1850 he worked as a millwright. In 1868 he and his family moved to Liberty Center, Ohio, where he began to manufacture dulcimers. Elon was listed in the 1870 census as "manufacturer of musical inst[rument]" and in 1880 as a cabinetmaker.[91] One instrument was reportedly marked "Hackett Brothers, Liberty Center, Ohio,"[92] indicating that Elon's brother Wheeler may have been involved in the enterprise for a while, but nearly all lack a maker's name. Elon's son Joseph Wheeler Hackett (1835-1908) continued manufacturing them until at least the 1890s. Clara Weirick (born about 1871), who played for dances in the late 1880s around Colton, Ohio, with her fiddling brother Bill, used to travel with Hackett and demonstrate his instrument.[93] Dulcimers made by the Hacketts are the most common variety of nineteenth-century instruments found in southeastern Michigan, western Ohio, and neighboring Indiana.[94] It seems unlikely that the Hacketts employed many salesmen, if any at all, since the distribution of the instruments was limited to this region.[95] "Wheel" Hackett did hire people, one of them Charles R. Barlow.[96] Players of Hackett dulcimers included the brother of William H. Balcom (born about 1860), of Reading Township, Hillsdale County, Michigan, who accompanied the latter's fiddling; Homer Wilbur (1881-1949), of Springport, Michigan, who learned from his father; Frank Wygant (1884-1974), a native of the Ohio-Hillsdale County border area; and Elgia C. Hickok, a native of Frontier, Hillsdale County, whose grandfather gave him his great-grandfather's dulcimer about 1905. Other families, like that of fiddler Jake Klump, of Saline, Michigan, who purchased one in the 1890s, bought them, but never learned to play.[97]

Although it lies some distance from the Great Lakes, northeastern Pennsylvania, in an area centering on Lycoming and Sullivan Counties, seems to have had a number of players in the nineteenth and early twentieth centuries. J. Lyman Jackson (1855-1929), of Hillsgrove, played the dulcimer as well as violin at dances and in the 1880s played a horn in the town band. He even had a tune published, "Hillsgrove Moonlight Waltz" (Philadelphia: J. W. Pepper, 1894). In his last years, Jackson played in the theater in Endicott, New York, where he lived.[98] Frank Watts (1876-1937), a lumberman of Millville, in neighboring Columbia County, played his dulcimer at dances in local hotels with hammers made with corset stays wrapped at the ends with wool; he also chorded on the piano and played the alto horn in the town band.[99] Other recollections of players in this area mention the dulcimer in association with dances.[100] This leaves little doubt that we should link the tradition in this area with that of the larger region.

The dulcimer seems to have been reasonably popular in northwestern Illinois during the 1860s. S. Hunter Smith (see illustration 21) was probably one of many players.[101] Born 29 January 1828 in Montgomery County, Indiana, Smith lost the use of his legs due to rheumatism at the age of twelve and for thirteen years could not sit upright. In 1853 he acquired a special wheelchair and in April 1854, when a resident of Knox County, began to play the dulcimer. In 1864, he began to tour with a "stereoscopic" exhibition, selling and autographing photographs of himself.[102] Daniel Leroy Van Antwerp (1848-1925), a brick mason of Vermont, Fulton County, Illinois, made and sold dulcimers and violins.

Van Antwerp traveled in the Midwest and South, operating a Punch and Judy show with a partner named Carpenter, and appeared in local opera houses as a ventriloquist and magician. He would play a few tunes and give instructions to purchasers of his instruments. At the time of his death, he had eight or ten unfinished dulcimers.[103] Van Antwerp's association with puppet shows recalls Pepys's seventeenth-century London reference. Whether he used the instrument in his shows is unknown, but it is not improbable that he did.

Migrants from western New York State, northern Pennsylvania and Ohio, and Michigan brought the dulcimer with them to new areas. In some areas the instrument was a novelty. A. B. Wood, recalling the late 1880s in western Nebraska, mentions Wellington Clark (born 1847), who came from Michigan to Minatare and Gering, Nebraska. Clark had a family orchestra which included a dulcimer, the only one the author ever saw.[104] David Green, who played the violin, guitar, and dulcimer, moved from the Petoskey, Michigan, area first in 1883 to White City, Kansas, and then in 1885 to LaGrace, Campbell County, South Dakota.[105] In Los Angeles, California, during the 1880s, residents were familiar with an eccentric, one Professor Brewster, known also by his stage name, "Savariej" or "Savarie J.," who, in Ralph E. Shaffer's words, "demonstrated a lack of talent" on his violin or homemade dulcimer and caused groups to heckle him and make him the butt of jokes.[106]

One of the more prolific, yet largely regional, manufacturers was James A. MacKenzie (1848-1905), of Minneapolis, Minnesota.[107] Born in Ogle County, Illinois, his family came to Minnesota in 1854 and soon afterwards settled in Hutchinson. MacKenzie was issued three patents (171,031; 440,601; and 461,915) in 1875, 1890, and 1891, on designs of dulcimers. He christened his instrument the "piano-harp" and fancied himself, in the age of Edison, its "inventor," as a photograph shows him seated at one of his instruments before a sign inscribed "Dont fail to see and hear the Piano-Harp played now in public only by the inventor."[108] He appears in the Minneapolis city directories of 1875 and 1876 as a manufacturer of musical instruments, but seems to have left the city afterwards, showing up in the 1884-1885 directory as a musician and then in 1888-1889 as selling musical instruments. The 1875 patent is for a "piano-harp" with two soundboards; the rectangular instrument could revolve in its case, so that the player could play two sets of strings, presumably one tuned in the sharp keys and the other in flats. It also had jacks under the strings to allow the pitch of those courses to be altered by a half-step. This variety, however, may not have been the usual model that he manufactured in 1875, as one instrument with two six-pointed star sound holes in a rectangular case, resembling those features in the patent drawing, did not have the second soundboard and set of strings.

Most of MacKenzie's manufacturing activity seems to date from 1888 to about 1904.[109] Curiously, at least some of these instruments, although they resemble the 1890 patent drawing, bear the stenciled inscription "J. A. Mackenzie's Piano Harp pat. Feb. 14. 1873," although he never was issued a patent on that date. This model incorporates a cast rectangular frame resting in a walnut case with turned legs. MacKenzie remarked in his patent application that

> my instrument may be called an "improved dulcimer"; but I have given it the new name of "piano-harp." This name is more appropriate than dulcimer as defining the invention, because, first, it may be played with hammers, and when so played it yields the full, deep tones of the piano-forte, and not the thin wiry tones of the old dulcimer; secondly, having placed each group of strings (giving the different tones) one-third closer to each other than they are on the ordinary dulcimer, the player is able to reach an octave of strings with the fingers, as upon the piano-forte, so that when playing with the hammers (one in each hand), the fingers may be also brought into play in the same strain of music either alternatively or without breaking the time, thus giving the results of both piano and harp.[110]

Indeed the tone of MacKenzie's "piano-harps" is deep and pleasing, but one cannot help but imagine his salesmanship and his demonstration techniques in making this claim. The inventor also wrote and published a tune book for the instrument, *J. A. Mackenzie's Piano Harp Book: The Piano Harp is here Played at Sight without a Teacher by using Letters: Children Learn Who Know Their A.B.C's,* in a numerical tablature of his own design.[111] The repertoire resembles other dulcimer books of the nineteenth century, with dance tunes and popular songs. MacKenzie clearly had a flair for self-promotion and salesmanship, but seems to have lacked a sales force that the Ransom, Wade, and Durand factories had. His second wife traveled with him and demonstrated the instrument,[112] and one "piano-harp" went to England, but he seems to have sold most of them in Minnesota and the neighboring states of Wisconsin, Iowa, and the Dakotas.[113]

Despite the maker's promotion of his instrument as no mere dulcimer, purchasers bought the "piano-harp" to play in the same contexts as
those of the dulcimer. Husband and wife Willie and Catherine Manley,
of Fillmore, Minnesota, used to take two "harps," as they called them,
on buckboards to play them together at local dances, around 1910.[114] In
a region where many European immigrants had settled during the late
nineteenth century, "piano-harp" technique must have owed much to
that of the American dulcimer style existing among native migrants from
further east.

Although located within the Great Lakes region, one manufacturer
differed from the others in providing dulcimers for the music trade and
mail order houses nationally. Lyon and Healy was established in Chicago in 1864 and by 1890 was the country's largest music store.[115] The
firm manufactured all types of musical instruments, and by 1880 had
begun to advertise dulcimers. In that year the Lyon and Healy catalog
offered a dulcimer with a black soundboard and heart-shaped sound holes
for $24, as well as a tuning hammer with oblong or square hole, and
hammers made of wood with buckskin-covered heads and "pliable"
handles.[116] Montgomery Ward, in its 1894-1895 catalog, offered American-made dulcimers in an imitation rosewood finish with heart-shaped
soundholes that likely were manufactured by Lyon and Healy.[117] Other,
presumably later, instruments were manufactured under the Washburn
"Perfection" label, with round sound holes and tuning pins on the left-
hand pin block. By 1897 the Sears and Roebuck catalog listed a newer
design, labeled "Improved Perfection" dulcimer, with a second bass bridge
to allow a partially chromatic tuning, for $22.90.[118] Lyon and Healy's
1898-1899 catalog shows the same instrument priced at $42, as well as
tuning hammers, hammers with flexible handles and felt-covered heads,
tuning pins, and wire.[119] In 1905, the company's catalog listed a dulcimer for $20, but it discontinued the instrument soon afterwards; in the
following year Sears and Roebuck no longer offered a dulcimer in its
catalog.[120]

In Brooklyn, New York, an immigrant maker seems to have created
a local fashion for the instrument around the turn of the century. Anton
Stonitsch, born 1842 in Germany, immigrated in 1876 and settled first
in Iowa. In 1900, he was in Brooklyn and reported his occupation as
cabinetmaker, but by 1902, he had a shop at 576 Broadway, in Brooklyn,
where he sold musical instruments.[121] Stonitsch manufactured dulcimers
not of traditional American or Austrian design, but with his own unique

chromatic tuning scheme. Some carry his name, while others, of similar design, bear decals with the label "Jos. F. Stroehlein, manufacturer, Brooklyn, N.Y." Since no Brooklyn directory carries a listing for such a person, Stonitsch likely made them. He was not above putting a decal on some instruments that claimed it had won a prize at the "National Exhibition" in Philadelphia in 1876, clearly a fiction, since Stonitsch arrived in America that year, and, as Nancy Groce has mentioned, the Centennial Exhibition did not list a Stroehlein as a medal winner.[122] Another maker of similar dulcimers was Alphons L. Henn, of Brooklyn.[123] Stonitsch probably sold most of his instruments from his shop, as surviving instruments turn up mostly in the New York City region. Players of these Brooklyn dulcimers may have tended to be German-Americans, such as John J. Strasser (born 1890), of Glendale, Long Island, who played popular tunes from the 1920s on his instrument, accompanied by guitar or banjo.[124] Whatever the ethnic origin of the makers or players, however, we should regard these instruments as an individual American development, rather than part of a tradition brought over from Europe.

Utah

Many early Mormons had origins in western New York State and had lived in northeastern Ohio before settling in Utah. The sect, unlike many others, did not discourage music or dancing, and a number of its members played the dulcimer. Don Carlos Shurtz (1836-1922), a native of Kirtland, Ohio, made a dulcimer in 1861 in Kanarraville, Utah, from local red cedar. It is now in the collection of the Pioneer Memorial Museum in Salt Lake City.[125] Ezra G. Ramsay (1844-1929), a native of McDonough County, Illinois, played the dulcimer with William Parker, Will Bond, and Hyrum Adams, and others, on violins, for dances in Kanosh, Utah.[126] Joseph Prows, of Kanosh, also played the instrument.[127] Ammon B. Reynolds (1853-1916), born in Adrian, Michigan, sometimes accompanied William Park, a fiddler, and Henry Howard, an accordion player, for dances near Salt Lake City.[128] Raymond Reynolds, of Ashley Valley, played it at dances.[129] At Christmas 1874, Nathan Adams played the dulcimer for a children's dance at Kanab, Utah, Esther Judd recalled many years later.[130]

Many Mormons came from Great Britain as well, and some of them played the dulcimer. Henry Clegg (1825-1894), who immigrated in 1855, settled at Springville, Utah. He played dulcimer in an orchestra consisting, besides him, of two violins and a cello, which played for theatricals and balls at the Camp Floyd Theatre in Springville from 1861 to 1868. Clegg also traveled around the state as a lecturer, and his two wives would entertain by singing to his dulcimer accompaniment.[131] His son Israel E. (1849-1923) played a dulcimer which his father had made in the "Shepherd-Clegg Orchestra" at dances in Weber County, Utah. Whenever he was late, he had to pay a fine of twenty-five cents, but was so often late that he had to quit playing.[132] Fredrick Weight (1828-1901), of Springville, a native of England who played cello in Clegg's orchestra, made a dulcimer in 1893 for his fourteen-year-old son Claude and a cello for his son Ralph, and the following year made another dulcimer. Weight's four sons Alfred, George, Claude, and Ralph, with the instrumentation of violin, piccolo, dulcimer, and cello, a combination which their father called "very good," played for their first dance in January 1895. The boys' mother wrote that the Weight brothers' "string band" played one afternoon in May 1895 for a local Relief Society program.[133] Fred Lewis, from Wales, played the dulcimer for dances near Salt Lake City.[134] The instrument was also played by descendants of these British immigrant Mormons. Frank Herbert (1861-1924) accompanied his fiddling brother John, as well as William Bate, second violin, Jefferson Eastmond, banjo, and Jeddie Eldredge, flute, in the "Herbert Orchestra," which played for dances around American Fork, Utah.[135] After moving to the vicinity of Idaho Falls, Idaho, the Herbert brothers played regularly for dances at a pavilion on their homestead.[136] Although the dulcimer tradition in Utah seems to have died out before the middle of the twentieth century, its use as an accompaniment for the fiddle places its style firmly with that of the Great Lakes region.

Midlands

This region, which we might define as stretching from southern Pennsylvania, Maryland, and Virginia in the east to Missouri and Kansas in the west, taking in the southern Midwest and Kentucky, was one in which the dulcimer was scarcer in the nineteenth century than in the Great Lakes region, although there were exceptions. This is rather surprising, in view of the fact that this region included the chief westward destinations of migrating Pennsylvania Germans. Although some Pennsylvania Germans did migrate westward with dulcimers,[137] it appears that the instrument largely died out among them by the middle of the nineteenth century. The areas within this region where the dulcimer was most numerous seems to have been in northern West Virginia and in southern Missouri. In both areas, the tuning and arrangement of the strings follows the broader general American variety, rather than those of the German *Hackbrett*,[138] and it is likely that the tradition was largely English in origin.

West Virginia

Russell Fluharty wrote that during the nineteenth century, around Mannington, in northern West Virginia, dulcimer players "were always in great demand at bean stringins, corn shuckins, wood gittins, house warmins, guiltin [sic] partys, and many other community activities."[139] Most instruments were made by individuals for sale limited to their region; factory-made examples seem to be rare. Groce lists a number of West Virginia makers about whom both Fluharty and H. E. Matheny, a West Virginia native from a family involved for several generations in making and playing the instrument, had learned. Matheny's great-grandfather Reuben (1809-1877), of Harrisville, made several, as did his youngest son, Reuben, Jr. (1857-1936), a shoemaker (see illustration 23).[140] The instrument was common enough for a dulcimer contest to be held at the Ritchie County Fair in Pennsboro in 1894. About a dozen players entered, and fifteen-year-old Joseph Edward Matheny, nephew of the last Reuben, won the prize. "Eddie" played the dulcimer as a solo instrument, rather than with other instruments.[141] Jesse Ash (born 1860), of Ashley, Doddridge County, made rectangular dulcimers, although his last, made in the 1920s, were trapezoidal. That community included several players who were elderly in the 1920s, including Philip Underwood and Mrs. Mary Underwood, who placed her rectangular instrument on her lap when in play.[142]

Southern Midwest

Moving west through the southern Midwest and Ohio Valley, we find occasional use of the dulcimer, such as in central Indiana. A Mrs. Carter, of Pittsboro, Indiana, who had bought a Durand dulcimer in 1873, played it at the Lebanon (Indiana) centennial about 1926.[143] Eli Wright, of Frankton, Indiana (born 1850), played "old-fashioned tunes" on his dulcimer at the centennial celebration in Anderson in 1916.[144]   Eliza

Jane Jones Jeffryes (1816-1869), of Smith Township, Whitley County, Indiana, and a native of Greenville County, Virginia, of Occaneechi Indian descent, willed her dulcimer to her daughter.[145] I once met a man who remembered a player in his hometown of Columbus, Indiana, who was active prior to 1915. The presence of nineteenth-century dulcimers in central and southern Indiana is further evidence of the instrument's use there.

Missouri

A dulcimer factory was active in Missouri, probably soon before or after the Civil War. According to Jean Granberry Schnitz, her grandfather C. A. Lee (1836-1896), of Lee Spring, Barry County, Missouri, bought a dulcimer in 1859 which had been built in a shop at Sedalia, Missouri.[146] An instrument identical to this was played by Nellie Chase McKinney, born in 1870 in neighboring McDonald County, and another, after 1936, by Ruth Tyler, of Joplin.[147] The location of these instruments in southeastern Missouri suggests that the factory may have been there. Indeed, Phillip Van Arsdale, of Clarksville, Arkansas, heard of a maker named Thomas at Pea Ridge, Arkansas, but I have been unable to verify this person. This factory may have come into being as a result of the activity of salesmen or agents from the Wade and Ransom factories in western New York, although the design is somewhat different, having ten, rather than eleven, treble courses. Bill McNeil, folklorist at the Ozark Folk Center at Mountain View, Arkansas, said there were at least two dulcimer factories in the Missouri Ozarks during the nineteenth century, and learned of a maker active at Damascus, Van Buren County, Arkansas, during this period as well.[148] Harvey Prinz writes of Joseph Fox, a fiddler of Greeley, Anderson County, Kansas, who heard a dulcimer in a traveling medicine show and made one in 1895 from memory.[149]

Daughters of the Lee family played mainly dance tunes on the dulcimer. Schnitz mentions the names of many tunes and writes that Dora Lee Scudder (1874-1970), her grandmother, played frequently with her husband Ira Scudder, a fiddler. Dora recalled that when her family moved to Texas in 1878 with a wagon train, her sister Ida played with Newton Meador, a fiddler, for dancing each evening.[150] As Schnitz makes no mention of playing an accompaniment part, it is likely that when members of the Lee family played it, the dulcimer part doubled that of the fiddle.

The South

North Carolina

A number of players lived in Randolph County, North Carolina, during the first half of the twentieth century, and the tradition went back into the previous century. The grandfather and father of Virgil Craven (1902-1980), of Cedar Falls, played the dulcimer as well as the fiddle. Virgil learned such fiddle tunes as "Forked Deer," "Chapel Hill Serenade," "Mississippi Sawyer," "Darling Chloe," and others, from his father.[151] He knew three others who played the dulcimer.[152] In an autobiographical sketch, Ida May Beard (born in 1862 in Forsyth County, North Carolina) recalled, during her childhood, a neighbor who played a couple of tunes, including "Dixie," on the dulcimer for her.[153] Beard does not describe the instrument further, but, since Forsyth County is close to Randolph County and farther from the locations in the western part of the state where the Appalachian dulcimer appeared in more recent years, we might assume she heard the hammered dulcimer.

Tennessee

The dulcimer enjoyed a certain popularity in Tennessee during the latter part of the nineteenth century, especially in the middle part of the state. The protagonist of George Washington Harris's *Sut Lovingood* (1867), an east Tennessee mountaineer, was familiar with the word, as he remarks "The 'perpryiter' anser'd in soun's es sof an' sweet es a poplar dulcimore, tchuned by a good nater'd she angel in butterfly wings an' cobweb shiff."[154] Salesmen from the Ransom factory at Newport, Kentucky, evidently sold many in the state before the Civil War, as Richard H. Hulan discovered five examples within forty miles of Gallatin.[155] One day in 1862 Colonel John Beatty, other officers, and a newspaper correspondent enjoyed supper at the home of a Nashville farmer loyal to the Union. Afterwards, reported Beatty, his daughter entertained them with a tune on the dulcimer, "an abominable instrument, which she pounded with two little sticks."[156] Local makers also satisfied the demand for the instrument. According to his relatives, Hulan's great-uncle Sam Hulan, who lived ten miles downstream from Nashville, became an agent for a dulcimer factory, perhaps located in Missouri, about 1885.

Shortly afterwards, he decided it would be more profitable to make them himself, and he and his two younger brothers, Minor and George, made them, and Sam and Minor sold them. About 1900 their business ended.[157] Another maker was Valentine Columbus (Lum) Scott, who lived across the state line at New Roe, Allen County, Kentucky, in the 1890s.[158]

More examples and information are needed in order for us to get a better understanding of the use of the dulcimer in Tennessee. Twentieth-century players played mostly dance tunes, and such was probably the case during the previous century. Charles Wolfe describes a pre-1900 photograph from Robertson County in which two people pose behind a dulcimer in a "fiddle band," and he notes that the instrument was "rather common in middle Tennessee rural stringbands."[159]

Elsewhere in the South the dulcimer seems to have been rather rare. Nevertheless, some examples show that the instrument was not unknown. James Wesley Samples (1845-1920), of Forsyth County, Georgia, played one that he made.[160] About 1873, Elum Cockrell, of Clay County, Alabama, purchased a dulcimer. His daughter Nancy played both that instrument and the fiddle after the family's migration to Itawamba County, Mississippi.[161]

Notes

1. For example, see Ruth Hoppin, "Personal Recollections of Pioneer Days," *Collections and Researches Made by the Michigan Pioneer and Historical Society* 38 (1912): 416.

2. Daniel Spillane, *History of the American Pianoforte: Its Technical Development and the Trade* (New York: D. Spillane, 1890), describes the growth of the piano industry in Boston, New York City, Philadelphia, Albany, Baltimore, and in other cities. Many of the manufacturers had learned the trade in England or Germany; Philip F. Gura and James F. Bollman, *America's Instrument: the Banjo in the Nineteenth Century* (Chapel Hill: The University of North Carolina Press, 1999) discusses antebellum banjo makers, mainly in New York, Baltimore, and other cities, and shows that many were immigrants.

3. C. Haight, *A Complete System for the Dulcimer* (New York: William Hall & Son, 1848), 5.

4. "Whigville Tavern, Once Scene of Schottische and Polka, Re-Opens After Years of Disuse," 1931 article, probably in *Flint Journal*, in scrapbook at Whaley Historical House, Flint, Mich., citing a letter from Elizabeth Waterous to Asahel Collins.

5. Henry Parker Smith Diaries, 25 Dec. 1848; 4 July 1850; 16 Aug. 1848; 26 Jan. 1849, Bentley Historical Library, University of Michigan.

6. Harry Ellsworth Cole, *Stagecoach and Tavern Days in the Baraboo Region* (Baraboo, Wis.: Baraboo News Publishing Co., 1923), 60. In the author's *Stagecoach and Tavern Tales of the Old Northwest* (Cleveland: Arthur H. Clark Co., 1930), 257, he mentions that the dulcimer and bass viol were favorite instruments used at larger parties.

7. "John S. Donald and Mother to Play Old Time Dulcimer for WIBA Fans Wednesday," *Capital Times*, 22 Mar. 1927, in John Sweet Donald Papers, 1811-1934, State Historical Society of Wisconsin.

8. Dulcimers with such tuning pins are held in the following collections, to my knowledge: Historic Deerfield, Deerfield, Massachusetts; Newark Museum, Newark, New Jersey (acc. no. 13.307); Rockingham Free Public Library, Bellows Falls, Vermont. A dulcimer in the Metropolitan Museum (acc. no. 1979.522.2), with pins having raised letters "WW" and "A" on opposite sides, may also belong to this group. See Laurence Libin, *American Musical Instruments in The Metropolitan Museum of Art* (New York: The Metropolitan Museum of Art, 1985), 103. Nancy Groce, *Musical Instrument Makers of New York: A Directory of Eighteenth- and Nineteenth-Century Urban Craftsmen*, Annotated Reference Tools in Music, no. 4 (Stuyvesant, N.Y.: Pendragon Press, 1991), 165, lists a piano maker, John F. Wake, who in 1855 was a maker of hardware for pianos; William Wake was a journeyman piano maker active at that time.

9. Until about 1970, Schaff Piano Supply Company of Chicago advertised 1/0 (.276 inch) tuning pins as "dulcimer pins."

10. Nancy Groce, *The Hammered Dulcimer in America*, Smithsonian Studies in History and Technology, no. 44 (Washington: Smithsonian Institution Press, 1983), 47f.

11. *History of Clark County, Ohio* (Chicago: W. H. Beers, 1881), 948; Sara Johnson, personal communication, who described such a dulcimer from Adams County, Ohio.

12. Reuben Beecher Hughes, *Genealogy of a Branch of the Beecher Family* (New Haven: Hoggson & Robinson, printers, 1889), 65.

13. 1855 New York State Census, Chautauqua County, Town of Harmony, Manufactures.

14. Marshall Wells, of Stow, N.Y., and his mother, Mrs. Byron Smith, have dulcimers which have been in the Wells family, which has resided in the neighborhood continuously since the time of the Wade factory; Floyd Darrow, *History of the Town of North Harmony, Chautauqua County, New York* (n.p.: The Town Board of North Harmony, 1955), book 2, 80-81.

15. Archie Cowles, his grandson, conversation with author, Stedman, N.Y., about 1972.

16. The only copy I have located is in the University of Pittsburgh Library.

17. *Some Events in the History of Sherman* ([Sherman, N.Y.]: 1923), 110, which says he had a factory on South Main Street in that year. As his enterprise was not recorded in the 1855 state census, I assume that it began the next year.

Wyllys C. Ransom, *Historical Outline of the Ransom Family of America* (Ann Arbor: Richmond & Backus Co., 1903), 382-383.

    18. *The Centennial History of Chautauqua County, New York* (Jamestown, N.Y.: 1904), 1: 438.

    19. Michael Rugg, "Early California Dulcimers," *Frets* 2 (Feb. 1980): 62. Either this instrument was not a Ransom instrument or it actually went to California after 1854, but the photograph shows a rectangular dulcimer with heart-shaped sound holes.

    20. United States Census of Manufactures, 1860, Kentucky, Campbell County, National Archives. This was the only dulcimer factory reported for the whole United States in this part of the census.

    21. Jack Metcalfe, of Lexington, Kentucky, owns such a dulcimer, which rests in a specially made case with a lid and four turned legs.

    22. James W. Kimball, personal communication.

    23. I bought one in Union Lake, Michigan, in 1969, and know of another that was in private hands in Howell, Michigan, in 1948; Jon Blasius, of Cedar Ridge, California, has the remains of one; and Richard Hulan, "Music in Tennessee," *Antiques* 100 (Sept. 1971): 419, illustrates one and writes that "four other hammered dulcimers by the maker of this instrument have turned up within forty miles of Gallatin, Tennessee."

    24. Russ Meyer, personal communication, 1998. Jim Kimball says there is one such dulcimer at the Sherman Museum, Sherman, N.Y.

    25. U.S. Census, 1860, New York, Chautauqua County, Town of Sherman, 270.

    26. The 1865 New York state census shows no dulcimer manufacture in Sherman.

    27. Andrew E. Ford, *History of the Origin of the Town of Clinton, Massachusetts, 1653-1865* (Clinton, Mass.: W. J. Coulter, 1896), 166, 429; Henry S. Nourse, ed., *The Birth, Marriage and Death Register, Church Records and Epitaphs of Lancaster, Massachusetts, 1643-1850* (Lancaster, n.p., 1890), 212, 263.

    28. 1860 census, Worcester Co., Mass., Town of Clinton, 557.

    29. This book accompanied dulcimers manufactured by Henry Ransom, owned by Vince Matthews of Shinglehouse, Pennsylvania, in 1974, and perhaps by Mortimer DeLano, at least in two cases.

    30. Groce, *Hammered Dulcimer in America*, 43.

    31. *Michigan State Gazetteer and Business Directory for 1863-4* (Detroit: Charles F. Clark, 1863), 435; Mrs. Edward Bossardet, conversation, 1976.

    32. Lloyd Kelly, conversation with author, Oil Springs, Ontario, 1979.

    33. U.S. Census, 1860, Michigan, Oakland County.

    34. U.S. Census, 1860, Michigan, Cass County, 3; Berrien County, 296.

    35. Internal Revenue Assessment Lists, Michigan, District 3, Division no. 11, Collection District No. 3, 1862, National Archives, microfilm.

    36. Ibid., 1863.

37. Ibid., 1864.

38. Washtenaw County, Michigan, deeds, 53: 724; 57: 388.

39. On a dulcimer owned by Lyle Schwall, Bay City, Mich., 1979.

40. *Michigan State Gazetteer and Business Directory for 1867-8* (Detroit: Chapin & Bro., 1867), 128.

41. Washtenaw County, Michigan, quitclaims, 1: 429, 492.

42. John W. Stedman, *Stedman's Directory of Norwich, Connecticut, 1868* (Norwich, Conn.: Norwich Printing Co., 1868), 94, 196.

43. David Durand, pension application, National Archives.

44. Andrew Boyd, *Boyd's American Musical Directory of the United States and Provinces* (Syracuse, N.Y.: [the author], 1882), 163; Portland Directory, 1884, 128; Portland Directory, 1891, 270. See also Paul Gifford, "Ezra Durand, William Vogel, and Their Dulcimers," *Dulcimer Players News* 23 (May-July 1997): 42-43, (Aug.-Oct. 1997): 42-43.

45. Ezra Durand, *Dulcimer without a Master* (Boston: Oliver Ditson & Co., 1867), 21.

46. According to Paul F. Wells, Center for Popular Music, Middle Tennessee State University, who has participated in compiling the National Tune Index.

47. Ann Branson, *Journal of Ann Branson, a Minister of the Gospel in the Society of Friends* (Philadelphia: William H. Pile, 1892), 137-138.

48. Jane M. Tillotson diary, 15 May 1858, in "Jane M. Tillotson Ohio Diaries Study Project," website, <http://www.geocities.com/Athens/Forum/6800/1858may.htm>.

49. Preble County, Ohio, wills, in "Ohio Wills," website, <http://freepages.genealogy.rootsweb.com/~hollowel/OhioWills.html>.

50. Annie R. Stuart diary transcript, 18 May 1861, 20 May 1861, MMS-1454, Center for Archival Collections, Bowling Green State University, website, <http://www.bgsu.edu/colleges/library/cac/mms1454a.htm>.

51. Robert S. Dilworth, personal journal, 5 July 1862, Robert S. Dilworth Papers, MS 800, Center for Archival Collections, Bowling Green State University, website, <http://campus.bgsu.edu/colleges/library/cac/ms0800tt04.html>.

52. Jacob Bruner to Martha J. Bruner, 7 May 1863, Jacob Bruner Papers, Ohio Historical Society.

53. Mrs. Basil Coltston, granddaughter of Julia Ellen Smith, conversation with author, Rochester, Mich., about 1979.

54. Julie Letendre, Curator, Fairbanks House, Dedham, Massachusetts, letter to author, 20 Apr. 1999.

55. Mrs. Franc L. Adams, *Pioneer History of Ingham County*, vol. 1 (Lansing: Wynkoop Hallenbeck Crawford Co., 1923), 409.

56. Marshall Wells, conversation with author, Stow, New York, May 1976.

57. Archie Barnes, interview by Charles Delamarter, tape recording, Sept. 1964, Okemos Historical Society collection.

58. Hans Nathan, *Dan Emmett and the Rise of Early Negro Minstrelsy* (Norman: University of Oklahoma Press, 1962), 149 n. 16. Robert Winans saw a minstrel show playbill in the Harvard Theatre Collection with an illustration of a dulcimer player.

59. Howard L. Sacks and Judith Rose Sacks, *Way Up North in Dixie: A Black Family's Claim to the Confederate Anthem* (Washington: Smithsonian Institution Press, 1993), 58, 63.

60. P. T. Barnum, *The Humbugs of the World* (New York: Carleton, 1866), 144-146.

61. Mary Hartwell Catherwood, *Old Caravan Days* (Boston: D. Lothrop, 1884), 37-38.

62. Wilbur Zelinsky, *The Cultural Geography of the United States* (Englewood Cliffs, N.J.: Prentice-Hall, 1973), 127.

63. I base this on conversations I had between 1972 and 1979 with Loy Swiger, Worley Gardner, Herman Matheny, and Russell Fluharty, all natives of West Virginia familiar with local traditions, and J. R. ("Peanut") Cantrell, of McMinnville, Tennessee, and a recording of Virgil Craven, of Cedar Falls, North Carolina, made in 1974 by Blanton Owen and Tom Carter, AFS 18690, American Folklife Center, Library of Congress.

64. Sir John Graham Dalyell, *Musical Memoirs of Scotland* (1849; reprint, Norwood, Pa.: Norwood Editions, 1973), 260f.

65. James W. Kimball, notes to *Sackett's Harbor: Nineteenth-Century Dance Music from Western New York State: The Tunes* (Rochester, N.Y.: Sampler Records Ltd., 1994), n.p., ix, x.

66. From a dulcimer owned by Robert Winans.

67. My father knew Merritt Barnes in the 1920s, then an elderly janitor at the Farmers and Mechanics Bank in Jamestown, and probably heard Barnes talk of his years playing for dances.

68. Floyd L. Darrow, *History of the Town of North Harmony, Chautauqua County, New York*, Book 1 (n.p.: Town Board of North Harmony, 1953), 130f.

69. The granddaughter of one of them, who played the dulcimer and later moved to Medford, Wisconsin, told me of them in 1976.

70. Article from *Watertown Daily Times*, undated, in Linda Milligan Oatman, Oatman genealogy, website <http://www.sentex.net/~cdoatman/1475.htm>.

71. W. Scott Munn, *The Only Eaton Rapids on Earth* (Ann Arbor: Edwards Brothers, printers, 1952), 283.

72. Reminiscences of Mrs. Della Tubbs, 1925, in *Byron, Michigan, Sesquicentennial 1824-1974* (n.p., 1974), 17.

73. *Milwaukee Journal*, 23 June 1946; William F. Shaw to Helen Stratman-Thomas, 15 July 1946, in Helene Stratman-Thomas (Blotz) Collection, Mills Music Library, University of Wisconsin. I would like to thank Jim Leary for this reference.

74. *Milwaukee Journal*, 23 June 1946; note with dulcimer, Michigan State Historical Museum.

75. See Groce, *Hammered Dulcimer in America*, 30.

76. "Early American Dance" radio show script, Feb. 5, 1944, Ford Motor Co., Advertising, general files, Acc. 149, box 43, Ford Archives, Dearborn, Michigan.

77. *Michigan State Gazetteer and Business Directory* (Detroit: 1883), 585.

78. Margaret Ford Ruddiman, reminiscences, in Allan Nevins and Frank E. Hill, *Ford: the Times, the Man, the Company* (New York: Scribner, 1954), 105. A poem by Harry McErlean, written for Ford's 75th birthday, mentions "Phelps and Brace" as musicians and Bill Cox as caller (Ibid., 308 n. 35). Race was buried in Woodmere Cemetery, Detroit.

79. William Finzel, reminiscences, Dec. 1955, Ford Archives.

80. John W. Fitzmaurice, *The Shanty Boy, or Life in a Lumbercamp* (1889; reprint, Upper Saddle River, N.J.: Literature House/Gregg Press, 1970), 54-60, for example gives a description of entertainment on a Saturday evening at a camp on the Rifle River in Michigan in 1883. Ray Hoffmeyer, of Atlanta, Michigan, worked in some of the last lumber camps in Michigan, and told me in 1975 about the same recreational activities that he witnessed in the 1920s.

81. *Morley Centennial 1869-1969* (n.p., 1969?), n.p.; Milton Weeks (his grandson), conversation with author, Mackinac Island, Mich., 1983.

82. Arch Bristow, *Old Time Tales of Warren County* (n.p., 1932), 129-130.

83. Henry W. Shoemaker, *The Music and Musical Instruments of the Pennsylvania Mountaineers* (Altoona, Pa.: Mountain City Press, 1923), 5f.

84. Henry W. Shoemaker, *Mountain Minstrelsy of Pennsylvania*, 3rd ed. (Philadelphia: Newman F. McGirr, 1931), 7.

85. For example, see Gary Eberle, "The Lumberjack's Piano," *West Michigan Magazine*, Feb. 1984, 18-20, 54; "The Bands of Summer," *Time*, 27 Aug. 1979, 67, which includes a photograph of a female player in a group called "Brandywine," playing on a street in Seattle with a poster in front of the dulcimer that says it "became known here as the whamadiddle or the lumberjack's piano (since it was easy to carry from one lumbering camp to another)."

86. Robert Spinner, conversations with author.

87. *Grand Rapids Press*, 26 Nov. 1947.

88. William Hogan's daughter, conversation with author, Hubbardston, Mich.

89. *Detroit Free Press*, 30 Jan. 1939.

90. Ronald R. Crump, letter to author, 28 Oct. 1985.

91. 1870 census, Henry County, Ohio, 32; 1880 census, Henry County, Ohio, Village of Liberty Center, 12.

92. Robert Spinner, conversations with author.

93. Robert C. Stykemain, letters to the author, 25 Apr. 1975, 27 Oct. 1978, the latter quoting from Robert Travis.

94. I have seen or know of over thirty.

95. Naturally their dulcimers have since become more widespread through migration. An instrument in the collection of the Museum of New Hampshire History (1974.65), for example, was originally owned by Mrs. Pius Krieg and

sold by an antique dealer in Epsom, New Mexico, to the museum. A Hackett dulcimer in the collection of The Metropolitan Museum of Art (1979.522.3) is incorrectly identified as "in the style of Perry Wight, South Alabama, New York" (Libin, *American Musical Instruments*, 102).

96. Janis Pahnke, a descendant of Elon Hackett, personal communication, 26 Jan. 1999.

97. This information is from surviving family members of the players, including Mildred Hickok, of Sears, Michigan, Helen Gross, of Saline, Michigan, and Homer Wilbur, Jr., of Springport, Michigan.

98. "Dryer Family Photographs," website <http://freepages.genealogy.rootsweb.com/~dryer/fu.jpg>; William Brenchley, great-grandson, personal communication, 18 Sept. 2000.

99. John C. Watts, grandson, telephone conversation with author, 18 Sept. 2000. I would also like to thank A. J. Bashore II for information.

100. Guy Bankes, letter to author, 20 Sept. 1998, who heard of a legless man who played the dulcimer at dances in eastern Lycoming County around 1900; Lynn Converse told me in 1973 of a neighbor he remembered who lived about ten miles from Williamsport about 1910 and played the dulcimer and mandolin; Bruce Henry, telephone conversation with author, 17 Sept. 2000, who once met a man in Hughesville, Pennsylvania, who had played, and also had heard of a Mr. Weed in Sullivan County who was active about 1950.

101. I also heard of a Mr. Cummings, of Geneseo, Illinois.

102. Taken from a printed inscription on the back of a photograph, for sale at Ebay.com (no. 181033523) by Stewart's Military Antiques, Mesa, Arizona, in October 1999.

103. Dennis Trone, telephone conversation with author, 1985; Lee Douglas van Antwerp, "The Van Antwerp Family in America," *New York Genealogical and Biographical Record* 80 (Oct. 1949): 206.

104. A. B. Wood, *Pioneer Tales of the North Platte Valley and Nebraska Panhandle* (Gering, Neb.: Courier Press, 1938), 116.

105. "Discover South Dakota," website. May Green Holmes Krueger, oral history, Daughters of Dakota Collection, <http://discoversd.tie.net/themes/continuing/resources/daughter/campbell/krueger.htm>.

106. Ralph E. Shaffer, "Letters from the People: Los Angeles Times, 1881-1889," online article, "'Crazy Shaw': Frederick M. Shaw's Letters to the Los Angeles Times, 1883-1887," website, <http://www.intranet.csupomona.edu/~reshaffer/shawx.htm>.

107. He signed his name "McKenzie" and "Mackenzie," but his gravestone and his son Douglas E. MacKenzie used the form "MacKenzie."

108. Groce, *Hammered Dulcimer in America*, 52. MacKenzie was not the only dulcimer maker to give it a new name; the Ransom and Wade Brothers instruments sometimes were called "piano dulcimers," the same name stenciled on an instrument in the author's collection that was probably made in Ontario in the 1880s.

109. His son Douglas E. MacKenzie, of Rockton, Illinois, born in 1898, told me that he vaguely remembered the workshop.

110. U.S. Patent, 440,601, dated November 11, 1890.

111. A copy is at the Hennepin County Historical Society.

112. Douglas E. MacKenzie, conversation with author, Rockton, Ill., 1976.

113. I have heard of players or owners in Armstrong, Iowa, Bancroft, Iowa, Balaton, Minnesota, Duluth, Minnesota, Mankato, Minnesota, Clark, South Dakota, and Kenosha, Wisconsin.

114. Granddaughter of Willie Manley, conversation with author, Mackinac Island, Mich., 1981.

115. Russell Sanjek, *American Popular Music and Its Business: the First Four Hundred Years*, vol. 2, *From 1790 to 1909* (New York: Oxford University Press, 1988), 354.

116. Lyon & Healy, *Illustrated Catalogue of Musical Merchandise, Imported, Manufactured, for Sale* ([Chicago]: Donnelley, Gassette & Loyd, printers, 1880), 16, 105, 107.

117. Montgomery Ward & Company, *Catalogue & Buyers Guide No. 56: Fall and Winter 1894-95* (Chicago: The Lakeside Press, printers, n.d.), 241.

118. *1897 Sears Roebuck Catalogue* (1897; reprint, New York: Chelsea House, 1968), 522.

119. Lyon & Healy, *Catalogue of Musical Merchandise* (Chicago: Lyon & Healy, 1897), 29, 318.

120. Lyon & Healy, *Lyon & Healy's Musicians' Hand Book* ([Chicago]: Lyon & Healy, 1905), 95.

121. U.S. Census, 1900, Kings County, N.Y., Brooklyn, e.d. 296, sheet 16; *Uppington's General Directory of Brooklyn . . . for the year 1902* (Brooklyn: George Uppington, 1902), 887.

122. Groce, *Hammered Dulcimer in America*, 57-58. She is probably wrong, however, in suggesting that these instruments were imported.

123. Saverio Minicucci, personal communication, 7 Apr. 1997.

124. John J. Strasser, Jr., letter to author, 1985. Groce, *Hammered Dulcimer in America*, 40, mentions Fred D. Kunz (born 1892), of Long Island and undoubtedly German-American, who played a "Long Island style" dulcimer, probably one of Stonitsch's, on WNYC in 1922.

125. *An Enduring Legacy*, compiled by Lesson Committee (Salt Lake City: Daughters of Utah Pioneers, 1978), 1: 71.

126. Kate Carter, *Heart Throbs of the West*, vol. 12: *The University of Utah and Other Schools of Early Days*: Millard County (Salt Lake City: Daughters of Utah Pioneers, 1947), database at <http://www.ancestry.com>; *An Enduring Legacy*, vol 4: *Pioneer Dancing*: Kanosh.

127. *An Enduring Legacy*, vol. 4: *Pioneer Dancing*: Kanosh.

128. Kate Carter, *Treasures of Pioneer History*, vol. 2; "Dancing—A Pioneer Recreation" (Salt Lake City: Daughters of Utah Pioneers, 1952), database at <http://www.ancestry.com>.

129. Carter, *Treasures of Pioneer History*, vol. 2; "Dancing—A Pioneer Recreation", database at <http://www.ancestry.com>.

130. "A Story of the Life of Esther Irene Judd Ford," website, <http://www.cache.net/~sungen/html/eijudd.htm>.

131. Carter, *Treasures of Pioneer History*, vol. 2; "Dancing—A Pioneer Recreation"; *An Enduring Legacy*, vol. 6: Immigrant Pioneers: Margarett Ann Griffiths Clegg, database at <http://www.ancestry.com>.

132. *Our Pioneer Heritage*, vol. 20: Bands and Orchestras: Utah County, Weber County, database at <http://www.ancestry.com>; Ida Clegg Bird, "History of Israel Eastham Clegg and His Wife Verona Noakes Clegg," website, <http://www.cclegg.com/family/history/israelclegg.htm>.

133. "Fredrick Weight," website, <http://pc38.ve.weber.k12.ut.us/Family/Pioneers/weight/weightf.htm>; "Elizabeth Bocock (Weight)," website, <http://pc38.ve.weber.k12.ut.us/Family/Pioneers/weight/bocock.htm>.

134. *Our Pioneer Heritage*, vol. 13: *The Mormons from Scotland and Wales*: Stalwart Citizen: Company E (Salt Lake City: Infobases, Inc., 1996), database at <http://ancestry.com>.

135. Carter, *Treasures of Pioneer History*, vol. 2: "Dancing—A Pioneer Recreation," database at <http://ancestry.com>.

136. Mary Jane Fritzen, *Idaho Falls, City of Destiny* [Idaho Falls: Bonneville County Historical Society, 1991], chapt. 3, website, <http://www.srv.net/~bchs/chap3.html>.

137. An early nineteenth-century dulcimer was brought by the Knittle family from Pennsylvania to Adams County, Indiana (Harold Zimmerman, letter to author, 1985). I also talked to a person in 1977 whose Kansas ancestor, a Civil War veteran from Pennsylvania Dutch country, had one, but unfortunately I did not get more details.

138. Although the Alpine and Volga German *Hackbrett* has a diatonic tuning, they generally have four strings per course, including bass courses, while the most common traditional design in West Virginia uses three strings per course, and the common Missouri factory-made instrument had two strings per bass course. Rosettes or multiple holes, typical of the German design, are absent in this region.

139. Russell Fluharty, "The Dulcimer Story: Dulcimer Over 100 Years Old" (Mannington, W. Va.: the author, n.d.), n.p.

140. Groce, *Hammered Dulcimer in America*, 65-67, 76-78.

141. David L. Taylor, "J. E. Matheny, an Early Hammered Dulcimer Player," *Dulcimer Players News* 3 (Spring 1977): 34-35.

142. Loy Swiger, interview by author, tape recording, Massillon, Ohio, 12 Oct. 1978; Mrs. Underwood's granddaughter, conversation with author, Mackinac Island, Mich., 1981.

143. *Indiana Daily Student*, 4 Sept. 1952, 3.

144. Harlow Lindley, ed., *The Indiana Centennial, 1916: A Record of the*

Celebration of the One Hundredth Anniversary of Indiana's Admission to State-hood (Indianapolis: Indiana Historical Commission, 1919), 198. I would like to thank Paul Tyler for this reference.

145. Whitley County, Indiana, will book 2: 12; Whitley County Historical Society, cemetery records, website <http://home.whitleynet.org/genealogy/cem63.htm>; Weston A. Goodspeed and Charles Blanchard, *History of Whitley and Noble Counties, Indiana* (Chicago: F. A. Battey Co., 1882), 340.

146. Jean Granberry Schnitz, "Hammered Dulcimers and Folk Songs: the Musical Heritage of the C. A. Lee Family," in *Corners of Texas*, Publication of the Texas Folklore Society 52 (Denton, Texas: University of North Texas Press, 1993), 160.

147. "Aunt Nellie McKinney," *Dulcimer Players News* 10 (Fall 1984): 6, reprinted from *The Knotty Post*, July 1954; Ray M. Lawless, *Folksingers and Folksongs in America* (New York: Duell, Sloan and Pearce, 1960), 226-227.

148. "Rackensack Group Revives Arkansas's Earliest Traditions," *Arkansas Democrat-Gazette*, 27 June 1986.

149. Harvey Prinz, "In Search of the Kansas Dulcimer," *Dulcimer Players News* 11 (Summer 1985): 14-15.

150. Schnitz, "Hammered Dulcimers," 160, 163-164, 167, 169.

151. Virgil Craven, audiotape, recorded by Tom Carter, 20 January 1974, AFS 1860, reel 217, Archive of American Folklife, Library of Congress.

152. "Hammer Dulcimer Virtuoso," *Greensboro Daily News*, 18 May 1977; Craven, audiotape.

153. Mrs. I. M. Beard, *My Own Life, or A Deserted Wife*, 5th ed. (n.p., 190-?), 72-73.

154. George W. Harris, *Sut Lovingood: Yarns Spun by a 'Nat'ral Born Durn'd Fool'* (New York: Dick & Fitzgerald, 1867), 176-177. No further description is given with which to identify the instrument, however.

155. Hulan, "Music in Tennessee," 419.

156. John Beatty, *Memoirs of a Volunteer, 1861-1863*, edited by Harvey S. Ford (New York: W. W. Norton & Co., 1946), 142-143. Thanks to Janet Cole for this reference.

157. Richard H. Hulan, "Hunting and Taming the Native American (or Hammered) Dulcimer," *Newsletter of the Greater Washington Folklore Society* 5, no. 6 (Feb. 1969): 6.

158. Hulan, "Music in Tennessee," 419; Richard Hulan, personal communication, 15 Nov. 1999.

159. Charles K. Wolfe, *The Grand Ole Opry: The Early Years, 1925-35*, Old Time Music, booklet 2 (London: Old Time Music, 1975), 87.

160. Bill Andre, personal communication, 1999.

161. "The Cockrell Family: A Concise History," website, <http://www.network-one.com/~robfra/cockr.htm>. In this case the author identifies the instrument as a "hammer" dulcimer.

· *14* ·

The Design of Nineteenth-Century
American Dulcimers

Although nineteenth-century American dulcimers vary tremendously in design, they share enough characteristics in common which both distinguish them from instruments of traditions of other countries and form a recognizable type. By the middle of the century a number of different designs were in vogue. Migrants and commercially made instruments both spread these designs. Although certain designs were more common in specific regions, they were not necessarily tied to those regions, and in some states, several designs existed side by side. Rather than breaking down the discussion of the designs by state or region, it is better to discuss them by type.

First, let us identify certain characteristics which distinguish American dulcimers from those in Europe and elsewhere.[1] One is the outer shape. American instruments are either rectangular or trapezoidal, the former being numerically rather common because many factories produced such instruments, while the trapezoidal shape is represented by a greater variety of builders. The rectangular outline is virtually unknown outside North America. It probably developed from dulcimers, used in homes, which rested in rectangular cases with lids. Transitional instruments, where the dulcimer is built into a rectangular case with lid, while still retaining a trapezoidal shape formed by the pin blocks, seem to date from about 1830 to 1850. They may represent a link to dulcimers from northern England, although the development could have arisen in both countries independently.[2]

Another characteristic is that bass courses are almost always fewer in number than treble courses and have fewer strings per course as well. Some designs lack bass courses entirely. On many European systems, the number of both the bass courses and the number of strings per course is the same as those of the treble courses. The usual number of strings per bass course on American instruments is two (less commonly three), while the total number of bass courses varies. Again, this characteristic may represent a link to northern English tradition. As we have mentioned, Kettlewell notes that Birmingham dulcimers, in contrast to those of East Anglia, have generally fewer bass courses than treble courses and fewer strings per bass course (usually three).[3]

Internal bracing systems, to the extent that we can study them, vary in design, but in most cases the back (baseboard) supports most of the lateral tension of the strings. As a result, it tends to be rather thick (usually three-quarters to one inch or more). This characteristic again bears similarity with English dulcimers and distinguishes American instruments from, for example, those of Appenzell and the Eastern European types of the cimbalom family, where the backs are as thin as one-quarter inch. On trapezoidal instruments, the pin blocks are joined directly to the baseboard, as on English instruments, rather than being joined to or mortised into the side rails or lengthwise braces, like some *Hackbrett*s and Italian *salterio*s, and forming a cavity between the baseboard and pin block. However, the pin blocks of most rectangular instruments are joined to the side rails or lengthwise braces in that manner and do not touch the baseboard.

Many American dulcimers, both rectangular and trapezoidal, feature hinged lids. Although exceptional, some older English dulcimers have them, and the older Chinese *yangqin* almost always incorporates a fitted lid into its design. Older Appenzell *Hackbrett*s always have unhinged lids, but in other traditions they are rare or do not exist at all. Lids appeared as early as about 1540 in English tradition,[4] so this feature might well be a survival from that period.

The wood used in construction of nineteenth-century American dulcimers frequently is pine or hemlock for the soundboard, sides, baseboard, and internal bracing. However, soundboards and baseboards often are also made of moderately soft hardwoods, such as whitewood or yellow poplar, and hardwoods like white ash appear occasionally. The sides, sometimes beveled or milled, may also be made of walnut, cherry, oak, or other hardwoods. Pin blocks are usually of maple, less often of oak or ash. Joints are usually glued and held by cut nails or, on later instruments, screws.

The finish and decoration varies considerably. Many of the commercial, factory-made varieties are veneered and varnished. Most others, however, are stained or painted, although some have a natural, varnish finish, and others may be completely unfinished. One regularly encounters instruments decorated with grain painting, a characteristically rural American technique also called graining or *faux bois*. Some versions imitate wood rather closely, while others produce more fantastic results. Soundboards are often painted black or stained. They may feature stenciled designs and note names, sometimes with numbers, under each course. Where this feature occurs, one can assume that the maker intended to sell the instrument.

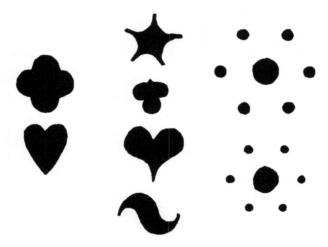

Figure 14.1: Selected sound-hole designs of nineteenth-century dulcimers. Left column, sound holes from trapezoidal dulcimers (from the top): unknown, but probably Mortimer DeLano, Oxford, Mich., c.1863; William Thurston, Farmington, Mich., c.1860. Middle column, sound holes from rectangular dulcimers with eleven treble courses and seven bass courses (from the top): unknown; Henry Ransom, Newport, Ky., c.1859-1861; Henry Ransom, c.1856-1859, or Lafayette Chesley, both Sherman, N.Y., c.1859-1860; Lewis S. and Harrison Wade, Stedman, N.Y., or Milton, Ky., c.1858-1860. Right column, sound holes associated with the variety with a trapezoidal outline, twelve treble and three to five bass courses (from the top): unknown; Elon or J. Wheeler Hackett, Liberty Center, Ohio, c.1868-1890.

The number and design of sound holes varies. Most instruments have two sound holes, but some have four or even six, while others lack them entirely. Sound hole designs fit into categories relatively neatly. Some consist of a center hole with four to twelve or more (but especially six) concentric holes, a design also found, curiously, on Hungarian, Romanian, and Belarusian instruments. Others are round or in the shape of tildes, f-holes, hearts, and other designs. One recurring characteristic found on some instruments with round sound holes is a simple decoration of veneer, wood, or cardboard attached to the margins of the underside of the sound hole. Cloth may also be similarly attached.

Let us now examine common types of American dulcimers and specific characteristics of commercial instruments. In order to arrive at something that approaches a reasonable scheme of classification, string layout is the most practical means to use. Other characteristics of design may be associated with particular layouts, but this is not always the case. We should remember that although differences in tuning may be associated with differences in design, none are so large that a player familiar with a dulcimer of one design could not play a dulcimer of a different design.

Nine Treble Courses, No Bass Courses

Figure 14.2: Dulcimer from middle Tennessee, mid-nineteenth century. Author's collection.

This variety seems to have been fairly widespread, although mostly limited to the Midlands and South. Associated characteristics of this design include a rectangular body, three (sometimes two) strings per course, and four sound holes, usually round. It appears that this was the most common design in northern West Virginia, used by such makers as Reuben Matheny, Jr., of Harrisville, and Jesse Ash, of Ashley. An instrument in the author's collection, purchased in Lebanon, Tennessee, was probably commercially made around 1870. This rectangular dulcimer measures 41 inches (104.5 cm) in length, 15 inches (38.1 cm) in width, and 2½ inches (6.7 cm) high, with a 2¾ inch (7 cm) deep lid. It is painted black, with a stained soundboard and unfinished bottom. Its four round sound holes measure 5/8 inch (16 mm) in diameter and are surrounded by stenciled blue sunburst designs. Russell Fluharty, of Mannington, West Virginia, had a dulcimer with nine treble courses which belonged in this category. The tuning pins, however, had probably been replaced with screws, and the number of strings per course had increased to six, while the bridges divided the courses into fourths instead of the usual fifths. This dulcimer measures 44 inches (111.8 cm) in length, 15 inches (38.1 cm) in width, and 3½ inches (8.9 cm) in height, with four round sound holes. A dulcimer made by James Wesley Samples (1845-1920), of Forsyth County, Georgia, for his own use, has nine courses of two strings each, four sideways f-holes, and measures 42½ inches (108 cm) in length, 18½ inches (47 cm) in width, and 3 inches (7.6 cm) in height.[5] Jesse Ash made rectangular dulcimers of this type, but his instruments in later years were trapezoidal. Loy Swiger, of Massillon, Ohio, had one made by Ash in 1928, and in the late 1970s, he made several following Ash's pattern. Ralph Campbell, of Mannington, West Virginia, made several after Fluharty's instrument in the 1970s. Asel Gardner, of Kingwood, West Virginia, made changes to this basic design, and in the late 1960s and 1970s, produced dulcimers in a rectangular outline with fourteen treble courses of five strings each, some of the bridges dividing the courses into intervals other than a perfect fifth.

Loy Swiger tuned his nine-course dulcimer so that the lowest course was d^1 to the right of the bridge and a^1 to the left, the remaining courses continuing in the usual fashion to the highest course, which was e^2 on the right and b^2 on the left. He learned the tuning from Jesse Ash, and it was probably the standard system for this type.

A late nineteenth-century trapezoidal dulcimer from Jackson, Tennessee, in the author's collection, has nine treble courses of four each, but unlike most other dulcimers with this number of treble courses, it has nine bass courses, with three strings each. Like other Tennessee dulcimers, the lowest bass course precedes the first treble course. Such an arrangement indicates that the lowest treble course was probably intended to be tuned a¹ | d¹. This dulcimer measures 42 (107 cm) and 25 inches (64 cm) in length and 12 inches (30 cm) in width.

Ten Treble Courses, Seven Bass Courses

Perhaps dulcimers with ten treble courses retain a southern English design. This arrangement was used in the first part of the nineteenth century by Philander Cogswell, of Bath, New York, but it was more characteristic of Tennessee. One variant of this type, from Middle Tennessee, has ten treble courses, seven bass courses, and a rectangular outline, perhaps an influence from the factory-made dulcimers sold in the state before the Civil War. Thus one might regard this type as a variant of the eleven treble courses-seven bass courses type described below. The father of J. R. Cantrell, a native of Putnam County and a resident of Smith County, Tennessee, made one about 1910 with ten treble courses of three each and seven bass courses of two each, with milled sides and a half-inch thick poplar upper surface. One played by Laura Lambert, of Fairfield, Tennessee, made by Lum Scott, of New Roe, Allen County, Kentucky, had the same number of courses, but the lowest bass course stands below the lowest treble course, rather than the position between the first and second treble courses usual in the North.[6]

Eleven Treble Courses, Six Bass Courses

Trapezoidal dulcimers with eleven treble courses of four strings each and six bass courses of two each comprise another design used during the middle of the nineteenth century. Instruments of this type have appeared in New York, New Jersey, Michigan, West Virginia, and Virginia. At least two examples exist of one model, perhaps from West Virginia, with this string arrangement and four tilde-shaped or sideways f-hole sound holes, two larger than the others. They have grain-painted sides and painted decoration on the soundboard. One instrument measures 42½ inches (108 cm) at its longer length and 15½ inches (39.4 cm) in width.[7] Another instrument, which came from a barn in Jackson County, Michigan, is made of poplar, its sides stained, and has the same string arrangement, hand-forged tuning pins, and two tilde-shaped sound holes. It measures 42¼ (107.3 cm) and 22¼ inches (56.5 cm) in length, 15 inches (38.1 cm) in width, and 3 inches (7.6 cm) in height.[8] The Smithsonian Institution has one with two round sound holes, individual bridges, handmade tuning pins, and a grain-painted finish, that came from Fulton County, New York. It measures 42¼ (107 cm) and 18¾ inches (47.4 cm) in length, 15½ inches (39.5 cm) in width, and 3½ inches (9.1 cm) in height.[9] A dulcimer in the Newark Museum, Newark, New Jersey, is veneered with mahogany and has two sound holes with inset, perforated rosettes and possibly hand-forged tuning pins; it measures 41¾ (106 cm) and 18½ inches (47.3 cm) in length and 3½ inches (8.9 cm) in height.[10] The Mercer Museum of the Bucks County Historical Society, Doylestown, Pennsylvania, has a dulcimer with this string arrangement that came from the Shenandoah Valley in Virginia. It has a grain-painted finish and six round sound holes around which are painted blue circles and eight-petaled designs, with margins of white dots. Rather remarkably, the notes are indicated by shape-notes.[11] This indicates a standard tuning, starting at g♯¹ | c♯¹ and with bass courses an octave below the treble course immediately above. These examples, made in small numbers by different hands, seem to date from the 1840s or 1850s, yet by their relatively similar dimensions demonstrate that this type had already found a wide circulation.

Later examples may derive from such relatively early examples. John Brown, of Torch Lake, Michigan, made a number of dulcimers in the 1890s and early 1900s. They are finished with a walnut stain and have six round sound holes. He tuned the lowest treble course to a¹ | d¹, tuning the bass courses a fifth lower than the neighboring treble course, rather than the usual octave. One of his instruments measures 43 (109.2 cm) and 19 inches (48.3 cm) in length, 14½ inches (36.8 cm) in width, and 3 inches (7.6 cm) in height.[12] A commercial instrument by an unknown maker, which came from Ontario and probably dates from the 1880s, bears the stenciled inscription "piano dulcimer." This has eleven treble courses of three strings each, except the lowest, which has two strings, and six bass courses of two strings each. Its soundboard, lacking sound holes, is decorated with bronze painted designs and has notes stenciled under each course. They indicate the common North American tuning, including bass courses an octave below the neighboring treble courses. Its front and rear sides extend one inch past the pin blocks and it sits on three scroll-cut legs. It measures 42 (106.7 cm) and 26 inches (66 cm) in length, 15½ inches (39.4 cm) in width, and 5 inches (12.7 cm) in height.[13]

Eleven Treble Courses, Seven Bass Courses

Figure 14.3: Dulcimer probably manufactured by the Wade Brothers, of Stedman, New York, or possibly Milton, Kentucky, c.1859. Author's collection.

This layout had appeared by the 1840s in New York State, as C. Haight's *A Complete System for the Dulcimer* (New York: William Hall & Son, 1848) shows a tuning diagram with this design. Usually associated with it are a rectangular outline, two sound holes, and sometimes a lid. The Wade brothers, of Stedman, New York, manufactured a model with eleven treble courses of three strings each and seven bass courses of two strings each, measuring 36¼ inches (92.1 cm) in length, 14¼ inches (36.2 cm) in width, and 3¼ inches (8.3 cm) in height. The soundboard lacks sound holes; its interior surface is painted black, while its sides and lid have a brownish grain-painted finish. A probable later model produced by the Wades' factory in Stedman and perhaps at the factory the brothers presumably owned in Milton, Kentucky, has the same number of courses and strings per course, but has two tilde-shaped sound holes and is finished with walnut or mahogany veneer on its sides and upper free surfaces.[14] This measures 38¼ to 39¼ inches (97.2 to 99.7 cm) in length, 15 to 15¼ inches (38.1 to 38.7 cm) in width, and 3¼ inches (8.3 cm) in height. The Wades' competitor Henry Ransom produced rectangular dulcimers of this type, with eleven treble courses of four strings each and seven bass courses of two strings each. His earlier models, made probably when his factory was located in Sherman, New York, from 1856 to 1859, measure 39 inches (99.1 cm) in length, 15 inches (38.1 cm) in width, and 3¾ to 4 inches (9.5 to 10.2 cm) in height, some with lids 2½ inches (6.4 cm) in height. They have two heart-shaped sound holes backed by cloth, with gold-painted margins, and are covered with mahogany, walnut, or bird's-eye maple veneer. Some of the models with lids have beaded molding around the edges of the soundboard, lid, and sides of the instrument.[15] Instruments perhaps made when the Ransom factory was located in Newport, Kentucky, from 1859 to 1861, have the same number of strings, but measure 37¾ to 38 inches (95.9 to 96.5 cm) in length, 14¾ inches (37.5 cm) in width, and 3¾ to 4 inches (9.5 to 10.2 cm) in height. These have two sound holes consisting of three lobes and a triangle (or a "club" shape), backed by cloth, with green and red painted decoration on the surface near the sound holes. Such instruments are covered with mahogany or bird's-eye maple veneer and the ones with lids have beaded molding like the earlier model. Ransom's successor in Sherman, Lafayette Chesley, seems to have continued Ransom's earlier design.

The Missouri factory instrument played by Nellie McKinney and described by Jean Granberry Schnitz has eleven treble courses of three strings each and seven bass courses of two strings each, the lowest bass course being placed between the second and third treble course instead of the usual first and second course. It is rectangular, with corner-lock joints on its corners, two round sound holes, and a hinged, two-piece lid with lock. The dulcimer rests on legs at an incline and measures 36 inches (91.4 cm) in length and 15 inches (38.1 cm) in width.[16]

Haight's tutor, and those written subsequently by Low and Rudisill, show that the lowest treble course was intended to be $g\sharp^1$ on the left and $c\sharp^1$ on the right, continuing up to c^3 and f^2 on the highest course. The bass courses were tuned an octave below the right-hand treble tones, starting with d^0 and continuing upwards to c^1. Makers preferred spring brass wire for the bass strings, although the scarcity of such wire meant that they sometimes used steel wire instead.[17]

Twelve Treble Courses, Three Bass Courses

Instruments with this system or some variation appeared in a wide area, from central New York State to North Carolina, westward to Ohio and Michigan, by the first half of the nineteenth century. Such a wide distribution points to a prototype that may have circulated through the seaboard colonies during the previous century. Associated with this layout are a trapezoidal outline, individual, turned bridges, and two sound holes consisting of a central hole and usually six concentric smaller holes.

Figure 14.4: Dulcimer of unknown manufacture, perhaps made in Ohio, c.1870. Author's collection.

The twelve treble courses have four strings per course, and the three bass courses have two each. Variants may have two, four, or five bass courses, but the placement of the bass courses is distinctive, as they usually lie between the first and second, second and third, and fourth and fifth treble courses. An early example of this type is a dulcimer in the Michie Tavern Museum, Charlottesville, Virginia, described in chapter 12. An instrument made by Philip N. Woliston, of Springfield, Ohio, has all the characteristics of this type, although it has four, instead of three bass courses, and is built into a rectangular case, measuring 42 inches (106.7 cm) in length and 16 inches (40.6 cm) in width, with a cloth-lined lid, resting on lyre legs 26 inches (66 cm) high.[18]

The most prolific manufacturers of dulcimers of this type were Elon and his son Joseph Wheeler Hackett, of Liberty Center, Ohio, active from the late 1860s until the 1890s. As the family had lived in Dryden, Tompkins County, New York, prior to moving to Ohio in 1838, it is perhaps no coincidence that this basic design seems to have been characteristic of dulcimers made in the southern Finger Lakes region and the adjacent part of Pennsylvania. At some point Hackett or his son increased the number of bass courses from three to five. Their instruments display minor variations in design, such as some, probably earlier, examples, with straight sides without lids, and perhaps other painted finishes. However, most have beveled sides wider at the bottom edge than at the upper edge, a fantastic grain-painted finish usually using red paint over a yellow ochre base, a natural finish on the soundboard and pin block surfaces, and individual nut rods. Most have lids and a lock. They measure

41½ to 43 inches (105.4 to 109.2 cm) and 19½ to 20¼ inches (49.5 to 51.4 cm) in length, 14½ to 16 inches (36.8 to 40.6 cm) in width, 3½ inches (8.9 cm) in height, with lids that are one-half inch (1.3 cm) high.[19] A dulcimer by another manufacturer, examples of which have turned up in Ohio, Michigan, and West Virginia, has twelve treble courses of four strings each and three bass courses of two strings each, with the same sound hole type and bridges, but has milled, stained sides and measures 46 (116.8 cm) and 23¾ inches (60.3 cm) in length, 15¼ inches (38.7 cm) in width, and 4½ inches (11.7 cm) in height.

Other unknown makers followed this general pattern, although with variations. The Henry Ford Museum has two examples of a commercial dulcimer, one of them coming from Millport, New York. These have four bass courses of two strings each, two f-holes, and beveled sides which are decorated with stenciled floral designs. They measure 44 inches (111.8 cm) and 43 inches (109.2 cm) and 22 inches (55.9 cm) and 21 inches (53.3 cm) in length, 14¾ inches (37.5 cm) in width, and 3½ inches (8.9 cm) in height.[20] Another commercial variety, one example of which its original owner, according to tradition, bought in Grand Rapids, Michigan after the Civil War, belong to this variety by virtue of the placement of their bass strings. This has twelve treble courses of four strings each, except the highest course, which has only two strings, and three bass courses of two strings each, which are placed between the first and second, second and third, and fifth and sixth (rather than fourth and fifth) treble courses. They rest on single-piece, rather than individual, bridges, and have four round sound holes, each seven-eighths of an inch (2.2 cm) in diameter. This instrument measures 41½ inches (105.4 cm) and 19¼ inches (48.9 cm) in length, 16¾ inches (42.5 cm) in width, 2¾ inches (7 cm) in height and lacks a lid. A dulcimer in the author's collection, from Blissfield, Michigan, belongs to this type, due to its four bass courses, placed between first and second, second and third, fourth and fifth, and fifth and sixth treble courses and its six sound holes consisting of a central hole and eight concentric holes, but its large size indicates that it was meant to be tuned a fifth lower than usual. It measures 59 (149.8 cm) and 27 inches (68.6 cm) in length at its bottom, the sides being beveled, 18¼ inches (46.3 cm) in width, and 4¼ inches (10.8 cm) in height. Although considerably altered, a dulcimer from Dundee, New York, with sixteen treble courses of four strings each and thirteen courses of two strings each, probably belongs to this type, as it seems to have had individual, turned bridges and two sound holes consisting of a center hole one-half inch in diameter with six 5/16-inch (8 mm) concentric holes. It measures 53 inches (134.6 cm) and 24 inches (61 cm) in length, 20½ inches (52.1 cm) in width, and 3½ inches (8.9 cm) in height, and its baseboard is carved.[21] Although the number of courses is unusual, its other design features place it within this type. Similarly, another dulcimer, from Pennsylvania, has three bass courses of two each placed in the usual position of instruments in this type and the typical sound hole design of a center hole and six concentric holes, but has eleven treble courses of four each resting on single-piece bridges. This instrument measures 38½ (97.8 cm) and 21 inches (53.3 cm) in length, 14½ inches (36.8 cm) in width, and 2½ inches (6.5 cm) in height.[22] Although even more removed from this basic design, a trapezoidal, veneered dulcimer, bearing the inscription "John Van Buskirk, maker, Jacksonville, N.Y., Jan. 8, 1861" has twelve treble courses of four each and five bass courses.[23]

The tuning of the treble courses was like the other varieties, starting at $g\sharp^1$ and $c\sharp^1$ for the lowest course and continuing upwards to d^3 and g^2 on the highest course. The tuning of the bass courses is uncertain. As the Hacketts generally used brass wire, it is unlikely that they would have been tuned a fifth below the neighboring treble courses (that is, g^0, a^0, and c^1), which would be logical, yet an octave tuning would result in d^0, e^0, and g^0, not the most used fundamental notes. Nevertheless, the three bass courses provide a clue for their function—to reinforce tonic notes at the cadences.

A variant of this design was used in Piedmont North Carolina. Although the characteristics are sufficient to form a separate type, its individual bridges and small number of bass courses link it to this geographically more widespread type. Edward Babel investigated the tradition in the 1970s and located six instruments and two players. An unusual feature of five of these dulcimers was that the tuning pins rest in the left, rather than the right pin block. Another is that both Virgil Craven, of Cedar Falls, and Harvey Jones tuned the bottom four-course set in the key of G, higher than the more normal D. The number of bass courses on these instruments ranged from three to twelve, but Babel felt that most originally had three courses and that some were added, mostly to give the appearance of symmetry. Bass courses had one wound string per course and were located next to the treble courses which on the right side were tuned to the cadential notes of G, C, and F. The soundboards of these instruments had two to six round soundholes, or in one case in the shape of six-pointed stars. Players used long hammers made of hickory or white oak curved at the ends and wrapped with yarn. The length of the dulcimers at their longest ends ranged from 35 inches (89 cm) to 47 inches (119 cm); the instruments that Craven and Jones played, which started with a G scale, were 35 inches (89 cm) and 39 inches (99 cm).[24]

A nineteenth-century photograph (see illustration 22) shows a man playing a dulcimer with eleven treble courses of three strings each resting on individual bridges and two bass bridges which rest on the left side of the instrument holding two strings each. Although the provenance of this photograph is unknown, it was sold by a North Carolina dealer, and the player and his instrument exhibit characteristics of the Piedmont tradition, including long hammers curved back at their ends and wrapped with yarn. Craven's dulcimer, which his grandfather used, also had eleven treble courses, of four strings each, and three bass courses, each with single, wound strings. Both Craven and the unidentified player in the photograph held their hammers between index and middle fingers. This might suggest a German source for the tradition here, but the hammers somewhat resemble the split-cane hammers used in southern England in recent times. That hammer grip was in use in England at one time as well; the painting *A Musical Gathering* (see illustration 17) shows an Essex gentleman holding hammers in this manner. The individual bridges and the G tuning of the lowest set of four courses on the dulcimers of the North Carolina Piedmont further suggest a southern English origin for this type.

Twelve Treble Courses, Eight to Eleven Bass Courses

Figure 14.5: Dulcimer made by William Thurston, of Farmington, Michigan, c.1860. Collection of Robert Hubbach.

Dulcimers with this string arrangement appeared mostly in the North, from New York and Pennsylvania to Michigan and Illinois. Associated design characteristics include a trapezoidal outline and single-piece bridges. Some have lids, but most do not. This layout appears on instruments from the middle of the nineteenth century, although it could have existed earlier. A dulcimer in the author's collection, from northwestern Pennsylvania, probably dates from around 1850 and has twelve treble courses of four strings each and eleven bass courses of three each, held by handmade tuning pins. Although rectangular, its pin blocks are visible. Its outside bottom measurements are 42 inches (107 cm) in length, 15¼ inches (38.7 cm) in width, and 4¾ inches (12.1 cm) in height, with a lid 2¼ inches (5.7 cm) high. Another early dulcimer of this variety is in the collections of Historic Deerfield, Deerfield, Massachusetts. It came from West Hawley, Massachusetts, and because of its tuning pins that carry the name "W. Wake," can be dated to the 1850s. This instrument likewise has visible pin blocks and two round sound holes and sits on two lyre legs. It has twelve treble courses of four strings each and eleven bass courses of two each and measures 46½ inches (118.1 cm) in length, 15 inches (38.1 cm) in width, and 4¾ inches (12.1 cm) in height, with a lid 2 inches (5.1 cm) high.

More typical of instruments with this string arrangement is a trapezoidal outline. Dulcimers made by Perry Wight, of South Alabama, New York, before his death in 1862 have twelve treble courses of four strings each and eleven bass courses of three each. The side pieces are of even thickness, but the outer edge on the pin blocks is beveled at a oblique angle to the baseboard. He used a grain-painted finish and stenciled his name. They measure 39½ and 42 inches (100.3 and 106.7 cm) at the longer length, 14¾ inches (37.5 cm) in width, 3 inches (7.9 cm) in height, with a lid 1¼ inches (2.9 cm) high.[25] Perhaps following a similar model, Mortimer DeLano, of Oxford, Michigan, made trapezoidal dulcimers with similarly beveled outer pin-block edges, but with twelve treble courses of three strings each and eleven bass courses of two each. His instruments sometimes carry the stenciled inscription "M. DeLano" and are otherwise painted black, with stenciled notes and numbers under each course. Two instruments bearing his name have two round sound holes, each backed with cardboard sunburst rosettes. One lacking his name, but in other respects identical to those with the name, measures 40¾ and 42 inches (103.5 and 106.7 cm) and 18¾ and 20 inches (47.6 and 50.8 cm) in length, 15 inches (38.1 cm) in width, and 3¾ inches

(9.5 cm) in height. Commercial instruments similar in design to those of DeLano, except that their two sound holes are in the shape of four joined lobes, are found in Michigan and Ontario. One instrument measures 43½ inches (110.5 cm) at its longest point, 19¾ inches (50.2 cm) at its shorter length, 14½ inches (36.8 cm) in width, and 3 inches (7.9 cm) in height.[26] Perhaps purchasers of this maker's dulcimer could order a specially made case with turned legs and a lid; such an example, together with John Low's method and whalebone hammers, exists in the Barnum House Museum in Grafton, Ontario. Dulcimers very similar to the preceding design were made commercially, in the 1870s, by Emerson Kelly, of Mount Forest, Ontario.[27] Jarvis G. Stocking, of Otisco Township, Ionia County, Michigan, made them commercially. One dulcimer, dated 1869, has twelve treble courses of three strings each and seven bass courses of two each, although it originally had eleven bass courses. Its sides are stained, while its soundboard is black, with gold and fantastic grain-painted decoration, and features two sound holes, consisting of center holes and twelve concentric holes.[28]

We might consider instruments with eight (and sometimes fewer) bass courses as a variant of this type. William Thurston, of Farmington, Michigan, was active about 1860 and made dulcimers on which the inscription "Wm Thurston / Farmington" appears stenciled on the front side. His instruments have beveled oblique sides, measure 43½ and 42 inches (110.5 and 106.7 cm) at the lower length, 19¾ and 18 inches (50.2 and 45.7 cm) at the upper length, 15½ inches (39.8 cm) in width, and 3¼ inches (8.3 cm) in height, and have twelve treble courses of three strings each and eight bass courses of two strings each. He grain-painted the sides of his dulcimers in a reddish pattern and painted the soundboards black, using two heart-shaped sound holes.[29] An unknown maker, who probably was active during the early 1870s in Michigan, made dulcimers with twelve treble courses of four strings each and eight bass courses of two each, with stained sides and pin blocks, black soundboards, and two round sound holes with a gold-painted border, measuring 37 (94.3 cm) and 16½ inches (42.2 cm) in length, 14¼ inches (36.2 cm) in width, and 3 inches (7.3 cm) high.[30] Another unidentified Michigan maker produced instruments with twelve treble courses of three strings each and eight bass courses of two each. This model measures 49 (124.5 cm) and 22½ inches (57.2 cm) in length and 16 inches (40.6 cm) in width, and has two sound holes, consisting of three holes one-half inch (1.3 cm) in diameter, with cloth backing.[31] Although presumably by a different maker, another Michigan dulcimer, probably from about 1875, which has twelve treble courses of three strings each and seven bass courses of two each, has a similar size. It is 49½ (125.7 cm) and 22¾ inches (57.8 cm) in length, 15½ inches (39.4 cm) in width, and 1¾ inches (4 cm) in height; its black soundboard is stenciled with bronze and red floral patterns and has two round sound holes.[32]

This variety was found elsewhere in the Great Lakes region. A trapezoidal dulcimer from Wisconsin, with a name George Ma . . . (the last name is illegible) and a date, 1876, with twelve treble courses of three strings each and eight brass bass courses of two each, sits inside a rectangular case with lid and, because of the inscription, may represent a commercial variety.[33] Lyon and Healy, of Chicago, produced dulcimers under the "Washburn 'Perfection'" label with twelve treble courses of three strings each and eight bass courses of two each, prior to 1897. This instrument's tuning pins are zither pins, placed in the left pin block. It has two round sound holes and measures 36 (91.4 cm) and 19 inches (48.3 cm) in length, 15 inches (38.1 cm) in width, and 3 inches (7.3 cm) in height. By 1897, the company's design had changed. Its "Perfection" dulcimer had thirteen treble courses of three strings each and twelve bass courses, each of two strings, divided into a lower bridge with seven courses and an upper bridge with five courses. Courses on the upper bass bridge were to be tuned to accidental notes missing in the treble courses. It measures 36 (91.4 cm) and 20¾ inches (52.7 cm) in length, 14¼ inches (36.2 cm) in width, and 3¼ inches (8.3 cm) in height.

The evolution of Lyon and Healy's design and the exceptions to the number of courses illustrates the difficulty in developing a typology for nineteenth-century American dulcimers. Although string arrangement provides an obvious criterion, other design features may be associated with certain string arrangements, and the addition or subtraction of a course to a design belonging otherwise firmly within one type may cause problems in its classification. In this sense, this last type is somewhat of a catchall.

Exceptions and Innovations

Most nineteenth-century North American dulcimers fall into one of the above categories, but others are exceptions. Although tradition acted to conserve the design, the dulcimer's many strings and informal use allowed and sometimes encouraged makers to alter traditional features. They might change the number and tuning of strings, experiment with the bracing, and try unusual materials. Makers made these attempts usually in order to increase the tonal range, improve the tone, and make the instrument's tuning more stable. During the nineteenth century the inventor became a kind of national hero, and certain dulcimer makers were quick to assume that role by taking out patents on their innovations and attempting to commercialize their ideas.

The instruments manufactured by Ezra Durand and William Vogel between about 1863 and 1869 in Chelsea and Niles, Michigan, and Stonington, Connecticut, do not fit into any of the above categories. The string arrangement on their dulcimers had eleven treble courses and eleven bass courses, both treble and bass courses having two strings each. This configuration is unusual enough, but more unusual is the placement of the bass bridge along the left edge of the soundboard. In addition, the makers intended the tuning to be a fifth lower than that used on most North American dulcimers (see appendix 1). Another contemporary cabinet dulcimer from Michigan has a bass bridge placed on the left, so this characteristic of the Durand-Vogel design may not have been their innovation, but that instrument has fourteen treble courses of four strings each and fourteen bass courses of two strings each.[34] Perhaps the placement of the bridge on the left was an attempt to make it more like the arrangement on a piano keyboard.

The usual model manufactured both in Chelsea and Stonington was a rectangular cabinet with a hinged, two-piece lid, finished with walnut veneer painted to look like rosewood. The edges around the lid and upper edge of the skirt around three sides of the instrument are decorated with beaded molding. The dulcimer has four walnut legs turned at the upper and lower ends with tapering octagonal centers. The upper surface of the instrument has a pine soundboard with a natural finish and two sound holes consisting of a center hole and ten concentric holes. Two cloth-covered candle rests lie in the upper corners. The case measures, at its bottom edges, 42 inches (106.7 cm) in length, 18 inches (45.7 cm) in width, and 6½ inches (16.5 cm) in height, with a one-half-inch (1.3 cm) thick lid. Variants include a model manufactured by Vogel at Niles, Michigan, with a stained upper surface and no candle rests, sound holes with twelve instead of ten concentric holes, and turned legs, measuring 41 inches (104.1 cm) in length, 18 inches (45.7 cm) in width, and 5 inches (12.7 cm) in height.[35] A portable model, probably manufactured at Stonington, lacks the lid and legs and has fluted molding around the lower surface on the sides of the dulcimer and beaded molding on the top edge.[36] Finally, by 1868, William Vogel was manufacturing a deluxe model, with cabriole legs and more elaborate molding, although otherwise similar to the standard model.[37] Vogel received a U.S. Patent, number 84,027, on November 10, 1868, for such a dulcimer which incorporated dampers operated by two pedals attached to a lyre underneath the instrument. The patent also was for an iron plate into which tuning and hitch-pins were held. The damper pedal design is significant, as Vogel developed the idea before Schunda, of Budapest, whose 1874 invention was widely publicized. Both Vogel and Schunda designed the pedal mechanism to push rods through the instrument, but Vogel's differed in that two pedals operated right and left damper independently and that the dampers rose up underneath the strings. The end of the Vogel-Durand enterprise in 1869 meant that the business undoubtedly manufactured few of these instruments, and the pedal soon became forgotten.

One might categorize James A. MacKenzie's "piano harp" as belonging to the type which uses twelve treble courses and eleven bass courses, but the "inventor" made so many innovations—which he was not shy to announce—that we should place it outside that category. Most of his surviving instruments have fourteen treble courses of three strings each and ten bass courses of two strings each, tuned to the standard North American scheme. The chief distinguishing feature is rectangular cast-iron frame with an arched upper surface. Pin blocks are fitted at each end at right angles to the sides, the treble pins sitting at a lower plane than the bass pins. The soundboard conforms to the arch of the iron frame, has two five-pointed-star-shaped sound holes, and is painted black, with stenciled bronze note names under each course, as well as the inscriptions: "J. A. Mackenzie's / Piano Harp / Pat'd Feb. 14. 1873." and "Manufactured / by the Inventor / Minneapolis, Minn." The frame sits in a rectangular walnut case with turned walnut legs and a hinged, two-piece lid. A removable wooden cover fits over the pins and unplayed portion of the instrument, forming a half-moon space where the strings and bridges lie.

However MacKenzie may have gotten the date 14 February 1873, the U.S. Patent Office did not grant him a patent until 14 December 1875, when he received number 171,031. This patent was for a "piano harp" with two soundboards attached on either side of a rectangular frame, arched on both sides in order to allow the bass strings to be played on either side of the treble bridge. This frame revolved in a rectangular case with scroll-cut legs. The patent drawing shows two six-pointed stars, but probably an unrealistic number of strings. Metal jacks were placed under each course (apparently of two and three strings) to allow the pitch to be raised by a half-step. MacKenzie's patent, number 440,601, granted on 11 November 1890, was for his usual model. Since most of his surviving instruments seem to have the 1873 patent date, he probably began manufacturing this model before 1890. MacKenzie's third and final patent, number 461,915, granted 27 October 1891, was for a large instrument with a fully chromatic range of over four octaves, from G^0 to a^3. Like his other piano harps, this model had a cast-iron frame, but he completely changed the tuning, so that a "treble" bridge divided twenty courses of three strings each into half-steps, while two series of bass courses of two strings each passed between each treble course over bridges on the left. Although the patent drawing shows the frame resting in a case resembling that of an upright piano, a surviving example of this model, in the Stearns Collection of Musical Instruments, University of Michigan, has the cast frame resting in an oak case conforming to the frame's outline, resting on three massive legs. An attached music stand confirms the inventor's wish that it would be "adapted for playing classical music as well as ordinary simple music, such as ballad music, waltzes, &c."[38] Such a complicated and heavy instrument, while no doubt pleasing the manufacturer, probably found, for those same reasons, few purchasers.

Other musical tinkerers took out patents on their ideas, although they did not seem to manufacture their instruments. Jesse Merrill (born 15 March 1825, Belmont County, Ohio, died 10 May 1902), of Kanopolis, Kansas, made a violin, guitar, and child's piano,[39] but received a patent (no. 582,537) on 11 May 1897, for a chromatically tuned dulcimer. This half-trapezoidal instrument had twenty-nine courses of three strings each, passing over two bridges parallel to the left side, with a range of two octaves and a major third. Courses tuned to the natural notes of the C scale rested on the inner bridge, while accidental notes rested on the outer bridge. Edwin G. James (born Feb. 1854 Illinois),[40] of South Milwaukee, Wisconsin, took out a patent (number 808,374) on 26 December 1905, for a dulcimer using an iron or steel frame, tubular steel bridges, and tension rods underneath the frame for support.

Other experimenters never bothered to apply for patents. John A. Snyder, a piano technician active in Grand Rapids, Michigan, in the 1880s, made an otherwise ordinary dulcimer with cast-iron bridges. A largely metal dulcimer with an unusual string arrangement is in the collection of the Eaton County Historical Society, Charlotte, Michigan. A "barrel" dulcimer, consisting of an ordinary instrument with a hole cut out of its bottom so that a barrel, on which it rested when in play, would aid its resonance, was played in a seedy tavern in Parkersburg, West Virginia.[41] In the early 1970s, Asel Gardner made a dulcimer with a round back in order to emulate the "barrel" dulcimer. Less experimental, perhaps, and more a result of lack of familiarity with the instrument, is an old dulcimer in western Michigan with its bass and treble bridges placed in mirror image and its pin blocks at right angles to its sides.[42]

Hammers

Hammers in much of the United States during the nineteenth century consisted of three parts: the head, shaft, and handle. Typically the head was about one-quarter inch thick and about one inch to one-and-one-half inch long and about three-quarter to one inch in width, forming a somewhat oval shape. A piece of leather or buckskin covered the circumference of the head and its ends were tied with thread at the point where the shaft entered the head. The shaft was usually made of whalebone, a readily available, flexible material commonly used for corset stays. Slots were cut into the heads and into the handles and the shaft fit snugly into them, the shaft perhaps being tightened by the use of waxed thread. The handle, perhaps two to three inches long, was made of hardwood and was held between thumb and index finger.

As spring steel replaced whalebone for corset stays between 1880 and 1890, spring steel increasingly found its way into use as the shafts of dulcimer hammers. Spring steel tends to be more flexible than whalebone, however, and other players used hacksaw blades (Jesse Martin and his grandsons, the Van Arsdale brothers), hickory (Chet Parker, Gardner brothers), willow, and bamboo. Handles tended to disappear.

American players usually held hammers between thumb and index finger, but there were exceptions. Loy Swiger held his between first and second fingers, as did Virgil Craven. This grip, however, does not necessarily indicate a German origin of the dulcimer tradition in West Virginia and North Carolina, because there is evidence that shows the

English players in the eighteenth century held them in the European fashion.

Other Paraphernalia

Players placed their dulcimers on tables, chairs, or their laps while in play, but collapsible stands were popular in the Great Lakes region. These generally allowed the dulcimer to rest at an angle, to permit easier playing. When the dulcimer rested on a table or other flat surface, the player usually placed an object under the dulcimer in order to allow the bottom to resonate. Tuning hammers varied in design, but were generally made by a local blacksmith or by the player himself.

Notes

1. This analysis is based on over one hundred unique examples of nineteenth-century American (including, in a few cases, some from Ontario) dulcimers that I have either seen directly, examined photographs or read descriptions thereof during the past thirty years. The actual number of instruments is much higher, but that number includes multiple examples by the same makers.

2. David Kettlewell, "The Dulcimer" (Ph.D. diss., Loughborough University, 1976), 249a, discusses such an instrument, made by Annabel Kerr after one in Hartington, Derbyshire. Sally Whytehead, of Birmingham, owns a dulcimer built into a rectangular case.

3. Ibid., 238, 242.

4. See the illumination in Henry VIII's Psalter, Royal MS, 2A XVI, f. 98v., British Library. See chapter 3, note 60 for references to reproductions of this illustration.

5. Bill Andre, personal communication, 1999.

6. Richard H. Hulan, "Hunting and Taming the Native American (or Hammered) Dulcimer," *Newsletter of the Folklore Society of Greater Washington* 5, no. 6 (Feb. 1969): 8. He gives the tuning, but places it a fourth lower than it undoubtedly was.

7. David Taylor, letter to author, about 1975. Patty Looman, of Mannington, West Virginia, has one that was bought at Arthurdale, West Virginia.

8. Formerly owned by Mike Berst, of Detroit, Michigan.

9. Acc. no. 94,871; see Nancy Groce, *The Hammered Dulcimer in America*, Smithsonian Studies in History and Technology, no. 44 (Washington: Smithsonian Institution Press, 1983), 5.

10. Acc. no. 27.173; Ulysses Grant Dietz, The Newark Museum, letter to author, 21 Apr. 1999.

11. Cory M. Amsler, The Bucks County Historical Society, letter to author, 2 Oct. 1997.

12. Robert Spinner, conversations with author. He learned this tuning from Ralph Sickles and others who had instruments made by John Brown.

13. Author's collection.

14. I am attributing this model to the Wade factory because of its wide distribution and its similarity to the Ransom instruments. Mrs. Byron Smith, of Stow, New York, had a dulcimer in 1969 with most of these characteristics, although with four strings per treble course, which she said was made by that factory.

15. Although Ransom's instruments are unidentified, the attribution of this model is made possible by a dulcimer in the collection of the New York State Historical Association, donated in 1947 by a descendant of Ransom, Helen Sainsbury, who identified it as a dulcimer manufactured by her ancestor in Sherman.

16. Jean Granberry Schnitz, "Hammered Dulcimers and Folk Songs: The Musical Heritage of the C. A. Lee Family," in *Corners of Texas*, ed. Francis Edward Abernethy, Publication of the Texas Folklore Society 52 (Denton, Tex.: University of North Texas Press, 1993), 160-161. In 1972, the Miles Mountain Musical Museum in Eureka Springs, Arkansas, had a dulcimer of this design, but it had twelve treble courses.

17. My father, born and raised around Sherman, New York, learned of the use of brass strings through local sources. It is impossible to determine in all cases whether the steel wire found on certain old instruments is original or was replaced by later owners.

18. Sara Johnson, personal communication, 1998.

19. The beveled sides account for the variations in measurement, the higher number indicating the measurement at the bottom, the lower indicating that at the upper edges.

20. The larger dimensions in length are from 33.73.1, the shorter from 00.4.393, which appears to have been altered at one time by adding more bass courses and single-piece bridges.

21. Bob Wey, letters to author, 19 Nov. 1977, 27 Nov. 1977.

22. Guy Bankes, letters to author, 6 Sept. 1998, 20 Sept. 1998.

23. Bruce Henry, telephone conversation with author, 17 Sept. 2000.

24. Edward Babel Collection, Southern Folklife Collection, Southern Historical Collection, University Archives, University of North Carolina at Chapel Hill.

25. This is based on a single example, at the Genesee Country Museum.

26. Measurements are from a dulcimer owned by Luke Kawecki, of Farmington Hills, Michigan. A similar one, owned by Ellen McHugh, of Rockford, Illinois, was bought by her ancestor, Hugh C. McNeil, of Edwardsburg, Michigan, who also had a copy of John Low's method.

27. Lloyd Kelly, conversation with author, Oil Springs, Ontario, 1977.

28. This was owned and played by Charles B. Huntington (1857-1959), of Chesaning, Michigan, and repaired by William T. White, Okemos, Michigan, in 1985.

29. Robert Hubbach, of Clarkston, Michigan, has one, and Karen Domanski, of Okemos, Michigan, another.

30. One was played by Albert Ives, born 1853, of Bailey, Michigan, which is in the collections of the Michigan State University Museum (1222 HM), the other was owned by Oren Snyder, of Hanover, Michigan, in 1976, and played by his grandfather.

31. One instrument of this variety is owned by William Kuhlman, of Midland, Michigan, and another was brought to me for repair about 1979.

32. This belonged to John Kemerling (1857-1921), of Barry County, Michigan, and is now in the author's collection.

33. Gary Scott, Madison, Wisconsin, personal communication, 1999.

34. This was for sale by Elderly Instruments, East Lansing, Michigan, about 1979.

35. An example of this is 2841CW, in the Michigan State University Museum, but without a label. Another, owned by Lyle Schwall, of Bay City, Michigan, in 1977, had a label identifying it as made by William Vogel in Niles, Michigan.

36. An example of such a variety is in the Peterborough Historical Society, Peterborough, New Hampshire.

37. See Groce, *Hammered Dulcimer in America*, 46 and cover illustration, for an illustration of this model, which is number 94,872 of the Smithsonian Institution's collection.

38. U.S. Patent no. 461,915.

39. Delores M. Young, Aurora, Colo., letter to author, 15 Apr. 1991.

40. U.S. Census, 1900, Milwaukee County, Wisconsin, e.d. 145, sheet 7.

41. H. E. Matheny, conversation with author, Uniontown, Ohio, 1970s.

42. This was owned by John Hawksley, of Alto, Michigan, about 1980.

The Dulcimer in North America, 1900-1975

In some ways it is wrong to break up the discussion of the dulcimer in the United States by creating another chapter and a periodization. During much of the twentieth century, the tradition established in the nineteenth century continued with little change. Some of the players active in the first part of the twentieth century learned to play in the previous century and passed their knowledge on to newer players. Nevertheless, new developments, both musical and social, brought change.

One of the newest technological changes, that of sound recording, captured the American dulcimer for posterity. Roy Gibson went to the Edison studio in 1901 to record four marches as dulcimer solos: "Gibson March," "Rosetzky March," "27th Ohio Regiment March," and "March Arcadia."[1] These brown wax cylinders are among the earliest recordings of any variety of American vernacular music. Although nothing is known about the performer, he probably played the dulcimer by ear. His repertoire probably consisted mainly of square dance tunes and waltzes, but his choice of selections at these recording sessions was probably influenced by Edison agents, who knew that their customers wanted marches. The fad for the two-step, which was danced to march music, was in full gear. Gibson's "March Arcadia" is a standard march in 2/4, played in G major, with two strains and a trio coda. Of the other titles, he may have composed "Gibson March;" "Rosetzky March" may be "Radetzky March," by Johann Strauss; and "27th Ohio Regiment March" may date from the Civil War. Although historians of country music generally refer to the 1922 Victor session of Texas fiddlers Eck Robertson and Henry C. Gilliland as the earliest evidence of traditional rural American music on record, Gibson may actually have an earlier claim.

William A. Moriarity followed in Gibson's wake, recording two cylinders for Edison: "Ain't Dat a Shame," a ragtime "coon" song, issued in 1902, and "Llewellyn March," a march in 6/8, issued in 1904.[2] Again, nothing is known of Moriarity, although his choice of tunes suggests a more commercial approach than that of Gibson. Certainly the "coon" song was a novelty.

Whatever changes the new technology offered and whatever interest Edison, who was born and raised in Ohio and Michigan at a time when the dulcimer was at the height of its popularity, had in the instrument, recording technology did not revive it. Apart from the recordings by Henry Ford's orchestra, discussed in chapter 16, the Anglo-American dulcimer did not appear on recordings commercially available in the United States until the 1960s.[3] Those early cylinders soon became forgotten.

The Sears and Roebuck catalog for 1906 no longer offered the instrument for sale. Presumably the company had made a decision to discontinue the item due to lack of sales, and its supplier Lyon and Healy probably stopped manufacturing it. This company was apparently the only firm which could supply new dulcimers to the music trade, so local music stores could no longer order them for their customers. In 1908, Boston's largest music dealer, Oliver Ditson Company, had one dulcimer in stock, but had not sold any for ten years, there being no demand for them.[4] The era of commercial dulcimers had now come to a close. Although the instrument had largely existed outside the conventional music trade, having been manufactured in large quantities only briefly and sold by traveling salesmen or made in smaller quantities and sold locally by the maker himself, anybody considering to learn to play the instrument would now need to know someone who had an old one or who might make one.

For most of the twentieth century, the knowledge of playing the dulcimer was passed rather intimately from individual to individual. This had probably been true in the latter half of the nineteenth century as well, but people could sometimes buy published tutors to help them learn to tune and play their new instruments. After 1900, someone new to the instrument needed someone to explain the tuning before he or she could start to play it. Without this direct instruction—available only through informal channels, such as family, neighbors, or acquaintances, not through professional music teachers or from published sources—nobody could make sense of it. It had now reverted to its older status as a true folk instrument.

Great Lakes Region

During the first part of the twentieth century, nearly all dulcimer playing in the Great Lakes region was confined to rural areas. As players migrated to cities and small towns, one might hear the instrument on occasion in those places, but its natural home was on farms. Where farmers gathered, such as at neighborhood parties and public dances at local halls and barns, one might hear the dulcimer, but the latter occasions were about the only times when an outsider might hear the instrument. In most cases the instruments never left the players' homes. Thus older people living in the 1970s and 1980s usually remembered the dulcimer in a rather intimate way, played by a family member or neighbor.

Michigan

The tradition of dulcimer playing was relatively strong in the state of Michigan. By assembling a list of names of players who various people I encountered in the 1970s and 1980s could recall, it is possible to draw a reasonably good picture of dulcimer players in Michigan in the early years of the century. I located 120 individuals who reportedly played the instrument in the 1910 census manuscript schedules, most of whom were probably actively playing at that time. It is impossible to know how representative this sample is, but the number is large enough to have some meaning. The sample underrepresents women players, who, in any case, were a minority (5.8%), and also people with common names, who are hard to identify. Nevertheless, from this list, we can draw certain conclusions about Michigan dulcimer players in the first part of the century.

In 1910, 52.8% of Michigan's population resided in "urban" locations, that is, in places with populations of 2500 or more.[5] Of the sample, however, 90.8% were rural. The players living in urban areas, like Muskegon, Lansing, and smaller cities, had recently migrated from farms. Most of the male players (56.6%) were farmers, more than two times the rate for the state as a whole, which was 20%. Others were farm laborers (15.9%), nonfarm laborers (8%), brick and stonemasons (3.5%), and carpenters (2.7%). Other individual occupations included barber, machinist, baker, automotive inspector, blacksmith, physician, mail carrier, pattern maker and butcher.

They were also overwhelmingly (98.3%) natives of the United States, in contrast to the state's population, which was 77.9%. Even more strikingly, 71.7% of the sample's parents were both natives, almost double the rate for the entire state, which was 43.6%. The majority (73.3%) was born in Michigan. Ranking after Michigan as birthplaces were Ohio (8.3%), New York (5%), and Indiana (3.3%); Pennsylvania and New England each accounted for 2.5%. The remainder were born in Illinois and Wisconsin. The two foreign-born players were born in Canada. Of the 15% who had one native and one foreign-born parent, England ranked as the leading birthplace of the foreign-born parent, followed by Canada, Germany, Norway, and Ireland. More significant is the number of players both of whose parents were foreign-born (10.8%). Children of immigrants from Canada and Germany accounted for 4.2% each, while the remainder were children of parents from Ireland and Holland.

Their ages ranged from fourteen to seventy-eight, with an average of thirty-eight. Given that their names were collected mostly in the 1970s and 1980s, one would assume that the sample would be skewed towards people who were relatively young in 1910. Since the average year of birth is 1871, it is reasonable then to conclude that in Michigan, the dulcimer began to decline after 1890. Young men learning to play the instrument tended to be in their late teens or early twenties, unless they had grown up in a house with a parent who played it. Sociability was, as always, a part of youthful life, and an ability to play for parties was an important way for one to gain popularity in a rural community. Still, in some neighborhoods, young people continued to learn to play the instrument well after 1890.

The map (see figure 15.1) shows the residence of players identified in the 1910 census. Despite clusters caused by particular families with a large number of players or particular neighborhoods where I have had more contacts, a pattern still emerges. Although players lived in most parts of the Lower Peninsula,[6] they were very scarce in the Thumb and area along Lake Huron, which was settled mainly by migrants from Ontario. Areas with heavy European settlement, such as the Dutch area of Ottawa County and the German areas of Saginaw, Macomb, Washtenaw, and Wayne Counties, were also underrepresented. On the other hand, central and western Michigan, largely settled by migrants

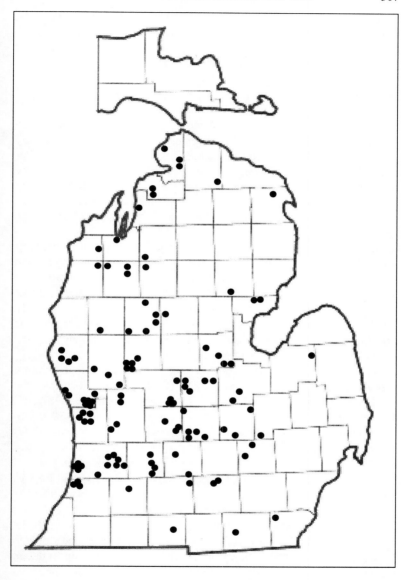

Figure 15.1: Residence of dulcimer players in Michigan identified in 1910 census. Each dot represents one player.

from western New York, was well represented. The list of players in the 1910 census reflects this. The same percentage of the fathers of the players were born in New York (25.8%) as in Michigan. For their mothers, Michigan ranks as the chief birthplace (25.8%), with New York second (16.7%), and Ohio third (14.2%). The low number of players with family origins in Canada is striking, given that Canadians accounted for a large part of the state's settlers.

We may conclude that by 1910 the dulcimer tradition in Michigan was long established, and that, although essentially local, its origins lay with the popularity of the instrument with settlers from New York. Between 1830 and 1860 the vast majority of the state's settlers came from the Empire State, especially the western part of the state, near Rochester.[7] Once established, the dulcimer continued to be used into the twentieth century in rural areas where the way of life had changed little in fifty years.

Individually, dulcimer players varied greatly in their ability and willingness to play in public. Some never took it outside the home, and others never even took it into the house. Lewis H. Brown (born about 1874), of Norwood Township, Charlevoix County, whose father Sylvester and uncle John had played the instrument, only played it in his barn on Sunday mornings, after his wife and children had left for church. One time his son Wilbur secretly watched him singing "In the Baggage Coach Ahead" while accompanying himself on the dulcimer.[8]

The dulcimer was commonly used as an instrument that a family member might use to play with another family member. Typically the father might play both the fiddle and dulcimer, and his children would learn those and other instruments. Thus Welcom D. Toms (1870-1949), of Greenwood Township, Wexford County, used to let his son Allan (1897-1969) accompany his fiddling on his dulcimer (see illustration 24), just as he had done with his father before him.[9] Daniel K. Gunn (1872-1957), of Allendale Township, Ottawa County, and later Grand Rapids, would let his son Howard play the fiddle while he played the dulcimer and his wife played the piano at family get-togethers.[10] Ada Johnston (1889-1985) accompanied her father Thomas A. Johnston (born 1853), of Brooks Township, Newaygo County, when he played the fiddle.[11] Gordon O. Batey (born about 1874), of Ganges Township, Allegan County, would play the fiddle while his daughter Dorothy accompanied on the dulcimer at home in the 1920s.[12] Cassius F. Bacon (1856-1941), of Northeast Corners, Monroe County, would play with his son Earl R.

(1886-1970), who also played the piano.[13] Although one could list many other examples of children playing the dulcimer with their parents, these suffice to show how players passed the instrument's techniques to the next generation. In all these examples, the father played both the violin and dulcimer.

Frequently brothers or a brother and sister played together regularly. In some cases, especially with a female family member, they may have grown up in a house with a dulcimer. Such was the case with Archie Barnes (1877-1966) and his sister Elizabeth Palen (1876-1960), of Alaiddon Township, Ingham County, who played together (Archie playing the fiddle and Elizabeth the dulcimer) as late as the 1950s for events such as a party for road construction workers or a local historical society.[14] Brothers Mark (1854-1934) and Lewis C. Sturgis (1860-1940), of Argentine Township, Genesee County, played the instruments regularly together until their last years. So did their relatives, brothers John and Edward Sturgis (1874-1952), of Byron, Shiawassee County. In Mount Haley Township, Midland County, Ray Brooks played the dulcimer with his brothers Dan, a fiddler, and Artie, who played the five-string banjo.[15] Again, this list is merely suggestive, as there were many other examples.

It was easy and almost natural for a child to learn to play an instrument that was lying around the house. Others developed an interest in the instrument from watching neighborhood friends. Acquiring a dulcimer might present a problem, however, since music stores did not sell them. A few individuals made them for sale, although not on a commercial basis. When Claus Borchers (1896-1990), a hired man on a farm in Sullivan Township, Muskegon County, about 1917, wanted a dulcimer, he bought one from Lewis Eckhoff, owner of a sawmill in Nunica, who had made a few "just for fun of it." He sold one to Claus for five dollars.[16]

Even players who learned at home might make one. Albert Hober (born 1878), of Ravenna Township, Muskegon County, had borrowed one from his neighbor Ned Golden, a fiddler, with whom he played for local dances. His son Albert Jr. (1907-1998) learned to play chords on it, and sometime in the 1920s, the son asked his father if they could make one together. The father declined, but encouraged his son to do so. Al recalled:

> I got all the stuff ready and made it, and do you suppose I could tune that? No. I had one heck of a time. I had it all strung up and everything.

Dad said, "Why don't you take that over to Ravenna?" Freddie White lived over there. He could play a violin, and he could play a dulcimer, and he could tune 'em. . . . I had a motorcycle with a sidecar on, and so I stuck that (it slides right into a grain bag pretty nice and tied a string around the end) in there down in the sidecar of the motorcycle and went over there. Freddie White lived down in a gully, like, in just a little shack down there, and he must've been seventy years old then, and I went down there. Of course as quick as I come, why, he got his violin out, and his dulcimer was always out, and we set down and played a little while. I said, "Fred, do you know I made one of them, but," I said, "I can't tune it." "Bring her in," he says. "I'll fix her." And, by God, he did. He says, "Boy, you know you done a nice job on that." So he picked around on the strings, and he got him a hammer, took them bridges around a little bit, and in about a half hour's time, he says, "Here, now play on it." He says, "You got a darn nice dulcimer there."[17]

Fred White, according to another old-time dulcimer player and fiddler from Hober's neighborhood, Pete Seba (1883-1986), sold the dulcimers he had made for five dollars apiece.[18]

The dulcimer enjoyed a certain popularity in the rural area of Ravenna Township, and a more detailed discussion of the tradition there may illuminate aspects of other local traditions. Settlers began to create farms there in the 1840s and 1850s, coming mainly from New York and Ontario. A substantial number of Germans followed, after the Civil War, so by 1894, 18.2% of the population of the township was foreign-born.[19] The oldest player remembered by Pete Seba and Al Hober was Freddie White, although undoubtedly other players preceded him. White, thought Hober, was "real good," as "he could play all them old-time tunes" on the instrument. He also had an unusual ability to play the fiddle and dulcimer at the same time. Hober recalled, "He'd do that whenever he felt right. You know, give him a few drinks, and he'd put the dulcimer right down on the floor and grab the violin, take his shoes off, stick the sticks between his toes—he had little short sticks—and, boy, he could really play it, too."[20]

Brothers Wes Anderson (1881-1971) and Glenn Anderson (1895-1959) also played the dulcimer, and their brother Charlie (1884-1936) played the fiddle. Glenn could "play 'Turkey in the Straw' and all that on the dulcimer. By God, he could hammer it all. Play the tune right on the dulcimer," according to Pete Seba.[21] Presumably their father Rinaldo E. Anderson (1856-1937) played both instruments.[22] Ned Golden (born about 1862) was the best fiddler in the area, according to Hober, but also played the dulcimer.

Several German families bought farms in the southern part of the township in the years after the Civil War. Pete Seba, whose parents came from Germany, recalled their parties before the turn of the century: "Them old Germans, they used to get a keg of beer, and then they'd get somebody to play the violin and waltz and sing them old German songs. They used to have a good time, them old farmers. They didn't have much— they worked hard, didn't have much, but God, they was happy!"[23]

Other children of German-speaking immigrants learned to play the locally popular instruments used for parties, the violin and dulcimer. Gustes A. Rollenhagen (1878-1943) learned at the age of fifteen, from watching local players, and also learned the violin. On the dulcimer he played tunes like "Turkey in the Straw," "Irish Washerwoman," and "Red Wing," as well as "chording" patterns to accompany fiddlers.[24] Albert Hober, Sr. played from a young age and, in the 1910s and 1920s, took his dulcimer to play with Ned Golden at local parties. Pete Seba began to play the violin at about fourteen or fifteen. Following his marriage in 1905, his father-in-law Jim Gleason, of Walkerville, made a dulcimer for him, which he continued to play to the end of his life. In 1984, I watched incredulously as Seba, at the age of 101, played the dulcimer at his home, accompanying fiddler August Hasted. Brothers Archie (1892-1965), Alfred, and Clarence Gutknecht (1914-1968) also learned to play the dulcimer.

In nearby Sullivan Township, Claus Borchers and August Hasted were hired hands on neighboring farms around 1914, when they combined their savings and ordered a violin kit from Sears and Roebuck. The only person who played the dulcimer that Borchers knew, besides Lewis Eckhoff, who made his instrument, was Pete Seba. Seba showed him how to "play the chords" on it, and shortly afterwards, Claus was playing with fiddler Clemo Shepherd at house parties around Spring Lake.

These German-American amateur musicians learned the square dance music of their neighbors. Al Hober, Jr., mostly chorded on the dulcimer, although he could play a nameless tune generally known as "Miss McLeod's Reel." On the mouth organ, he played "On the Road to Boston," but without a name, and knew the tunes "Finnegan's Wake" (probably "Haste to the Wedding") and "Fisher's Hornpipe" by name. Other older dance tunes played or mentioned by Seba and Hasted included

"Devil's Dream," "Irish Washerwoman," "Soldier's Joy," and "My Love She's But a Lassie Yet." Their German tunes included "O du lieber Augustin" and a couple of other nameless waltzes. Thus the local repertoire was a complementary mixture of music brought by the area by their parents and grandparents and the dance music of their American neighbors.

Before 1920 music at local house parties was usually provided by a fiddle and a dulcimer. Around 1900, at nearby Fruitport, Charles F. Peterson told a reporter that country dances were held nightly and the dulcimer was "one of the favorite instruments" at those dances.[25] Claus Borchers remembered that three or four teams of horses would lead two or three sleigh loads to Cloverville towards Muskegon and parties would start about eight o'clock and last until three or four in the morning. Al Hober recalled that his father would take his dulcimer under his arm and walk with Ned Golden five or six miles to play at a house. Some of these parties were not the sober affairs of their more temperance-minded neighbors. Albert Hober, Sr., told his son

> Ned would set there and fiddle when he was so drunk that he couldn't hardly walk. . . . He was a-playin' away there one time and pretty quick he stopped fiddlin' and he said 'All ass end up' and he fell right on backwards with the chair. That was the end of the dance. It was all done then. As long as he could set on the chair it was all right.[26]

One could hear the dulcimer occasionally at public dances held at local halls, but changes in dance styles and the popularity of the piano doomed it in those places. Claus Borchers played the dulcimer with Clemo Shepherd for dances at the West Crockery Grange Hall in 1919. The next year the Grange purchased a piano, which put an end to the dulcimer.[27] Still, Gustes Rollenhagen played the dulcimer, fiddled, and called, with his brothers George and Andy, in combinations that included violin, dulcimer, and piano, or violin, dulcimer, and drums, at Oddfellows halls in Nunica, Ravenna, and Coopersville, as well as the Grange hall in Nunica.[28] Al Hober, Sr., played the dulcimer with fiddler Pat Gibbs and a piano player for dances at a hall in Coopersville, and with Pete Seba at the Bunny Club, a community hall in Ravenna. In later years, the dulcimer disappeared from most of the local public dances, such as at George Howard's barn, which featured violin, piano, and drums.[29] Claus Borchers remarked that the old fiddle-dulcimer duo common at dances in the teens and earlier gave way to four-piece "orchestras" with piano. He mentioned the Ralya family orchestra, which had its origins with Leonard Ralya, who played the fiddle (as well as the dulcimer) while his son Harold (1907-1989) accompanied him on the accordion at the Gleaners' hall in Robinson Township, Ottawa County. His other son Lawrence Ralya (1897-1979) learned the dulcimer from his father, and played "chords" on the dulcimer at parties with his brother, but later played the piano in a group which generally consisted of violin, saxophone, piano, and drums. The Ralya brothers continued to play for dances at the Eagles hall in Grand Haven and at wedding receptions into the 1960s.[30] Although they adapted to the newer tastes in dance music, they needed to switch from the dulcimer to piano in order to stay in demand.

Until the 1920s, rural house parties were the typical venue for the dulcimer and its associated music. Neighbors came to dance, eat supper, perhaps play cards, and leave early in the morning. Often held in the winter, sleigh rides were part of the fun. Harley Sinclair remembered going with his parents and brothers and sisters to local parties around Bushnell Township, Montcalm County, where his father Eugene (1872-1925) would bring his dulcimer to accompany a local fiddler, Frank Pearson:

> It was in the twenties, early twenties, and he used to play. . . . Course we was just young kids then and used to go when they played 'til four o'clock in the morning. We have went with horses over there, when they used to throw the dulcimer in the sleigh, and everybody would put a bunch of straw in the bottom of the sleigh, over heavy quilts with soapstones. . . . At that time, when they went, they stopped every place. They come out and get in the sleigh with us, all the neighbors, so they went where they was gonna dance.[31]

The host of the party would clear out the rooms and remove the carpets. Young children would have places reserved for them to sleep. In most cases there was only enough room for one set (four couples) of dancers. In the 1910s and 1920s, most of the dancing consisted of square dances, but there were also round dances, such as the two-step, schottische, waltz, Put Your Little Foot, and heel-and-toe polka, although the last was in decline. Contradances, such as the Virginia Reel and Irish Trot, were popular in some neighborhoods until the 1920s. Around Ravenna, Claus Borchers and Pete Seba recalled the Money Musk and Opera Reel still being danced in the 1910s.

The instrumentation of the music for the dancing was variable, as it depended on the instruments the local musicians played. Bill Bigford (1898-1986), of Marion, sometimes played his fiddle alone at house parties, because, he recalled, "there wasn't too many who'd get out of bed away for the night and go away and play. I'd have 'em get me out of bed many a night to go and play for a house party or something. Take up a collection and maybe get a dollar or two."[32] In many areas of Michigan, a typical combination was two fiddles, one playing the lead and the other playing second. Stewart Carmichael (1899-1990), of Chippewa Township, Mecosta County, said that was the usual combination in his neighborhood about the time of his birth. In Trowbridge Township, Allegan County, John Annis and Manny Daggett played in that combination in the 1920s, as they had for many years before.[33] If the host had one, someone might play second on a reed organ, fiddle and reed organ being a popular combination. The lead instrument was usually a fiddle, and the "second" was provided by various other instruments, including a fiddle, organ or later piano, five-string banjo, guitar, or accordion. The dulcimer was one of the "seconding" instruments.

Dancing took place in circumstances even more impromptu than at house parties, which did involve some planning. Alida Chapman, recalling her childhood in Delhi Township, Ingham County, early in the century, writes: "After the oxen or horses were fed and all the dishes washed, Uncle Alvin would bring out the dulcimer and Johnny would tune up the fiddle for the 'Money Mush,' 'Old Irish Washwoman,' or 'Arkansas Traveler.' Then Uncle Bob would holler, 'Two more couples right this way.'"[34]

Fenton Watkins (1885-1980) told of "maple sugar" parties in his rural neighborhood near South Haven, around 1900. He played the dulcimer at those events, when local youth would gather to taste the newly made maple syrup and dance to their homemade music.[35] Harley Sinclair remembered Christmas dinners with his uncles visiting. After dinner, they would take up the rug and start dancing, his father and uncles providing the music with dulcimer and fiddles. Each spring, when his mother took the carpets out of the house to clean them, the family would have a little dance.[36]

Although in decline, youth still played the dulcimer in informal groups, much as they probably did in the nineteenth century. Around Frontier, Hillsdale County, Elgia C. Hickok (1894-1967) began to play a dulcimer, which had belonged to his great-grandfather, at the age of nine. Hickok wrote:

Shortly afterwards a group of neighborhood boys organized a string band [the "Tough St. String Band," consisting of Guy Hickok, violin; Bill Gaffney, violin; Everett Hickok, guitar; Frank Gaffney, mandolin; Elgia Hickok, dulcimer] and soon we were playing for neighborhood parties. Within a few years we were going as far as 20 miles by horses and wagon to play for dances. At the beginning of World War I the group continued [*sic*, discontinued] playing.[37]

Most such groups lacked a formal name. One exception was the "Skunk Hunters' Band," of Portland, formed around brothers Alton (1880-1963) and Bill Barnes, who played the fiddle and dulcimer respectively.[38]

The dulcimer might also appear at public dances. Shortly after the turn of the century, an interurban company developed Lake Lansing, several miles from Lansing, where it built a casino for skating and dancing. Rather than hiring a professional orchestra from the city, the promoters engaged a local group from Meridian Township. Fred Sherman played the lead fiddle, Ed Hardy the second fiddle, and Carlton Sherman played the dulcimer.[39]

More typically, dances at which the dulcimer might appear were held at Grange or Oddfellows halls. Leslie Raber recalled that the music for dances at the Grange hall in Trowbridge Township, Allegan County, about 1917, was provided by Erie B. Torrey, a fiddler, and his wife Cora (1864-1944), who played the dulcimer.[40] Albert A. Woodmansee (1875-1938), of Baltimore Township, Barry County, played the fiddle, dulcimer, and drums, in a group usually consisting of four or five pieces that played for dances at Grange halls in the area as late as the 1930s. The group included his cousin Harry A. Woodmansee, a fiddler, Freeman Kemerling, on cello, and Harry's daughters on banjo and piano.[41] Harry Keirnan and his brother Tom Keirnan, both of whom played the fiddle and dulcimer, played for dances at the Oddfellows hall in Glenn, Allegan County, around 1930.[42] Around 1950, one could still hear the dulcimer at dances at the Oddfellows hall in Pullman, in Allegan County.[43] Chet Parker played his dulcimer at dances at Grange halls north of Grand Rapids well into the 1950s. Artie W. Brooks (1883-1959), of Mount Haley Township, Midland County, played second on the dulcimer (see illustration 31), as well as five-string and later tenor banjo, with his family orchestra, which included his sons Lloyd on violin, Eugene on

tenor saxophone, and daughter-in-law Natalee on piano, at dances at the
Homer Township Grange Hall and other places in Midland County as
late as the 1950s.[44] Around 1960, Alton ("Aldie") Barnes played his
dulcimer with fiddler Bill Bigford and a guitar player at the Portland
Hotel.[45]

Where the dulcimer appeared at public dances after 1920, it was a
rarity. When Grace Ryan, of Portland, was surveying rural Michigan
dances in the 1920s, she found the most common combinations to be
violin and piano; violin, banjo, and piano; violin, banjo, and guitar; and
violin, piano, guitar, and banjo. She remarked "the dulcimer is rather
rare now, but it is sometimes found playing with any of the above combinations."[46]

Although dancing and dance music was associated with the dulcimer, the instrument also appeared occasionally in public strictly as entertainment. In the 1920s, Louis Walker (1867-1955) played his dulcimer with fiddler Nelson Louks at Pomona Grange meetings at Orono,
near Reed City, for example.[47] During that same decade, a woman used
to play the dulcimer alone at the annual Garfield Township fair, in
Newaygo County.[48] About that time, a blind man, recalled by some as
"Blind Charlie," used to play the dulcimer at the Grand Traverse County
Fair in Traverse City as well as in front of lines at theaters in Cadillac.[49]
That was as close as the instrument got to the stage, however.

Typically, most Michigan dulcimer players used the instrument as a
"seconding" instrument. They might play a few tunes on it, but mostly
they "chorded." Their need for melody was often fulfilled by a fiddle,
many of whom played that instrument. Frank Stevens (1889-1977), of
Sand Lake, learned both instruments as a teenager. He played a large
number of tunes on the fiddle, but on the dulcimer, he played only "Turkey in the Straw" and a nameless 6/8 tune in D, besides chording. Peter
Reames (1888-1980), of Muskegon Heights, who learned the dulcimer
at Shelby Township, Oceana County, about 1904, mainly played chords,
besides lead on a few tunes like "Red Wing" and "Soldier's Joy." Stewart
Carmichael bought a secondhand dulcimer in 1922, gave it a chromatic
tuning, and only played chords on it, although he played many tunes on
the fiddle. Elgia Hickok played only a few lead tunes on it, including
"Golden Slippers" and "Darling Nelly Gray," yet had a great interest in
the instrument and liked to accompany fiddlers. Delbert Schrader (1896-
1980), of Au Gres, learned the dulcimer from his Indiana-born father
and never played anything more than second on it, content to accompany fiddlers like Charles Moran of Mount Morris on the instrument.

Chording was common to the Great Lakes area but was apparently unknown in other areas. Since players learned the technique orally, the exact notes varied from player to player. In play, the fiddler would usually announce the key and begin playing, the dulcimer player and other accompanying instruments joining in. The caller would start "Allemande left" at the end of the first phrase, and the square dance would begin.

A few players, however, cultivated playing lead on the dulcimer. This was exceptional, although not likely an innovation. Ernest E. Brown (1891-1946), of Davison, learned the dulcimer from his father, Murray Brown, at Prescott, Arenac County, as a child. Following a house fire in 1913 which destroyed the dulcimer, he had a cabinetmaker in Flint replace the instrument. His son recalled him playing tunes like "Soldier's Joy," "Red Wing," "Irish Washerwoman," "Turkey in the Straw," "Arkansas Traveler," "Bye Bye Blackbird," and the obscure "Elephant Walk" and "Race Horse."[50]

Chet Parker made his dulcimer in 1904. Unlike most other players in the area, he "never played no second."[51] His father was a fiddler, and he learned the violin as well, favoring tunes like "High Level Hornpipe" and "Constitution Hornpipe." He learned to read music and was proud to have memorized all of the quadrille changes in the series *Gems of the*

Example 15.1: "Moonglow Schottische," played by Archie Barnes. Recorded at Okemos, Michigan, in 1965 by Charles Delamarter, Okemos Historical Society Oral History Collection.

Ballroom (Chicago: E. T. Root, 1896), a popular publication sold through the Sears catalog. In addition to these tunes, he learned tunes from other publications, such as O. F. "Cub" Berdan's *Pride of the Ballroom* (Detroit: O. F. Berdan, 188-?), and by ear. He continued to play for dances at Grange halls until the 1960s and kept up with the changes in styles by adding two-steps, fox-trots, and polkas to his repertoire. In his last years, he played regularly with Warren ("Killer") Waid, who accompanied him on an electric guitar, at Rockford bars and at the Driftwood Inn at Croton. His 1966 Folkways recording documents a substantial, but nevertheless small, portion of his repertoire.[52] Although his dulcimer had become a novelty by that time, it was firmly based in local tradition.

Western New York and Northwestern Pennsylvania

The dulcimer barely survived into the twentieth century in western New York State and northwestern Pennsylvania. Despite thousands of instruments produced before the Civil War by two or more factories in Chautauqua County, New York, by 1930 only the old-timers were familiar with it. As in Michigan, a few families and individuals continued to play it.

At Sherman, where Henry Ransom's concern was located, Charles W. Stanton, Jr. (1856-1936) played the fiddle and a Ransom dulcimer, which he lent for the 1903 county centennial exhibition. By the 1920s, he had moved to Ithaca, and no one there actively played it. My uncle Walter D. Gifford (1902-1984), of Sherman, who played clarinet and saxophone for dances during that decade, bought a dulcimer in 1928 and played it occasionally at local affairs, but the instrument was a novelty then. In the neighboring town of North Harmony, Merle Wells, a fiddler who lived at Stow, played for many dances, and taught his son Marcus to play second on the dulcimer to accompany him. They were active as late as the 1940s playing at local square dances. More typically, the instrument was played at home, as Velma E. Messinger (1866-1942), or her son Jake, who made one, did.[53] In the town of Harmony, John Gunton (1878-1954), of Watts Flats, played the fiddle with his brother Glen (1882-1948), who generally played the dulcimer. Their father Matthew (born 1858) played both instruments as well, but John learned the dulcimer from Adrian Bagley, of Watts Flats. John and Glen both read music, favoring *Gems of the Ballroom* as a source for dance music.[54]

Frank Young (1882-1974), of Union City, Pennsylvania, played a Ransom dulcimer and made two copies of it, as well as a squarish guitar he made himself. Hibbard Swan, also of Union City, played the fiddle and dulcimer. His sister Kimmie accompanied him on the dulcimer at a fiddler's contest in Erie or North East, probably in the 1920s. Hibbard's sons Lewis (1908-1973), who moved to Samaria, Michigan, and Floyd (1910-1986), of Corry, Pennsylvania, also played the dulcimer, limiting themselves to playing second, and continued to do so at family reunions until the 1970s.[55]

The best-known and the most talented player in the area was Jesse R. Martin (born 9 June1854 Kiantone, New York, died 1 January 1939 Frewsburg, New York), of Frewsburg, New York. His older brother Albert probably introduced him to the instrument and, against his father's wishes, he began to learn it at about the age of ten. By fourteen he was playing for local dances. Presumably he played second to different fiddlers, and it was in this way that he learned a large repertoire of dance tunes, since he played by ear. These included tunes for square dances, contradances (Money Musk, Opera Reel, Chorus Jig, Crooked S), lancers, schottisches, and waltzes. Marvin Thayer played with him at dances and liked to tell

Example 15.2: "Lancers Quadrille" played by Paul Van Arsdale. Recorded at Dunkirk, New York, in July 1975 by the author. (This transcription does not convey all the variations he might play.)

a story how at one dance Martin had passed out after drinking too much hard cider, yet kept on playing his dulcimer.[56] Starting in 1918, when he worked in a furniture factory in Jamestown, he played at parties with Laura Biers, who accompanied him on the Hawaiian guitar. He also played frequently for dances at the Frewsburg Grange Hall and the Crystal Ballroom in Jamestown. In his later years, concerned about the decline of the dulcimer, he taught the instrument and the many dance tunes he knew to his grandsons, Phillip and Paul Van Arsdale (born 1920), and to young people in his neighborhood.[57]

Ohio

Most Ohio players active in the first part of the twentieth century seem to have lived in the northern part of the state. Luther Battles (1889-1985), of Hambden, Geauga County, began to play at the age of fourteen, learning from Will Ostrander, of Ashtabula County. He played an early Lyon and Healy dulcimer, using corset-stay hammers, and, like most other players in the Great Lakes region, only played second. For many years, until 1971, his group, consisting usually of fiddle (played by Keston Peters or Art Grootegoed), dulcimer, and bass, played at the annual Maple Sugar Festival, at Chardon, Ohio (see illustration 32), and Apple Butter Festival, at Burton, Ohio.[58] Their trio preserved what had been a locally popular instrumentation well into the twentieth century.

A number of players lived in northwestern Ohio, due probably in no small part to the activity at the end of the nineteenth century of "Wheel" Hackett, of Liberty Center. Around Millbury, during the early part of the century, a woman used to accompany her brother at dances.[59] Al Cromer (born about 1865), of Tiffin, played the dulcimer regularly with his brother Virgil (died 1914), who played the fiddle, mandolin, and harmonica. They played at the Ohio State Fair in the 1910s.[60]

Indiana

In the northern part of Indiana there were a number of players, whose playing probably followed the general style of the region. During the 1920s, dulcimer players appeared at dances around Crown Point, Mill Creek, and Lafayette.[61] Tracy W. Redding, in his reminiscences of his childhood early in the century in Porter County, described the local parties:

> Two uncles always provided the music for the dancing, Uncle Pete with his fiddle and Uncle Bob with his dulcimer. I don't know whose uncles they were. Everybody called them "uncle." Uncle Andrew was always the caller, and how he could call those changes! He would always start with the "Virginia Reel." Then came the "Washerwoman," "Turkey in the Straw," "Pop Goes the Weasel," "Dovie Gets Out and Duckie Gets In," "The Girl You Left Behind You." Uncle Pete was good at jigging, and he would give a dance between changes if we asked for it; he nearly shook the house down doing it. About midnight cider and doughnuts were always served. Then the dance was on again until time to go home for the morning milking at about four o'clock.[62]

The association of the dulcimer with the fiddle and with dancing in these references indicate that the same style and function that existed in Michigan, Wisconsin, northern Ohio, northwestern Pennsylvania, and western New York was probably common to northern Indiana. Certainly Delbert Schrader's father, who came from around South Bend, Indiana, played only second on his dulcimer, which was the way Delbert played.[63]

Wisconsin

In the 1920s and 1930s, a number of dulcimer players were active in the state, including at Ashland, Elroy, and Fond du Lac.[64] Tommy Nelson, of Knapp, used to accompany a fiddler with his dulcimer. Emil Meixner, of Madison, chorded on the dulcimer with a fiddler named Boehm.[65] John S. Donald (1869-1934), of Madison, a farmer and politician who was state superintendent of education, developed an interest in the instrument in the 1920s, after recovering his mother's almost forgotten instrument.

The instrument was relatively popular in Columbia County. Mary Schmidt Wagner, of the Columbus area, who died about 1923 in middle age, played a rectangular dulcimer at house parties with her son Bill, who played accordion and mouth organ, and her son Art, who played drums; her daughter Laura also played the dulcimer.[66] Bennie Olson, of Lodi, played chords on the dulcimer at local dances in the 1920s and 1930s. Frank Cross, of Poynette (born about 1872), played "second" on the dulcimer with his brother Jim, a fiddler. Frank made six or seven

rectangular dulcimers, and Jim made two or three. Frank's son told me
he had never heard anyone play lead on the dulcimer before.[67] Although
some Wisconsin dulcimers were trapezoidal, it appears that most were
rectangular in shape. Such was the dulcimer played by Ragna Holten, of
Menomonie, who was photographed accompanying her fiddling husband Otto at home in 1980.[68]

Iowa

There were players scattered in different parts of the state; Thomas
Mann, of Adel, in central Iowa, who learned from his English-born fa-
ther, is mentioned in chapter 11. In southeastern Iowa, Mabel Cox, of
Fairfield, played the instrument, as did Mrs. Adam Gephart, of
Keosauqua, who in 1929 and 1934 entertained at family reunions with
her sixty-year-old dulcimer, which she had played since childhood.[69]
Players who seem to be part of the Great Lakes tradition, however, lived
mainly in the northeastern part of the state. Bert McCann, for example,
played a trapezoidal dulcimer with a fiddler at house parties around
Waubeek about 1930.[70] Peter Getzinger, of Luxemburg (died 1939),
played the dulcimer and other instruments, including flute, in an orchestra for local dances in the 1910s and 1920s.[71] Nearby, brothers William A. White (1871-1916) and Nelson White, of Turkey River, made
three dulcimers, one from an old kitchen table. William's son Reuben
chorded on one of the dulcimers with his brothers Martin, who generally
played the violin, but also dulcimer, and Dewey, who played the bass, for
dances in the 1920s. Their aunt Amy and sister Marvel chorded on the
reed organ and uncles Nelson and Grant played the banjo, as well. One
could hear their old-fashioned sound at local parties and at dances at
Millville Hall.[72]

Further West

Arthur Ambroson (1908-1979) played the fiddle and piano-harp for
dances around Flandreau and Sioux Falls, South Dakota in the 1920s
and 1930s. He normally played second on the piano-harp, in a style
similar to that used in the Great Lakes region.[73] No doubt there were
others. For example, Eva Conklin, of Sioux Falls, South Dakota, was
active in the 1940s and 1950s, playing her Hackett dulcimer for women's

groups and the like. Whether people like Henry Johnson, a player in Ashland, Nebraska, living in 1939, or Edwin Ayers (1901-1976), of Mossyrock, Washington, who inherited a dulcimer which he played, as well as other stringed instruments, or others scattered in the West, played in this style or perhaps belonged to a more Southern tradition, is unknown.[74] One can say the same of Milt Campbell, who played the dulcimer with a fiddler and a banjo player at local "musicals" organized in the neighborhood of Poosey, Livingston County, Missouri, in the 1920s to celebrate birthdays and other occasions.[75]

Chording

The defining feature of dulcimer playing in the Great Lakes region was its use as an instrument for accompaniment. Its traditional range extended at least from Chautauqua County, New York, and Warren County, Pennsylvania, in the east, through northern Ohio and Indiana into Michigan and Wisconsin, to parts of Iowa and South Dakota in the west. Players in Ontario, central Illinois, and West Virginia did not seem to be familiar with the style.[76] While the fiddler or perhaps accordion player played the melody, or "lead," other instruments—which might include another fiddle, a banjo, guitar, organ, piano, or any other instrument at hand capable of harmony—played "second." "Lead" and "second" formed the basis of American vernacular music theory, at least in the latter part of the nineteenth and early part of the twentieth centuries.

More specifically, the technique of playing second on the dulcimer was called "chording" or "playing chords." This terminology also applied to accompaniment on keyboard instruments. Although the exact notes varied from individual to individual, the concept was the same. Most players followed a fixed harmonic progression in an eight-bar tune: I-I-V-V-I -IV-V-I (tonic in the first two measures, dominant in the next two measures, tonic in the fifth measure, subdominant in the sixth measure, dominant in the seventh measure, and tonic in the eighth measure). Some players did not use the subdominant chord. Even if proper harmonization of a particular tune might call for another chord, the progression remained the same. The dulcimer's tuning lent itself easily to this progression. Once the player had learned only two patterns, he or she could chord in A, D, G, and C major, merely by moving up or down the strings.

Chording was done in three rhythms: common time (2/4), 6/8, and 3/4. These three rhythms covered most tunes used for dancing, including tunes for square dancing and contradancing, waltzes, and some other round dances. Once the player had mastered the harmonic pattern, altering the notes to fit the rhythm was easy.

The earliest written examples appear in a manuscript of the Wight family, of South Alabama, New York, now in the possession of James W. Kimball,[77] and a broadside written in a numerical tablature that was attached to the lid of a dulcimer probably manufactured by Elon Hackett, of Liberty Center, Ohio, in the possession of Robert Winans. Both date from the mid-nineteenth century, the latter probably from a few years after the Civil War. Example 15.3 shows the "dulcimer second" in the Wight manuscript, meant to accompany the tune "Money Musk."

Example 15.3: "Dulcimer Second" for the tune "Money Musk," from Wight manuscripts, in possession of James W. Kimball; facsimile in James W. Kimball, *Sackett's Harbor: Nineteenth-Century Dance Music from Western New York State* (Rochester, N.Y.: Sampler Records Ltd., 1994).

The next examples show "Accompaniment in D" and "Accompaniment in A" from the Hackett broadside, realized from the numerical tablature. Although the specific notes vary from the Wight manuscript, both examples suggest an improvisatory type of accompaniment, rather than a fixed pattern, since the patterns of the broken chords in the two parts of Example 15.3 and those in the D and A accompaniments in Example 15.4 show variety.

Example 15.4: "Accompaniment in D" from "A Collection of Choice Tunes Prepared Expressly for the Dulcimer!" (broadside, c.1870), which accompanied a contemporary dulcimer presumably made by Elon Hackett, of Liberty Center, Ohio.

Example 15.5: "Accompaniment in A" from "A Collection of Choice Tunes Prepared Expressly for the Dulcimer!"

Further transcriptions are illustrated here to demonstrate both how the dulcimer was used in ensemble playing and how the particular chording pattern might vary from person to person. First are demonstrations of chording in common time by four Michigan players, Frank Stevens, of Sand Lake, Elgia Hickok, of Sears, Allan Toms, of Lansing, formerly of Manton, and Pete Seba, of Ravenna. Although the exact notes differ from player to player, the basic style is the same.

Example 15.6: Frank Stevens, demonstrating "chording" in A. Recorded June 1971 at Sand Lake, Michigan, by the author.

Example 15.7: Elgia Hickok, demonstrating "chording" in D. Recorded in 1963 at Barryton, Michigan, by Eugene A. Cox.

Example 15.8: Allan Toms, demonstrating "chording" in F. Recorded in 1963 at Barryton, Michigan, by Eugene A. Cox.

Example 15.9: Pete Seba, "chording" in D. Recorded in 1981 at Ravenna, Michigan, by the author.

The next examples are of actual ensemble playing. It should be noted that, as these performances were played by ear, the actual notes may vary slightly the second or third time around. The groups here consist of violin, dulcimer, and tuba; button accordion and dulcimer; and violin and dulcimer. The geographical range of the players extends from western Michigan to northwestern Pennsylvania.

Example 15.10: Nameless quadrille (first strain). Keston Peters, violin, Luther Battles, dulcimer, unknown, tuba. Recorded about 1960 at Chardon, Ohio.

Example 15.11: "Turkey in the Straw" (first strain). Peter Reames, diatonic accordion, and his granddaughter Eleanor Sorenson, dulcimer. Recorded in 1973 at Grand Rapids, Michigan, by the author.

Example 15.12: "Rickett's Hornpipe" (first strain). Lewis Swan, violin, and brother Floyd Swan, dulcimer. Recorded about 1968 at Corry, Pennsylvania.

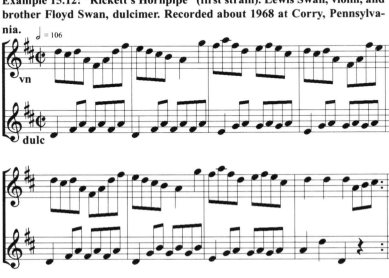

Other Areas

New England

Information on dulcimer playing in New England is scant. There were some players in the first part of the twentieth century. I once met a man who said his father, who lived on Cape Cod, played it. Charlie Krull, a blacksmith of Douglas, Massachusetts, made a rectangular dulcimer, which he played by himself in the 1930s and 1940s.[78]

Canada

Although this chapter intends to treat the United States, Canada is listed here for the sake of convenience. A few dulcimer players lived in southern Ontario. Elmer Earls, of the London area, played "jigs" on his dulcimer, as well as the violin and piano.[79] Colon Love (died 1980), of Grand Bend, used to played the dulcimer and fiddle with his brother.[80] The family of Donald Mackenzie, of Swift Current, Manitoulin Island, played the dulcimer as late as the 1920s.[81]

The most active player in the province, however, was probably Paul Bertrand, of Connaught, in northern Ontario. Born about 1872 near Ottawa, he also played the violin, mandolin, and piano, all by ear. His family did not know where he learned the dulcimer, but in Connaught, there was another player, Bob Hiteman, a forest ranger, and other lumberjacks in the area may have played it in the late nineteenth century. In any case, he played his "dulcimore" (or, in French, *musique à baguette*) regularly at local square dances. He designed and built a dulcimer with a chromatic range, which he named a "carolino," after his wife Caroline. In the 1920s, he moved to Montreal, intending to promote and manufacture his "invention" with a partner. The partners had a falling out, however, and nothing came of Bertrand's plan. Nevertheless, Paul and his daughter Blanche in 1928 recorded a duet on the "carolino," *Danse carrée* (Starr 15511), probably playing on the same instrument. Paul placed his dulcimer on a stand and played it with hammers made of balsam fir, curled on the ends, with felt on the tips. His sister, who married a Chevrier, also played the dulcimer, as did most of her children. Ted DeLorme (born 1919), of North Bay, whose brother married one of the Chevrier girls, is the last player of this local tradition.[82]

In 1949, Henri Granger, made several recordings of French-Canadian reels for the Starr label in Montreal on his *xylopiano*. These include *Reel Langelier* and *Reel Canrobert* (Starr 16844). He may have been active as late as about 1960.[83] Granger must have been one of the few in that province who played the instrument.

There were dulcimer players on Prince Edward Island. One was John Chisholm, active around 1920.[84] The Prince Edward Island Museum also holds a dulcimer. Chisholm's grandson also knew a player in Antigonish, Nova Scotia, named Angus Macdonald. In the 1930s, a Mrs. Cromwell, a black woman in Nova Scotia, played the dulcimer as well as reed organ.[85] The tradition in the Maritimes probably derived more directly from the British Isles, rather than that in Ontario, which was more closely connected to that across the border.

Example 15.13: Nameless tune, played by Ted DeLorme. Recorded in 1979 at North Bay, Ontario, by the author.

Illinois

Daniel L. Van Antwerp seems to have influenced a tradition of dulcimer playing around his home of Vermont, in Fulton County. M. Asa Trone (1878-1968), a farmer of Bater, Schuyler County, had made a fiddle for himself as a teenager. He soon bought a dulcimer from Van Antwerp and spent the night at his house, learning the basics. Trone usually played sitting down, with the instrument resting on his lap. He played the dulcimer with a fiddler and sometimes a guitar for dances at Kinderhook School and various town halls, as well as for box socials at country churches. Some of his favorite tunes were "Over the Waves," "Under the Double Eagle," and "When They Ring Those Golden Bells for You and Me," and schottisches. He also liked to entertain people with novelty techniques, such as playing on the dulcimer covered with a bandana or playing with two hammers in the right hand and one with the left. In later years, he made about four dulcimers, which he gave to friends.[86] Trone's contemporary in his area, Emma Van Fossen Robinson, bought a dulcimer from Van Antwerp and played it at the Baptist church which her husband pastored. She passed the skill on to her son Ross. The latter's son Bill Robinson learned some of her old tunes, and since the 1960s he has been active playing the dulcimer, as well as five-string banjo, fiddle, and guitar, in bluegrass groups.[87]

The tradition in west central Illinois may be somewhat transitional between that of the Great Lakes region and that further south. The instruments, like many in the former region, were trapezoidal, with three treble strings per course, and the Robinsons used corset-stay hammers. On the other hand, chording seems not to have been a practice. The tradition in this area dates back to the 1850s, but Daniel Van Antwerp may have had a considerable hand in shaping it.

John Lambert (born 1870), of DuQuoin, in southern Illinois, made about a dozen "dulcimer-harps," as he called them. Some were trapezoidal, some oblong, and one combined both shapes. He made his last one about 1935.[88] The curious term he used was not unique. Around 1910 or 1920, a man from around Springfield, Missouri, played a trapezoidal "dulcimer-harp."[89] This suggests a particular tradition in southern Illinois and southern Missouri that perhaps may have resulted from some enterprising nineteenth-century maker who gave a new name to his product. Given the origins of most of the settlers in this region, the term may have come from Kentucky or Tennessee.

Ozarks and Westward

Nellie R. Chase McKinney (born 11 January 1870 in McDonald County, Missouri, died 31 March 1962 in Orange County, California) owned and played one of the Missouri factory-made dulcimers described in chapter 14. She married Dr. A. J. McKinney, a physician and druggist, and, after his death in 1903, she ran his drugstore. About 1920, she and her two children moved to California, and in her last years lived with her daughter in Santa Ana. In 1949, she began to play her dulcimer at Knott's Berry Farm, a theme park in Buena Park, settling into a log cabin in the park's "Ghost Town." She became a popular attraction, remaining at the park until about 1957. Without doubt more people heard her play than any other dulcimer player of the postwar period. People purchased postcards with her photograph, and some still remember her fast renditions of dance tunes.[90]

Dora Lee Scudder, a native of Barry County, Missouri who was raised in Comanche County, Texas, played as a child a dulcimer manufactured by the same factory as Nellie McKinney's. In 1931, living in Abilene, Texas, she got the instrument back, repaired it, and began to play it again. She played it with her husband, a fiddler, and performed for church groups, teas, luncheons, in parades, and at schools. She continued to play it in other towns in Texas through the 1950s and 1960s, and played it at home until 1969, the year before her death. Her granddaughter Jean Granberry Schnitz learned the tunes she played on her dulcimer and has written an article about her family's musical tradition.[91]

There were other players in this tradition, as well. Jim Schell, of Mountain, Barry County, Missouri, born in the 1890s, played "real good," according to a relative.[92]

West Virginia

Dulcimer playing in northern West Virginia survived tenuously into the middle of the century. Worley Gardner (1919-1992) recalled an elderly neighbor, Simon Myers, who visited his rural Monongalia County home as a child, playing his dulcimer in return for dinner.[93] In the 1920s, Loy Swiger, then a child, learned to play from Jesse Ash, of Ashley, in Doddridge County. In 1928 Russell Fluharty (born 13 December 1906, died 29 March 1989), of Mannington, acquired an antique, out-of-repair dulcimer which his uncle had stored in his grain house. Not knowing anyone who played it or could show him how to tune it, he devised his own unique tuning system, with treble bridges dividing the courses into fourths, rather than the customary fifths. Fluharty said that for forty years, he felt that he was the only person playing the dulcimer, only hearing reports of antique instruments.[94]

Unlike the instrument in the Great Lakes region, the dulcimer in northern West Virginia seems not to have been part of an established ensemble playing music for dancing. Swiger, however, played tunes familiar to fiddlers in that area, like "Golden Slippers," "Buffalo Gals," "Go Down to Johncock's" (his version of "Irish Washerwoman"), "Eighth of January," "Cindy," and "Girl I Left Behind Me," and a local favorite, "Phoebe Ice," as well as tunes of play-party origin, like "Skip to My Lou," and older popular songs, such as "When You and I Were Young, Maggie," "Listen to the Mockingbird," and "Marching Through Georgia." Fluharty played a similar repertoire, but perhaps with more popular songs, and often sang with his dulcimer. Since he learned in isolation, however, it is hard to know how much his playing resembled that of other West Virginia players of the nineteenth century, when the tradition was more vigorous.

Example 15.14: "Phoebe Ice," played by Loy Swiger. Recorded 12 October 1978 at Massillon, Ohio, by the author.

Tennessee

A few people who learned to play the dulcimer from family members or neighbors continued to play the instrument into the mid-twentieth century. They lived in middle Tennessee, where the instrument clearly had enjoyed a certain popularity in the previous century. Still, by 1952, Charles Faulkner Bryan could write that "since their function has been forgotten, they are usually discovered in the attics of Southern homes or perhaps in antique shops, where, in many cases, they have not been recognized. The coverall word *zither* is incorrectly used by the dealer to describe the hammered dulcimer."[95]

In the early 1930s, someone used to play it at reunions of migrants from Claiborne County who lived in Carroll County, Indiana.[96] Richard Hulan met a woman, Laura Lambert, of Fairfield, Sumner County, in 1966, who could play "Soldier's Joy" on a locally made instrument.[97] J. R. ("Peanut") Cantrell (born 1897), of McMinnville, played one that his father had made, as well as one that he himself had made. He placed the dulcimer on a table or on his lap and could play a number of tunes: "Sail Away Ladies," "Play Girl," "Dixie," "Walkin' in the Parlor (Susie, Won't You Come?)," "Sugar Gal," "Soldier's Joy," "Turkey in the Straw," and "Needle in the Haystack," a tune he wrote. He also sang a song in a free meter, "Blind Child," which he accompanied by playing the melody with his right hammer and droning a low bass string on the far left side, with the left hammer. Although the bass bridge on his dulcimer lay on the right-hand side, there was enough space at the left side to allow him to hit the lowest bass course.[98]

Cora Denning Cline (born 25 July 1876, Sumner County, Tennessee, died 10 March 1973), of Westmoreland, Tennessee, played for a wider, if invisible, audience than almost any other dulcimer player in her day (see illustration 27). In 1928, she responded to a request that radio station WSM in Nashville made for musicians to audition for a new show, the "Grand Ole Opry." She brought her dulcimer and played with a relative, Edgar Cline, a fiddler. After four or five appearances with him, the station's manager asked him to drop out, and she continued playing on the radio for perhaps four or five more years. During this period, she earned a dollar for each minute of air time, which she used to pay the neighbors who drove her to Nashville. She received a large amount of fan mail during her years on the radio. After coming upon a car which had gone into the Cumberland River, she became afraid of long drives and stopped playing for the station. Cora's dulcimer was made by Lum Scott, of New Roe, Allen County, Kentucky, and she began playing as a child, since she had to stand on a chair to reach it when she first started. She played tunes like "Sally Goodin," "Chippie Get Your Hair Cut," "Lexington," "Airplane," "Going Up Cripple Creek," "When the Saints

Go Marching In," and "Arkansas Traveler." Even as an elderly woman, when her occasional playing had long been restricted to her home, her playing impressed Richard Hulan as "lightning-fast."[99]

Example 15.15: "Walkin' in the Parlor (Susie, Won't You Come?)," played by J. R. ("Peanut") Cantrell. Recorded in 1975 at McMinnville, Tennessee, by the author.

Notes

1. "Gibson March," Edison 7769; "Rosetzky March," Edison 7770; "27th Ohio Regiment March," Edison 7771; "March Arcadia," Edison 7933.

2. "Ain't Dat a Shame," Edison 8021; "Llewellyn March," Edison 8065.

3. Commercial recordings appeared, however, on the Canadian label Starr during the 1920s and 1930s. The Library of Congress issued a 78 r.p.m. recording of Thomas Mann playing dulcimer solos made in 1937; an unknown West Virginia player's "Drunken Sailor," recorded in the mid-1940s, appeared on a 1959 set, *Folk Music U.S.A.*, Ethnic Folkways FE 4350.

4. A. T. Sinclair, "Gypsy and Oriental Musical Instruments," *The Journal of American Folk-lore* 21 (1908): 207.

5. Bureau of the Census, *Thirteenth Census Taken in the Year 1910*, vol. 2: *Reports by States* (Washington: Government Printing Office, 1913), 932.

6. I only heard of one player in the Upper Peninsula. This person lived in Naubinway and had migrated from the Lower Peninsula.

7. See Gregory S. Rose, "South Central Michigan Yankees," *Michigan History* 70 (Mar.-Apr. 1986): 32-39, for further discussion of the origins of Michigan settlers from New York State.

8. Wilbur Brown, conversation with author, Harbor Springs, Mich., 1977.

9. Viola Cox, Eugene Cox, conversations with author.

10. Granddaughter of Daniel Gunn, conversation with author, Mackinac Island, Mich., 1976.

11. Nelda Newton, letter to author, 25 Oct. 1985.

12. Dorothy Burrows, conversations with author, Mackinac Island, Mich., 1976, 1983.

13. Ruth Miller, letter to author, 1985.

14. *[Lansing] State Journal*, 29 Sept. 1957.

15. D. Eugene Brooks, telephone conversation with author, 9 Oct. 1999.

16. Claus Borchers, interview by author, tape recording, Spring Lake, Mich., 22 Sept. 1985.

17. Al Hober, interview by author, tape recording, Pewamo, Mich., 28 Sept. 1980.

18. Pete Seba, interview by author, tape recording, Ravenna, Mich., 4 Sept. 1981.

19. *Census of the State of Michigan, 1894* (Lansing: 1896), vol. 1.

20. Hober, interview.

21. Seba, interview.

22. Hober, interview; Seba, interview.

23. Seba, interview.

24. Ellis Rollenhagen, letter to author, 1985.

25. *Detroit News*, 19 Dec. 1926.

26. Hober, interview.

27. Borchers, interview.

28. Ellis Rollenhagen, letter to author, 1985.

29. Hober, interview.

30. Borchers, interview; Harold Ralya, letter to author, 1985.

31. Harley Sinclair, interview by author, tape recording, Evart, Mich., 19 July 1986.

32. Bill Bigford, interview by author, tape recording, Pewamo, Mich., 28 Sept. 1980.

33. Les Raber, interview by author, tape recording, Evart, Mich., 20 July 1986.

34. Alida Chapman, *Looking Back* (n.p.: Delhi Township Bicentennial Commission, 1976), 96f.

35. Fenton Watkins, conversation with author, Birmingham, Mich., 1970s.

36. Sinclair, interview.

37. Elgia Hickok, scrapbook, in possession of Mrs. Mildred Hickok, 1976.

38. *Portland Review*, 29 Dec. 1925; Bill Bigford, conversations with author, 1970s.

39. Evelyn H. Raphael, *A History of the Haslett-Lake Lansing Area, Meridian Township, Ingham County, Michigan* (n.p., 1958, rev. 1975), 44.

40. Raber, interview.

41. Leslie Raber, Bud Pierce, Varsel Fales, Robert Babcock, conversations with author.

42. Informant, conversation with author, Mackinac Island, Mich., 1983.

43. Informant, conversation with author, Mackinac Island, Mich., 1980.

44. Silas Braley, Robert Spinner, conversations with author.

45. Bill Bigford, conversations with author.

46. "Pioneer Dances Live On," paper, in Grace Ryan Papers, Clarke Historical Library, Central Michigan University.

47. Max Louks, interview by author, tape recording, Evart, Mich., 19 July 1986.

48. Jesse Lummen, interview by author, tape recording, Evart, Mich., 19 July 1986.

49. Maurice Hulett, conversation with author; James Herald, interview by author, tape recording, Evart, Mich., 19 July 1986.

50. Fred Brown, letter to author, 1985.

51. Chet Parker, conversation with author, Edgerton, Mich., 1971.

52. *The Hammer Dulcimer Played by Chet Parker*, Folkways Records FA 2381.

53. My father Norman Gifford knew all these people and talked with them in the 1930s and 1940s.

54. Norman Carlson, "The Dulcimer in Chautauqua County," unpublished paper, version of article in Jamestown (N.Y.) *Post-Journal Magazine*, 15 Jan. 1977.

55. Frank Young, conversation with author, Union City, Pa., July 1972; Mrs. Lewis Swan, conversation with author, Samaria, Mich., 1975; Floyd Swan, conversation with author, Stedman, N.Y., May 1976.

56. Sterl Van Arsdale, conversation with author, Jamestown, N.Y., May 1973.

57. Carlson, "The Dulcimer in Chautauqua County"; Nicholas Hawes, notes to *Paul Van Arsdale: Dulcimer Heritage*, Folk-Legacy Records FSA-87.

58. Luther Battles, conversations with author, Hambden, Ohio, 1972, 1975, 1984.

59. Robert Stykemain, letter to author.

60. Informant, conversation with author, Mackinac Island, Mich., 1981.

61. Informants, conversations with author, Mackinac Island, Mich., 1977, 1978.

62. Tracy W. Redding, *Hoosier Farm Boy* (Philadelphia: Dorrance & Co., 1966). I would like to thank Paul Tyler for this reference.

63. Delbert Schrader, conversation with author, Dearborn, Mich., May 1974.

64. Informants, conversations with author, Mackinac Island, Mich., 1976; Guy E. Peterson, "An Old Dulcimer," *The Wisconsin Magazine*, Aug. 1927, 18. I would like to thank Jim Leary for pointing out this reference.

65. Informants, conversations with author, Mackinac Island, Mich., 1978, 1983.

66. Clarence Sennhenn, telephone conversation with author, 1983.

67. Harold Cross, conversation with author, Mackinac Island, Mich., 1980. E. C. Beck, *They Knew Paul Bunyan* (Ann Arbor: University of Michigan Press, 1956), 30, mentions "Cross, of Lodi, Wisconsin."

68. Philip Martin, *Farmhouse Fiddlers: Music & Dance Traditions in the Rural Midwest* (Mount Horeb, Wis: Midwest Traditions, Inc., 1994), 8, 123.

69. Informant, conversation with author, Mackinac Island, Mich., 1976; McIntosh family reunion minutes, 1929, 1934, in Clan McIntosh home page, <http://www.mcintoshweb.com/clanmcintosh/reunion/min1920s.htm> and <http://www.mcintoshweb.com/clanmcintosh/reunion/min1930s.htm>.

70. Informant, conversation with author, Mackinac Island, Mich., 1980.

71. Informant, conversation with author, Mackinac Island, Mich., 1976.

72. Reuben White, letter to author, 1985; *1984 History of Clayton County, Iowa* (Elkader, Iowa: Clayton County Genealogical Society, 1984), 778.

73. Donald Ambroson, letter to author, 22 Oct. 1979.

74. Charles W. Huyck, interview, Lincoln, Nebraska, 1939, Nebraska WPA project, *American Memory Project*, website, <http://lcweb2.loc.gov/cgi-bin/query/D?wpa:1:./temp/~ammem_2Z75::>; informant, conversation with author, Mackinac Island, Mich., 1983.

75. Anna Dockery Burgess, *A Place Called Poosey,* Livingston County Library website, <http://www.livcolibrary.org/History/Community/poosey.htm>.

76. Although a larger number of players would need to be interviewed in order to establish the boundaries of this regional style better, Lloyd Kelly, of Oil Springs, Ontario; Dennis Trone, of Petersburg, Illinois, who was familiar with his grandfather Asa Trone's playing; Russell Fluharty, of Mannington, West Virginia; and Loy Swiger, originally of Ashley, West Virginia, were all unfamiliar with chording. The *accordes* played by Ted DeLorme, of North Bay, Ontario, were not broken chords, but played on the downbeat and upbeat, suggesting an invented style.

77. James W. Kimball, notes to *Sackett's Harbor: Nineteenth-Century Dance Music from Western New York State: The Tunes* (Rochester, N.Y.: Sampler Records Ltd., 1994), n.p.

78. Player's son, conversation with author, Cambridge, Mass., Oct. 1975; informant, conversation with author, Mackinac Island, Mich., 1977. Margaret MacArthur, interview by Madeline MacNeil, Doug Berch, and Larkin Bryant, *Dulcimer Players News* 7, no. 1 (Winter 1981): 6, said that when she was investigating music in Vermont in the 1950s and 1960s, "there was lots of evidence of the hammered dulcimers, but no evidence of mountain dulcimers in New England."

79. Informant, conversation with author, Mackinac Island, Mich., 1985.

80. Informant, conversation with author, Mackinac Island, Mich., 1980.

81. Informant, conversation with author, Mackinac Island, Mich., 1977.

82. Albert Bertrand, interview by author, notes, Connaught, Ontario, Sept. 1980; Ted DeLorme, interview by author, notes, North Bay, Ontario, Sept. 1979.

83. Bob Kamen, personal communication, 3 Oct. 1996. He saw a dulcimer player in a group in Montreal about 1960 playing with a fiddle, accordion, and guitar. Whether he was Granger is impossible to say.

84. Grandson of John Chisholm, conversation with author, Petrolia, Ontario, June 1973.

85. Grandson, conversation with author, San Francisco, Cal., Feb. 1980.

86. Dennis Trone, grandson, telephone conversation with author, 1985.

87. "Bill Robinson: Aural Tradition, Illinois Style," *Dulcimer Players News* 22 (May-July 1996): 24-25; H & R Dulcimer website, <http://ghostlight.com/hr-dulcimers/H&R14.htm>.

88. Grandson, conversation with author, Mackinac Island, Mich., 1981.

89. Daughter, conversation with author, Mackinac Island, Mich., 1976.

90. "Aunt Nellie McKinney," *Dulcimer Players News* 10 (Fall 1984): 6, reprinted from *The Knotty Post*, July 1954.

91. Jean Granberry Schnitz, "Hammered Dulcimers and Folk Songs: The Musical Heritage of the C. A. Lee Family," in: *Corners of Texas*, Publication of the Texas Folklore Society 52 (Denton, Texas: University of North Texas Press, 1993), 162-172.

92. Martha Schell, letter to author, 28 Oct. 1975.

93. Mark Crabtree, "Worley Gardner: Mountain Music, Dance and Dulcimers," *Goldenseal* 18 (1992): 9.

94. Ken Sullivan, "Russell Fluharty: The Dulcimer Man," *Goldenseal* 12 (1986): 23-24.

95. Charles Faulkner Bryan, "American Folk Instruments: II. The Hammered Dulcimer," *Tennessee Folklore Society Bulletin* 10 (June 1952): 46. Indeed in 1999 I bought such a "zither" from an antique dealer in West Tennessee.

96. Informant, conversation with author, Mackinac Island, Mich., 1983.

97. Richard H. Hulan, "Hunting and Taming the Native American (or Hammered) Dulcimer," *Newsletter of the Folklore Society of Greater Washington* 5 (Feb. 1969): 7-8.

98. J. R. Cantrell, interviews by author, McMinnville, Tenn., 1972, 29 Sept. 1975.

99. Charles K. Wolfe, *The Grand Ole Opry: The Early Years, 1925-35*, Old Time Music, booklet 2 (London: Old Time Music, 1975), 87; *Nashville Tennessean*, 1962 article in vertical file, Archive of American Folklife, Library of Congress, "Ramblin' Rhodes: TV Show to Salute Pioneers," *Augusta Chronicle Online*, 10 July 1997, website, <http://augustachronicle.com/stories/071197/fea_rhodes.htm>; Dot Gudger, her granddaughter, personal communication, 7 Mar. 1999; Hulan, "Hunting and Taming," 6.

The Dulcimer's American Revival

Unlike other forgotten American instruments, such as the Appalachian dulcimer or the five-string banjo, which Jean Ritchie, Pete Seeger, and Earl Scruggs introduced to mass audiences in the 1950s and 1960s, the hammered dulcimer's revival was sparked by a number of people in different parts of the country. By the late 1970s, when the instrument began to show the effects of a revival, "American folk music," as popularly conceived during the Folk Revival in the late 1950s and 1960s, had lost its mass appeal and had diverged into different categories. Although it continued to exist, traditional, locally based music was in decline and subject to greater influence from the mass media, and, as in earlier times, people were familiar with such music often only if they happened to know someone who played it. As described in the previous chapter, this was the status of dulcimer music throughout most of the century.

We might consider the revival of the instrument to have been carried out by two different groups, "insiders" and "outsiders." Although in practice the difference between the two groups may sometimes be hard to distinguish, the characteristics of each are rather simple to define. Insiders are those people who are introduced to the instrument by family or someone in the neighborhood and usually know something about the musical traditions of which the dulcimer was a part, though this knowledge might be fragmentary. Outsiders, on the other hand, are introduced to the instrument by strangers, in such contexts as folk festivals, street performances, recordings, or workshops. They may already have developed an interest in "folk music" or may even have a large collection of recordings of types of folk music. Just as likely, they may have interests in other types of music and find interest in the dulcimer only in its tone and method of playing. Given the right circumstances, an outsider might become an insider.

Before we discuss the beginnings of the present revival, which occurred in the 1960s, we should look at earlier attempts to revive the instrument. Although they met with small successes here and there, they were generally unsuccessful. All were carried out by insiders.

Henry Ford and the Dulcimer

Henry Ford, a fiddler, mouth organ, and jew's harp player himself,[1] found his spirits suddenly lifted by hearing the fiddling of Jasper ("Jep") Bisbee, of Paris, Michigan, on a camping trip in 1923 with Thomas A. Edison and Harvey Firestone.[2] Soon he began to buy up old taverns and play the fiddle (see illustration 29, one of two known photographs of him playing) and call to the spontaneous dancing of his intimate friends and family.[3] He recalled the pleasant days before his industrial and political activities occupied so much of his time, when he went to local parties where the music was provided by a fiddler and dulcimer player (see chapter 13). In 1924, determined to recreate the music, dances, and atmosphere of his youth, he began to hold auditions for musicians who could play regularly for his dances.

The distinctive part of the dance music of his youth was the dulcimer, and he was determined to find a player to hire. Word spread through the Ford organization and Detroit professional music circles. A dulcimer player, no doubt, would be hard to find, at least in the world of professional music. A Ford bus driver first appeared with a "rather rude czymbalom."[4] By the end of the year, a professional cimbalom player, William Hallup, was hired. Hallup was part of the community of Gypsies with origins in Šariš, Slovakia, discussed in chapter 6, and had grown up in Pennsylvania in an immigrant Slovak and Hungarian environment. He was living in Cleveland at the time he was hired but soon moved to Dearborn.[5]

During the winter of 1925, Hallup accompanied many fiddlers and violinists who came to Dearborn both to audition for the position in Ford's orchestra and to play for private dances. Some played by ear and others by note.[6] Clayton A. Perry, a professional violinist with experience and familiarity with square dance fiddling, was hired at the beginning of 1925. But Ford still lacked a dulcimer player. Perhaps there was initial confusion over the instrument, as the first to appear were cimbalom players. This is not surprising, however, since Detroit had attracted a large Hungarian immigrant population, and Gypsy cimbalom players were part of a professional, rather than amateur, tradition. Dulcimer players, on the other hand, were amateurs and generally not known outside the neighborhoods in which they lived.

One day in late 1924, Roy Baxter, a food-service worker in the Ford organization who drove Ford home from a dance, mentioned to his employer that his cousin played the instrument. At the beginning of 1925, the manufacturer hired Edwin F. Baxter, then working as an interurban rail conductor. Baxter, a native of Tower, Cheboygan County, Michigan, learned to play at the age of twelve from his father, James G. Baxter, who in turn was said to have been the third generation in his family to play the instrument. Ford paid the younger Baxter $225 a month, gave him a house, and expected him to play each morning for an hour or two. He was not satisfied with the instrument Baxter had, and he ordered a new instrument made, with some chromatic notes, probably by his violin maker, Austrian immigrant John Hitter.[7] This instrument's case resembled those made commercially by Ezra Durand and William Vogel in the 1860s.

Clayton Perry wrote that the orchestra (see illustration 30) had various duties. They included searching out old published music and trying out new tunes (tunes were also collected from oral tradition), playing an hour or two each morning in the "Experimental Room" at Ford's residence, "Fairlane"; playing for Ford's guests after lunch in the engineer's room; playing for a weekly dance at the Botsford Inn, at the Dearborn Country Club, or at his home. The orchestra had begun to play for children's dancing classes in Dearborn and at many Detroit public schools.[8] In later years it played for dances at the Michigan State Fair.

The orchestra continued to practice daily, frequently with Ford in attendance, sometimes playing along on a fiddle or jew's harp. Dancing master Lovett arranged the dances, some of which were Ford's favorites in his youth, and compiled a manual, one of Ford's intentions being to "standardize" the dances which had local variants in different parts of the country.[9] During 1924 and the first part of 1925, these activities went on without publicity. Then in May 1925, with the advance release to newspapers of *"Good Morning": After a Sleep of Twenty-five Years, Old-fashioned Dancing Is Being Revived by Mr. and Mrs. Henry Ford*, a publicity campaign ensued.[10] The book, a collection of older ballroom dances, resembled those produced commercially in the previous century.

By this time, Ford had gained skill in dealing with the press. He knew when to talk and when to stay quiet. The press was intensely curious about this somewhat aloof and eccentric character, and when he chose to talk, the press ate his words. *Good Morning* appeared in July, 1925, and, on 16 August 1925, the *New York Times* published a lengthy interview with Ford about his dancing and music.[11] Shortly afterwards the dance manual was serialized in many newspapers around the country. Feature stories followed in magazines and newspapers.

Although one Ford executive thought this campaign was a shrewdly conceived publicity gimmick,[12] Ford himself, although using the press for his plan to "replace the jazz dances popular in the cities with the more graceful steps," approached the matter with an anti-commercial (although xenophobic and racist) bias. After all, part of his dislike for fox trots and jazz was the commercial nature of the idiom.[13] He did not copyright *Good Morning*. Except for one national radio broadcast, Ford never permitted the orchestra to appear in commercial situations and once refused to allow Baxter to appear in a Hollywood Western.[14]

By the end of 1925, local fiddle contests, perhaps spurred on by the publicity over Ford's latest interest, appeared with greater frequency. Mellie Dunham (1853-1931), of Norway, Maine, won a local contest and wrote to Ford for an audition.[15] His subsequent trip to Detroit, in which he played for a private dance for Ford and his friends, became a media spectacle. Local boosters, who felt they knew fiddlers equal or better, then began to sponsor fiddle contests in much of North America, from the Maritimes to Pennsylvania to Tennessee to Iowa and New England. Elderly fiddlers were in great demand on vaudeville, radio and records, and some theater owners now felt threatened by the competition of local shows sponsored by fraternal organizations and the like, featuring old-time performers.[16] This was an entirely grass-roots phenomenon. Ford himself (or the Ford Motor Company) never sponsored any contests.[17]

This phenomenon reached a peak during the winter of 1926 but soon declined. The Depression certainly curtailed most of the commercial activity. Certain effects, however, lasted. Some fiddle contests developed into annual events, and the Nashville radio station WSM, which began broadcasting fiddler Uncle Jimmy Thompson, developed the show into the "Grand Old Opry."[18]

The dulcimer benefited from the phenomenon only in those areas where it had been a part of the local tradition. In other words, Ford's interest in the instrument did not seem to draw new audiences to it and create a phenomenon similar to the revival which began in the 1970s. Players did receive some exposure at local shows, which were primarily fiddler's contests, but which also included jig dancers, singers, and other entertainment.

The Junior Chamber of Commerce organized a fiddler's contest in February, 1924, in Flint, Michigan, to be held the following month, one of the first which followed in the wake of Ford's visit to Bisbee. Fiddler Mark Sturgis, of Byron, went to the manager of the Junior Chamber of Commerce and told him, "I see you're putting on another fiddlin' contest. But if you want to make the thing a success you should include a dulcimer." The manager, a native of Lebanon, Kentucky, was unfamiliar with the instrument. Sturgis replied "Yep, they used to be all the rage at the dances years ago."[19] His brother Lewis Sturgis, who began playing the instrument about 1874 and who said the instrument had been in his family for one hundred years, played it at the contest. The Sturgis brothers were in demand during this period. Lewis accompanied all but one of the fiddlers at the Flint contest on 5 January 1926, part of a series leading to a statewide contest, despite rules which forbade accompaniment.[20] Soon afterwards, they became part of the orchestra, consisting of three fiddles, two pianos, a dulcimer, cornet, bass horn, and clarinet, which played for a series of dances sponsored by the local newspaper and the Industrial Mutual Association, a factory-sponsored recreational organization. The large orchestra was necessary, as the dances drew as many as three thousand people.[21]

Ferreting out all the incidents of dulcimer playing at these local events is an impossible task, but a few other examples of local appearances may be mentioned. William Jordan played a few dulcimer solos at a fiddler's contest sponsored by the Knights of Columbus in Lansing, Michigan, on 12 January 1926.[22] William McDonald played it at a fiddler's contest in Rice Lake, Wisconsin, in February 1927.[23] Kimmie Swan accompanied her brother Hib at a fiddler's contest in North East, Pennsylvania, during this period.[24]

Some dulcimer players appeared on the radio. John S. Donald played with his mother on WIBA and WHA, Madison, Wisconsin, in March and April 1927.[25] William Amick (1860-1949), of Stanwood, Michigan, played with a fiddler on a radio broadcast.[26] In the late 1920s, Freeman Kemerling (1878-1951) played the dulcimer on a Battle Creek, Michigan, radio show sponsored by Sweet's music store.[27] Undoubtedly other players also appeared on local radio stations.

This grass-roots phenomenon benefited no dulcimer player more than it did Jesse R. Martin, of Frewsburg, New York. A planer at a furniture factory, he had played the instrument since the age of fourteen and was well known in his area. Martin, learning of Ford's interest, wrote to him on 24 November 1925, and soon received an answer inviting him to come to play. Mellie Dunham's visit between December 8 and 13, and the phenomenal publicity which ensued, led to Dunham's signing a vaudeville contract on December 16. Martin went to Detroit that same day. Although the *New York Times* reported the trip, his visit did not generate the same kind of local activity that Dunham's did.[28] Unlike old-time fiddlers, which could be found in every community, dulcimer players were relatively rare, and Martin did not face the same kind of challenges local boosters made to Dunham to show that their favorite fiddlers were better.

Martin "rehearsed" with the Ford orchestra on the afternoon of the day after his arrival and did so the next day. In the evening he played with the orchestra for a dance at the Dearborn Country Club. He talked with Ford and his wife at some length about old-fashioned dances and the dulcimer. The next day he returned home and told a reporter that he "had the time of [his] life" and that, unlike Dunham, he was not interested in vaudeville, content to continue playing at local dances.[29]

But events soon caught up with Martin, and he toured on the vaudeville circuit (see illustration 26), traveling as far as Maryland, but generally staying close to home, in northeastern Ohio, Pennsylvania, and western New York. In these performances, he played with Laura Minkley Biers, who accompanied him on the Hawaiian guitar. He played on stations WLDB in Erie, Pennsylvania, and WKBN in Youngstown and for many local dances and shows. He even endorsed a tonic.[30]

In 1927, he returned to Dearborn to play for Ford. Martin told my father in 1938 that he could recall all but one tune which Ford asked him to play, and it bothered him that the tune came to him only later. This may have happened on the second trip. Martin's busy schedule declined in a few years and he retired to the home of his daughter, where he taught his grandsons Phillip and Paul Van Arsdale his large repertoire of old dance tunes as well as others. He never recorded, but his family has remarkably preserved his music.

In the 1920s, Ford was busy collecting all kinds of Americana, from watches to buildings, and he assembled what remains the largest collection of American-made dulcimers. He or his agents purchased many

from antique dealers and attempted to buy others from individuals.[31]
Charles F. Peterson, of Muskegon, Michigan, a dulcimer player for twenty-four years, wrote to Ford in 1926, asking if he would be interested in a dulcimer he had made, patterned after an antique instrument. Ford wired Peterson to "send one along by express."[32]

The Victor Talking Machine Company sent a recording crew to Dearborn in December 1925, and the Ford orchestra went to New York the next month. In between performances on radio station WEAF, a broadcast connected to thirteen other stations with hookups to radios at Ford dealers around the country (which coincided, not accidentally, with the introduction of new models),[33] the orchestra went to recording sessions for Victor, Columbia, and Edison. Further sessions followed in May 1926 and January 1927. Henry Ford subsidized part of the recording expenses.[34] Ultimately the companies released a total of 44 sides (including cylinders), under the names "Henry Ford's Old-Time Dance Orchestra" (Victor and Edison) and "Henry Ford's Old-Fashioned Dance Orchestra" (Columbia). Baxter's dulcimer solo, "Medley of Reels," appeared on both Victor and Columbia.

The records indicate that the orchestra varied its arrangements little. Baxter doubled the melody on the dulcimer and Hallup played accompaniment on the cimbalom. Gino Caporali, who replaced Maurice Castel as bassist in 1938, said that the dulcimer also sometimes played an accompaniment part,[35] so apparently later the orchestra varied their arrangements. In any case, the choice of dances was probably in the hands of Ford and Lovett and perhaps some of the music as well. About 1943 and perhaps later, the orchestra recorded a series of records at the Ford Engineering Laboratory under the "Early American Dances" label. Baxter's playing is less audible on these recordings, as the playing of guitarist Roy Austin, who replaced Baxter following his retirement due to illness in the winter of 1945,[36] is rather prominent.

From 22 January 1944 to 7 July 1945, the orchestra played on a weekly radio show, "Early American Dance," which appeared twice a day in fifteen-minute segments on the NBC Blue Network. Surviving scripts show that Baxter occasionally played solos, such as on the first show, when he played "Father O'Flynn" and "Stack of Barley," on the second week, with "Rory O'More" and "Dashing White Sergeant," and the succeeding week, when he played "Larry O'Gaff" and "Neil Gow."[37]

With the death of Ford in 1947, the dancing and music stopped. As time passed, it became more and more forgotten. Ford's interest in the dulcimer did renew some interest in the instrument in those areas where it had been known, but, with very few exceptions, it found no new players.[38] However, a small increase in outside interest in the instrument and its music did occur in central Michigan from the 1930s to the early 1950s.

The "Michigan Lumberjacks"

Earl Clifton Beck, a Nebraska native and professor of English at Central Michigan State Teachers' College in Mount Pleasant, had developed an interest in the ballads still sung by elderly former lumberjacks living in the area. Besides collecting and publishing them, he organized troupes of performers, including fiddlers and dulcimer players, who appeared at various public venues. Beck had organized a "lumberjack's contest" in 1934, and that year the Michigan Tourist Bureau contacted him to help choose Michigan's representation to the first National Folk Festival in St. Louis, Missouri. Henry Babcock, of Alma, a fiddler, singer, and guitarist who had won the contest, led a group of musicians at the festival that year, and they also played on radio station KSD there.[39] The group of musicians had developed from a group of people who started getting together casually in the late 1920s to play music.[40] Perhaps this activity was one of those local responses to Henry Ford's efforts to promote old-time fiddling and dancing.

Beck's "Michigan Lumberjacks" was an informal grouping that varied over time. Beck, the outsider, acted as the emcee. The typical program featured two or three ballad singers (acetate recordings made in the early 1950s show that the singers were accompanied by a nontraditional piano and other singers on the choruses) and recitations in French-Canadian or Swedish dialect, interspersed with music which might accompany a jig dancer or general square dancing. The musicians included a number of fiddlers and a dulcimer player, along with perhaps guitar, mandolin, tenor banjo, bass, and spoons. They performed at several events in other states, such as broadcasts on NBC and CBS from Washington in 1937, including an appearance on a show called "We the People," a performance in New York City, the Indianapolis Sport Show, and the Chicago Tribune Music Festival, but most events were closer to home. Typical venues might be outdoors shows, lumberjack shows, town homecomings, and teachers' conferences.[41]

The first dulcimer player associated with the group was Arthur J. Mulford (born about 1877), of St. Louis, Michigan, who was also the first player Beck ever heard. He seems to have accompanied the group led by fiddler Henry Babock, of Alma, to the National Folk Festival. Beck writes that Mulford, who stood as he played (see illustration 28), was a "great favorite of the folklorists at the folk festivals." John Samuel Rouse (born about 1878), of Wheeler, replaced Mulford after his death and accompanied the troupe at the Chicago Folk Festival. Beck called him "a different sort of dulcimer player, but he is one of the finest soloists among a fine lot."[42] Donald L. Baker (born 1904, died 1950s), of Ithaca, Gratiot County Superintendent of Schools, played regularly with the group in the late 1940s and early 1950s. His father Daniel Baker had played it, having purchased the instrument from its maker for six dollars, in Ovid, Michigan, in 1885.[43] Don began playing only in 1945 and played only a few tunes and only lead, according to Bob Spinner, one of his favorite tunes being "Haste to the Wedding," others including "Peek-a-Boo Waltz" and "Buffalo Girls." In 1950, he traveled to New York City and took part in a program with Jean Ritchie that she describes in her book *Dulcimer People*. She quotes a reviewer for the *New York Herald Tribune*, who called his instrument a "hammer" dulcimer, the earliest example of this modifier yet found.[44]

Other players helped from time to time. Jay B. Mudge was one. Rather than the traditional chording accompaniment, however, he played lead, with his wife accompanying him on piano.[45] Mudge went to the National Folk Festival in St. Louis with dance instructor Grace Ryan, of Central Michigan College. A. Otis Fish, of Mount Pleasant, was another. This "southpaw whanger"[46] was the fiddler who posed for a photographer in 1899 with dulcimer player Curtis O. Render and guitarist Lewis Dunlap.[47]

Beck mentions two others, Elgia C. Hickok, of Sears, who "played a loose-strung dulcimer and played it well,"[48] and Bob Spinner, "the speed kid from Elk Rapids."[49] The association of these two individuals with Beck's "Michigan Lumberjacks" is significant, because they figure in the organization of the Original Dulcimer Players Club and with other aspects of the instrument's revival.

Although he played dulcimer in the traditional manner, Hickok liked to promote the instrument and was not afraid to play it in non-traditional situations. For example, he performed in a play, "Sump'n Like Wings," by Lynn Riggs, at the Detroit Playhouse in 1931. In the late

1930s, he played for thirteen weeks on the radio in Mount Pleasant, in a group consisting of one or two violins, accordion, dulcimer, guitar, and electric guitar.[50] Beck recalled in the fall of 1950 that he helped Hickok arrange a dulcimer program to take on tour, and Hickok "reported that his program went very well."[51] The tour seems to have coincided with the Baker's appearance in New York City, but it is unclear whether the two events were related. In the 1950s and 1960s, Hickok and other dulcimer players performed at the Saginaw County Fair.

At Early Folk Festivals

As noted above, the dulcimer was present at the first National Folk Festival, organized by Sarah Gertrude Knott, in 1934. This series of festivals featured a wide variety of music, from different regions and different ethnic groups in the United States. Although some of the performers were recorded by Alan Lomax and other workers for the Library of Congress, most never recorded or achieved any sort of stardom. While they offered outsiders a chance to hear music peculiar to a particular tradition, they never created a popular movement to re-create music of those traditions. Nevertheless, they contributed much to forming the popular conception of "American folk music."

Since the instrument had largely been limited to homes and local halls, these events were the first true occasions for outsiders to hear the dulcimer. Players with the "Michigan Lumberjacks" went two or three times. Henry Ford's "Early American Dance Orchestra" went to the 1946 festival in Cleveland, although without a dulcimer player.[52]

Perhaps the first player influenced by folk festival music was Ruth Tyler (1894-1976), of Neosho, Missouri, who began playing her antique instrument about 1938, when she was well into middle age. A dialect columnist for the *Ozark Guide*, she played tunes like "Old Joe Clark," "Buffalo Gals," "Skip to My Lou," and "Go Tell Aunt Rhody" at the National Folk Festivals in 1948 and 1950, and at the Ozark Folk Festival in Eureka Springs, Arkansas. In 1951, she performed at the University of Arkansas, receiving extensive publicity, and played on NBC radio's "Monitor" show and KMBC in Kansas City.[53]

The West Virginia State Folk Festival, in Glenville, was organized on an annual basis in 1950 by Patrick W. Gainer, a professor at West Virginia University who had given lectures and recitals on the Appalachian dulcimer or "rebec," as he preferred to call it, since 1928.[54] Performers on the hammered dulcimer appeared in the early years of the festival. They included Ira Mayfield (1886-1972), of Rhinehart, who played a dulcimer made by Jesse Ash, and Russell Fluharty, who appeared many times. In the 1950s and 1960s, Fluharty played widely around West Virginia, at colleges, schools, churches, nursing homes, and different festivals. He helped organized the Ripley festival and was employed by the West Virginia Department of Commerce as an entertainer.[55]

Around 1966, Worley Gardner, of Morgantown, West Virginia, purchased an antique dulcimer and, recalling a neighbor in his childhood who played it, began to learn to play the instrument. He convinced his brother Asel, who had retired to Kingwood, Maryland, to start making the instruments, and by the early 1970s, he had made over twenty.[56] In the 1970s, Worley and his brother Willis performed regularly and sold Asel's instruments at the West Virginia Art and Craft Fair at Ripley. In 1971, Russell Fluharty organized the Mountaineer Dulcimer Club, which began with five members. Two years later, there were six or seven players, all of whom played instruments made by Asel Gardner or Ralph Campbell, who made them after Fluharty's instrument.[57]

The instrument occasionally appeared in other public spheres. Carol Zeiss, of Burkburnett, Texas, played "Red River Valley," with full studio orchestra accompaniment, on a dulcimer her grandfather had made in 1912 on "Ted Mack's Original Amateur Hour" in the late 1950s for a national television audience.[58] Paul Van Arsdale played on a local television broadcast in Buffalo about 1950.

The Original Dulcimer Players Club

Robert C. Spinner (1932-1990), of Elk Rapids, first saw the dulcimer when he was in eighth grade and Jay Mudge played at his school. He was immediately stricken with the instrument and made several over the next few years. He would skip school and hitchhike around the state, looking for people with dulcimers. He learned old-time square dance music from playing at dances with fiddler Emma (Brown) Warner, of Charlevoix, whose father and uncles played fiddle, dulcimer, and five-string banjo. In 1951 Bob sat in at a Michigan Lumberjacks' show for the Michigan Retired Teachers' Association.[59] Later, while at school in

Kalamazoo, he played at square dances in that vicinity. Bob did not read music and played tenor banjo, piano, and other instruments by ear. Spinner was practically unique as the one of the few of his generation in Michigan to take to the instrument. Such public activity as there was did not seem to generate new playing.

Hickok, younger than most of the players with the Michigan Lumberjacks, was aware that the instrument was dying. Still, his organizing of a dulcimer program in 1950 and later programs at the Saginaw County Fair demonstrated his early interest in reviving the instrument. Perhaps Hickok's awareness of clubs of players of other instruments, such as a banjo club (somewhere in Michigan) and a fiddler's club, as well as Spinner's knowledge of the Milwaukee Zither Club, suggested to him the idea of starting a dulcimer club. In any case, in 1963 a critical mass of players and people interested in the instrument living in the central part of the state began to form. Hickok personally contacted people he had heard about. He drove up to the house of Viola Cox in Manton one day and asked her about the "zither" she played. She showed it to him, and in short order he mentioned his idea for the club and asked her if she would be secretary.

Jim Herald, of Cadillac, had grown up hearing about the dulcimer that his father, John Herald, had played as a young man. Around 1950, Jim acquired an old dulcimer from a friend who worked with him, fixed it up, and presented it to his father. In the early 1960s, he got another one, and in order to learn more about the instrument, contacted Hickok and Spinner. Herald became treasurer of the club.[60]

The first meeting took place at the Barryton Community Hall, a rustic place with outdoor toilets, on September 28, 1963. Fifteen postcards which announced the meeting brought in about seventy-five people, including fourteen dulcimers. Ten people played, although Hickok and Spinner were almost the only ones who could produce more than a few tunes or play the instrument comfortably with others. The instruments were nearly all antiques, each had slightly different tunings, and most had never been played outside of the family circle. It was a demonstration of a true traditional art, one that the general public had forgotten.

The players at the first meeting of the Original Dulcimer Players Club were some of the last carriers of the tradition, not only in the state of Michigan, but in the United States. For some, it was an opportunity to demonstrate some knowledge or ability to play the instrument which they had learned years ago. Others had more recently become interested

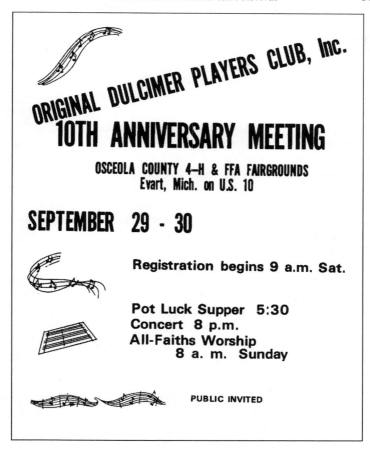

Figure 16.1: Poster announcing the 10th Anniversary Meeting of the Original Dulcimer Players Club at Evart, Michigan, in 1973.

in it and were still learning. But in all cases their playing was linked to an earlier tradition. In this sense the organization of the club was an insiders' revival. For the first ten years or so of the club's existence, most of the players who attended were elderly or had learned to play the instrument from a family member. In some cases, this revived interest caused younger members to learn to play the dulcimer or to make one, but, like Eugene Cox or Lilah Hickok Gillett, their older relatives had

already played it. Publicity was limited to advertisements in local newspapers and spread by word of mouth. The people who were likely to
attend were those people who already had some familiarity with the instrument, although, like Harley Sinclair, who came for the first time in
1970, they may not have played it for many years.

The usual format of the meetings was a short business meeting followed by individual performances, usually demonstrations of "chording" or playing three tunes or so, ending with a jam session, in which
fiddlers and other instrumentalists joined in, which sometimes accompanied a change of square dances. The club expanded to two meetings a
year in 1967, and the venues began to expand beyond small rural halls
by 1970, when a meeting was held at the Grand Rapids Public Museum.
Eugene Cox became president after Elgia Hickok's death and effectively
managed to keep the organization together. In 1973, the club sponsored
a two-day event at Evart, Michigan, in honor of its tenth anniversary.
About one hundred people attended, and the following summer the club
held a "Fun-Fest" there. This event grew rapidly, but still for several
years, the "Fun-Fest" remained more or less another meeting, the number of which expanded to three per year in 1975.[61] By this time a sub-
stantially large number of new players began to attend. The insider nature of the members also began to change.

In the Folk Revival

New forms of popular music developed in the 1950s as a reaction to
the long-standing, commercial Tin Pan Alley tradition. One of these
was rock 'n roll, where teen idols adapted forms of Afro-American popular
music and built their appeal on youthful rebellion. Another was "folk"
music, in which singers like Harry Belafonte incorporated traditional
songs from different cultures to the accompaniment of guitars and other
acoustic stringed instruments. This movement built on the left-wing,
activist music of Woody Guthrie and Pete Seeger, which in turn had
been influenced by New Deal-era programs which recorded music that
appeared at the folk festivals of the 1930s. "Folk" music tended to appeal to college students, who learned to play the guitar and five-string
banjo and sing the songs popularized on the radio by groups such as the
Kingston Trio. Although it developed from several traditions, including
local and family-based music, it was a thoroughly popular music in the

sense that it was spread by radio, television, and recordings, as well as touring professional performers.

The Newport Folk Festival, held for the first time in 1959, differed from earlier folk festivals in that it also included younger professional performers of the new popular variety of "folk" music, such as Bob Dylan and Joan Baez, as well as the traditional blues singers, ballad singers from the Appalachians, and Cajun musicians, who might have appeared at the earlier festivals. The Newport festival also introduced the workshop, in which a performer might explain aspects of his music in an informal setting.[62] Given the high number of college students in the audiences, the workshop—a term and concept originally developed in educational and arts circles in the 1930s and 1940s—developed into a successful format.

The Appalachian dulcimer was prominently featured at the Newport Folk Festival. Although its traditional range extended well outside the high Appalachians, into southern Tennessee, Missouri, and even Nebraska, commercial makers like Charles N. Prichard, of Huntington, West Virginia, and J. Edward Thomas, of Bath, Kentucky, seem to have popularized the instrument in the late nineteenth century in the Appalachians.[63] By the early twentieth century, settlement schools in eastern Kentucky promoted and taught the construction of the instrument, and outsiders were performing on it as early as the 1910s.[64] In the same period, an Englishman, Cecil Sharp, collected songs from the Appalachians and had a great deal of influence on the emerging popular conception of American folk music. However the players of the older tradition may have used the instrument, ballads and the Appalachian dulcimer developed a close association, at least to those who by 1940 had developed an interest in American folk music. In the late 1940s, Jean Ritchie, a native of eastern Kentucky and an insider to the tradition who lived in the New York City area, began to play regularly at concerts of folk music. She appeared at the first Newport Folk Festival in 1959 (and was a member of the festival's board at its reorganization in 1963), as did John Jacob Niles, an outsider who had popularized the instrument as an accompaniment for his songs in the 1930s and 1940s. Other players appeared at the festival and held workshops, and in 1963 Jean Ritchie published a method.[65]

All this might be incidental to the introduction of the hammered dulcimer to the world of the Folk Revival were it not for the fact that the two instruments shared the same name. It is unclear when Elgia Hickok

first learned of the Appalachian dulcimer, but it was probably through
the mass media's reporting on music at the Newport Folk Festival. In
any event, Hickok wanted to show the people at the festival the instrument he had played for many years and had always known as a dulcimer,
so he wrote the organizers and went in 1963. The following year, he
brought Chet Parker, and they performed "Golden Slippers" together,
followed by Chet's introductory joke before his playing the "Temperance
Reel." Although all of the seventy thousand people who attended this
festival (the vast majority of whom were drawn by the big-name pop-
folk performers) did not hear them play, a record of the performance did
introduce the instrument to others, this time as the "hammer" dulcimer.[66]

Having appeared at the Newport Folk Festival, Chet Parker's reputa-
tion now extended into what had been the unlikely world of college cam-
puses and folk music aficionados. Patrick R. Murphy, of Kalamazoo,
Michigan, recorded his playing and sent the tape to Folkways Records,
who issued it as *The Hammer Dulcimer Played by Chet Parker*, in 1966.[67]
Parker appeared at the 1969 Smithsonian Festival of American Folklife,
at the Kalamazoo Folk Festival in 1970, and at the "Ark" coffeehouse in
Ann Arbor, Michigan, in 1970. By this year, a group of young musicians
in Kalamazoo, who comprised a bluegrass band, "Sweetcorn String
Band," had developed an interest in this instrument, and T. William
Smith, and, after his departure from Kalamazoo, Mark Sahlgren began
to play it with the band. Another instrument maker in Kalamazoo, Sam
Rizzetta, originally from Chicago, had started making the instrument.
Parker's playing in his home area had also influenced brothers Jack and
Jerry Korcal, of Pierson and Belmont, Michigan, to make and play the
instrument, and by 1970, they were attempting to make dulcimers com-
mercially.

Russell Fluharty, advertised as "America's greatest hammered dulcimer player,"[68] appeared at the first Beers Family Festival of Traditional
Music and Arts in Petersburg, New York, in 1966. One of the performers there, Howard Mitchell, a Washington, D.C., teacher who had been
making Appalachian dulcimers for the previous ten years (having been
introduced to that instrument about 1954 by hearing Jean Ritchie on
record), heard Fluharty and the instrument for the first time at that festival. Mitchell had been holding workshops on making Appalachian
dulcimers and had recently authored a record and book with his ideas on
making and playing the instrument.[69] He immediately began to make

hammered dulcimers, first after Fluharty's instrument, then through experimentation. A complete outsider to the instrument and its traditions, Mitchell was able to learn more about the instrument through hearing Ray Baca's playing of a dulcimer in the Texas Moravian tradition at the Smithsonian Festival of American Folklife in 1967 and from English and American books at the Library of Congress. By 1968 he had made sixteen and written a paper detailing his experiences.[70] In 1972, he issued a book and record set, *The Hammered Dulcimer: How to Make It and Play It*.[71] Mitchell held workshops on making the instrument at the Beers Family Festival and in other locations. Although he failed to learn much from living traditions and learned mostly through trial and error, his book was influential.

The substantial number of individuals who had already tried their hands at making an Appalachian dulcimer were now ready to try to make a dulcimer of another sort. Certain settlement schools had promoted construction of the Appalachian dulcimer early in the century, and by 1967, several how-to-build articles and books had already appeared.[72] Mitchell's 1966 book and record set was widely distributed in the small but growing network of folk music-oriented businesses, as well as record stores, so many makers were already familiar with his name.

Another maker of Appalachian dulcimers, Dennis Dorogi, of Brocton, New York, also developed an interest in the instrument, and in 1970 made his first one, copying an old one from Michigan. He traveled around to folk festivals and sold a number of instruments.

Conclusion

By 1970, a revival was underway, although at the time one could hardly tell. A small number of people around the country had taken a renewed interest in the instrument and had begun to make them on a regular basis, but the vast majority of people who were familiar with the instrument were still those who had seen them played by family members and neighbors at local parties and dances. The Folk Revival, although widespread and influential, was largely limited to younger, educated, urban people who had little connection to existing traditions of playing, and to larger college communities and eastern cities. The popular conception of folk music, fed by the Folk Revival, consisted of singing. Guitars and five-string banjos, and to a lesser extent, Appalachian dulcimers, because they accompanied singing, were thus the main instruments that benefited from this new interest. Instrumental music still largely remained outside the Revival. Furthermore, "source" music was limited to music of parts of the Appalachians and the Mississippi Delta. Thus the Folk Revival largely ignored the hammered dulcimer, which had been connected to traditions in areas mostly outside the favored source regions. Nevertheless, it set the stage for the outsider revival in succeeding decades. But the insider revival began first and made it possible.

Notes

1. Benjamin Lovett, reminiscences, 17, Ford Archives, Dearborn, Mich.

2. *New York Times*, 13 Oct. 1923.

3. "Ford Jigs for Joy at Old-Time Party," *Detroit News*, 9 Feb. 1924; "Henry Ford Stages Fete at Wayside Inn," *Detroit Free Press*, 10 Feb. 1924.

4. Harold Cordell, reminiscences, 74, Ford Archives.

5. *Detroit News*, 27 July 1924; Martin Hallup, grandson, conversations with author, Detroit, Mich., 1980s.

6. Mrs. Stanley Ruddiman, reminiscences, 4, Ford Archives. She said "some of those musicians were regular breakdown callers, and some were more or less finished."

7. "Dulcimer and Its Player Joins Ford's Orchestra," *Detroit Evening Times*, 19 or 20 Feb. 1925.

8. Clayton A. Perry, "Fiddling for Henry Ford," *The Musical Observer*, July 1926, 11.

9. E. G. Liebold, reminiscences, 1367, Ford Archives.

10. Evidence that Ford and his associates planned such a campaign can be assumed from the lack of newspaper stories in the clip books maintained by the Ford organization between February and July 1925; "Mr. Ford's Page," *Dearborn Independent*, 6 June 1925, is an editorial on old-time dancing which was incorporated into *Good Morning*. This seems to have launched the campaign.

11. "Ford Revives the Old Dances," *New York Times*, 16 Aug. 1925.

12. Charles E. Sorensen, with Samuel T. Williamson, *My Forty Years with Ford* (New York: W. W. Norton & Co., 1956), 20.

13. *Detroit Free Press*, 12 July 1925.

14. James Baxter, conversation with author, Taylor, Mich., Sept. 1975.

15. A. M. Dunham to Henry Ford, 23 Oct. 1925, Office of Henry Ford, Correspondence files, 1927, Ford Archives.

16. Paul F. Wells, "Mellie Dunham: 'Maine's Champion Fiddler,'" *JEMF Quarterly* 12 (Autumn 1976): 112-118; *Vaudeville*, Jan. 1926 (in clip book for that period, Ford Archives).

17. This point cannot be stressed enough. A contest involving Tennessee, Kentucky, and Indiana, was sponsored by Ford dealers, and the winner, Bunt Stephens, subsequently toured, claiming falsely to have been personally chosen by Ford as champion. Ford's personal involvement with the contests was limited to his attendance at the Michigan state contest in Detroit on 19 January 1926 and providing trophies at that contest and for the North Atlantic States Radio Fiddler's Contest, held in Boston on 13 March 1926. Joe Wilson's analysis of these contests (in Joe Wilson and Lee Udall, *Folk Festivals: A Handbook for Organization and Management* [Knoxville: University of Tennessee Press, 1982], 157-158) is based mainly on the chicanery of Stephens or his promoter, rather than the facts of the very local nature of most of these contests.

18. See Charles K. Wolfe, *The Grand Ole Opry: The Early Years, 1925-35*, Old Time Music, booklet 2 (London: Old Time Music, 1975).

19. "Another Fiddlers' Contest Staged," *Greater Flint* 2 (Mar. 1924): 12-13.

20. "Nine Old Fiddlers in Concert Here," *Flint Journal*, 6 Jan. 1926; "Cowles Wins Old Fiddlers' Contest Here," *Flint Journal*, 14 Jan. 1926.

21. "Old-Time Players Form Band for I.M.A., Journal," *Flint Journal*, 21 Jan. 1926.

22. "County Farm Jig Champion Wins on Home-Made Fiddle," *Lansing State Journal*, 15 Jan. 1926.

23. *Rice Lake Chronotype*, 2 March 1927, in James P. Leary, "Ethnic Country Music on Superior's South Shore," *JEMF Quarterly* 19 (Winter 1983): 224. This photograph also appears in Philip Martin, *Farmhouse Fiddlers: Music & Dance Traditions in the Rural Midwest* (Mount Horeb, Wis.: Midwest Traditions, Inc., 1994), 97.

24. Frank Young, conversation with author, Union City, Pa., July 1972.

25. "John S. Donald and Mother to Play Old Time Dulcimer for WIBA Fans Wednesday," *Capital Times*, 22 Mar. 1927; John S. Donald to Jessie [sic] R. Martin, 22 Apr. 1927, in John S. Donald, Papers, 1811-1934, State Historical Society of Wisconsin.

26. Daughter, conversation with author, Mackinac Island, Mich., 1975.

27. Note with dulcimer, in possession of the author.

28. *New York Times*, 13 Dec. 1925, 6.

29. *Jamestown Journal*, 11 Dec. 1925, 15 Dec. 1925, 19 Dec. 1925, 21 Dec. 1925.

30. Nicholas Hawes, notes to *Paul Van Arsdale: Dulcimer Heritage*, Folk-Legacy Records FSA-87, based on Jesse Martin's scrapbook, in possession of Paul Van Arsdale.

31. I have heard at least two stories of dulcimer owners refusing to sell to him.

32. *Detroit News*, 19 Dec. 1926.

33. *New York World*, 11 Jan. 1926.

34. Liebold, reminiscences, 1367, Ford Archives. He said that it cost Ford $100 or $120 per mother record. On the other hand, Walter W. Clark, Victor Talking Machine Co., to E. G. Liebold, 19 Nov. 1925, Acc. 285, Ford Archives, asks what the company should pay the musicians, and in Liebold to Clark, 23 Nov. 1925, Acc. 285, Ford Archives, Liebold writes "Mr. Ford will make no charge for the use of the orchestra."

35. Faye Witt Moreland, *Green Fields and Fairer Lanes: Music in the Life of Henry Ford* (Tupelo, Miss.: Five Star Publishers, 1969), 13.

36. Advertising, General files, Acc. 149, Box 45, Ford Archives.

37. Advertising, General files, Acc. 149, Boxes 43, 45, Ford Archives.

38. My uncle's purchase of a secondhand dulcimer in 1928 may have resulted from his seeing Jesse Martin play, although he had always been familiar with the instrument. This is the only such example of renewed interest in the instrument during this period that I have encountered.

39. Earl Clifton Beck, *It Was This Way* (Ann Arbor: 1963), n.p.

40. Earl Clifton Beck, announcing, on acetate recording, acc. 91.156.1, Michigan State University Museum.

41. Beck, *It Was This Way*, n.p.

42. Earl Clifton Beck, *Songs of the Michigan Lumberjacks* (Ann Arbor: University of Michigan Press, 1941), 3.

43. Robert M. Hodesh, "Recording the Sounds of America: 3 - Songs from the Sawdust," *Ford Times* 43, no. 3 (Mar. 1951): 18.

44. Jean Ritchie, *Dulcimer People* (New York: Oak Publications, 1975), 10.

45. *Grand Rapids Press*, Nov. 26, 1947.

46. Earl Clifton Beck, *Lore of the Lumber Camps*, (Ann Arbor: University of Michigan Press, 1948), 7.

47. Nancy Groce, *The Hammered Dulcimer in America*, Smithsonian Studies in History and Technology, no. 44 (Washington: Smithsonian Institution Press, 1983), 30.

48. Beck, *It Was This Way*, n.p.

49. Earl Clifton Beck, *They Knew Paul Bunyan* (Ann Arbor: University of Michigan Press, 1956), 30.

50. Mildred Hickok, conversation with author, Sears, Mich., 1975.

51. Beck, *It Was This Way*, n.p.

52. Twelfth Annual National Folk Festival program, Cleveland, Ohio, May 22-26, 1946, in Helene Stratman-Thomas Papers, Mills Music Library, University of Wisconsin Library. William Hallup did play a cimbalom solo. Thanks to Jim Leary for this reference.

53. Questionnaire and correspondence, Ray Lawless Papers, Archive of American Folklife, Library of Congress. The tunes and ballads (others were "Barbara Ellen," "The Poor Wayfarin' Stranger," and "The Gypsy's Warning") that she mentioned in her questionnaire resemble more the kinds of tunes repre-

sented by the contemporary conception of folk music than did the tunes played by Dora Scudder, a native of the Ozarks, as described in Jean Granberry Schnitz, "Hammered Dulcimers and Folk Songs: The Musical Heritage of the C. A. Lee Family," in: *Corners of Texas*, Publication of the Texas Folklore Society 52 (Denton, Texas: University of North Texas Press, 1993), 162-172, who mentions more obscure songs and ballroom, rather than play party, tunes.

54. Ritchie, *Dulcimer People*, 56.

55. Ken Sullivan, "Russell Fluharty: The Dulcimer Man," *Goldenseal* 12 (1986): 24; Loy Swiger, interview with author, 1979.

56. Mark Crabtree, "Worley Gardner: Mountain Music, Dance and Dulcimers," *Goldenseal* 18 (1992): 12-13.

57. I attended in 1973 with a "delegation" from Michigan, which temporarily augmented the number of players.

58. Peter Henderson fortunately tape-recorded this segment of the show.

59. Beck, *It Was This Way*, n.p.

60. James Herald, interview by author, tape recording, Evart, Mich., 19 Aug. 1986.

61. For more history of the Original Dulcimer Players Club, see *Michigan Hammered Dulcimer: 25 Years with the Original Dulcimer Players Club* (n.p., 1988), and Paul Gifford, "Origins and Early Years of the Original Dulcimer Players Club," *Dulcimer Players News* 25 (Feb.-Apr. 1999): 20-21, 25 (May-July 1999): 40-41.

62. Ritchie, *Dulcimer People*, 12.

63. See L. Allen Smith, *A Catalogue of Pre-Revival Appalachian Dulcimers* (Columbia: University of Missouri Press, 1983) and Ralph Lee Smith, *Appalachian Dulcimer Traditions*, American Folk Music and Folk Musicians, no. 2 (Lanham, Md.: The Scarecrow Press, 1997), for more information.

64. Ralph Lee Smith, "Mountain Dulcimer Tales & Traditions," *Dulcimer Players News* 24 (May-July 1998): 46-47, describes Loraine Wyman, who gave recitals of French and British songs, as well as songs she had collected in Kentucky, and evidently played the Appalachian dulcimer, with which she posed for a photograph for a 1917 *Vogue* article. Better known, of course, was John Jacob Niles, who began to do the same about 1930.

65. Ritchie, *Dulcimer People*, 9-15.

66. *Traditional Music at Newport 1964: Part 1*, Vanguard VRS-9182.

67. Folkways Records FA 2381.

68. *Sing Out!* 16, no. 3 (July 1966): 32, advertisement.

69. Howard Mitchell, *The Mountain Dulcimer: How to Make It and Play It (After a Fashion)*, Folk-Legacy Records FSI-29; Howie Mitchell, interview by Kevin Roth, *Dulcimer Players News* 2, no. 2 (Spring 1976): 15.

70. Howard Mitchell, "The Hammered Dulcimer," dittoed paper, 1968.

71. Howard Mitchell, *The Hammered Dulcimer: How to Make It and Play It*, Folk-Legacy Records FSI-43.

372 *Chapter 16*

72. Red Bell, "Build a Dulcimer," *Stray Notes*, 1, no. 6 (1 Nov. 1965): 13; John Bailey, *Making an Appalachian Dulcimer* (London: Cecil Sharp House, 1966); Tom Adler, "How to Make an Appalachian Dulcimer," *Autoharp*, no. 30 (20 Oct. 1967): 8-10; and Mitchell, *Mountain Dulcimer*.

Dulcimer to "Hammer(ed) Dulcimer": Transformation of the Instrument since 1970

Although elements of a revival had begun, in 1970 the vast majority of people in the United States who were familiar with the dulcimer or could play it were of rural origin and had learned about it through firsthand contact from family or neighbors, or perhaps through exposure to an elderly player at a community dance, fair, school presentation, or similar event. Familiarity with the instrument, however, was low in absolute numbers and confined mostly to elderly people in certain areas of the country. Thirty years later the situation has changed completely. Today the instrument, now generally identified with the modifier "hammered" or "hammer," is familiar to a wide audience, even if only in general terms, throughout the United States. The process by which it reached this stage is complicated; to do it full justice would require a study much longer than space here allows.

The Folk Revival of the 1960s focused on singing and vocal music, yet covered a wide, if limited, variety of styles of music. Under the rubric of "folk music," its semiofficial organ *Sing Out!* featured articles on newly written political songs, blues, Appalachian music, Cajun songs, bluegrass, Irish songs, and on performers of those kinds of music. A circuit of coffeehouses and festivals grew up around the country, mostly catering to college students, where touring performers, who likely would follow one variety or another but might also combine elements of different genres, could perform. Small companies produced records of these performers and distributed them to record stores, probably largely in college towns or in "alternative" areas of large cities. "Folklore centers," or businesses catering to the folk music trade, selling musical instruments (especially guitars) and instruction books oriented to this variety of music, sprouted up around the country.

This environment—which by 1970 had been heavily influenced by the anti-Vietnam War movement, Civil Rights movement, and recreational drugs and elements of the so-called "hippie" movement—was, somewhat ironically, a favorable one for the dulcimer. The Baby Boom produced a large number of college students during the late 1960s and early 1970s, and, as the anti-war movement declined, as Nixon and the Congress tried to extricate the military from Vietnam, many of these former college students romanticized about a simpler, rural way of life. Some moved to the country; others lived in the city and bought organic vegetables at the local food co-op. The mountain dulcimer grew rapidly in popularity during this period. Already heavily infused with Appalachian mystique through its association with Jean Ritchie at folk festivals, craft fairs, and tourist destinations such as the Smoky Mountains, the instrument's simplicity and delicate form appealed to amateur musicians who wanted to try to play something besides the guitar.

A survey conducted in 1975 by John F. Putnam revealed that 53 shops, involving 71 persons, produced an annual output of 22,000 mountain dulcimers. Their increasing total production, mostly within the previous ten years, had accounted for 120,000 instruments. Of that number, over two-thirds were produced in kit form.[1] This growth in popularity was astonishing in its sheer quantity, but the fact that kits had exposed thousands of individuals to the elements of instrument making had even more implications. The phenomenon would probably have had little effect on the instrument that is the subject of this book, however, were it not for the fact that it shared the same name. Sooner or later some of the mountain dulcimer fanciers would learn about the dulcimer which they read about in dictionaries and books on musical instruments.

In the course of research towards a directory of contemporary American instrument makers, Susan Caust Farrell sent out questionnaires between 1974 and 1980. Of the responses she received from those sent in 1974, thirty reported that they made or had made hammered dulcimers. Of that group, twenty-three had made mountain dulcimers, and twelve of those had produced more than fifty mountain dulcimers. Thus only seven of the hammered dulcimer makers had not made a mountain dulcimer. The most prolific makers of hammered dulcimers in 1974, each having made more than fifty instruments, were Asel Gardner, of Kingwood, West Virginia; Hughes Dulcimer Company, of Denver, Colorado; and the Round Family Dulcimer Company, of Grandville, Michigan. In the next tier, with twenty-five to fifty instruments, was Dennis Dorogi, of Brocton, New York, and in the next group, with ten to twenty-five instruments each, were Nicholas Apollonio, of Tenants Harbor, Maine, J. Ralph Campbell, of Mannington, West Virginia, Charles Maxson, of Volga, West Virginia, Brian Mumford, of Santa Barbara, California, Michael Murphy, of St. Clairsville, Ohio, and Sam Rizzetta, of Barboursville, Virginia. The number of makers canvassed by Farrell increased to eighty by 1980.[2] Although not a comprehensive list, Farrell's research established that a small, but growing number of people around the country had begun to make them on a commercial, if mostly part-time, basis, and none had made them prior to 1966.

A significant center for the spread of the dulcimer was the annual Beers Family Festival at Petersburg, New York, where Russell Fluharty had introduced the instrument at the first festival in 1966. Howard Mitchell, having begun to experiment with its construction, subsequently presented workshops on making and playing it, and in 1969 Bill Spence, an enthusiast from the Albany area, discovered the instrument there. Spence began to make them commercially and continued Mitchell's workshops. Other performers, like Walt Michael, a young guitarist in a bluegrass group, Mitzie Collins, and Guy Carawan, an established folksinger and political activist, discovered the instrument at this festival between 1968 and 1972.[3] In the latter year, nine dulcimer owners participated in a workshop there. Spence began to play in 1972 with a group, "Fennig's All-Star String Band," at dances and festivals, and in 1973 made a record, *The Hammered Dulcimer*, which, though self-produced, was distributed widely and became very influential in the early part of the revival. The tunes on the record had come from a variety of recorded and printed sources.[4] Spence's success with the record led his wife Andy to start a mail-order business selling records, instruction books, instruments, and similar items.

Elsewhere the dulcimer began to receive exposure in other contexts, both for Folk Revival and general audiences. In 1972 *Sing Out!* published articles by Ed Trickett, a folksinger who got a dulcimer from his friend Howie Mitchell in 1967 and used it to accompany his singing, and Dave Williams, an English maker.[5] Guy Carawan started to include it in 1972 at his presentations in San Diego and, for example, at a workshop on "mountain movement music" in October 1972 at the Highlander Research and Education Center in New Market, Tennessee.[6] T. William Smith, who had learned the instrument in Kalamazoo, Michigan, played at Eisteddfod, a folk festival at Southeastern Massachusetts University in 1973, and in subsequent years his friend Sam Rizzetta played there.[7] Rizzetta, then employed at the Smithsonian Institution, wrote two pamphlets on constructing and playing the instrument, which the Smithsonian published in 1972.[8] He gave demonstrations at the National Folk Festival, in Vienna, Virginia, in 1974 on making his "two-hour" dulcimers.[9] In 1972 and 1973 I played at coffeehouses and festivals in southern Michigan, and in 1974 I wrote an article on nineteenth-century dulcimer manufacturers and traditions, something I felt was lacking in this incipient revival.[10] Street musicians began to appear about this time, such as Dorothy Carter, who, from 1973 to the late 1970s, accompanied her singing with a *yangqin* in New York City and Boston,[11] Robb Goldstein, who played his Dorogi dulcimer at Key West, Florida, and Nantucket, and William White, who played in Florida and Michigan from 1973 to about 1980. Worley and his brother Willis Gardner continued to play regularly at the annual festival at Ripley, West Virginia.

In the larger Folk Revival, the trend in the 1970s was getting away from all-inclusive festivals, such as those modeled after the Newport Folk Festival, which offered a wide variety of music and performers, and towards smaller festivals. At the same time, their number declined. According to Joe Wilson, "the 'sixties' ended for folk festivals in 1978-80," noting that "in a two-year period the popular audience for individual folk festivals dropped by 40 to 60 percent for virtually all festivals."[12] Ironically, this happened during a period in which interest in both mountain and hammered dulcimers grew rapidly—especially outside the relatively narrow confines of Folk Revival venues.

During the middle and latter part of the 1970s interest in the hammered dulcimer grew from the activities of several different players and makers in different parts of the country. Public familiarity developed as particular festivals featured the instrument and became annual events. Beginning players, who might have first fleetingly seen the instrument played on the street or by a touring musician at a local show or festival, could attend regularly and learn from more experienced players and makers. Some of the dulcimer festivals had stronger links to the Folk Revival than others and probably drew their audiences from the same socioeconomic group, but in general the new dulcimer gatherings attracted an audience that was more socially diverse. Rather than relying on the counterculture-leaning college students of the Folk Revival, the new gatherings brought retired farmers and laborers together with book-keepers and engineers from the suburbs and small cities.

Centers of Diffusion

The first festival with the hammered dulcimer as its focus began as a ten-year anniversary meeting of the Original Dulcimer Players Club at the Osceola County 4-H and Future Farmers of America Fairgrounds at Evart, Michigan, on September 29-30, 1973. The next year in June the club sponsored a "Non-Electrified Musical Fun-Fest." Most of the orga-nizers were traditional dulcimer players and fiddlers and had little fa-miliarity with the Folk Revival, and they intended the event as a partici-patory affair, in which all but electrified rock and country musicians would be welcome to play. Although publicity was minimal, word of mouth gradually drew bigger audiences, and by 1979 there were over five thousand who attended. Although the atmosphere was much like a county fair, they came not to see the latest Nashville stars, but mostly to hear the hammered dulcimer, and the names of the players mattered little to them.[13]

In most other parts of the country, the emerging festivals tended to group the hammered dulcimer with the mountain dulcimer. This pairing indicates a strong outsider approach, since organizers grouped the two instruments together based on what one might see in a dictionary defini-tion rather than on their musical traditions. These events differed in their origins. Some were organized by enthusiasts, both individual and in organized groups, others by museums or academic institutions, and still others by commercial interests.

The linkage of the two instruments and the creation of an informal network was spurred by the creation of a new publication. In 1975, Phillip Mason, a dulcimer maker living in Bangor, Maine, with a special inter-est in hammered dulcimers, started *The Dulcimer Players News*. By this time there were enough makers and players of the mountain dulcimer to make this publication feasible, and most of the articles for the first few years were submitted by mountain dulcimer players. The following year Mason was joined in the enterprise by Madeline MacNeil, of Front Royal, Virginia, and in 1978 she became sole editor and publisher. The success of this magazine was made possible by the continued growth of interest in both mountain and hammered dulcimers. It created interest in the hammered dulcimer among the much larger number of readers who had an interest in the mountain dulcimer and promoted the growth of festivals which featured both instruments. MacNeil continues to publish the periodical, not a small achievement in a world filled with short-lived small magazines.

Festivals and gatherings specifically intended by their organizers to feature the hammered dulcimer also started to grow. Bob Wey, of Horseheads, New York, Ben Stone, and John Kleske organized "The First and Hopefully Not Last Northeastern Cranberry Hammered Dulcimer Gathering," at the Unitarian Universalist Church in Binghamton, New York, on 30-31 July 1977. Its initial format consisted of numerous workshops, discussing aspects of construction and playing, with an evening concert with performances by individuals selected by the organizers from the participants.[14] Although intended for the hammered dulcimer, many brought mountain dulcimers, about fifty or seventy-five attending.[15] The Cranberry festival continues, but the focus has widened to include mountain dulcimers and autoharps.

Another organization began when Lilah Hickok Gillett, daughter of Elgia Hickok, and Harvey Prinz, of the Kansas City area, organized the Prairie Dulcimer Club. Its first meeting, in March 1977, drew about forty-five people, of which only three had hammered dulcimers, while over thirty-five brought mountain dulcimers.[16] In addition to regular meetings, the club has continuously sponsored a "Dulcimer Days Festival," with workshops, and the relative interest in the hammered dulcimer has increased.

Other events started primarily as mountain dulcimer festivals or workshops and expanded to include hammered dulcimers as interest in the latter instrument increased. The first annual "Roscoe Village Spring Festival and Dulcimer Contest" at Coshocton, Ohio, was held in 1975, but with only one hammered dulcimer player, David Taylor, no contest on that instrument was held.[17] The next year there were three contestants, and a contest was held, as it was in subsequent years. Jean and Lee Schilling, of Cosby, Tennessee, dulcimer makers whose nonprofit Folk Life Center of the Smokies had been holding the "Folk Festival of the Smokies" since 1969, began sponsoring an informal "Convention of Hammered and Plucked Dulcimer Makers, Players, Lovers" in 1977. By 1984, this had expanded to include harps, and it featured concerts as well as informal workshops and jam sessions.

Davis and Elkins College, in Elkins, West Virginia, organized the first Augusta Heritage Arts Workshops in 1973, which were formal, four-week classes emphasizing traditional crafts, such as pottery, basket making, and weaving. Dulcimer makers Charles Maxson and Paul Reisler were involved from the beginning, and Reisler developed much of the music program in the following years. One person who learned to make a hammered dulcimer in 1974 gave it to her friend John McCutcheon, who learned to play it. He soon began to make them commercially and appeared at many festivals in Appalachia, including a regular stint teaching Appalachian music at the Augusta Heritage Workshops. In 1981, Sam Rizzetta taught a class, with help from Bob Shank, and did so for several years thereafter. In 1989, the college inaugurated "Spring Dulcimer Week," which included classes by as many as four instructors each in both hammered and mountain dulcimers.[18] The formal educational program of Augusta influenced other summer programs and appealed to the same, well-educated, upper-middle-class audience that might participate in Elderhostel programs and continuing education classes at local universities.

Other centers of dulcimer diffusion gradually arose. Having begun to make dulcimers commercially, Donald Round and his sixteen-year-old son Jay, of Grandville, Michigan, began to attend festivals of various sorts in Indiana and other states in 1973. Jay made two recordings, with a bluegrass group, the Williams Family, by 1975, and Jay began to tour widely, including with Grandpa Jones, the banjo-playing comedian of television's "Hee Haw." Within a few years the Rounds then began to spend much of their summers at Silver Dollar City, a theme park in Branson, Missouri, and the Ozark Folk Center at Mountain View, Arkansas. Both places became centers for the diffusion of the instrument in the southern Midwest.

In 1977, the National Flat-Picking Championship Folk Arts and Crafts Festival in Winfield, Kansas, which began in 1972, introduced a hammered dulcimer contest, which has continued every year since. Bob Wey took first prize the first year; Donald Gillett, son of Lilah Gillett, placed third. The following year the festival hired touring performers, including Malcolm Dalglish and Mary Faith Rhoads, and the format proved very successful. Affiliated regional contests are held in Texas, Ohio, Iowa, and Arkansas.

Formation of a Revival Repertoire

Records and instruction books gradually started to increase in the latter part of the 1970s. Although the first recordings reflected individual preferences and influences, they influenced the development of subsequent playing and the formation of a certain repertoire. Most of the tunes on these recordings were traditional, but they had little connection to dulcimer tradition. Local musical tradition generally includes a core of older tunes that are commonly if not universally known by carriers of the tradition, as well as a mixture of tunes of later styles, both of a folk and a popular nature, that may or may not be commonly known. Dulcimer players in the United States traditionally played no tunes specific to their instrument, although the accompaniment style was. However, the influences from records on the emerging revival determined the choice of tunes and type of repertoire played by many of the new players.

Bill Spence's first record, for example, included a mixture of tunes whose sources probably included records by a Canadian fiddler, Jim Magill and His Northern Ramblers; a Washington fiddler, Joe Panczerzewski; Chet Parker and Elgia Hickok; the Hollow Rock String Band, a revivalist group from North Carolina; the New Lost City Ramblers; a Texas fiddler, Benny Thomason; and tunes and medleys of Appalachian, Scottish, English, and Irish origin. Some of them probably came ultimately from the *Fiddlers' Tunebook*, a publication of the English Folk Song and Dance Society, through the influence of Dudley Laufman and his New England contradance revival. The 1975 record of "Trapezoid," a Virginia group consisting of Sam Rizzetta, Paul Reisler, Pete Vigour, and Paul Yeaton, who played dulcimers in three sizes, includes some tunes from the New England contradance repertoire and two tunes by the Irish harper Turlough O'Carolan, among others. John McCutcheon's 1977 *The Wind That Shakes the Barley* includes tunes from various Appalachian fiddlers, tunes from English sources, two tunes by O'Carolan, and Bach's *Jesu, Joy of Man's Desiring*. The widely sold *Banish Misfortune* (1977), featuring Malcolm Dalglish, of Cincinnati, on the dulcimer, included jigs and reels of Irish and Northumbrian origin.

Later recordings varied more in repertoire, but the vast quantity issued, especially after 1980, prevents a thorough analysis here. Although their repertoire was primarily American, the performers chose many Irish,

English, and Scottish tunes—some clearly even of nationalist tone, like "Scotland the Brave" or "British Grenadiers." Presumably their intentions in choosing such tunes was based merely on personal tastes, but the effect was to create an identity for the dulcimer in the minds of many Americans as a "Celtic" instrument. This was also influenced by the success, beginning in the mid-1970s, of the "Chieftains" (whose harpist, Derek Bell, occasionally used a small cimbalom, which he christened a *tiompan*) and other Irish groups, such as the "Boys of the Lough," in American tours and record sales.

Another influence was Christmas music. Many of the carols heard during this season are themselves a product of the Victorian revival of Christmas celebrations, which sought to introduce customs, such as caroling, which Puritan influence had eliminated in America. The older carols and newly composed hymns and popular Christmas songs are mostly diatonic and readily playable on a dulcimer. As players were hired by local museums and the like for "Victorian Christmas" celebrations, they learned Christmas carols and made Christmas recordings, which proved popular. Mitzie Collins, of Rochester, New York, a church organist, made the first, and many others followed. Most performers today with three or four recordings will usually have one Christmas recording. They are common enough to be heard as background music piped in on store sound systems during the shopping season. Particularly popular recordings have led performers to tour with special Christmas programs. Maggie Sansone, of Baltimore, Maryland, whose Christmas recordings became the biggest selling recordings of her own label, organized a tour in 1998, "Scottish Christmas," featuring dulcimer, fiddle, guitar, Celtic harp, and bagpipes, and two dancers.[19] "Magical Strings," a group consisting of Philip and Pam Boulding, of Seattle, Washington, on dulcimer and Celtic harp, tour with their children each December, giving "Celtic Yuletide" concerts.[20]

The "Celtic"/Christmas orientation also readily absorbed Renaissance music, although the latter remains a minor influence. In the popular mind, nevertheless, images of the Renaissance conjure up visions of Merrie Olde England, so the connection should not surprise us. The popularity of "Renaissance" fairs and festivals, profit-making ventures which involve actors and entertainers creating a mock sixteenth-century English village, has grown throughout the United States since the 1970s. In 1976, Barbara Mendelson played her dulcimer at the original Renaissance Faire near San Francisco. Her success caused organizers of Renaissance festivals in other parts of the country to seek out dulcimer players as entertainers. Their continued commercial success will probably encourage more players to arrange and popularize Renaissance tunes.

Making, Manufacturing, and Marketing

It was typical in the 1970s for individuals to attempt making a dulcimer after having seen one played. Although by 1980 there were a number of full-time makers, all made them on order. The few stores which might have an interest in the instrument rarely sold them, and the potential buyer would either have to order one from a maker or try to make one himself. Howard Mitchell's book and record set and Sam Rizzetta's Smithsonian pamphlet were very influential in this regard.

Rizzetta's pamphlet provided a design for a dulcimer which was closer to the traditional design. Many instruments made in the 1970s, however, differed from older instruments in that they were uniformly trapezoidal and, contrary to custom, often had tuning pins on the left-hand pin block. Both Mitchell and Rizzetta provided a tuning chart where the bass courses were tuned a fifth below the neighboring treble course, rather than the more usual octave of the older instruments, and this tuning became standard, as methods and instruction books used this tuning. Rizzetta liked to experiment with different designs, and many makers incorporated particular features he used at one point in time, such as tuning pins placed in the pin block at a plane with the soundboard, as on the Iranian *santur*; two strings per course; Delrin bridge rods; and an adjustable inner bridge support.

However, others incorporated many innovations. Donald Round added an interior metal frame to a dulcimer of traditional design. Bill Webster, of Detroit, used aluminum tubing as supports inside a traditional design. Roderick L. Cramer, of The Beriyth Company, Wytheville, Virginia, was issued the only patent on a dulcimer design during this period, no. 4,388,852, on 21 June 1983, on tubular bracing. Although earlier makers of American dulcimers had followed certain patterns by custom, few revival makers felt any connection to them. However, like the nineteenth-century makers who took out patents on their inventions, they felt free to experiment with new bracing designs and materials. The perennial problems associated with the instrument—excessive sustain, lack of tuning stability, and tone—always presented challenges for those makers inclined to face them.

As interest in the instrument increased during the 1970s, some mountain dulcimer makers also produced hammered dulcimers. Some makers took the kit concept and applied it to the hammered dulcimer, but, in contrast to the success with mountain dulcimer kits, hammered dulcimer kits were generally unsuccessful. By 1980 there were perhaps as many as fifty makers in the United States actively producing hammered dulcimers, some on a full-time basis; the number increased during the 1980s.

The trend in the 1980s was towards a more commercial approach, as competition increased, requiring a serious investment in machinery and marketing. The earliest major attempt at marketing dulcimers at wholesale prices to the music trade was that of Breezy Ridge Instruments (Mary Faith Rhoads and John Pearse), of Center Valley, Pennsylvania, in 1981. The design of this instrument used the double-course string arrangement which was becoming common to most revival dulcimers, but radically departed from tradition in that the instrument lacked a baseboard. Its pin blocks were attached to three rails, the outer rails forming the sides. Although the design was adopted by at least one other maker, the enterprise stopped promoting its dulcimers after a few years.

Ray Mooers organized the Dusty Strings Dulcimer Company, of Seattle, in 1979 and by 1984 was offering three models to the music trade. This company has had considerable success and remains in business. It has probably produced a larger number of instruments than any other single manufacturer, with a "unibody" design (the soundboard attaches to the upper surface of the pin blocks), like some of the manufactured dulcimers of the middle of the nineteenth century. Like other manufacturers, it produces a number of different models, which differ mostly in the number of courses and in diatonic and chromatic tuning schemes.

Russell Cook, of Bennington, Oklahoma, first assembled a kit in 1978. He began to make dulcimers commercially in 1981, and by 1984 offered three different models commercially, under the name Wood 'N' Strings, in Arlington, Texas.[21] His business expanded, and in 1991, with Mark Tindle, opened a factory, Master Works, in Estes Park, Colorado, moving later to Bennington, Oklahoma. Cook used the earlier name as a business to market his recordings. Master Works, employing five workers, had, according to Cook, produced 4,300 instruments by 1998.[22]

Other makers active in the 1980s and 1990s (listed here in no particular order) included William Webster, of Detroit, who began in 1974 and produced over a thousand dulcimers; Folkcraft Instruments, of

Winsted, Connecticut; Rick Fogel, of Chesapeake, Virginia, and Seattle, Washington (Whamdiddle Dulcimer Company); R. L. Tack and Son, of Hastings, Michigan; Jean and Lee Schilling, of Cosby, Tennessee; Jim Miller, of Hampton, Tennessee; Michael C. Allen, of Ostrander, Ohio (Cloud Nine); Jerry Read Smith, of Black Mountain, North Carolina (Song of the Wood); Lee Spears, of Salisbury, North Carolina; James Jones, of Bedford, Virginia; Nicholas Blanton, of Shepherdstown, West Virginia; Jim Hudson, of Britton, Michigan (J & K Hammered Dulcimers); Jerry Hudson, of Whitney, Texas; David Lindsey, of Bennington, Oklahoma; John Kelly, of DeWitt, Michigan (Maple Valley Dulcimers); William Walker, of Elkhorn, Kentucky (Green River Dulcimers); Chris Foss, of Summersville, Missouri (Songbird Dulcimers); and Linda Foley, of Muskegon, Michigan (Lost Valley Dulcimers). This is not meant to be an exhaustive list; many other makers were active as well. They set up booths at dulcimer festivals and arts and crafts festivals and demonstrated their instruments. Competition became fierce as they had to explain the qualities of their dulcimers to potential customers, who tended to buy the instruments recommended by performers.

By the late 1980s, most makers produced dulcimers with two strings per treble course, a departure from American and European tradition. This appealed to potential buyers, because such instruments needed less bracing, resulting in a lighter instrument (an important consideration, since many of the new players were women and many carried them to festivals) and less time to tune, which was also made easier by the introduction of the electronic tuner. Another development was a chromatic tuning, developed by Rizzetta, Webster, Tack, and others, which retained the traditional diatonic tuning but added chromatic intervals through the use of agraffes or hold-down rods in the bridges which divided courses that were placed between existing treble and bass courses.

Retail businesses which specialized in selling dulcimers produced by others also grew. Some were tied to the tourist industry, as Jean and Lee Schilling, in Cosby, Tennessee (Smoky Mountains), the Mountain Music Shop, in Branson, Missouri, or Eddie and Anne Damm's Song of the Sea, in Bar Harbor, Maine. Others, like Music Folk, of suburban St. Louis, House of Musical Traditions, of suburban Washington, and Elderly Instruments, of Lansing, Michigan, were part of the larger phenomenon of retail businesses which had grown out of the "folklore centers" of the Folk Revival era. These establishments sold recordings, sheet music, and sometimes offered lessons.

Methods and Instruction

In the 1970s, people learned to play by watching others, listening to recordings (sometimes at slow speed), and teaching themselves. This was much the same method of learning as had been practiced for hundreds of years. With the growth of interest in the instrument in the United States, however, it was inevitable that instruction books and sheet music began to multiply. Unlike the development of the Salzburg *Hackbrett* in the curricula of the state music schools of Germany and Austria in the 1950s and 1960s, which was aimed at children, compilers of the American books intended them for self-instruction. Eventually regular lessons became commonplace, however, though methods designed for a formal course of study have yet to appear.

Phillip Mason wrote the first, *The Hammered Dulcimer Instruction Book* (Washington, D.C.: Communications Press, 1977). This was followed in 1979 by three: Lilah Gillett's *Easy Chord Playing Method for Hammered Dulcimer* ([Overland Park, Kans.: the author]); Norman Hughes's *Mel Bay Presents the Hammered Dulcimer* (Pacific, Mo.: Mel Bay, 1979), and Peter Pickow's *Hammered Dulcimer* (New York: Oak Publications, 1979). Mel Bay and Oak Publications distributed their publications widely, and the last two appeared in music stores. Lucille Reilly wrote *Striking Out . . . and Winning! An Unabridged Guide for the Hammered Dulcimer* (Moorestown, N.J.: Shadrach Productions, 1984) and Karen Ashbrook compiled *Playing the Hammered Dulcimer in the Irish Tradition* (Silver Spring, Md.: Foolscap Publications, 1984). Others followed in subsequent years; one trend was for Mel Bay to issue sheet music in conjunction with a performer's recording.

By the mid-1980s, several people were active around the country giving lessons. Lilah Gillett taught hundreds in the Kansas City area, Judi Morningstar was active in the Detroit area, and Karen Ashbrook in the Washington, D.C., area. There were many others. At dulcimer festival workshops, one began to notice the regular appearance of sheet music about this time.

Books with tunes intended for the dulcimer began to appear in this decade. Linda Lowe Thompson published *Tunes for Hammered Dulcimer* in 1982 and followed with several other books, containing Christmas songs, hymns, and classical pieces. Sara Johnson began her *Kitchen Musician's Occasional Collection* series in the early 1980s, containing a variety of Irish and Scottish jigs and reels, Christmas carols, and older country dance tunes. Mel Bay, which began as a publisher of popular guitar materials, expanded their selection of hammered dulcimer books. The firm published some of these in conjunction with compact disc recordings by Carole Koenig, Maggie Sansone, and others. Finally, videotaped instructional courses by John McCutcheon, Walt Michael, Madeline MacNeil, and Kendra Ward appeared in the 1980s and 1990s. This is again not intended to be a comprehensive list; many others produced tune books.

Clubs

In Michigan, local dulcimer clubs began to sprout up after 1980. Unlike most such organizations in other parts of the country, which had the mountain dulcimer as their primary instrument, Michigan clubs focused on the hammered dulcimer. By this time, the Original Dulcimer Players Club, which still met around the state three times a year, was spending more of its energy on the annual Evart "Fun-Fest." Local clusters of beginning players felt a need for regular meetings near their homes. In the early 1980s, beginning players organized Uncle Carl's Dulcimer Club (named after Carl Hakes, of Hanover, Michigan, who made most of their instruments), around Jackson. This group learned the same tunes and played together at local museums and festivals. The Silver Strings Dulcimer Club, of the western suburbs of Detroit, was organized soon afterwards. Ten years later over fifteen local dulcimer clubs in the state of Michigan had formed.

In other areas, dulcimer clubs grew as well. Although some were specifically for the hammered dulcimer, most were primarily for the mountain dulcimer. As some hammered dulcimer players or people interested in learning that instrument came to meetings of those organizations, they expanded their field of interest.

Clubs meet regularly, perhaps once a month, often in a church, school, or other public facility. They may issue a newsletter and sponsor workshops or a festival, although not every group has such ambitions. Some perform as a group at museum events, parks, or campgrounds, while others remain only a participatory activity for the members themselves. The focus really is on group learning, naturally with a strong element of socializing. At the larger festivals, such as Evart, members of local clubs may camp near each other and set up areas for practicing and jam sessions.

The Changing Nature of Dulcimer Festivals

Dulcimer festivals have evolved according to the needs of their audiences. The Evart "Fun-Fest" began as a participatory event without stars or workshops. The first Cranberry Gathering also had no paid performers, although workshops were a primary feature from the beginning. Around 1977, some Evart attendees, aware of the workshops at other festivals, began to demand them. Gradually participants offered to hold them, and they increased in number to the point that within ten years workshops dominated the festival.

Typically performers on both hammered dulcimer and mountain dulcimers appear on concert schedules at the festivals. They have established their names and reputations by making recordings and touring, having feature stories written about them in the *Dulcimer Players News*, and make at least a substantial part of their income by playing. They may also give workshops, but others may limit their appearances to teaching at workshops. Workshop topics may be limited to "beginning," "intermediate," and "advanced," at smaller festivals, or they may be divided into any number of topics: "theory and chord substitution," "fancy embellishments," "chromatically classical," "beginning chording," "Scandinavian tunes," and "jazz chords revisited" are actual examples.[23]

The success of the Augusta Folk Arts Workshops has influenced other tuition-paid classes. The Swannanoa Gathering, at Warren Wilson College, in Asheville, North Carolina, hosts an annual "Dulcimer Week," with workshops in "both" dulcimers, and, curiously, included a hammered dulcimer in its "Celtic Week" program but not in its "Old-Time Music & Dance Week," at least in 1998.[24] The number of festivals continued to increase in the 1990s. A complete list would be difficult to record here; those interested might look at a recent issue of the *Dulcimer Players News*.

The Changing Player and Playing

The population of the United States is overwhelmingly located in urban areas, so it is not surprising that urban (or rather, suburban) areas are where most dulcimer players live. In 1970, as discussed earlier, the vast majority who were familiar with the instrument came from rural origins. As the revival progressed, it found a home with people who had neither the ethnic, cultural, social, or geographic ties to the people who were associated with the instrument before 1970. The earliest of the new players tended to be younger males, often in college communities, who had an interest in folk or traditional American music. Women, a minority at first, gradually became a majority.[25] Many of them had taken piano lessons in their youths but had given up music, only to start playing the dulcimer in middle age. Some of the new players could afford to pay a thousand dollars or more for a new instrument and sometimes the tuition for week-long classes. They might also have the disposable income and leisure time to own recreational vehicles and to travel to distant campgrounds to pursue their hobby.

The result was a drastic change in the social environment associated with the instrument. The individualism of the odd person who learned to play from his (and at least in most cases, it was *his*) relatives or neighbors and who tended to follow custom, as far as style and repertoire went, had evolved towards a social outlet involving clubs and gatherings of various types.

Some players sought to separate themselves from the pack through innovation in the types of music they played. Already in 1966, Patrick Murphy's liner notes to Chet Parker's recording set the tone, when he wrote "most of the music is the old time dance tunes represented in this album, but I have heard classical and semiclassical music played. It would be interesting to see if someone can come up with some dulcimer playing in the jazz medium."[26]

Jay Round recorded an album using the dulcimer to play swing tunes in 1980, but the general trend was towards "Celtic" music (a deliberately imprecise term covering traditional or national music of countries or regions of Celtic origins, but chosen by Americans outside those traditions). Dance tunes of native provenance, of the sort recorded by Chet Parker, tended to recede.[27] In some quarters music of the New England Contradance Revival, already flavored by Irish and Scottish jigs and reels rather than by the older Yankee tradition, influenced the new players. Others took a more classical, or light classical approach, arranging standard melodies for the dulcimer, or playing newly composed music in a "New Age" or popular vein, as Cecelia Webster, Malcolm Dalglish, Dan Duggan, and Steve Schneider and others have done.

The number of new players continued to increase during the 1990s, and in some areas (as in many parts of Michigan) the instrument was familiar to most people. Indeed, in 1999, following a "demonstration" of over fifty dulcimers at the state capitol in Lansing, one Michigan legislator introduced in committee a bill to make the instrument the "state" instrument.

Although a substantial number of new players sought to set themselves apart from the pack through recordings, most were content to practice in the confines of their homes or at club meetings, festival workshops, and jam sessions. In this sense the instrument still resembled its old self, although the Grange meetings and house parties had become transformed into events focusing on the music itself. Local events might also foster regional styles, something that players in some areas appreciated, but the nature of commerce and the mobility of the American population made local styles something that would not likely endure.

Once its revivers took the dulcimer out of its old haunts and into contemporary view, the dulcimer lost its folk status. Gradually it became an instrument of a variety of popular music. The instrument also tended to branch off from the mainstream of "folk music," a form of popular music usually involving songs accompanied with guitar. Many of the dulcimer's earliest performers who made recordings were unfamiliar with the traditions of the instrument, though they might have been familiar with traditional music. Each subsequent generation became further removed from both the instrument's tradition and traditional music as well. Still, many of tunes that are likely to be common at least to beginning players in different parts of the United States (and, to some extent, in the English-speaking world) have origins in traditional musical environments.

One musical strand among American dulcimer players prefers "native" music. In this sense the identification of the instrument with native tradition, which is universal with all forms of the dulcimer around the world, endures. The "Celtic" orientation of many others may seek to find an ancestral spirit to traditional Anglo-American tunes. Others will continue to innovate and play styles of music that set themselves apart. What kind of repertoire and what music the instrument's players will develop fifty years from now is impossible to predict. Many of today's players are well into middle age or older; few young people seem to take an interest in the instrument. It is entirely possible that interest will gradually fade until the dulcimer again passes into obscurity. But the solid revival of the last three decades of the twentieth century indicates that a return to obscurity is a long way off.

Notes

1. John F. Putnam, "Plucked Dulcimers Hit a High Note," *Sing Out!* 25, no. 2 (1976): 35.

2. Susan Caust Farrell, *Directory of Contemporary American Musical Instrument Makers* (Columbia: University of Missouri Press, 1981), passim.

3. Stephanie P. Ledgin, "Walt Michael: Beyond the Hammered Dulcimer," *Sing Out!* 35, no. 4 (Winter 1991): 4; Guy Carwan, interview by Evan Carawan, *Dulcimer Players News* 22, no. 1 (Feb.-Apr. 1996): n.p.; Mitzie Collins, "Notes from a Personal Collection of Dulcimers and Dulcimer-type Instruments," *Dulcimer Players News* 3, no. 3 (Summer 1977): 32. In 1972, Spence and Dorogi had booths; I met Carawan, but saw otherwise little evidence of dulcimer activity.

4. Bill Spence with Fennig's All-Star String Band, *The Hammered Dulcimer*, Front Hall Records FHR-01.

5. Ed Trickett, "Teach-In: Hammered Dulcimer," *Sing Out!* 21, no. 4 (1972): 18-19; Dave Williams, "Teach-In: A Simple Hammered Dulcimer for Home Construction," *Sing Out!* 21, no. 4 (1972): 47.

6. *Sing Out!* 21, no. 6 (1972): 39; Malcolm Dalglish, conversation with author, 1977.

7. *Sing Out!* 22, no. 4 (1973): 43.

8. Sam Rizzetta, "Hammer Dulcimer: History and Playing," Smithsonian Institution Leaflet 72-4; Sam Rizzetta, "Making a Hammer Dulcimer," Smithsonian Institution Leaflet 72-5.

9. A. McD. Davis, letter to author, 28 June 1974.

10. Paul Gifford, "Developement [sic] of the Hammer Dulcimer," *Mugwumps* 3, no. 5 (Sept. 1974): 19-23.

11. "Our Local Correspondents: Five New York Street Musicians," *The New Yorker* (29 Sept. 1975): 39-40.

12. Joe Wilson, The National Council for the Traditional Arts, website, <http://www.ncta.net/national1.htm>.

13. In the 1970s, only a minority of the performers on the stage included a dulcimer, and one of the frequent requests was that there be "more dulcimer." I was closely involved in those days as a regular performer and secretary of the club.

14. Flyer for "The First and Hopefully Not Last Northeastern Cranberry Hammered Dulcimer Gathering."

15. Bob Wey, "In Memoriam," *Dulcimer Players News* 25, no. 3 (Aug.-Oct. 1999): 5.

16. "KayZing," email to Hammerd-L mailing list, 13 Oct. 1996.

17. David L. Taylor, "Annual Dulcimer Contest-Convention Information," *Dulcimer Players News* 1, no. 6 (Sept.-Oct. 1975): 26.

18. John Lilly, "Augusta: A Living Tradition," in Augusta Heritage Center, *1997 Catalog: 25th Anniversary Commemorative Issue* (Elkins, W. Va.: Augusta Heritage Center of Davis & Elkins College, 1997), 3-6; Michael Kline, "Augusta: A Reaffirmation of Homemade Values," *Dulcimer Players News* 9, no. 1 (Winter 1983): 30-31.

19. "Plaid You Like It: 'Scottish Christmas' Offers Seasonal Salute to Kilts, Haggis and Ho Ho Ho," *Tulsa World*, 19 Nov. 1998.

20. Magical Strings, website, <http://www.magicalstrings.com/Bio-Long.html>.

21. Wood 'N' Strings, *1984 Catalog* (Arlington, Tex., [1984]).

22. Shirley Jenkins, "The String Beat; Dulcimer Devotee Brings New Life into Old-Time Instrument," *Fort Worth Star-Telegram*, 29 Nov. 1998, 34.

23. Original Dulcimer Players Club, *25th Annual Dulcimer Musical Funfest* program.

24. Advertisement, *Dulcimer Players News* 24, no. 1 (Feb.-Apr. 1998): 12.

25. This is difficult to judge accurately. One measure is a survey made by Barb Cummings in February 1997 of subscribers to Hammerd-L, an internet mailing list, which showed that women comprised 51.7% of the respondents (which numbered 143 which could be identified by sex) to her survey. This is a small, perhaps meaningless sample, but as internet users tended to be males more often than females, the likely proportion of females to males is higher. The survey also revealed that the average age of the respondents was 44.12 years and that the average age at which they began to play was 38.58 years. A subsequent informal survey on the same mailing list, made by Brett Ridgeway in February 2000, showed that of the 164 respondents, 55% were female and that 36% had begun to play the instrument in their forties and 28.7% in their thirties.

26. Patrick R. Murphy, notes to *The Hammer Dulcimer Played by Chet Parker*, Folkways Records Album no. FA 2381.

27. Ironically, his inclusion of some old tunes of Irish or pseudo-Irish origin, like "Temperance Reel" and "St. Patrick's Day in the Morning," may have influenced the "Celtic" direction later players took.

• *Appendix 1* •

Tunings

This appendix contains selected tuning arrangements for dulcimers of different traditions. They follow the same order as the discussion of the traditions in the main text. The numbers refer to the sources in back.

The pitches are represented by octaves starting at C. Thus:

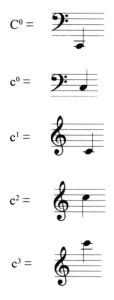

1.

b^2*	c^3		
g^2	a^2	$g\sharp^1$	
e^2	f^2	$d\sharp^1$	
d^2	$g\sharp^1$	$c\sharp^1$	$c\sharp^0$
$c\sharp^2$	$f\sharp^1$	b^0	B^0
c^2	f^1	$a\sharp^0$	$A\sharp^0$
b^1	e^1	a^0*	A^0
$a\sharp^1$	$d\sharp^1$	g^0*	G^0
a^1	d^1	f^0*	F^0
g^1	c^1	$d\sharp^0*$	$D\sharp^0$
		d^0*	D^0
$\mid c^0*$			C^0

2.

g^2	b^1	$d\sharp^1$
$f\sharp^2$	$a\sharp^1$	d^1
e^2	$g\sharp^1$	$c\sharp^1$
d^2	$f\sharp^1$	b^0
$c\sharp^2$	f^1	a^0
c^2	e^1	$g\sharp^0$
b^1	$d\sharp^1$	g^0
a^1	d^1	$f\sharp^0$
g^1	c^1	f^0
f^1	$b\flat^0$	e^0
e^1	a^0	c^0
$\mid d^0$		

3.

f^2	$b\flat^1$	
e^2*	a^1*	
d^2*	g^1	
c^2	f^1	-0-
b^1*	e^1*	-0-
a^1*	d^1*	-0-
g^1	c^1	-0-
f^1	$b\flat^0$	-0-
$d\sharp^1$	$g\sharp^0$	-0-

4.

f^2*	$b\flat^1*$	
$e\flat^2*$	$a\flat^1*$	$e\flat^1$
$d\flat^2*$	$g\flat^1*$	$c\sharp^1$
c^2*	f^1*	b^0
$b\flat^1*$	$e\flat^1*$	a^0
$g\sharp^1*$	$c\sharp^1*$	g^0
$f\sharp^1*$	b^0*	f^0
f^1		$e\flat^0$
$e\flat^1$	$a\flat^1$	$c/c\sharp^0$

5.

c^3	f^2	
$a\sharp^2*$	$d\sharp^2*$	g^1
a^2	d^2	f^1
g^2	c^2	$d\sharp^1$
f^2*	$b\flat^1$	d^1
e^2	a^1	c^1
d^2	g^1	$a\sharp^0$
c^2*	f^1	a^0
b^1	e^1	g^0
a^1	d^1	f^0
g^1	c^1	e^0
$f\sharp^1$	b^0	d^0
e^1	a^0	c^0
d^1	g^0	B^0
		A^0

6.

g²	c²	f¹
f♯²	b¹	e¹
e²	a¹	d¹
d²	g¹	c¹
c♯²	f♯¹	b⁰
b¹	e¹	a⁰
a¹	d¹	g⁰
g♯¹	c♯¹	f♯⁰

d⁰
A⁰
e⁰ |

7.

a²	
g²	g♯²
f²	f♯²
d♯²	e²
c♯²	d²
b¹	c²
a¹	a♯¹
g¹	g♯¹
f¹	f♯¹
d♯¹	e¹
c♯¹	d¹
b⁰	c¹
a⁰	a♯⁰
g⁰	g♯⁰

8.

f³	f²	
e♭³	e♭²	f¹
d³	d²	e♭¹
c³	c²	d¹
b♭²	b♭¹	c¹
a♭²	a♭¹	b♭⁰
g²	g¹	a♭⁰
f²	f¹	g⁰
e♭²	e♭¹	f⁰
		e♭⁰

9.

f♯²	b¹	
e²	a¹	e¹
d²*	g¹*	d¹
c♯²	f♯¹*	c¹*
c²*	f¹	b⁰
b¹*	e¹	a⁰*
a♯¹	d♯¹	g⁰*
a¹	d¹	f⁰*
g¹	c¹	e⁰

c⁰
A♯⁰
F⁰
d♯⁰
d⁰*

10.

f²	g²	d♯¹
e²	a♯¹	c♯¹
d²	g♯¹	b⁰
c♯²	f♯¹	a♯⁰
c²	f¹	a⁰
b¹	e¹	g♯⁰
a¹	d¹	g⁰
g¹	c¹	f♯⁰

f⁰
d♯⁰
c♯⁰
e⁰
d⁰
c⁰

11.

c^3 $a\sharp^2$

$g\sharp^2$ | b^2 | e^3 $c\sharp^3$
$f\sharp^2$ | a^2 | $d\sharp^3$ $d\sharp^2$
f^2 | g^2 | d^3 $d\sharp^1$
e^2 | $a\sharp^1$ $c\sharp^1$
d^2 | $g\sharp^1$ b^0
$c\sharp^2$ | $f\sharp^1$ $a\sharp^0$
c^2 | f^1 a^0
b^1 | e^1 $g\sharp^0$
a^1 | d^1 g^0
g^1 | c^1 $f\sharp^0$
    e^0
f^0 d^0
$d\sharp^0$ c^0
$c\sharp^0$ $A\sharp^0$
B^0 - - - - -
A^0 $G\sharp^0$
G^0 $F\sharp^0$
F^0 E^0
D^0

12.

f^2 | $a\sharp^1$
e^2 | a^1
d^2 | g^1 $a\sharp^0$
$c\sharp^2$ | $f\sharp^1$ b^0
c^2 | f^1 a^0
b^1 | e^1 g^0
a^1 | d^1 f^0
g^1 | c^1 e^0
$g\sharp^1$ | $c\sharp^1$ d^0

13.

b^2 | c^3 c^1
$g\sharp^2$ | a^2 b^0
$f\sharp^2$ | g^2 $a\sharp^0$
e^2 | f^2 a^0
d^2 | $d\sharp^2$ $g\sharp^0$
$c\sharp^2$ | $f\sharp^1$ g^0
c^2 | f^1 $f\sharp^0$
b^1 | e^1 f^0
$a\sharp^1$ | $d\sharp^1$ e^0
a^1 | d^1 $d\sharp^0$
g^1 | c^1 d^0
$g\sharp^1$ | $c\sharp^1$

14.

e^2	a^1	$d\sharp^1$
$d\sharp^2$	$g\sharp^1$	$c\sharp^1$
$c\sharp^2$	$f\sharp^1$	b^0
b^1	e^1	a^0
a^1	d^1	g^0
g^1	c^1	

15.

		$a\sharp^2$	b^2
e^2	g^2	$g\sharp^2$	a^2
$d\sharp^2$	$f\sharp^2$		
d^2	f^2		
$c\sharp^2$	$f\sharp^1$		
c^2	f^1		
b^1	e^1		
$a\sharp^1$	$d\sharp^1$		
a^1	d^1		
$g\sharp^1$	$c\sharp^1$		
g^1	c^1		

Right column (15): b^0, $a\sharp^0$, a^0, $g\sharp^0$, g^0, $f\sharp^0$, f^0, e^0, $d\sharp^0$, d^0, $c\sharp^0$, c^0

Left lower (15): B^0, $A\sharp^0$, A^0, G^0

16.

e^2	a^1	c^1
$d\sharp^2$	$g\sharp^1$	$c\sharp^1$
d^2	g^1	b^0
$c\sharp^2$	$f\sharp^1$	$a\sharp^0$
c^2	f^1	a^0
b^1	e^1	g^0
$a\sharp^1$	$d\sharp^1$	$f\sharp^0$
a^1	d^1	f^0
g^1	c^1	e^0
$g\sharp^1$	$c\sharp^1$	d^0
$f\sharp^1$	b^0	

17.

e^2	g^2	$a\sharp^2$
$d\sharp^2$	$f\sharp^2$	a^2
d^2	f^2	$g\sharp^2$
$c\sharp^2$	$f\sharp^1$	
c^2	f^1	
b^1	e^1	
$a\sharp^1$	$d\sharp^1$	
a^1	d^1	
$g\sharp^1$	$c\sharp^1$	
g^1	c^1	

Right column (17): b^0, $a\sharp^0$, a^0, $g\sharp^0$, g^0, $f\sharp^0$, f^0, e^0, $d\sharp^0$, d^0

Lower left (17): $|c^0$

18.

$d\sharp^2$	f^2
d^2	e^2
$c\sharp^2$	$f\sharp^1$
c^2	f^1
b^1	e^1
$a\sharp^1$	$d\sharp^1$
a^1	d^1
g^1	c^1
$g\sharp^1$	$c\sharp^1$

Right column (18): b^0, $a\sharp^0$, a^0, $g\sharp^0$, g^0, $f\sharp^0$, f^0, e^0, d^0, c^0, B^0

Lower left (18): A^0, G^0

19.

b^2	$g\sharp^2$
$a\sharp^2$	g^2
a^2	$f\sharp^2$
$d\sharp^2$	f^2
d^2	e^2
$c\sharp^2$	$f\sharp^1$
c^2	f^1
b^1	e^1
$a\sharp^1$	$d\sharp^1$
a^1	d^1
$g\sharp^1$	$c\sharp^1$
g^1	c^1

B^0
A^0
G^0
D^0

b^0
$a\sharp^0$
a^0
$g\sharp^0$
g^0
$f\sharp^0$
f^0
e^0
$d\sharp^0$
d^0
$c\sharp^0$
c^0
$A\sharp^0$
$G\sharp^0$
$F\sharp^0$

20.

$d\sharp^2$	f^2
d^2	e^2
$c\sharp^2$	$f\sharp^1$
c^2	f^1
b^1	e^1
$a\sharp^1$	$d\sharp^1$
a^1	d^1
$g\sharp^1$	$c\sharp^1$
g^1	c^1

d^0
c^0

b^0
$a\sharp^0$
a^0
$g\sharp^0$
g^0
$f\sharp^0$
f^0
e^0
$d\sharp^0$
$c\sharp^0$

21.

e^3	$a\sharp^2$
d^3	$g\sharp^2$
c^3	f^2
b^2	$d\sharp^2$
a^2	$c\sharp^2$
g^2	c^2
$f\sharp^2$	b^1
e^2	a^1
d^2	g^1

g^0

f^1
$a\sharp^1$
$g\sharp^1$
$d\sharp^1$
$f\sharp^1$
e^1
d^1
c^1
b^0
a^0

22.

$f\sharp^3$	$d\sharp^3$
e^3	$a\sharp^2$
d^3	$g\sharp^2$
c^3	f^2
b^2	$d\sharp^2$
a^2	$c\sharp^2$
g^2	c^2
$f\sharp^2$	b^1
e^2	a^1
d^2	g^1

g^0
d^0

f^1
$a\sharp^1$
$g\sharp^1$
$c\sharp^1$
$d\sharp^1$
$f\sharp^1$
e^1
d^1
c^1
b^0
a^0

23.

f♯³	d♯³
e³	c³
d³	a♯²
c♯³	g♯²
b²	f²
a²	d♯²
g²	c²
f♯²	a♯¹
e²	g♯¹
d²	g¹
c♯²	f♯¹
b¹	e¹
a¹	d¹

f¹
d♯¹
c¹
a♯⁰
g♯⁰
c♯¹
b⁰
a⁰
g⁰
f♯⁰
e⁰
d⁰
c⁰

f⁰
d♯⁰
c♯⁰
B⁰

24.

c³	f²
b²	e²
a²	d²
g²	c²
f+²	b-¹
e²	a¹
d²	g¹
c²	f¹

g¹
f¹
e¹
d¹
c¹
b⁰
a⁰
g⁰

25.

a♭²	d♭²
g²	c²
f²	b♭¹
e♭²	a♭¹
d♭²	g♭¹
c²	f¹
b♭¹	e♭¹

d♭¹
c¹
b♭⁰
a♭⁰
g♭⁰
f⁰
e♭⁰

26.

-0-	-0-
-0-	-0-
-0-	-0-
-0-	-0-
e♭²	a♭¹
d²	g¹
c²	f¹
b♭¹	e♭¹

-0-
-0-
-0-
-0-
-0-
d¹
c¹
b♭⁰
-0-

27.

$d\flat^2$	$g\flat^1$	
c	f^1	$g\flat^0$
$b\flat^1$	$e\flat^1$	f^0
$a\flat^1$	$d\flat^1$	$e\flat^0$
g^1	c^1	$d\flat^0$
f^1	$b\flat^0$	c^0
$e\flat^1$	$a\flat^0$	$B\flat^0$
		$A\flat^0$

28.

$d\sharp^3$	e^3	$g/g\sharp^3$					
$c\sharp^3$	d^3	$f/f\sharp^3$					
	c^3	$g\sharp^2$	c^2	f^1	c^1		
	b^2	f^2	$a\sharp^1$	$d\sharp^1$	$a\sharp^0$		
	a^2	$d\sharp^2$	$g\sharp^1$	$c\sharp^1$	$g\sharp^0$		
	g^2	$c\sharp^2$	$f\sharp^1$	b^0	$f\sharp^0$		
	f^2	b^1	e^1	a^0	e^0		
	e^2	a^1	d^1	g^0	d^0		
	d^2	g^1	c^1	f^0	c^0		
	c^2	f^1	$b\flat^0$	$e\flat^0$	B^0		
	$b\flat^1$	$e\flat^1$	$a\flat^0$	$d\flat^0$	A^0		
	$a\flat^1$	$d\flat^1$			G^0		

29.

c	f	
$b\flat$	$e\flat$	$g\sharp$
a	d	$b\flat$
g	c	$g\sharp$
$f\sharp$	b	f
e	a	e
d	g	$c\sharp$
$c\sharp$	$f\sharp$	c
b	e	b
a	d	a
$\mid d$		g

30.

g^3	c^3	
$f\sharp^3$	b^2	b^1
e^3	a^2	a^1
d^3	g^2	g^1
c^3	f^2	f^1
b^2	e^2	e^1
a^2	d^2	d^1
g^2	c^2	c^1
$f\sharp^2$	b^1	b^0
e^2	a^1	a^0
d^2	g^1	g^0

31.

e^3	$c\sharp^3$	
$d\sharp^3$	$a\sharp^2$	$a\sharp^1$
d^3	$g\sharp^2$	$g\sharp^1$
c^3	f^2	f^1
b^2	$d\sharp^2$	$f\sharp^1$
a^2	$c\sharp^2$	e^1
g^2	c^2	d^1
$f\sharp^2$	b^1	c^1
e^2	a^1	b^0
d^2	g^1	a^0
		g^0

32.

f^3	$b\flat^2$	
e^3	a^2	$b\flat^1$
d^3	g^2	g^1
c^3	f^2	f^1
b^2	e^2	e^1
a^2	d^2	d^1
g^2	c^2	c^1
$f\sharp^2$	b^1	b^0
e^2	a^1	a^0
d^2	g^1	g^0
$c\sharp^2$	$f\sharp^1$	f^0
b^1	e^1	e^0
a^1	d^1	d^0
$g\sharp^1$	$c\sharp^1$	A^0

33.

f^2	$b\flat^1$	
g^2	c^2	d^1
$f\sharp^2$	b^1	c^1
e^2	a^1	b^0
d^2	g^1	a^0
$c\sharp^2$	$f\sharp^1$	g^0
b^1	e^1	$f\sharp^0$
a^1	d^1	e^0
$g\sharp^1$	$c\sharp^1$	d^0

34.

c^3	f^2	$c\sharp^2$
b^2	e^2	b^1
a^2	d^2	a^1
g^2	c^2	g^1
$f\sharp^2$	b^1	$f\sharp^1$
e^2	a^1	e^1
		d^1

35.

b^2	b^1	
a^2	a^1	b^0
g^2	g^1	a^0
f^2	f^1	g^0
e^2	e^1	f^0
d^2	d^1	e^0
c^2	c^1	d^0
		c^0

36.

c^3	$[f]^2$	
b^2	$[e]^2$	$a^1]$
a^2	$[d]^2$	$[g^1]$
g^2	$[c]^2$	$[f^1]$
$f[\sharp]^2$	$[b]^1$	$[e^1]$
e^2	$[a]^1$	$[d^1]$
d^2	g^1	c^1
$c[\sharp]^2$	$f[\sharp]^1$	b^0
b^1	e^1	a^0
a^1	d^1	g^0

37.

b^2	e^2
a^2	d^2
g^2	c^2
$f\sharp^2$	b^1
e^2	a^1
d^2	g^1
$c\sharp^2$	$f\sharp^1$
b^1	e^1
a^1	d^1

38.

c^3	f^2	
b^2	e^2	
a^2	d^2	
g^2	c^2	
$f\sharp^2$	b^1	c^1
e^2	a^1	b^0
d^2	g^1	a^0
$c\sharp^2$	$f\sharp^1$	g^0
b^1	e^1	$f\sharp^0$
a^1	d^1	e^0
$g\sharp^1$	$c\sharp^1$	d^0

39.

d^3	g^2	
c^3	f^2	
b^2	e^2	
a^2	d^2	
g^2	c^2	
$f\sharp^2$	b^1	
e^2	a^1	
d^2	g^1	
$c\sharp^2$	$f\sharp^1$	$[g^0/c^1]\,|$
b^1	e^1	
a^1	d^1	$[e^0/g^0]\,|$
$g\sharp^1$	$c\sharp^1$	$[d^0]\,|$

40.

c^3	$[f^2]$	
b^2	$[e^2]$	
a^2	$[d^2]$	
g^2	$[c^2]$	
$f\sharp^2$	b^1	
e^2	a^1	b^0
d^2	g^1	a^0
$[c\sharp^2]$	$f\sharp^1$	g^0
$[b^1]$	e^1	$f\sharp^0$
$[a^1]$	d^1	e^0
$[g\sharp^1]$	$c\sharp^1$	d^0

41.

d^3	g^2	g^1
c^3	f^2	f^1
b^2	e^2	e^1
a^2	d^2	d^1
g^2	c^2	c^1
$f\sharp^2$	b^1	b^0
e^2	a^1	a^0
d^2	g^1	g^0
$c\sharp^2$	$f\sharp^1$	$f\sharp^0$
b^1	e^1	e^0
a^1	d^1	d^0
$g\sharp^1$	$c\sharp^1$	

42.

	g^2	c^2
d^1	$f\sharp^2$	b^1
b^0	e^2	a^1
a^0	d^2	g^1
g^0	$c\sharp^2$	$f\sharp^1$
$f\sharp^0$	b^1	e^1
e^0	a^1	d^1
d^0	$g\sharp^1$	$c\sharp^1$
c^0	$f\sharp^1$	b^0
B^0	e^1	a^0
A^0	d^1	g^0
G^0		

43.

e^3	c^3	$a\sharp^2$
d^3	$a\sharp^2$	e^2
c^3	$g\sharp^2$	$d\sharp^2$
b^2	f^2	$a\sharp^1$
a^2	$d\sharp^2$	$g\sharp^1$
g^2	c^2	c^1
$f\sharp^2$	b^1	b^0
e^2	a^1	a^0
d^2	g^1	g^0
$c\sharp^2$	$f\sharp^1$	$f\sharp^0$
b^1	e^1	e^0
a^1	d^1	d^0
$g\sharp^1$	$c\sharp^1$	

c³	f²	
b²	e²	
a²	d²	
g²	c²	
f♯²	b¹	c¹
e²	a¹	b⁰
d²	g¹	a⁰
c♯²	f♯¹	g⁰
b¹	e¹	f♯⁰
a¹	d¹	e⁰
g¹	c¹	d⁰
f♯¹	b⁰	G⁰

44.

d³	g²	
c³	f²	
b²	e²	
a²	d²	
g²	c²	c¹
f♯²	b¹	b⁰
		d¹
e²	a¹	a⁰
d²	g¹	g⁰
c♯²	f♯¹	f♯⁰
b¹	e¹	e⁰
a¹	d¹	d⁰
g♯¹	c♯¹	

45.

e³	g²	
c♯³	e²	
b²	d²	
g²	b¹	e¹
e²	a¹	d¹
d²	g¹	a⁰
b¹	e¹	g⁰
a¹	d¹	-0-
g¹	c¹	-0-
e¹	a⁰	-0-

46.

f³	b♭²	
e³	a²	
d³	g²	
c³	f²	
		f¹
b²	e²	
e²	d²	
d²	c²	
		c¹
f♯²	b¹	
e²	a¹	
d²	g¹	
		g⁰
c♯²	f♯¹	

47.

e²	b¹
d²	a¹
c²	g¹
a¹	e¹
g¹	d¹
f¹	c¹
e¹	b⁰
d¹	a⁰
c¹	g⁰

48.

a²	d²
g²	c²
f♯²	b¹
e²	a♯¹
d²	g♯¹
c♯²	f♯¹
b¹	e¹
a¹	d¹
g¹	c♯¹
f♯¹	b⁰
e¹	a⁰
d¹	g⁰
c¹	f⁰
a⁰/b⁰	d⁰/e⁰

49.

50.

d³	g²	
c³	f²	c²
b²	e²	b♭¹
a²	d²	a¹
g²	c²	g¹
f♯²	b¹	f¹
e²	a¹	e¹
d²	g¹	d¹
c♯²	f♯¹	c¹
b¹	e¹	b⁰
a¹	d¹	a⁰
g♯¹	c♯¹	g⁰

51.

d³	g²	
c♯³	f♯²	
b²	e²	
a²	d²	
g²	c²	
f♯²	b¹	
e²	a¹	d¹
d²	g¹	c♯¹
c♯²	f♯¹	b⁰
b¹	e¹	a⁰
a¹	d¹	g⁰
g♯¹	c♯¹	f♯⁰

52.

	b
b[♭]	a
a[♭]	g
f[♮]	f
	e
e[♭]	d
c[♯]	c
	b
b[♭]	a
a[♭]	g
f[♮]	f
	e
e[♭]	d
c[♯]	c
	b
b[♭]	a
a[♭]	g

53.

a	g♯	
g	f♯	b
f	e	[a♯]
d♯	d	[a]
c♯	c	[g♯]
b	a♯	[g]
a	g♯	[f♯]
g	f♯	[f]
f	e	[e]
d♯	d	[d♯]
c♯	c	[d]

54.

d♯	d
c♯	c
b♭	b
g♯	a
f	g
e♭	f♯
c♯	e
b	d
a	c
g	b♭
f♯	g♯
e	f
d	e♭
c	c♯

Sources

Hackbrett

1. Holland. Source: Joos Verschuure Reynvaan, *Muzijkaal Kunstwoordenboek* (Amsterdam: W. Brave, 1795), 356.

2. Switzerland: Appenzell. Source: adaptation for an instrument made by Hans (John) Kegel in 1906 from tuning used by Johann Fuchs, Appenzell.

3. Switzerland: Wallis. Source: Amadé Salzmann, *Das Hackbrett im Wallis* (Visp: Rotten-Verlag, 198-), 66. Asterisks indicate the presence of jacks which can raise the pitch by a semitone.

4. Austria: East Tyrol. Source: Florian Pedernig, "Das Hackbrett im Osttirol," in *Beiträge zur Volksmusik in Tirol*, ed. Walter Deutsch and Manfred Schneider (Innsbruck, 1978), 174.

5. Austria: Styria. Source: Walter Kainz, *Hackbrett-Fibel: eine Anleitung zum Schlagen des steirischen Hackbrettes*, 2nd ed. (Graz: Verlag der Arbeitsgemeinschaft für Volksmusikpflege in Steiermark, 1954), 3.

6. Volga German. Source: an instrument owned by the widow of Henry Maser, of Au Gres, Michigan, 1976.

7. Germany: "Salzburg" Hackbrett. Source: Karl-Heinz Schickhaus, *Hackbrett-Fibel: Eine Unterweisung für das Spiel auf dem chromatischen Salzburger Hackbrett* (Munich: Musikverlag Josef Preissler, 1963), 7.

Santur

8. Iran. Source: Faramarz Payvar, *Dastur santur: Talif ve tasnif* (Tehran, 1346 = 1967), 37. The struck-through flat symbol represents a tone less than one semitone. This tuning would be for the dastgah *bayat turk*.

Cimbalom family

9. Austria: Upper Austria. Source: Othmar Wessely, *Die Musikinstrumenten-Sammlung des oberösterreichischen Landesmusems* (Linz, 1952), n.p.

10. Czech Republic: Moravia. Source: Ludvik Kunz, *Die Volksmusikinstrumente der Tschechoslowakei*, Handbuch der europäischen Volksmusikinstrumenten, series 1, vol. 2 (Leipzig: VEB Deutscher Verlag für Musik, 1974), 63.

11. Hungary. Above the dotted line is the range of the three-quarter-size portable cimbalom of the late nineteenth century; the range below the line is for the full-size instrument manufactured by Lajos Bohak from the 1920s to the 1950s. The lowest tone on instruments by Schunda and his contemporaries was D^{0}, while the range of later Bohak instruments was increased to a^{3} and, on some instruments, down to A^{1}. For the "Jewish" tuning (so called because of its "reversed" tuning), in use around Szeged, see Balint Sarosi, *Die Volksmusikinstrumente Ungarns* (Leipzig: VEB Deutscher Verlag für Musik, 1967), 43.

12. Poland: Rzeszowskie. Source: William Henry Noll, "Peasant Music Ensembles in Poland: A Culture History" (Ph.D. diss., University of Washington, 1986), 207. Noll gives three other tunings he collected as well.

13. Belarus. Tuning used by Semyon Lepyansky, of Vitebsk, and sons. Source: N. F. Findeizen, "Evreiskie tsimbaly i tsimbalisty Lepianskie," *Muzykal'naia etnografie*, 1926, 40. An example of a tuning used by a Jewish player.

14. Belarus: Borisov district. Source: I. D. Nazina, *Belorusskie narodnye muzykal'nye instrumenty: strunnye* (Minsk: Nauka i Tekhnika, 1982), 32. This was collected by Yosif Zhinovich and is illustrated to show a tuning on a *tsimbaly* with a small number of courses.

15. Belarus. Standard tuning for the model developed by Sushkevich in the 1930s and manufactured by the Belarusian Industrial Amalgamation of Musical Instruments in Minsk.

16. Ukrainian-Canadian. Source: Mark Jaroslav Bandera, *The Tsymbaly Maker and His Craft: The Ukrainian Hammered Dulcimer in Alberta*, Canadian Studies in Ukrainian Ethnology, vol. 1 (Edmonton: Canadian Institute of Ukrainian Studies Press, 1991), 46-47. Bandera says that this tuning, variously called "Gypsy," "Bukovinan," "Romanian," or "Wallachian," is the most common in western Canada. Some use variations of it.

17. Ukraine. Tuning for the model produced in the Chernihiv Musical Instruments Factory.

18. Romania. Source: Tiberiu Alexandru, *Instrumentele muzicale ale poporului romîn* (Bucharest: Editura de Stat pentru Literatură i Artă, 1956), 103.

19. Greece. Source: Dimitris V. Kofteros, *Dhokimio yia to elliniko santouri* (Athens: Ekdhoseis "Dhodhoni," 1991), 96.

20. Turkey: *santur fransiz*. Source: Raouf Yekta Bey, "La musique turque," in *Encyclopédie de la musique*, ed. Albert Lavignac (Paris: Librairie Delagrave, 1922), 3: 3021.

Salterio

21. Italy. Source: "Regola pratica del saltero," Civico Museo Bibliografico Musicale, Bologna. An eighteenth-century manuscript.

22. Brazil. Source: Antonio Vieira dos Santos, *Cifra de musica para salterio*, ed. Rogério Budasz (Curitiba, 1996), n.p. This dates from the early nineteenth century.

23. Mexico: *salterio tenor*. Source: Jorge Alberto Jara. The *salterio requinto* is tuned an octave higher.

Yangqin family

24. China: Guangzhou (Canton). Source: Josephine Ng, "The Chinese Dulcimer: Yang Ch'in" (master's thesis, University of Washington, 1978), 73-75.

25. Korea. Source: *Survey of Korean Arts: Traditional Music* (Seoul: National Academy of Arts, 1973), 37.

26. Tibet. Source: Geoffrey Samuel, "Songs of Lhasa," *Ethnomusicology* 20 (Sept. 1976): 416.

27. Uzbekistan. Source: Viktor Beliaev, *Muzykal'nye instrumenty Uzbekistana* (Moscow: Muzgiz, 1933), n.p. In his *Ocherki po istorii muzyki narodov*

SSSR, vol. 1, *Muzykal'naya kul'tura Kirgizii, Kazakhstana, Turkmenii, Tadzhikistana i Uzbekistana* (Moscow: Gosudarstvennoe Muzykal'noe Izdatel'stvo, 1962), 192, Beliaev gives the tuning of the *chang* a semitone lower than in his earlier book.

28. China. For the large model manufactured today. Source: Lee Yuan-yuan, "Yangqin," *Chinese Music* 4, no. 1: 10.

Dulcimer

29. England. Seventeenth century. Source: a handwritten chart in John Playford, *Select Musicall Ayres* (1653), Ewing Music Collection, Glasgow University Library, in David Kettlewell, "The Dulcimer" (Ph.D. diss., Loughborough University, 1976), 184a-184b.

30. England: East Anglia. Source: "Diagram and Scale of the Dulcimer, with 32 Notes" (London: for Ihlee & Sankey, 1885).

31. England: East Anglia. Source: Paul N. Hasluck, ed., *Violins and Other Stringed Instruments: How to Make Them*, Cassell Work Handbook Series (London: Cassell, 1906; Philadelphia: David McKay, 1907, 1912, 1914), 157.

32. England: Birmingham. Source: Kettlewell, "The Dulcimer," 240b. Bill Fell.

33. Scotland. Source: John McCutcheon, "Jimmy Cooper: Dulcimer Player: A Review and Musings," *Dulcimer Players News* 4, no. 3 (summer 1978): 17. Jimmy Cooper.

34. Ireland: Ulster. Source: Kettlewell, "The Dulcimer," 275b. John Leach.

35. United States: Ohio?. Source: Dulcimer from Darrtown, Ohio, c.1815, in the Metropolitan Museum of Art, New York City. Examined in 1975; the tuning was written on the upper part of each individual bridge.

36. United States: New York. Source: Dulcimer made by P. Cogswell, probably Bath, New York, 1830. Ontario County Historical Society, Canandaigua, New York, acc. no. 1979.369x.

37. United States: West Virginia. Source: Loy Swiger, Massillon, Ohio. This is probably the standard tuning meant for nine-course dulcimers.

38. United States: western New York, 1850s. This is the tuning meant for the dulcimers made in the factories in Chautauqua County, New York, and others with the same configuration. Source: C. Haight, *A Complete System for the Dulcimer* (New York: William Hall & Son, 1848), 5.

39. United States: Ohio and elsewhere. Presumed tuning for dulcimers with this configuration. As the original bass strings were sometimes brass, they would probably be tuned an octave below the neighboring treble course, but this is uncertain.

40. United States: Virginia. Tuning for a dulcimer from the Shenandoah Valley, c.1850. Shaped notes painted on soundboard. Source: Mercer Museum, Bucks County Historical Society, Doylestown, Pennsylvania.

41. United States: Michigan, New York, and elsewhere. Tuning for nineteenth-century dulcimers with this configuration; stenciled notes appear on many

dulcimers of this variety, such as those made by Mortimer DeLano, Oxford, Michigan, in the 1860s.

42. United States: Michigan-Connecticut. Dulcimer manufactured by Ezra Durand and William Vogel, c.1864-1869, in Niles, Michigan, Chelsea, Michigan, and Stonington, Connecticut. Source: E. Durand, *Dulcimer without a Master* (Boston: Oliver Ditson & Co., 1867), 20.

43. United States: "Perfection" dulcimer manufactured by Lyon & Healy, Chicago, Illinois, c.1895-c.1905. Source: Henry Ford Museum.

44. United States: Michigan. Source: Fenton Watkins, Birmingham, Michigan; dulcimer made about 1949 by Ed Johnson, Kalamazoo, Michigan.

45. United States: New York. Source: Paul Van Arsdale, North Tonawanda, New York; dulcimer made by Jesse Martin, Frewsburg, New York.

46. United States: Tennessee. Source: J. R. Cantrell, McMinnville, Tennessee.

47. United States: North Carolina. Virgil Craven, Cedar Falls, North Carolina. Source: Edward Babel Collection, Southern Folklife Collection, University Archives, University of North Carolina at Chapel Hill.

48. United States: West Virginia. Source: Russell Fluharty, Mannington, West Virginia.

49. United States: West Virginia. Source: Worley Gardner, Morgantown, West Virginia.

50. United States. Source: Sam Rizzetta, "Hammer Dulcimer: History and Playing," Leaflet 72-4, Smithsonian Institution.

51. Canada. Source: Ted DeLorme, North Bay, Ontario; dulcimer made by Jean Tremblay, c.1920.

52. United States. Dulcimer patented by Jesse Merrill, of Kanopolis, Kansas, 11 May 1897, no. 582,537.

53. United States. Dulcimer patented by John Low, of Clinton, Massachusetts, 19 June 1860, no. 28,811. Source: patent model, Smithsonian Institution, cat. no. 331,204.

54. United States. Dulcimers manufactured by Anton Stonitsch (under name "Jos. F. Stroehlein") and A. L. Henn, Brooklyn, New York, c.1900-1905.

Michigan Dulcimer Players Identified in 1910 Census

me	age	bp	fbp	mbp	occupation	type	county	township/city
lams, Harry	40	US	US	US	stonemsn.	—	Ionia	Portland
nick, William	47	WI	PA	NY	farmer	carpenter	Mecosta	Austin
nidon, Henry E.	42	MI	NY	VT	farmer	gen. farm	Shiawassee	Hazelton
derson, Charles	25	MI	MI	IN	—	—	Muskegon	Ravenna
derson, Glen	14	MI	MI	IN	—	—	Muskegon	Ravenna
derson, Rinaldo	53	MI	OH	PA	farmer	gen. farm	Muskegon	Ravenna
derson, Wesley	28	MI	MI	IN	barber	o. shop	Muskegon	Ravenna
drews, William	29	MI	MI	MI	farm labor	gen. farm	Gratiot	New Haven
acon, Cassius P.	53	OH	OH	OH	farmer	gen. farm	Monroe	Milan
iliff, Edmund	41	MI	OH	OH	farmer	own farm	Allegan	Clyde
ker, Daniel	37	MI	US	OH	farmer	own farm	Gratiot	Lafayette
rker, Nihil	30	MI	MI	VT	machinist	motor fy.	Muskegon	Muskegon
rlow, William	39	MI	MI	CA	farmer	hm. farm	Ottawa	Robinson
rnes, Alton	29	MI	MI	MI	farmer	gen. farm	Clinton	Westphalia
rnes, Archie	31	MI	NY	OH	farmer	gen. farm	Ingham	Alaiedon
rnes, William C.	27	MI	MI	MI	laborer	gen. farm	Ionia	Portland
tchelder, Perley	32	IL	NH	NH	farm lab.	hm. farm	Wexford	Colfax

y: bp = birthplace; fbp = father's birthplace; mbp = mother's birthplace; Alb. = Albert; Aug. = gustus; Chas. = Charles; Thos. = Thomas; CA = Canada; EN = England; GR = Germany; HL = olland; IR = Ireland; NR = Norway; carp. = carpenter; cmt. plt. = cement plant; com. = mmon; cy. = country; dry. = dairy; fy. = factory; gen. = general; h. & s. = house and sign; hm. home; lab. = laborer; msn. = mason; mtrwks. = motor works; o. shop = own shop; patternmkr. patternmaker; pr. = practice; sltr. ho. = slaughterhouse; stonemsn. = stonemason; syr. = wyer; tr. = thresher; wh. = warehouse; w.o. = works out.

Batey, Gordon O.	36 MI MI NY	farmer	gen. farm	Allegan	Ganges
Baxter, Edward	29 MI MI NY	laborer	syr. mill	Alpena	Maple Ridge
Baxter, James	52 MI CA CA	farmer	gen. farm	Cheboygan	Forest
Belgraph, Frank	23 IN GR GR	farmer	gen. farm	Allegan	Monterey
Bennett, Edson	24 MI OH EN	farmer	gen. farm	Montcalm	Bushnell
Bentley, Andrew	53 NY NY EN	farmer	gen. farm	Osceola	Highland
Berghorst, John	30 MI HL HL	farmer	gen. farm	Kent	Solon
Borst, William	32 MI MI IN	laborer	railroad	Manistee	Cleon
Brooks, Artie W.	26 MI EN MI	laborer	farm	Midland	Mount Hale
Brown, Ernest M.	19 MI OH MI	none	—	Arenac	Mason
Brown, John	58 MI NY US	farmer	gen. farm	Antrim	Torch Lake
Brown, Lewis H.	35 MI MI PA	farmer	gen. farm	Charlevoix	Eveline
Brown, Murray	65 OH NY MA	farmer	gen. farm	Arenac	Mason
Burdick, Mary M.	36 MI NR MI	—	—	Oceana	Hart
Carpenter, Byron	43 MI NY NY	farmer	gen. farm	Allegan	Watson
Chaddock, Edward	33 MI NY MI	farm lab.	w.o.	Van Buren	Geneva
Clark, Edson J.	46 MI NY MI	carpenter	house	Branch	Coldwater
Coon, Bert	28 MI MI MI	laborer	farm	Saginaw	St. Charles
Crump, Martin E.	34 MI CA MI	farmer	gen. farm	Emmet	Littlefield
Daniels, John N.	41 MI NY PA	laborer	farm	Allegan	Hopkins
Davis, John A.	24 MI MI MI	painter	h. & s.	Newaygo	Fremont
Dickerson, Oria	21 MI MI MI	farm lab.	on farm	Newaygo	Ensley
Doherty, Albert B.	48 MI IR MA	farmer	dry. farm	Kalkaska	Springfield
Dunshee, Fred E.	39 MI MI NY	—	—	Kent	Grand Rapids
Echoff, Louis	27 MI GR GR	laborer	on farm	Ottawa	Crockery
Eggleston, Allen	26 MI MI MI	farmer	gen. farm	Montcalm	Ferris
Evilsizer, Otis A.	31 OH OH OH	farmer	gen. farm	Ogemaw	Horton
Fletcher, Hiel J.	55 MI CA CA	carpenter	home	Kent	Grandville
Frost, Ben	40 MI PA PA	butcher	sltr. ho.	Oceana	Ferry
Gifford, Otto	23 MI MI MI	laborer	odd jobs	Newaygo	Brooks
Gilbert, Robert M.	39 MI OH OH	farmer	farm	Emmet	Maple River
Golden, Edward	48 PA IR IR	farmer	gen. farm	Muskegon	Ravenna
Gunn, Daniel K.	38 MI MI EN	mason	stnmsn.	Ottawa	Allendale
Hathaway, Sam. J.	33 NY NY NY	farmer	gen. farm	Benzie	Inland
Herald, John	29 MI NY MI	baker	o. shop	Muskegon	Muskegon
Hober, Albert P.	41 MI GR GR	farmer	gen. farm	Muskegon	Ravenna
Hogan, William	28 MI MI MI	salesman	hardware	Ionia	Hubbardston
Holbrook, Walter	35 MI NY GR	farmer	gen. farm	Eaton	Brookfield
Huntington, C.B.	52 VT NY VT	farmer	gen. farm	Saginaw	Brady

es, Albert	55	NY	NY	NY	farmer	gen. farm	Muskegon	Casnovia
ck, Robert	38	NY	CA	CA	laborer	mill yard	Clare	Redding
hnston, Thos. A.	57	OH	PA	PA	laborer	corset fy.	Barry	Hastings
rdan, Henry	38	MI	IR	CA	farmer	gen. farm	Shiawassee	Perry
rdan, William	49	MI	NY	NY	laborer	auto fy.	Ingham	Lansing
eene, James B.	53	MI	MI	MI	mor. msn.	plastering	Allegan	Cheshire
eirnan, Harry	27	MI	MI	MI	farmer	gen. farm	Allegan	Ganges
eirnan,Thomas W	30	MI	MI	MI	farmer	gen. farm	Allegan	Ganges
emerling,Freeman	29	MI	US	US	farmer	gen. farm	Barry	Johnstown
emerling, John H.	53	IL	OH	OH	mail carrier	RFD	Barry	Baltimore
napp, Claud D.	32	MI	MI	US	farmer	gen. farm	Gratiot	Emerson
anning, Otto	22	IN	IN	IN	farmer	gen. farm	Missaukee	Bloomfield
ghthill, John	38	IN	IN	IN	farm lab.	w.o.	Gratiot	New Haven
ttle, Ed	57	OH	OH	OH	laborer	odd jobs	Gd. Trav.	Traverse City
aybee,Milton W.	63	MI	CA	NY	farmer	gen. farm	Van Buren	Geneva
cCain, Frank	31	MI	PA	PA	farmer	gen. farm	Osceola	Sylvan
cCleary, Martha	35	IN	PA	IN	none	—	Wexford	Wexford
cDonald, James	70	PA	PA	PA	physician	own pr.	Lenawee	Clayton
udge, Jay B.	34	CA	CA	CA	farmer	seed wh.	Charlevoix	East Jordan
ulford, Arthur J.	33	MI	NY	OH	laborer	farm	Gratiot	Sumner
elson, Jessie	22	MI	CA	CA	none	—	Ionia	Ionia
lson, Holly	26	MI	NR	MI	inspector	mtrwks.	Muskegon	Muskegon
sborn, James	55	CA	NY	CA	farmer	gen. farm	Emmet	Readmond
addock, Archie S.	38	MI	NY	MI	farmer	gen. farm	Van Buren	Geneva
arker, Chester	18	MI	NY	NY	none	—	Kent	Algoma
armelee, Fred L.	37	MI	NY	MI	farmer	gen. farm	Osceola	Middle Br.
ase, Coit D.	35	OH	OH	OH	farmer	gen. farm	Allegan	Hopkins
uick, Jullie Anna	64	ME	NH	ME	—	—	Tuscola	Novesta
alya, Leonard	37	MI	PA	NY	farmer	hm. farm	Ottawa	Robinson
eames, Peter	21	MI	MI	MI	laborer	farm	Oceana	Shelby
ender, Curtis O.	36	OH	EN	OH	farmer	gen. farm	Midland	Geneva
ollenhagen, Aug.	32	MI	GR	GR	carp.,msn.	—	Muskegon	Ravenna
ouse, John S.	27	MI	CA	MI	farmer	gen. farm	Midland	Lee
eba, Peter C.	26	MI	GR	GR	farmer	gen. farm	Muskegon	Ravenna
erman,Carlton L.	44	MI	NY	NY	thresher	grain tr.	Ingham	Meridian
ores, Fannie N.	44	MI	EN	MI	—	—	Osceola	Evart
houp, Dan F.	68	OH	OH	OH	patternmkr.	cmt. plt.	Lake	Marlborough
nclair, Eugene	37	MI	NY	MI	farmer	gen. farm	Montcalm	Bushnell
oan, Charles	50	MI	VT	NY	farmer	gen. farm	Clinton	DeWitt

Smith, Albert A.	34	OH	OH	OH	com. lab.	—	Kalamazoo	Kalamazoo
Smith, Byron	40	MI	EN	NY	farmer	gen. farm	Livingston	Handy
Smith, Casper V.	32	MI	NY	NY	farmer	gen. farm	Montcalm	Bushnell
Spicer, Frank	22	MI	MI	MI	farm lab.	farm	Clinton	Eagle
Stoner, Dillas	38	MI	PA	NY	farmer	gen. farm	Livingston	Cohoctah
Sturgis, John	32	MI	MI	MI	farmer	gen. farm	Genesee	Argentine
Sturgis, Lewis	50	MI	MI	MI	farmer	gen. farm	Genesee	Argentine
Thayer, Arthur T.	35	MA	MA	MA	farmer	gen. farm	Midland	Ingersoll
Throop, Al	47	MI	NY	NY	laborer	teamster	Shiawassee	Laingsburg
Tilley, Francis A.	60	OH	MD	MD	farmer	gen. farm	Allegan	Martin
Toms, Welcom	39	MI	MI	MI	farmer	gen. farm	Wexford	Greenwood
Torry, Cora	45	MI	PA	NY	—	—	Allegan	Allegan
Towe, Edna G.	19	MI	OH	MI	none	—	Eaton	Chester
Walker, Lewis H.	42	PA	NY	PA	farmer	gen. farm	Osceola	Richmond
Weeks, Burrell B.	19	MI	NY	OH	laborer	hm. farm	Mecosta	Aetna
Weeks, George O.	22	MI	NY	OH	laborer	farm	Mecosta	Aetna
Weeks, James B.	32	MI	NY	OH	blacksmith	cy. shop	Mecosta	Aetna
Weeks, John S.	66	NY	NY	NY	farmer	gen. farm	Mecosta	Aetna
White, Fred	49	MI	NY	NY	farm lab.	w.o.	Ottawa	Polkton
Wilbur, Edmund S.	78	NY	MA	MA	farmer	gen. farm	Jackson	Rives
Wilbur, Homer E.	31	MI	NY	OH	farmer	gen. farm	Jackson	Rives
Wirth, Arthur A.	28	MI	MI	GR	farmer	gen. farm	Clinton	Riley
Wise, Samuel	46	MI	—	—	farmer	gen. farm	Calhoun	Clarence
Woodmansee, Alb.	34	MI	US	US	mason	stone	Barry	Baltimore
Worden, Charles	37	MI	MI	EN	laborer	farm	Oceana	Shelby

Select Bibliography

Origins and Beginnings

Books

Bernard, Nelly van Ree. *The Psaltery: An Annotated Audio-Visual Review of Different Types of Psaltery*. Buren: Frits Knuf, 1989.

Denis, Valentin. *De Muziekinstrumenten in de Nederlanden en in Italie naar hun Afbeelding in de 15eeuwsche Kunst: Hun vorm en Ontwikkeling*. Antwerp: Uit gever smij N. v. Standard-boekhandel, 1944.

Galpin, Francis W. *Old English Instruments of Music: Their History and Character*. 3rd ed., rev. London: Methuen, 1932.

Kuret, Primož. *Glasbeni instrumenti na srednjeveških freskah na Slovenskem*. Ljubljana: Slovenska Matica Ljubljana, 1973.

Le Cerf, G., with E.-R. Labande, eds. *Instruments de musique du XVe siècle: les traités d'Henri Arnaut de Zwolle et divers anonymes*. Paris: Editions Auguste Picard, 1932.

Marcuse, Sybil. *A Survey of Musical Instruments*. New York: Harper & Row, 1975.

Mersenne, Marin. *Harmonie Universelle: the Books on Instruments*. Translated by Roger E. Chapman. The Hague: M. Nijhoff, 1957.

Sendrey, Alfred. *Musik in Alt-Israel*. Leipzig: Deutscher Verlag für Musik, [1970].

Stauder, Wilhelm. *Alte Musikinstrumente in ihrer vieltausendjährigen Entwicklung und Geschichte*. Braunschweig: Klinkhardt & Biermann, 1973.

Articles

Dick, Friedrich. "Bezeichnungen für Saiten- und Schlaginstrumente in der altfranzösischen Literatur." *Giessener Beiträge zur romanischen Philologie* 25 (1932): 98-105.

Farmer, Henry George. "The Canon and Eschaquiel of the Arabs." *Journal of the Royal Asiatic Society* (1926): 239-256.

Heyde, Herbert. "Frühgeschichte des europäischen Hackbretts (14.-16. Jahrhundert)." *Deutsches Jahrbuch für Musikwissenschaft* 18 (1973-1977): 135-172.

Howell, Standley. "Paulus Paulirinus on Musical Instruments." *Journal of the American Musical Instrument Society* 5-6 (1979-1980): 9-36.

LaPointe, Claude. "A Case Study in Iconographic Research." *RIdIM/RCMI Newsletter* 4, no. 1 (Jan. 1979): 3-12.

Leach, John. "The Dulcimer." *The Consort* 25 (1968-1969): 390-395

———. "Psalteries (Plucked and Struck)." *The Consort* 39 (1983): 507-514.

———. "The Psaltery and Dulcimer." *The Consort* 34 (1978): 293-301.

Santur

Books

Caron, Nelly, and Dariouche Safvate. *Iran: collection de l'Institut International d'Etudes Comparatives de la Musique publiée sous le patronage du Conseil international de la musique*, Les traditions musicales. [Paris]: Buchet/Chastel, 1966.

During, Jean. *La musique iranienne: tradition et évolution.* Institut Français d'Iranologie de Téhéran, Bibliothéque iranienne, no. 29. Paris: Editions Recherche sur les Civilisations, 1984.

Feldman, Walter. *Music of the Ottoman Court: Makam, Composition and the Early Ottoman Instrumental Repertoire.* Intercultural Music Studies, ed. Max Peter Baumann, vol. 10. Berlin: Verlag für Wissenschaft und Bildung, 1996.

Hassan, Scheherazade Qassim. *Les Instruments de musique en Irak et leur role dans la societé traditionnelle.* Cahiers de l'homme: ethnologie, geographie, linguistique, n.s., vol. 21. Paris: Mouton, 1975.

Khaliqi, Ruhallah. *Sar-guzasht-i musiqi-i-Iran*, vol. 1. (Tehran, 197-?).

Pacholczyk, Jozef M. *Sufyana Musiqi: the Classical Music of Kashmir.* Intercultural Music Studies, ed. Max Peter Baumann. Berlin: Verlag für Wissenschaft und Bildung, 1996.
Touma, Habib Hassan. *La musique arabe.* Paris: Editions Buchet/Chastel, 1977.
Zonis, Ella. *Classical Persian Music: An Introduction.* Cambridge: Harvard University Press, 1973.

Articles

Pacholczyk, Jozef. "The Status of Sufyana Kalam in Kashmir." *Asian Music* 12 (1979): 159-163.
———. "Sufyana Kalam, the Classical Music of Kashmir." *Asian Music* 10 (1978): 1-16.
Yekta Bey, Raouf. "La musique turque." In *Encyclopédie de la musique et Dictionnaire du Conservatoire*, edited by Albert Lavignac, 3: 3021-3022. Paris: Librairie Delagrave, 1922.

Hackbrett

Books

Bachmann-Geiser, Brigitte. *Die Volksmusikinstrumente der Schweiz.* Handbuch der europäischen Volksmusikinstrumente, ed. Ernst Emsheimer and Erich Stockmann. Leipzig: VEB Deutscher Verlag für Musik, 1981.
Boone, Hubert, and Wim Bosmans. *Volksinstrumenten in Belgie.* Louvain: Peeters, 1995.
Deutsch, Walter, and Harald Dengg, eds. *Die Volksmusik im Lande Salzburg*, 11. Seminar für Volksmusikforschung, 1975. Vienna: A. Schendl, 1979.
Engeler, Margaret. *Das Beziehungsfeld zwischen Volksmusik, Volksmusiker und Volksmusikpflege: am Beispiel der Appenzeller Streichmusik.* Herisau/Trogen: Verlag Schläpfer, 1984.
Halmbacher, Hans. *Sänger und Musikanten im bayerischen Oberland: aus Vergangenheit und Gegenwart der Landkreise Miesbach und Bad Tölz-Wolfratshausen.* Hausham: Fuchs-Druck, n.d.

Hartinger, Walter. *Volkstanz, Volksmusikanten und Volksmusikinstrumente der Oberpfalz zur Zeit Herders.* Quellen und Studien zur musikalischen Volkstradition in Bayern, ser. 4, Studien zur musikalischen Volkstradition, vol. 1. Regensburg: Gustav Bosse, 1980.

Hürlemann, Hans. *Brummbass, Geige, Hackbrett: 100 Jahre Appenzeller Streichmusik Alder.* Appenzeller Brauchtum, vol. 2. St. Gallen: VGS Verlagsgemeinschaft, 1984.

Kainz, Walter. *Hackbrett-Fibel: Eine Anleitung zum Schlagen des steirischen Hackbrettes.* 2nd ed. Graz: Verlag der Arbeitsgemeinschaft für Volksmusikpflege in Steiermark, 1954.

Klier, Karl M. *Volkstümliche Musikinstrumente in den Alpen.* Kassel: Bärenreiter Verlag, 1956.

Kumer, Zmaga. *Die Volksmusikinstrumente in Slowenien.* Handbuch der europäischen Volksmusikinstrumente, ser. 1, vol. 5. Ljubljana, 1986.

Meer, John Henry van der, Brigitte Geiser, and Karl-Heinz Schickhaus. *Das Hackbrett: ein alpenländisches Musikinstrument.* Herisau/ Trogen: Verlag Schläpfer, 1975.

Salzmann, Amadé. *Das Hackbrett im Wallis: Instrumentenbau und Spielanleitung.* [Brig]: Rotten-Verlag, 1989.

Schickhaus, Karl-Heinz. *Hackbrett-Fibel: eine Unterweisung für das Spiel auf dem chromatischen Salzburger Hackbrett.* Mit Beiträgen von Tobi Reiser, Wastl Fanderl und Georg v. Kaufmann. Munich: Josef Preissler, 1962.

———. *Über Volksmusik und Hackbrett in Bayern.* Munich: BLV Verlagsgesellschaft, 1981.

Warren, Mark, and Marilyn Hehr Fletcher. *Hochzeit: Dutch Hops: Colorado Music of the Germans from Russia, 1865-1965.* Evergreen, Colo.: Shadow Canyon Graphics, printer, 1990.

Articles

Birsak, Kurt. "Das Hackbrett," *Salzburger Heimatpflege* 4 (1980): 106-116.

Boone, Hubert. "Beknopte Bijdrage tot de Geschiedenis van het Hakkebord in de Lage Landen." *Volkskunde: Tijdschrift voor Nederlandsche Folklore* 77 (1976): 203-216.

Cherbuliez, Antoine E. "Quelques observations sur le 'psaltérion' (tympanon) populaire suisse 'Hackbrett'." *Journal of the International Folk Music Council* 12 (1960): 23-27.

Christen, Hanny. "Unser Hackbrett." *Volkshochschule* 25 (1956): 37-42.

Fletcher, Marilyn Mehr. "The Dutch Hop in Northern Colorado." *Viltis* 44 (May 1985): 16-19.

Gössmann, Ferdinand. "Das Hackbrett—Neubesinnung auf ein traditions-reiches Musikinstrument." In *Quaestiones in musica: Festschrift für Franz Krautwurst zum 65. Geburtstag*, edited by Friedhelm Brusniak and Horst Leuchtman, 159-165.Tutzing: Hans Schneider, 1989.

Gstrein, Rainer. "Tanzmusik-Ensembles in Österreich im 19. Jahrhundert: Ein Beitrag zur Frage der 'Authentizität' der Besetzungspraxis instrumentaler Volksmusik." In *Tanz und Tanzmusik in Überlieferung und Gegenwart: Bericht über die 12. Arbeitsgang der Kommission für Lied-, Musik- und Tanzforschung in der Deutschen Gesellschaft für Volkskunde e. V. vom 12. bis 16. September 1990 in der Otto-Friedrich-Universität Bamberg*, ed. Marianne Bröcker, 419-427. Schriften der Universitätsbibliothek Bamberg, vol. 9. Bamberg, 1992.

Hurdes, Franz. "Wesen und Bedeutung des Hackbrettes." *Heimatland: Monatschrift für Volksleben und Volkskunst in Österreich* (1934): 2-3.

In der Gand, Hanns. "Volkstümliche Musikinstrumente der Schweiz." *Schweizerisches Archiv für Volkskunde* 36 (1937): 92-94.

Omerzel-Terlep, Mira. "Cimbale - opsase ali orphica - na Goriškem in v Brdih." *Etnolog: Glasnik Slovenskega Etnografiskega Muzeja* 53, no. 1 (1992): 197-210.

———. "Das Hackbrett in Slowenien." *Sänger– und Musikantenzeitung* 34 (1991): 426–429.

———. "Oprekelj na slovenskem etničnem ozemlju." *Traditiones: zbornik Inštituta za Slovensko Narodopisje* 19 (1990): 177-210.

———. "Oprekelj na Slovenskem." *Muzikološki zbornik* 16 (1980): 93-107.

Pedarnig, Florian. "Das Hackbrett in Osttirol." In *Beiträge zur Volksmusik in Tirol*, edited by Walter Deutsch and Manfred Schneider, 171-174. Innsbruck: n.p., 1978.

Reiser, Tobi. "Wie das Hackbrett zu neuem Leben kam." *Sänger– und Musikantenzeitung* 2 (Jul.-Aug. 1959): 52-53.

Rosenzopf, Max. "Der Bau des steirischen Hackbrettes in Köflach 1970." *Instrumentenbau-Zeitschrift* 25 (1971): 148-149.

Sackett, S. J. "The Hammered Dulcimer in Ellis County, Kansas." *Journal of the International Folk Music Council* 14 (1962): 61-64.

Schneider, Max F. "Ein Kongress der Hackbrettler im Wallis." *Schweizer Volkskunde* 42 (1952): 55-59.

Cimbalom Family

Books

Alexandru, Tiberiu. *Instrumentele muzicale ale poporului romîn.* Bucharest: Editură de Stat pentru Literatură şi Artii, 1956.

Anoyanakis, Fivos. *Greek Popular Musical Instruments.* 2nd ed. Athens: n.p., 1991.

Baca, Cleo R. *Baca's Musical History.* LaGrange, Tex.: LaGrange Journal, 1968.

Baltrėnienė, Marija, and Romualdas Apanavičius. *Lietuviu liaudies muzikos instrumentai.* Vilnius: Mintis, 1991.

Bandera, Mark Jaroslav. *The Tsymbaly Maker and His Craft: the Ukrainian Hammered Dulcimer in Alberta.* Canadian Studies in Ethnography, vol. 1. Edmonton, Alberta: Canadian Institute of Ukrainian Studies Press, 1991.

Beregovskii, Moisey. *Evreiskaia narodnaia instrumental'naia muzyka.* Moscow: Sovetskii Kompozitor, 1987.

Berov, L. *Moldavskie muzykal'nye narodnye instrumenty.* Kishinev: Gosudarstvennoe izdatel'stvo "Cartea Moldovenească," 1964.

Czekanowska, Anna. *Polish Folk Music: Slavonic Heritage, Polish Tradition, Contemporary Trends.* Cambridge: Cambridge University Press, 1990.

Famintsyn, Aleksandr Sergeyevich. *Skomorokhei na Rusi.* St. Petersburg: Izdvo "Aleteia," 1995.

Geist, Troyd. *From the Wellspring: Faith, Soil, Tradition: Folk Arts from Ukrainian Culture in North Dakota.* Bismarck: North Dakota Council on the Arts, 1997.

Humeniuk, Andrii Ivanovych. *Ukrainski narodni muzychni instrumenti.* Kiev: Naukova Dumka, 1967.

Kofteros, Dimitris V. *Dhokimio yia to elliniko santouri.* Athens: Ekdhoseis "Dhodhoni," 1991.

Kunz, Ludvík. *Die Volksmusikinstrumente der Tschechoslowakei.* Handbuch der europäischen Volksmusikinstrumente, ser. 1, vol. 2. Leipzig: VEB Deutscher Verlag für Musik, 1974.

Leng, Ladislav. *Slovenské l'udové hudobné nástroje.* Bratislava: Vydavatel'stvo Slovenskej Akadémie Vied, 1967.

Manga, Janos. *Hungarian Folk Song and Folk Instruments.* Hungarian Folk Art, no. 2. Budapest: Corvina Press, 1969.

Mierczynski, Stanisław. *Muzyka huculszczyzny.* Cracow: Polskie Wydawnictwo Muzyczne, 1965.

Morgenstern, Ulrich. *Volksmusikinstrumente und instrumentale Volksmusik in Russland.* Berlin: Verlag Ernst Kuhn, 1995.

Nazina, Inna D. *Belorusskie narodnye muzykal'nye instrumenty: strunnye.* Minsk: Nauka i Tekhnika, 1982.

———. *Belaruskiya narodnyya muzychnyya instrumenty.* Minsk, 1997.

Nezovibatko, Olexander. *Ukrains'ki tsymbaly.* Kiev: Muzychna Ukraina, 1976.

Noll, William Henry. "Peasant Music Ensembles in Poland: A Culture History." Ph.D. diss., University of Washington, 1986.

Priedite, Trisa. *Tautas mūzikas instrumenti.* Latvijos etnogrāfiskais brīvdabas muzejs. Riga: Arots, 1988.

Salmen, Walter. *Jüdische Musikanten und Tänzer vom 13. bis 20. Jahrhundert.* Innsbruck: Edition Helbling, 1991.

Sarosi, Balint. *Die Volksmusikinstrumente Ungarns.* Handbuch der europäischen Volksmusikinstrumenten, ser. 1, vol. 1. Leipzig: VEB Deutscher Verlag für Musik, 1967.

———. *Folk Music: Hungarian Musical Idiom.* Budapest: Corvina Press, 1986.

———. *Gypsy Music.* Budapest: Corvina Press, 1978.

Szydłowska-Ceglowa, Barbara. *Staropolskie nazewnictwo instrumentów muzycznych.* Wroclaw: Zakład Narodowy Imienia Ossolińskich Wydawnictwo Polskiej Akademii Nauk, 1977.

Vertkov, K., G. Blagodatov, and E. Yazovitskaya. *Atlas muzykal'nykh instrumentov narodov SSSR.* Moscow: Gosudarstvennoe Muzykal'noe Izdatel'stvo, 1963.

Vizitiu, Zhan. *Moldavskie narodnye muzykal'nye instrumenty.* Kishinev: Literatura Artistică, 1985.

Articles

Bandera, Mark J. "'The Western Canadian Championships': *Tsymbaly* Competitions at the Red Barn." *Canadian Folk Music Journal* 11 (1983): 28-33.

Borgó, András. "'Pharao barna ivadékai' és a klezmorim." *Muzsika* 36, no. 9 (Sept. 1993): 32-40.

Cherwick, Brian. "Ukrainian *Tsymbaly* Performance in Alberta." *Canadian Folk Music Journal* 23 (1995): 20-27.

Dahlig, Piotr. "Das Hackbrett im Nordosten Polens." *Studia instrumentorum musicae popularis* 8 (1985): 118-121.

————. "Das Hackbrett und Hackbrettspieler im Südosten Polens." In *Chetverta konferentsiya doslidnykiv narodnoi muzyky chervonorus'kykh (halyts'ko-volodymyrs'kykh) ta sumizhnykh zemel' (Lviv, 1-3 kvitnya 1993 roku): Materialy.* Lviv, 1993, 52-60.

Findeizen, N. F. "Evreiskie tsimbaly i tsimbalisty Lepianskie." *Muzykal'naia etnografie* (1926): 37-44.

Freyer, Helen. "The Hungarian National Instrument: the Czimbalom." *The Etude* 48 (1930): 695-696.

Hartmann, Arthur. "The Czimbalom, Hungary's National Instrument," *Musical Quarterly* 2 (1916): 590-600.

Kaptain, Laurence. "The Hungarian Cimbalom." *Percussive Notes* 28 (Aug. 1990): 10-14.

Kara, I. "Lăutari evrei din Moldova." *Revistă cultului mozaic*, 15 Apr. 1974, 3.

Kroó, György. "The Hungarian Cimbalom." *The New Hungarian Quarterly* 16, no. 59 (Autumn 1975): 218-220.

Lang, György. "A cimbalom fejlődéstörtenete." *Muzsika* 16 (Nov. 1973): 37-41.

Leach, John. "The Cimbalom." *Music & Letters* 53 (1972): 134-142.

Michalovič, Peter. "Die Streicher–Hackbrett–Ensembles in der Westslowakei." *Studia instrumentorum musicae popularis* 11 (1995): 139-142.

Mikušová-Ukropcová, Lýdia. "Cimbal—nástroj a jeho hudobnotechnické využitie na Slovensku." *Musicologica Slovaca* 13 (1988): 51–57. Abstract in German, 94–96.

————. "Das Hackbrett: zur Erforschung der instrumentalen Volksmusik in der Slowakei." *Musikforum* 33 (1988): 41-46.

Pintér, Emőke. "The Hungarian Dulcimer." *The New Hungarian Quarterly* 20, no. 76 (Winter 1979): 217-220.

Shramko, I. K. "Ukrain'ski tsymbaly." *Narodna tvorchist'a etnografia* 4 (1989): 13-22.

————. "Z istorii tsymbaliv." *Muzyka*, 1983, no. 6, 13-14.

Sinclair, A. T. "A Hungarian Gypsy Tzimbal-Player." *Journal of the Gypsy Lore Society*, new ser., 3 (1910): 228-232.

Vicol, Adrian. "Contribuţii la cercetarea monografică a ţambalului."
    Revistă de etnografie şi folclor 15 (1970): 355-374.
Wolf, Albert. "Fahrende Leute bei den Juden." *Mitteilungen zur jüdischen
    Volkskunde* 27 (1908): 89-96, 150-156, 28 (1909): 4-29, 40-91.

Pantaleon

Articles

Ahrens, Christian. "Pantaleon Hebenstreit und die Frühgeschichte des
    Hammerklaviers." *Beiträge zur Musikwissenschaft* 29 (1987): 37-
    48.
Egerland, Annedore. "Das Pantaleon." *Die Musikforschung* 23 (1970):
    152-159.
Hanks, Sarah E. "Pantaleon's Pantalon: An 18th-century Musical Fash-
    ion." *Musical Quarterly* 55 (1969): 215-229.

Salterio

Books

Valdrighi, Luigi Francesco. *Musurgiana: scràndola-pianoforte-salterio*.
    Modena: Tipografia Cesare Olivari, 1879.

Articles

Budasz, Rogério. "A Nineteenth-Century Brazilian Dulcimer Tablature."
    Electronic Musicological Review 1 (Sept. 1996) <http://cce.ufpr.br/
    ~rem/REMv1.1/vol1/salting.html>.
Kenyon de Pascual, Beryl. "Los salterios españoles del siglo XVIII."
    Revista de musicología 8 (1985): 303-321.
———. "The Spanish Eighteenth-Century *Salterio* and Some Comments
    on Its Italian Counterpart." *Musique-Images-Instruments* 3 (1997):
    33-62.
Vilar, J. M. "Un mètode d'afinacio del salteri del segle XVIII," *Recerca
    Musicologica* 3, no. 19 (1983): 201-209.

Yangqin and Asian Forms

Books

Belyayev, Viktor. *Muzykal'nye instrumenty Uzbekistana*. Moscow: Muzgiz, 1933.

Eckhardt, Andre. *Musik, Lied, Tanz in Korea*. Bonn: H. Bouvier & Co., 1968.

Howard, Keith. *Korean Musical Instruments*. Hong Kong: Oxford University Press, 1995.

Korean Music. [Seoul]: Ministry of Culture and Information, n.d.

Kraus, Alexandre, fils. *La musique au Japon*. Florence: L'Arte della Stampa, 1879.

Laloy, Louis. *La musique chinoise*. Les musiciens célèbres. Paris: Henri Laurens, n.d.

Miller, Terry E., and Sean Williams, eds., *Southeast Asia,* The Garland Encyclopedia of World Music, vol. 4. New York: Garland Publishing, 1998.

Moule, A. C. *A List of the Musical and Other Sound-Producing Instruments of the Chinese*. 1908. Reprint, Buren: Frits Knuf Publishers, 1989.

Ng, Josephine. "The Chinese Dulcimer." M.A. thesis, University of Washington, 1978.

Soulié, Georges. *La musique en Chine*. Paris: Ernest Leroux, 1911.

Survey of Korean Arts: Traditional Music. Seoul: National Academy of Arts, 1973.

Trân Vân Khê. *La musique vietnamienne traditionelle.* Annales du Musée Guimet, Bibliothéque d'études, vol. 66. Paris: Presses Universitaires de France, 1962.

Van Aalst, J. A. *Chinese Music.* 1884. Reprint, New York: Paragon Book Reprint Corp., 1964.

Vyzgo, Tamara S. *Muzykal'nye instrumenty Srednei Azii: Istoricheskie ocherki*. Moskva: Izd-vo "Muzyka," 1980.

Vyzgo, Tamara S., and A. Petrosyants. *Uzbekskii orkestr narodnykh instrumentov*. Tashkent: Gosudarstvennoe Izdatel'stvo Khudezhestvennoi Literatury UzSSR, 1962.

Articles

Chang Sa-hun. "On the Interpretation of the Dulcimer Score and the Problems of Phyeong-Si-jo." *Asea Yon'gu* 1 (1958): 107-127. In Korean; English summary, 126-127.

Courant, Maurice. "Chine et Corée," in *Encyclopédie de la musqiue et dictionnaire du Conservatoire*, edited by Albert Lavignac, 1: 180-181.

Ho, Edward. "Yangqin and Its Music in China in the Period of 1949-1979." *Chinese Music* 20 (1997): 17-20, 24-31.

Ho, Edward, and Xu Pingxin. "The Manchurian Yangqin." *Chinese Music* 18 (1995): 50-55.

———. "The Manchurian Yangqin II." *Chinese Music* 19 (1996): 9-15.

Lee Yuan-yuan. "Instrumental Music in the Chinese Society." *Chinese Music* 4 (Dec. 1981): 69-71.

———. "Yangqin." *Chinese Music* 4, no. 1 (1981): 10-14.

Samuel, Geoffrey. "Songs of Lhasa." *Ethnomusicology* 20 (Sept. 1976): 415-417.

Xiang Zuhua. "The Development and Schools of Performing Arts of the Chinese Yangqin." *Chinese Music* 5, no. 3 (1982): 50-53, 74-76.

———. "An Examination of the Origin of the Yangqin." Translated by Lee Shuk-ming and Lai Chun-yue. *Chinese Music* 4, no. 1 (1981): 15-18.

———. "The Tradition and Development of the Music of the Chinese Dulcimer—Yangqin." *Chinese Music* 15 (Dec. 1992): 64-68.

Dulcimer in the British Isles

Books

Hasluck, Paul N. *Violins and Other Stringed Instruments: How to Make Them*. London: Cassell, 1906; Philadelphia: David McKay, 1907, 1912, 1914.

Kettlewell, David. *"...All the Tunes That Ever There Were...": An Introduction to the Dulcimer in the British Isles*. Tisbury, Wilts.: Spoot Books, 1975.

———. "The Dulcimer." Ph.D. diss., Loughborough University, 1976.

Articles

Bennington, Billy. "Billy Bennington." Interview by John Howson. *English Dance and Song* 46, no. 1 (1984): 2-6.

Cooper, Jimmy. "Jimmy Cooper: the Great Dulcimer Player from Coatbridge near Glasgow Tells His Own Life Story." Interview by Alan Ward. *Traditional Music* 7 (1977): 21-23.

Couza, Jim. "An Introduction to the Chromatic Hammered Dulcimer as Played in East Anglia." *Dulcimer Players News* 10, no. 1 (winter 1984): 20-22.

Donnelly, Seán. "A German Dulcimer Player in Eighteenth-Century Dublin." *Dublin Historical Record* 53, no. 1 (Spring 2000): 77-86.

Feeney, John. "The Dulcimer Player of Clonmeen." *Treoir* 10, no. 5 (1978): 11.

Kettlewell, David. "First Steps on the Dulcimer." *Early Music* 2 (1974): 247-253.

———. "Leslie Evans: Dulcimer Player." *English Dance and Song* 41 (1979): 4-6.

———. "'That's What I Call a Striking Sound': The Dulcimer in East Anglia." *English Dance and Song* 36 (1974): 50-51, 96-97.

McCutcheon, John. "Jimmy Cooper, Dulcimer Player: A Review and Musings." *Dulcimer Players News* 4 (Summer 1978): 17.

Southgate, T. L. "Evolution of the Pianoforte." In *English Music [1604 to 1904]: Being the Lectures Given at the Music Loan Exhibition of The Worshipful Company of Musicians, Held at Fishmongers' Hall, London Bridge, June-July, 1904.* London: Walter Scott Pub. Co., 1906.

Summers, Keith. "Sing, Say or Pay! A Survey of East Suffolk Country Music." *Traditional Music* 8 & 9 (late 1977/early 1978): 5-54.

Wortley, Russell. "Chromatic Tuning for Dulcimer as Used by Traditional Players in Norfolk." *English Dance and Song* 39 (1977): 75.

———. "The Traditional English Dulcimer." *Folk Review* 5 (Nov. 1975): 13-15.

Dulcimer in America

Books

Groce, Nancy. *The Hammered Dulcimer in America.* Smithsonian Studies in History and Technology, no. 44. Washington: Smithsonian Institution Press, 1983.
Hawes, Nicholas. Notes to *Paul Van Arsdale: Dulcimer Heritage: Traditional Hammered Dulcimer Music from New York State.* Sharon, Conn.: Folk-Legacy Records, 1983.
Kimball, James W. *Sackett's Harbor: Nineteenth-Century Dance Music from Western New York State: the Tunes.* Rochester, N.Y.: Sampler Records Ltd., 1994.
Michigan Hammered Dulcimer: 25 Years with the Original Dulcimer Players Club. N.p: 1988.
Shoemaker, Henry W. *The Music and Musical Instruments of the Pennsylvania Mountaineers.* Altoona, Pa.: Mountain City Press, 1923.

Articles

"Aunt Nellie McKinney." *Dulcimer Players News* 10 (Fall 1984): 6. Reprinted from *The Knotty Post*, July 1954.
Collins, Mitzie. "The Elizabeth Garbutt Reed Dulcimer." *Dulcimer Players News* 10 (Spring 1984): 22-24.
———. "Notes on a Personal Collection of Dulcimers and Dulcimer-Type Instruments." *Dulcimer Players News* 3, no. 3 (Summer 1977): 32-34.
Crabtree, Mark. "Worley Gardner: Mountain Music, Dance and Dulcimers." *Goldenseal* 18, no. 2 (Summer 1992): 9-15.
Dulcimer Players News, 1 (1975-present), passim.
Gifford, Paul. "Development of the Hammer Dulcimer." In *The Hammer Dulcimer Compendium*, edited by Michael J. Holmes, 8-16. Silver Spring, Md.: MIH Publications, 1977.
———. "Ezra Durand, William Vogel, and Their Dulcimers." *Dulcimer Players News* 23 (May-July 1997): 42-43; (Aug.-Oct. 1997): 42-43.
———. "Henry Ford and the Dulcimer." *Dulcimer Players News* 24, no. 1 (Feb.-Apr. 1998): 26-29.

Hulan, Richard. "Hunting and Taming the Native American (or Hammered) Dulcimer." *Newsletter of the Folklore Society of Greater Washington* 5 (Feb. 1969): 6-9.

———. "Music in Tennessee." *Antiques* 100 (1971): 418-419.

Prinz, Harvey. "In Search of the Kansas Dulcimer." *Dulcimer Players News* 11 (Summer 1985): 14-15.

Rizzetta, Sam. "A Profusion of Hammer Dulcimer Tunings." *Dulcimer Players News* 23 (Feb.-Apr. 1997): 14-15, (Nov. 1997-Jan. 1998): 48-49, 24 (Feb.-Apr. 1998): 44-45, (Aug.-Oct. 1998): 18-21.

Rugg, Michael. "Early California Dulcimers." *Frets* 2 (Feb. 1980): 62.

Schnitz, Jean Granberry. "Hammered Dulcimers and Folk Songs: The Musical Heritage of the C. A. Lee Family." In *Corners of Texas*, ed. Francis Edward Abernethy. Publication of the Texas Folklore Society, vol. 52. Denton, Tex.: University of North Texas Press, 1993.

Sullivan, Ken. "Russell Fluharty: The Dulcimer Man." *Goldenseal* 12, no. 4 (Winter 1986): 16-26.

Taylor, David L. "J. E. Matheny, an Early Hammered Dulcimer Player." *Dulcimer Players News* 3 (Spring 1977): 34-35.

Unpublished Material

Alm, Jan. "Michigan's Hammered Dulcimers." Paper, Western Kentucky University, 1980.

Babel, Edward. Collection, 197-?. Southern Folklife Collection, University of North Carolina at Chapel Hill.

Original Dulcimer Players Club. Records, 1963-1980. Bentley Historical Library, University of Michigan.

Index

cittern, 39, 68, 73, 105, 107, 108, 176, 214, 215, 239
Ciuciu-Marinescu, Iani, 126
clarinet, 70, 71, 74, 76, 80, 110, 116, 120, 123, 128, 251, 252
Clark, Wellington, 270
Clauss, Adam, 84
clavichord, 36, 37, 38, 39, 73, 176, 214
clavicymbalum, 103
Clegg, Henry, 228, 273
Clegg, Israel E., 274
Cline, Cora Denning, **27**, 344
Cloughley, Dave, 228
cobza, 125
Cockrell, Nancy, 278
Codolban, Nitza, 126
Cogswell, Philander, 246–248, 253, 294
čögür, 48
colascione, 38
Collins, Mitzie, 375, 381
Conklin, Eva, 332
Conley, John C., 242
Cook, Russell, 383
Cooper, Billy, 222, 223
Cooper, Jimmy, 224, 225, 227
cornet, 66, 220
Coula, Madame, 135
Couza, Jim, 227
Cox, Eugene, 363–364
Cox, Mabel, 332
Cox, Viola, 362
Cramer, Roderick L., 382
Cranberry Gathering, 378, 387
Craven, Virgil, 277, 300, 309
Cromer, Al, 330
Cromwell, Mrs., 340
Cross, Frank, 331
Cross, Jim, 331
crowd, 37
crumhorn, 68
Crump, Martin E., 268

Cummings, Donald, 225
Cymbal: of German speakers in Austria, Bohemia, and Germany, 69, 71, 87, 92, 109, 110, 111–112, 137, 138, 166; in America, 129, *138*; in Holland, 108; tuning, 395
cymbal, Slovak, 116
cymbal (hurdy-gurdy), 216, 217
cymbały, Polish: 106, 117, 120, 121–122, 145; tuning, 396

dabbuddà, 15, 38
daf, 52
Dalglish, Malcolm, 379, 380, 388
Dall'Olio, Giovanni Battista, 173, 175
Damm, Eddie, 384
damnyen, 202
dàn ban nguyêt, 202
Davis, Meyer, 130
Deines, Adam, 92
DeLano, Mortimer, 257, 302
DeLano, Oscar, 257
DeLorme, Ted, 339, 340
demi canon, 13
dokra, 53
dolcemèle, 38–39, 171
dolzaina, 214
domra, 104
don-min, 203
Donald, John S., 331, 355
Dorogi, Dennis, 367, 375
douçaine, 214
Douglass, Robert, 226
doulcemèr, 28, 31, 40; design, 35; early illustrations, **5**, **6**, 32, 34, 37
Dowling, Andy, 226, 227
Dowling, John, 225
drum, 71, 123, 251
Duggan, Dan, 388
dulce melos, 26, 27, 31

lute, 35, 37, 39, 66, 72, 73, 104, 106,
107, 108, 190, 214, 215, 217
Lyon and Healy, 272, 304, 330

MacArthur, Bill, 229
Macdonald, Angus, 340
Mackenzie, Donald, 339
MacKenzie, James A., 18, 270–
271, 306–307
MacNeil, Madeline, 377, 386
Maga, John, 133
mandolin, 181, 217
mandore, 191
Manley, Catherine, 272
Manley, Willie, 272
Mann, Thomas B., 228
Mann, Thomas P., 228, 332
Marta, Dick, **14**, 131
Martin, Jesse R., **26**, 267, 308, 329–
330, 356
Martini, Giovanni Battista, 172
Maser, Henry, **12**, 92
Mason, Malchart D., 265
Mason, Phillip, 377, 385
Matheny, H. E., 5
Matheny, Joseph Edward, 275
Matheny, Reuben, **23**, 275, 293
Mattheson, Johann, 68
Maxson, Charles, 375, 379
Mayfield, Ira, 361
McCann, Bert, 332
McCutcheon, John, 379, 380, 386
McDonald, William, 355
McKinney, Nellie Chase, 276, 297,
341
McNally, Dominic, 229
McNally, William, **19**, 224
medio cano, 12
Meixner, Emil, 331
melodeon, 251
Mendelson, Barbara, 381
meo canon, 13
Mercado, Angel, 181

Mercado, Sara, 181
Merrill, Jesse, 307
Messinger, Jake, 328
Messinger, Velma E., 328
metzkanon, 13
mezzo cannone, **2**, 13
micanon, 13
Michael, Walt, 375, 386
Michigan Lumberjacks, **28**, 358–359
Mickiewicz, Adam, 120
Mikova, Veronica, 130
Miller, Jim, 384
minstrels, 3, 34, 35, 37, 38, 65, 67,
68, 73, 105, 218
miskal, 48
Mitchell, Howard, 366, 375–376,
382
Mogyoróssy, Gyula, 115
Mohammed Hasan, 51
Mohammed Sadeq Khan, 51
Mongolia, 201
monochord, 12, 19
Montgomery Ward, 272
Mooers, Ray, 383
Moral, Pablo del, 177
Moriarity, William A., 314
Morningstar, Judi, 385
Moskowitz, Joseph, 132
mountain dulcimer. *See* Appalachian
dulcimer
Mountaineer Dulcimer Club, 361
Mozart, Leopold, 112
Mudge, Jay B., 268, 359, 361
Mulford, Arthur J., 359
Mumford, Brian, 375
Murphy, Michael, 375
Musâhib Santûrî Hüseyin, 48
Music Folk, 384
musique à baguette, 339
Myers, Simon, 342

Namyniuk, Bill, 133
Nasolini, Sebastiano, 173

About the Author

Paul M. Gifford, born in 1950 in Detroit, became interested as a teenager in the dulcimer and its associated music through his father Norman, a pianist and flutist, who had known dulcimer players and fiddlers in the 1920s and 1930s near his hometown of Sherman, New York. He played it extensively around Michigan in the 1970s and 1980s, while also exploring the musical traditions of other immigrant groups and countries. A graduate of the University of Michigan (B.A., 1983, M.L.S., 1984), since 1987 he has been an archivist and librarian at the University of Michigan-Flint, Flint, Michigan.